D1551925

Rolling Rivers

Rolling Rivers

An Encyclopedia of America's Rivers

Richard A. Bartlett
EDITOR

McGraw-Hill Book Company
New York St. Louis San Francisco Auckland
Bogotá Hamburg Johannesburg London
Madrid Mexico Montreal New Delhi
Panama São Paulo Singapore
Sydney Tokyo Toronto

Library of Congress Cataloging in Publication Data
Main entry under title:

Rolling rivers.

1. Rivers—United States.   I. Bartlett, Richard A.
GB1215.R64 1984   333.78'45'0973   83-18745
ISBN 0-07-003910-0

1 2 3 4 5 6 7 8 9 DOC/DOC 8 9 0 9 8 7 6 5 4

ISBN 0-07-003910-0

*Thomas H. Quinn and Michael Hennelly were the editors of this
book. Naomi Auerbach was the designer. Sara Fliess supervised
the production. It was set in Aster by Santype-Byrd, Inc.*

Printed and bound by R. R. Donnelley and Sons, Inc.

Contents

Preface

From a jetliner 30,000 feet over Omaha the Captain informs his passengers of the presence below of the Missouri River. There it is, a black, serpentine artery twisting north by northwest across the American landscape, disappearing far off in a cold, gray mist.

How many passengers on the airliner will have thoughts about two army officers named Lewis and Clark who in 1804 led an expedition up that mighty river? How many will contemplate the achievement in rowing and pulling those heavy boats, the men encouraged ever onward by the curiosity of what lay around the next bend? Probably very few on board will muse about such happenings in our American past.

For more and more people, like the jet passengers, see the United States as a maze of cities connected by airlines and airports or by wide, straight-as-an-arrow, concrete interstate highways. They have forgotten the nation's history and geography, its mountains and valleys, lakes, forests, prairies, and, above all, its rivers. Concrete ribbons and black-topped Tarmacs have replaced visits to places of quiet natural beauty, while road maps and airline schedules have taken precedence over histories or travelogues about the nation's places of local and regional interest.

It is to offer in a single volume much of the excitement, romance, adventure, hardship, challenge, tragedy, and charm of the local and regional history affiliated with selected American rivers that this compilation has been made. Most especially it is hoped that present and future generations of Americans, many of them restless and even rootless, will discover in these essays the richness and variety of America's colorful, varied local and regional heritage. By reading them perhaps they will gain pride in region and nation.

I owe very special thanks to the generosity of the contributors to *Rolling Rivers*. They accepted their tasks cheerfully and worked many hours over their essays. Many swallowed hard and accepted without protest deletions due to space restrictions of their favorite paragraphs or subject matter. But above all they deserve my gratitude because of their incredible knowledge of their rivers. Because they have shared this knowledge with us, it can be stated positively and accurately: nowhere else is there so comprehensive a history of America's rivers in a single volume.

Rolling Rivers

General Introduction

When Europeans first touched America's shores, its rivers flowed free. Deep and placid and clear, they supported millions of fish, bird life so abundant it occasionally covered the streams with a feathery carpet, and verdant shores where a Noah's Ark of animals thrived. On the waters Indians paddled gracefully shaped canoes that glided effortlessly over the liquid highways, be their destination a friendly village for trade or an enemy village for attack. The rivers beckoned Europeans whose own watercourses were already dirty and utilized to a state of ugliness. Explorers gazed up the rivers into the mists seeking the Northwest Passage, a short, easy water route to the Pacific.

From the St. Lawrence River French explorers and *coureurs de bois*, led by Indian guides, discovered the Niagara and its falls, coasted the south shore of Lake Erie to a portage that brought them to French Creek, which in turn emptied into the Allegheny. Down that river they floated until they reached the Forks where the Monongahela emerges like an exposed artery from the forest-covered hills of Appalachia to fuse with the Allegheny. Now they were paddling down the ever-widening Ohio. From its right and left banks navigable rivers such as the Muskingum, Scioto, Miami, and Wabash from the north and the Kanawha, Big Sandy, Licking, Kentucky, and Tennessee from the south, debouched into the southwest flowing stream which finally entered the Father of Waters, the Mississippi, flowing toward the Gulf of Mexico.

As the French probed the vast arterial riverways of the interior valley, British colonists settled along the coastal rivers. They forged into a new "west" up the south-flowing Connecticut and Delaware. When they captured New Amsterdam (New York) they also took Fort Orange (Albany) and from there, where the east-flowing Mohawk enters the Hudson, challenged the French who controlled the fur trade via the St. Lawrence.

Settlers of the south Atlantic colonies expanded westward along the sluggish rivers draining the coastal plain, building a plantation society using the streams for communication with the outside world. Even farther south the Spanish, French, and finally British again, settled along the St. Marys and St. Johns rivers of Florida.

Rivers were the key to settlement and trade; they were also links to the interior. Cresting the Appalachians, the wanderers discovered the southwest flowing headwaters of the Watauga, Holston, Nolichucky, and French Broad, rivers that coalesced and led men to the mighty Tennessee.

Southward the Chattahoochee, Flint, Tombigbee, Black Warrior, Alabama, Pearl, and other streams drifted casually southward, their waters eventually ending in the Gulf of Mexico. Along these streams lived sedentary Creek, Chickasaw, and Choctaw Indians, their towns strung like beads along the rivers in a land of plant and animal abundance.

West of the Mississippi, the rivers challenged men to search upstream for the Northwest Passage. Lewis and Clark embarked on the Missouri, followed its headstream which they called the Jefferson to its headwaters struggled over the divide, finally embarking on the Clearwater which flows into the Snake, down the Snake to the Columbia and so to the Pacific. Thomas Jefferson had hoped the portage between Missouri and Columbia headwaters would be so narrow and easy that it would inspire a brisk trade by water from the Orient to St. Louis. He was wrong, but his emphasis on river transportation bears evidence of its importance prior to the coming of the railroads.

After Lewis and Clark came the traders and trappers, up the Missouri, Platte, Cheyenne, Yellowstone, and Bighorn. Other mountain men forged up the Arkansas or the Red River of the South. When traders reached Santa Fe they were entering upper Rio Grande country, already settled by the Spanish who had worked upstream beginning with Don Juan Oñate in 1598. West of there to California, Spanish missionaries learned of the Colorado, Salt, Verde, and Gila—life-giving streams in a desert land.

Then came American far west migration. Oregonians and Californians trudged along the Platte and North Platte to the Sweetwater to the Sandy to the Green to the Bear; if bound for Oregon they then pointed their teams toward the Snake. If California-bound they headed southwest and west along the Humboldt and then up the Walker, Carson, or Truckee to California. It was on a tributary of the American River on the western slope of the Sierras that James Marshall discovered gold in 1848.

When settlement began it was usually along river valleys where the soil was rich, timber prevalent, water available, and communications made easy by the flowing stream. Like the people in the riverside town, the river was a living, changing personality whose temperament and physical condition was of constant concern. Its floods caused death and destruction;

its droughts brought economic hardship; its waters provided fish for food and sport; its banks supported fur-bearing animals; its rapids threatened boats but challenged mill owners to harness the power; its wintry solidity offered ice skating frolics; its waters provided potable liquid for thirsty humans; and its free flow offered easy disposal of the community's industrial and human wastes.

Residents along a river were proud of it, boasting of "their" stream, and creating mythical characters who lived along it. Mike Fink worked the Mississippi. Pecos Bill, who as a child had fallen off a wagon as it crossed Texas' Pecos River, was rescued and raised by coyotes; his childhood pets were centipedes and tarantulas. Up Nebraska's Dismal River was Febold Feboldson's ranch; he sold frozen post holes. The legendary lumberjack Paul Bunyon is credited with the meanderings, gorges, and rapids of many northern rivers. Washington Irving's Rip Van Winkle and Ichabod Crane lived near the Hudson, and Mark Twain's Tom and Huck rafted the Mississippi.

But today modern transportation has dulled the conscious existence of our rivers and led us to forget the richness of the local history made along them. A heritage is being forgotten. *Rolling Rivers* has attempted to capture some of the disappearing lore. Consisting of 117 essays on some of America's most historic rivers, written primarily by professional historians, and emphasizing the human story, *Rolling Rivers* serves to remind us of the link between humanity and its environment, and to renew our interest in protecting our rivers as both a great national resource and a precious historical heritage.

East Coast Rivers

When their creaking little sailing ships dropped anchor in the estuaries of
the New World, crew and passengers felt an exhilaration that overcame
their physically emaciated bodies and their emotionally exhausted minds.
Up to nine weeks of close-quarters shipboard living, and a seafaring diet
of moldy hardtack, salt pork, and stale water had weakened everyone's
constitution. Close to twenty-four-hour-a-day contact with shipmates
had frayed everyone's nerves and storms and the ship's seaworthiness
had tested everyone's courage. Would they make it?

Then one day the westerly breeze brought the fresh scent of green
growing things. Some branches and leaves floated by while land-based
birds were observed overhead. A bucket dipped into the water brought up
fluid more fresh than salt. The distant cloud bank materialized into a
forested landscape. Gradually land was observed to right and left as the
ship entered an estuary. Landfall had been made. Now new hopes, new
plans, new beginnings lay ahead. Weakened bodies gained renewed
strength, a psychosomatic reaction to the mental relief.

Whether they were French, sailing up the cold St. Lawrence or the
semi-tropical St. Johns, Dutch investigating the Delaware or Hudson, or
English settling along the Charles or James, the relief was the same.
Indeed the newcomers had reason to be joyful. The streams were of fresh,
clear water and teemed with fish; their banks abounded with game and
birds dotted the sky. Trees, vines, ferns and flowers bore evidence of a
fertility that could be made to produce the white man's crops. And where
did the rivers lead? To exotic peoples with gold and silver? To a
Northwest Passage to the Pacific?

Rapidly men landed, settled, probed up the rivers, established towns
and cities, farms and plantations, and lines of communication into the
headwater country. For 400 years the migration continued using the
rivers until today the streams are taken for granted and in that sense are
virtually forgotten. Yet the East Coast Rivers have played an enormous

role in America's story and their importance continues. Part I offers a sampling of the history of these streams, the first ones observed by newcomers to the New World.

Richard A. Bartlett

The Altamaha River

Source: Juncture of Ocmulgee and Oconee Rivers in Southeast Central Georgia
Length: 137 miles
Tributaries: Ohoopee River
Mouth: Forms delta into Atlantic between Sapelo and St. Simons Islands
Agriculture: Timber farming, soybeans, peanuts, corn
Industries: Lumbering, naval stores, shrimping

The Altamaha River is formed by the junction of the Oconee and Ocmulgee rivers, which meet head-on at the "Forks" in southeast central Georgia. The mighty Altamaha then flows 137 miles southeastwardly to the Atlantic Ocean. Through most of that distance it meanders through "wire-grass" Georgia, joined by the Ohoopee River and numerous creeks. Approximately twenty-three miles from the Atlantic the river forms a delta and divides into several branches, namely, the Altamaha, the South Altamaha, and the Darien rivers. Ocean tides affect these streams up to thirty-five miles inland. Sapelo and St. Simons islands, lying on either side of the river's estuary, like the other major off-shore islands of the Georgia coast, are closely connected with the history of the Altamaha.

The coastal area was home for about 4,000 Guale Indians, a Muskogean tribe linguistically linked to the Yamassees and Creeks with whom they eventually merged. The Guales were sedentary, living from hunting, fishing, and primitive agriculture.

Almost from the beginning of European colonization Georgia was a "debatable land." By 1568 Spanish Jesuits had introduced Christianity along the Georgia coast. In 1573 Franciscans resumed missionary activities and their missions remained until Spain's Guale outposts were pushed south of the Altamaha by the British in 1680.

For several decades Guale remained uninhabited by whites and undisturbed except for occasional pirate activities. In 1721 South Carolinians built Fort King George on high ground where Snow Creek entered the old meander of the Darien River. Constructed as a barrier against the Spanish in Florida and the French from the interior, it was the first English fort on Georgia soil. It was abandoned in 1727 because of mutinous garrisons, a destructive fire, and high maintenance costs.

The original grant to the "Trustees for Establishing the Colony of Georgia in America" embraced that territory between the Savannah and Altamaha rivers from the coast northward to their headwaters, and thence westward to the Pacific Ocean. General James Oglethorpe founded Savannah in 1733 and subsequently won the friendship of the local Indian chiefs, convincing them to cede the lands designated in the charter of 1732.

In 1736 Scotch Highlanders, recruited for their fighting abilities, settled Darien at the mouth of the Altamaha, while Fort Frederica was at the same time nearing completion on St. Simons Island. By 1740 the town of Frederica had a population of 1000 and the fort was perhaps the most costly citadel erected by the English in North America. Oglethorpe resided there until 1743. John and Charles Wesley, the founders of Methodism, preached at this remote corner of the British empire. Other outposts, with connecting roads and waterways, were constructed in the vicinity.

Oglethorpe's defensive strategy was soon tested in the War of Jenkin's Ear (1739–1742), a phase of the imperial rivalry between England and Spain that developed into King George's War. Land operations of this conflict were fought largely on St. Simons Island in July, 1742. Following several skirmishes the British surprised a Spanish detachment, killing or capturing 200 soldiers in the Battle of Bloody Marsh. While it was far from a decisive victory, the battle sufficiently demoralized the Spaniards to cause them to return to Florida.

Georgians continued to face serious difficulties from the Spanish, South Carolinians, and Creek Indians before gaining undisputed control over the region south of the Altamaha. While in limbo the area became a refuge for outlaws and a target for schemers. By 1763 South Carolina's claims had been settled, the Creeks had ceded their lands along the coast from the Altamaha to the St. Marys River, and the region lay open for settlement. The rising spirit of revolution, however, postponed this development for years.

Although few major Revolutionary battles were fought on Georgia soil, widespread devastation was caused by invading British regulars and bitter conflicts between Whigs and Tories. The region between the Altamaha and Florida became a haven for Tories, runaway slaves, and hostile Indians. For three years Georgia troops marched up and down the coast in what historian E. Merton Coulter described as "a border war game, half-comic though tragic enough." The infamous Florida Rangers, operating from St. Augustine, remained an ominous threat to Fort Howe (Fort Barrington) on the Altamaha. By the end of January, 1779, Georgia had fallen to the British. However, guerrilla resistance on land and sea kept the patriots' cause alive. By July, 1782, British troops had evacuated Savannah and the rebel government of Georgia had been restored to power.

From the beginning of English settlement agriculture, cattle raising, and lumbering were the main economic interests along the Georgia coast. The *Constitution*, famous as "Old Ironsides," was built of oak grown on St. Simons Island. In the early nineteenth century sea-island cotton became the leading crop of the coastal islands. First grown on St. Simons by the Scots as early as 1778, the staple quickly spread to other islands along the coast and replaced indigo as the principal crop. Thomas Spalding's

plantation on Sapelo Island produced the first sugar cane in Georgia. By 1830 sugar cane culture had spread upriver as far as Milledgeville and Macon. Other crops common to the sea islands included corn and sweet potatoes.

The limited zone marked by the ebb and flow of the tides was the preeminent domain of the great rice plantations—an expansion of the South Carolina rice plantation culture. Local planters developed an extensive hydraulic engineering system of dikes, canals, sluice gates, and dams that controlled the flow of river water into the fields at high tide and drained them at low tide.

A short distance upriver from Hopeton the tidewater region gives way to wire-grass country. Here in the vast forests of long-leaf pine early settlers made small clearings in which they planted corn, tobacco, sugar cane, and patches of vegetables. Their main livelihood was derived from cattle and hogs that ranged freely through the piney woods, grazing on wire grass, shrubs, acorns, and pine mast. The naturalist William Bartram, who visited the region in the 1770s, referred to the settlements as "cowpens." A regional writer, Caroline Miller, won the Pulitzer Prize in 1934 for her novel, *Lamb in His Bosom*, a story of pioneer life in wire-grass Georgia during pre-Civil War Days. This sparsely settled region still retains its unique cultural identity; its residents still farm, harvest timber, and sell pulp wood and naval stores.

For most of the nineteenth century the Altamaha system was the main artery of commerce between middle Georgia and the coast, with Darien the seaport. Flatboats carried cotton downriver where the craft were dismantled and sold for lumber. Poleboats, manned by crewmen thrusting long poles into the river bed to propel the craft, carried passengers and freight in both directions. Traveling upstream from Darien to the "Forks" by poleboat required fifteen to twenty days.

Along the river one still encounters colorful place names like Hell's Shoal, Stooping Gum, Marrowbone Round, Hog Pen Slough, and Doctortown. Upriver was Rag Point where a raftsman on his first trip down to Darien customarily left a piece of his shirt tied to a tree. As for the lilting name Altamaha, it is apparently of Indian origin, and was mentioned by some of De Soto's chroniclers in 1540.

Although its population was never large, Darien prospered throughout the nineteenth century. The first steamboat to travel the Altamaha left Darien late in 1818 and arrived in Milledgeville early in 1819. Actually steamboats never completely replaced poleboats because the latter could navigate in low water. The Macon-Atlantic Navigation Company, the last line to operate on the river, continued until the 1930s. When the Central of Georgia Railroad reached Macon in 1843, steamboat lines were forced to reduce freight rates; other rail lines and a network of highways doomed the surviving steamboats. Today the river is used largely by pleasure craft and fishermen.

For about forty years prior to the First World War log rafting thrived on the Altamaha and its tributaries. The virgin yellow pine forests of the interior with trees sixty to a hundred feet high were harvested, formed into rafts sometimes 200 feet long, and floated downstream by raftsmen partially controlling the craft with a long sweep at bow and stern. From Darien the rough, colorful rivermen walked back home. Depletion of the forests ended Darien's booming prosperity; the old town has never recovered.

Just south of Darien lies Butler Island where for a brief period lived Fannie Kemble, the beautiful British actress. It was here that she began writing her *Journal of a Residence on a Georgia Plantation*, a passionate denunciation of slavery. After a brief, stormy marriage she divorced her husband and returned to the British stage, but her daughter inherited the plantations and managed them for four years during the Reconstruction era. Her experiences are recorded in *Ten Years on a Georgia Plantation Since the War*, a major study of the problems of coastal planters without slaves.

Along the south branch of the Altamaha were baronial estates tended by hundreds of Gullah slaves whose descendants still speak a distinctive dialect. For decades scholars have been fascinated by the Gullah culture, a unique blend of European and African traits. One can still discover believers in "conjuring," "haints," and "root doctors." Some still dance frenetically to the beat of drums and tamborines.

Reconstruction brought a new social order to the Altamaha. Along the lower river one of the most controversial personalities was Tunis G. Campbell, a black carpetbagger from New Jersey. After an unsuccessful attempt to establish a black separatist regime on St. Catherines Island, Campbell became labor and political boss of the former Gullah slaves, served in Georgia's constitutional convention in 1867–1868, and was later elected to the state senate.

By 1900 shortages of labor and capital, destructive hurricanes, and competition from Louisiana had ended rice culture in the Altamaha delta. Naval stores, lumbering, and later shrimping replaced agriculture as sources of livelihood. The region languished economically and culturally although a few towns along the railroads and automobile roads gradually developed a measure of prosperity. Slash and loblolly pine forests were planted and harvested for lumber and paper products produced by big corporations. The Edwin I. Hatch Nuclear Plant near Baxley, about twenty miles below the "Forks" was recently built. The plant, utilizing river water in a closed circulatory system, has a generating capacity of 1,600,000 kilowatts. It represents an investment of nearly a billion dollars and gives energy to the upper Altamaha region.

Major changes have occurred also in the lower reaches of the Altamaha. Beginning with Thomas Carnegie's purchase of the greater part of Cumberland Island in 1881, the coastal islands of Georgia soon became the playground of northern millionaires. In 1886 Jekyll Island became one of the world's most exclusive winter resorts.

Today Georgia's coast remains a "debateable land" as conservationists, real estate developers, and industrialists eagerly covet its natural resources, beauty, and history. The unspoiled region drained by the mighty Altamaha constitutes a rich legacy—one of the nation's best-kept secrets.

FURTHER READING: Brainard Cheney, *River Rogue* (novel, 1941). Burnette Vanstory, *Georgia's Land of the Golden Isles* (1956). Betsey Fancher, *The Lost Legacy of Georgia's Golden Isles* (1971).

R. F. Saunders, Jr., and George A. Rogers

The Ashley and Cooper rivers

Source: Sand Hills and swamps above Charleston
Length: Cooper: 32 miles; Ashley, 40 miles
Mouth: Charleston Harbor
Cities: Charleston, South Carolina
Industries: Lumber, textile manufacturing

Until relatively recent geologic ages the coastal plain of South Carolina was covered by ocean waters. The Sand Hills, approximately sixty miles inland from the shore, mark the former coastline. Just east of the Sand Hills a long, sinuous swamp system winds through the coastal plain paralleling the ocean for sixty-five miles. In a low-lying area known as Ferguson Swamp, south of the Santee River basin, small, ill-defined channels indicate the origins of the East and West Branches of the Cooper River. The branches wind their way seaward until they join together thirty-two miles north of the Cooper River's outlet in Charleston harbor. Farther south, on the eastern slopes of a sand hill ridge, the headwaters of the Ashley River are found.

Along their upper sections the Ashley and Cooper rivers follow a narrow, winding course through the swamplands. The water flow is relatively swift, channel depths range from one to six feet, and many side or back channels are formed as the water leaves the stream bed to flow through the adjacent swamps. Before the English colonists cleared great stretches for farming, the land, except for occasional savannahs, was heavily forested along the rivers' course with large mature hardwood forests, including groves of oak and hickory, and stands of pine sheltered birds and game. The preserved remnants of the great swamp giants—big black gum, tupelo, and ancient bald cypress trees as tall as a ten-story building—stand today as monuments to an earlier age.

As the river waters approach the sea, wooded swamplands give way to low-lying marshlands. The river channels widen considerably and follow an easy, winding course. In the midst of vast tidal swamps, the Ashley and Cooper rivers form the peninsula upon which the city of Charleston is built. Joined by the Wando, the rivers come together to form Charleston harbor.

The geographical configuration—fertile lands mixed with unyielding water wilderness, slow-moving rivers that penetrate only a short way into the interior, and immense stretches of marshland, shaped the economy and culture of low-country South Carolina.

The Indian tribes of the Carolina low country were numerous and small, perhaps because the land is cut up by numerous tidal creeks and small rivers, while the tribes of the interior were larger and fiercer. The Kiawahs, hoping to gain protection from their hostile neighbors and their Spanish allies, invited the English colonists to settle upon Kiawah lands. The settlers to whom this invitation was tendered were part of an expedition outfitted by the Carolina Proprietors, a company whose most versatile and brilliant member was Anthony Ashley Cooper, Earl of Shaftesbury. Accepting the offer, the colonists established a settlement, Charles Towne, (as it was first called) on a tidal creek of a river they named the Ashley. The site was a place of elevated ground, guarded on one flank by an inaccessible marsh and on another by a steep creek bed, and densely timbered. The land was fertile, but that was a secondary consideration; the location had been picked because it could be defended. Shortly afterward, the colonists further honored their chief proprietor by bestowing his surname upon the second of the two rivers that later generations of Charlestonians would allege "flow together to form the Atlantic Ocean."

Within a decade the settlement was relocated on the peninsula. In time, the colonists discovered that the wet black mold of the swamps was ideal for the production of rice. The crop speedily became the staple of the province. The constant need of rice for water caused some planters to dam small streams for reservoirs from which they periodically watered the fields. By the end of the colonial period, attempts had been made to control the growth of plants and weeds by alternately flooding and draining the rice fields. Transferred to the freshwater portion of the tidelands after the American Revolution, this method of cultivation developed into the famous water culture.

Rice growing demanded adequate amounts of high land and desirable swamp, plentiful labor, and access to navigable water. This combination was hard to secure except by taking up large tracts of land along the low country rivers. The consequence was to make South Carolina a region of large plantations worked by slaves. The plantations themselves turned their backs to far-off or inadequate roads in favor of the ease and neighborliness of river transportation. Water travel was safer, cheaper, and more common, and the rivers carried people from plantation to plantation and goods to and from Charleston. Here was the sustenance provided by the rice fields formed from the marshes and watered by the floods; here too was government, for the planter families, isolated in their domains, ruled over the lands their slaves worked. Collectively, the planters ordered the affairs of South Carolina.

In wartime the Ashley and Cooper Rivers became vital components of defense. In colonial times, when the Indians, Spanish, and French threatened Charles Towne, fortifications were erected in the harbor and along the river banks. During the American Revolution the Cooper River served as a sanctuary for the tiny American navy, and it and the Ashley formed the flanks defended by the American army which locked itself into Charleston in a futile attempt to withstand the British siege. In the Civil War the Ashley and Cooper were Charleston's fortified outposts, each with an interlocking complex of guns, forts, garrisons, mines, booms, sunken pilings, floating batteries, gunboats, and deliberately sunken obstructions that guarded the approaches to the city.

The prosperity of the low-country depended upon commerce in the ante bellum period, and commerce required that Charleston harbor be accessible to ocean-going vessels. The sea entrance to Charleston harbor, a little more than a mile and a quarter wide, lies between Sullivan's Island and Morris Island. Their presence forms the spout of a gigantic funnel through which pours the Atlantic Ocean. The dynamic of the tides and the angular movement of the breaking waves deposits sand to form an outer or drift bar that stretches across the Charleston harbor entrance like a great bow. For three hundred years or more, tidal and river action carved several channels through the bar, a caprice of nature which enabled Charleston to become colonial America's most important southern port.

For reasons unknown the harbor channels began filling in during the 1840s—just the moment when steam power was revolutionizing oceangoing commerce by making ships larger and faster. Harbor improvements, jetties which would control the flow of the ebb tide and keep the main channel clear by sweeping sand away, were clearly necessary. But the construction was not completed until 1895, and low-country South Carolina did not have a modern outport until then. In the aftermath of the Civil War, nature added to the woes of an economy devastated by the fighting.

The only bright spot was afforded by the "Fish Bed of the Charleston Basin," a stratum along the Ashley River, ten miles above Charleston, named for the abundance of marine animal remains, including sharks' teeth of enormous size and weighing from two to two and a half pounds each. The rocks of the stratum were first subjected to chemical analysis in 1867 and proved to be phosphates. A fertilizer industry quickly developed, shot to first rank among low-country manufactures, and shipped a sizeable proportion of its product upcountry. The addition of fertilizer to the cotton fields caused production to soar and cotton prices to fall. A consequence was that South Carolina was gripped more tightly by an economy geared to the production of a single staple crop.

The pattern of slow economic growth broken only by recessions in the predominately agricultural economy might have been changed by industrialization, but factors did not permit that. Instead, because of the harbor improvements, military installations began to be located in and around Charleston; first coastal defense batteries and a garrison, then a naval base, then, later, modern docks and facilities for shipping troops and supplies overseas. The presence of these installations required river and harbor improvements. Upcountry, in Piedmont, Carolina, textile manufacturing had spread rapidly, greatly aided by progress in hydroelectric technology. Hydropower was generated by impounding river waters in man-made lakes. One of the more ambitious plans, the Santee-Cooper Project, diverted the waters of the Santee River into the Cooper River to construct a set of two dams for the generation of power and, secondarily, provide a navigation route. Completed on the eve of American entry into the Second World War, Santee-Cooper shouldered the burden of providing power for defense industries and Charleston's rapidly expanding military facilities. The electrical power became crucial to life and economic development; manufacturing, municipalities, and the area's residents depended upon the system. Meanwhile, in mid-country South Carolina a huge recreation industry centered upon the Santee-Cooper lakes sprang up.

With the completion of the Santee-Cooper Project the drainage of the "new" Cooper River increased from 1,200 square miles to over 15,000

square miles. The average flow from the river into Charleston harbor rose from about 72 cubic feet per second to about 15,600 cubic feet per second. Every day the additional fresh water flowed on top of salt water, carrying into the tidal estuary tons of fine, inorganic silt. The Cooper River estuary changed from a vertically mixed river to a salt-wedge stratified type, creating an ideal environment for the deposition and entrapment of sediments in the harbor, whose inner structure was now altered. Instead of being a wide natural harbor, Charleston harbor now resembled a river port with narrow channels dredged through shallow mud flats. Environmental change had taken place. The phenomenal increase in the rate of shoaling made frequent redredging necessary. The dredged material, spoil, had to be dumped in designated marshlands. The disposal areas

Charleston, South Carolina sits on a peninsula framed by the Ashley River (left) and Cooper River (center) which flow together with the Wando River (far right, above the bridge), to form Charleston Harbor. (U.S. Army Corps of Engineers photo.)

proved to be excellent habitats for the breeding of saltmarsh mosquitoes. The rising cost of harbor maintenance coupled with the health hazards made more engineering necessary.

Plans, proposals, and studies dealing with the problem occupied 25 years. At the core of the complex problem lay a simple fact: construction of the Santee-Cooper system had changed the natural environment in ways that affected Charleston harbor adversely. Thus the natural environment had to be restored. But the hydroelectric facilities had also brought into being a new industrial-residential-municipal-recreational-defense industry complex which sustained normal life. This social environment could not be disturbed. As the options narrowed educated opinion settled upon a plan to redivert the water flow to the Santee River. Construction of a canal and dam system to return the Cooper River to its natural state while preserving the recreational lakes and hydropower facilities began in 1977 (to be completed in June, 1984).

Today, in their upper stretches, flat bottom boats glide back and forth along the Ashley and Cooper rivers in ways as timeless as the cypress and oaks that shade them. Downstream, nearer Charleston harbor, the savannahs and marshlands surround new industries settled near old, preserved plantations. Charleston harbor is a cluster of facilities of a modern port and naval base. Container ships and nuclear submarines make their way amid fleets of pleasure craft, modern successors to the sailing ships of a bygone time, while tourist boats follow routes once traveled by pirate ships on their way to rendezvous with Charleston's traders. In the harbor, the waters of the Ashley and Cooper meet, mix, and flow with the ebb tide past Forts Sumter and Moultrie, the menace of their guns a source of interest to the tourists who visit the reconstructed monuments. Somehow, somewhere along the course of the Ashley and Cooper past and present have met.

FURTHER READING: Jamie W. Moore, *The Lowcountry Engineers, Military Missions and Economic Development in the Charleston District, U.S. Army Corps of Engineers* (Charleston, 1981).

Jamie W. Moore

The Catawba, Wateree, and Santee rivers

Source: Blue Ridge Mountains of North Carolina near Grandfather Mountain and Linville Gorge
Length: c. 395 miles
Tributaries: South Fork River; Congaree
Mouth: Into Atlantic Ocean south of Georgetown, South Carolina
Agricultural Products: Cotton, tobacco, lumber
Industries: Cotton textiles, furniture

The first "Mark Twain" was not Samuel Clemens, but Isaiah Sellars, who called Iredell County, North Carolina, his home. (Later, using the pseudonym, he did a column for the New Orleans *Picayune* from whence Clemens borrowed the name.) Had Mark Twain né Isaiah Sellars written of his native river, the Catawba-Wateree-Santee, he would have needed a geography and an intricate map to determine the configuration of the many streams of the system.

Waters spilling off the rocks on the southern slopes of Grandfather Mountain, highest point on the Blue Ridge, form the Linville River, a clear mountain stream that begins the system. After it spills over an eighty foot falls and splashes through Linville Gorge, its waters merge with a smaller mountain stream already named the Catawba.

The Catawba flows eastward for about sixty miles and then bends south before a large Piedmont ridge in Iredell County. The South Fork River, rising in the South Mountains to the west, swells the Catawba near Charlotte, North Carolina. The river remains known as the Catawba until it is about thirty miles into South Carolina.

Then it becomes the Wateree at the great falls of the river near Rock Hill. The Wateree, after passing Camden, joins the Congaree—a short river created by the merger of the Broad and Saluda rivers—and the combined waters become known as the Santee. It passes out of the sandhills region into the low country of cypress swamps and savannahs before entering the Atlantic south of Georgetown, South Carolina.

When the first whites explored the region they found a number of tribes who, it was later determined, spoke a language similar to that of the Siouan tribes who lived much further West. Some anthropologists believe the Catawbas, as they came to be called, originated in the Ohio Valley and crossed the Appalachians to their new habitat not too many centuries before the European discovery of America.

The earliest white explorers—Herdinand De Soto and Juan Pardo—found most of the tribes concentrated on the upper reaches of the river. Catawba tradition relates that their power declined after a series of wars in the early 1600s with their mountain neighbors, the Cherokee. By the time of white settlement, however, the Catawbans had settlements along most of the river system.

Actually, none of the tribes called themselves "Catawba." Early settlers called them by their own name, "Iswa" or "Esau." Relatives of the main groups of these Siouan peoples included the Waxhaws, the Congarees, the Santees, the Pee Dees, and the Cheraws, all of whom would lend their names to later geographical points in the Carolinas.

Neither did the Indians call the river by any of its present three names. To them the stream was "eswa-taroa," the river. John Lawson, an English explorer, in 1700 applied the Indian words "watera," meaning "to float on water," and "santa," meaning "to run": thus Wateree and Santee. Most authorities believe the word Catawba is derived from the Choctaw dialect, "katapa," meaning to divide, separate, or break. The earliest known use of the world is "Catamba" (rather than Catawba) on a French map in 1712.

The Catawbans concentrated in semipermanent towns along the river. Most lived in wooden and bark huts, and although farming was practiced, they depended largely upon hunting for subsistence. Early white settlers considered them fierce warriors, but their towns on the lower river declined after the Yamassee uprising in 1715–1716, although the Yamassees were Muskogean, not Siouan. War with the Cherokee and white diseases, particularly smallpox, also decimated the Siouan Catawbas until by 1763 the remnants were segregated on a tract near present Fort Mill, South Carolina, close to the North Carolina border. During the nineteenth century the Catawba reservation was reduced until only about one square mile and 100 Indians remained. In 1977 tribal officials sued the state of South Carolina for return of lands lost when old treaties were broken. A tentative, out-of-court financial settlement has been reached.

White settlement came first to the lower river area. French Huguenot families moved to the lower Santee about 1689. There the Marions, Moultries, Horrys, Hugers, and Laurenses established prosperous plantations in the cypress swamps. Black slaves imported from the West Indies worked the fields of rice and indigo. The planters' fortunes made them influential in the politics and society of Charlestown.

Other settlers reached the upper area of the Catawba by the 1740s. Most came from Pennsylvania and Maryland by the Great Wagon Road. At Salisbury on the Yadkin River, these Scotch-Irish and German families fanned westward over buffalo traces and Indian paths. George Davidson and John Oliphant had by the mid-1740s registered land claims on the east side of the Catawba. Adam Sherrill is said to have been the first white man to lead his family west across the Catawba, establishing a homestead in 1747 in what would become Catawba County. Before the Cherokee raids during the French and Indian War, settlement had reached Catawba headwaters. North Carolina colonial officials erected Fort Dobbs near present-day Statesville in 1760 to protect settlers from the Cherokee.

With the outbreak of the American Revolution most communities up and down the river formed new local governments supporting the Continentals. Elders of the Scotch Irish Community of Charlotte on the lower Catawba reputedly passed a series of resolves (known as the Mecklenburg County Resolves) in May, 1775, which condemned the acts of Parliament and had set a pattern of local sentiment for independence by the time Congress declared it in 1776.

In 1775 most of the Catawba area militia joined in an expedition to put down a Tory uprising in South Carolina. Many of the same men in 1776 invaded Cherokee lands in the mountains to eliminate the threat of Indian attack. A Santee planter, William Moultrie, commanded South Carolina forces which repelled the first British invasion at Fort Sullivan, on Sullivan's Island at the mouth of Charlestown harbor.

Civil war never entirely left the Carolina backcountry during the Revolution. Each side, in a spirit not quite as romantic and heroic as later portrayed by South Carolina author William Gilmore Simms, fought the other with vengeance. The Whigs finally ended Loyalist attacks with a victory at Ramseur's Mill near the South Fork of the Catawba in 1780.

Lord Cornwallis used the river basin as an invasion route in 1780 and 1781. He first destroyed a Continental army at Camden on the Wateree in 1780 and then headed for Charlotte to claim North Carolina. The steady resistance of the Catawba area militia caused Cornwallis to leave what he called a "hornet's nest." In October of 1780 Catawba area militia gathered at Quaker Meadows near the mouth of the Linville and on the South Fork joined with the Overmountain Men to destroy a part of the British army at Kings Mountain (October 7, 1780). Cornwallis returned to North Carolina in January, 1781, chasing the Continental army across the Catawba at Cowan's Ford and scattering the local militia.

When Cornwallis left South Carolina he retained there a chain of defensive outposts, but they were not much of a barrier against the forays of such Patriot leaders as Francis Marion, a Santee planter who led raiding parties out of the Santee swamps to play havoc with British troop movements, earning him the name "Swamp Fox." British domination of most of South Carolina ended with the Battle of Eutaw Springs on the Santee in 1781.

The area around Eutaw Springs became the center of South Carolina's cotton plantation system in the nineteenth century. French Hu-

guenots, after frequent flooding caused by upstream settlement ruined their rice fields, moved to the English Santee area whereupon much of the lower Santee returned to swamp and wilderness.

Fewer plantations were found along the Catawba. Poor transportation both by road and river hindered the development of the Carolina backcountry in the antebellum period. All legislative efforts to make the Catawba navigable fell short of success. Farmers generally practiced subsistence planting, growing all they needed. Many, like future presidents Andrew Jackson and James Knox Polk, sought better prosperity in the West. Some of the most prosperous planters established cotton mills to stem outmigration. The Long Island and Granite Shoals mills in North Carolina began operation in the 1850s and continued to operate for the next 100 years. The railroad reached the area in the 1850s and led to greater development.

Except for the burning of Columbia, South Carolina, by General Sherman and the Union Army, the Civil War had little military effect on the river basin. More important was the postwar economic impact. Many of the plantations of the lower Santee were broken up into tenant farms, and the area lost much of its antebellum prominence. Upriver the small farmers fell into overdependence on cotton as a cash crop and often lost their land. Many tenants and debtors joined the migration to the many cotton mills opening on the streams that feed the Catawba and Wateree. Spartanburg and Greenville in upper South Carolina dominated the area's industrial growth. Rock Hill quadrupled its size by building cotton mills. Columbia became one of the south's largest mill communities.

Before 1900 textile manufacturing centers on the upper Catawba lingered behind other South Carolina towns. After 1900 many communities such as Hickory and Morgantown prospered with the establishment of furniture factories. The foothills area also gained a steadily increasing tourist trade in the late Victorian period. Many hotels offered cures for various ailments at springs in the Thermal Belt south of the Catawba.

The prosperity of a tobacco magnate, James Buchanan Duke, led to the many dams and lakes which altered the Catawba's course. Duke, who had invested much of his wealth in the cotton mills of the Piedmont, became convinced after 1900 that hydroelectricity offered the best source of power for the mills. His Southern Power Company began a comprehensive program to dam the Catawba in 1903. The first dam, "Old Catawba Station," provided power to its first customer, the Victorian Cotton Mill, in 1904.

Southern Power had hardly begun additional dams when in July, 1916, rains from two hurricanes dumped as much as nineteen inches in a twenty-four-hour period in the mountains, turning the Catawba tributaries into raging torrents. Flood waters smashed bridges, engulfed homes, and endangered riverside towns. At least eighty persons lost their lives.

The Southern Power Company replaced the foundations of Lookout Shoals dam, lost in the flood, and in the next decade constructed ten more hydroelectric dams creating lakes along 217 miles of the Catawba. Duke Power, successor to Southern Power, pioneered the engineering of the comprehensive transmission high-voltage power to a regional network. By the 1960s Duke Power had put to use more than 85 percent of the river fall of the Catawba. One plant, Marshall Steam Station of Mooresville, North Carolina, has been rated the most efficient steam power plant in the United States.

Hydroelectric development also altered the lower Santee. In 1939 Lake Marion and Lake Moultrie were constructed on the sites of the old antebellum cotton plantations. Lake Marion, covering 100,000 acres, is the largest manmade body of water in the eastern United States. A canal, patterned after the 1786 idea, leads from Lake Moultrie to the Cooper River.

Recreational lakes ended much of the lifestyle of old time river folk along the Catawba which, as "the most electrified river in the United States," consists mostly of lakes and memories. It nevertheless serves those near it in comprehensive ways just as it did the first settlers on the Santee swamps and the Piedmont foothills long ago.

FURTHER READING: Douglas Sumner Brown, *The Catawba Indians* (1966). Henry Savage, Jr., *River of the Carolinas: The Santee* (1956).

Gary Freeze

The Congaree River

Source: Formed by merger of Broad and Saluda rivers at Columbia, South Carolina
Length: 62 miles
Tributaries: None of consequence
Mouth: Joins Wateree River to form Santee River in Lake Marion southeast of Columbia, South Carolina
Agricultural Products: None of significance
Industries: Lumbering, fishing, recreation

The Congaree River flows for 62 miles through the center of South Carolina from the confluence of the Broad and Saluda Rivers at the state capitol, Columbia, to its confluence with the Wateree River forming the Santee River in the headwaters of Lake Marion. The name "Congaree" is thought to have been an early Indian word for the "Scraping Place" referring to the rocky outcrops at Columbia on the Fall Line. The drainage area feeding the Congaree comprises 7,850 square miles (20,330 square kilometers) covering most of the upper part of South Carolina. Both of the major tributaries, the Broad and Saluda rivers, are controlled and produce an average discharge of 9,333 cubic feet per second (264 cubic meters per second) at the head of the Congaree. The maximum discharge recorded before the period of record was established was 364,000 cubic feet per second (10,300 cubic meters per second) in 1908.

Once the Congaree leaves the rock outcroppings at Columbia, it enters a gently curving course through an alluvial floodplain bordered by a section of extensively cultivated land. At the Lexington/Calhoun county line ten miles below its start, it begins to enter the Congaree Forest. For the next fifty-two miles, the Congaree curls and winds through a dense river floodplain averaging three miles in width. The present course of the river lies close to the southern edge of the plain on the Calhoun County side. This southern boundary is characterized by a series of massive bluffs rising 100 to 200 feet above the river. These bluffs are believed to have been inhabited by various groups of Indians (enjoying the rich resources available in the bottomlands) for as long as 10,000 years. Buyck's Bluff, approximately halfway along the course of the river, has been nominated for the National Register of Historic Places due to the significance and richness of its Indian artifacts.

The soil of the cutoff islands and deposition banks along the Congaree has attracted farmers from pre-historic times to the eighteenth century. The fields, some of which have been in continuous cultivation for over 100 years, produce outstanding yields without fertilizer and are still in use despite the difficulties of getting agricultural equipment to them.

The most significant feature of the Congaree floodplain is a 12,000 acre expanse of river forest on the north, or Richland County side of the river. The Congaree, though changing its channel continuously, has remained close to the southern edge for at least the last 500 years. This factor, plus the periodic flooding of the whole plain, has produced some of the most spectacular stands of large trees in the eastern United States. The predominant species are oaks and gums with trees three to four feet in diameter frequently encountered. A number of the trees are listed as being National Champions, such as: Possumhaw (Ilex decidua), Swamp Privet (Forestiera acuminata), Sugarberry (Celtis laevigata), Swamp Cottonwood (Populus heterophylla), Butternut Hickory (Carya cordiformis), and Sweetgum (Hiquidambar styraciflua).

Because of the diversity, health, and size of the trees in the forest, the National Park Service is purchasing large tracts for inclusion in the Congaree National Monument on the Richland County side. The South Carolina Water Resources Commission is in the process of trying to preserve the quality of the southern bank of the river through the State Scenic River program. Development pressure from the Columbia Metropolitan Area and the activities of major forest products corporations make the Congaree a subject of critical concern for the preservation of this last great river floodplain forest in South Carolina.

The Congaree provides the citizens of South Carolina with a good fishing resource. Thirty- to forty-pound catfish are regularly caught and the spawning run of rockfish is a major yearly event. While not suitable for most pleasure boating due to numerous sand banks and the loopings of the channel, the Congaree is and will continue to be an exciting river for float trips. Access to the river for the public is rather limited, with one boat ramp at Cayce on the south side across from Columbia and a boat ramp at the Highway 601 bridge near the confluence with the Wateree River. While private ramps are available, the access limitations tend to restrict the use of the river.

Historically, the Congaree was a major source for bulk transport of agricultural products to the coast. Steamboats plied the river until the railroads drove them out of business. The last major use of the river for transport was during the construction of the Santee-Cooper Project on Lakes Marion and Moultrie when granite blocks were floated down the Congaree from up-state quarries on wooden flats. These flats were left in the river and constitute, if not a hazard to navigation, at least a link to the river's past.

In colonial times the Congaree River Forest presented a major obstacle to communication and this in turn may have contributed to its preservation with major activities routed around and away from it. During the revolution, the two major crossing points on the Congaree came to be the focus of some military activity. Granby, a now defunct village on the south shore across from present day Columbia, was a major convoy stop on the route to the up country. Ft. Motte, a fortified mansion on a bluff overlooking the other crossing at McCords Ferry near the confluence with the Wateree, earned a small but unique place in the history of the War for Independence.

The mansion was built by Thomas Motte, a wealthy landowner, on a high ridge overlooking the river. Motte was killed at the siege of Savannah, Georgia, in 1779, and when the Crown's forces overran South Carolina in 1780, his house was taken and fortified by the British. Mrs. Motte was removed to an outlying building to make room for the British garrison. In May of 1781, Francis Marion and "Light Horse" Harry Lee besieged the Fort. Unable to take it by assault, they were faced with a lengthy siege they could ill afford. Mrs. Motte, rising to the occasion, produced a set of East Indian fire arrows given to her husband by a sea captain. The arrows were fired from muskets at the roof of the mansion and the British efforts to extinguish the flames were met with an intense fusillade preventing them from getting to the roof. The British commander thereupon surrendered and the patriot forces assisted the British in putting out the flames. Mrs. Motte's willingness to sacrifice her own home for the cause of liberty is an outstanding tribute to her courage and determination.

FURTHER READING: Edward C. L. Adams, *Congaree Sketches* (1927).

George S. Saussy III

The Connecticut River

Source: The Connecticut Lakes in extreme northern New Hampshire
Length: 345 miles
Tributaries: Passumpsic, White, Deerfield, Farmington, Ammonoosuc, and Chicopee rivers
Mouth: At Old Saybrook, Connecticut, into Long Island Sound
Agricultural Products: Shade tobacco, poultry, dairying
Industries: Machine tools, diversified manufacturing

The Connecticut River, the longest stream in New England, starts its 345-mile journey to the Atlantic from the Connecticut Lakes in extreme northern New Hampshire. It flows south, forming the border between Vermont and New Hampshire. The right tributaries (those entering from the west) are the Passumpsic, White, Deerfield, and Farmington rivers; its left tributaries are the Ammonoosuc and Chicopee rivers. As it journeys toward the Atlantic, the Connecticut River flows across Massachusetts and Connecticut to its mouth at Old Saybrook on Long Island Sound.

The Connecticut is the only major river in the United States without a city at its mouth. An obstructing sandbar has allowed only the towns of Old Saybrook and Old Lyme to develop. Old Saybrook, founded in 1635 by English colonists, was named for Lord Say and Lord Brooke, the Plymouth Company's proprietors. The major cities located on the river are Hartford, Connecticut; Springfield, Massachusetts; and Brattleboro, Vermont.

The first European to view the Connecticut was Adrian Block, a Dutch fur trader, explorer, and ship captain. In 1614 aboard his ship, the *Restless*, he explored Long Island Sound and sailed upriver as far as Enfield Falls. He named this newly discovered ribbon of water "De Versche Riviere"—"Freshwater River." Prior to this, the local Indians had called the river "Quoneklacut," "Quonehtacet," or "Ouinnituket," which means "long river" or "the river without end." The Pequot Indians inhabited the lands along Long Island Sound. Block and his countrymen later established trade with other nearby tribes: the Niantic, Podunk, Poqunock, Mohegan, Massacoe, and others.

Captain Block explored most of the river which today lies in the state of Connecticut, but he was destined to see it never again. Back in Holland, his enthusiastic report caused Amsterdam merchants to form the Amsterdam Trading Company which was given a three-year monopoly to trade in the area, dubbed "New Netherland." Subsequently they built a palisaded post called the "House of Hope" and a stronger fort near present Hartford.

Pilgrims from Plymouth were the first Englishmen to exploit the rich potential of the Connecticut River region. In 1631 Edward Winslow and an English crew sailed into the river, exploring it for possible future colonization. Winslow was later credited with discovering the river due to this voyage. In 1633 colonists from Plymouth built a trading post near present Windsor, Connecticut, successfully defying Dutch threats. Subsequently an Englishman, John Oldham, established a trading post near present Wethersfield and returned a year later with colonists from Watertown, Massachusetts.

In England certain lords and gentlemen had received a grant of territory from Point Judith on the Atlantic coast of southern Rhode Island, southward to New York and west to the Pacific, a territory that included Connecticut and a section of Massachusetts. The "Old Patent of Connecticut" was bestowed upon a syndicate that included among its members Lord Say and Sele, John Pym, Sir Richard Saltonstall, and John Hampden. John Winthrop, son of Massachusetts's governor, established another colony at the mouth of the Connecticut River. He named it Saybrook after Lord Say and Sele and Lord Brooke. Also in 1635 a group of colonists led by Roger Ludlow joined the established settlement at Windsor. In 1636 Thomas Hooker brought colonists from Newtown (present Cambridge, Massachusetts) into Connecticut, establishing a settlement at Hartford. Through this steady infiltration the English colonists soon came to outnumber the Dutch.

Throughout its history the Connecticut River has been navigated by everything from canoes to steamboats. The river was an important highway in colonial times, and although its navigational use was at first confined to sixty miles from its mouth, the development of the flatboat by English colonists extended travel upriver to Springfield, Massachusetts. These flatboats were equipped with a mainsail set in the middle, and a topsail which could only be used before the wind. When the breeze failed, flatboats were propelled by poles twelve to twenty feet long.

The first colonist to utilize the river's trade potential was William Pynchon, who established a trading business in 1636. Pynchon had exclusive privileges, granted by the standing council of Massachusetts Bay, to trade with the

Indians. Another industry, shipbuilding, was encouraged from the very start of the Connecticut settlements, and by the 1650s ships built in Connecticut were sailing far from the river. To facilitate the development of upriver settlements in New Hampshire, and new trading posts, the system of river transportation by flatboats and shore teams around the various falls was extended northward by the end of colonial times. Because there were no bridges across the Connecticut until after the Revolutionary War, ferries were used to facilitate passenger transportation across the stream.

Initially the Indian tribes along the Connecticut were friendly to the colonists but friction soon developed. The Pequots spoke an Algonquian language and lived in communal longhouses in the upper Connecticut Valley. They lived by hunting and growing small vegetable gardens. Trouble with the colonists over alleged massacres led to the Pequot War of 1637. Colonists formed an alliance with the Mohegans and defeated the Pequots. Most of the tribe was killed. Those who survived merged with the neighboring tribes. They were mistreated, however, and eventually resettled with the aid of the colonists along the Mystic River.

Throughout the seventeenth century Indian tribes in the Connecticut River valley, often spurred on by the French, clashed with white settlers. In 1675 the northern settlement of Deerfield, Massachusetts, was attacked by sixty Indians but its inhabitants successfully drove off the invaders. Shortly after members of the Nipmuck tribe attacked Northfield, forcing the settlers to seek refuge in a blockhouse where they were besieged for a week before the militia arrived from downriver and lifted the siege. Northfield was soon abandoned and Deerfield became the northernmost outpost on the Connecticut River. From Hadley the militia was sent back to harvest Northfield's crops. They were ambushed and nearly annihilated near a stream which, reddened by the militiamen's corpses, was given the name of "Bloody Brook." Soon after this massacre Deerfield was abandoned due to another Indian attack, and in the winter of 1675 Springfield, Massachusetts was burned by the Indians as its settlers looked on from Major Pynchon's barricaded warehouse.

To avenge themselves against the tribes, representatives from the river settlements met in December, 1675, to plan a military campaign. The result was the Great Swamp fight, one of the bloodiest battles fought in New England between the red man and the white man. The tribe targeted for this military attack was the Narragansett, who inhabited a large blockhouse in the swampy regions of lower Rhode Island. In December, 1675, a strong colonial militia surprised them, slaughtered over a thousand Narragansett, and seized their winter corn supply. The Great Swamp Fight broke the red man's power in the Connecticut River valley though for the next fifty years occasional skirmishes occurred between Indians and settlers.

For example, Deerfield, which had been reoccupied, was attacked in 1704 by Indians from Canada. Fifty settlers were killed and 116 taken captive. Only the toughest of them survived the long trek to Canada. In 1725 the Indians and the English signed a treaty in Boston that brought twenty years of peace to the Connecticut Valley. Until 1763 sporadic clashes with the Indians occurred, however, but with the signing of the Peace of Paris, French influence in the New World, and over the Indians, ended.

Soon after the end of the American Revolution, plans for improving the navigability of the Connecticut River were formulated by men seeking to establish a series of canals around the principal falls. A rivalry between Massachusetts' seaports and the lower river towns of Springfield and Hartford helped stimulate interest in the new enterprise. Creation of the South Hadley Canal proved a costly venture. This canal extended for two and a half miles along the Connecticut and entered it above a wing dam which projected outward. South Hadley Canal was completed in 1795 and the Turner's Falls Canal in 1800. The Bellows Canal, a short one with eight locks, was opened in 1802. Two smaller canals were dug along the Connecticut but did not open until 1810.

The construction of a canal system helped make the Connecticut a popular transportation artery. In 1825 a meeting of 200 delegates from the river towns resulted in a petition to Congress for help in financing upriver canal plans. At the same time Massachusetts was promoting a canal to connect Boston harbor with the Connecticut and Hudson rivers. New Haven also planned

a canal from tidewater to Northampton in order to share in the wealth of the lower river towns. The Enfield Canal was completed in 1829 with the first steamboats on the river commemorating the event, but none of the other plans reached completion. When Vermont granted its first railroad charter in 1840, the death knell was sounded for the Connecticut River canal system.

Popular history has awarded Robert Fulton the honor of developing the first steamboat. A closer examination of the historical records will reveal that two Connecticut River men, John Fitch and Samuel Morey, developed steamboats before Fulton. Fitch was the first in America to have exhibited a steamboat with movable paddles, and Morey is credited with creating the mechanism Fulton later used in the *Clermont*. The steamboat services which developed along the Connecticut River were doomed like the canals after the advent of the railroads, but one can still enjoy steamboat travel below Hartford.

Throughout its recorded history the Connecticut River has been transformed occasionally from a beautiful ribbon of water into an enraged force of nature. The first recorded flood occurred in 1635. Another in 1815 wrecked lands and houses and cost many lives. A flood in 1840 cut Hadley in two, and later a protective rampart was erected around the town's most exposed sections. The devastating flood of 1927 was caused by abnormal amounts of rainfall; it resulted in the deaths of twenty-five people. A 1936 flood which occurred in two separate weeks of March caused eleven deaths. After this flood the public clamored for flood control dams and other measures which were taken by the Army Engineers.

Nor has the valley been spared from fierce Atlantic hurricanes. In 1938 a storm born in the West Indies caused extensive damage. In 1954 and 1955 severe hurricanes lashed the Connecticut River valley again, and the floods of 1955 resulted in Connecticut being declared a disaster area. More than 100 persons died and damage was estimated at $200 million.

The Connecticut River valley has witnessed great industrial development throughout its long history. In 1781 Eli Whitney, the inventor of the cotton gin, acquired a government contract to make muskets. His plant in New Haven produced thousands of these military items. Simeon North also began to produce pistols using mass production of interchangeable parts in that year. In 1788 the first woolen mills in New England were built at Hartford. Later, in 1848, Samuel Colt opened a factory in Hartford for the production of the famous Colt revolver.

The National Hydraulic Company began to manufacture rotary pumps in 1829. In Vermont the city of Springfield gradually became the industrial center of the northern Connecticut River area and also an important tool manufacturing center. The development of canals,

steamboats, and railroads all helped make the Connecticut River valley states become heavily industrialized by the end of the nineteenth century. The river remains an important source of water power, especially for Hartford, Connecticut, and Springfield and Chicopee, Massachusetts. Adrian Block's "Freshwater River" continues to provide power for industry and pleasure for the millions who take the time to enjoy it.

FURTHER READING: Edwin M. Bacon, *The Connecticut River and the Valley of the Connecticut* (1906). Walter Hard, *The Connecticut* (1947).

Kathy J. Nelson

The Delaware River

Length: 390 miles
Tributaries: Neversink; Lehigh; Schuylkill
Mouth: Head of Delaware Bay (Liston Point)
Agricultural Products: Truck gardening
Industries: Electronics, chemicals, food processing— the Delaware Valley is one of the most industrialized river valleys in the world.

The Delaware River is formed by the coalescing of two headwater streams, the East Branch and the West Branch, at Hancock, in southern New York. The river then flows southeast to Port Jervis, in southeastern New York, and then south, forming boundaries between Pennsylvania and New York, Pennsylvania and New Jersey, and Delaware and New Jersey, before it enters Delaware Bay. It is navigable as far upriver as Trenton, New Jersey, and for many miles before entering the Bay the river is at places three miles wide.

It seems strange that this important river should be so little known. No literary genius has written of its placid waters, no ditties of its rivermen have gained widespread popularity, no terrible catastrophes have marred its course through history. Yet it serves parts of heavily populated New York, New Jersey, Delaware, and Pennsylvania. So subject is the Delaware River region to such internal improvements as

freeways, railroads, canals, airports, factories, and cities, that few people even know its geography.

Some of the oldest fossil-bearing rock in the world is found along the Delaware. In more recent geologic times ice caps advanced southward to within sixty miles of Trenton. They left a deposit of fine sand which, when mixed with clay and organic matter, created a rich soil, the basis of the extensive agriculture practiced in the Delaware Basin. Traces of the saber-toothed tiger, wooly mammoth, and ground sloth have been found along with paleolithic and pre-Indian occupation.

At the time of white arrival the region was inhabited by the Lenni-Lanapes, an Iroquoian tribe that came to be known as the Delaware. They were a sedentary, rather peaceful people, hunting deer, bear, turkeys, and pigeons, and taking shad, sturgeon, and oysters from the river. They raised corn, squash, beans, pumpkins, and sweet potatoes in abundance. Their homes were wattled huts of corn husks and bark and their villages were protected by palisades.

To early explorers such as Henry Hudson, who explored the mouth of the Delaware in August, 1609, or Lord De La Warr, the governor of Jamestown who visited the Bay in 1610 and gave it, and the river, his name, the Delaware was a lovely stream flowing through a bounteous Eden. Even today, in spite of the industrialization along its banks, some of that primeval beauty can still be observed.

The upper half of the Delaware flows through the Atlantic Highlands. On clear days the soft blues of the Catskills entice the eyes up and away from the river. The thirty-nine-mile span from Hancock to Sparrow Bush is so scenic that it has recently been placed under the protection of the Federal Wild and Scenic Rivers Act. The most famous attraction along the upper Delaware, however, is the Delaware Water Gap, now a National Recreational Area. It is in extreme northwestern New Jersey where the river retained its channel even though the Kittatinny Mountain Ridge rose athwart it in past geologic time. The lower half of the river flows through a coastal plain that in earlier times was heavily timbered. Low ridges separate the fertile valleys of tributary streams: the Neversink, which flows in at Port Jervis; the Lehigh, which comes in from the west at Eason, Pennsylvania; and the Schuylkill, joining the Delaware at Philadelphia.

From 1623, when Cornelis Jacobsen May established Fort Nassau on the east bank near present Gloucester, New Jersey, until 1664 when the British took their settlements, the Dutch were along the Delaware. The settlers were Protestants, many of them Belgian Walloons or German Moravians. They did not enjoy great success, and some were massacred by Indians.

Swedes also settled along the river. Their settlements dated from 1638 when Peter Minuit, though a Dutchman, set up Fort Christina, at the present site of Wilmington, with Swedish Protestants. The Swedes constructed log cabins, thus setting style for the dwellings that American pioneers would use all the way across the continent. In 1655 the Dutch forcibly took over the Swedish settlements.

When the British occupied the villages the Duke of York, who had the title, gave the region to two men, Sir George Cartaret and Lord Berkeley. Cartaret, whose old world home had been on the Island of Jersey, named his new possession New Jersey. Berkeley sold out, one of the purchasers being William Penn. New Jersey was split into East Jersey, which Cartaret retained, and West Jersey, which began to be settled by

Quakers. The New Jersey towns of Burlington and Salem were founded.

Meanwhile, William Penn had heard of the beauties of the Delaware country. In payment of a debt of £16,000, King Charles in 1681 granted Penn what became the present state of Pennsylvania. Penn was still not satisfied. The Duke of York still held the three lower counties on the west side of the Delaware. From them he could, if he so chose, tax shipping to and from Penn's upriver colony. Somehow Penn prevailed upon the Duke to give the counties to him. This was done, beginning "at a point on a circle twelve miles north of New Castle"—and to this day Delaware's northern boundary is a half circle above Newcastle. The people of these counties were fretful that their rights would be infringed upon by Pennsylvania, so in 1704 Penn gave the people of these lands home rule with their own Assembly, although Penn remained their Governor. Thus did Delaware come into being.

With fertile land easily obtainable in a salubrious climate, freedom of worship, mild taxation, and a humanitarian proprietor, it is little wonder that, at a time of religious intolerance in Europe, refugees flocked to Pennsylvania. From the holds of hundreds of ships, often sickly and more dead than alive, came the first of tens of thousands of immigrants into the Delaware region. Even before the year 1682 closed, twenty-three shiploads had arrived and probably 3,500 people were living in the Delaware Valley. They were Welsh, English, Finns, Swedes, and French Huguenots. A generation or two later two other groups, Germans (who came to be called Pennsylvania Dutch) and the Scotch-Irish, flocked to the ports in the Delaware region. After the American Revolution still other peoples sought a new, free, and more abundant life along the Delaware: Irish, Jews, Italians, blacks from the Southern states, all of whom added to the richness of the region's culture.

The Delaware Valley was the scene of many decisive events during the Revolutionary War and the Federalist periods (1776–1800). At Philadelphia the First and Second Continental Congresses met, the Declaration of Independence was signed, and the Constitutional Convention was held. The Valley suffered through more warfare than any other region. Battles were fought at Trenton, Princeton, Brandywine, Germantown, and Monmouth, while Washington's winter camp at Valley Forge became a symbol of American tenacity, suffering, and patriotism.

When most Americans think of the Delaware they conjure up the image of Washington standing in the bow of an open boat, leading his men through the sleet of a winter night to the British side. This is due partly to the many reproductions of the German artist Emanuel Leutze's painting of "Washington Crossing the Delaware," and partly to the victory which is of significance to the outcome of the war.

Washington had retreated across New Jersey before the onslaught of forces under Sir William Howe and Lord Cornwallis. By December, 1776, Washington had 6,000 troops in very poor condition on the west bank of the Delaware. Even the persuasiveness of Thomas Paine's pamphlet, "The Crisis," failed to convince many soldiers that they should remain loyal to the cause. Something had to be done.

Washington decided upon a surprise attack. Between midnight and 3:00 A.M., December 25, 1776, his army of 2,400 crossed the ice-filled river, marched in two separate columns to Trenton, captured over 800, most of whom were Hessian mercenaries, and many guns, cannon, and supplies. No Americans were killed, morale was restored, and faith in Washington's abilities was revived.

During 1777–1778 the Delaware Valley was the scene of much of the war's military activity. Then the theater of war changed to other sections of the thirteen states. Yet the people of the Delaware Valley retained keen interest in events. Robert Morris and Haym Solomon of Philadelphia continued to help finance the war. On October 24, 1781, Tench Tilghman clattered into Philadelphia with news of the victory at Yorktown. He had ridden more than 400 miles in five days to convey the news of the surrender.

The Delaware Valley adjusted rapidly to peace-time living. Peopled with industrious folk from many lands, the region invited ingenuity, speculation, and experiment, John Fitch launched his steam-propelled vessels on the Delaware. In July, 1788, he began scheduled runs between Philadelphia and Burlington, New Jersey. The American Philosophical Society served as a meeting place and publishing house for an increasingly prestigious scientific community.

Robert Fulton's shipyards, Baldwin's locomotive works, and John Robeling's wire works attested to the rapid growth of industry. Woolen and cotton textile industries expanded, aided by Oliver Evans' inventions. Du Pont's powder works expanded rapidly. John Ross's seamstress wife Betsy at least received credit for designing the American flag. Yet all this industrial activity was not without cost, and during the nineteenth century pollution killed off most of the shad, perch, herring, and sturgeon in the Delaware River.

People along the Delaware have always approached their river pragmatically, with a view to its usefulness. It was linked by canals with the Raritan in 1834 (now abandoned), the Hudson in 1828 (now abandoned), and with Chesapeake Bay by a short canal that is still in operation. Better than 22 million people, about one-tenth the population of the United States, live within reach of its waters.

The four Delaware Basin states (New York, New Jersey, Delaware, and Pennsylvania) have been competing for the water for over fifty years. New York City draws about a third of its water from Delaware headwaters, Philadelphia relies on the river for half its supply, while Trenton, New Brunswick, and other New Jersey cities consume another 100 million gallons a day. In 1936, by legislation in each of the four states, the Interstate Commission on the Delaware Basin (INCODEL) was created. Although it did have some success in preventing communities from dumping untreated sewage into the river, it failed at about every other undertaking. Industries continued to pollute the river. Then in 1961, in spite of incredible obstacles, the Delaware Basin Commission came into being. It included representatives of the four states plus the federal government.

It was not operational a moment too soon. In August, 1961, a drought set in which lasted forty-six months (until June, 1965) in which period the region lost the equivalent of a full year's normal rainfall. It was the worst drought since 1820, one so bad that meteorologists estimated a recurrence of the same magnitude would not happen for another 100 to 200 years.

New York City, faced with a water crisis, halted the flow of some water into the Delaware, thus threatening the water supplies of Trenton,

Philadelphia, and other cities. These cities protested. Even as discussions and recriminations were going on, the rain finally came and the drought was ended.

In a Supreme Court case involving the Delaware decided in 1931, Justice Oliver Wendell Holmes stated that "a river is more than an amenity, it is a treasure. It offers a necessity of life that must be rationed among those who have the power over it."

Once, the Delaware was an amenity, a pleasant attraction, and it still is in its upper reaches. There its waters run placidly through gentle farm and dairyland. But from Trenton down to the sea, 75 percent as much tonnage passes as the entire Mississippi carries over a 2,000-mile course. Along the Delaware's banks are smelters, warehouses, oil tank farms, chemical plants, food processors, and electronics firms, all to serve a busy world. In serving them the Delaware is not romantic, nor pure, nor clean, nor pretty, nor even appreciated: it is *used*.

FURTHER READING: John Palmer Garber, *The Valley of the Delaware and Its Place in American History* (1934; 1969). Harry Emerson Wildes, *The Delaware* (1940).

Richard A. Bartlett

The Hackensack River

Source: Rises in Rockland County, New York
Length: c. 35 miles
Tributaries: None of major importance
Mouth: Flows into Newark Bay west of Jersey City
Agricultural Products: Truck vegetables
Industries: Diverse manufacturing, oil depots, public utilities

The Hackensack rises near Haversack in Rockland County, New York, and flows in a generally southerly direction before emptying into Newark Bay, thirty-five miles distant. The river drains an area of 202 square miles, sixty-four of which are in New York and the remainder in New Jersey. It is navigable to New Milford, twenty miles from its mouth. Above this point the river flows through gently rolling terrain rising gradually to the north.

The lower portion of the Hackensack Valley is occupied by a glacially created tidal marsh and meadowland roughly ten miles long and four miles wide, with about one mile of higher land on the eastern and western borders of the meadows. The 19,846 acres of the meadows are only a few inches above sea level at high tide.

In its upper reaches the river's maximum elevation is 400 feet and drops to zero in the meadows of the lower valley. A traprock ridge forms the eastern and northern boundary of the watershed. Throughout most of its length the drainage area extends to within one half mile of the Hudson River on the east. To the west, a traprock ledge separates the drainage areas of the lower Hackensack and Passaic Rivers.

Rockland Lake in Palisades Interstate Park is the only natural lake of substantial size in the Hackensack watershed. There are, however, four large reservoirs of the Hackensack Water Company, namely, Lake De Forest near Congers, New York, Lake Tappan at River Vale, Woodcliff Lake at Park Ridge, and the Oradell Reservoir, all in New Jersey. These provide much of the potable water supplies for fifty-nine New Jersey and New York communities.

Before the arrival of white settlers, the Hackensack Valley was inhabited by two sub-tribes of the Lenni Lenapes. In the lower valley the Achkinheshacky (Hackensacks) controlled much of the land between the Hudson River and the First Mountain range to the west. To the north, and extending into New York, was the territory of the Tappans, who had their main village at the present site of Tappan.

The most important villages of the Hackensacks were located at Communipaw and along Overpeck Creek near today's Ridgefield Park. The latter was the center of tribal activities, where provisions were cultivated and stored, wampum was made, and tribal ceremonies took place. Oratam, a Sachem, or Chief, was a notable leader of the Hackensacks during the period of white settlement in the seventeenth century: many sales of land to the Dutch and English were transacted under his jurisdiction.

The Hackensacks and Tappans were generally friendly and peaceful in relations with the early settlers. When provoked by aggressive white actions, however, they resisted strongly and once destroyed all the early Dutch settlements in New Jersey.

Colonization of the Hackensack Valley grew out of Dutch occupancy of Manhattan and the efforts of the West India Company to establish patroonships in New Jersey and elsewhere. It began on November 22, 1630, when Michael Pauw, a patroon, obtained an Indian deed for lands along the western shore of the Hudson River extending from Communipaw north to Hoboken and inland to the Hackensack River. Pauw named the tract Pavonia, in recognition of his patroonship, and arranged for settlers from Holland to build homes and lay out farms.

Indian troubles precipitated by William Kieft, then Director General of New Netherland, who in 1639 demanded tribute from the natives, caused serious friction. This increased and, on the night of February 25, 1643, led to the slaughter of more than eighty Indians seeking the protection of the Dutch at Pavonia. This brutal affair, now identified historically as the Pavonia

Hackensack River, showing development in the meadowlands along the banks of the river. New Hilton Hotel complex in the background. (Photo by N. F. Brydon.)

Massacre, resulted in bitter Indian retaliation. By the end of August, 1643, they had completely wiped out all traces of Dutch settlements in Pavonia and killed most of its inhabitants. A final peace was not negotiated until August, 1645, after which the Dutch gradually returned to the devastated area.

Colonization of lands along the Hackensack then expanded rapidly. The important town of Bergen was settled in the early 1650s and, in 1664 became the capital of New Jersey for a brief period. In that year, under a treaty of peace between England and Holland, the English were ceded possession of all of New Netherland. Grants then made to English claimants led to colonization of lands between the Hackensack and Passaic rivers. English, German, Scottish and others made homes along the Hackensack with the predominant Dutch. Among the newcomers was a group of Huguenots under David des Marest who in 1676 established a colony north of Hackensack.

The fertile Hackensack Valley by the mid-1700s was occupied by prosperous farmers who conducted a thriving trade with villages along the river as well as with Manhattan, Bergen, and other towns. The forests disappeared as the lands were cleared. Timber for fuel and building purposes became an important item of trade.

Roads were constructed across the meadows, with ferries for river crossings, opening up trade to Newark and the west. The New Bridge near Hackensack provided a link with Bergen and the Hudson River ferries to Manhattan. A wooden drawbridge across the lower river was completed in 1795 as part of a new road between the Hudson River and New Jersey.

During the Revolution residents of the Hackensack Valley had sharply divided loyalties. Most of the leading citizens supported rebellion and desired independence, but many remained loyal to England. This division caused bitterness and resulted in many acts of violence by both loyalists and patriots throughout the conflict.

The war came to the Hackensack Valley following the defeats of American armies on Long Island and Manhattan late in 1776. In November its defenders abandoned Fort Lee on the New Jersey side of the Hudson after a strong British force made a surprise landing at Closter and moved on the fort. The garrison joined the ragged Continental troops encamped on the green in Hackensack. Two days later, Washington, seeing that his position was indefensible, began the historic retreat to the Passaic and down that river to Newark, and across New Jersey to the Delaware. The British waited two days before beginning an unsuccessful pursuit.

With the British in control of northeastern New Jersey, there began a period of looting and destruction of properties of known supporters of the rebellion. In retaliation, an American force under General Heath raided Hackensack on December 15, 1776, and captured prisoners and much needed supplies. This was but one of a series of similar actions by both sides, which caused much suffering to inhabitants of the valley throughout the war.

In September, 1777, Sir Henry Clinton with 5,000 regular and irregular troops, made a major advance into the upper Hackensack Valley, confiscating large numbers of cattle, sheep, grains and other supplies before withdrawing to Manhattan. A somewhat similar sortie occurred in September, 1778, when Lord Cornwallis, with several thousand troops, landed at Paulus Hook and moved north. Out of this came one of the war's most gruesome episodes: 150 American men and officers under Colonel Baylor, who were bivouacked on a farm near Old Tappan, were surprised in a night attack by British troops under General Gage. Many were ruthlessly killed and the remainder captured.

A successful raid heartened the Americans. In the early morning of August 19, 1779, Major Henry (Light Horse Harry) Lee with some 500 men captured almost the entire British garrison at Paulus Hook in a surprise attack, Lee succeeded, with much difficulty, in marching the prisoners back to the American lines. In another action, General Anthony Wayne, with a large force and artillery, set off on July 21, 1780, to capture a blockhouse manned by refugees near Bull's Ferry on the Hudson. Despite the Americans' great numerical superiority, the blockhouse was successfully defended. Wayne, much chagrined, withdrew with some captured cattle as his only reward.

For the remainder of the war the Hackensack Valley was generally under control of the British stationed on Manhattan. Raids and counter-raids continued. General Benedict Arnold's desertion to the British and British Major John Andre's trial and execution at Old Tappan as a spy took place during this period. As the war drew to a close many Tories fled the valley and their properties were confiscated. Victory was celebrated and peaceful ways were resumed.

From early Colonial times and well into the 1800s sailing vessels of all descriptions plied the Hackensack. These conducted most of the trade between the towns along the river and to Manhattan and other markets. Freight-carrying vessels transported merchandise and food supplies of many types to settlements as far upriver as the head of navigation at New Milford. On the return trips, farm produce, bricks and lumber were carried downstream. Lumber, then used for fuel as well as construction, was especially important to the cities: for example, at River Edge, one of the major ports-of-call, thousands of cords of firewood were stored during the winter awaiting shipment as soon as the river was opened for navigation in the spring.

During the 1800s the windjammers were gradually replaced by steam-propelled vessels. River steamers in turn lost trade to the railroads and oil burning vessels, and by the early 1900s had all but disappeared from the scene. One of the last steamboats operated by the Hackensack River men was a tug, the *Elsie K*, which was used until 1915 when she sank and her captain was drowned.

The waters of the Hackensack also attracted private sailboats and yachts of many types. Sailing races were weekly features on a course laid out between Hackensack and Secaucus. Much of this activity was centered at the La Favorita Boat Club in Hackensack.

Private motor craft and sailboats still may be seen on the middle and lower Hackensack, while the many industrial plants, oil depots, and utilities along the lower river keep busy ocean-going and coastal vessels.

At various times during the nineteenth century there were more than forty grist and lumber mills and several chair factories using the water power of the Hackensack and its tributaries. These were located in the higher country of northern Bergen County. By the end of the century most of these had ceased operations or converted to steam or other power sources. Replacing them in the early 1900s were oil refineries,

utilities, and coke processing and other industrial plants, attracted by the navigable waters of the lower river and their accessibility to other ports. Tankers, freighters, tugs and barges, and other marine craft formed part of a major metropolitan transportation complex. New highways and bridges crossing the Hackensack were vital components of this complex.

Following America's entrance into World War I, the War Department, after surveying the region and considering a number of possible sites, decided to use a tract of 770 acres on a wooded ridge near Tenafly between the Hackensack and Hudson Rivers for the site of a pre-embarkation camp. The first troops were received for processing on August 30, 1917. Between that date and the end of the war in November, 1918, some 600,000 men passed through the camp on their way to the war zones. Almost 500,000 passed through on their way home after the war ended. Its purposes served, the camp was razed. A memorial marker for this facility has been erected in Cresskill. Camp Shanks near Orangeburg, New York, served a similar purpose during World War II.

By the mid-twentieth century the Hackensack River and its meadowlands suffered from many environmental problems. Much of the tidal portion of the river ran through marshy meadows filled with every describable form of sight pollution. Two thousand acres were covered with garbage from some 150 municipalities. Organic and metal pollutants were being dumped as wastes by a variety of industries. Overtaxed municipal waste treatment plants discharged inadequately treated sewage. Oil spills and fish kills were frequent. And there was thermal pollution from two large utilities.

After years of controversy, the New Jersey Legislature, in December, 1968, enacted legislation creating the Hackensack Meadowlands Development Commission. This body was given authority to promote environmental cleanups and control industrial and residential development in the meadowlands.

A master plan was placed in effect in 1971. Since then toxic waste discharges have been reduced, dissolved oxygen levels have risen, oil spills and fish kills have diminished, and increases in fish and other aquatic life have been encouraging. Solid waste dumping by municipalities has all but stopped and its end is in sight. The Commission's land use and zoning programs provide for setting aside 6,210 acres of open space for recreation, education, and conservation purposes.

A major development took place in 1976 when the New Jersey Sports and Exposition Authority opened its Giants Stadium and Meadowlands Race Track. Additional sports and recreation facilities are planned, subject to Commission approval.

The accomplishments of the Commission, fed-eral action under the Water Pollution Control Act Amendments of 1972, and the upgrading of many municipal waste water treatment plants along the river auger well for a better future for the Hackensack River. There is still much to be done, but there is good reason to anticipate much better days ahead for the river and its people.

FURTHER READING: James and Margaret Cawley, *Exploring the Little Rivers of New Jersey* (1942; 1971).

Norman F. Brydon

The Housatonic River

Source: **Berkshire Hills of northwest Massachusetts, junction of South and West Branches, south of Pittsfield**
Length: **c. 115 miles**
Tributaries: **Shepaug; Naugatuck**
Mouth: **Flows into Long Island Sound at Stratford**
Agricultural Products: **Negligible**
Industries: **Aircraft, pens and cigarette lighters, diversified manufactures**

The Housatonic begins its 115-mile journey to the ocean in the beautiful Berkshire Hills. It then winds through the peaceful meadows and valleys of Stockbridge, Massachusetts, and Kent, Connecticut, past the sprawling factories of Derby and Shelton, Connecticut, between the Connecticut harbor towns of Stratford and Milford, into Long Island Sound. From its headwaters at Pittsfield to the Sound, the river descends from 1,600 feet above to sea level. Varying in width from 50 to 100 yards, the Housatonic has never been navigable by large craft more than 12 miles inland.

Within the Housatonic Valley have lived poets and inventors, farmers and industrialists, soldiers and diplomats, Puritan émigrés from England and native Americans descended from the Algonquins of New York. Since man first settled on its banks, the Housatonic has been fished in, sailed on, dammed up, and polluted into. In the latter half of the 20th century the river revenged itself with a flood which caused enough devastation to create a disaster area below Kent, Connecticut. This is the Housatonic.

Excluding the Stone Age relics discovered in Washington, Connecticut, there are no real sources of information about the men who lived within the valley prior to the white man. The Puritans are the earliest available historians of the valley's red men. The Indians and legends documented by these first white settlers described red men who had contact with white men. Thus, as far as can be documented, the Indians of the "At the Place Beyond the Mountain" Valley sprang into existence when the sachem Ansantaway sold part of present-day Milford to some Puritans for "six coats, ten blankets, one kettle . . . hoes, knives, hatchets, and glasses" on February 12, 1639.

Each of the six Indian tribes of the Housatonic Valley had their own sachems with one being a "sagamore," or first among equals. The most famous valley sachem was Waramaug who had a "palace" just below the Great Falls near New

Milford. His residence was described by one settler as an

> edifice ... built in the Indian style ... about one hundred feet in length and ... twenty in breadth, covered with bark curiously wrought and embellished with portrait paintings ... [of] every kind of four footed beast, flying birds and creeping things down to the ant and covey-fish all drawn much to the life. ...

According to Indian, or Puritan, legend, Lillinonah, Waramaug's daughter, encountered a lost white man in the woods near New Milford. She returned with him to her village, saved him from possible murder by her tribesmen, and ultimately pledged her troth to him. He begged leave from Waramaug to return for a short time to his own people. Waramaug assented. When the young man had been gone almost a year, Waramaug promised the hand of the pining Lillinonah to a young brave. Just before the wedding Lillinonah paddled toward the Great Falls in a canoe. Her white lover, who was returning at that time, saw Lillinonah's plight and leapt from a nearby cliff, now called "Lover's Leap." The young couple then joined the Great Spirit beneath the Housatonic.

It was in 1613, a half century before Waramaug, that Captain Adrian Block became the first European to touch the shore of Connecticut. He anchored at the mouth of the river, which he christened the "River of the Red Hills," and claimed all land north of this spot for Holland. However, since the Dutch of New Amsterdam never built any settlements in the area, the Puritans were the first whites to colonize the Housatonic Valley. Expanding westward from the New Haven, Connecticut, and Massachusetts Bay colonies, the Puritans spread imperturbably upriver.

The Milford plantation and the Stratford settlement took root at the mouth of the river simultaneously in 1639. In 1648 Moses Wheeler of Stratford received a concession to conduct a ferry across the Housatonic. By 1651 that town had become "civilized" enough to hang its first convicted witch, Goody Bassett, at Witches Rock. In 1655 five families from Milford moved to form a small village in the heights of Paugasset, contemporary Derby, Connecticut. This group started the first industry on the river when they began shipbuilding, a trade which flourished for over two centuries.

In April of 1673 Stratford colonists on rafts and canoes proceeded farther up the Great River to establish a settlement at Southbury. In 1685 another flock of Puritans moved northward onto a tributary of the Housatonic, settling adjacent to a huge swamp. Their desire to have their town incorporated two years later as Swampfield was stymied by Connecticut governor Robert Treat who approved the incorporation but changed the name to the more euphonic Danbury.

The most utopian settlement on the Housatonic was initiated in 1714 at New Milford. Here Indians and colonists coexisted peacefully on two hills a mile apart, separated only by the river. Eleven years later the Massachusetts General Court bought land from Sachem Konkapot in Berkshire County. This land was divided and incorporated as Sheffield in 1722 and Stockbridge in 1736. Sheffield was divided again in 1742 when Housatonuck [sic] gained its own parish.

In 1737, the same year that New Milford built the first bridge across the Housatonic, an Indian Mission was started at Stockbridge. John Sargeant, a graduate of Yale, was the first minister. He held this position until his death in 1749. During this period the Indians in Stockbridge were not only enfranchised but also held office in local government. Sargeant has been acclaimed as an exemplary leader in Indian relations. He supported Indian participation in local politics and attempted to ensure that the Indians be allowed to retain control of their land. Sargeant's rapport with Konkapot's people was enhanced by his ability to communicate fluently in their language.

Three years after Sargeant's death, in 1751, Johnathan Edwards, a leader of the evangelical "Great Awakening," was appointed to succeed him. More interested in writing his treatises such as "Freedom of the Will," Edwards was not able to fulfill the needs of the Stockbridge Indians as well as Sargeant. Yet, his outspokenness in letters to the General Assembly made him a thorn in the side to Stockbridge patriarch Euphraium Williams in that man's efforts to create a land monopoly. In 1758 Edwards left to accept the presidency of Princeton.

While the northern valley had been dealing in various ways with the Indian "problem," the inhabitants of the lower valley had been faced with annoyances caused by the presence of British troops garrisoned in the area to fight the Seven Years or French and Indian War. In 1757 British soldiers outraged the pious residents of Stratford by using Christ Church's golden weathervane for target practice. A year later drunken soldiers billeted in a Milford townhouse burned that house to the ground. These and similar incidents were the only intrusions on the peace of the valley during the war.

In the late eighteenth century the valley was prosperous and still expanding. In 1761 Great Barrington, the former site of the Indians Great Wigwam, was incorporated. The rapid population increase in that area might be illustrated by the tombstone of Mrs. John Paell of Litchfield. It states:

> She died November 11, 1768 aged 90, having had 13 children, 191 grandchildren, 247 great-grandchildren, and 49 great-great grandchildren—total 336 survived her.

Prosperity, however, did not lead to complacency. In July of 1774 the Berkshire County Convention meeting at the Red Lion Inn in Stockbridge passed an unconditional act of non-intercourse with Britain—this nation's first declaration of independence. Valley residents participated in the Boston Tea Party and the First Continental Congress. Roger Sherman, a one-time resident of both Milford and New Milford, was the only man to sign the Articles of Association, the Declaration of Independence, the Articles of Confederation, and the United States Constitution. Ethan Allan led the sneak attack on Fort Ticonderoga which helped to arm the Continental Army. David Humphreys of Derby was an aide to General Washington. After the war Humphreys served as a minister to Spain and Portugal. Upon his return to the valley, Humphreys was a leader in another revolution. That revolution was industrial.

During the 17th and 18th centuries the area in the Housatonic watershed had been primarily rural and agricultural. In the 19th century much of the river valley developed into factory towns. When David Humphreys returned to Derby from Spain he brought the first merino sheep to the United States. He also started the first valley textile mills. In 1830 Derby had the first United States hoop skirt factory, in 1836 the first factory which machined tacks, and in 1837 the first factory to manufacture paper from straw. Upriver in 1837 Charles Goodyear accidentally discovered the process of vulcanizing by dropping India rubber mixed with sulfur onto a hot stove. In 1836 the Berkshire Woolen Company had opened a water-powered mill at Great Barrington. And by 1840 the Pittsfield region was manufacturing half the paper used in the United States. In nearby West Pittsfield the Shaker community, which had been established in 1780, had invented over twenty-six "labor saving" devices, including a threshing machine, the circular saw, the washing machine, and the first one-horse wagon in the United States.

Mines in the Salisbury region of the state were producing so much iron ore that colliers had to be imported from Europe to keep the nearby furnaces stoked with fuel. In 1853 the Lenox Glass Works had been built at Lenox Furnace. Marble was being quarried in Egremont, Alford, and Barrington. Marble from a quarry in Lee was used to construct the extension to the U.S. capitol building. This heavy industrialization initiated the development of the Housatonic Railroad from Canaan to Bridgeport. This line was chartered in 1836 and completed in 1842.

While the industry in the lower valley thrived, the upper valley's died. By 1850 the iron forges at Lakeville, which had manufactured the guns for the New York Battery and the anchor for Old Ironsides, and Mt. Riga had failed. By 1855 many marble quarries had closed. Even the Lenox Glass Works, "the largest factory under one roof" went under. Yet these failures were not the death knell of Housatonic industries. Two men in Great Barrington, Franklin Pope and William Stanley, in 1886 created power transformers which could allow electricity to be carried great distances and in 1894 transformed current from a Housatonic dam to generate electric power. A fellow inventor, Stephen Dudley Field of Stockbridge, demonstrated his overhead trolley system at the Chicago World's Fair. In the early 1890s a dam was built across the Housatonic from Derby to Shelton for the generation of electric power.

This heavy industrialization of the Housatonic

which began in the early 19th century continues to the present, especially in the lower valley. While the old Indian Mission of Stockbridge has become a colony of artists, poets and craftsmen, Derby, Shelton, Milford, and Stratford's major industries have nestled on their shores. While Stockbridge and Lenox hosted the great writers of the late 19th century American Renaissance such as Nathaniel Hawthorne, Herman Melville, and Henry Wadsworth Longfellow, the lower valley prefers to shelter Sikorsky Aircraft, a major producer of military helicopters; Bic Pen, creator of a 19¢ pen guaranteed to write the "first time, everytime"; and any number of more minor industries.

The factory towns which border the southern Housatonic region suffered an enormous blow when a flood unparalleled in the river's history struck on August 15, 1955. Temporarily paralyz-ing any manufacturing on the river from Cornwall to the ocean, this deluge caused over $4 million worth of damage to the area. Yet, even despite a second, lesser flood on October 19, 1955, those businesses staged a remarkable recovery through the 1960s and 1970s.

Since that time the upper and lower sections of the Housatonic Valley have continued developing in their unparalleled directions. It seems somehow logical that 1978 headlines should feature a Stratford story that Sikorsky Aircraft had secured a renumerative government military contract while Stockbridge reporters should note that distinguished townsman and artist Norman Rockwell died while in the process of working on a picture entitled "John Sargeant and the Indian."

FURTHER READING: Harold J. Bingham, *History of Connecticut* (4 vols., 1962). Richard D. Birdsall, *Berkshire County* (1959).

Mary Ellen Forbes

The Hudson River

Source: Lake Tear of the Clouds in northeastern New York State
Length: 316 miles
Tributaries: Mohawk
Mouth: Flows into Atlantic at New York City
Agricultural products: Truck crops, apples
Industrial Products: Many and diversified

If New York City's teeming millions were reduced to a few thousand, and the region of eastern New York State was equally reduced in population, the forces of nature would soon return the Hudson River country to its original Edenlike beauty. Indeed, even with heavy population, industrial abuse, and water pollution, much of the Hudson River Valley remains as beautiful as it was in the nineteenth century when artists painted landscapes based upon scenes in the region. They had a wide choice, from the stunning cliffs of the Palisades to the tree-covered Catskill Mountains to the rugged but peaceful Highlands. Even the river changed character as it coursed south from its place of origin as a trout fishing stream to a waterway for oceangoing ships and an estuary debouching into the Atlantic.

By any measure the Hudson is a mighty waterway. It is in no small part responsible for New York City's greatness. Yet its origin, only 316 miles north-northwest of New York City, is so isolated that until 1872 geographers incorrectly credited its source as Lake Avalanche. In that year it was discovered that a tiny, two-acre pond, Lake Tear of the Clouds, was the Hudson's true, ultimate source. The tiny body of water lies at 4,293 feet in the Adirondacks, close to 5,344-foot Mount Marcy, the highest point in New York State.

The upper Hudson is a mountain stream with rapids and waterfalls that have long been harnessed for water power. By the time it has reached Troy, New York, with the addition of the Mohawk's water which flows in from the west at Cohoes, just north of Albany, the Hudson has become an impressive stream. It continues to deepen and widen and is, in fact, a tidal estuary for 150 miles above its mouth. In glacial times when more land was above sea level the Hudson dug a deep channel another 120 miles out into the Atlantic. Today the Hudson is navigable to ocean vessels to Albany and by smaller boats another fifty miles north to Fort Edward. The New York Barge Canal System, using the Hudson and Mohawk rivers, links the region with the St. Lawrence Seaway which in turn serves the Great Lakes and Lake Champlain.

The span from Albany down to Newburgh is considered as the middle Hudson Valley. Eighty-five or ninety miles long, it is rugged and scenic. On the west are the Catskill and Shavangunk mountains while east across the river are beautiful estates some of which date back hundreds of years to when Dutch landed aristocrats, called patroons, dominated the region. Franklin Roosevelt's Hyde Park is one of those estates.

Below Newburgh the river flows through the Highlands, a deep gorge in a region of green mountains. Within eight miles, on the west side, the United States Military Academy at West Point comes into view. Still further downstream is spectacular Bear Mountain Bridge. Then, just below Tarrytown, the Hudson widens to as many as three miles in what is known as the Tappan Zee. This has narrowed again by the time the river reaches Yonkers, just north of New York City. Now the river is protected on its west side by the cliffs known as the Palisades and has become the boundary between New York and New Jersey. The two states are linked by the George Washington Bridge and the Holland and Lincoln tunnels.

When whites first arrived in the Hudson Valley they found it sparsely populated by Indians of the Hokan-Siouan linguistic stock. Known as the Iroquois, their five nations (later six) had been joined into a loose confederation in about 1570 by a prophet Deganawida and his disciple Hiawatha. Palisaded villages extended up the Hudson toward the St. Lawrence and west to the Genesee River and Lake Ontario. The Iroquois were among the most advanced Indians in North America. They blocked English emigration west along the Mohawk and also served as barriers to French expansion out of Montreal and Quebec.

From 1524 on, the Hudson estuary attracted explorers. The first to sail up it was Giovanni da Verrazano, an Italian navigator in the employ of King Francis I of France. The very next year (1525) a Portuguese, Estevan Gomez, sailing under the flag of Spain, apparently observed the river. However, since these discoveries were not followed with exploitation or settlement, the real credit for Hudson River discovery goes to Henry Hudson, an English navigator in Dutch employ. With a mixed Dutch and English crew aboard the eighty-ton *Half Moon*, Hudson in early September, 1609, dropped anchor near Staten Island. While he traded with the local Indians he sent a small crew to explore further; they passed through the Narrows between Staten Island and present Brooklyn and entered the Upper Bay. When the men returned with the news of a great estuary extending northward Hudson raised anchor, threaded the *Half Moon* through the Narrows and sailed north. By mid-September he had reached Yonkers; then Hudson sailed his little ship on up to West Point and northward past the Highlands until he reached the limits of navigation. Correctly he concluded that he had failed to find the Northwest Passage so the *Half Moon* sailed downriver and back to Holland.

Hudson and his men had traded profitably with the Indians, bartering liquor in exchange for valuable furs. The enterprising Dutch sensed the lucrative profits from the fur trade in the Hudson Valley and were quick to take advantage of their knowledge. For a brief time prior to 1618 they even had a fur trading post above Albany. There was a brief hiatus and then in 1824 the Dutch West India Company launched a program of settlement and trade that took their merchant adventurers to the Delaware, Hudson, and Connecticut rivers. In a short time the most lucrative points of trade were at New Amsterdam on Manhattan and at Fort Orange, present Albany.

In order to persuade the comfort-loving Dutch to settle in the new land the West India Company offered patroonships—feudal grants of land along the Hudson—to any Company member who would bring over fifty persons for settlement. The patroon was allowed an estate of four leagues along one bank or two leagues on each bank of the river, reaching as far into the interior as he wished. A few of these estates, such as Rennsaelerwick south of Fort Orange, existed into recent times. More important, the system established a pattern of settlement along the valley in the form of large landed estates such as the Roosevelt home at Hyde Park, founded in 1740. From the mid-nineteenth century on, the valley was home for such business tycoons as the Vanderbilts and the Goulds. The early, concentrated ownership along the Hudson prevented settlement by the common pioneer, who had to work west along the Mohawk or Genesee to find cheap or free land. Finally, Dutch settlement along the Hudson created local color in the form of Dutch towns, Dutch architecture, and Dutch folklore.

Fortunately much of the lore of Dutch times has been preserved through the writings of Washington Irving (1783–1859). From his home at Sunnyside overlooking the Tappan Zee from the east, Irving wrote tales about the lanky schoolmaster Ichabod Crane and the Headless Horseman, of Rip Van Winkle, and the humorous *A History of New York* that spoofs the Dutch government and society.

In 1664 the British took New Amsterdam, renaming the colony New York in honor of the Duke of York. Fort Orange became Albany and the fur trade continued unabated with many of the Dutch traders continuing their activities. It was from Albany that Sir William Johnson dealt successfully with the Iroquois in the 1740s, 1750s, and 1760s, keeping those tribesmen generally on the side of the British during the long conflict with the French. New York City continued to grow, and the Hudson became ever busier as a trading waterway.

In the early years of the American Revolution the Hudson was of strategic concern. In 1776 British General Howe landed with troops at Staten Island, outflanked Washington at Brooklyn Heights, occupied New York City, and subsequently defeated the Continentals at Fort Lee, on the west bank of the Hudson, at Fort Washington on the north end of Manhattan Island, and at White Plains; when the war ended at Yorktown in the fall of 1781 the British were still in New York. The Hudson also figured in British strategy in 1777. This called for General Burgoyne to come down the river thus cutting off New York and New England from the rest of the colonies. Burgoyne, however, was defeated at Saratoga. In 1780 Benedict Arnold's traitorous plans to place West Point in British hands were intercepted, and the scheme did not succeed.

After 1783 a part of the United States of America, the Hudson River region flourished peacefully for many years. Always present in the minds of New Yorkers, however, was the possibility of tapping the productivity of the expanding West. From earliest times perceptive explorers and traders had conceived the practicability of a canal linking Lake Erie with the Hudson River. In 1817 the digging of such a waterway began; when it was completed in 1825 the 364-mile-long Erie Canal began a new era for the entire region. Now all manner of goods, but especially grain, could pass cheaply from the Great Lakes by way of the Erie Canal and down the Hudson to New York Harbor. Now the Hudson was busier than ever and the population of New York City boomed.

The natural beauty along the river was still such as to inspire an entire generation of painters known collectively as the Hudson River School. One of its leading artists was Thomas Cole, born in England but raised in America. In 1825 he made a trip up the Hudson and saw the region as the untamed America he had dreamed of in his childhood. Cole, and other members of the School, painted huge landscapes in which humans, if they did appear, ranked no more conspicuously than animals. Another prominent painter was Frederick E. Church, from whose castle-home, Olana, one has an extraordinary view of the Hudson and the Catskills. Other painters of the genre which lasted from 1825 until about 1875 were Thomas Doughty, Henry Inman, and Albert Bierstadt.

Until it leaves the Adirondacks the Hudson is a wild river with deep pools and swift rapids offering the fly fisherman hours of intensive casting. Then the river flows calm and smooth. As such it has become one of the world's most heavily used waterways with oceangoing vessels steaming as far as Albany and smaller vessels on up to Fort Edward. More than a thousand factories line its banks, and even the banks have been damaged by railroads asserting a right-of-way up most of the length of the river.

With usage came incredible pollution. A stream which is one of the world's greatest spawning grounds was by 1960 becoming a sterile, stinking sewer. Pollution began even before the river left the Adirondacks and reached its worst between Fort Edward and Troy. The polluted Mohawk's waters, residue from huge pulp and paper mills, and the waste from about 600,000 people created a putrid area known as the Albany Pool. The Hudson was dying and its scenery was disappearing. But the Palisades were saved from being blasted into building stone, and Storm King Mountain was denied to a utility's plan for development. Organizations came into being to act as watchdogs over the Hudson, save swamps, establish river-side parks, and force factories to obey anti-pollution regulations. Fishermen organized to campaign for clean water in order to increase the edible fish that spawn in the river. The federal Environmental Protection Agency stepped in to help. Today more shad, sturgeon, and blue crabs are being caught in the Hudson while more and more of its water flows fresh and clean. Thanks to citizens' organizations, the future of the beautiful Hudson looks bright.

FURTHER READING: Robert H. Boyle, *The Hudson River* (1968). John Reed, *Hudson River Valley* (1960).

Thomas Allan Bartlett

The James River of Virginia

Source: Convergence of Jackson and Cowpasture rivers in Botetourt County in southwestern Virginia
Length: c. 200 miles to widewater at Richmond and another 140 miles to mouth.
Tributaries: Appomattox; Chickahominy
Mouth: Into Atlantic Ocean at Hampton Roads, Virginia
Agricultural Products: Truck vegetables, apples
Industries: Fishing, chemicals, manufactured products

The James River traverses about 340 miles of varied Virginia terrain and links the Allegheny Mountains with the Atlantic Ocean. The river then flows southeastward through the Blue Ridge, dropping precipitously at scenic Balcony Falls; then it flows northeast and then east to its mouth at Hampton Roads, where it enters Chesapeake Bay. Tidewater extends 100 miles up the estuary to Richmond. The James's two principal tributaries are the Appomattox, which flows in at Bermuda Hundred, and the Chickahominy, which enters at a point about ten miles west of Williamsburg.

The Indians named the river for their chief, Powhatan, and the English called it King's River after their monarch, James I, but it soon acquired its present name. In 1607 the English were induced to build Jamestown, their first permanent settlement in the New World, on a peninsula jutting into the river. (Today Jamestown is an island reached easily by ferry boat.) One of their reasons for this choice was their belief, based upon the river's depth, width, and direction, that the stream crossed the continent. Despite its failing as a pathway to the Orient or as a route leading to gold, the James River and the valley through which it passed supplied the necessary elements for the creation of a vibrant civilization.

For many years the history of Virginia remained little more than a record of activities along the James. At the peak of their wealth the planters of the lower James built some of the most impressive estates in America, some of which still exist. Important in peacetime, the river was even more vital in times of war. During the Revolution the Virginians operated a foundry at Westham and a navy yard at Warwick, above and below the fall line respectively. Although these were destroyed during the war, the existence of such enterprises reinforced a belief that the James River basin had an excellent economic potential. During the Civil War the river was of extreme strategic importance, with General McClellan trying to take Richmond and the siege of Petersburg by the Army of the James.

In a more routine fashion the James, like many rivers, assisted the settlement process. Although Indian attacks held back speedy development, mining efforts were nevertheless underway over a hundred miles upstream within five years of initial settlement. Not until 1675, however, did the harbinger of white civilization, the Indian trading post, reach the river's fall line. Four years later William Byrd secured the right to settle the head of navigation. Up to that time, and until numerous settlers moved into the Piedmont portion of Virginia above the fall line, the river retarded urban development because tobacco growers of the lower James, with the river navigable for ocean-going vessels, did not need to carry their tobacco to a town for shipment. Soon the tobacco culture passed above the fall line, beyond the reach of sailing ships, and many merchants, particularly Scotsmen, set up stores near colony-owned tobacco warehouses. The resultant commercial centers, such as Manchester and Rockett's, eventually became part of Richmond. Lynchburg, a Piedmont town, also emerged as a riverport late in the 18th century.

Although not without perils for shipping, the lower part of the James in its natural state permitted 18th century square-riggers to reach Bermuda Hundred. Smaller vessels of up to 150 tons could ascend the James to the rapids. In 1745 the colonial assembly forced fishermen and mill owners to clear passageways for vessels through their stone steps and dams. The existence of such diverse activities, along with the presence of the Midlothian coal mines southwest of Richmond, whose products were transported down the James, shows a varied and sometimes conflicting use of the river.

Long before the Revolution, businessmen called for the removal of the natural obstacles, particularly those in the fall line. After the war, George Washington recommended a survey of the Potomac and James rivers. In 1785 the state chartered the James River Company which canalled around the falls to Westham and cleared the waterway to a depth sufficient to allow rafts to come all the way from Buchanan across the Blue Ridge. An 1812 commission headed by John Marshall urged the construction of a major

canal and a system of turnpikes to develop commercial relations with the Ohio Valley through the Greenbrier and Kanawha rivers. In 1820 this company became an agent of the state and ultimately a state-owned corporation. It achieved major improvements, including the construction of a seven-mile long canal through the Blue Ridge at Balcony Falls, a thousand-foot gorge.

Before the projects were completed, however, the state embraced a far more visionary scheme to build a canal to the Kanawha River. The James River and Kanawha Company, chartered in 1832, completed the task of building a major canal from Richmond to Lynchburg, some 148 miles, by 1840, and reached Buchanan, almost another fifty miles, eleven years later. At that time the company owned nearly 160 miles of canal and almost thirty-seven miles of slackwater. The next step in the scheme—to construct a canal past Covington, Virginia, to the Kanawha River—foundered in spite of Herculean efforts to build underground waterways and aqueducts. The company did successfully erect canals along several of her tributaries, but even in comparatively prosperous times such as the 1850s, the company found its debt excessively burdensome. The construction of east-west railroads and the Civil War, along with the ruggedness of the terrain, eliminated any chance of completion. Sheridan's troops in 1865 knocked out miles of the banks which separated the canal from the river. Fifteen years later the Richmond and Allegheny Railway Company, itself later absorbed by the Chesapeake and Ohio, bought the stock of the canal company.

Interest in the navigability of the lower James did not entirely flag in the antebellum period. The James River and Kanawha Company developed the Richmond docks to permit oceangoing freighters to secure their cargos directly from canal packets. The capital of Virginia became a large exporter of tobacco and flour. Some of the latter was made from wheat brought to the large flour mills at Richmond from farms along the river valley. The river between Bermuda Hundred and Richmond left something to be desired, however, because of its serpentine character. During the Civil War, Union Major General Benjamin Butler tried to eliminate one of these curves by digging the Dutch Gap Canal. Under heavy Confederate fire, engineers set a charge which, upon detonation, lifted a huge amount of soil and sand, but the whole mass fell right back into its original position and James River mariners waited another ten years before the project, which cut off seven miles of travel, could be completed. By then the ever-growing network of railways and the constant increase in the size of oceangoing ships had sharply reduced freight traffic along the lower James.

Steamboat passenger business remained feasible well into the 20th century. Steamers initially appeared on the James in 1815, an event which opened up an era of near open warfare among owners of the fragile vessels. The James River Steam Boat Company played a central role in these controversies which peaked in the 1840s when Virginia's railroads, competing bitterly with each other, used the steamers in their own struggles. Major lines emanating from New York took over the Norfolk to Richmond route in the 1850s.

With the demise of the James as a major link in transportation the communities along the river continued to rely on their stream for a wide variety of purposes—recreation, drinking water, drainage, and fishing. The tiny commercial communities evolved into large industrial centers. In addition to Richmond, the city of Petersburg, located on the Appomattox River, emerged as a 19th century textile milling center and Lynchburg as a pre-Civil War iron milling town. The area near Lynchburg experienced a brief burst of iron mining around 1880. On the Jackson River (another tributary), Covington became a 20th century lumber town. During World War I the port at the confluence of the Appomattox and the James, formerly known as City Point, used by the Union Army as its logistical center for the siege of Petersburg, became the chemical-industrial city of Hopewell. After World War II, the Allied Chemical Corporation contracted Life Science Products Company to produce Kepone, a poison. When workers showed symptoms of poisoning, scientists studied the lower James and found Kepone residue which appar-

ently had entered the river through the Hopewell sewage system. In 1975 the state banned some fishing, and the once extensive crab industry, focused in Hampton Roads, the eastern terminus of the James, endured reduced production and sales. Oystering, with a harvest annually of over two million bushels plus huge amounts of seed oysters, also became imperiled.

Eighteenth-century documents reveal the existence of a large number of shad in the lower James. Shad fishing became an important industry during the 1700s, and the countryside south of the James has long been known for its shad plankings, occasions of both social and political significance. In the more recent past shad for these affairs have come from rivers other than the James.

The James, and the varied nature of the country through which it runs, provided the basis for a broad-based economy, but each use of the resources created problems. Farming along the river established the basis for much wealth, but at the same time exhaustive farming practices led to erosion, especially for the Piedmont countryside. The regular flooding of the James (major freshets occurred in 1771, 1877, and 1972 resulting in considerable loss of buildings and land), along with poor farming techniques, sent much soil down the river. Extensive lumbering which peaked in the early part of this century stimulated the economy but altered the nature of the forest cover and probably contributed to the erosion problem. Full-scale oyster harvesting likely reduced the accessibility of this resource. These endeavors conflict with each other and with mining, manufacturing, and transporting of materials along the James. The use of the river for drinking water and for sewer drainage present an obviously conflicting use of the waterway. Efforts to clean up the James were progressing until the Kepone crisis overshadowed these accomplishments.

FURTHER READING: James River Project Committee (Comp.), *The James River Basin: Past, Present and Future* (1950). Blair Niles, *The James: From Iron Gate to the Sea* (1945).

Peter Stewart

The Merrimack River

Source: Confluence of Pemigewasset and Winnipesau-
kee rivers
Length: 110 miles
Tributaries: Contoocook, Concord
Mouth: Into Atlantic Ocean at Newburyport, Massa-
chusetts
Agricultural Products: Truck farming, poultry, dairy-
ing
Industries: Textiles, diversified manufacturing

The Merrimack River is formed in the lakes region of central New Hampshire by the confluence of the Pemigewasset River, an indistinguishable continuation of the Merrimack, and the Winnipesaukee River, which flows out of New Hampshire's largest lake of the same name. The Merrimack drains into the Atlantic Ocean at Newburyport, Massachusetts, having descended 110 miles through a succession of waterfalls whose power gave rise to New England's textile industry.

The headwaters of the Pemigewasset are found at Profile Lake in the White Mountains of northern New Hampshire. The lake is aptly named for its reflection of the Old Man of the Mountain, a natural granite profile that protrudes from a mountain cliff 1,500 feet above the lake. From this picturesque beginning the Pemigewasset flows southward through the White Mountain National Forest, a vast wilderness preserve containing the highest mountain ranges in the Northeast. The Pemigewasset descends rapidly, growing in volume and power from tributary streams that drain the mountains of snow and rain. From Profile Lake to Ashland the river plunges 1,400 feet in forty miles. Below Ashland the Pemigewasset widens considerably, flowing through wooded hills and meadows until it reaches Franklin, where Daniel Webster was born in 1782.

At Franklin the Merrimack is born where the Pemigewasset comes together with the Winnipesaukee River. It is at this juncture that the waters from Lake Winnipesaukee find an outlet. With seventy-two square miles of water surface the lake adds significant volume to the Merrimack River system. Lake Winnipesaukee, a major vacation attraction in New England, was discovered in 1642. Problems had arisen at that time over the Merrimack being used as a borderline in various colonial charters. The General Court of Massachusetts sent out an expedition to locate the northern limits of the river. In 1832 a boulder bearing the inscription of these explorers was found in the Winnipesaukee River near the lake entrance.

From Franklin the Merrimack flows 110 miles to its mouth at the Atlantic Ocean. Derived from an Algonquian Indian word meaning "strong and swift water," the river certainly lives up to its name. Fed by numerous tributaries, and punctuated by rapids and waterfalls, the Merrimack presents a formidable power source for both energy and industry.

Fifteen miles south of Franklin, on the west bank of the river, is the largest of the Merrimack's tributaries, the Contoocook River. Having its source in Massachusetts, the Contoocook is a river that has preserved the beauty and atmosphere of an earlier New England. It was at Hillsborough, New Hampshire, on the banks of the Contoocook, that Franklin Pierce, fourteenth President of the United States, was born in 1804.

South of the Contoocook, the Merrimack flows past the city of Concord, the state capital of New Hampshire. Established in 1635 by the Massachusetts Bay Colony, Concord originally served as a defensive outpost on the French and Indian frontier of the upper Merrimack. Below Concord the Merrimack is characterized by torrents and waterfalls. The most considerable of the cascades is the Amoskeag Falls, around which grew the textile mills and city of Manchester. Dropping fifty-four feet, these falls today contain the Amoskeag dam, a hydroelectric project that generates much of the energy for the surrounding region. Flowing southward through gently rolling pine forests the Merrimack crosses into Massachusetts where it changes course toward the northeast. It is during this great bend that the Merrimack encounters the most famous of its tributaries, the Concord River. Flowing tranquilly from the south, the Concord opens into the Merrimack at Lowell, Massachusetts.

Fifteen miles south on the Concord is the village of Concord, Massachusetts. Founded in 1635, it had become by 1775 a focal point of pre-Revolutionary War activity. Military supplies were harbored there and troops were trained in the surrounding countryside. When British forces moved on Concord to destroy these munitions, they were driven back by the "Minute Men" at North Bridge, which spans the Concord River. Here, on April 19, 1775, occurred the first forcible resistance of the American Revolution. Concord subsequently became a major cultural center in the nineteenth century. Writers such as Ralph Waldo Emerson, Louisa May Alcott, Nathaniel Hawthorne, and Henry David Thoreau lived and gained inspiration in this peaceful village. In 1839 Thoreau traveled up the Concord and Merrimack by rowboat, later recording his thoughts and observations. *A Week on the Concord and Merrimack Rivers* offers a glimpse of the Merrimack in its natural state, before progress and pollution had taken their toll.

Moving downstream past the textile cities of Lowell and Lawrence, the Merrimack descends its last series of falls at Haverhill, Massachusetts. These falls act as a barrier to the advancing Atlantic tide, twenty-two miles on downstream. At the mouth of the Merrimack is the venerable and elegant city of Newburyport. Its harbor, now filling with sand, was in the eighteenth century one of the busiest in North America.

Founded in 1635 by Puritans, Newburyport represented the first colonial expansion into the Indian territory along the Merrimack. The natives there were members of two Algonquian tribes, the Pennacook and the Abenaki. The Pennacook were a confederacy of related bands whose villages lined the banks of the lower Merrimack and its tributaries. This confederacy was organized in order to defend against hostile encroachment by the Mohawk, members of the Iroquois league in northern New York. The Abenaki, found throughout northern New England, were important allies of the French during the Colonial wars. Abenaki war parties seriously impeded Colonial expansion along the upper Merrimack until 1763.

During the late seventeenth century, homesteads spread along the lower Merrimack in Massachusetts, on the edge of the wilderness frontier. These settlements were never far from garrison houses where refuge could be sought during Indian attacks. Although the Indians of the Merrimack were usually friendly and cooperative, encouragement from the French and increasing colonial encroachment into Indian territory often brought disastrous results. In 1675 Wampanaug raiding parties reached the Merrimack settlements during King Phillip's War. On the Nashua River, a Merrimack tributary, the Massachusetts settlement of Groton was completely destroyed. During King William's War (1689–1697) the Abenaki, having been incited by the French, spread a reign of terror along the settlements of the lower Merrimack Valley.

In a raid on Haverhill, Massachusetts, in 1697, twenty-seven colonists were killed and thirteen others carried off toward Quebec. One of these captives was Hannah Dustin, whose infant child had been killed before her eyes. On an island in the Merrimack, close to the mouth of the Contoocook, she escaped, but not before she had killed and scalped her sleeping captors. Today there stands a monument on that island commemorating her courage and frontier spirit.

With the signing of the Treaty of Paris in 1763, the last threat of Indian attack was effectively removed along the Merrimack. It was during this period that Newburyport gained preeminence as a major commerical port. Located at the deep-channeled mouth of the Merrimack, and surrounded by a ready supply of lumber, shipbuilding in Newburyport inevitably gained distinction. Whaling ships embarked from there for the southern seas and trading packets sailed regularly for the West Indies. This diversified economy of trade, shipbuilding, and manufacturing brought to Newburyport both wealth and reputation. However, Jefferson's Embargo of 1807–1809 suddenly interrupted the flourishing activity. Newburyport's rapid decline in importance was put to verse by an anonymous poet:

Our ships all in motion once weathered the ocean
They sailed and returned with a cargo
Now doomed to decay they have fallen prey
to Jefferson, worms, and the Embargo.

Newburyport was affected no more by the Embargo than were Boston or Gloucester. What prevented Newburyport from regaining its importance was the building of the Middlesex Canal. Boston merchants at the turn of the eighteenth century were competing with Newburyport for the inland products of the Merrimack Valley. These merchants in 1793 commissioned the building of a canal between the Merrimack at Lowell, and the Charles River at Boston. This canal effectively cut off Newburyport from much of the timber and agricultural produce of the Merrimack country.

Completed in 1803, the Middlesex Canal was the first great accomplishment of canal engineering in the United States. With twenty locks over its twenty-seven mile length, the Middlesex inaugurated an ambitious canal age on the Merrimack. Canals were built in order to bypass such obstacles to navigation as the Amoskeag Falls. By 1815 the Merrimack system was navigable from Boston to Concord, New Hampshire, enabling both increased expansion and commerce. At the head of navigation, Concord became the commercial center of the upper Merrimack; from it roads fanned out into the surrounding agricultural and lumbering regions. It was along these roads that the Concord coach first traveled. Designed and produced in New Hampshire's capital, this passenger coach was celebrated throughout the world for its engineering and comfort. Today the Concord coach is most familiar to us as the stagecoach of Hollywood westerns.

The turbulent character of the Merrimack, which had previously presented obstacles to expansion, had become in the nineteenth century the greatest single factor in the economy of New England. The river's harnessed power gave birth to textile and manufacturing complexes that marked the beginnings of the industrial growth of the United States.

In 1789 Samuel Slater, a young apprentice in the growing textile mills of England, carried to the New World a version of Richard Arkwright's water frame. The introduction of this water-powered spinning wheel gave rise to the cotton spinning industry in America. In 1825 Slater built a cotton spinning mill which utilized the power of the Amoskeag Falls. The mills expanded rapidly, attracting a growing work force that transformed the country village of Derryfield into the industrial city of Manchester, New Hampshire. By 1850 the Amoskeag mills had become the largest textile complex in the world. This boom spread through New England, particularly along the southern Merrimack in Massachusetts. Utilizing the river's waterpower, the industrial cities of Lowell and Lawrence grew rapidly in importance, transforming the social and economic character of the surrounding countryside.

The textile mills along the Merrimack reached their peak production just after the First World War. Postwar depression and southern competition brought an end to their supremacy. Wage cuts and increasing work hours brought about massive strikes which seriously weakened textile production. By 1935 the mills along the Merrimack had become incapable of keeping their priority in the world market.

Today these mills have been reorganized, successfully expanding into a variety of manufacturing concerns. Other problems along the Merrimack have yet to be answered. For years, city dwellers and textile mills alike have contributed to the river's pollution. What begins as a clear mountain stream has become by its entrance into the Atlantic Ocean a convenient receptacle for society's refuse. Ecological concern has lately made some headway in alleviating the Merrimack's pollution, but there is still a long way to go.

FURTHER READING: Raymond P. Holden, *The Merrimack* (1958). Elizabeth Forbes Morison, *New Hampshire* (1976).

Edward T. McCarron

The Niagara River

Source: Flows out of Lake Erie at Buffalo
Length: 36 miles
Tributaries: Buffalo, Cattaraugus, Tonawanda, Cezenovia, and Cayuga creeks
Mouth: Into Lake Ontario at Youngstown, New York, and Fort Niagara
Agricultural Products: Apples, peaches, and truck vegetables
Industries: Hydroelectric power, ceramics, abrasives, chemicals, steel, food processing, and diversified manufactures

The short, north-flowing Niagara River is proof that a river does not have to be long to be important. The stream flows out of Lake Erie, separating Buffalo, New York, from Fort Erie, Ontario. It forms the United States–Canadian boundary and after thirty-six miles flows into Lake Ontario near the village of Youngtown, New York, and restored Fort Niagara. At Niagara Falls the river bed drops spectacularly, creating one of the best-known scenic spectacles in the world. The American Falls are 182 feet high and about 1,000 feet wide. On the Canadian side, separated from the American Falls by American-owned Goat Island, the Horseshoe Falls are 176 feet high and about 2,500 feet wide. Strictly speaking the Niagara is not a river but a strait, a length of water connecting two larger bodies, but the river name has been used since Western man first set eyes upon it.

The first widely read description of Niagara Falls was that of the French Recollect Father Louis Hennepin. He had set out from Montreal in 1678 on an exploration of the Great Lakes basin. In December he arrived at the mouth of the Niagara and said the Christian Mass along its waters for the first time. Then, accompanied by Seneca Indians who had told him of the falls, he set out to see them. "Betwixt the Lake Ontario and Erie," he wrote, "there is a vast and prodigious Cadence of Water which falls down after a surprising and astonishing manner, insomuch that the Universe does not afford its parallel. . . ."

Father Hennepin's account was first published in 1683 and was soon translated into a number of languages; the English edition was first published in 1698. Thus it has been well over 300 years since Western man first visited the banks of the Niagara. In that time it has become a well-known stream. For the 150 years after Father Hennepin's visit, few people were able to see its wonders or know all its advantages. The next 150 years, however, were a different story: since 1,820 millions of people from every part of the world have observed at least the falls part of the Niagara. Today the site is more popular than ever before and its power potential has been put to use.

The French well realized that their ownership of the vast interior valley of North America depended upon their control of the strategic points along the lakes, rivers, portages, and transfer points west and south from the upper St. Lawrence River Valley. They quickly grasped the strategic significance of the Niagara River and in 1679, took positive steps to ensure control of the waterway.

It was the ambitious French explorer, Robert Cavelier, Sieur de La Salle who, with the help of his second in command, Henri de Tonti, in January, 1679, chose a site on a bluff overlooking the Niagara's mouth for a fort. Though Fort Condé, as they named it, was just a blockhouse that would soon be abandoned, the location was so good that subsequent fortifications were built there.

In the same year, along the banks of the upper Niagara where the Cayuga enters the main stream, La Salle built the *Griffon*, the first large vessel to sail on the upper lakes. His intention was to sail the *Griffon* through the wilderness waterways seeking a connection to the Mississippi and then down that river in search of a trade route with Mexico. The vessel started on a fur trading expedition across the lakes all the way to Green Bay, on the west side of Lake Michigan, only to have the vessel vanish on the return voyage. Late in the same year (1679) Fort Condé was abandoned. The first French attempt at control of the Niagara had not been auspicious.

Nor was the second attempt any more successful. As a part of the warfare being conducted by the French against the Iroquois, Fort Denonville was built in 1687 on the site of old Fort Condé; it had to be abandoned the next year. Only an eighteen-foot high cross, commemorating the deaths of eighty Frenchmen in the embattled wilderness, was left at the site.

For the next several decades Niagara was used by white fur traders—*coureurs de bois*—who existed precariously, trading with tribes that were pawns in the great rivalry between the British and the French. One of the most successful of these French traders was Louis Thomas de Joncaire, who in 1721 established a fur trading post named Magazin Royal on top of the escarpment above present Lewiston, below the falls. The British retaliated with a trading post at Oswego far to the east on the southern shore of Lake Ontario. In 1726 still another stage of Anglo-French rivalry was reached when Chausegros de Léry constructed the stone fortress, defended with cannon, known as Fort Niagara, where Forts Condé and Denonville had previously stood.

For thirty-three years thereafter the French expanded their control over the portages and

Niagara Falls, River and Gorge, have long been scenic attractions. Canada's Horseshoe Falls are at lower right. (Photo © Philip Mason.)

rivers from Niagara, along the southern shore of Lake Erie, down French Creek and the Allegheny to the forks of the Ohio (Fort Duquesne) and beyond. As every schoolchild knows, in 1754 young George Washington and his Virginians clashed with the French at Fort Necessity, near the Forks, beginning the Seven Years War.

In July, 1759, the British laid siege to Fort Niagara and after a decisive battle captured the fort on July 26. British soldiers continued to occupy the fortress and thus control the Niagara region down through the years of the American Revolution. Raiders led by John Butler, Sir John Johnson, and Chief Brant left the fort to penetrate deep into New York and Pennsylvania, striking terror through the Mohawk, Genessee, and Wyoming valleys and disrupting food supplies for General Washington's army. The Continentals, in return, under General John Sullivan attempted to retaliate by capturing Niagara. Although Sullivan succeeded in pillaging Iroquois lands, he never got within ninety miles of the fort.

By the Treaty of Paris (1783) the middle of the Niagara River constituted a part of the United States–Canadian border, and Fort Niagara went to the Americans. However, the British failed to honor the treaty and continued to occupy the fort. Not until the Jay Treaty of 1794 did they give it up; Fort Niagara was finally occupied by American forces on August 11, 1796.

The Niagara country was a busy part of the westward movement between 1783 and the War of 1812; then it became a principal scene of action. By the fall of 1812 about 5,200 New York militiamen were encamped on the lower Niagara and an additional 1,500 to 2,000 regulars and naval personnel were in the Buffalo area. An attempt was made to take Queenston Heights on the Canadian side, but the American forces under General Stephen Van Rensellaer were badly defeated. Throughout 1813 there was bloody fighting on both sides of the Niagara and on December 19, Fort Niagara fell to the Canadians. In 1814 the Battle of Chippewa was won by the Americans and three weeks later (July 25) the bloodiest battle of the war, Lundy's Lane, was likewise considered an American victory; it was fought just a mile from the falls. By the Treaty of Ghent the Niagara country was restored to the status quo antebellum.

Settlers returning after the ravages of the War of 1812 saw the advantages of catering to others who had the leisure time to travel to the falls, already becoming renowned through paintings, prints, and the printed word. Soon hotels and taverns proliferated. By the time of the Civil War the pattern was well set. Visitors made the overnight trip by railroad from the eastern population centers. They strolled the river banks and savored the beauties of the river and the falls. Those who came in wintertime, particularly after a number of low-degree February days, visited a fairyland of frozen spray covering every inch of the nearby trees and land. Below, the gorge was choked with an ice jam known locally as the ice bridge; for years in winter it was used as a means of communicating between Canada and the United States.

The first suspension bridge spanned the Great Gorge in 1848 but the great wonder of the age was the one designed by John August Roebling (father of Washington Roebling who built the Brooklyn Bridge) in 1855. The Niagara Bridge was a double-roadway railroad and vehicular suspension bridge which became a marvel of the engineering world and rivalled the very falls as an attraction.

The peacefulness of the growing tourism industry was interrupted in 1837 during the Canadian rebellion when a dilapidated steamboat, the *Caroline*, which was transporting men and supplies to the Canadian rebels, was captured while moored on the American shore and set afire and adrift, eventually going over the falls. War hysteria again swept through the Niagara country, but the matter was settled amicably by Colonel Winfield Scott and later by the Webster-Ashburton Treaty (1842). Until the Civil War the Niagara served as a corridor to freedom for runaway slaves headed for Canada.

Niagarans soon learned that tourists like thrills, and by the end of the 1850s daredevils were furnishing them. Jean Frances Gravelot, better known as Blondin, crossed the Niagara regularly in the summers of 1859 and 1860 to the cheers of thousands while walking on a three-quarter-inch rope. In 1860 tightrope walker Farini was a magnificent rival. After the turn of the twentieth century a Michigan school teacher, Annie Edson Taylor, successfully went over the Horseshoe Falls in a wooden barrel and started a parade of others who would attempt the same feat.

In the 1880s men began making plans to use some of Niagara's water to turn the wheels of industry. Water wheels along the river and along a hydraulic canal had long used a fraction of that potential. Now plans were more ambitious. In 1895 the Adams Station, the first large-scale hydroelectric plant in the world, was producing alternating current; the next year that same power was running street cars in Buffalo. Today with power plants on both sides of the river using one-half of the river's water, the Niagara produces about 23 million kilovolts of electricity per year, the largest in the free world. This cheap power has spawned industries on both sides of the Niagara: ceramics, abrasives, chemicals, steel, grain milling, and a thousand other manufactures.

Tourism continued to grow. After the land near the falls became New York's first state park in 1885 it was easier than ever to see Niagara Falls. The hotels became not only more numerous but bigger. Perhaps as many as ten million visitors a year can be at present accommodated on both sides of the river.

Buffalo is the commerical center for two million nearby residents in both countries. The lower Niagara, at Lewiston, New York, and Queenston, Ontario, where the Great Falls started 12,000 years ago, passes through the rich lake plain agricultural country known for its apples, peaches, and farm crops. The Niagara's waters flow peacefully here, stirring to the movement of pleasure craft as they flow past restored Fort Niagara and into Lake Ontario.

The Niagara is short in length, fast moving, strategically located, and attractive to both industry and tourism. It is a river whose name is generally known throughout the world only for its great falls. But it is much more than just that spectacular natural phenomenon.

FURTHER READING: Robert West Howard, *Thundergate: The Forts of Niagara* (1968). Donald E. Loker, *Visitors Guide to Niagara Falls* (1969).

Donald E. Loker

~~~~~~

The Ocmulgee River

Source: Lake Jackson, southwest of Atlanta
Length: 255 Miles
Tributaries: Towaliga, Falling Creek
Mouth: Joins Oconee to become Altamaha at "the Forks" in southeast-central Georgia
Cities: Macon
Industries: Lumbering, pulp and paper, kaolin products
Agriculture: Soy beans, cotton, peanuts

Ocmulgee is an Indian word meaning "bubbling waters." Its three headwater streams, one of them rising in the heart of Atlanta and the other two in the mountains of north-central Georgia, are fed by bubbling springs. As these streams approach each other they flow into Lake Jackson, a reservoir some forty miles southeast of Atlanta. Out of the lake emerges the Ocmulgee. It flows swiftly southward through red hills, receiving additional waters from such tributaries as Towaliga and Falling creeks.

At Macon, the largest city along its course, the Ocmulgee reaches Georgia's fall line and becomes sluggish. Then it twists and winds southward, makes a big bend, and flows eastward. At the bend its flow is swollen by the addition of cold blue waters from deep springs on both sides of the river. Finally it joins the Oconee at "the Forks" near Lumber City, thereby creating the Altamaha which flows to the Atlantic. In all, the Ocmulgee is about 255 miles long.

Geographically it lies in central Georgia, with the Oconee, Ogeechee, and Savannah rivers to the east and the Flint and Chattahoochee lying to the west. When the land was new and only narrow Indian paths connected settlements, these rivers were the real trails through the wilderness. In the westward movement, the Ocmulgee played a significant part.

From prehistoric times on, the river was used by the Indians. The systematic earthen structures of the Mound Builders, called the Hitchites, have been found along the river and especially at Ocmulgee Old Fields near Macon. In historic times they gave ground to a fierce, invading people called the Muscogees, later known as the Creeks. They extended their domains until they controlled lands from the Savannah River on the east to the Chattahoochee on the west. An aggressive, intelligent people, they too were centered at Ocmulgee Old Fields.

The first whites to see the Ocmulgee were De Soto's men who in 1540 probably crossed at a convenient point near Abbeville, at the big bend, and then advanced upriver to present Hawkinsville. Only then, having observed heavy Indian settlement along the way, did De Soto turn eastward.

In the late sixteenth century the Spanish converted the Indians of Apalache (north Florida) and carried on trade with the Creeks. However, English traders from South Carolina soon enticed the Creeks from the Spanish. By 1703 they were willing to unite with the English under Governor James Moore of South Carolina to march into Apalache and destroy the Spanish missions there.

Yet the Creeks themselves were chastised by the English as a result of the Yamassee War (1715), and by 1730 had settled in two general regions. The Upper Creeks were in Alabama along the Alabama, Coosa, and Tallapoosa rivers. The Lower Creeks spread westward across Georgia from the Savannah River across the Oconee and Ocmulgee to the Flint and Chattahoochee rivers and south to the Gulf of Mexico. In spite of the appearance of French traders from the lower Mississippi and Spanish traders working up from the Gulf, the English retained control of the Indian trade.

In 1733 the English philanthropist James Oglethorpe assumed direction of the new colony of Georgia. In 1739 he met with Indians at Coweta Town on the Chattahoochee, camping on the way near present Macon. Oglethorpe was a diplomat and a man of integrity. He maintained good relations with the Indians which continued until the 1760s.

Yet trouble was simmering, for each year the Indians were aware of more encroachments by whites upon their territory. During the Revolutionary War they turned on the whites, and when with the end of the war more white intruders preempted their lands, the Indians raised the tomahawk. Previously ratified treaties were repudiated by the half-blood Creek leader Alexander McGillivray. The Treaty of New York between McGillivray for the Creeks and the new United States was supposed to end the troubles, but the savage fighting went right on. Only when the federal government sent Benjamin Hawkins among the Creeks in the early 1800s was a semblance of peace established on the westward-creeping frontier.

In 1805 the Creeks agreed that the Ocumulgee River would constitute the dividing line between the whites and the Indians. Both peoples could navigate and fish the stream, though whites could not use fish traps and, if they used nets, they must be hauled to the east bank. The Indians allowed the whites to stake out and use a pathway from the Ocmulgee west across Creek lands to the Mobile River.

Almost immediately a flood of settlers inundated the fertile, green lands east of the Ocmulgee. What had been a region heavily populated by Indians became an equally heavily populated agricultural land inhabited by whites. By 1809 seven counties had been created in the Ocmulgee Fork—the land between the Oconee and Ocmulgee. Because the Indians were just across the latter river on the west bank, the whites organized militia companies and in times of Indian troubles erected stockades at strategic places.

Usage soon turned Indian trails into wagon roads. The River Road was especially important: it twisted along the east bank of the Ocmulgee from Fort Hawkins (present-day Macon) southward past the Indian trading post at Durham's Bluff, on past Buzzard's Roost Bluff, down to Jacksonville (Georgia) and finally to the juncture with the Oconee. Sometimes the road wound through giant oaks with so much shade that the traveler rode for miles in a sort of gloaming.

Even more important as a "road" was the Ocmulgee itself, and, after it joined the Oconee, the Altahama down to the Atlantic at Darien.

From the first white occupation these rivers were used for transportation. Rafts were constructed from nearby timber and, loaded with the produce of the frontier—salt pork, beeswax, tallow, hides, turpentine, corn, and cotton—floated down to Darien. Only long poles, dexterously manipulated by the raftsmen, prevented accidents. If all went well, Darien was reached, the raft and all its produce was sold, and the men returned on foot upstream along the narrow, shaded River Road.

Soon poleboats made their appearance. These flat-bottomed vessels demanded the muscular energies of ten or twelve men. Downstream was hazardous because of the serpentine route; upstream was slow and toilsome. In deep water where poles were useless the raftsmen used an iron hook. It was caught on an overhanging tree, then the boat pulled up to it, and then the procedure was repeated. It was a three to four weeks' journey up the Altamaha and Ocmulgee to Fort Hawkins. At times of Indian troubles there was danger of ambush.

It is too bad more folklore has not been retained about those days. It is known that the rivermen sang chanties in unison as they poled along. The boat was a conveyer of news as well as commodities from the outside world. Many a youth remembered all the rest of his life the haunting sounds of the chanting river men as they poled closer and closer to a plantation landing.

In the 1840s, as cotton became king in the Ocmulgee country, the need for larger and better boats rose apace until boat building became an important industry. Some of the larger boats could carry up to 700 bales of cotton. The Georgia legislature, not unmindful of the Ocmulgee's importance as a trade artery, appropriated funds to clear the river of snags and otherwise aided navigation.

Even though the Indians had title to the lands on the west bank, the prevalence of whites caused them to move further west. By 1810 the Federal Road from Fort Hawkins to Fort Stoddert on the Mobile River was being heavily used by immigrants pushing into "the foreign country of West Georgia." It was inevitable that the Indians would put up a last stand, and this came during the War of 1812. A substantial number of Creeks, accepting Tecumseh's pleas for a united Indian front against the whites, took up the tomahawk. Indian depredations along the Ocmulgee increased. Then in March, 1814, General Andrew Jackson defeated the Indians at Horseshoe Bend. Not until 1821, however, by the Treaty of Indian Springs, did the Indians finally give up the territory between the Ocmulgee and the Flint River.

In 1829 the steamboat *North Carolina* reached Macon and within a few years steamboats were making regular runs between Darien and Macon. Most were sternwheelers drawing up to 20 ft. of water. Cotton and steamboats now rapidly transformed the frontier Ocmulgee country into the fabled land of the antebellum South. Beautiful homes appeared, and the River Road carried visitors to white-columned mansions. Macon, Hawkinsville, Abbeville, Jacksonville (Georgia), and Lumber City were leading river ports.

The most important center of population along the Ocmulgee was Macon. It was situated at Ocmulgee Old Fields, which in 1806 had been chosen as the site of Fort Hawkins, named for the Indian agent Benjamin Hawkins. In 1823 the town of Macon was laid out. It soon became the focal point for pioneers seeking fame and fortune. It served a fertile agricultural region and was the railroad, manufacturing, and geographical center of the state. The Southern poet Sidney Lanier was born there in 1842.

When the Civil War came, the idyllic life along the Ocmulgee came to an end. Macon was taken by Union troops in 1865 and the entire area subsequently fell into post-war decline. Sharecropping and the crop lien system replaced the plantation economy. Railroads displaced river transportation. Then gradually lumbering, pulp and paper factories, and kaolin products made from tremendous deposits of the fine, white clay revived much of the region's economic activity.

Today Macon has 150,000 people and is known as a city of great beauty, history, and culture. Wesleyan Female College, the first college in the world chartered to grant degrees to women, and Mercer University are located there. Many of Macon's Greek Revival mansions and decorative Victorian cottages have been preserved along its winding, tree-lined streets. Nearby is Warner Robins Air Force Base. And there are still old mansions along the oak-enshrouded River Road along the Ocmulgee, reminding visitors of the slow-moving, gentle way of life of a century and a quarter ago.

The Ocmulgee is an example of a waterway that was once of great importance, but in our own age of technology and rapid land communication has lost much of its usefulness. In some ways this is fortunate, for in an age of rapidly disappearing wilderness long stretches of this beautiful river remain in a natural state. For those who fish its waters for bass weighing up to thirty-five pounds, and hunt along its banks where they may see panthers, wildcats, wild turkeys, alligators, water moccasins and rattlers, this is just fine. They like its swamps, its high bluffs, and its primitive silence broken only by the sounds of nature. Most of them hope it stays that way.

FURTHER READING: Fussell M. Chalker, *Pioneer Days Along the Ocmulgee* (1970). E. Merton Coulter, *Georgia, A Short History* (1960).

John J. McKay, Jr.

The Oconee River

Source: South of Athens, Georgia, at junction of North Oconee and Middle Oconee Rivers
Length: 229 Miles
Tributaries: Apalachee, Middle Little
Mouth: Joins Ocmulgee in southeast central Georgia to form Altamaha River
Cities: Milledgeville, Athens
Agriculture: Cotton, dairying, poultry, pecans, peaches, soybeans, peanuts, corn, wheat
Industries: Wood products, textiles, kaolin products

Many of Georgia's rivers, like the Oconee of middle Georgia, bear Indian place names—names with music and poetry in them. The Oconee winds 229 miles through central Georgia draining a basin that is a microcosm of the state's interior geography. Bisected by the fall line—an irregular shoreline of the Atlantic Ocean in the geologic past—the Oconee region sprawls northward into the Piedmont Plateau and southward into the Coastal Plain. The river has its source a few miles south of Athens where the North Oconee and the Middle Oconee merge to form the larger stream.

After the merger of its two main tributaries, the Oconee flows generally southward through the Oconee National Forest where it is fed by the Apalachee River. The enlarged stream, along with another tributary, Little River, is slowed by the man-made Lake Sinclair a few miles north of Milledgeville. Below the power dam it continues southward, crossing the fall line at Rock Landing. From here it flows southeastward through Dublin to its terminus at the "Forks" near Lumber City. Joined by the Ocmulgee, the combined rivers become the Altamaha. Together this network forms the largest watershed in Georgia, draining a vast hinterland to the Georgia coast.

William Bartram, the naturalist-explorer who crossed the region in the 1770s, described the flora and fauna in his *Travels*. In its virgin state the sandy sedimentary soils below the fall line supported a vast forest of long-leaf pine and the red clay soils of the Piedmont sustained a mixed forest of pines and hardwoods. Erosion, caused by the clearing and cultivation of the rolling terrain, gave the Oconee its "muddy red" color, its most distinctive feature. While the modern visitor might not notice many of the diverse species of natural vegetation, it would be difficult for one to ignore the rampant, cascading kudzu vines, a questionably valuable introduction from Asia.

From the first settlement of the Oconee region in the early 1800s until the disastrous invasion of the boll weevil about 1920, cotton dominated the region's economy. While other agricultural products and livestock made the area practically self-sufficient even in antebellum days, "King Cotton" supported a society romanticized in

Gone With the Wind. The white-columned mansions of Milledgeville, Eatonton, Sparta, and Athens survive as monuments to this prosperous age. After the Civil War the cotton economy persisted in spite of declining profitability until prices plummeted in the Great Depression. Forced to diversify, farmers turned to dairying, beef cattle, poultry, and other crops like pecans, peaches, corn, and soybeans. Abandoned fields reverted to woodlands; three-fourths of the area is now devoted to commercial forestry.

Manufacturing began before the Civil War. As early as 1829 Judge Augustin S. Clayton established a cotton mill on the Oconee near Athens. By 1855 cotton textile mills were operating in Milledgeville, Sparta, and Eatonton. It was not until the mid-twentieth century, however, that large-scale industry became significant. Presently, lumber, wood products, textiles, and kaolin are the main manufactures of the region.

The location of towns in the Oconee region was affected by factors such as proximity to navigable streams, shoals, fords, Indian trails, and later railroads and highways. Sandersville was originally the site of an Indian trading post and Milledgeville was founded near the fall line at the junction of several Indian trails. From settlements like Milledgeville and Dublin on the Oconee, flatboats floated cotton down to Darien. Incapable of returning upstream, the vessels were dismantled and sold for lumber. Pole boats, operated by thrusting long poles into the bottom of the river, navigated the river in both directions. The first steamboat made its way from Darien to Milledgeville in 1819. The next year obstructions in the river were cleared as far north as Athens. While optimists envisioned a thriving commerce on the Oconee, steamboating was hampered by low water, a winding course, and the hazard of fire. Consequently, flatboats, wagons, and later the railroads carried the bulk of the freight. Another use of the Oconee involved log rafting which peaked in the decades 1880–1910.

Little is known of the pre-Columbian peoples who lived in the Oconee region. Effigy mounds located at Rock Eagle (Putnam County) and in the vicinity of Little Shoulder Bone Creek (Hancock County) are as mysterious as Stonehenge or the pyramids of Egypt. These mounds are the only known effigies constructed of stone in North America. Rock Eagle is considered by some experts to be the most perfect mound in America today.

Hernando De Soto, the first white man known to explore the region, crossed the Oconee at Carr Shoals (Laurens County) in 1540. The Oconees, a sub-tribal group of the Creeks, inhabited the river and these lands. Their chief village was Oconee Town located near Rock Landing. According to a local historian, a Spanish mission called San Francisco de Oconee was established here in 1680. The Yamassee War forced some of the Oconees to migrate to the Chattahoochee River; others went to Florida where they founded the town of Cuscovilla and later merged with the Seminoles. The Lower Creeks then expanded their hunting grounds to include this area.

General James Oglethorpe, Georgia's founder, negotiated a treaty with the principal Creek tribes in 1739. After the War of Jenkin's Ear (1739–1742) eliminated the Spanish menace, the Indians remained peaceful until the last quarter of the eighteenth century when white settlers began to encroach on Indian lands.

Apparently the region was so remote and sparsely settled that it was little affected by the major operations of either side during the Revolution, but once the war ended pressure mounted for the opening of Indian lands between the Ogeechee and Oconee rivers. This clash of interests caused the Oconee War. Indian depredations and retaliatory campaigns by white settlers ravaged the middle Georgia frontier for more than a dozen years. Alexander McGillivray, a half-blood Creek chief, united his people in opposition to white expansion. In 1790 President Washington finally enticed McGillivray to New York where, after generous gifts and promises, the chief acceded to the cession of lands east of the Oconee.

While the Treaty of New York reserved lands west of the Oconee for the Creeks, Elijah Clarke and a motley band of followers laid claim to an illegitimate buffer state in that region. They erected forts along its borders in defiance of federal law under the pretense of protecting Georgia from Creek depredations. The new Trans-Oconee Republic, as it was called, supposedly framed a constitution and organized a government. When President Washington ordered Clarke's arrest, he surrendered to friends who acquitted him without questioning his motives. Governor George Mathews was ordered by federal authorities to destroy the forts and settlements, but all efforts to convict Clarke of treason failed.

The United States Government soon negotiated the Treaties of Fort Wilkinson (1802) and Flint River Agency (1804) which extinguished Creek claims to the lands between the Oconee and the Ocmulgee. White settlers poured into the new lands and began to transform the Oconee basin into a productive agricultural region. Georgia's capital was moved to the west bank of the Oconee and named Milledgeville for then Governor John Milledge. The state legislature held its first meeting in November, 1807, although the Statehouse was not completed until 1836. The rowdy frontier capital reflected the ascendancy of the backcountry Piedmont over the more cultured coastal area.

By mid-century Milledgeville was graced by a new executive mansion that was designed by Charles B. Cluskey. It was also the site of the Georgia State Penitentiary, the State Arsenal, and the Georgia Lunatic Asylum. While Milledgeville's population grew slowly, reaching only 2,313 by 1870, its society gradually became more refined. The removal of the capital from Milledgeville to Atlanta in 1877 was an irrevocable loss to the old antebellum town.

The decades from 1830 to 1860 were the most prosperous years for the cotton planters of the Oconee "black belt." While planters were never as numerous as yeoman farmers, the slavocracy dominated the social, economic, and political life of the entire state. In 1860 the 832 planters of Hancock and Putnam counties, situated in the Oconee heartland, together produced 24,651 bales of cotton. These same planters collectively owned 15,275 slaves. In defense of this economic, cultural, and racial system and as a reaction to the sectional crises of the 1850s, Southern nationalism matured. Georgia was swept into secession by a special convention that assembled in Milledgeville in January, 1861.

The pivotal historical event of the Oconee region was the Civil War. Although Georgia experienced only limited military operations prior to 1863, Georgians rallied to the cause by organizing numerous volunteer units. An illustration of the casualties suffered by these units is provided by the Baldwin Blues; of their original roster of sixty men only seven were present at Appomattox.

Not until Sherman's infamous march to the sea after the burning of Atlanta on November 5, 1864, did middle Georgia experience the full impact of war. With an army of 65,000 men and the intent to live off the land, Sherman headed for Savannah. The left wing of his army, commanded by General Henry W. Slocum, marched along the west side of the Oconee through Madison and Eatonton to Milledgeville. After a minor scouting skirmish at Oconee Station, the main force entered Milledgeville on November 23. Sparing most of the private residences, Sherman ordered the burning of a number of public buildings though the Statehouse was only vandalized. The whole region through which the army passed was terrorized and pillaged by undisciplined "bummers."

The era of Reconstruction brought a social revolution to the region. Widespread sharecropping and farm tenancy, the crop lien system, absentee ownership, and declining cotton prices fostered poverty and deprivation. Henry W. Grady, from Athens, and Joel Chandler Harris, from Eatonton, exemplified the contradictions of the Southern mentality. Grady, editor of *The Atlanta Constitution*, was chief advocate of the "New South," while Harris created the nostalgic image of the "Old South" in his Uncle Remus stories. World Wars I and II, the Great Depression, the experiments of the New Deal, shifts in population, industrialization, declining provincialism, and changing race relations drastically altered land use and the quality of life.

Athens and Milledgeville emerged as the main cultural centers of the Oconee region. The University of Georgia at Athens, adjacent to Cedar Shoals on the Oconee, has become an educational and research center of national renown with an enrollment of over 25,000.

Today the residents of the Oconee Basin, rich in culture, natural resources, and a fascinating heritage, confront optimistically the greater demands and accelerating changes of the present.

FURTHER READING: James C. Bonner, *Milledgeville, Georgia's Antebellum Capital* (1978). E. Merton Coulter, *Georgia, A Short History* (1960).

R. F. Saunders and George A. Rogers

The Passaic River

Source: Eastern slope of a hill near Morristown, New Jersey
Length: About 100 miles
Tributaries: Rockaway, Pompton, and Saddle rivers
Outflow: Newark Bay
Agriculture: Minimal
Industry: Diverse, heavy manufacturing activity

The Passaic was once described as the most crooked, most sluggish, and the longest river in New Jersey. It has its source in a group of springs at an elevation of some 600 feet on the eastern slope of a hill in Mendham near Morristown. From this point a small stream meanders across open fields, is joined by others, and proceeds toward Newark Bay almost 100 miles distant. En route, the river winds in every direction of the compass and flows through seven new Jersey counties and forty-five municipalities.

From its source, the river descends rapidly in a southeasterly direction, passing through Morristown National Historical Park at Jockey Hollow and the Great Swamp National Wildlife Refuge. Ten miles beyond the Great Swamp, after dropping some 400 feet, it is turned to the north by the Watchung Mountain range. The river, to this point, is swift-moving, beautiful, and relatively unspoiled.

The Passaic then follows a generally northerly course for approximately thirty miles, moving slowly through a broad valley. A number of swamps and marshlands border the river in this section, alternating with numerous residential and industrial developments. After passing the Great Piece Meadows, a major wetland, it veers to the east and gathers speed as it nears the Great Falls at Paterson. It tumbles some seventy feet at the falls, then curves around the city of Paterson and begins its final phase, flowing south toward Newark Bay and the Atlantic Ocean.

Between its source and Newark Bay, the Passaic and its tributaries drain an area of approximately 950 square miles. This comprises much of northern New Jersey and a portion of southern New York state. A network of smaller streams contributes in three principle tributary systems to this vast basin drainage area. The Rockaway, which rises in Sussex County, flows southeast and receives the waters of the Whippany river before uniting with the Passaic near Caldwell. The Pompton river is a complex of three river systems, the Ramapo, the Wanaque, and the Pequannock, all of which unite to form the Pompton ten miles north of its confluence with the Passaic. The Saddle River, which rises in Rockland County, New York, drains much of central Bergen County before emptying into the Passaic at Lodi in the lower Passaic Valley.

For several thousand years before the arrival of the white man the Passaic River basin was inhabited by the Leni Lenape, a semi-nomadic, peaceful Indian sub-tribe of the Algonquian nation. Never very numerous, they offered little resistance to the early Dutch and English settlers of the area. By the time of the American Revolution there were but a few scattered remnants of the Leni Lenape in northern New Jersey.

Dutch colonization of Manhattan and the adjacent portion of New Jersey began in the early 1600s. However, the vast wetlands of the Hackensack and Passaic rivers acted as barriers to westward expansion, postponing settlement along the Passaic until 1666. In May of that year a group of thirty English colonists from Connecticut led by Robert Treat sailed into Newark Bay, entered the Passaic River and dropped anchor near the west bank at the present site of Newark. They purchased a large tract from the Hackensack Indians and established a small village. The colony grew rapidly as more settlers arrived; it expanded northward along the river and westward beyond the Watchung Mountains. Meanwhile, Dutch colonization had spread along the Hudson and into the interior of northeastern New Jersey. The Dutch settlers finally reached the Passaic some fifteen miles above Newark and moved upstream to the present Paterson area and beyond.

Dutch and English colonial expansion in the

Passaic Valley eventually met, first to the north of Newark, and later near present Caldwell. Above this point a large part of the early development along the Passaic resulted from the outgrowth of English settlements at Elizabethtown, Perth Amboy, and New Brunswick south of Newark. By the time of the Revolution most of the lands along the river had been claimed, villages had been established, farms were in full production, and there was active trading between the outlying settlements and the towns.

Throughout the Revolutionary War the Passaic River, because of its peculiar geographical situation, played an important role in the conflict. In November, 1776, following the British successes on Long Island and Manhattan, it was witness to the disastrous retreat of Washington's defeated army across New Jersey. Newark, on the lower river, was readily accessible by water to British forces stationed on Staten Island and in Manhattan: four major raids by British troops and many lesser forages kept the town in a state of seige and turmoil during much of the war.

Within its broad middle valley beyond the Watchung Mountains, the river served as an effective defense barrier to the movement of British armies toward Morristown and the Continental encampments and supplies in that area. American forces stationed behind this barrier formed a reserve available when needed to help thwart British troop movements east of the mountains. The availability of these reserves was an important factor in the failure of British assaults near Springfield in July, 1780. The river also helped screen Continental troop movements from Morristown to the northern or central New Jersey sectors.

The winter sufferings of Washington's ragged soldiers in and around the Jockey Hollow encampment along the upper reaches of the Passaic River are an unforgettable saga of the war. The general's success in maintaining his army there played a vital part in the ultimate success of the American cause. From Jockey Hollow the armies marched to Yorktown, the defeat of Cornwallis, and victory in the struggle for independence.

At Paterson, the Great Falls of the Passaic present a scene of awesome beauty long considered one of the natural wonders of the eastern states. First discovered by white trappers in the mid-1600s, stories of their majesty spread and attracted visitors from many parts of America and Europe. General Washington and his staff often visited the falls and the General is said to have carved his initials in the traprock there in 1780. Spring runs of shad and sturgeon yielded large catches at the foot of the falls. Today, in spite of residential and industrial development nearby, the falls are still an awe-inspiring sight at full flood following spring freshets and heavy rains at other seasons.

Water power provided by the Passaic and its tributaries was an important source of energy from Colonial days until the late 1800s. Mills were to be found at many points, especially in the upper and middle valleys, and at the rapids at Little Falls, the Great Falls, and Passaic. Smaller tributary streams also had their share of saw, grist, and other mills.

It was inevitable that the potential of the Great Falls as a major power source would attract attention. In 1791, on application from Alexander Hamilton and others, a charter was granted by the Governor of New Jersey for a society for Establishing Useful Manufactures. The Society selected the Great Falls as the best location for its operations, raceways and mills were constructed, and the machinery for spinning hemp and wool was installed. In spite of early financial problems, the Society survived and, stimulated by military needs of the War of 1812, eventually flourished. Out of this beginning grew the industrial city of Paterson, with its once famed textile industry, its rolling mills and factories producing machinery, tools, locomotives, and a wide range of consumer goods. For many years Paterson was the center of the American silk industry and became widely known as the "Silk City."

The Passaic's water power was also an important factor in the industrialization of the city of Passaic several miles down river from Paterson. There a series of rapids marked the head of navigation to which ships plying the river transported materials and products from Newark and beyond, and carried agricultural and other merchandise on the return trip. A dam at the head of the rapids was completed in 1859, and, with an adjacent canal, marked the beginning of an industrial era for Passaic. After early difficulties the Passaic area became a major center for woolen and worsted goods, cotton prints, chemicals, artificial leather, and a variety of other manufactured products.

Newark, which was to become New Jersey's principal city, lacked the advantages of significant water power. However, with its location near the mouth of the Passaic and its accessibility to New York and other eastern seaboard cities, it early became a major trading and shipping center. Agricultural products, lumber, and coal and iron from the interior formed the basis for its exports, while imported and locally manufactured goods were shipped up the river to meet the needs of the ever-increasing population there. The completion of the Morris Canal to Newark in 1832 increased that city's commercial importance. Through the first half of the nineteenth century and for a number of years thereafter the Passaic teemed with river traffic between Newark and Passaic. Gradually, however, this was superseded by the railroads.

During this period the Passaic's natural beauty made it a residential and recreational paradise. Homes with spacious and well-landscaped grounds lined its banks, pleasure boats of many descriptions plied its waters, fishing was excellent, and hockey and skating were popular winter pastimes. Passenger steamers furnished well-patronized daily commutation service between the river communities and Newark.

Unfortunately, the discharges of industrial wastes and raw sewage led inevitably to the Passaic's deterioration. By the late 1800s pollution had taken its toll and the lower Passaic had lost much of its former charm. Pleasure boat cruising ceased, the once-abundant fishing resources disappeared, and the water became unsafe for human use. The stately homes along the river were gradually abandoned as the polluted waters and foul odors increased. Potable water supply requirements had to be met by the construction of reservoirs along the major tributaries in the northern Passaic River basin.

In recent years, due to greater public awareness of the environment and resultant pressures, some reduction in the pollution levels of the Passaic has been achieved. This has come about largely because of stricter enforcement of state-enacted legislation, backed by programs initiated under the Federal Water Pollution Control Act Amendments of 1972. While these actions have been slow to take effect and there is still much to be accomplished, continued improvement is anticipated.

The control of another and in some respects much more serious problem still appears to be many years distant. Since early Colonial times the river and some of its tributaries have been subject to frequent floods. Over the years flood prevention has been sought at local, state, and federal levels. Specially authorized commissions have studied all aspects of the situation. Recommendations have been made, but little has been done. Largely unimpeded development along the river and in the flood plains, resulting in increased runoff during times of heavy rains, has accentuated the severity of the flooding and related property damage. The Army Engineers, which entered the picture in 1936, has made exhaustive studies and submitted four major reports. None of these have received Congressional approval, due largely to a lack of the required local support. Completion of a study begun in 1978 and positive action to control flooding appear to be several years in the future.

The Passaic River is similar in many respects to other rivers in various sections of the United States. It has serious problems and is threatened by the pressures of constantly increasing population. On the other hand, it still has many recreational values and much beauty, with a potential for greater future assets. Time and human determination and ability to cope with its needs will decide its fate.

FURTHER READING: Norman F. Brydon, *The Passaic River* (1974). Harry Emerson Wildes, *The Raritan and the Passaic* (1943).

Norman F. Brydon

The Patuxent River

Source: Eastern slope of Parr's Ridge in northwest Howard County, in central Maryland
Length: 100 miles
Tributaries: None of significance
Outflow: Chesapeake Bay
Agriculture: Tobacco
Industry: Fisheries

Maryland, though a small state, stretches from the forested foothills of the Appalachians eastward to the salt marshes, bays, and estuaries of the Atlantic Ocean. Prior to the coming of the whites there was heavy Indian settlement around the Chesapeake Bay area of the state. The whites likewise prospered from the fish and mollusks that flourished in the Bay. They also found the land fertile and the climate mild. The whites also profited from the religious toleration of the colony, which was first settled by George Calvert, Lord Baltimore, in 1634. He was a Catholic.

The principal river that flows exclusively through Maryland is the Patuxent. It originates on the eastern slope of Parr's Ridge, the western segment of a drainage divide that separates streams flowing into the Chesapeake Bay to the east from those flowing into the Potomac River to the south and west.

From its source, the Patuxent flows southeast about 100 miles before flowing into Chesapeake Bay. For the first thirty miles it flows in a winding course through the rolling piedmont to the fall zone. This is close to present U.S. Highway 1 between Washington, D.C., and Baltimore. Then the river meanders downstream through the softer coastal plain sediments to the village of Queen Anne. This abandoned tobacco inspection and transshipment point was at an earlier time the head of navigation on the river. Below it the Patuxent flows more than fifty miles to its mouth at Chesapeake Bay. It widens noticeably below Benedict, some twenty-five miles up-river from the mouth.

The pre-history of occupancy in Maryland is similar to that of other mid-Atlantic states. The fluted points of hunters who were in the region at least 8,000 years ago, after the last Ice Age, have been found in many parts of the state including along the Patuxent. At the time of the white intrusion the Indians were of Algonquian stock, farming, fishing, and hunting. So overwhelming was white occupancy of the region, however, that by 1700 the Indians were gone from the colony.

Learning from the experience of their neighbors to the south, the settlers of Virginia, the Maryland colonists began tobacco culture immediately and met with quick success. To this day the largest concentration of rich tobacco-producing land in southern Maryland lies along the Patuxent's middle course between Queen Anne and Benedict. From the beginning the river functioned as the critical transportation link for this rich core of tobacco production. It remains important to the tobacco industry to this very day.

The main stem of the Patuxent River was deep enough to permit passage of colonial ocean-sailing vessels upstream to Queen Anne. During the early colonial era, bartering of goods between planters and shipmasters was the most common method of marketing tobacco and other agricultural commodoties. These activities took place at numerous private and the few public town landings. Many smaller planters without river frontage had to rely upon one of the larger plants, located on the river, for transshipment of their tobacco. There were many disadvantages to these marketing procedures. Of particular concern was smuggling, especially of tobacco, the colony's most important export.

The first effective regulation of exports came with the passage of the Maryland Tobacco Inspection Act of 1747. This law required that all tobacco be shipped through designated inspection warehouses along the Patuxent River and other watercourses in the colony. The 1747 act and its successors remained in effect into the 1800s. As a result, tobacco collection was concentrated at a dozen strategic locations along the Patuxent. These inspection warehouses and their adjacent landings proved useful locations for the establishment of stores and the concentration of other economic activities.

The Patuxent Basin came into increasing competition with Baltimore after the American Revolution. By 1790 that growing community had become the primary port of call for the larger ocean-sailing vessels and increasing quantities of tobacco were being shipped to that city prior to export from the state. Consequently, tobacco inspection was progressively located in Baltimore, to the detriment of Patuxent business. The old public landing and warehouse sites and some private landings along the river continued in use only for local and regional traffic. They supplied Baltimore with tobacco and other agricultural commodities.

After the War of 1812, shallow-draft steam-powered vessels, drawing three and one-half to four and one-half feet of water, gradually came into use and were able to service the Patuxent landings more efficiently. However, the poor farming practices of that era caused erosion of the land and siltation of the river; this began to impede navigation before 1850. The situation was not severe in most of the main stem of the river except, perhaps, near Queen Anne, in the upstream reaches of the previously navigable channel. Tidal movements in the lower reaches of the Patuxent River probably helped maintain the channel by scouring out the silt deposited there. However, sedimentation was more severe in some of the tributaries. These could be negotiated only by small vessels by the mid-1800s.

The last significant carrier to operate on the Patuxent was the Weems Steamship Line, which continued to serve the landings until 1929. By then, increasing competition from the railroads and, later but more significantly, the expanding highway network, led to the demise of steamship service.

Widespread changes have occurred in the Patuxent Basin since the cessation of steamship service fifty years ago. In the Piedmont, westward and upstream from U.S. Route 1, the river has been altered by the construction of two dams. These formed the Rocky Gorge and Tridelphia reservoirs, used to supply potable water to Maryland suburbs of Washington, D.C.

Increased supplemental irrigation and better cropping practices have reduced erosion of agricultural soils in the Patuxent Basin. Supplemental irrigation to augment natural rainfall has gained favor on the tobacco and other specialty crop farms. On-farm impoundments provide virtually all of this water and help reduce local runoff. Furthermore, improved cropping practices, such as planting cover crops to hold the soil when other crops are not being grown, have gained acceptance.

Tobacco remains the most important cash crop in southern Maryland. Its limited acreage in comparison with corn, soybeans, winter wheat, fallow fields, and woodland may deceive the casual observer concerning the crop's economic importance. The most visible, widespread year-round evidence of the dominance of tobacco are the characteristic barns, with vertical ventilation slats. These slats are opened to permit air-drying of the leaves which are suspended on sticks inside the barn during the curing process.

Today, marketing of Patuxent River basin tobacco is again concentrated in southern Maryland, particularly along U.S. Route 301. Most tobacco is sold by auction during the major marketing season, from April to June. This takes place in large privately owned warehouses where the tobacco is displayed in open baskets. These warehouses were established in the 1930s as an alternative to marketing in Baltimore. Domestic tobacco companies largely buy the Maryland type 32 tobacco for blending with other cigarette tobaccos because of its excellent burning qualities. Continental Europe has long favored Maryland tobacco for pipe and cigar smoking. Consequently, some tobacco is exported in the traditional hogsheads (large oak barrels).

As in years past, commerical fishermen—locally known as watermen—are actively tonging oysters and netting fish in the Patuxent River. But other areas in Maryland's Chesapeake Bay region have more economically viable fisheries.

Since World War II the rural tranquility of the basin has been disturbed by rampant land speculation resulting from urban pressures of the Washington, D.C.-Baltimore-Annapolis triangle. Accelerated erosion of top and subsoil has resulted. Poor building practices, now officially prohibited, did little to contain runoff water and the soil it carried from being washed into the river and its tributaries.

Unkempt fields overgrown with weeds, run-down fences, and dilapidated farm buildings nearing collapse all testify both to earlier careless use of the soil and to the land speculators' desire for "quick-kill" profits. Proliferation of subdivisions and highways further detracts from the rural charm of the Patuxent Basin. Maryland authorities have enacted land-use legislation providing some tax advantages to preservation of open space in rural areas, but these are not strong enough to preclude further development. Perhaps the current and continuing energy crisis will forestall further "progress," which is viewed with disdain by many long-time residents.

FURTHER READING: Alice J. Pippson, ed., *The Chesapeake Bay in Maryland: An Atlas of Natural Resources* (1973). Arthur P. Middleton, *Tobacco Coast: A Maritime History of Chesapeake Bay in the Colonial Era* (1953). John Barth, *The Sot-Weed Factor* (1960) (fiction).

Basel H. Brune

The Pee Dee River

Source: Confluence of Yadkin and Uwharrie rivers near Albemarle in south-central North Carolina
Length: 233 miles
Tributaries: Little Pee Dee, Lumber, Black, and Lynches rivers
Mouth: Winyah Bay at Georgetown, South Carolina
Agricultural Products: Lumber and naval stores, small farming
Industries: Lumber mills, paper mills, textiles, recreation

When composing the lyrics for "Old Folks at Home," Stephen Foster first wrote, "Way down upon the Pedee ribber/ Far far away. . . ." Unfortunately for the Pee Dee, he switched to the Suwannee River in subsequent drafts of the lyrics. Even though Foster decided against using the Pee Dee, it has found its way into literature. Walt Whitman twice referred to the Pee Dee river in *Leaves of Grass*. As might be expected, the river also figures in the folklore of the region through which it flows.

The origin and correct spelling of the river's name are issues upon which scholars have disagreed. Most think that the name derived from the Pedee Indians who were living along a portion of the river when the first white settlers arrived. Some have argued, however, that the name is a mutation of an African word, "mpidi," which black slaves brought into the area and which means "a species of viper." The name was generally spelled as one word ("Pedee" or "Pee-dee") until into the nineteenth century when "Pee Dee" became the accepted version. The river is also sometimes referred to as the Great Pee Dee or Big Pee Dee to distinguish it from its principle tributary, the Little Pee Dee.

The Pee Dee River begins at the confluence of the Yadkin River and the Uwharrie River, near Albemarle in south-central North Carolina. It flows for 233 miles in a southeasterly direction (64 miles in North Carolina and 169 miles in South Carolina) until it enters Winyah Bay at Georgetown, South Carolina. The fall line is six miles above Cheraw, South Carolina, where the river passes from the Piedmont onto the Coastal Plain. For its short span in the Piedmont the river is vigorous, but below it the Pee Dee becomes sluggish, meandering, and is bounded by a wide flood plain, much of which is permanently inundated. The flow of the river is along one main channel except for the lower twenty-eight miles. Tidewater is thirty-eight miles above the mouth. The Pee Dee is muddy yellow because of clay washed into it from the Yadkin.

The drainage basin of the Pee Dee is immense. It drains 9,280 square miles of North Carolina, 180 square miles of Virginia, and 6,880 square miles of South Carolina where it is the second largest of the state's four drainage basins. The river has four major tributaries. Little Pee Dee River, the largest, originates in Scotland County, North Carolina, and joins the Pee Dee near

Yauhannah in Georgetown County, South Carolina. Lumber River rises in Moore County, North Carolina, and flows into the Little Pee Dee near Mullins, South Carolina. Black River, the second largest tributary, originates near Bishopville, South Carolina, and enters the Pee Dee four miles above Winyah Bay. Lynches River begins in Union County, North Carolina, and joins the Pee Dee in Florence County, South Carolina.

When Europeans began coming to the area, the river served as a natural route for settlers seeking homesteads in the Carolina interior. Welsh settlers, attracted by the bounties offered by the colonial government and by the opportunity to practice their religion, made one of the first settlements on the river in 1737 near present day Society Hill, South Carolina. During the Revolutionary War, the swamps along the river provided General Francis Marion and his band of Patriot guerrillas numerous hiding places and contributed to Marion's sobriquet, the "Swamp Fox." The river also played a role in the Civil War. The Confederate Navy established a ship yard at Mars Bluff (Florence County, South Carolina) and constructed a gunboat christened, *C.S.S. Pedee.* The only action the vessel saw was protection of Confederate troops who crossed the Pee Dee at Cheraw in early 1865. The crew scuttled the boat at Mars Bluff in March, 1865, to prevent its capture.

The river was an important transportation route from colonial times through the nineteenth century. As early as 1784, South Carolina appropriated funds for clearing obstructions from the river's mouth to the state line. In 1785, 1791, 1805, and 1815 the state enacted legislation which appropriated funds, levied special taxes, or required male residents of the counties adjoining the stream to labor six days each year in removing hazards to navigation. A survey conducted by the Confederate government during the Civil War reported that the average depth of the channel from Cheraw to Georgetown was eight feet. Acting under the commerce clause of the constitution, Congress authorized projects in the late nineteenth century for clearing portions of the river.

Products of farm and forest went downriver while manufactured goods traveled upstream, and Georgetown served as the main port. During the eighteenth and nineteenth centuries, there were many plantations along the river, and planters used the stream to ship their products (particularly cotton and rice) to market. By the 1820s, steam vessels were plying the waters of the Pee Dee. A high point for commerce on the river came in the period 1895–1907 when traffic averaged 156,000 tons per year. In 1896 and again in 1907 river commerce reached 230,000 tons. A breakdown of the commodities shipped on the Pee Dee in 1896 reveals the nature of the commerce:

	Tons	Value
Downstream		
Rosin	4,000	$ 40,000
Spirits of turpentine	1,750	105,000
Cotton	1,250	200,000
Crude turpentine	620	7,750
Timber	180,000	360,000
Shingles	4,000	40,000
Rough rice	2,178	90,000
Lumber	12,666	112,500
Wood	3,000	6,000
Crossties	10,000	40,000
Miscellaneous	500	15,000
Upstream		
General merchandise	10,000	300,000

River commerce declined rapidly in the twentieth century as alternative modes of transportation were developed in the basin. During the first third of the century the Atlantic Coast Line and the Seaboard Air Line railroads laid tracks which paralleled the Pee Dee and criss-crossed the basin. Construction of highways and bridges provided additional routes for transportation. By the 1930s the volume of commerce on the river was only 25% of what it had been when the century began. Today, commerce on the Pee Dee is slight, and the river is considered commercially navigable only as far as Georgetown.

Although the Pee Dee above the fall line was not well suited for navigation, it provided sites for hydroelectric development. Carolina Power and Light Company constructed a hydroelectric generating facility in 1912 at Blewett Falls, North Carolina, which was only twenty miles above the fall line. The present capacity of the site is 24.6 megawatts, and the 2,500 acres of water behind the dam forms Blewett Falls Lake. In 1928 the same power company completed a dam further upstream near Norwood, North Carolina. That dam impounds 5,000 acres of water, known as Lake Tillery, and the generating capacity of the facility is 84.4 megawatts.

There was talk in the 1930s of a hydroelectric dam at Mars Bluff which is well below the fall line. The Army Corps of Engineers investigated the site and concluded that development would require not only a dam across the river but also a high dike of 4 to 6 miles in length on the left bank. In view of the expense of the project, the engineers recommended against it. Water power developed by the Pee Dee, both above and below the fall line, has been utilized to drive grist, lumber, and textile mills.

Flooding has been a persistent problem on the Pee Dee which usually overflows its banks several times each year. Because the river's channel is relatively adequate in the Piedmont, flooding has never been as severe in that region as in the Coastal Plain where the river's channel is simply insufficient to carry off flood waters. Farmers in particular have long struggled against freshets on the Pee Dee. In 1809, for example, David Rogerson Williams completed a dike some five miles long to protect his cotton plantations near Society Hill. The Project was not entirely successful, however, because flood waters sometimes managed to break through the embankment.

A survey conducted in the 1930s estimated that 616,000 acres were subject to flooding in the Pee Dee basin. The inundated areas provide natural storage basins which serve to reduce the crest of a flood as it passes downstream. Most of the area subject to flooding is swamp and timber land. Very little is under cultivation, industrialized, or urbanized. As a consequence, most flood damage is ordinarily restricted to crops, highways, railroads, and bridges. Federal and state surveys have concluded that the cost of systematic flood control would exceed the benefits.

Unusually heavy rainfall in the basin has caused several major floods on the Pee Dee. Quite often the rain is the result of tropical storms and hurricanes reacting upon weather patterns over the basin. The earliest account of major flooding on the Pee Dee was recorded in 1796. Significant flooding occurred at least five times in the nineteenth century, and five times so far in the twentieth century. A freshet on the Pee Dee in 1865 which delayed for several days the crossing of Sherman's army at Cheraw is still known as "Sherman's freshet." One of the worst floods on record struck the Pee Dee in August, 1908. During the second week of the month excessively heavy rainfall thoroughly saturated the soil, and another downpour came in the third week. Monroe, North Carolina, for example, reported 7.15 inches of rain in one twenty-four hour period. At the height of the flood (August 27), the gauge on the Pee Dee at Cheraw registered 44.3 feet which was 17.3 feet above flood stage. Although no reliable estimates remain, property damage wrought by the flood was extensive.

Swamps commonly parallel the river on both sides of the channel in the Coastal Plain. Natural surface drainage is poor, and the characteristics of the soil are such that subsurface water movement is minimal. Historically the swamps have acted as a barrier to transportation across the river and served as a habitat for various creatures, including the American alligator. The large stands of gum, cypress, oak, pine, and other trees made the swamps of the Pee Dee an important source of lumber and naval stores. These swamp forests are still being harvested for saw mills and paper mills.

The mosquitoes which breed in the swamps have sometimes presented a threat to human health. During the eighteenth and nineteenth centuries, the planters along the river generally left the lowlands in the summer which they termed "the sickly season." In more recent times various state, federal, and private agencies have been involved in swamp drainage projects. The Rockefeller Foundation, for example, provided matching funds in the early twentieth century which South Carolina used to drain swamps, particularly in Marion County.

The Pee Dee basin has traditionally been agricultural and rural, but in the years since World War II industry has become increasingly important. Among the industries which depend upon water from the Pee Dee are E. I. Dupont and South Carolina Industries in Florence County, South Carolina, and J. P. Stevens Company in Marlboro County, South Carolina. Industries, small businesses, at least one city, and private individuals dump pollutants into the river. In the eighteenth and nineteenth centuries, rice planters along the lower Pee Dee used a system of dikes and flood gates to flood their rice fields with water from the river. With the exception of rice, the river has never been an important source of water for irrigation of crops because farmers have relied upon the rainfall which averages 46 inches each year.

Only a few municipalities rely upon the Pee Dee River for water. Norwood, North Carolina, draws water from Lake Tillery, and Anson County, North Carolina, has a county-wide water system which uses water from Blewett Falls Lake. Cheraw withdraws water directly from the river.

The Pee Dee River and its tributaries provide opportunities for various forms of water recreation. The Pee Dee is a favorite among sport fisherman, and North Carolina has identified the river as one of the best fishing streams in the Yadkin-Pee Dee basin. Hunters take advantage of opportunities afforded by the wildlife which inhabits the swamps, and South Carolina has established game management areas at various places along the river. Numerous boat landings dot the river banks.

Portions of the Pee Dee and its tributaries are noted for their scenic beauty. The Little Pee Dee retains today much of the appeal described by a traveler in 1801: "We crossed the Little Pee Dee at the Potato Bed Ferry. Beautiful deep sands, live oaks, lofty pines, pimeta [palmetto] swamps, with intermingled gums and cypress, variegated by evergreens of bay and laurel, and twining Jessamine flinging its odors far and wide around; lawns and savannahs—such is the country, and such the charming scenes through which we have frequently passed in our late rides." Stretches of the Little Pee Dee River and Black River have been surveyed for possible inclusion in the National Wild and Scenic Rivers system.

FURTHER READING: James A. Rogers, *Theodosia and Other Pee Dee Sketches* (Columbia, S. C.: R. L. Bryan Company, 1978). James McBride Dabbs and Carl Julien, *Pee Dee Panorama* (Columbia, S. C.: University of South Carolina Press, 1951).

Latty E. Nelson

The Penobscot River

Source: Convergence of West Branch and East Branch at Medway in northeast central Maine
Length: 150–350 miles depending on branch considered as main stream
Tributaries: Piscataquis, Passadumkeag, Mattawaukeag, East and West Branches of Penobscot
Mouth: Penobscot Bay
Agricultural Products: Truck crops, apples, potatoes
Industries: Sawmills, paper mills, textiles, tanneries

The Penobscot River system, Maine's largest, contains 8,200 square miles, or about one-fourth of the total area of the state. The Penobscot basin extends 150 miles from the Atlantic to the remote north woods and has an extreme width of 115 miles. Its headwaters rise on the Quebec frontier northwest of Moosehead in the North and South Branches. On the eastern boundary the Mattawamkeag draws water from within five miles of the international boundary with New Brunswick. From these wilderness streams the Penobscot begins a twisting run to the ocean, swelling with the passing miles from the contributions of hundreds of streams to a vast rolling river nearly 1,000 feet wide above the falls at historic Old Town.

The Penobscot has been a central factor in the lives of the people, both Indian and white, who have dwelt on its banks through many centuries. Sprinkled throughout this vast area are 467 lakes and ponds, all connected to the main branch by no less than 1,604 rivers, streams, and brooks. Major tributaries, large rivers in their own right, are the Piscataquis, Passadumkeag, Mattawamkeag, and the East and West Branches whose junction at Medway form the main branch, Penobscot. Near the center of Penobscot country rise the mountains of Katahdin, "the highest place," enfolded by the East and West

Branches. Katahdin is the northern anchor of the Appalachian chain. Visible for miles in any direction, this range is a striking feature noted by travelers and natives alike as a handy landmark and rugged symbol.

To the first permanent Penobscot inhabitants, the Algonquin speaking Woodland Indians, the river system served as a spiritual core and provided the political boundaries separating them from their Abnaki neighbors. With birch bark abundant, canoe making became a native art which provided a means of easily penetrating the wilderness. Fishing, hunting, and other forest pursuits depended on canoe travel and the river, so it is not surprising that Penobscot Indian creation tales closely link all human life with the creation of this beautiful river system. Their life style was the product of thousands of years of observation and trial-and-error experimentation. The harvest of fall-run eels is a good example of how keenly these people were in touch with natural processes. In the fall, eels, after maturing in northern ponds, run south to the sea to begin a journey of thousands of miles to ocean spawning grounds. The Penobscot Indians used dried and powdered jack-in-the-pulpit root, that, when vigorously mixed by splashing in the water, rendered the eels unconscious. It was then a simple matter to pluck them from the surface and preserve many pounds for winter use by either smoking or salting. The root can only be used if gathered at a certain time and the fish are available for a relatively short time, testifying to the Indians' formidable powers of observation and deduction. Waterfalls and rapids, natural barriers to fish migration, particularly salmon, were favored fishing spots and the sites of the Penobscot's permanent villages, such as Old Town, Mattawamkeag, and Kenduskeag.

Much Indian history and many clues to their lifeways remain in the aboriginal names still found in Penobscot country. Kenduskeag means "eel weir place" and, while applied to a tributary stream today, was meant to describe the confluence of that stream with the Penobscot. Other names recollect bloody skirmishes. Scalp Rock, a ledge a short way up Passadumkeag River, was the site of a Mohawk massacre of unprotected Penobscot women. The men were upriver hunting and the women were surprised, slain, and scalped, then left on this ledge propped in life-like positions by the marauding Mohawks.

Most names can aid birchbark navigators, unguided by formal maps, since they describe geographic features from a canoeman's point of view. For example, Mattawamkeag means "at the mouth a gravel bar", Passadumkeag means "entering above a gravel bar" thus describing streams which enter the main branch. These names, and others, provided early Indian canoemen with mental maps.

European explorers, notably Samuel de Champlain in 1604, commented on the river's beauty, the natives' friendliness, and the resources of this vast wilderness. The fur trade thrived, followed by permanent settlers moving up river. Penobscot power slipped after many years of cruel war, inspired by European rivalries carried on to the New World.

One of our earliest descriptive accounts of the Penobscot wilderness and Mt. Katahdin came from the memoirs of John Gyles. Gyles was captured in 1689 in the French-led Indian raid on Pemaquid. Only eleven years old at the time of his capture, he, with other captives, were taken by canoe from Pemaquid up the Penobscot to serve as slaves for their Malecite captors. During eight years of captivity Gyles endured severe abuse and great privation. During his first winter he amputated the frozen first joints of both big toes following severe exposure during a moose hunt. In his account he also describes Mt. Katahdin and the fear and reverence his Indian masters displayed toward the granite massif.

The destruction of French power in 1759 by Wolfe's capture of Quebec marked the end of war between the surviving Maine tribes and English settlers on the coast. With peace, pioneers ventured into the eastern wilderness and along the Penobscot where they wreaked ecological havoc. The principal attraction was cheap land and vast stands of white pine and spruce which could be easily converted into a cash crop. A man would log his tract, floating out the harvest on an adjacent stream. To "let daylight into the swamp" was a noble calling as cutover timberlands, it was thought, would make farming easy, attracting still more settlers. Power sites for dams needed for saw and grist mills were plentiful, and by the 1840s a massive lumbering industry flourished along the Penobscot and Bangor was the boom town.

The first settler of what is modern Bangor, Jacob Buswell, hacked a clearing on the river bank near the head of tide. By 1832 that small clearing had grown into a port town that in that year shipped over 37 million board feet of lumber. Between Bangor and Old Town, only a dozen miles or so, nearly 200 saw mills had sprung up. In September, 1846, Henry David Thoreau, on one of several jaunts into the Maine woods, observed something of the importance of the industry but questioned some basic underlying values: "Think how stood the white pine on the shore of Chesuncook," he commented, "its branches soughing in the four winds, and every individual needle trembling in sunlight,—think how it stands with it now—sold perchance to the New England Friction Match Company! . . ."

With a lumber industry of this magnitude on the Penobscot the state of Maine experienced what historians have called "Maine's Golden Age." The demand for more lumber created demand for more efficient tools of the trade such as Peaveys or cant dogs, driving boats and Bangor Snubbers. Lumbermen cooperated rather than competed as the demand was unlimited. The most notable development of this "Golden Age" was river driving. In her classic, *Penobscot Man*, Fannie Hardy Eckstrom recounts her image of these lumbermen: ". . . never again shall I behold men looking like these I used to see when they came off the river—white and Indian crisped almost to blackness by the sun, baked with the heat, bitten by black flies, haggard, gaunt, sure footed. . .and above all sleepy, . . . [for] in those days they worked both day and night. . . ."

While evidently not much to look at, these "Bangor Tigers" helped to create a modern industry of prime importance to the nation. The work was sometimes exciting but always dangerous. Death could come to a lumberman in the form of a falling tree or a dead branch. A loaded sled and team might be "sluiced" on a steep icy slope or perhaps an inattentive worker might be crushed by rolling logs. Death came most frequently on the drive when rivers were swollen with icy water from melting snow. Armed with cant dogs, pickpoles, and reckless courage, the riverdrivers guided the winter's cut of logs down

the brooks, streams, and rivers to the boom above Old Town. An old song captures some of the flavor of those old days on the Penobscot:

> Come all ye gallant shanty boys and listen while I sing!
> We've worked six months in cruel frosts but now we'll have our fling.
> The ice is black and rotten and the rollways is piled high.
> So boost upon your peavey sticks while I do tell you why.
> For it's break the rollways out me boys, and let the big sticks slide!
> And file your calks and grease your boots and start upon the drive!
> A hundred miles of water is the nearest way to town,
> So tie into the tail of her and keep her hustling down!
> When the drive comes down, when the drive comes down,
> Oh, it's then we've paid our money and it's then we own the town!

The Penobscot has its ghosts. At the numerous falls and pitches, logs would jam, dangerously piled and tangled by the swift current. There are many unmarked graves along the river banks in Penobscot country, final resting place for a driver, Yankee, Indian, or French.

"No man has ever come out of Rappogenus alive" is a maxim on the West Branch. Ripogenus Gorge, a 2-mile stretch likened to a "little Niagara," was one of the principal obstacles to river driving on the West Branch. But the logs were brought down by the millions, and the drive is a testament to the perseverance of men who worked daylight to dark, six or seven days a week, for the princely sum of two dollars and four meals a day. They also got a chance to sleep on the cold, wet ground devoid of protection save a common quilt, long enough to accommodate the entire crew!

One of the less heroic chapters in Penobscot history is the story of the polluting of this magnificent resource by sawmills, towns, and especially paper mills. Fish, notably salmon, were severely affected. Back in the 1860s fresh water commercial fisheries took 15,000 salmon per year, but because of industrial pollution and power dams only 1,500 were taken in 1920, a drop of 90 percent in fifty years. Things got much worse. By 1947 only forty fish were taken and commercial fishing ceased. Yet causes of the problem were long recognized. In 1868 the Commissioner of Fisheries pointed out that dumping of lime used in papermaking could depopulate fish in rivers and streams. During the 1890s the Army Corps of Engineers had to dredge sawdust and slabs, refuse from hundreds of sawmills, from the channels below Bangor, as it obstructed that port.

The economic growth of the Penobscot triggered the growth of upriver towns which became sources of further pollution. Textile mills, tanneries, dye houses, and finally municipal sewerage had a devastating cumulative effect. A factory at Millinocket (a town created by and for the industry in 1900) was dumping 500 tons of effluence daily from their mills astride the West Branch. By 1960 the Penobscot River was carrying a pollution load equivalent of 3,264,460 people although there were only 151,077 permanent residents. Public concern was translated into political action during the 1960s and pollution control and abatement plans were slowly implemented. Millions of dollars have been spent in the Penobscot region by private and public enterprise with good results. Trends during the late 1970s indicate that the rivers are cleaner. The Atlantic salmon are returning to their former haunts.

Today most of the Penobscot region is still wild. Towns dot the river banks and its tributary streams but much remains the same. The river still flows steadily. The people of the Penobscot are noticeably different from the tourist-service-oriented coastal dwellers. One senses a proud independence in these fresh-water Mainers, bred in through long years of work and the old Maine attitude of "make, make over, make do, or do without!"

Moose still wade in the West Branch, the salmon are ascending the river once again and canoes still ply Penobscot headwaters lakes and streams as they have for centuries. The future of this great river has not been brighter since the coming of European man. Every year thousands enjoy the great fishing on the numerous tributary streams or hunt along the banks. The river is still a valuable source of power. The many lakes hold over thirty billion cubic feet of water used for hydroelectric generation. The lakes have been enlarged and the virgin forests cut, but the wilderness qualities of the Penobscot are still visible. The new respect for the environment will guarantee that future generations will be able to work and play in an area unique to Maine.

FURTHER READING: Fannie Hardy Eckstrom, *Penobscot Man.* (1904). Frank G. Pseck, *Penobscot Man.* (1926).

Dave S. Cook

The Potomac River

Source: Confluence of North Branch and South Branch rivers southeast of Cumberland, Maryland
Length: c. 285 miles
Tributaries: Shenandoah, Wills Creek
Mouth: Chesapeake Bay below Washington, D.C.
Agricultural Products: Truck products, tobacco
Industries: Coal mining, tourism, center of federal government

The Potomac is one of the most impressive rivers flowing out of the Appalachians and eastward to the Atlantic. It is about 285 miles long, formed by the confluence of a North Branch and South Branch southeast of Cumberland in western Maryland. From there the river constitutes the boundary first between Maryland and West Virginia, yet at its northernmost point nearly cutting Maryland in two as it almost touches Pennsylvania. After passing through a number of Appalachian ridges the stream emerges through an impressive water gap at Harper's Ferry where its waters are swollen by the confluence with the Shenandoah flowing in from the south; it is the Potomac's largest tributary. The river then flows southeast serving as the boundary between Maryland and Virginia and then between Virginia and the District of Columbia. The Potomac estuary begins above Washington,

D.C., and runs into Chesapeake Bay. On its lower reaches, on the Virginia side, are Mount Vernon, George Washington's home; and Quantico, a U.S. Marine Corps base.

In the early 1600s several Algonquian tribes resided in palisaded villages near the banks of the Potomac and its numerous tributaries. In 1608 Captain John Smith, while exploring the Potomac, mapped the location of several villages along the river banks. The Conoy (or Piscataway) tribe or tribal confederacy, claimed territory extending northward from the Potomac almost to the present city of Baltimore and eastward to Chesapeake Bay. These Indians played an influential role in the early history of Lord Baltimore's proprietary colony.

It is clear that the Indians lived a good life along the lower reaches of the Potomac and around Chesapeake Bay. Firsthand accounts of early European visitors emphasize the importance of marine and animal life to the natives. Sir Richard Grenville stated that "the savages disband into small groups and disperse to different places to live upon shell fish. Other places afford fishing and hunting while their fields are being prepared for the planting of corn."

Methods of fishing included the use of seines, set lines, and weirs. One way of trapping fish was to construct V-shaped rock structures on the river, forcing the fish into a narrow chute from which they could be netted, scooped, or speared. While performing a photoarchaeological analysis of the Potomac, two investigators recently discovered the remnants of these Indian fishtraps. The size and number of middens (heaps of bones, shells, and artifacts marking the site of a prehistoric dwelling) are indicative of the importance of shellfish, oysters, and clams for foodstuffs by the Indians along the Potomac.

When Lord Baltimore's first contingent arrived in Maryland in 1634, they negotiated with Piscataway Indians for the purchase of land. In the early years strong efforts were made to maintain amicable relations with the aboriginal population, but soon the need for more land became a source of contention. After a half-century of land encroachment, disease, and warfare, most of the remaining Indians along the north shore of the Potomac had been forced to migrate to Virginia and Pennsylvania.

Although Maryland at first exhibited a diversified agricultural economy, by the close of the seventeenth century tobacco had become the staple crop. Continued emphasis on tobacco production created economic conditions that retarded expansion into Maryland's backcountry. Most merchants and planters knew that tobacco could be grown profitably only in the tidewater region, since a suitable transportation network so vital to inland production was precluded by the vast number of creeks and small rivers winding through Maryland.

The early inhabitants of Maryland had only the vaguest geographic notions of the interior of their colony; to all but a few individuals Maryland's backcountry was unknown. Some maps drafted prior to 1732 depicted the Potomac as flowing directly north and intersecting the fortieth parallel. Apparently most Marylanders confused the Monocacy, which rises in Pennsylvania and flows southeast through Maryland, with the Potomac. As a result of this error in geographical knowledge, even the proprietary officials thought Maryland's western boundary was much farther east than it really is.

When, after about 1732, settlers from Pennsylvania began to penetrate the backcountry, endless boundary disputes plagued Maryland's officials. The northern boundary of Maryland with Pennsylvania was settled with the running of Mason's and Dixon's line in 1767. The western boundaries between Maryland and Virginia were the subject of bitter litigation, finally decided in 1745 by the Privy Council in London in Virginia's favor. (Today that part of the region is in West Virginia.)

In the late eighteenth century people became aware that in Maryland's western reaches, along streams flowing into the Potomac, was "black gold"—coal. In 1816 a perceptive traveler, Uria Brown, noticed some twelve miles west of Cumberland, an abundance of good coal. He noted that although the well-watered land was thin and worn-out, the hills abounded with the black fuel. "Hills which had been purchased for taxes," exclaimed one investor, "suddenly were as valuable as gold mines." The price of coal at that time averaged between eight and twelve cents per bushel in Cumberland. Although much of the fuel was consumed locally, the inhabitants also shipped small quantities of coal and farm produce in time of high water on the Potomac to

Georgetown, just west of Washington, D.C. In exchange for their goods, they brought back in their boats commodities such as plaster, herring, shad, and manufactured products.

By 1820 large shipments of coal were being floated down the Potomac from Allegany County, Maryland, to the major seaports. The standard craft used in the trade was a flatboat type, rectangularly shaped with raking ends. It was usually eighty feet long, thirteen feet wide, and three feet deep, with a load capacity ranging from 1,500 to 1,800 bushels of coal. While the boats were being constructed along Wills Creek—a tributary flowing in from the north at Cumberland—the coal was transported to the point of river shipment where it was stockpiled. When weather conditions promised a "boating stage"—high water required to ship out—the boats were quickly loaded and sent off on a perilous journey to the tidewater markets. At trip's end the boats sometimes were sold, along with their cargoes, and the crews walked back to Cumberland; more often the boats were loaded with cargoes of salt and general supplies and were poled back upriver. Such trips could prove profitable with coal selling at fifty and sixty cents a bushel at Georgetown and Washington, D.C.

From Fort Cumberland on the North Branch of the Potomac General Edward Braddock launched his campaign in 1755. He built a road through the wilderness to the forks of the Ohio and there planned to wrest Fort Dusquesne from the French and Indians. Although his force was ambushed just short of its goal, July 9, 1755, and Braddock was mortally wounded, the road he had forged across the Appalachians became a highway of emigration into the Ohio Valley.

When, more than a generation later, a successful revolution had taken place and there was a new government of the United States of America, the necessity arose for a national capital. George Washington carried out Congressional mandates of 1790 and 1791 and, with geographical and political considerations in mind, chose a ten miles square area straddling the Potomac as the national capital, the District of Columbia. Originally it included the town of Georgetown in Maryland and the County of Alexandria in Virginia. In 1846, at its citizens' behest, Alexandria was permitted to return to Virginia jurisdiction; but the town of Washington on the north side of the river continued to grow. In 1878 Georgetown became a part of the city though to this day that section retains its original name.

The construction of an inland transportation system developed very slowly in Maryland. Settlers entering south from Pennsylvania, often by way of the Monocacy, helped settle north-central and eastern Maryland. Those who moved inland from tidewater tended to settle close to the Potomac and its tributaries. As land routes increased, people began to query the possibility of linking Baltimore to the Ohio Valley for trade purposes. Washington, D.C. residents wanted a cheap route into the interior in order to lessen the expense of fuel. Moreover, a canal would bring flour, wheat, rye, oats, barley, and whiskey into the the city at reduced cost.

After much debate a Baltimore committee decided that a railroad was far better suited to the situation than a canal across the mountains. In Washington, however, the demand for a canal continued unabated. Despite the staggering estimated cost of twenty-two million dollars, Washington's inhabitants pressed on with plans for construction of the Chesapeake and Ohio Canal. Both cities launched their ambitious enterprises on July 4, 1828.

In addition to a plague of legal problems, the C & O's construction was hindered by widespread labor unrest along the canal line, the increased cost of construction due to the inflation of the 1830s, and limited financial resources. By 1842 all hope of reaching the Ohio had been abandoned and company officials decided to end the canal at Cumberland. Not until October 10, 1850, after twenty-two years of labor strikes, flood damage, cholera epidemics, and shortages of capital was the C & O Canal opened to there. Baltimore's great hope, the Baltimore and Ohio Railroad, reached Cumberland on November 5, 1842, and pushed on through to Pittsburgh. For the time, it was a masterpiece of engineering and for many decades was a profitable railroad.

The Canal people tried in vain to compete with the railroad. Frequent interruptions due to floods, breaches, poor crops, and the exhaustion of the western Maryland coal fields all contributed to its eventual failure. The C & O continued to function commercially until 1890 when after a series of bankruptcies it went out of business. Today portions of the old canal are maintained by the National Park Service, offering to visitors a nostalgic glimpse into the past.

It was at Harpers Ferry that John Brown staged his abortive raid in October, 1859. During the Civil War the Potomac was a boundary between Confederate and Union land. Harpers Ferry was occupied by both sides and was destroyed several times before war's end; subsequent floods also did serious damage. Today it is a National Historic Park.

Intensive agricultural land use, especially the cultivation of tobacco; the mining of coal; and increased industrial activity have resulted in massive erosion, severe siltation, and pollution of the river. Many of these problems, unfortunately, are carry-overs from earlier exploitative activities. Along the North Branch severe acid mine drainage from abandoned coal mines has drastically restricted aquatic life. Downstream the water quality of the Potomac ranges from poor to excellent, depending on the amount of nutrients, bacteria, and sediments resulting from the discharge of raw sewage from municipal areas and industrial wastes.

Most of the population residing in the Potomac River basin, which includes the Washington Metropolitan area, depend on the Potomac for their water supply. Proposals to supply water with dams and reservoirs have met with opposition. Alternate methods are required. Recently it has been suggested that the Potomac estuary, which is essentially a large freshwater reservoir stretching 108 miles from Great Falls, above Washington, down to Chesapeake Bay, be tapped. Use of the Potomac estuary has been questioned, however, because of opposition to drinking from a body of water considered highly contaminated.

It seems readily apparent that the solution to the problems of the estuary and the protection of its biological resources will require all local jurisdictions to take actions within the shape of a regional biological resources management plan. Such efforts have been undertaken and positive goals are being achieved. A Sedimentation Specialist in the Maryland Department of Natural Resources has restated the goals for controlling erosion and sediment in the Potomac: (1) establish a sediment control program; (2) protect vital land resources from erosion; (3) protect vital water resources, aquatic life and wildlife from sediment pollution; and (4) provide high-quality water for human use.

The goals of river basin planning are more easily agreed upon than the strategy for reaching them. The shape of things to come will be determined by the growing number of people who are becoming aware that an old river is facing new problems. For almost 350 years the Potomac River has served the needs of Maryland and Virginia. Whether the people continue to use it as a source of water and as a recreational area in a dwindling wilderness, or whether they exploit and pollute it, is a question not yet answered.

FURTHER READING: Frederick D. Gutheim, *The Potomac* (1949). Paul Wilstach, *Potomac Landings* (1921).

Frank W. Porter III

The Rappahannock River

Source: Rises east of Front Royal, Virginia, in the Blue Ridge
Length: 212 miles
Tributaries: Rapidan
Agricultural products: Dairying, apples, corn, wheat, tobacco
Industries: Fishing, recreation, research

The Rappahannock River (named by Indians meaning "alternating stream") runs from deep in central Virginia to the Chesapeake Bay on the Atlantic. It is one of the most beautiful rivers in Virginia or, for that matter, on the east coast. Passing gently through the Tidewater region of the Old Dominion, it was linked closely to the history of Virginia from the state's earliest days. At many points it is seven miles wide and navigable for small ships from the Atlantic to Fredericksburg. The river runs over 200 miles in length with high banks and clear water well stocked with fish almost all the way down to the Chesapeake Bay. At its meeting point with the Chesapeake it abounds in oysters. The region it passes through, called the Tidewater, received its name from the influence of tides on all rivers emptying into the Chesapeake Bay.

For thousands of years, Indians have lived along the river's banks in the area between it and the James River to the south in the northeast corner in Virginia. In time, European explorers going through the area discovered the river and found it a useful way to travel into the interior. From the early 1600s people lived on the banks of this quiet river and since then it has played a central role in the life of most Virginians. Captain John Smith in his travels through the region in the early 1600s was fascinated by the river and told one of the first "fish stories" about it: "We found in divers places that abundance of fish, lying so thicke with their heads above water, as for want of nets we attempted to catch them with a frying pan." The famous Captain "sported himself by nayling them to the ground with his sword." More important, his

Rappahannock River—View of Fredericksburg from the Washington Farm. (Henry Howe, Historical Collections of Virginia. *Charleston, S.C.: Babcock & Co., 1845.)*

trip proved that the river was navigable and thus encouraged the settlement of the Tidewater region much like the Lewis and Clark Expedition fostered the settlement of the Far West.

Englishmen quickly moved into the Tidewater area during the first half of the 1600s. The flat rich land they found and the convenience of transportation along the river quickly led to the establishment of towns and large, profitable plantations growing tobacco. In fact, during the 1600s this region became the main area of economic and political development in Virginia. Large plantations sprang up quickly along its banks producing tobacco, shipping it to England, and, in exchange, receiving a wealth of furniture, art objects, clothes, wines, supplies, tools, and more settlers. The colony's early leaders all came from the Tidewater region and the banks of the Rappahannock.

Since navigation was possible and the land fertile and inexpensive, if not free, the area developed a rich culture and high standard of living by the mid-1600s. On the banks of the Rappahannock were the ancestral homes of the Carters, unquestionably one of the most important families in North America during the 1600s. "King" Carter, famous for being an important plantation owner, politician, and president of the council that ruled Virginia Colony came from the region. When he died he left an estate of 300,000 acres of land and over a thousand slaves. Plantations and properties of enormous sizes belonging to other families were nearby creating a baronial aristocracy of the land.

Rosegill Plantation, along the river, built by Ralph Wormeley, housed perhaps the largest library in the colonies by the start of the 1700s. He was part of a family dynasty that lived on the property from 1649 to 1806. Other leading families in the area near Rosegill also had large homes and substantial collections of books and paintings. Into this genteel background was born Mary Ball in 1708, the mother of George Washington. His father and other relatives also came from that area. During the 1700s plantation society had become a way of life along the Rappahannock for generations and counted the cream of Virginia's families among its members. James Monroe practiced law in Fredericksburg, at the falls of the Rappahannock River, while it is said that George Washington swam in the river during the 1750s not far from where he was born.

During this period other great homes were built along the banks of the river. Sabine Hall was the home of Landon Carter, son of King Carter, erected in 1730. Mount Airy, constructed in 1758, had twenty-five rooms and was built by Colonel John Taylor, a member of one of the oldest English families in the New World.

Small towns sprang up all along the river to support the commerce between England and the Tidewater area. Warehouses and wharfs, inns and restaurants, stores and churches, some of which can still be seen today were constructed throughout the 1600s and 1700s. Leedstown, a warehouse point, was incorporated in 1681—the same year as Philadelphia—and during its long history managed to be in five different counties as Virginia reorganized herself over a period of 200 years. Most famous of all was Fredericksburg, considered by many to be the most historic city in North America. Captain John Smith visited the site in 1608. In 1727 it was incorporated by the government at Williamsburg, which named it after Prince of Wales Frederick, who was to become the father of George the Third, king at the time of the American Revolution.

During the period from 1721 to the start of the American Civil War in 1861, the town continued to grow as a political and economic center. Anti-British activities took place there during the 1770s while the community maintained its leadership as the economic hub of the Tidewater. The town had many famous residents. Rev. Patrick Henry, uncle of the famous Patrick Henry, preached there; George Washington's family called the community home. A relative of Washington built Kenmore in 1746 and during the American Revolution had it decorated by German prisoners of war. James Monroe, President of the United States, lived in Fredericksburg as did Matthew Fontaine Maury who, in the 1800s, helped to lay the first Atlantic telegraph cable. General Robert E. Lee often visited Fredericksburg and fell in love with his wife in the area. In recent years, the city has restored many of the eighteenth century and early nineteenth century buildings of the community located on the banks of the river. Visitors today can thus have a sense of what a Tidewater town looked like to some of the most important figures in American history.

During the Civil War (1861–1865), the Rappahannock River played its traditional role as convenient transportation. During the course of the four years of battling between the Union and Confederate armies, attempting either to seize Richmond or protect it, the river was used to transport troops and supplies, mainly for the Union. Skirmishes were fought up and down its length and some old stately plantation homes to this day have the scars of bullets and shells from Union gunboats while others were used as field hospitals.

The area around Fredericksburg provided the setting for some of the heaviest fighting of the war. During 1862 alone, almost all the fighting in Virginia took place in and around Fredericksburg. Within a twelve-mile radius of the town were fought the battles of Chancellorsville, the Wilderness, Bloody Angle, Spottsylvania Court House, and others. Both armies faced each other across the river throughout the spring and summer of 1862. During May, ferocious fighting in the area took place and the city of Fredericksburg was heavily bombarded. The Union forces were supplied by way of the river. General Robert E. Lee defended the city with 60,000 men while General Burnside and later "Fighting Joe" Hooker led a Union army of about 130,000 soldiers. The city was kept under Confederate control but more men died in and around the area than anywhere else during the Civil War. Eventually General Ulysses S. Grant cleaned out all Confederate resistance near the Rappahannock toward the end of the Civil War.

At the end of the war, at a point on the river called Port Royal, the last drama of the conflict was played out. In April, 1865, John Wilkes Booth, after killing President Abraham Lincoln, came to Port Royal, crossed the Rappahannock here, only to be killed a few days later nearby.

After the Civil War, residents on the Rappahannock rebuilt Fredericksburg and other towns damaged by the fighting. They also developed a new economy no longer based on slaves and plantations. The river, however, continued to play its traditional role as an important source of easy, inexpensive transportation to and from central Virginia even though by now railroads competed with it. Farms still sent produce out of

the state to other parts of the Union on the stream. Lumbering also became a significant industry. By the end of the century, daily steamer transportation up and down the river was normal, carrying tourists and businessmen. The Tidewater plantation life which had been through a Golden Age in the 1600s and 1700s and struggled to maintain a bygone past in the 1800s, was no longer active and slipped into a quieter era. During the early part of the twentieth century, oyster fishing in the Chesapeake Bay became an important economic activity. With the introduction of the automobile, bridges of size and strength were constructed over the river. The first bridge to cross the river below Fredericksburg was built during the 1920s while above the town others were improved.

Since World War II, the Rappahannock has also become a playground. Tourists swarmed into the Tidewater area and to Fredericksburg. Fishing and boating became extremely important for the local economy and influenced the lives of all its local residents. By the 1960s, many of the old plantations along the river had been rebuilt or restored with a considerable number now open to the public. During the celebration of the Centennial of the Civil War and later the Bicentennial of the American Revolution numerous ceremonies took place along or near the river.

Other homes were being constructed during the twentieth century either as summer vacation spots or for citizens working in Fredericksburg and in Washington D.C. Nearby the U.S. Navy established a research and development complex. All told, the number of people living near the river continued to rise throughout the 1960s and 1970s.

Today the citizens of Virginia, very aware of the historical and ecological beauty of the Rappahannock, are working to keep it clean and as attractive as it was when Captain John Smith first saw it. The banks are still lined with trees and remain neat. Fish are very abundant as are the large variety of birds and other wildlife. Canoeing and pleasure craft are common as are swimmers and hikers. The lush vegetation nurtured in the red Davidson soil to the west and sandy dirt to the east all watered by the Rappahannock gives the entire area a beauty equal to that of any place along the Atlantic seaboard. No major obstacles stop the normal ebb and flow of this great river as it continues down to the Ocean. As it always has, the Rappahannock influences profoundly the lives of many Virginians. They understand its important historical role in their state's life, and its significance in making central and northern Virginia green and ecologically rich.

The river is today as always:

> Virginia's flow, from her tidal rim,
> Sweeps out on Atlantic's crest
> To call, as of yore, the mariner in
> To the havens of peaceful rest.

FURTHER READING: Edmund Randolph, *History of Virginia* (1970). Dora Chinn Jett, *In Tidewater Virginia* (1924).

James W. Cortada

The Raritan River

Source: Confluence of two branches of Raritan at Raritan, New Jersey.
Length: c. 35 miles
Tributaries: South River, Lawrence's Brook, Millstone River, Stony Brook, Bound Brook, and Middle Brook
Outflow: Raritan Bay between Perth Amboy and South Amboy, New Jersey
Agriculture: Truck farming
Industries: Coal freighting, metals, diverse manufactures

The mainstream of the Raritan River is formed by the junction of its two branches at Raritan, New Jersey. The longer of these, South Branch, has its source in Budd Lake near Hackettstown in Warren County. Forty-two miles in length, it flows through the mountains of western New Jersey in a southerly direction to Flemington, where it turns to the northeast before joining the Raritan. The average elevation of the drainage area is 750 feet, with a maximum of 1,200 feet. Two major reservoirs, Spruce Run and Round Valley, lie along its course near Clinton.

The North Branch of the Raritan rises as a spring-fed stream on a hill near Mendham in Morris County and flows almost due south for twenty miles. Much of its upper course is through hilly terrain with an elevation above 750 feet, while the lower portion is on a red sandstone plain having a general elevation of 250 feet which drops to fifty feet at Raritan.

From the junction of the South and North Branches, the Raritan's course is to the east for

twenty-five miles. It flows by way of Somerville, Piscataway, and New Brunswick to Perth Amboy, where it empties into Raritan Bay. The river is navigable to New Brunswick and tidal to a point two miles above that city. The total watershed area of 1,105 square miles makes it the largest of any rivers wholly within New Jersey.

Major tributaries are the South River, Lawrence's Brook, Millstone River, and Stony Brook, which drain areas to the south, and Bound Brook and Middle Brook, which flow to the north above New Brunswick. A network of smaller streams feed North and South Branches as they course through the traprock hills and red sandstone plains before converging.

Prior to the coming of white settlers to the Raritan Valley it was the home of several sub-tribes of the Lenni Lanape. These relatively peaceful Indians hunted and fished and cultivated native corn and a few other food crops near their villages. The Minisink Path, the great Indian trail from the Delaware River to the New Jersey coast crossed the Raritan near the mouth of South Rivers: along the ancient trail members of the Indian villages in northwestern New Jersey made their annual treks to the seashore to catch and cure fish and make wampum from the shells of oysters, clams, and mussels. As the influx of whites increased, the Lenape gradually ceded their lands to them and over a period of years vanished from the New Jersey scene.

The first significant effort toward white colonization of the Raritan River area took place in 1664 when Sir George Carteret and Lord John Berkeley, as proprietors, were granted a tract of land extending some thirty miles along the river into the interior. The proprietors encouraged settlers and, after reserving 1,000 acres at Amboy Point for their own use, divided 1,500 acres into 150 lots of ten acres each. The settlement was promoted as a planned utopia, and by the year 1684 a flourishing village had been established. The name was then changed to Perth in honor of James, Lord of Perth, a proprietor, to which Amboy was later added. In that same year Perth Amboy replaced Elizabeth as the capital of New Jersey.

Meanwhile, in 1666, John Pierce and others from Newbury, Massachusetts, obtained a deed for lands between the Rahway and Raritan rivers as far inland as Bound Brook. They established a village at Woodbridge. A short while later a second group settled in Piscataway.

In 1686, John Inian, after exploring the upper Raritan Valley and laying out trails and roads, founded the village of New Brunswick. A ferry service known as "Inian's Ferry" was established across the Raritan. New Brunswick pros-

pered and within a few years had become an important trading post serving the interior and downriver points. Raritan Landing, two miles above New Brunswick at the tidal limit, also became a busy trading center, with warehouses, water-powered mills, and a bridge, the first across the Raritan, contributing to its prosperity.

The number of villages in the Raritan Valley increased rapidly. By the year 1700 most of the lands along the mainstream and its tributaries in present Somerset and Hunterdon counties had been settled. The years preceding the Revolution saw the emergence of an area of prosperous farms covering the fertile countryside.

Along the mainstream from Perth Amboy to Raritan Landing, vessels of many descriptions were engaged in lively trade. Numerous mills helped meet the ever-increasing demands for food and lumber products as well as wrought iron items for home or farm uses.

As it did elsewhere, the coming of the Revolution brought dissension and conflict among neighbors, relatives and friends in the Raritan Valley. A majority favored, but many strongly opposed, the movement toward independence. Among the latter was New Jersey's Governor William Franklin at Perth Amboy who quarreled bitterly with his father, Benjamin Franklin, regarding the developing break with England. Their views proved irreconcilable.

When the war began Perth Amboy was garrisoned by a strong American force. Governor Franklin, still nominally the state's chief executive officer, continued to occupy the governor's mansion and perform official functions until June 17, 1776, when he was arrested as a result of a condemnatory action by the Provincial Congress. In the late summer of 1776 the British occupied New York City and Staten Island. Military and naval pressure then exerted on the garrison at Perth Amboy forced its abandonment on December 1, 1776. The British occupied the town until June 30, 1778, two days after the Battle of Monmouth, when they withdrew and American forces occupied it for the balance of the war.

A similar situation prevailed at New Brunswick. An American garrison was maintained there until late November, 1776. On the twenty-ninth and thirtieth, the fleeing remnants of

Raritan River—South Branch. The old grist mill at Clinton. The mill is in operating condition and serves as a museum for the local historical society. (N. F. Brydon Photos.)

Washington's army arrived from Newark, pursued by the British under Cornwallis. They remained at New Brunswick only long enough to regroup, partially destroy the covered bridge at Landing, and make a rear guard defense with a few pieces of artillery. The next day the tattered army of three thousand men was on its way to Trenton. The British, after crossing the river, renewed their futile pursuit. New Brunswick, like Perth Amboy, remained in British hands and served as a supply center until June 30, 1778, when it was evacuated following the Battle of Monmouth.

That inconclusive struggle was fought on June 28, 1778, near the source of South River, a Raritan tributary. The British army, enroute to New York after giving up Philadelphia, was intercepted at Tenant in Monmouth County. After a gruelling fight in intense heat, the British withdrew in the early morning hours on June 29. The Americans were left in possession of the field but had failed to achieve their objective of halting the British march to New York.

During the period of British occupancy of the Raritan area there were numerous raids by both sides. Americans attacked British garrisons at various points and fired on ships carrying supplies on the river. British foragers were a constant threat to the farms and villages in the surrounding countryside. A major British raid took place October 25, 1779, when Colonel John Simcoe crossed from Staten Island and attempted to capture Governor William Livingston. Failing in this the raiders rode into the back country, burned boats and several buildings, and were finally intercepted by the militia. Simcoe was severely wounded and the raiders escaped after suffering a number of losses and much harassment.

From 1780 to 1782 New Brunswick was headquarters for whaleboat privateers under Captain William Marriner and Captain John Huyler. They preyed on British shipping along the coast and Staten Island, capturing ships, crews and supplies and bringing them to New Brunswick. They became such a thorn in the British side that on January 4, 1782, the royal navy sent a force upriver to New Brunswick. The whaleboats were destroyed and prisoners were taken, thus ending the exploits of the whaleboat privateers.

The Raritan basin has the distinction of providing homes to two of America's oldest universities, Princeton and Rutgers. The former, chartered in 1746 as the College of New Jersey, is located near the Millstone River at Princeton. Rutgers, the State College on the Raritan at New Brunswick, was chartered in 1766 as Queen's College. Both universities are renowned for their outstanding educational programs. In the field of athletics they are noted as having been contestants in the first intercollegiate football game, played at New Brunswick on November 6, 1869. The game combined soccer and English rugby, with special rules for the occasion. There were twenty-five players to a side, with no referee or umpire. The rival captains settled any disputes. After a spirited contest, the lighter but quicker Rutgers boys were victorious by six goals to four.

Throughout the nineteenth century Perth Amboy and New Brunswick remained important trading and shipping centers. This accelerated when, on June 25, 1834, the Delaware and Raritan Canal was completed from the Delaware River to New Brunswick, thus permitting shipment by water of Pennsylvania anthracite and other products directly to New York City.

Industrialization along the Raritan's mainstream began in the early 1800s. Perth Amboy, with large deposits of usable clays nearby, became the center for the manufacture of clay and ceramic products, including bricks, housewares, terra cotta, and later, tiles and porcelain bathroom and kitchen fixtures. During the latter half of the century came chemical manufacturing, copper refining, drydock facilities, and many other industries. The twentieth century witnessed heavy industrialization, with oil refineries and storage facilities and plants manufacturing a wide variety of products.

A similar pattern has unfolded at New Brunswick. A carriage factory was established in 1810. The manufacture of rubber goods by the United States Rubber Company began in 1839. A factory for absorbent and surgical dressing materials began operations in 1887 and, much expanded, remains today as one of New Brunswick's leading businesses.

Water power for the use of mills was plentiful, especially in the upper Raritan watershed. Mills of many types (flouring, grist, saw, paper, snuff, etc.) as well as foundries, began to appear in Colonial times. Some 200 were still in operation at the beginning of the twentieth century. By the 1950s nearly all had ceased to function.

The industries along the mainstream led to serious pollution. Efforts directed toward its reduction were relatively unproductive until 1972, when the Federal Water Pollution Control Act Amendments became effective. Since then, due to federal and state enforcement work, improvement has slowly taken place.

Two large military installations in the Raritan Valley have been of national importance. The Raritan Arsenal was established along the north shore of the river between Fords and Highland Park during World War I. It served as a munitions depot and testing and proving area until it was phased out in 1964. Middlesex County College now occupies a portion of the former arsenal land.

Camp Kilmer, named to honor the New Brunswick poet Joyce Kilmer, was constructed in 1942. Its 1,120 buildings were used during World War II to serve and house men and women brought to the camp for final staging before going overseas. Approximately four and one-half million military personnel were processed there between 1942 and December, 1949. It was reactivated for the Korean War, and in 1956 and 1957 was used for the resettlement of some 32,000 Hungarian refugees who fled their homeland following the unsuccessful revolt

there. Today, Livingston College of Rutgers University occupies more than 500 acres of former camp property and a federally funded Job Corps Center uses some of the buildings for its activities.

Citizen concern with the non-tidal portion of the Raritan's watershed is reflected in the activities of three watershed associations, one for Millstone River and Stony Brook, another for the North Branch, and a third for the South Branch. Each association conducts programs aimed at insuring good potable water by means of water quality analyses, natural resource inventories, and environmental zoning analyses. Environmental education programs are coordinated with local schools, staff assistance is provided to municipal conservation commissions, zoning boards and other public officals. Complaints are referred to responsible parties and followed through to disposition. Publicity programs are initiated when appropriate on matters of environmental concern in the watershed. The work of these associations and the interest of their members helps assure continuance of good water quality, open space, and wholesome recreation opportunities throughout much of the Raritan watershed.

FURTHER READING: Wall and Pickersgill, *History of Middlesex County, NJ. 1664–1920* (1921). William E. Benedict, *New Brunswick in History* (1925).

Norman F. Brydon

The St. Croix River (Maine)

Source: Cheputneticook (or Schoodic) Lake near Houlton, Maine
Length: 75 miles
Tributaries: West Branch
Agriculture: Dairy products, blueberries
Industries: Lumber, pulpwood, tourism

The St. Croix River rises in Cheputneticook (or Schoodic) Lake, near Houlton, Maine, and flows south and east seventy-five miles as the Maine-New Brunswick boundary before it flows into

St. Andrews Bay, an arm of Passamaquoddy Bay. The river's principal tributary, the West Branch, flows out of Kennebusic and Grand Lakes and flows forty-two miles before it joins the St. Croix at Baileyville. Tidewater on the St. Croix is at Salmon Falls, about sixteen miles above the river's mouth.

From the lakes in which they rise to the Atlantic Ocean the land bordering the St. Croix and its tributaries is low, providing storage for freshets—sudden overflows due to melting snow or heavy rain. For ten miles above the tide the river is 500 feet wide and for fully half its length the St. Croix appears as one continuous lake; the West Branch is likewise often compared to a lake in motion. In all there are sixty-one lakes in the St. Croix system.

The river drains 800 square miles of Maine and 375 square miles of New Brunswick. The Indian name "Schoodic" means "low, swampy ground" and is applied to the St. Croix region in general. While the river is sluggish, Passamaquoddy Bay is superactive, having tides averaging nineteen to twenty feet with great whirlpools. It is a strong tourist attraction. Yet many beautiful islands dot the Bay. Campobello, New Brunswick, was the summer home of Franklin Delano Roosevelt; it is now a museum. Moose Island in Maine and Deer Island in New Brunswick are other beauty spots. They all complement the natural beauty of the St. Croix Valley with its rocks, great rolling hills, woods, and lakes.

The first explorer of this region was a Frenchman, Sieur de Monts. In 1603 Henry IV of France granted him all the territory in America between the 40th and 46th parallels north latitude; it was held for him under the name of Acadia. The first colonists included Samuel de Champlain and 100 others who sailed from Havre de Grace on April 7, 1604. They landed at the mouth of a beautiful river. Because two of its branches suggested the form of a cross they named an island in the estuary as well as the river St. Croix. On this island, near the present town of Calais, they laid the foundations for a great city—foundations which still exist. But their hopes exceeded their luck. Seventy-nine of the colonists remained there through the first winter, but by spring thirty-five of them had died of scurvy. In August, 1605, all of the survivors abandoned the settlement and returned to France or to Port Royal, Nova Scotia. Sieur de Monts was later deprived of his patent.

Recently the National Park Service has recovered the bones of the thirty-five dead. They have also identified the foundations of the 58-foot long storehouse. At the Monts site, which is now a national historic monument, the Park Service maintains a visitor's trail and a museum.

The adventures of these early Frenchmen were

St. Croix River. "Four Mile Deadwater between Dacey Dam and Orrin Falls." (Avery Collection, Maine State Library.)

soon forgotten. Samuel de Champlain's map of the St. Croix gathered dust in archives and the foundations of the early French settlement were forgotten. As a result the St. Croix became sort of a "lost river," and as such it was the subject of fifty years of wrangling between British and American authorities who disputed the route of the international boundary as it was described in the Treaty of Paris, 1783.

In 1792 Samuel Titcomb made a survey of the region for the Commonwealth of Massachusetts, mapping the Schoodic (St. Croix). He made use of Rufus Putnam's map of 1784 that showed the Schoodic branching westerly at the northeast corner of Baileyville; the North Branch (which is today considered a part of the St. Croix) he marked as the Passamaquoddy River. Titcomb recommended the North Branch of the Schoodic as the main course of the river, but England protested that this constituted a changing of the river course which, in turn, would deprive her of thousands of miles of land. Thus did the matter end still unsettled by the so-called Jay Commission of 1797.

In 1827 the dispute was referred for a decision to the Netherlands, acting as a neutral party, but no settlement was made. It was not until 1842, in the Webster-Ashburton Treaty, that the United States received 7,000 of the 12,000 miles in dispute including the Aroostook River valley, a fertile potato-growing region northwest of the St. Croix region. The North Branch of the Schoodic was recognized as the main branch of the St. Croix.

When the whites arrived the St. Croix was sparsely inhabited by eastern Woodland Indians. The Malecites of New Brunswick and the Penobscots of Maine called these people, and the St. Croix River along which they lived, Etechims, an early name for the Passamaquoddies who today still live on reservations within the state of Maine. These "Etechims" were expert canoeists, using the rivers as their highways. They went by way of the St. Croix to the upper St. John, the Machias, and the Union River, and they intermingled with the Penobscots to the west.

The early Indians had two principal camping grounds, one at the mouth of the St. Croix at St. Andrews, New Brunswick, and the other opposite in Maine at Pleasant Point. In the spring they came downriver for salmon and alewives which they took at Salmon Falls. In spring and summer they also dug clams and harvested shellfish on the flats; in the fall they moved upriver to hunt. Because their earliest contacts were with the French, they were converted to Catholicism, and they have remained staunchly Catholic ever since. In 1794 the Commonwealth of Massachusetts set aside for them 23,000 acres of land in Washington County—approximately a six-mile square township—and to this day it is a part of the Passamaquoddies' reservation. While the Indians continued to hunt and fish, they also adapted their lifestyles to farming and maple syruping.

The region's earliest white settlers came from Machias, a village about thirty miles south of Calais, through the woods, guided by an Indian; others came by water. Still others came from Nova Scotia. After the Revolutionary War the Loyalists who had fled from the States to Nova Scotia moved down to St. Stephen, New Brunswick, across the St. Croix from the town of Calais.

On the American side, Washington County which borders the St. Croix was organized in 1789 with Rufus Putnam surveying and dividing the area into townships; Calais was in Township No. 5 and until 1806 was known merely as "No. 5." Soon boats were being built there, and sawmills and lumbering became important. After 1827 Calais became two villages, Calais and Milltown. At that time there were 120 houses and 35 stores in the area, a gothic style Congregational church and a Methodist church. By 1830 there were 1,686 inhabitants and the communities were prospering. The real source of income was the tall stands of pine needed for masts and naval stores. Lumbering and its manufactures peaked in the period 1857–1873.

Industry brought dams for water power and log driving operations. From Calais to the wild, inaccessible area of Vanceboro to the north, and on both sides of the river, there were dams. The one at Salmon Falls was the most important and the last developed. It was the last dam at the head of tidewater. Lumber mills operated on both sides of the river at this point.

But along the St. Croix since 1895 sawmills and lumbering companies have been gradually disappearing. Pulp mills replaced the lumber mills. They manufactured newsprint, especially for the *Boston Globe*. Today most of the pulp mills are owned by the Georgia Pacific Corporation, although the St. Croix Paper Company name remains.

Besides pulp mills, some cotton textile mills, shoe, chemical, and food processing plants are in operation in the region. The International Bridge from Calais to St. Stephen, the easternmost bridge in the United States, connects U.S. 1 with Canada. With its opening in 1959, tourism has become the most profitable industry of Calais. The people of this quiet niche of North America enjoy lives dominated by the river and the forest and the area's attraction to urban dwellers escaping from the cities.

FURTHER READING: Harold A. Davis, *An International Community on the St. Croix, 1604–1930* (1950). Guy Murchie, *Saint Croix, The Sentinel River* (1947).

Shirley Thayer

The St. Johns River (Florida)

Place of Origin: Florida Everglades
Length: 285 miles
Mouth: Atlantic east of Jacksonville, Fla.
Agricultural Products: Citrus, truck products
Industries: Cattle ranching, tourism, space research

Among the great rivers of America the St. Johns is distinctive for its northward flow and the brevity of its course, confined wholly to the Florida peninsula. The river rises in Blue Cypress Lake, slightly north of the Everglades. For its first fifty miles the St. Johns runs hidden in the watery amorphousness of the land. Not until marshland yields to firm earth in Brevard County just east of the space complex at Cape Canaveral does the St. Johns become a discernible line on the geological survey maps. For another 200 miles the river, never more than thirty miles inland, hugs the coast on its northward course before turning abruptly eastward near the city of Jacksonville and emptying into the Atlantic.

The waters of the St. Johns are lazy; they meander haphazardly in and out of lakes and swamps, acquiring ever greater proportions after each until near journey's end the river exhibits in places an imposing width of five miles. The stream drops only twenty feet along its entire course. So low does it lie in relation to the sea that at Lake George, 161 miles upstream, ocean tides have appeared. At times the river seems to sit still, its downstream flow neatly balanced by the incoming tide. At other times the influence of wind, tide, or drought cause the river actually to flow backwards.

The first people to inhabit the St. Johns region entered Florida some 10,000 years ago. The river basin has remained occupied ever since, though the original discoverers moved on and were replaced over time by other peoples. By about 1000 A.D. the Indians in south Georgia and northeast Florida had developed a highly structured society with well-defined village sites, earthen temple mounds, chieftains, and priests. They belonged to a linguistic family known as the Timucuas. The largest tribe in that family was the Saturiwa, who inhabited the lower St. Johns Valley and numbered in the low thousands when the Europeans arrived. Within two centuries the Timucuas were extinct.

The circumstances and date of the St. Johns's European discovery remain unknown. John Cabot may have sailed far enough south in 1497 to have seen the river's mouth, and Ponce de Leon may have looked upon its waters when he set foot on the Florida coast in 1513. Many explorers followed in their wake. In 1564 a French expedition of Huguenots began construction of a log fort at the base of a sharp bluff on the south bank of the river, about five miles from the sea.

The Spanish monarch, Philip II, recognized the military value of the area and regarded the French activity as a particular menace to the

Crown's treasure fleets which followed the Gulf Stream, skirting the east coast of Florida. Having decided to plant a Spanish settlement in Florida, Philip ordered his commander, Pedro Menéndez de Avilés, to attend to the French as well. This Menéndez did, capturing and destroying the French force and the fragile settlement the Frenchmen had named Fort Caroline. Forty miles south of there, on September 8, 1565, the Spanish founded St. Augustine, the oldest permanent European settlement in the United States.

For the next two centuries the history of the St. Johns River valley remained inextricably woven to the fate of St. Augustine. It was not a pretentious settlement, simply a missionary and military village that clung precipitously to life on the edge of a hostile frontier. Additional mission sites arose at Picolata, twenty miles east of St. Augustine on the banks of the St. Johns, and at San Juan del Puerto, on Fort George Island at the river's mouth. From these and other bases Franciscans foraged the peninsula for Indian converts. Native revolts, frontier violence, and disease intermittently ravaged the missions. Traditional enemies of the Spanish, English slave traders, pirates, and merchants incited constant ferment among Indians. On three separate occasions British forces assaulted St. Augustine; after a 1702 raid only the massive stone fortress of Castillo de San Marcos survived. A century of hostility ended in 1763 when the Spanish and English exchanged Florida for Cuba.

An ensuing twenty-year hiatus of British rule produced indelible changes in the St. Johns valley. The government lured settlers and encouraged propagation schemes. One of these was Rolleston, named for its founder, Denys Rolle, a former member of Parliament. Populated by slaves, prostitutes, indentured servants, and London indigents lured to Florida by exaggerated promises, Rolleston, located near current Palatka, endured fitfully throughout the British occupation. A plantation called "New Switzerland" was established by Francis Philip Fatio, who emigrated from Switzerland through England and expanded his Florida tract into a veritable empire of citrus and timber holdings.

When the Revolutionary War ended, Great Britain returned Florida to Spain, but the colonial pattern of the earlier Spanish period had been irrevocably transformed. A plantation economy had emerged, and farmers, merchants, and traders replaced soldiers and missionaries in the valley's human fabric.

An enfeebled Spanish Crown, its imperial system on the verge of collapse, was ill-prepared to contend with the border chaos that embroiled post-revolutionary Florida. Angry, homeless Indians, escaped slaves, British arms merchants and slave traders, irrepressible frontiersmen thirsting for new land, and adventurers galore stirred constant trouble. Impetuous Americans organized several secession efforts, including an attempt in 1811 to establish a "Republic of East Florida" that wreaked havoc among the river plantations. In 1821 Spain relinquished Florida to the United States.

This did not bring peace and stability. Like its predecessors, the United States was troubled by Indian relations and, in fact, even less disposed than the Spanish or British to treat the natives benevolently. Florida's provisional (or first American) governor, Andrew Jackson, envisaged Indian removal from lands coveted by the whites. The exterminated Timucuas had been replaced by Seminoles, a polyglot tribe of refugee Indians fiercely determined to make a final stand in Florida. The United States fought three wars with the Seminole nation between 1817 and 1858. The bitterest was the seven-year struggle that began in 1835. Warfare swept the valley, resulting in destruction of more than a dozen plantations. The Seminoles were led by a dynamic warrior chief, Osceola, who was captured near Fort Peyton, southwest of St. Augustine, while parleying under a flag of truce. At the close of the war many Seminoles agreed to emigrate, but others melted into the Everglades.

Less than a year after the firing on Fort Sumter, Union troops occupied Jacksonville and St. Augustine, where they were content to close off major avenues of commerce and harass river plantations from gunboats plying the St. Johns. Confederate irregulars, often commanded by a gaunt, legendary cavalryman, Captain J.J. Dickison, harassed the Union flanks, but to no avail. Bitter defeat finally came, but it brought welcome peace to the St. Johns.

The first description of the North American continent published in Europe contained illustrations of Timucua Indians and Florida alligators drawn by a French artist, Jacques Lemoyne, who accompanied the expedition that built Fort Caroline. A classic account of the region's flora and fauna was written by a young American naturalist, William Bartram, who traveled up the St. Johns in 1774. Later visitors included Ralph Waldo Emerson and William Cullen Bryant. John James Audubon painted in unforgettable colors the splendid birds he found along the St. Johns. The river and the land about it were cast in an aura of mystery and romance that beckoned the adventurous like a beacon.

Railroads were hastily lengthened into Jacksonville while along the river hotels were constructed to accomodate the visitors they brought in. Picolata, Palatka, and Sanford became familiar stopping places for sightseers indulging in one of nineteenth-century America's most popular luxury vacations, a trip by steamboat up the St. Johns and its tributary, the Oklawaha, to the central Florida resort of Silver Springs. In 1885 there were thirty excursion boats operating on the river, carrying the rich and curious to view the dazzling birds, sullen alligators, and lush scenery along the way. Ulysses S. Grant toured the river in 1880 and Grover Cleveland spent his honeymoon in Palatka six years later. Entranced by the river she called "America's Nile," Harriet Beecher Stowe and her preacher husband purchased a small orange grove fronting on the water at Mandarin, just south of Jacksonville.

The St. Johns valley accordingly experienced considerable change and population growth in the second half of the nineteenth century. Palatka and Picolata, the latter St. Augustine's back door to the St. Johns, thrived on the tourist trade. In the 1880s Henry Flagler brought the Florida East Coast Railway into St. Augustine and built several ornate hotels in the little town, turning it into a winter watering place for the industrial north's idle rich. Oranges were exported principally from Sanford, the southern terminal of navigation for the St. Johns. None prospered like Jacksonville. Known in the 1820s as Cowford, it had flourished during the Seminole and Civil wars. By the twentieth century the city had become Florida's foremost industrial, commercial, and financial center.

After 1900 construction of railroads south to Palm Beach and the new city of Miami and the passing of the steamboat era deprived the St. Johns of much of its tourist industry. Citrus production likewise moved deeper into south and central Florida, driven out of the St. Johns valley by killing frosts in the winter of 1894-1895. Highways and trucks cut even more into the river's commercial traffic, and the great depression hit hard there as elsewhere in Florida.

After World War II the region experienced a remarkable resurgence. Agriculture, cattle raising, recreation, and a growing population, many of whom are retirees, have all spurred the economy. Brevard County is the site of the Kennedy Space Center, the launching pad for America's rocket missions.

Rapid growth has brought troubles to the St. Johns. In 1884 a South American water hyacinth was introduced for decorative reasons. In a few years it covered whole sections of the river, choking off its oxygen and prohibiting passage of boats; the battle to control the plant continues today. Waste pollution begins near the river's source from cattle grazing and fertilizer from agricultural lands. Municipal and industrial sewage enter the river in appreciable volume. By 1965 an estimated 16.8 million gallons of raw sewage was being dumped daily into the St. Johns. The Federal Water Quality Control Act, passed that year, forced the State of Florida to begin cleaning up the rapidly expiring river. By 1978 enough progress had been made that lower portions of the river were again being used for recreational purposes.

The environmental movement that developed in the 1960s came none too late to save the St. Johns. Alligators have returned to its banks, birds flock upon its quiet waters, and fish are still plentiful. Possibly it will become again, in the words of the French explorer Jean Ribault, "the fairest, frutefullest, and pleasantest in all the worlde. . . ."

FURTHER READING: James Robertson and Dana Snodgrass, *Old Hickory's Town* (1982).

William R. Adams

The St. Lawrence River

Source: Lake Ontario (northeast side)
Length: c. 760 miles
Tributaries: Oswegatchie, Ottawa, Richelieu, Sague-
   nay, St. Francis, St. Maurice, and others
Mouth: Gulf of St. Lawrence
Agricultural Products: Dairying, truck vegetables,
   fruits
Industries: Lumbering, paper mills, hydroelectric, and
   extensive manufacturing

The St. Lawrence River is the water link between the Great Lakes and the Atlantic, between
one of the world's most heavily industrialized
areas and the lanes of ocean commerce with
Europe, Africa, and Asia. One may stand at the
visitors's area of the Eisenhower Lock at Masse-
na, New York, and watch a downbound "salty"
working through the canal gate. She may have a
German name, a Chinese crew and fly the flag of
Singapore. Dwellers of the St. Lawrence Valley,
whether Canadians or "North Country" Americans, can watch the world go by whenever they
wish from May to December. The great waterway still closes down in ice season despite recent
discussions of year-round operation.

It is a 650-mile waterway from Lake Ontario
to the Gulf of St. Lawrence. Taken as a total
system it covers 2,480 miles, from the Lakehead
to the Strait of Belle Isle, both its termini in
Canada but washing the shores of seven of the
United States. A relief map shows it rounding
the northern end of the Appalachian barrier,
then veering southwest to the continental heartland. For 114 miles it forms part of the United
States-Canada boundary, crossed today by three
international suspension bridges at Massena-
Cornwall, Ogdensburg-Prescott, and the Thousand Islands. It abounds in scenery from the
Thousand Islands on the west to the Gaspé
Peninsula on the east, and it is the main street of
eastern Canada.

No one knows for sure how long people have
lived along the river. When the first French
explorer, Jacques Cartier, coaxed his ships upstream he found Indians living in villages at
what would later be called Quebec and Montreal. Cartier's visits did not lead to permanent

settlement, partly because of internal strife in
France and partly because there were no precious metals in Canada. Nor was the St. Lawrence part of a Northwest Passage to the Pacific
and the Orient. (A reminder of this search for a
Northwest Passage is the name of the Lachine,
or "China" rapids at Montreal.)

For years French fishermen had been dropping anchor in the mouth of the river and
landing to dry their fish. They had made contact
with Indians who traded them beaver pelts for
metal tools and European clothing and ornaments. By 1600 in Europe the beaver felt hat had
come into vogue and the resultant demand for
beaver furs renewed French interest in Canada.
Some thought there was enough money to be
made in the fur trade to pursue it as more than a
sideline of the fishery. One of these men was the
Huguenot de Monts who, after founding a post
in what is now Nova Scotia, and beginning the
colony of Acadia, established another one at
Quebec under command of his chief geographer,
Samuel de Champlain. The Algonquins at Quebec and the Hurons to the west in Ontario
became the middlemen of this French fur trade.
The Indian's canoes plied the rivers and lakes
between the inland trapper Indians and the
French at Quebec.

Champlain envisioned for Canada a permanent colony with farmers producing enough to
supply its needs, ending the dependence on the
annual spring convoy to France. In this plan he
had company opposition, for its philosophy was
pretty much one of "make the money and run."
Not until 1633 when Canada was returned to
France after a brief English occupation did a
serious effort at settlement begin. The French
crown required the fur company, as a condition
of its monopoly charter, to bring in settlers and
establish them on the land, to plant a new
France in the woods along the St. Lawrence. But
it was hard to recruit settlers. Frenchmen lacked
the economic desperation that drove many English to America, and the French crown determined that Canada would be restricted to
Frenchmen of the Roman Catholic faith. So New
France grew slowly along the river. Trois Rivi-

ères, upriver from Quebec, was established in 1634. Missionaries and fur traders under the soldier de Maisonneuve founded Montreal at the confluence of the Ottawa and St. Lawrence rivers in 1642.

Champlain quickly formed an alliance with the Algonquins and Hurons against the Five Nations of the Iroquois who occupied present northern New York. These fierce warriors found their own European allies in the Dutch at Fort Orange (Albany), thus beginning three centuries of economic rivalry between the two river systems, the St. Lawrence and the Hudson-Mohawk which led through the Appalachians, with its ocean base at Manhattan (New Amsterdam). Now the Iroquois, with their advanced village life and relatively sophisticated political federation, had guns as did the Indian friends of the French.

The Iroquois aim was to destroy the middlemen, the Algonquins and Hurons, and thus control the whole western fur supply. In 1648 they wiped out Huronia between Lake Ontario and Georgian Bay. In the 1650s they seemed likely to wipe out the tiny settlements of New France along the river. When Louis XIV came to power in 1663 he took Canada away from the fur company, made it a royal colony, and sent a French army under the Marquis de Tracy to crush the Iroquois. Although the Iroquois remained a threat, the great river was made once again a highway of French commerce.

From Montreal armies of *coureurs de bois* (bush rangers) in large canoe fleets went out to the Indians. The French established a chain of posts westward: Frontenac (Kingston, Ontario). Niagara, Detroit, Michilimackinac, Green Bay, and south along the Mississippi and west along the Saskatchewan, probing for the retreating beaver. The St. Lawrence was the trunk of a spreading tree of trade.

Along the river were settled the seigneurial grants from the French crown. Since each farmer wanted river frontage, farms were laid out in strips stretching back from the shore, the houses ranged in rows. This gave the incoming traveler the curious sense of a continuous village from Quebec up past Montreal. But it was not a village; it was a thin line. The population of Canada remained small compared to that of the rival English colonies to the southeast. Canada's economy remained preoccupied with the fur trade and suffered all the vicissitudes of one-crop economies elsewhere.

The French simply overextended their North American empire; it was more than they could defend. As Anglo-American land speculators and fur traders moved into the Ohio country a collision was inevitable. Quebec fell to General Wolfe's forces on the Heights of Abraham above the town on September 18, 1759; after the Treaty of Paris, 1763, the Union Jack flew the length of the St. Lawrence waterway system. Crowns and constitutions have changed, but even today along the lower St. Lawrence French is spoken and the motto of Quebec, "Je me souviens"—I remember—ties the region to the New France of over two centuries ago. Militant Franco-Quebecers propagandize for independence.

Twelve years later, at the start of the American Revolution, American troops under Richard Montgomery and Benedict Arnold failed to take Quebec on the night of December 31, 1775. In the spring a British fleet raised the Americans's siege of Quebec and chased the army from Canada. Most of the French Canadians declined to join either side in what they saw as a civil war among "the damned English."

The real impact of the American Revolution on Canada came after the shooting stopped. The crown rewarded American loyalist veterans and their families with lands in Nova Scotia and Canada, especially along the north shores of the St. Lawrence and Lake Ontario from east of Cornwall, Ontario to Niagara. This loyalist American settlement marked the beginning of an English Canadian people. In 1792 the British split Canada into two provinces, Upper Canada (Ontario) for the loyal Americans and Lower Canada (Quebec) mainly for the French.

As far as is known, the first vessels on the St. Lawrence were Indian bark canoes. Europeans brought large sailing ships up to Quebec and smaller ones on to Montreal. Between Montreal and Lake Ontario the French developed their own canoes following the Indian pattern. These grew to the large cargo-bearing "master canoes" built at Trois Rivières, sometimes forty feet long and carrying up to 4,000 pounds of cargo; such canoes were manned by fourteen men. The famed St. Lawrence skiff is a light, graceful variant of the canoe adapted for rowing.

Ocean ships found the St. Lawrence a treacherous entryway. Shoals and rocks in combination with dense fog near the river mouth brought many a ship to grief and even wrecked a large part of an English invasion fleet in 1711. Jesuits at Quebec founded a river pilots' school to train men to guide ships upriver. Today's Seaway pilots are part of a long tradition.

The first steamboat to run on the St. Lawrence was the *Accommodation* in 1809, owned by Montrealer John Molson. With its six horsepower motor, *Accommodation* was unsuccessful, but Molson, undaunted, followed up with *Swiftsure* in 1811 with twenty-eight horsepower. He began regular service between Montreal and Quebec, adding boats over the years. Steamers appeared upriver as far down as Ogdensburg and Prescott in 1817. These boats ran regularly between the upper river ports of Ogdensburg, New York, and Prescott, Upper Canada, and the western end of the lake. Their numbers increased with the years.

When New York began construction of the Erie Canal in 1817, Montreal merchants looked on in alarm. They had staked their fortunes on the carrying trade which would funnel grain and other goods through Montreal and Quebec to the sea. There was only one answer: canals around the St. Lawrence rapids. Between 1821 and 1845 they dug eight canals—the first St. Lawrence "Seaway" (although that term was not used). At the upper end of the system was the Welland Canal linking lakes Ontario and Erie; it met the threat of the Erie Canal at Buffalo. Steamboats ran the rapids to Montreal and returned upriver, via the canals, to Toronto, Hamilton, and Niagara and through the Welland to Erie ports. Later the canals were enlarged.

Propeller steamers rather than the more bulky sidewheelers appeared in the 1850s. After 1856 and the completion of the Grand Trunk Railway between Montreal and Toronto, passenger traffic declined although some passenger lines continued to operate into the 1940s. Bulk cargo shippers preferred, as they still do, the more economical water transport. For this trade there evolved a vessel unique to the St. Lawrence: the "canaller." Plain, tublike vessels with their engines aft and pilothouses forward, the canallers were tailored to fit the locks.

While a few small oceangoing freighters from northern Europe used the seaway into the 1950s, larger steamships on the Lakes as well as larger ocean ships could not use the canals. They had to transship at Cornwall or Prescott downbound, and at Montreal or Quebec upbound. The United States and Canada concluded a treaty in 1932 which provided for joint construction of a new seaway which had been discussed since 1900; however, the United States delayed action.

Finally, in 1954, after Canada had decided to build the Seaway alone, the Eisenhower administration agreed to cooperate and the project was begun; it opened officially in 1959. Today large ocean ships traverse the river and locks along with huge "lakers" carrying grain and iron ore. The river is busy as ever including, in the summer, pleasure craft of all sizes and descriptions.

The Rush-Bagot Agreement of 1817 stipulated that there be no warships on the Great Lakes and Lake Champlain beyond a few police boats; however, the British built forts along the river and the Americans built military roads to the river border and maintained a garrison at Sackets Harbor. In 1837 and 1838 popular uprisings in Canada attracted American sympathy. Guerrilla groups called "Hunter's Lodges" sought to assist the rebels. One such raid, remembered in northern New York as the "Patriot War," embarked from Ogdensburg and tried to "liberate" Upper Canada. Instead of rising to join them, the local militia turned out under the Union Jack and squashed the attempted filibuster. American guerrillas under the river bandit Bill Johnston burned the Canadian steamer *Sir Robert Peel* in 1838 in reprisal, they said, for the burning of the American steamer *Caroline* in the Niagara River the previous December. But there was no war. By the 1870s fortifications along the St. Lawrence were no longer manned.

The St. Lawrence system could never overcome the natural advantages of New York City and the Hudson-Mohawk route, for it was much cheaper to ship from New York than from Montreal. But the St. Lawrence has flourished even with seasonal operation. The river route, including parallel road- and railways and airlines, remains the main street of the most heavily populated region of Canada.

FURTHER READING: Alida Sims Malkus, *Blue-Water Boundary* (1960). Donald G. Creighton, *Empire of the St. Lawrence* (1958).

Arthur L. Johnson

The St. Marys River (Florida)

Source: Okefenokee Swamp of Southeast Georgia
Length: 175 miles
Tributaries: None of significance
Mouth: Cumberland Sound above Jacksonville
Agricultural Products: Cotton, corn, peaches, figs, pecans
Industries: Lumbering, naval stores

One of the most unusual boundaries in the United States is the imaginary line in the middle of the St. Marys River that separates northeastern Florida from coastal and southeastern Georgia. While Florida and Georgia are not the only states in the Union to designate a river as the official state boundary, no political units can claim a more crooked line than the body of water which defines the boundary of these two southern states.

The St. Marys has been described as wild, mysterious, beautiful, and "too crooked to be parallel to anything." Its headwaters, often referred to as the River Styx, originate as a slight current in the eastern interior of Georgia's Okefenokee Swamp. With hundreds of crooks, bends, and curls, the St. Marys flows about 175 miles altogether: first westward, then south as it develops from a stream into a river. It then meanders north and finally east to the Atlantic. Since it receives no large tributaries, the St. Marys is fed by small streams and the rainwater that flows from Trail Ridge, a hump or backbone formed in the Pleistocene epoch that runs over 100 miles through the Okefenokee Swamp. The river drops just 100 feet on its way to the Atlantic.

In addition to its crooked quality, the river corridor is heavily canopied with dense stands of cypress, oak, and pine. This heavy concentration of woodlands has made the corridor a center of timber-farm activity with the river serving as the principal transportation artery.

The St. Mary's current is placid, but the channel can be deceptively dangerous during the rainy season or in the event of an approaching storm. There are other dangers: many river travelers have been startled by abruptly snag-ging a partially submerged log or by peering up and seeing a cluster of hornet nests hanging three or four feet above the water. As the channel begins to widen, between Stokes Bridge and Folkston, the river is characterized by white sandbanks and tidal movements. From Folkston to the coastal town of St. Marys the water becomes increasingly brackish, and white sandbanks give way to the tidal salt marsh; the river's mouth is over 1,000 feet wide as it empties into the Atlantic. St. Marys river water, which has always had a reputation for being of the highest quality, is either black or tea-colored because of the presence of tannic acid and chemical solutions from palmetto roots and sand bottoms.

The semi-tropical climate of the river region and the Okefenokee is conducive to year around animal and plant life. Palmetto, cypress, inkberry, sumac, wisteria, and button bush abound, not to mention the extensive stands of slash and longleaf pine, which are concentrated on the low sandy bluffs, and oak and black gum which are more numerous in the coastal area. The region is also a veritable haven for raccoon, deer, bobcat, bear, bats, fox, shrew, owl, armadillo, osprey, a host of amphibian and reptilian creatures, and almost every imaginable variety of North American bird. As one observer remarked, there is "nothing exactly like it in the world."

Prior to the appearance of Europeans, Indians, including Timacuan and Creek, called the river Phlaphlagaphgaw or Thlathlothlaguphka (meaning "rotten fish"). The first white man to explore the St. Marys was the French Huguenot adventurer Jean Ribaut who landed at the river's mouth in 1562. French designs on the St. Marys proved to be brief, for Spain asserted dominance in the region. The river received its present name from a Spanish mission, Santa Maria de Guadeloupe, which was established in 1568 near the present town of St. Marys by Pedro Menéndez de Aviles, who also founded St. Augustine, Florida.

In spite of the Spanish presence the English began to probe the area in the early eighteenth century. During Queen Anne's War (1701–1713), Colonel James Moore, Governor of South Carolina, and his Creek allies drove the Spanish southward to the St. Johns River. In order to protect the St. Marys, James Oglethorpe constructed Ft. William in 1738 on Cumberland Island east of the river's mouth. Spain never recovered the Georgia coastline.

With the founding of Georgia in 1733 and British victories over the French and Spanish by 1763, the population of English-speaking settlers increased in the St. Marys river corridor. Although there were no large towns, sizeable plantations appeared, one of which, the Pagan Plantation, served as a base of operations for loyalists during the American Revolution.

The region's economy was based on agriculture, timber production, and to a lesser extent naval stores. Timber was floated down the river. Settlers hauled their cotton and naval stores in ox-drawn wagons to St. Marys and other river settlements. The town of St. Marys was also a favorite port-of-call for sailing vessels in need of fresh water. For decades seamen who sailed the oceans of the world were familiar with the quality of the water from the St. Marys. One old salt even claimed that the water would remain fresh and pure for two years. In the nineteenth century St. Marys river water was transported to communities along the Florida coast including Fernandina and Jacksonville, and sold for one penny a gallon.

Another economic activity along the Georgia coast was smuggling. Smugglers and pirates from Florida and the Caribbean often landed their contraband at St. Marys. With its "brawling, riotous" waterfront it was a smugglers's paradise.

Following the American Revolution the southeastern Georgia frontier communities were subjected to frequent attacks and harassment from Spanish authorities in Florida. This situation was partly ameliorated by the Treaty of San Lorenzo in 1795 by which the United States and Spain determined that the St. Marys would serve as the boundary between East Florida and Georgia. In 1800 U.S. Commissioner Andrew Ellicott led a team of surveyors up the St. Marys until he found what he considered to be the headwaters near Moniac. Since then the St.

Marys has been recognized as the official boundary line for southeast Georgia and northeast Florida. In the opinion of historian E. Merton Coulter, this was the "worst possible river boundary in all North America . . . because it was the most crooked river on the continent."

Notwithstanding the 1795 treaty and Ellicott's survey, Georgia frontiersmen and Spanish authorities continued to distrust one another, and border conflicts did not diminish until Spain ceded Florida in 1821. Indian problems persisted until the conclusion of the Seminole Wars. Yet the early nineteenth century was a period of unparalleled growth along the St. Marys. Small river trading posts suddenly developed into thriving market communities from St. Marys on the coast to Centersville and Traders Hill on the west.

It was at St. Marys, with its strategic position, that the United States government established a customs office in 1785. Because of the salubrious climate and abundant timber, vessels constructed there could be launched without seasonal interruptions. It was not uncommon for residents to christen a new craft amid gala festivities such as shad fishing, horse racing, and alligator, possum, and coon hunts.

In January 1815 British forces, unaware that the War of 1812 was over, landed at St. Marys, causing most of the local citizenry to retreat upriver. Opposition stiffened, however, as the British attempted to ply the river and capture Archibald Clarke's sawmill. Taking advantage of the dense forest cover and the crooked waterway, Captain William McCone and twenty-eight militiamen forced twenty-three barges loaded with British regulars to return to St. Marys. When the British heard that the Treaty of Ghent had been signed, the occupation forces withdrew.

While struggling against the British, residents of St. Marys were also casting a covetous eye on Spanish Florida. For years local settlers had blamed the Spanish for inciting the Indians and encouraging slaves to run away. Consequently local settlers along the Georgia-Florida frontier waged an undeclared war against Spanish Florida. This was in reality the first phase of the bloody, protracted Seminole Wars.

The sticky Florida problem was eventually

resolved through aggressive diplomacy, and the Adams-Onis Treaty accelerated the economic growth that had begun two decades earlier. Cultivation on both sides of the river of cotton, rice, corn, peaches, figs, quince, oranges, mulberry, and pecan tress, combined with the shipbuilding and timber industry, enabled St. Marys to flourish until the Civil War. While it did recover from the physical devastation of the conflict, St. Marys was unable to regain her prosperity. The advent of iron-clad and steel ships made wooden vessels obsolete, and lumber and turpentine interests utilized the railroads. Accordingly, St. Marys until recently was consigned to the status of a sleepy, picturesque fishing village.

A similar cycle of prosperity and decline took place at Center Village (or Centerville), founded in 1800 and in close proximity during the Seminole Wars to U.S. Camp Pinckney. The oldest major settlement after St. Marys was Traders Hill. It consisted of a trading post, a few rustic saloons, and Fort Alert, a military garrison established in the early nineteenth century to protect river settlers from hostile Indians. In 1854 Traders Hill became the county seat of Charlton County; it continued to flourish into the 1920s from sawmill operations and the turpentine industry.

No history of St. Marys would be complete without some reference to several grandiose—although unsuccessful—canal projects. Citizens of Georgia and Florida have long dreamed of a canal to link the Atlantic with the Gulf of Mexico. Since 1870 the Georgia legislature, and since 1878 the U.S. Congress, have occasionally enacted legislation looking to the construction of such a waterway. When public funds were not forthcoming, a wealthy Atlanta lumberman, Harry Jackson, tried to accomplish the project beginning in 1891, but "Jackson's Folly" was a colossal failure. A result of the continuing interest was the creation of the Okefenokee National Wildlife Refuge in 1937.

With the proliferation of automobile highways after World War I it was impossible for the nineteenth century. Sawmill and turpentine operations continue to play a role in the area's economy, however, while chemical and wood product industries have increased, creating some pollution and environmental problems.

Yet St. Marys could be on the verge of a new boom. The Navy looks with favor on King's Bay, just north of St. Marys, as a future base for nuclear-powered submarines. Meanwhile a less welcome boom has taken place: an increase in drug smuggling operations. The new smugglers use every possible stratagem including the use of dozens of obscure river inlets, coves, and tributaries.

Regardless of its future, the St. Marys remains one of the most picturesque rivers in the United States. We are fortunate that Jackson did not succeed in draining the Okefenokee because that mysterious swamp and the crooked old St. Marys are a wilderness paradise to be admired and respected by all. And let us hope that the tea-colored water—known for its purity and healthful qualities by seafaring adventurers many years ago—will be available for generations to come.

FURTHER READING: Eloise Bailey, et al. *Historical St. Marys, Georgia* (1974). Spencer B. King, *Georgia Voices: A Documentary History to 1872* (1966). Burnette Vanstory, *Georgia's Land of Golden Isles* (1956).

Carlyle Ramsey

The Savannah River

Source: Convergence of Tugaloo and Seneca rivers near Hartwell in northeast Georgia
Length: 314 miles
Tributaries: Broad River, two Little Rivers; Briar Creek, Stevens Creek
Mouth: Into Atlantic near Savannah, Georgia
Agricultural Products: Cotton; truck vegetables
Industries: Lumbering, papermills, textiles, petroleum refineries, chemicals, and gypsum

The Savannah River officially begins where the Tugaloo and Seneca rivers converge near Hartwell, in northeast Georgia. The Tugaloo, which serves as part of Georgia's northeast boundary with South Carolina, is formed by the waters of the Chatooga and Tallulah rivers. The Seneca (also known as the Keowee) has its origins in the merger of the Toxaway and Whitewater rivers in North Carolina. In turn, these headwaters streams are formed from springs and brooks on the high forested slopes of the Blue Ridge Mountains in North Carolina, South Carolina, and Georgia.

From the 5,500-foot altitude at the headwaters of the Tallulah the Savannah watershed descends to the 1,000-foot altitude of the Georgia-South Carolina Piedmont, gradually descending to about 200 feet by the time it reaches Augusta, Georgia; it then continues to fall through gently rolling country down to the Coastal Plain and sea level where it enters the sea. The Savannah serves as the state boundary between Georgia and South Carolina as it flows 314 miles in a southeasterly direction, finally discharging near the city of Savannah. The stream's major downstream tributaries are the Broad River and Briar Creek in Georgia, the two Little Rivers in Georgia and South Carolina, and Stevens Creek in South Carolina.

Rainfall is generally abundant in the Savannah watershed reaching an annual average of eighty inches; runoff averages about fifteen inches annually for the entire drainage area. The Savannah River basin is predominantly forested and supports a variety of wildlife, especially game animals, the swamps and marshes abound in wild ducks and geese.

The Indians were the first to exploit its navigable waters, calling the river the Keowee. A very old Indian trail which extended from a Cherokee Indian village in western North Carolina followed the banks of the Savannah on the Georgia side down through the present city of Savannah, ending on Skidaway Island just outside the city. The name Keowee was later changed by the Indians to Isundiga, then to Westobou or Westo for a fierce tribe of that name. In 1683, the Westos were defeated and practically annihilated by the Shawnee or Savannah Indians who changed the name of the river to Savannah.

The first Europeans known to have viewed this fair river were the Spanish explorer Hernando De Soto and his army who crossed its waters in 1540 in upper Georgia at Cofitachequi, an Indian village today known as Silver Springs. The Spanish called the river Rio Dulce, meaning soft or quiet river. The French explored the mouth of the river in 1562, calling its entrance the Bay of Bajos as they proceeded under the leadership of Jean Ribaut to settle Port Royal, South Carolina. The French were the first Europeans to engage in commerce on the Savannah River, trading with the Indians for sassafras; sassafras tea, as a medicinal drink, swept Europe as a fashionable fad. Sassafras may be said to have caused the first naval battle on the river. In 1603, while the French bartered with the Indians for sassafras roots and bark, a Spanish fleet entered the harbor and, being irate at what they deemed French aggression in Spanish New World territory, fought and defeated the French traders and captured their cruiser.

Carolina was chartered in 1663 and the English colonists of this province were soon using the Savannah River to engage in trade with the Indians, bartering guns and cloth for furs and deerskins. Canoes and Indian tradeboats were used to transport these commodities along the Savannah River and through the inland water-

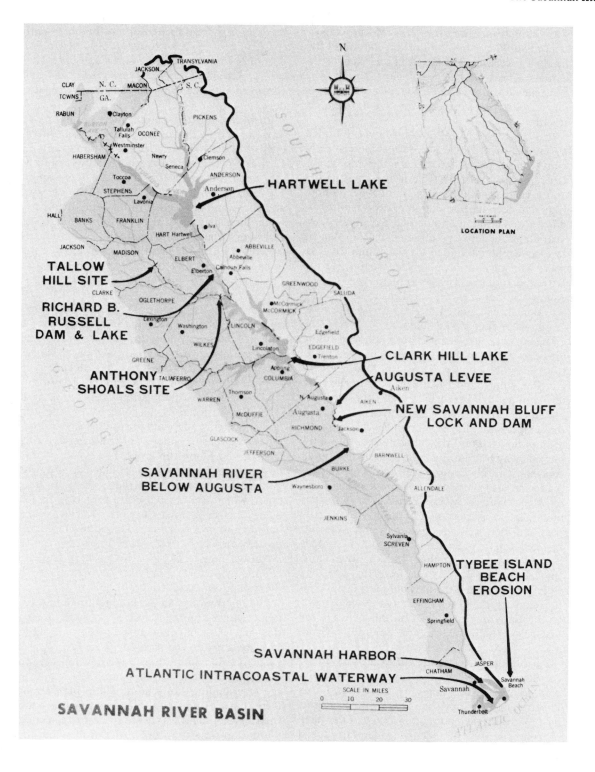

TRANSYLVANIA
JACKSON
MACON
CLAY
N. C.
TCWNS
S. C.
GA.
RABUN
Clayton
PICKENS
Tallulah
Falls
OCONEE
Westminster
Newry
HABERSHAM
Clemson
Seneca
Toccoa
ANDERSON
STEPHENS
Anderson
Lavonia
HALL
BANKS
FRANKLIN
HARTWELL LAKE
JACKSON
MADISON
HART Hartwell
Iva
ABBEVILLE
ELBERT
Abbeville
TALLOW HILL SITE
CLARKE
Elberton
Calhoun Falls
GREENWOOD
SALUDA
OGLETHORPE
Lexington
McCormick
McCORMICK
RICHARD B. RUSSELL DAM & LAKE
Washington
LINCOLN
Edgefield
GREENE
WILKES
Lincolnton
EDGEFIELD
Trenton
CLARK HILL LAKE
ANTHONY SHOALS SITE
TALIAFERRO
COLUMBIA
AUGUSTA LEVEE
Aiken
WARREN
Thomson
N. Augusta
AIKEN
NEW SAVANNAH BLUFF LOCK AND DAM
McDUFFIE
Augusta
RICHMOND
Jackson
GLASCOCK
JEFFERSON
BARNWELL
SAVANNAH RIVER BELOW AUGUSTA
BURKE
Waynesboro
ALLENDALE
JENKINS
Sylvania
SCREVEN
HAMPTON
TYBEE ISLAND BEACH EROSION
EFFINGHAM
Springfield
SAVANNAH HARBOR
JASPER
ATLANTIC INTRACOASTAL WATERWAY
CHATHAM
Savannah Beach
Savannah
Thunderbolt

SCALE IN MILES
0   10   20   30

SAVANNAH RIVER BASIN

N

SOUTH CAROLINA

GEORGIA

ATLANTIC OCEAN

LOCATION PLAN

way to and from Charleston. In 1715, the Yamas-see Indian War in South Carolina convinced the English government of the need for river fortifications. The following year, Fort Moore was constructed on the Carolina banks of the river about 200 miles upstream (by water) from its mouth.

In 1733, the province of Georgia was founded by James Edward Oglethorpe and nineteen associates who acted as Trustees for the colony. For Georgia's first settlers, Oglethorpe chose a site on the river about ten miles inland where a high bluff and deep harbor offered many advantages; a town was laid out and named Savannah. Two years later, Oglethorpe directed that a town be laid out at the fall line of the Savannah River to serve as a defense outpost and trading station with the Indians. The settlement was named Augusta in honor of the royal princess of Saxony. Augusta is situated directly across the river from where Fort Moore stood.

During Georgia's early history, other communities appeared on the Savannah River but were short-lived. These were Abercorn, Mount Pleasant, Purysburg, and Ebenezer. Oglethorpe sent ten families to Abercorn in 1733; the location was fifteen miles above Savannah on a creek that empties into the Savannah River. Abercorn did not flourish and the inhabitants eventually moved away but the site later became a popular spot for church camp meetings. Steamboats made special excursions to Abercorn to accommodate travelers. Mount Pleasant was settled under Oglethorpe's direction to serve as an outpost and fort between Savannah and Augusta. Located thirty miles above Savannah, it had been formerly a Euchee Indian town and English trading post. It was from this site that Oglethorpe began a memorable journey in 1739 to treat with the Creek Indians at Coweta Town on the Alabama side of the Chattahoochee River just below the present city of Columbus, Georgia.

Purysburg was founded on the Carolina side of the Savannah River in 1731 by Baron Pury who was granted 12,000 acres by the Swiss Lords Proprietors. Purysburg had nearly 100 dwellings by 1735 when the community reached the peak of its prosperity, but a lack of leadership caused its demise shortly thereafter. In the nineteenth century, however, the location became an important steamboat landing and stagecoach stop where passengers were transferred from one conveyance to the other to continue their journeys.

Ebenezer, located about thirty miles above Savannah, directly across the river from Purysburg, was settled by Salzburger immigrants in 1734 and became a prosperous trading community until the era of the American Revolution. The Salzburgers were noted for their industry and thrift and succeeded in manufacturing silk while their neighbors at Savannah failed in the endeavor. The British occupied Ebenezer between 1779 and 1783 and destroyed most of the town. The handsome brick Jerusalem Lutheran Church built in 1769 was not destroyed; it stands today as a testimony to these stouthearted Germans. Descendants of the original communicants worship in it at the present time. A church school and museum have recently been constructed and two original Salzburger houses have been moved to the site and restored.

By 1740, Augusta had become an important trading center with an estimated population of 600 or more inhabitants. Poleboats came into use as Indian tradeboats proved to be too small for the increasing amount of trade goods being transported along the river. The poleboat was larger than the canoe or tradeboat and was guided downstream with the current by long poles, which were also used to push or pole the boats upriver against the current. The vessels had regular crews; some belonged to plantation owners, others to individual river men or to factorage houses engaged in marketing staple commodities and supplying individuals with manufactured goods from abroad.

The restrictions against land tenure and slave labor which stunted Georgia's growth during the early years of colonization were removed in 1750; as a result, the economy grew rapidly and extensive rice plantations were developed from swamplands along the Savannah River and in the surrounding hinterland. These plantations were based upon capitalistic enterprise and their development was quite similar to the great plantation-slave units of South Carolina and the

West Indies. During the American Revolution, the great rice plantations of Loyalists and Americans fell into disrepair and their slaves absconded, about 7,000 fleeing to the British lines where they were granted freedom. After the war, the plantations were rehabilitated in a surprisingly short time and once again became thriving units.

In 1808, the first steamboat appeared on the Savannah River, built by William Longstreet of Augusta. In 1815, the first commercial steamboat, the *Enterprise*, was launched. It was a 152-ton boat constructed at Savannah in John Watts's shipyard. In 1819, the steamer, *Savannah*, financed by local businessmen, was the first such ocean liner to make a transatlantic crossing, leaving the Savannah River in May and arriving in Liverpool, England, the following month. By 1835, steamboats had supplanted poleboats and tradeboats as a more effective means of transporting freight between Savannah and Augusta. Steamboats were a great innovation for they carried mail and passengers in addition to freight. Prior to the era of the steamboat, the stagecoach was the only means of conveyance for persons wishing to travel between Savannah and Augusta.

The first commercially successful iron-hull steamboat in the United States, the *John Randolph*, was launched on the Savannah River in 1834. Other iron-hull steamboats which operated on the river were the *Chatham*, the *Lamar*, the *Mary Summers*, and the *De Rosset*. These vessels, unlike the flimsy wooden steamboats, were extremely well built and later were used by the Confederate government during the Civil War. During the war, before the Federal blockade became complete, the steamer *Fingal* slipped into the Savannah harbor with the richest contraband cargo of the Civil War: 14,000 Enfield rifles, 1,000,000 ball cartridges, 2,000,000 percussion caps, 1,000 short rifles, 500 revolvers, and 400 barrels of cannon powder.

After the Civil War, lumbering and naval stores gradually superseded cotton in value of exports transported on the Savannah River. By 1900, the need for wood had created a tremendous lumbering business. Gradually rafting was the only activity on the river for the railroad had

taken the place of the steamboat. In 1915, representatives of the sugar industry came to Savannah to find a site for a sugar refinery and chose a location several miles upriver. Since that time, industries have multiplied to include paper and paperboard, petroleum, chemicals, and gypsum. Upstream from Savannah is the giant Savannah River plant of the Nuclear Energy Commission where materials for man's most destructive weapons are made, and where studies are conducted on nuclear benefits for peaceful purposes.

Of all the traditions on the riverfront, the most widely known among mariners of the seven seas was the "Waving Girl." In 1887, Florence Martus started waving at every vessel that passed Elba Island, where her brother was lighthouse keeper. She waved a handkerchief in the daytime and a lantern at night. Today, a handsome bronze statue of the "Waving Girl" stands on River Street in Savannah as a memorial to this remarkable woman.

A comprehensive study of the Savannah's upper basin was completed in 1943. As a result, the 1944 Flood Control Act approved a general plan of comprehensive development of the Savannah River for flood control and other purposes. The plan, which included eleven reservoir sites, also authorized construction of the Clark Hill Lake as the initial step in this development. This project, completed in 1955, created a 70,000-acre lake behind the dam. The 1950 Flood Control Act authorized construction of Hartwell Dam, the second project in the approved plan; it was completed in 1962 and has a lake area of 56,000 acres.

The Trotters Shoals site replaces two sites in the general plan. This project, which has been renamed for the late Senator Richard B. Russell, was authorized for construction by the 1966 Flood Control Act. Construction was begun in 1974 and when completed, the dam will create a lake area of 26,000 acres, extending from the headwaters of Clark Hill Lake to the Hartwell Dam to form a chain of lakes 120 miles long. The other projects planned are not yet begun.

Savannah, the port city of Georgia, is located on a bluff with an average elevation of 41 feet above the river, differing sharply from other

South Atlantic cities which are located practically at sea level. The high bluff and surrounding salt marshes assure virtual freedom from damage by floods or tides. Because of the superior advantage offered by the Savannah River, the city has been a principal seaport since colonial times and today might well be called the "Mar-seilles of the Southeast" since it is the leading general cargo port for this section of the United States.

FURTHER READING: George Hatcher, (ed.), *Georgia Rivers* (1962). Thomas L. Stokes, *Rivers of America; The Savannah* (1951).

Julia F. Smith

The Shenandoah River

Source: **Rises north of Lexington, Virginia (as the North Fork)**
Length: **1,150 miles (or 55 miles from convergence of North Fork and South Fork near Front Royal)**
Tributaries: **None of significance**
Agricultural Products: **Dairying, apples, peaches**
Industries: **Lumber, manufacturing, tourism**

> Oh Shenandoah, I hear you call me
> Away, you rolling river
> Oh Shenandoah I'm going to leave you
> Away, away I'm bound to go
> Across the wide Missouri

The origins of this plaintive song lie deep in American folklore. It is a sea chanty, about a river far from the sea; it is an old U.S. cavalry song; it encompasses the homesick longing of the westering pioneer for his beloved valley; and it symbolizes the historic and cultural significance of the Virginia lands beyond the Blue Ridge Mountains.

The word "Shenandoah" may be translated as "beautiful (or clear-eyed) daughter of the stars". It is an Indian name. About the time that John Smith was leading the English settlers at Jamestown, an Iroquois Chief named "Sherando" fought against a "son" of Powhatan after agreeing that the eastern Virginia Indians could share in the trade of the valley. Powhatan's forces in turn captured (and possibly killed) Chief Sherando. Perhaps the name originated here. Or, it may have come from an obscure Algonquin tribe living in the lower valley called Senedoes who were all massacred by the Iroquois on one of their marauding expeditions. It may be a version of the Shawnee Indian word "cenantua." Some believe that the word is Iroquoian, in which case it should be translated as "Big Meadow." Whatever its origin, the valley and the river have both been called "Shenandoah" for three centuries.

The river rises north of Lexington, Virginia, and drains seven counties as it flows northeast for about one hundred fifty miles before plunging spectacularly into the Potomac at Harpers Ferry, Virginia. Thomas Jefferson wrote in his *Notes on Virginia* (1782) that this was "perhaps one of the most stupendous scenes in nature... wild and tremendous... [it] is worth a voyage across the Atlantic..." to see it.

The Shenandoah flows from a height of about 1,500 feet above sea level down to 500 feet at Harpers Ferry, between two parallel mountain ranges, one geologically very old (the Blue Ridge), the other, comparatively younger (the Allegheny). Much of the river is shallow, broken by occasional rapids; since it flows through a plateau-like limestone-floored valley, it is characterized by some spectacular meanders—notably the seven bends near Woodstock. Here the river takes thirty miles to cover a distance of ten. For much of its course, the river is divided into the North and South Fork by a forty-five-mile-long isolated hill called the Massanutten Ridge. The two river branches come together north of Front Royal at Riverton and thence flow to the Potomac as one.

The Shenandoah Valley is part of the great

Appalachian Valley system. It is a large area of broadly rolling, well-watered fertile land varying in width from twenty-six miles (at Winchester) to eight miles (at Lexington). The area is rich in limestone, creating vast caverns (such as Luray, Endless, Grand, and Shenandoah) with dramatic formations beneath the earth and rich pasture and farmlands on the surface. The Blue Ridge Mountains (to the east) are not high (3,000 to 4,000 feet) and have several wind gaps, but the valley was easily accessible to the first settlers only in the north where it joins the Potomac and south at Buchanan where the James River breaks through the mountain chain. It was thus a lovely, but isolated valley with lush deep grasses, oaks and chestnut trees, beeches and poplars, maple and pine forests, perfumed with fruit blossoms in the spring and aglow with color in the fall.

Not many rivers in North America run, for any length of time, from the south to the north: only the St. Lawrence in Canada, the St. Marys in Florida, the Red River, and the Shenandoah. Because of this, the usual descriptive terms are inverted; for example, the upper valley (Staunton) is south, the lower valley (Winchester) is to the north, the headwaters of the river are to the south, the mouth of the river is north.

Because of its strategic location between the fall line and the eastern continental divide and its unique north-south orientation, the region was already a significant crossroads long before European colonization. Archaeological evidence reveals ancient Indian settlements (some perhaps quite large) as well as hunting, salt collecting, and fighting grounds. There were apparently two principal Indian trails: one along the top of the Blue Ridge, roughly parallel to the present Skyline Drive, used by war parties for strategic observation; the other in the valley, used by hunting parties. The latter became the Great Wagon Road of the 18th century and later the Valley Pike (Route 11) and eventually Interstate 81.

Most of the Indians appear to have been Algonquins—Shawnee, Occoneechee, Catawbas. Here they met their enemies, the Delawares, the Cherokees, the Susquehannas, and the Iroquois, often, legend says, in fierce battle. Myth has also been the foundation of the oft-repeated story that the Indians used the valley for a vast pasture and regularly burned it over so that grass would grow for the buffalo. Modern ecologists no longer accept this, and pioneer testimony bears witness to the heavily wooded areas of much of the valley as well as its open meadows. It does appear, however, that it is historically accurate that few Indians made their permanent home in the Shenandoah Valley at the time of the beginnings of white settlement. The rapid progress by which this took place in the eighteenth century makes this frontier unlike many others.

The first white man to record seeing the Shenandoah River and the valley was a German medical doctor and explorer, John Lederer, who made three trips into the region during the 1670s. His voluminous reports and crude maps were dismissed by his English sponsors (including Sir William Beverley) as lies. But other explorers and fur traders followed, the most flamboyant being the expedition organized by the governor of Virginia, Alexander Spotswood, in September, 1716. Spotswood, dressed in green velvet with boots of Russian leather, accompanied by fifty "gentlemen," rangers, horses, and pack animals, climbed the mountains at Swift Run Gap. They descended into the valley and camped beside the river not far from present-day Port Republic. They fired a volley into the air, drank a toast to the King, buried a bottle with a message claiming all the land west to the Mississippi in the name of George (I) of England, and returned to Williamsburg where, legend says, the governor commemorated the occasion by giving each of his companions a small golden horseshoe. Spotswood had, incidentally, named the lovely river "Euphrates," but subsequent settlers fortunately preferred the more melodious name of Shenandoah.

Serious European settlement began in the early 18th century. From the east came English settlers, Huguenot, and some German colonists as well. By the 1730s, southward from Pennsylvania, hundreds of Scotch-Irish (John Lewis "who slew the Irish lord"), Swiss (Jacob Stover), and German (Adam Muller and Joist Hite) came seeking cheap and fertile land, religious toleration, and ethnic identity. Control by Virginia persisted, however, particularly under such leaders as Governor William Gooch. The Shenandoah was regarded as a valuable buffer against aggressive frontier Indians and later the assertive French. Professional promoters and enthusiastic large-scale land grant speculators (including Lord Fairfax, William Beverley, James Patton, and Dr. Thomas Walker) were generous with credit and land titles; the colonial government required only minimal observance of religious restrictions and, until the French and Indian War (1754), the Indians were relatively peaceful. Andrew Burnaby, an English traveller, observed that the settlers had "health, content and tranquillity of mind" (1760).

The valley settlers were of many religious persuasions: Quakers near Winchester, Lutheran, German Evangelicals, Mennonites in the area between Winchester and Harrisonburg, and south to Lexington the Scotch-Irish Presbyterians. These settlers had no intention of remaining "back country" impoverished pioneers. In addition to churches, county government was soon established (Augusta and Frederick in 1745), trading areas began to develop (Winchester, Front Royal, and Staunton), and a more diversified economy characterized the second generation of settlers. In the 18th century the chief route for trade was by wagon down the valley to the outlet cities of the east—Baltimore, Alexandria, Falmouth, and Fredericksburg. Immigration into the area was slowed by the ravages of the French and Indian War and some of the most colorful legends and myths tell of Indian captives and the victims of Indian outrages. After Braddock was ambushed near Fort Dusquesne, George Washington was placed in charge of the defense of the Virginia frontier. He struggled to maintain security with limited resources, and many valley people retreated east across the Blue Ridge. Prosperity and population returned with peace (1763), and in the years preceding the Revolution, paticularly in the northern valley, well-defined and socially central estates began to serve as the focus for political, religious, and urban development. To the Revolution (which was impressively supported by the valley families), the area contributed generals Andrew Lewis, Daniel Morgan, and Peter Muhlenberg. The latter was a Lutheran minister whose moving sermon, "there is a time for peace and a time for war," was followed by his throwing off his clerical garb, revealing his uniform as a Virginia colonel, and his recruitment from his congregation of the "German Regiment."

After the American Revolution the Shenandoah region became an administrative and travel center for westward expansion over and through the mountains into the nearby Ohio Valley. The population expanded so greatly that inhabitants complained bitterly about their powerlessness in state affairs under the eastern-oriented state constitutions.

The valley was a rich agricultural area, producing wheat, some tobacco, cattle, sheep, and hogs; linsey-woolsey and even a bit of cotton cloth were manufactured. Later there would be modest but flourishing iron, limestone, and lumber industries. Still later in the 19th century apples and peaches were produced commerically. Agricultural production increased with the introduction of the iron plow, the systematic use of fertilizers, and mechanical devices such as the reaper invented by Cyrus McCormick of Rockbridge County in the Valley in 1831.

The river provided the power for waterground flour and cornmeal mills and the saw mills. Numerous fords allowed passage from one side to the other. Ferries were much in demand; McKay's at the Page-Warren County Line, Chester at Riverton, Castleman's Ferry at Berryville, and Harper's at the junction with the Potomac, are best known.

Although the economic role of the river has never been outstanding and many of the cities of the valley are on the turnpike rather than the river, it was used for serious commerce in the years before the intrusion of the railroad (1854). Flatboats transported goods northward and contemporary tiny villages still bear names (Newport, Port Republic) indicating how deep into the valley such commercial enterprise reached. In 1798, the Virginia Assembly granted a charter to a Shenandoah Company to operate a fleet of barges and these remained important until the 1890s. Rivermen called their barges "gundalows." They might be as large as nine feet wide and seventy-five feet long. It took fourteen to eighteen men to pole these unwieldly monsters and their cargo of millions of dollars worth of lime, mill feed, corn, flour, leather, sumac, brandy, and dried fruit that were sent downriver to

Harpers Ferry. From Riverton, the trip took four days going down and three days to walk back. The barge would be sold for timber once it reached Harpers Ferry. In the 1880s one would bring as much as twenty-five dollars.

The river has been spanned by many bridges, often destroyed by war and flood. Most are undistinguished, but an interesting old covered bridge remains at Meems Bottom near Mt. Jackson. It is a single span, 204-foot covered bridge still carrying traffic on its wooden planks. The massive arch-supports and stone abutments were quarried nearby. Stonewall Jackson burned an earlier bridge at this site to delay advancing Union troops.

In the years before John Brown's raid on Harpers Ferry (1859), transportation in the valley vastly improved. Not only was the river used, but canals were built around the falls of the Potomac and the James (bringing partial fulfillment to a long-standing dream of George Washington); the valley turnpike was macademized (1834–1840); and finally railroads were introduced into the valley, coming in from the north to Winchester and from the east to Staunton.

Not unexpectedly, the Shenandoah Valley was vitally important during the Civil War. Inhabitants had not used slavery extensively and had voted moderately pro-Union in 1860, but they became loyal southerners after sectional lines were fixed. The valley became a significant military corridor, particularly for the Confederate invasion of the north; conversely the Union invaded the valley to destroy supplies and checkmate Confederate invasion plans. Following early campaigns by T. J. ("Stonewall") Jackson, whose Valley Campaign of 1862 remains a classic in the tactics of rapid troop movement and the element of surprise, the Union undertook, first under Hunter and then under Sheridan, invasions of the valley. One episode of the later war was the Battle of New Market (May 15, 1864) where youthful cadets from VMI fought to hold back the "Yankee invaders." By the last year of the war the valley had been reduced to ruin and much of the countryside was bare. Grant had ordered that crows flying over the land "will have to carry their provender with them. . . . We want the Shenandoah Valley to remain a barren waste." And so it was. To add to

the bitter Reconstruction years, the river flooded in 1870, taking out all the bridges, swamping the railroad lines, and destroying mills and ironworks to Harpers Ferry where forty-three people drowned. Farming declined, there was an increase in orchards and pasturelands, and population declined.

In the 1890s came a great land boom resulting from the end of Reconstruction and the revival of prosperity in Virginia. But the dream collapsed with the depression of 1893, and the valley entered the twentieth century quietly and without major change until World War II.

A strong commitment to education has been characteristic of the valley people since the 18th century, part of their religious and ethnic orientation. Some truly distinguished colleges and universities are located in the Shenandoah Valley—Washington and Lee and Virginia Military Institute at Lexington, Mary Baldwin College at Staunton, Bridgewater College and James Madison University in Rockingham County. It has only been in recent decades that major industry has been introduced, supported in part by the river's waters. Population has revived around the old urban centers of Winchester, Harrisonburg, Waynesboro, and Staunton. Industry has brought the threat of water and air pollution, and, as always, compromises between economic necessity and environmental purity have had to be made. But, in large part, the valley and its river remain relatively uncontaminated—their beauty intact.

Tourism and recreation have flourished since the mid-20th century. The Shenandoah National Park and Skyline Drive was begun in 1936 and linked to the Blue Ridge Parkway south of Rockfish Gap. These magnificent automobile highways along the mountain ridges, the hiking trails, camping sites, and mountain lodges allow a bird's-eye view of the Shenandoah previously available to only a few hardy mountain folk. The river itself provides superb fishing, swimming, picnicking, and canoeing. There is some challenging white water for the rafting enthusiast. Geologists marvel at the rock formations along the river banks, in the caverns, and at such natural wonders as the Natural Chimneys, now a regional park.

There are several modest hydroelectric dams along the Shenandoah River. Twice in this century, once in the 1940s and again in the 1970s, the river has been threatened by major flood control and power projects. The valley people protested successfully against such major physical alterations of what is surely one of the most beautiful rivers in America.

Many famous Americans have had their roots in the Shenandoah Valley. Sam Houston, John Sevier, Ephraim McDowell, and Woodrow Wilson were all born here. Thomas Lincoln (father of Abraham), Ida Stover Eisenhower, and "Grandma" Moses belong to the Shenandoah; Washington, Jefferson, Madison, Lee, and Stonewall Jackson lived and worked within its perimeters. But the real strength of the valley has been its ordinary people—strong, independent, family-centered, inclined to political conservatism (Federalist in the 1790s, Unionist in 1860, the Byrd homeland of the early 1900s, and Republican since 1950), and religious commitment. The northern valley in particular offers a unique test tube for students of cultural history and anthropology because of the survival of Germanic arts and customs and even linguistics, surrounded as they were by alien cultures from the eastern English and the immigrating Scotch and Irish.

In spite of modern changes, the land is still mostly rural, in philosophy if no longer totally in fact. In the relatively isolated foothills and stream-carved gaps of the two mountain ranges, there remain pockets of traditional culture, poverty, and pride. The people of the valley reflect their heritage, the magnificent physical surroundings of their land, their mountains and their river.

FURTHER READING: Julia Davis, *The Shenandoah* (1945); William Couper, *History of the Shenandoah Valley*, Three Volumes (1952).

Robert Lafleur
Patricia Menk

The Susquehanna River

Source: Otsego Lake, near Cooperstown in central New York
Length: 444 miles
Tributaries: Chenango, Chemung, West Branch, Juniata
Mouth: Upper Chesapeake Bay at Havre de Grace, Maryland
Agricultural Products: Truck farming, dairying
Industries: Anthracite coal, diversified manufacturing

The Susquehanna River rises in Otsego Lake near Cooperstown in central New York and flows 444 miles, first southwesterly through New York, then primarily south through eastern Pennsylvania, finally draining into Chesapeake Bay in northeastern Maryland. Its watershed exceeds 27,000 square miles including most of the eastern half of Pennsylvania. Flowing through hills and valleys, with tributary streams draining lush agricultural country, the Susquehanna evokes thoughts of an Indian word, perhaps meaning "long and crooked river" or "river of the winding shore," but apparently the word means simply "muddy river," "stream," or just plain "water."

The main river, in its upper reaches sometimes called the North Branch, is joined at Binghamton by the Chenango, and a little farther downstream just across the border into Pennsylvania, by the Chemung. It then twists through Pennsylvania's Endless Mountains, from whence drivers along paralleling highways have many spectacular overlooks. The river begins to straighten out as it passes down the Wyoming Valley past Scranton and Wilkes-Barre. At Northumberland, Pennsylvania, it is joined by the West Branch, which has twisted eastward 238 miles from its source in the Allegheny Plateau. Just above Harrisburg the Juniata, also from the Allegheny Plateau to the west, enters. From there to the upper Chesapeake Bay in Maryland the Susquehanna is a mighty river averaging a mile in width.

The Susquehanna drains a region which in the geologic past was covered by great glaciers which, upon retreating, left behind hundreds of feet of sand and gravel. During the spring freshet in March and April the river runs thick and brown, indicating that it has cut deeply into the sand and gravel of the glacial drift. Thousands of years ago the river carried the melted glacial waters, along with the drift, seaward in a massive flood. Visions of its prehistoric volume were easily conjured by witnesses and victims of the floods of 1936, 1972, and 1975.

In historic times the Indian population of the Susquehanna drainage area was small; little else but resonant place-names survive as reminders of these first Americans. War parties of Iroquois left their home grounds in central New York and followed the river southward, leaving it to push on into the Carolinas. The few natives of the river, called Susquehannocks, were in 1676 overwhelmed by the Iroquois, who looked upon them as competitors in the fur trade and forced them to relinquish most of their territory to the more powerful tribesmen from central New York.

Then the Iroquois confronted their own unshakeable antagonists, the European settlers. As population increased along the eastern seaboard, pioneers eyed the valleys of the West and North branches and especially the beautiful Wyoming Valley where Scranton and Wilkes-Barre are now located. The valley is about twenty-five miles long and three to four miles wide. Although today smoke and industrial blight have destroyed much of its beauty, its natural flora of meadowlands and open forests carpeted with lush grasses and wildflowers provided clues to the richness of the soil.

During the 1760s pioneers from Connecticut led the vanguard, claiming the region on the grounds of western lands granted the colony in its charter. However, Pennsylvania disputed these claims and, on several occasions, called up its militia to drive off the New Englanders who, however, always returned. With the coming of the Revolution both claimants suffered. The Iroquois aligned with the British, who promised to protect Indian territory from further encroach-

ment. In June, 1778, a force of 1,100 Loyalist rangers and warriors marshalled at Tioga Point, east of present Elmira, and, on June 30, started downriver.

Settlers in the Wyoming Valley took refuge at Forty Fort, a two-acre stockade near Wilkes-Barre. On July 3, believing that the best defense is a good offense, 300 of the defenders marched out to meet the foe, were ambushed, massacred, and Forty Fort was subsequently captured. In what came to be called the "Great Runaway" hundreds of families in the Susquehanna region then fled to safety downriver.

Not until the following summer (1779) could Washington release troops to mount a counter-offensive. From the south General John Sullivan marched upriver, past Forty Fort and through the Wyoming Valley to Tioga Point where he joined General James Clinton who had come down the North Branch from Otsego Lake. Now 3,500 strong, the troops marched up the Chemung and on August 29 defeated a force of Loyalists and warriors at the Battle of Newtown. Subsequently the army marched into the Iroquois heartland in the Finger Lake region, destroying forty villages and marking the beginning of the end of Iroquois power.

Even more fatal to Iroquois security were the reactions of the troops to the country through which they had fought. As peace came to the Susquehanna Valley in 1783, many veterans returned to settle. More lands were cleared of Iroquois Indian title in treaties of 1784 and 1790. One settler was William Cooper who founded Cooperstown, near Lake Otsego, and whose son, James Fenimore, wrote the great American epic, the *Leatherstocking Tales*. Today Cooperstown is the site of the Baseball Hall of Fame and the nearby Farmer's Museum.

With peace restored, settlement advanced rapidly into the Valley. The white pine and oak forests were cut down, the logs floated in great rafts downstream. Once the lands were cleared and fields in production, farmers had a transportation problem in exporting their grain to market. The solution was the ark, a rather clumsy craft averaging seventy-five feet long and sixteen feet wide. Its advantage was volume, for it could transport a great deal of grain; its drawback was that it had to be abandoned or sold for lumber when its one trip was ended. The coming of the steamboat was of no great help, for although in 1826 the *Cordorus* reached Binghamton, it took four months and the journey was recognized as being so hazardous as to be uneconomic.

Then came the railroad which by 1860 was serving the Susquehanna Valley. At about the same time the discovery was made that beneath the verdant farmland lay perhaps the largest deposit of coal (anthracite) in the United States. By 1960 the mining had ended, leaving in its wake 500 foot-high coal rock wastes, barren of vegetation. Elsewhere the dingy dwellings and shabby coal towns attested to an industry that left in its wake unemployment and waste.

Worst of all was the damage not seen. Hundreds of tunnels were dug fifteen to 2,000 feet below the surface and the hard coal removed; later companies did "pillar robbing," cutting away at the coal pillars that had been left to support the tunnels and chambers. Houses and business buildings, basements, and sections of streets have fallen into these unsupported caverns. Worse still, the hundreds of miles of tunnels have filled with water which has combined with residual carbons to form acid. Residents use the tunnels as sewers and corrupt industrialists have dumped dangerous chemical wastes into the remote tunnels. As a result, on occasion they have filled with poisonous, inflammable fumes. At one time an oil slick appeared on the river thirty-five miles long. A carcinogen, dichlorobenzine, was found in drinking water taken from the Susquehanna sixty miles downstream from where the chemical was spilled into the stream. The United States Bureau of Mines has been trying to cope with the problem. Meanwhile environmentalists are working to get passed a stringent industrial waste law for Pennsylvania.

Hardly were steps toward control of the vacant mine problem getting under way before the people of the lower Susquehanna Valley were frightened by a new problem. On March 28, 1979, at Three Mile Island in the Susquehanna, close to Middletown, Pennsylvania, a pressurized reactor at Metropolitan Edison's plant malfunctioned. At this time (July, 1983) cleanup efforts are continuing. Catastrophe was averted, but it was a narrow escape.

Although it has been exploited and abused, much of the Susquehanna region remains a land of quiet beauty close to great centers of population. The North Branch around Elmira, New York, appealed to Samuel Clemens (Mark Twain) while James Fenimore Cooper gained inspiration for his *Leatherstocking Tales* from a happy boyhood along the banks of Otsego Lake. Yet neither the North Branch nor the West Branch were included in the Scenic Rivers System as created by Congress in October, 1968. The urge for industry was too strong. Nevertheless, in 1970 environmentalists won approval of the Susquehanna Basin Compact. One of its provisions restricts the power of the U.S. Army Engineers. It is hoped that they will concentrate more on strip mine reclamation, sewage treatment, and control of acid mine drainage and less on constructing even a few of the 120 dams they have proposed to control flooding. Such dams, by inundating such historical sites as Azilium, founded in 1793 by exiles from France, and farms, towns, and beauty spots, would be more devastating than the damage done by an occasional flood.

In 1879 Robert Lewis Stevenson, observing the Susquehanna from a railroad coach, described the region as "a shining river and desireable valley." Let us hope our descendants a hundred years from now will still find the Susquehanna a "shining river and desireable valley."

FURTHER READING: Walter F. Burmeister, *The Susquehanna River and Its Tributaries* (1975). Carl Carmer, *The Susquehanna* (1955).

Alfred Runte

Rivers of the Northeast
Mississippi Valley

Although the Spanish from the time of De Soto's wanderings (1540–1542) possessed an impression of the great Mississippi Valley, it was the French who first comprehended the potentialities of the marvellous water links between their settlements along the St. Lawrence, through the Great Lakes, and southward along the rivers to the warm waters of the Gulf of Mexico. For the French these waterways were the keys to control of a vast inland empire extending from the western slopes of the Appalachians–the Northeast Mississippi Valley especially–all the way west to the Rockies.

Unfortunately the peripatetic English soon discovered the same keys and began using them to unlock the overmountain trade. Enterprising merchants began spilling over the mountains from Pennsylvania and Maryland into the Ohio River country, while other English colonists from Virginia and North Carolina began settlements along the headwaters of the Tennessee.

In 1763 the British and in 1783 the Americans gained control of the Northeast Mississippi Valley. They overwhelmed the Indians under Pontiac, Little Turtle, Tecumseh, and Black Hawk north of the Ohio, and chastised the Cherokees in the Tennessee country. Pioneers floated down the Ohio and Tennessee and worked up the Cumberland and Kentucky, Muskingum, Miami, and Wabash, establishing farms and communities at such strategic points as the mouths of rivers or at fords.

In time they made of the Northeast Mississippi Valley an interior empire so wealthy it would have aroused Midas' envy. And they accomplished it with the help of their waterways. Barges carried millions of tons of corn, wheat, flour, coal, iron ore, petroleum, and a myriad of other products from point of origin to point of processing to place of consumption. In spite of pollution, dams, and overuse, the vast region still needs the rivers; it could not exist without them.

Save for the St. Louis River, which flows into Lake Superior, the

Grand which flows into Lake Michigan, and the Cuyahoga, which flows into Lake Erie, all the waters of the Northeast Mississippi Valley find their way into the Mississippi and the Gulf of Mexico. Herein is a sampling of the history of these all-important arteries of trade and communication.

Richard A. Bartlett

The Allegheny River

Source: Potter County in North Central Pennsylvania
Length: 321 miles
Tributaries: Kiskiminetas, Clarion, French Creek,
  Conewango Creek
Mouth: Joins the Monongahela at Pittsburgh to form
  the Ohio
Agricultural Products: Truck products
Industries: Coal, iron and steel products, chemicals,
  glass

The Allegheny rises high on the western slope of the Allegheny ridge in north-central Pennsylvania, enters New York state more than fifty miles, then turns generally south and southwest to Pittsburgh, where it joins the Monongahela to form the Ohio. Its total length is almost exactly 321 miles, to reach a point approximately 125 miles away as the crow flies.

Of its many tributaries, the most important are the Kiskiminetas River, its largest; Clarion River, its second largest; French Creek, which in early days was the principal course of transit between Pittsburgh and Lake Erie; and Conewango Creek, which receives the drainage of Lake Chautaqua in New York.

Prior to the time of the great Kansas glacier, some 600 million years ago, the Allegheny drainage area was occupied by three smaller streams running northwards into Lake Erie. A considerable part of the present course of the river is along the lateral moraine of that ice flow while some of its tributaries still run along courses of pre-glacial streams.

The Allegheny is a steep river, especially for the first thirty miles, with an average fall per mile of twenty-seven feet. From Port Allegany it averages from one to four feet except for a few short stretches, one of the worst being at Pithole Creek, where it reaches seven. The banks are mostly low, with a fairly wide flood plain, and the bottom is of rocks and glacial gravel.

Through this gravel, protected in the lower river from the main stream by a thin layer of clay, flows an aquifer of remarkably pure water, often referred to locally as "the underground river." It moves so slowly through the glacial drift—about three miles a day—that it is coldest at the river's mouth in midsummer, and warmest in midwinter. A few miles down the Ohio it runs into the main river, being forced upwards by a slanting wall of bedrock. Above this point, however, it has provided many towns and industries with an almost inexhaustible water supply.

The origin of the river's name is uncertain. Some early authorities believe it was named for the Alleghewi, a semilegendary tribe of Indians (perhaps ancestors of the Cherokee) who were crowded southwards at an early date by the Iroquois and Delaware. According to this theory the word might mean something like "going far away." Others derive it from words meaning "fair river." This would be in line with the name given it by French explorers and their Indian allies, "Oh-ye-o," and "La Belle Riviere," both meaning "beautiful river." Both French and Indians considered it the same river as the Ohio, and with some reason, as it supplies more than eighty percent of the water for that stream at Pittsburgh, where the Allegheny and Monongahela join.

French explorers, possibly under La Salle in 1669, appear to have been the first Europeans to view the Allegheny, but by 1720 many British fur traders were crossing the mountains to trade in its valley. The French, seeking to consolidate their hold on the area west of the mountains, planned a line of forts down the Ohio and Mississippi to connect their holdings in Canada and Louisiana. In the spring of 1749 a party of considerable size, led by Celeron de Blainville, came down the Allegheny, formally laying claim to the area and burying lead plates at principal junctions with tributaries, among them Conewango and French creeks.

When Governor Robert Dinwiddie of Virginia learned of the French plans, he sent the youthful George Washington late in 1753 to warn the French of the English claim to the region. Washington's party visited Forts Machault (Franklin) and LeBoeuf (Waterford), both on or near French Creek on the road to Presque Isle (Erie). Rebuffed, Washington almost lost his life twice on the return journey.

Already Governor Dinwiddie had a small party at the forks building a little bastion dubbed Fort Prince George. But the work crew had scarcely started when a thousand French and Indians arrived down the Allegheny and demanded their immediate surrender. They allowed the British to take all their possessions and go in peace. Then the French rebuilt and enlarged the stockade, renaming it Fort Duquesne. Washington, with a small colonial force, and Edward Braddock with two British regiments, were both defeated (1754, 1755) but when General John Forbes approached in November 1758 with a large force, the French blew up their fort and retired from the scene. The British made peace with the Indians, then used them to harry the western border during the Revolutionary War. The Allegheny continued to be the line between settled and "Indian land" until after "Mad Anthony" Wayne's victory at Fallen Timbers in northwestern Ohio in 1794.

Most of the land in the Allegheny Valley was set aside by Pennsylvania for her Revolutionary War veterans. These Donation and Depreciation Lands were an excellent idea, but unfortunately more than half of them were grabbed by gigantic land companies, the result being years of litigation. Some lands were given to the friendly Indian, Cornplanter.

Many west-bound emigrants came across southern New York and then down the Allegheny, either past Chautauqua Lake and down French Creek, or by taking to the water at Port Allegany (the Indian "canoe place," or head of navigation). At that point in 1788 Rufus Putnam and one segment of the Connecticut group which made the first Ohio settlement at Marietta, built their canoes and began their journey south. About the same period another New Englander, John Chapman, a Swedenborgian missionary, paused for a year or so at Broken Straw to plant

Allegheny River. Pittsburgh in 1817. (Historical Society of Western Pennsylvania.)

a nursery before going west to carry on his work as the eccentric but beloved "Johnny Appleseed." In 1793 David Mead founded Meadville, an early cultural center. Settlers were flocking into the valley, but it was still a dangerous area until 1795.

Early commerce on the Allegheny was by flatboats downstream and by keelboats in both directions. These were large wooden craft of ten to twelve tons burden, pushed upstream and guided downstream by poles pressed by the crewmen against the bottom and banks of the river. As early as 1779 Robert Miles and his crew took the first cargo from Pittsburgh up to Warren. Later many such craft operated commercially until the beginning of steam navigation, and afterwards during periods of low water.

From a very early period industry flourished along the Allegheny. By around 1800, settlers, guided by salt licks and springs, were drilling wells for salt water and boiling it down to make salt, a critical need west of the mountains. The Pennsylvania Salt Company (now Pennsalt) laid out Natrona in 1850 and built an immense chemical plant which operates today, but with raw materials imported from other areas.

Lumbering was another early industry in the valley. Black walnut made strong ship planking and the tall white pines were ideal for masts, spars, and interior work. These sailing ships could only go downstream to New Orleans, but on reaching the sea were capable of going almost anywhere. The brig *Dean*, 170 tons, was built on the lower Allegheny at Pittsburgh in 1801. In 1803 it arrived at Liverpool, believed to be the first ever sailing to Europe from the interior waters of America.

By this time towns were springing up which needed lumber for all sorts of purposes. Hundreds of sawmills operated in the valley, and on every freshet the Allegheny and its principal tributaries were filled with rafts of sawed timbers and planks—even sometimes of laths. Most of this came from the immense forests of white pine and hemlock. The hemlock bark provided acid for another industry, and for years the valleys of the Allegheny and Clarion provided most of the tanneries and leather for the nation.

Steam-powered vessels were slow in coming to the Allegheny because of its curving, rocky shores and dangerous floor, but in 1827 the *Albion* reached Kittanning; the following year the *William D. Duncan* ran up to Franklin, and in 1830 the *Allegheny* made it to Warren. On its third trip that year this boat reached Olean, New York, which has proved the limit for such navigation. Regular service was maintained to Franklin and sometimes to points above until the building of the railroads drove out the steamboat shortly before the Civil War.

The success of the Erie Canal inspired the building of the Pennsylvania main line canal, which crossed the Alleghenies on a Portage Railroad, and followed the Conemaugh and Kiskiminetas to reach the Allegheny at Freeport. There it crossed the Allegheny on an aqueduct and ran down the right bank to Pittsburgh, where it recrossed on another aqueduct, to a basin in the city. The canal was an important artery of commerce until the building of the Pennsylvania Railroad, which reached Pittsburgh in 1851.

The Allegheny Valley was rich in iron ore, with plentiful forests to supply the charcoal with which smelting was done until about 1860. The area had more than a hundred furnaces casting pots, stoves, and other useful articles. However, a large proportion was sent as pig iron to Pittsburgh, whose refining furnaces, rolling and slitting mills, naileries, foundries and other factories quickly made it the "Birmingham of America."

The petroleum industry was born on Oil Creek, an Allegheny tributary, near Titusville, Pennsylvania, in August, 1858, when a well drilled by Edwin L. Drake came in at sixty-nine feet. In 1865 a large strike at Pithole City set off a wild frenzy of speculation and caused Pithole City to spring up. Within less than a year it had a population of more than 15,000, but the oil wells went dry, and the town was soon deserted. So many wells were struck far up and down the river that its course was dubbed "the valley of oil."

Joseph M. Fox II, son of a wealthy landowner, learned to play golf in England and in 1884 laid out a course at Foxburg. It is the oldest continuously used course in America, and site of the American Golf Hall of Fame. In the summer of 1874 Lewis Miller, an Akron manufacturer, and Bishop John Vincent, of the Methodist Church in Ohio, launched a Sunday School Institute at

Chautauqua Lake which quickly grew into the Chautauqua Institution, one of the most famous religious and cultural foundations of America.

As the years passed, many industries flourished along the Allegheny. The first practical typewriter was invented in Kittanning in 1881 and manufactured there for a number of years. In 1887 Captain John B. Ford established the plate glass industry at a nearby site now named Ford City. For years this plant was the largest plate glass factory in the world. New Kensington was laid out in 1891 and quickly became the "Aluminum City."

In spite of railroad competition river boats continued to haul sand and gravel, coal, oil and gasoline, iron and steel and limestone. In 1897 a Boatmen's Association was organized to press for improvements. Today eight locks and dams provide a nine-foot channel to East Brady and there is considerable barge traffic.

Pollution was another serious problem, so bad that around the turn of the century typhoid deaths in lower river communities using its unfiltered water averaged over 1,800 a year. Since World War II, however, clean streams legislation has restored Allegheny water to a reasonable degree of purity, and people fish in the river at Pittsburgh.

The Allegheny was long subject to flooding, especially at and near its mouth. Deforestation and encroachment aggravated the situation until at least in 1936 a rise—principally from the Kiskiminetas—brought the crest at Pittsburgh to forty-six feet—twenty-one above flood level. Since that time many dams have been built to impound flood waters and maintain dry weather flow in its watershed.

The flood-control lakes provide recreation facilities for several million visitors a year. Moreover, since their completion the Allegheny has been rather well behaved. In spite of all its history and the extensive industry along its banks, the river remains an attractive stream. Today, with the new awareness of ecological values, there is hope that the years ahead will bring about still more restoration of its natural beauty.

FURTHER READING: Frederick Way, *The Allegheny* (1942). Solon J. and Elizabeth A. Buck, *The Planting of Civilization in Western Pennsylvania* (1939).

George Swetnam

The Clinch River

Place of Origin: Southwest Virginia
Length: About 300 miles
Mouth: Into Tennessee River at Kingston, Tennessee
Principal Cities: Oak Ridge, Tennessee
Principal Tributaries: Powell River, Emory River
Industry: Coal mining, atomic energy, hydroelectric power

Both the Clinch and the Powell river, its principal tributary, rise in the mountains of southwest Virginia and flow down southwest-running valleys into Tennessee. At points the creeks which feed these twin rivers are formed within yards of each other on the steep slopes of the ridges dividing the watersheds. The precipitous terrain and heavy annual rainfall make for swift streams with large volumes of water, and both the Clinch and the Powell are impressive arteries when they enter Tennessee about twenty miles apart. At places in Tennessee the rivers widen and slacken as they flow through broad, fertile valleys, but always in the distance are the high ridges which seem to march abreast of the rivers.

The Clinch and Powel converge north of Knoxville in the lake formed by TVA's Norris Dam. Emerging from the dam's spillways the Clinch flows south, receiving the waters of another tributary, the Emory, just before joining the Tennessee at Kingston, just west of Knoxville.

The Clinch is about 300 miles long; the Powell about half that length. Pioneers crossed Powell Valley to reach Cumberland Gap on the west side and through the Gap entered Kentucky.

The Cherokees are said to have called the Clinch the Pelissippi, meaning "like a river," but the original name is preserved only in the name given the main highway that crosses the Clinch connecting Knoxville with Oak Ridge. The stream was already known as "Clinche's River" when Dr. Thomas Walker in 1750 toured the area on behalf of the Loyal Company, a group of Virginia speculators. Walker crossed the Clinch near the site of present Sneedville, Tennessee, and remarked that the river was named for "a

hunter who first found it." The naming of the Powell River is easier to document. Originally known as the Beargrass, it took the name of Ambrose Powell, a member of Walker's party.

Besides the five counties in Virginia which it drains, the Clinch claims all or parts of twelve East Tennessee counties in its watershed. The Clinch-Tennessee junction is therefore the key point in the upper Tennessee River system since the mouths of the Holston, French Broad, and Little Tennessee are above this junction.

The strategic value of the site was not lost on the pioneers of the late eighteenth century. When the Tennessee country was organized in 1790 as Southwest Territory, William Blount,

Oak Ridge, Tennessee, on the Clinch River, was built during the Second World War to construct atom bombs. This photo shows the graphic reactor under construction in 1944. (Courtesy Photographic Services, Oak Ridge Operations, U.S. Department of Energy.)

the territorial governor, selected a site on the Clinch at the mouth of the Emory—where he owned 5,000 acres—as a likely location for his territorial capital. However, the Treaty of Holston with the Cherokees (1791) limited white settlement to the area east of the Clinch, and so the capital was located at White's Fort, renamed Knoxville.

The Clinch-Tennessee junction did become the site of Fort Southwest Point where Cherokee Indian Agency headquarters was located from 1801 to 1807, and, in a ruse to persuade the Indians to cede more land, nearby Kingston was for one day in 1807 the state capital. It continued to be an important point in the land and water transportation system. Here the great road to the West paused at the Ferry across the Clinch, and thousands of emigrants passed here on their way to new homes on the receding frontier.

After the American Revolution the Clinch country was opened to white settlement, and soon the better valley lands were occupied by farms and budding villages. On the high ridges that parallel the river the early settlers found a people who appeared to be neither white, nor black, nor Indian. These were the Melungeons, a mysterious race of olive or coppery complexion with straight, dark hair. Whether the Melungeons were already there when the pioneers arrived in the 1780s or whether they crept unnoticed onto their ridges at the same time other immigrants were settling in the valleys is unknown, but for over a century the Melungeons and their origins have been a subject of romantic surmise and conjecture. Some say they are descended from shipwrecked Portugese sailors who sought refuge in the mountains; others have speculated that the Melungeons sprang from Welshmen who "discovered" America in 1170. In the last fifty years, however, the Melungeon communities have been largely dispersed and the Melungeons themselves, as well as their history, seem more obscure than ever.

Most of the Clinch Valley people are of English, Scotch-Irish, and German stock; they settled the region as farmers. In the Powell Valley and elsewhere along the Clinch there are great brick mansions which attest to the wealth of the region in the antebellum era. One of these mansions, now called "Speedwell," has been careful-

ly relocated in Knoxville where as a house/museum it occupies a hilltop overlooking the Tennessee River.

The Clinch country experienced no major Civil War battles, but the area south of Cumberland Gap was a thoroughfare for Confederate and Union armies using the famous passage through the Cumberlands. In sentiment the people were divided: most of those in the Tennessee part of the Clinch Valley supported the Union, while the Virginians in the upper watershed were more Confederate in sympathy. Besides the destruction wrought by war itself the region was plagued by bands of guerrillas or bushwhackers who often carried out private vendettas which had no connection with the great conflict.

In the wake of the war the Clinch country seemed to slumber, a forgotten corner of remote Appalachia. The river itself provided the readiest access to the outside world, and for many years the rafting of timber was one of the few ways to earn cash. Beneath the forest floor, however, lay more riches. Dr. Walker, the first explorer into the region, had noticed black "stones" in the bed of Powell River, and near the mouth of the Clinch coal was mined as early as the 1840s for shipment down the Tennessee. Large-scale mining began in the Cumberlands as early as 1868. But since most of the Clinch Valley had no railroads, there was little realization of the region's mineral wealth. The great Wilderness Road down the valley and through Cumberland Gap had once been a major American thoroughfare, but in 1886 it took a day's hard ride on horseback to reach the Gap from the nearest rail junction at Morristown, Tennessee.

All was changed by the rediscovery of the mountain region in the late 1880s. Exploitation of the coal resources was in harmony with the spirit of the robber baron era. Additionally there was the romantic appeal of the remote, the primitive, and the unspoiled which the promoters stressed along with the mines and mills that were to be built in the "Magic Cities."

Two new towns sprang up in the Clinch country: Big Stone Gap at the forks of the Powell River in Virginia, and Middlesboro, Kentucky, just across Cumberland Gap from the Powell Valley. The former owed it existence to John D. Imboden, a former Confederate general, whose eloquence persuaded capitalists to build a railroad to Big Stone Gap. By 1890, when the railroad was completed, many other capitalists were investing in the area. A number of "large and elegant" residences were constructed, though a planned $150,000 hotel was never built. The depression of the early 1890s, together with the low quality of the area's iron ore, ended the boom and dealt Big Stone Gap a blow from which it never recovered. It would be forgotten but for John Fox, Jr.'s *The Trail of the Lonesome Pine*. Fox lived at Big Stone Gap and wrote vividly about the people of the Clinch and the Cumberland Mountains.

Like its Virginia counterpart, Middlesboro was brought to life by a railroad built by a romantic outsider who fell in love with the Clinch country, Alexander Allan Arthur, a Scottish engineer. He organized a company of British and American investors, the American Association Ltd., to buy 80,000 acres in the vicinity of Cumberland Gap, while another company built a railroad from Knoxville through the Gap to "Middlesborough," as the projected city was originally named. The Kentucky boom town suffered a fate similar to that of Big Stone Gap. So rapid was the deflation that the splendid 700-room Four Seasons Hotel which overlooked Powell Valley below Cumberland Gap was demolished and sold as salvage in 1895 only three years after it was opened. Even the railroad to Middlesboro seemed jinxed by accidents and tunnel cave-ins.

In spite of these failures the production of energy has been a most important part of economic life in the Clinch Valley since the 1880s. The Clinch and its sister streams of the Tennessee River system were at once dangerous enemies and potential servants of the valley people. Largely unregulated by dams, the rivers often swelled to flooding torrents in autumn and spring, sweeping bridges, buildings, and animals to destruction. To control flooding, generate power, and make the streams navigable, the Tennessee Valley Authority was established in 1933. Senator George Norris of Nebraska introduced the bill which set up the Authority, and the first dam TVA built was named Norris in his honor.

Situated on the Clinch near the mouth of Cove Creek just north of Knoxville, Norris Dam rises

265 feet above the valley floor and extends 1,860 feet in length. TVA purchased 152,000 acres for the project and removed about 3,000 families and 6,000 graves from the reservoir site. Relocation of both the living and the dead required a sometimes traumatic adjustment on the part of the valley people, but the benefits which the dam brought helped to ease the pain of transition. The thousands of jobs generated by the Norris project were a godsend to the region, already impoverished and suffering still more from the depression. Moreover, TVA sought to develop human resources and to make life healthier and more comfortable and prosperous for the valley's inhabitants. A new town named Norris was built near the dam site to accommodate workers and their families and also to provide an example of a planned residential community.

In the years since its genesis TVA has fostered industrialization and improved the living standards of the region. In 1945 on the lower Clinch a federal installation—locally known as the Clinton Engineer Works or the Kingston Demolition Range—manufactured the first atom bomb and as a byproduct had created Oak Ridge, a city with a peak population of 75,000. An outgrowth of research there is the proposed Clinch River Liquid Metal Fast Breeder Reactor which would produce plutonium 239, a material useable as fuel in other reactors. It is a dangerous process, however, and the plans have not yet been approved.

Today the Clinch Valley combines exciting industrial activity with unspoiled reaches which resemble the environment of the primeval river. In sum, this Appalachian river and its tributaries—such as the Obed, designated a Wild River—are characterized by history and modernity, by wildness and development. The Clinch is thus truly representative of that region of which it is a part.

FURTHER READING: Stanley J. Folmsbee, et al., *Tennessee: A Short History* (1969). Robert L. Kincaid, *The Wilderness Road* (1947). Tennessee Valley Authority, *The Norris Project: A Comprehensive Report on the Planning, Design, Construction, and Initial Operations of the Tennessee Valley Authority's First Water Control Project* (1940). John Fox, Jr., *The Trail of the Lonesome Pine* (1908)—fiction.

William J. MacArthur

The Cumberland River

Source: Harlan, Kentucky, at junction of Poor Fork, Clover Fork, and Martin's Fork
Length: 687 miles
Tributaries: Laurel, Rock Castle, South Fork, Obey, Caney Fork, Stones, Harpeth, and Red Rivers
Mouth: Smithland, Kentucky, into Ohio River
Principal Cities: Nashville
Agricultural Products: Corn, wheat, hay, livestock
Industries: Iron, coal

The Cumberland River begins where the Poor Fork, Clover Fork, and Martin's Fork meet at Harlan, Kentucky, in the southeast corner of the Bluegrass State. From its birthplace the river flows crookedly westward, snaking its way through the folds of the Cumberland Mountains. In Daniel Boone National Forest in eastern Kentucky, the river drops sixty-eight feet at Cumberland Falls in a spectacular display of rushing waters, spray, and muted rumbling. This is the only natural waterfall of significance in the 687-mile length of the Cumberland.

Not far below the falls the Laurel and Rockcastle rivers flow in from the north, and further still, the South Fork River flowing north out of east Tennessee joins the Cumberland. From its juncture with the South Fork River to the Tennessee border, the river's most distinguishing feature is Lake Cumberland, a thirty-mile-long empoundment created by the Corps of Engineers' Wolf Creek Dam.

From its point of entry into Tennessee, the river follows a curved course similar to the outline of a drawn Indian bow, flowing first southwest, then west, and finally northwest to a juncture with the Ohio River at the town of Smithland in western Kentucky. The Obey, Caney Fork, and Stones are all major tributaries that empty into the Cumberland as it crosses the plateau region of the Volunteer State and enters the fertile central basin region. Here, just above Nashville, the Cumberland has been dammed by the Corps of Engineers, creating Old Hickory Lake, named for Andrew Jackson, the state's foremost citizen. Nashville, the state's capital, is the oldest and largest community on the banks of the river.

West of Nashville the Cumberland turns to the northwest and receives the waters of the Harpeth River and the Red River. As the river re-enters Kentucky, it begins to spread into Lake Barkley, a thirty-mile-long body of water named for Kentucky's famous United States Senator and Vice President, Alben Barkley. This is the last of the man-made alterations to the river that combine to curb the disastrous spring flooding which used to characterize the Cumberland and to provide river traffic with a minimum depth of nine feet of water from the Ohio River to the town of Carthage upstream from Nashville. Army Engineers not only dammed the Cumberland to form Barkley Lake but also constructed a canal between the lake and Kentucky Lake to the west, allowing the river traffic to flow between the Cumberland and Tennessee rivers without entering the Ohio to the north. Thirty miles downstream from Lake Barkley in the west Kentucky plain region the Cumberland merges with its larger sister, the Ohio River. The river and all its tributaries drains a land basin of approximately 17,750 miles.

The river's role in the history of man in North America is an ancient one. Probably the earliest human inhabitants were prehistoric hunters. Some of the most important of the later arrivals were the mound builders who were in the region as early as 1000- 500 B.C. In the eighteenth century, when Europeans began to make regular contact with the tribes of the Cumberland, they found Indians whom they called by names we use today. The river country was a game-rich area continually fought over by the Shawnee, Cherokee, Chickasaw, and Creeks. It was the Cherokee who proved the most formidable barrier to white hunters and settlers who began entering the Cumberland country in the eighteenth century.

The name of the first European to set eyes on the Cumberland will likely never be known. The French explorer Louis Jolliet drew a map in 1674 that showed the Ohio River branching off the Mississippi to the east and a branch of the Ohio that appears to be the Cumberland. A young man named Gabriel Arthur, hired in 1673 to establish trade contacts with the Cherokee, crossed the Cumberland and re-crossed it on his return to Virginia. More than three-quarters of a century later another visitor would give the river its name.

In the spring of 1760, Dr. Thomas Walker, a representative of the Virginia-based Loyal Company, and five friends were attempting to establish the location of land granted to the company by King George II and located in the region known as "Kentokee." Doubtlessly wanting to honor the King's son, the Duke of Cumberland, whom he had met on a trip to England, Dr. Walker named the stream in the Duke's honor. The river he christened has carried the designation ever since.

In the 1760s and 1770s parties of Virginia and North Carolina hunters were drawn to the area by the plentiful game, but Indians were a constant threat. Daniel Boone and his friends were returning in 1771 from a two-year hunt on the upper Cumberland and in present-day central Kentucky when a Cherokee band took their rifles, skins, horses, and everything else of value

and warned them not to return to the hunting grounds.

The Revolutionary War years set the stage for the permanent settlement of the middle Cumberland area in Tennessee. Richard Henderson, a North Carolina land speculator, turned to the Cumberland River land claimed by North Carolina and began plans for settlement. He found two experienced men, James Robertson and John Donelson, in the Watauga River settlements of upper east Tennessee. Both men were eager to work with Henderson to settle the central Cumberland region.

In the winter of 1779–1780, Robertson and Donelson led a two-pronged movement of settlers westward bound for French Lick on the Cumberland. Robertson led a group westward overland to central Kentucky and then south to the Lick. Donelson commanded a flotilla of flatboats down the Tennessee River to its mouth, then navigated the Ohio River upstream to the mouth of the Cumberland, and ascended it to the Lick. Robertson left in October and had a relatively uneventful trek, arriving on the banks

Nashville, Tennessee, on the Cumberland, was already a flourishing city when this engraving was made in 1859. (Credit: Tennessee State Library & Archives. Source: Albigence Waldo Putnam, History of Middle Tennessee; or Life and Times of Gen. James Robertson, *Nashville, printed by the author, 1859.)*

of the Cumberland at Christmas of 1779. Donelson set out at the end of December. The boats were repeatedly attacked by Indians; one with smallpox aboard was lost to the Cherokees with all hands when it lagged behind the rest. When the Donelson party arrived at the Lick in April they were gaunt and near exhaustion. Overcoming all the trials of their 1,000 mile river trip the men, women and children in the party were at last united with their relatives in the Robertson group.

The first few years of the Cumberland settlement's existence were filled with progress in the face of peril. Because they were over 200 miles from settlements to the east, the pioneers drew up the Cumberland Compact outlining a temporary form of government for the eight stations (stockades) that comprised the community.

Through 1789, Indian attacks led to the death of a settler every ten days. Much of the credit for the settlement's survival goes to Robertson, who led defense efforts against the Indians and recruited new settlers to augment the original group. The community was known as Fort Nashborough, the name given the first stockade built on the river bank and christened in honor of Revolutionary War General Francis Nash of North Carolina. In 1783 the Cumberland Association received permission to organize a local government. The first county court met in the fall of 1783, and the next year they changed the name of the county seat from Davidson to Nashville.

Statehood came for Tennessee in 1796. Its capital was moved from Knoxville to Murfreesboro in middle Tennessee on the Stones River, a Cumberland River tributary, and then to Nashville in 1826, still the capital of Tennessee. Its most famous resident was Andrew Jackson.

In the first half of the nineteenth century the waters of the Cumberland were tamed first by the hardy breed of men who manned barges, flatboats, and keelboats, and soon after by crews of an increasing number of steamboats. The first steamboat to navigate the Cumberland to Nashville was the *General Jackson*; it arrived in March, 1819. By 1830 seventy-nine different steamboats had traversed the Cumberland. The boats brought all forms of general merchandise to Nashville and carried away cargoes of cotton,

tobacco, meat, and hides. In 1847 river cargo worth $13,000,000 passed through Nashville.

In the decade 1850–1860 steamboat activity peaked as an estimated 400 steamboats saw service on the river. An average of almost 800,000 tons of cargo passed through Nashville each year during the decade, and total river tonnage for the period has been estimated at 1,000,000 tons per year, worth almost $40,000,000. The most important freight was cotton; boats were sometimes so burdened with the fleecy cargo that their decks were nearly awash. Because travel on the Tennessee River to the south was blocked by Muscle Shoals, merchants and farmers to the south and southwest looked to Nashville and the Cumberland for shipment and receipt of their goods.

During the Civil War the banks of the Cumberland and its tributaries were the setting for some of the conflict's fiercest engagements. On January 19, 1862, at Mill Springs, Kentucky, on the banks of Fishing Creek, a small encounter opened the path to Union advances into east Tennessee. On the lower Cumberland and the Tennessee, Forts Henry and Donelson barred Union access to the Tennessee and Cumberland rivers just south of the Kentucky border. Fort Henry fell on February 4, 1862, after a few hours' bombardment. Fort Donelson, twelve miles to the east on the Cumberland, offered stiffer resistance. Located high on a bluff overlooking the river near the town of Dover, it fell to General Grant's troops on February 15.

The fall of Fort Donelson was the most serious setback suffered by the Confederacy to that point in the war. A little over a week later, stunned Nashvillians witnessed the occupation of their city by Union troops who now controlled the Cumberland as far as the state capital. The capture of Nashville opened the door to a southeastward thrust by the Union army that eventually took it to Chattanooga, Atlanta, and then the Atlantic coast.

After the battle of Stones River which left Chattanooga open to Union forces (January, 1863), the war passed beyond the Cumberland country only to return in the last months of 1864, when Confederate General John B. Hood led the Army of Tennessee northward from Georgia toward Nashville. He was determined to cut General William T. Sherman's supply lines and end the Union army's triumphant progress through Georgia. But Hood lost 6,000 men in a battle on the banks of the Harpeth River (November 30, 1864) and on December 15 and 16, Nashville-based Union forces, some 70,000 strong, struck the Army of Tennessee and drove it from the field. The Battle of Nashville was the last important military engagement of the war in Tennessee. Stillness returned to the Cumberland region; its role in the bloody sectional struggle was over.

Peace brought slow but steady change to the Cumberland. River traffic rose steadily in response to new peacetime demands. In 1880 there was a minimum of twenty-seven steamers making regular trips out of Nashville, and total river tonnage for the year was possibly in excess of 1,000,000. Lower river cargoes changed as middle Tennessee planters and farmers turned away from cotton planting and toward a more diversified agricultural industry based on such products as corn, wheat, hay, tobacco, and livestock. In the late 1880s, the river town of Clarksville became the second largest tobacco market in the United States. The upper Cumberland was the setting for a thriving lumber and timber industry that reached its peak soon after 1900. When the water was high, skilled rivermen navigated hardwood log rafts averaging 200 feet long by 30 feet wide down tributaries such as the Obey or the Caney Fork into the Cumberland and then to Nashville sawmills. The most famous of these raftsmen was Cordell Hull, Congressman and Secretary of State, who rode log rafts to the state capital as a young man. Depletion of the hard-wood forests doomed the raftsmen's era, and by the 1920s competition from railroads and motor trucks spelled the death knell for steam packets on the waters of the Cumberland.

The resurgence of commercial traffic on the river since 1930 and the development of the Cumberland's recreational potential has been due to the development of the modern towboat and the construction of dams by the Army Corps of Engineers. By 1976 powerful diesel-driven towboats pushing strings of barges raised river tonnage to 11,500,000. Army Engineers have built eight dams on the Cumberland and its major tributaries for flood control, navigational improvement, hydro-electric power generation, and recreation. These dams have enabled the taming of the river. Gone are the sudden tides, shifting sandbars, and treacherous snags that threatened generations of rivermen and settlers. Corps dams have established a constant channel depth for a significant portion of the river and created lakes whose recreational use has boosted the economies of Tennessee and Kentucky.

From the late Ice Age to the present, our world has changed in astonishing ways, but one thing that has not changed has been the Cumberland's significant role in the history of the people who have come into contact with it. Predictions are hazardous in our fast-paced world today, but the continuing importance of the Cumberland to the people of Tennessee and Kentucky in the years to come seems certain.

FURTHER READING: Byrd Douglas, *Steamboatin' on the Cumberland* (1961). James McCague, *The Cumberland* (1973).

Robert B. Jones

The Cuyahoga River

Source: Two separate springs in northern Geauga County, Ohio.
Length: 100 miles
Tributaries: Little Cuyahoga River
Mouth: Flows into Lake Erie at Cleveland, Ohio
Agricultural products: Insignificant
Industries: Petroleum, tire manufacturing, and diversified manufacturing

The Cuyahoga (pronounced kī-e-hō-ge—Indian for "crooked river") in northeast Ohio is unusual in several respects. It is only 100 miles long and yet is the most important watercourse in the area. The Indians named it so because of its unique U-shaped course. The upper sections of the stream run parallel to and in an opposite direction from the lower sections. Originating from two separate springs in northern Geauga County, the small brook wanders away from its final destination, Lake Erie. Both of these south-flowing sources are north of the river's mouth and less than fifteen miles from the lake. Near Akron an escarpment turns the Cuyahoga westward and then north. Following this abrupt turn, the river enters a valley which is a natural dividing line between the Appalachian Plateau and the Central Lowlands physiographic provinces. This valley is a "botanical crossroads" and contains plants indigenous to both regions. The river finally meanders into Lake Erie, in the process forming Cleveland's harbor. Because of its U-shaped course, the river's watershed is less than 800 square miles and the only significant tributary is the Little Cuyahoga River.

The area's earliest inhabitants were the Adena and Hopewell Indians, both Mound Builders. Archeologists have found evidence in several hundred archeological sites that these peoples lived in the valley from 300 B.C. to 600 A.D. The Erie Indians then occupied the valley. In the mid-seventeenth century Indians from the Five Nations (the Iroquois) destroyed the Eries, whereupon several tribes inhabited the region. They peacefully agreed that the Cuyahoga was neutral ground because it was an integral part of an inland river highway system. Where the river turns sharply northward, Indians had for years portaged their canoes eight miles to the headwaters of the Tuscarawas River which flows on to the Muskingum and the Ohio. This "carrying place," as white settlers called it, was the shortest portage between the Great Lakes and the Ohio River. Strategically important, it appeared on European maps well before the Great Lakes were accurately drawn. George Washington, writing in 1784, said this route was the "shortest, easiest and least expensive communication with the invaluable back country."

General Anthony Wayne's defeat of the Indians at Fallen Timbers in 1794 and the subsequent Treaty of Greenville was important to the Cuyahoga watershed. These events removed the danger of Indian attack, opened the area for settlement, and established a western boundary for the United States. A line running from Lake Erie up the Cuyahoga, across the portage, down the Tuscarawas to Fort Laurens, westward across Ohio to Fort Recovery, and then southwest across Indiana separated the Indians from the white men. West of this line was Indian territory; east of the line was the United States. Connecticut was extremely interested in this boundary agreement because the state owned a large tract in northeast Ohio—the Connecticut Western Reserve—that was now open for settlement.

Connecticut sold the land to a group of speculators who, in 1796, sent Moses Cleaveland to survery the Western Reserve into five-mile-square townships. While his men surveyed, Cleaveland explored the Cuyahoga Valley, established his headquarters at the river's mouth, and planned the city which bears his name. He was scrupulously careful not to cross the Cuyahoga and violate the treaty agreement. In 1805 a new treaty (Fort Industry) pushed the Indians farther west and opened the west bank of the Cuyahoga to settlers.

Settlement of the Western Reserve was slow and sporadic. Although the Cuyahoga was a major route to the interior, no cities developed along its course. Cleveland, ideally located to become an important economic center, repelled people because of water-borne diseases, and a large sandbar blocking the river's mouth thwarted commercial activities. Lack of local markets and no easy access to the East strangulated the area economically. The tremendous success of New York's Erie Canal prompted Ohio to construct a similar waterway from Lake Erie to the Ohio River. The Ohio and Erie Canal, started in 1825, chiefly followed the old Indian river route along the Cuyahoga and up the portage to the Tuscarawas, down that river, then overland to the Scioto River and the Ohio. Constructed in a piecemeal fashion, the first completed section paralleled the Cuyahoga.

The canal brought prosperity and people to the valley. Cheap transportation to eastern and southern markets opened the Reserve hinterlands and cities developed. Cleveland, following a harbor and river dredging, suddenly became a major port and mushroomed within a few years. Akron, on heretofore uninhabited land, grew because the series of stepped locks at the Portage Summit created a bottleneck for canal boats. Superseded in the 1850s by the railroads, the Ohio and Erie Canal nevertheless remained in operation until 1913 when a major Cuyahoga flood destroyed part of the waterway. Much of the Cleveland and Akron Canal section remains intact today.

The strategic locations of Cleveland and Akron led to the development of major industries. Coal from Pennsylvania and iron ore from Minnesota was brought to the banks of the Cuyahoga, and Cleveland became a large iron, later steel, producing center. Following the discovery of oil in western Pennsylvania, small refineries developed among the steel mills. John D. Rockefeller consolidated these refineries under the Standard Oil Company name. The last six miles of the river is today lined with heavy industries, and Cleveland is a major international port. Akron, meanwhile, became the rubber capital of the world. Benjamin Franklin Goodrich brought his rubber vulcanizing process to the city because of the abundant water supply. The development of the auto industry spurred the expansion of the tire industry and many of the largest rubber manufacturers located in Akron.

The expansion of industry and urbanization along the Cuyahoga altered the river's use. Ak-

ron draws its water supply from Lake Rockwell, a dammed section of the stream north of Kent. Industries and municipal sewer systems dumped noxious effluents, raw sewage, harmful chemicals, and oil into the river unchecked. Once a river which supported some fifty species of fish, the lower Cuyahoga by 1969 had no visible life, not even leeches or sludge worms that live on wastes. The river became a joke to Cleveland residents: "Anyone who falls into the Cuyahoga does not drown," citizens said, "he decays." On June 22, 1969, the river became a symbol of environmental degradation when its oily surface burst into flames and nearly destroyed two railroad bridges spanning the river.

Since this national embarrassment, businessmen and government officials have worked to clean up the river. Steel companies began cooling their water before dumping it into the river; oil spills were reduced; chemical pollutants declined; and sewage was cleansed. The difference is apparent: six types of fish now live in the river and the water is a muddy brown, not black as before. The Cuyahoga will never return to its pristine state because of the heavy industry and large surrounding population. Nevertheless the river cleanup is significant for its environmental progress.

A major step in protecting the Cuyahoga River came in December, 1974, when the 30,000-acre Cuyahoga Valley National Recreation Area was established. Encompassing nearly twenty miles of the river from the northern edge of Akron to the southern edge of Cleveland, it is designed to preserve "recreational open space necessary to the urban environment." This area is relatively undeveloped and yet within thirty miles nearly four million people reside. The Recreation Area is not a place for amusement parks or large organized sports; rather, it is a place to observe nature and keep a link with the past. The National Park Service, which administers the area, has many plans for the valley aimed principally at preserving the existing primitive setting and historical sites, but progress has been slow. The future of the Cuyahoga Valley, however, is very bright.

Indeed the Cuyahoga is an unusual river. Physically unique and short, it nevertheless was instrumental in the early development of interior Ohio. Used by the Indians as a route from the

Great Lakes to the Ohio River, the stream became significant with the opening of the Ohio and Erie Canal. People built industries along the banks which made the river of greater importance, but they also polluted the river and made it a national disgrace. Finally, the river serves as a model for environmental cleanup and open-space preservation within the urban milieu.

FURTHER READING: William Donohue Ellis, *The Cuyahoga* (1966). Harlan Hatcher, *The Western Reserve: The Story of New Connecticut in Ohio* (1949).

Raymond M. Hyser

French Creek

Source: Junction of East Branch and West Branch south of Wattsburgh in northeast Pennsylvania
Length: 140 miles
Tributaries: South Branch
Mouth: Joins Allegheny at Franklin, Pennsylvania
Agricultural Products: Truck farming
Industries: Recreation, diversified manufacturing

French Creek, the most important stream in northwestern Pennsylvania, was known to the Seneca Indians as In-nun-ga-ch. This word has some reference to a crude and indecent figure carved upon a tree which they found after their arrival in the region. Later came the French and they gave it the name *Riviere aux Boeufs*, since buffalo ranged in the valley. The names "Beef River" and "Buffalo River" appear on maps in the Pennsylvania Archives. Most European visitors, however, called the stream Venango, a name allegedly derived from the Delaware term *Winingus*, meaning "mink." But it was George Washington who gave it the simple name that the Americans came to use—French Creek.

Anyone looking at a map has to be impressed with the Creek's complex and rambling character. There are three branches which were once called Forks. The junction of the East and West branches, south of Wattsburg in northwest Pennsylvania just west of the New York boundary, creates the main stream. The East Branch rises in extreme southwest New York near the town of Sherman, while the head of the West Branch is at Findley's Lake, about two miles over the New York line in the same county. The Southern Branch enters the main stream several miles southeast of Waterford. After this the Creek flows south about 100 miles until it unites with the Allegheny River at Franklin. By this time French Creek has widened considerably and looks more like a river than a stream. In all, it is considered as being 140 miles long.

The historical significance of French Creek was determined by its geography. Located between the Great Lakes and the Ohio River basin, it was at first a target of control by French, English, and Indians. Later it became the lifeline between the established American communities in the East and the sparsely settled lands of northwestern Pennsylvania.

The French plan was simple: to connect their possessions in the St. Lawrence-Great Lakes area with those in the Mississippi Valley. This would provide permanent protection from penetration of the trans-Appalachian region by the English. Expeditions into the upper Ohio Valley by the Baron de Longueuil in 1739 and Celoron de Blainville in 1749 underscored the seriousness of the French intent. Then in 1753 the French sent troops to occupy the Ohio country and fortify strategic locations. Several new forts were to be built between Lake Erie and the Forks of the Ohio, where the Allegheny meets the Monongahela. Two forts, Le Boeuf and Machault, were built where the cities of Waterford and Franklin now stand.

This French move was a threat to the security and expansion of the English colonists, whose claim to this area was based on early charters and Indian purchases. The French argued that their discovery of the St. Lawrence and Mississippi entitled them to the territory bordering those rivers and their tributaries. To them the Ohio constituted a natural avenue of communication between Canada and Louisiana while the Appalachians to the east separated the English colonies from the Ohio country. French logic, however, failed to impress Virginia's governor, Robert Dinwiddie. When he learned that the French were implementing their plan of conquest he dispatched young George Washington in late 1753 to deliver a letter to the French commander in the Ohio country advising him that he was there in violation of English territorial sovereignty.

Among the earliest accounts of French Creek and its contiguous lands, and the first in the English language, are the journals kept by Washington and Christopher Gist (a frontiersman with Washington) on this painful and dangerous mission. The two men first saw French Creek when they encamped at the Indian village of Venango, near the place where it empties into the Allegheny. It was here that they met French officers who boasted how their nation intended to take command of the entire Ohio country. They also directed Washington northward along the Creek to find the French commandant at Le Boeuf, a several days' journey. In his journal Washington mentioned "several extensive and rich meadows" between Venango and another Indian village on French Creek, Cussewago, the present site of Meadville. The Virginians followed the Indian trail up the east bank and reached Le Boeuf on December 11th. They remained there until the 16th, meeting with the French commandant, Legardeur de St. Pierre, and assessing the French troop strength and military equipment, which was greater than they had imagined. After receiving a written reply, Washington's party started down French Creek in a canoe. The young commander later wrote: "We had a tedious and very fatiguing passage down the creek. Several times we had like to have been staved against rocks; and many times were obliged all hands to get out and remain in the water half an hour or more, getting over the shoals. At one place, the ice had lodged, and made it impassable by water; we were, therefore, obliged to carry our canoe across the neck of land, a quarter of a mile over. . . . This creek is extremely crooked. I dare

say the distance between the fort (at Le Boeuf) and Venango cannot be less than one hundred and thirty miles to follow the meanders."

After Washington's return to Virginia, events moved quickly. His published journal received international attention and alerted the London government to the implications of the French invasion. Meanwhile, the French completed their forts. In early 1754 Washington returned to the Ohio country, a confrontation took place, and diplomacy gave way to fire power and the French and Indian War began. For the next three decades French Creek would assume a military importance as the English battled the French, and then the Americans in their struggle for independence fought the British and their Indian allies.

Squeezed between the warring intruders were the Indians. There were various tribes, some loyal to the British and some to the French. Fort Machault at Venango served as a rallying place for those who remained friendly to the French even after the English had succeeded in capturing Fort Duquesne at the Forks of the Ohio. The French built boats on French Creek for a massive assault against the English at the Forks, massing an estimated 1,000 Indians at the mouth of French Creek to take part in the expedition. But the project was abandoned in the summer of 1759 in order to allow the forces instead to rush to the defense of the important French bastion at Niagara. Seizing the forts at Venango and Le Boeuf, the English finally achieved control of French Creek valley only to see their grip temporarily vanish in 1763. In that year the Conspiracy of Pontiac released hostile tribes who swept through the valley, driving back the English and burning the two forts they had recently captured. The entire garrison at Venango suffered torture and death at the hands of the Senecas.

The close of the Revolutionary period did not bring lasting peace with the Indians of northwestern Pennsylvania. Sporadic raids harassed the pioneers who trickled into the area. At best, the first settlements, including David Mead's at Cussewago in 1788, were a gamble. The government did build Fort Franklin near the mouth of French Creek, but it was not until Anthony Wayne's defeat of the western tribes at Fallen Timbers in 1794 that the Indian threat finally ended. With peace and plenty of cheap land available, settlers poured in. By 1800 many small communities dotted the countryside, most of them on streams that accommodated grist and saw mills.

The very survival of these communities, including Meadville, Waterford, and Franklin, depended upon the waterways since roads were few. Until local industries could develop, most of the supplies came in keelboats from Pittsburgh with the larger boats going generally no further than Waterford. On smaller streams canoes were used. Sometimes goods reached the region by way of Erie and Waterford. A good example of this was the salt trade—one of the earliest and most lucrative enterprises. The source of this salt was the Lake Onondaga area of western New York. It was hauled to Buffalo by oxen and from there shipped in sailboats to Erie. Then it was transported by wagon across the portage to Waterford, where it was often stored awaiting a freshet. When the water reached the desired level the entire community loaded the barrels of salt on the boats. In 1807, following a rise in the Creek, twenty-two keelboats loaded with 4,000 to 5,000 barrels of salt were observed passing a point on the river.

In addition to salt, choice timber, skins, and foodstuffs from the upcountry were loaded on large flatboats and floated downstream to cities as far south as New Orleans. Many of these flats, sometimes called French Creeks, were made at Meadville. By 1830 the value of trade on French Creek was estimated at $100,000 per year—a fair amount for that day.

The merchants and pilots were an aggressive, versatile group who inspired a rich body of popular literature and song. Legendary boatmen like Marcus Hulings, Edward FitzRandolph and Luke Hill made the keelboat age the exciting era that it was. There were the dangers of natural disaster, river pirates, and marauding Indians to add spice to a day's labor. When William Magaw in 1809 sailed from Meadville with five flatboats destined for New Orleans, he ran into trouble typical of such a long journey. Long before he reached his destination his original crew had deserted him because of the con-

stant harassment from thieves. The river roughs sneaked aboard and broke into the food and whiskey even after Magaw spiked the flour with ashes. Because some of the robbers were Indians who got drunk on the whiskey, Magaw ended up in jail for contributing to their delinquency!

With poor roads, and heavy river shipping confined to times of freshets, French Creek merchants turned to canals to solve their problems. The opening of the Erie Canal in 1825 presented great possibilities. In August, 1827, ground was broken in Meadville for a feeder canal from French Creek to the summit level of Conneaut Lake some ten miles west of the city. This lake is on the divide which separates the Mississippi River system from that of the Great Lakes. Conneaut Lake was therefore made the reservoir for feeding the canal in both directions, and it gave the city all the advantages of the Erie's main line.

The era of the feeder canal also marked the height of the commercial importance of French Creek. Then came the railroads, and interest in canals quickly waned; French Creek likewise lost much of its importance. Its purpose evolved into something new—a fisherman's paradise, a canoeist's challenge, a camper's hideaway. Some of Pennsylvania's finest fishing is done in its waters and those of its tributaries.

But one thing about the Creek has always been remembered: the ferocity of its waters. Probably no other stream of its size has had such a consistent record as a flood maker. The Army Engineers have done their best, but as late as 1959, when the region was struck with a paralyzing flood, residents were reminded of French Creek's capacity for destruction. Two new dams, one at Union City and the other at Woodcock, have reduced flood hazards considerably. And only a few people hear the strange names affiliated with the Creek—Cussewago, Le Boeuf, Woodcock, Conneaut—and pause to recall its early history.

FURTHER READING: John E. Reynolds, *In French Creek Valley* (1938). Samuel Bates, R.C. Brown, *et al.*, *History of Crawford County* (1885).

Robert D. Ilisevich

The Grand River

Source: Spring-fed lake near Jackson, Michigan
Length: 270 miles
Tributaries: Maple River, Red Cedar
Mouth: Lake Michigan
Agricultural Products: Dairying, fruits and vegetables, tulips and other flowers and shrubs
Industries: Furniture, automobiles and parts, printing and publishing, musical instruments, tourism

The Indians called it Owashtonong—"the faraway waters." Today it is known as the Grand, a wide majestic river that flows through Michigan's lower peninsula. The longest and most important river in the state, the Grand rises from a spring-fed lake near Jackson and makes its way over a 270-mile course, passing through eighteen cities and towns before it empties its waters into Lake Michigan.

The Grand was formed more than 13,000 years ago by the cold rushing waters of a melting glacier. At first its banks were barren, but the climate warmed, and animals and then people made their way into the region sustained by the river, which dominated their lives and those of many who came after. They adjusted their annual routine to its changing moods. When it flooded and flowed fast and angry, they moved back and waited. When the Grand was placid and calm, they moved close and took the sustenance if offered. Even crossing the stream was a major challenge, for these wandering hunters had no canoes or boats, although they may have floated on logs. Over thousands of years, adaptations in the lifestyle of these early residents reflected the changing environment of the postglacial forests. Evergreens were supplanted by broadleafed hardwoods, and smaller game such as deer and bear replaced earlier mastodons and mammoths.

About 3,000 years ago, a particularly vigorous culture emerged. People known today as Early Woodland and Middle Woodland (Hopewell) came into the region from the south. They wore clothing of skins or woven fabric, and brought with them an assortment of stone and copper tools and ornaments. They also brought trade items from distant areas: mica from the Appalachians, shells from the Gulf of Mexico, and flint from the Ohio River valley. Most important, perhaps, is the fact that the earliest of these people introduced domesticated plants and pottery to the valley. They raised squash and sunflowers, and later corn, to supplement their basic diet of nuts, berries, and seeds, and meat from hunting and fishing.

The Hopewell are best remembered for the large burial mounds they built. These early monuments were a place to inter dead leaders together with carefully prepared ceremonial vessels, pipes, projectile points and pottery. Practices of this sort suggest a well-organized social structure. The relationship between these people and those who lived along the Grand River at the time European adventurers first

Artist's conception, based upon archaeological evidence, of a Hopewell burial scene along the Grand River, near present-day Grand Rapids, about 2,000 years ago. (Pictorial Materials Collection, Grand Rapids Public Museum.)

arrived is unclear. It is known that mound building had disappeared.

Just as the river enabled the Indians to travel from one place to another, so too, did it permit explorers from Europe to enter the region. Adventurers from France were the first to enter, and by 1650 they had made their way to lakes Superior and Michigan and were fanning out into the lands around them.

No one is certain when a European first dipped his canoe paddle into the waters of the Grand, but it may have been Father Pierre Marquette who passed the mouth of the river when he explored Lake Michigan's west coast in 1675, or it may have been Robert Cavalier de la Salle who built a stockade on the St. Joseph River a little more than fifty miles to the south in 1679. The following spring he set out across the lower Michigan peninsula for Lake Huron to the east. He and his men followed the Grand River for a time, charting its course. It is La Salle, the earliest European to sense the magnitude of the river, who is credited with giving it the name by which it is still known.

During the French period Ottawa Indians controlled the western river valley and Ojibwas lived along its banks in the interior. Both tribes carried on a vigorous fur trade with French, and later English and American, traders. This trade had a deleterious effect on the valley's animal population. Beaver, marten, and other fur-bearers nearly disappeared, and deer and bear were no longer seen with their earlier regularity.

In 1783 Michigan became a part of the new United States of America and the first permanent Grand River settlements by white people were established. When the French and British had claimed the area, Indian title was uncontested, but it was American policy to extinguish Indian title to western land, thereby opening it to anxious migrants from the east. In 1821 and again in 1836 treaties were signed with the Ottawa and Ojibway, transferring land north and south of the river to the public domain. Land purchases and migration to Michigan reached a high point in the mid-1830s, and for many, it was the Grand River valley that beckoned most strongly.

In short order a series of communities of log and board buildings made their appearance. By 1836, Grand Rapids had several hundred people and was an incorporated village, while Grand Haven, Walker, Lowell, Ionia, Lansing, and Jackson followed in the next two decades. The river was a crucial factor when these sites were selected. It provided a transportation route for rafts and boats, it was a water source, and most important, it soon became a power source for sawmills, flour mills, and cabinet shops. Later it provided power for the first electrical companies. A sawmill was built in the late 1820s at Reverend Leonard Slater's Indian Mission where Grand Rapids now stands. For the first time, people were not only living along the river, they were harnessing its strength.

Although stories of the origin and growth of these river cities seem similar, a closer examination reveals local variations. Grand Haven, founded in 1854 at the river's mouth, quickly developed as the entrepot for West Michigan. Shipments that came from the East via the Erie Canal and Lake Michigan were transshipped there for stops upriver, and goods from the valley were gathered there and sent east.

Thirty miles upriver from Grand Haven were the rapids, the furthest point for easy navigation. Here Reverend Leonard Slater's Indian Mission and Louis Campau's trading post were established in 1826. Ten years later Lucius Lyon and Louis Campau plotted lots and promoted two adjoining "towns." Settlers responded, and the water power available led to the development of a variety of manufacturing efforts, primarily associated with lumbering, cabinet-making, and milling. These firms prospered and grew until by the later decades of the nineteenth century, Grand Rapids boasted of being the "Furniture City." Its fine furniture was shipped throughout the United States. Although today its economic base is diversified, the city still boasts a large number of companies making both home and commercial furniture.

Further east, where the Red Cedar River joins the Grand, Lansing was founded. It claims two distinctions. Since 1847 it has been the capital of Michigan, and since 1857 the home of Michigan State University. It was named the seat of government because legislators supporting other towns were forced to settle on a compromise site. Many did not feel that Lansing, which at the time had one two-story cabin, could meet their requirement for a capitol building on short notice, and were surprised when it succeeded. The city has grown into a governmental and manufacturing center for over 130,000 people.

South of Lansing about forty miles, near the source of the Grand, grew yet another community, and here too, the drama was played with local variations. Jackson, named after President Andrew Jackson, was founded in 1836. Mills and mercantile stores took root, but the city's most famous seed was planted "under the oaks," on the edge of town, in 1854. There a group of dissident anti-slavery Democrats, ex-Whigs, and Free-Soilers met and adopted a platform centering on their opposition to slavery, selected a slate of candidates, and chose for themselves a new name: Republicans. Their candidates were elected in that year's fall election and thus a new party was born. The finest hour for the Republican party in the Grand River valley came when one of its own, Gerald R. Ford, assumed the Presidency of a troubled nation in 1974 and was only narrowly defeated for election in 1976.

Throughout the 1800s settlers came to the Grand River valley from all parts of the globe. First were the New Englanders and New Yorkers. Then in 1837–38, Canadians fleeing the effects of a short-lived rebellion against British authority found refuge in the valley. Irish laborers were digging canals along the river near Grand Rapids by 1835, and ten years later a large number of their countrymen joined them when Ireland was swept by famine. Similarly unrest and revolution brought immigrants from Germany, Poland, and other northern European countries.

A few miles from the mouth of the river a Dutch group led by Dr. Albertus Van Raalte, a vigorous advocate of Calvinism, made their home. Holland, Michigan, grew steadily, sending its children to surrounding communities. Today, the large number of Christian Reformed churches and the many Dutch surnames in telephone books attest to their presence.

After the Civil War another oppressed group, Southern blacks, came north to the Grand River valley. Another influx of these people came during and after World War II when a demand for laborers and Federal judicial rulings opened previously closed doors.

Steamboats began plying the Grand shortly after the first settlers arrived. For eighty years the shrill sound of their whistles echoed along its banks. The *Governor Mason*, constructed in Grand Rapids in 1837, was the river's first steamer. It did not last long, sinking in 1840, but others followed. State and local funds provided for deepening and widening the channel, and by 1855, exports from the valley had a value of $1,500,000. Railroads ended the steamboat era when they entered the valley in the last decades of the nineteenth century. The last whistle pierced the air in 1917.

Steamboats were not the only nineteenth-century traffic on the Grand. From 1869 to 1889, large rafts of logs were floated to Grand Haven where they were transferred to lake schooners. The greatest logging year was 1883, when spike-booted loggers brought nearly two million feet of logs to the river's mouth. Occasionally a log jam would create a dam. If not broken quickly, it would pile up in a spaghetti jumble before letting go with an awful roar. Bridges and shore installations were damaged in the wake of the broken jam.

Residents along the river feared floods as much as log jams. On several occasions, heavy precipitation combined to send the river far over its banks. In the 1904 flood, the greatest of all, electricity was cut off, factories were closed, and rowboats plied Grand Rapids' streets. The river is now dammed, flood walls protect homes and businesses, and the threat of floods is minimal. However, even now the Grand can undo people's best efforts at control. Seldom does a spring pass without residents being displaced at some point along the river by high water.

As time went on the communities along the Grand River passed from rambunctious youth into robust adulthood full of industrial, economic, social and governmental growth. Farming produced cattle, dairy products, and fruits and vegetables for local and national markets. Manufacturers produced items as diverse as furniture, automobiles and parts, pianos, pool tables, and jukeboxes.

By 1970, settlement in the valley's main cities had reached over 400,000. Another 650,000 lived in small towns and rural areas. At first glance, theirs was a good life. The standard of living was high and unemployment was low.

However, there were problems hidden in this prosperity. The river, in so many ways the source of their prosperity, was dying. Factories and farms, cities and towns, all produced waste that was turning the Grand River into a conduit for sewage. People disregarded and even feared the dirty river. They no longer looked upon it as a friend and partner in their lifestyle. Few dared eat the fish that survived its waters.

Fortunately, not everyone was willing to let the river die. Concerned citizens and government leaders passed control measures to manage discharges into the river. By 1972 the flow of industrial wastes had been reduced and trout and salmon reintroduced into the stream. In subsequent years, sportsmen found the river an increasingly desirable place to wet their lines,

and canoeists and boaters returned to the river as more boat ramps were built. Volunteer groups picked up debris along the banks.

The increasingly complex technology of recent decades has given people new power over the Grand. At first, they misused the power, and the river suffered. But today the river is recognized for its central role in the lives of those who inhabit its shores. Now they carefully watch over it to make sure that it will survive to serve future generations.

FURTHER READING: Z.Z. Lydens, ed., *The Story of Grand Rapids* (1966). Donald Chrysler, *The Story of the Grand River* (1975).

Gordon L. Olson

The Greenbrier River

Source: Two forks joining at Durbin, Pocahontas County, eastcentral West Virginia
Length: c. 165 miles
Mouth: Flows into New River
Agricultural Products: Vegetables, livestock
Industries: Tourism

The Greenbrier is one of the few remaining streams in Appalachia that has largely escaped the outrages of coal mines, factories, and large city sewers. It is clear, free running, and sweet smelling. It is a challenging opportunity for each generation to pass on to future ones the legacy of an unspoiled, beautiful river.

The Greenbrier has its source in two forks which head in east-central West Virginia in the general area known as the "birthplace of rivers." This highland region is the source not only of the Greenbrier but also of the Gauley and Elk rivers, the Jackson, the South Branch of the Potomac, the Cheat and the Tygart.

The West Fork of the Greenbrier heads in the red spruce and northern hardwood forests on Shaver's Mountain at an elevation of 3,625 feet. The East Fork heads in Blister Swamp, elevation

3,637 feet, on the west slope of Allegheny Mountain.

The East and West Forks merge at Durbin to form the main stream of the Greenbrier which then flows southward through the steep, timbered hills of northern Pocahontas County. Further south the hills give way to beautiful limestone farmlands. The river then meanders westward to join the New River below Hinton, West Virginia. The Greenbrier travels a distance of over 160 miles and drains 1,600 square miles. The total drop in elevation is about 2,500 feet—an average of almost sixteen feet per mile.

It is not known when humans first entered the Greenbrier Valley. For thousands of years it provided the Indians a bountiful harvest of deer, elk, bison, bear, wild turkey, and abundant lesser game. Fish, mussels, and crayfish added variety to their diet. Small Indian towns were widely scattered along the river as evidenced by flint points and other artifacts. These towns were all gone by 1749 when white settlers first arrived and the area was considered common hunting ground by Shawnee, Delaware, and Mingo tribesmen.

The Greenbrier Valley contained numerous deeply rutted trails used jointly by the Indians and the bison. The main trail connected the Seneca of the north with the Cherokee of the south and was known as the Seneca Trail. Other trails branched eastward and westward. They were of extreme importance during the bloody Indian raids in the latter part of the eighteenth century.

The first white men to slake their thirst in the Greenbrier River were French explorers and traders. Little is known of their experiences, but at least one native plant made a lasting impression. This is a spiny, woody vine that formed almost impenetrable thickets along the river banks. The French called the pesky plant "Ronceverte," which was translated "Greenbrier" by the English. In addition to the river, the name Greenbrier is applied today to a county in West Virginia, to a large limestone formation in the area, to a famous hotel located at White Sulphur Springs, and to other local points of interest.

It was not until 1749 that Jacob Marlin and Stephen Sewell settled on the Greenbrier River near the mouth of Knapps Creek where the town of Marlinton now stands. They were the best of friends except on the subject of religion. Quarrels on this topic convinced them to separate; Sewell set up his abode in a hollow sycamore tree nearby, leaving the cabin to Marlin.

Within a few years other settlers had followed Marlin and Sewell, and the lower Greenbrier Valley rang to the sound of axes and the falling of trees as farms were cleared. These were uneasy times on the western frontier and many forts were established where settlers could gather for protection from Indian attacks.

From 1755 until 1780 Indian attacks continued sporadically throughout the valley. Typical of these attacks was that on the Clendenin homestead near present Lewisburg. Here, on July 15, 1763, the Clendenins were preparing a feast for their neighbors. A group of Indians led by the young chief, Cornstalk, quietly appeared. They seemed friendly and wandered about looking at the young pigs in the pen and at the garden vegetables.

Suddenly the busy domestic scene was shattered by a scream as one of the Indians with his tomahawk split the skull of an old lady sitting on the kitchen steps. Clendenin and his little son were both killed. Mrs. Clendenin was tied and gagged, while three boys working in the corn field were captured. The Indians, having looted and burned the homestead, then left the scene with their captives.

Settlers in the Greenbrier Valley suffered many similar raids until the Indians were decisively defeated in 1778 when they attacked Fort Donnally near the present site of Frankfort. After cessation of Indian hostilities, settlement along the Greenbrier accelerated. Water mills for grinding grain and sawing lumber were built on many of the tributary streams, and a strong rural economy developed.

The Civil War had little effect on this region. Most of the people in the valley were from further east in Virginia and had strong ties with the South. There was little of military value in the Greenbrier area; however, further north the important railroad center at Grafton, West Virginia, was a prime target of the Confederates. This led in 1861 to a campaign by Robert E. Lee to drive the Federal troops from Cheat Mountain and continue northward to capture the railroad. Lee led his troops northward along the Greenbrier by way of Marlinton and established headquarters at Linwood. After several delays the plan was abandoned and Lee returned to Richmond.

By 1862 all of Virginia west of the Alleghenies was in Federal hands except the Greenbrier Valley. The Confederates, under the command of W.L. Jackson and General John Echols, retreated before a force under Union general William W. Averell as far as Droop Mountain, in east-central West Virginia. There they fortified the top of the mountain and awaited the Federal forces. Averell attacked from the Confederate's front and left flank. Finding their position untenable, Echols and Jackson retreated through Lewisburg and southward. Droop Mountain was the largest of the Civil War battles to be fought in present West Virginia.

The event that brought the first major changes to the Greenbrier Valley was the construction in 1872–1873 of the Chesapeake and Ohio Railroad. This line crossed the Greenbrier several times on its route from Richmond to Huntington. According to tradition, it was in the construction of Big Bend Tunnel near Talcott, along the Greenbrier, that John Henry, one of America's foremost folk heroes, performed his famous contest with the steam hammer. The railroad opened the vast timber lands of the region to exploitation.

The Greenbrier Valley contained over 600 million board feet of prime white pine timber. In 1875, Colonel Cecil Clay and others organized the St. Lawrence Boom and Lumber Company and built a large, circular, steam-powered sawmill on the Greenbrier at Ronceverte. Experienced loggers were brought in from Nova Scotia and New England to organize a work force to cut this timber and drive (float) it downstream to the mill.

The next twenty-five years were filled with excitement and activity. Skilled workers began cutting the white pine, peeling the logs and stacking them along the Greenbrier and its major tributaries; later they were floated downstream to the mills. A log drive would require three weeks to travel the eighty miles from Cass, then south down the river to Ronceverte. The work was dangerous and disagreeable. Nevertheless, the pay was good, $3.50 to $7.00 a day in 1898, and the food was excellent. There was much competition for places on the drive.

Just after the turn of the century another event took place that was to have a profound effect on the Greenbrier and the surrounding countryside. This was the building of the Greenbrier Division of the Chesapeake and Ohio Railroad. This track left the main line of the C. & O. near Caldwell on the Greenbrier River and followed the course of the stream northward to Durbin, a distance of ninety-four miles. When this line opened in 1902, it gave access to the entire Greenbrier watershed and provided an outlet for the extensive timberlands on Cheat Mountain west of the upper Greenbrier.

Lumbermen built such towns as Wildell, May, Gertrude, Olive, Dunlevie, Cass, Raywood, Stillwell, Seebert, and Watoga. These led a riotous existence for the next several years until the original timber was cut. After this the mill was moved out and the town quickly fell into disrepair and in many cases totally disappeared. In 100 miles along the Greenbrier, twenty-nine lumber towns flourished during the period 1905–1920. Only five of these towns exist today.

The C. & O. Railroad also stimulated other industries to locate in the Greenbrier Valley. Among these are two tanneries located at Frank and Marlinton, a manufacturing plant at Ronceverte, and numerous small mills and businesses. It also stimulated growth of the Greenbrier Hotel at White Sulphur Springs. Here as early as 1780 the mineral spring attracted people to bathe in its curative mineral waters. In 1800, cottages were built near the springs. These were followed by a tavern in 1808, and for nearly a century the spa that developed there, in the coolness of the Allegheny Mountains, became the summer capital of the United States. At least thirteen presidents from Andrew Jackson in the early 1800s have spent vacations there.

The Greenbrier has been many things to many people in its colorful past. To the Indian it was a source of food and transportation as he glided through the dense forest of white pine. At the turn of the present century, to the hardy timbermen who cut these same pines and drove them downstream to the sawmills, it was the rushing excitement of log drives. To many the Greenbrier was the old swimming hole where, as youngsters, they first learned the delights of swimming. These swimming holes helped bring strength and tranquility to many others who were baptized in its limpid waters. Today, it is excitement to the canoeist riding the rolling spring flood, and healing relaxation to the fisherman wading its clear water tantalizing trout, black bass, rockbass, and walleyed pike into a creel.

Today the Greenbrier still flows through a rural area. The towns along its route are neither large nor highly industrialized. There is occasional pressure to dam its flow to protect low-lying areas from periodic flooding, but alternatives are available that will allow the Greenbrier to flow unimpeded in all its beauty and tranquility as it has done for millions of years.

FURTHER READING: Charles H. Ambler and Festus P. Summers, *West Virginia, the Mountain State* (1958). Phil Conley and Boyd B. Stutler, *West Virginia Yesterday and Today* (1952).

Roy B. Clarkson

The Hiwassee River

Source: In Towns County in northeast Georgia
Length: 150 miles
Tributaries: Nottely, Valley, Toccoa-Ocoee rivers (the latter is called the Toccoa in Georgia and the Ocoee in Tennessee)
Mouth: Tennessee River at Chickamaugua Reservoir
Agricultural Products: Vegetables, grain
Industries: Lumbering, copper sulfide mines, paper

The Hiwassee River rises in Towns County in northeast Georgia, flows across the western tip of North Carolina, then follows a generally west-northwesterly course to the communities of Charleston and Calhoun. It then flows on to its junction with the Tennessee River thirty-five miles upstream from Chattanooga at the site of the Chickamauga Reservoir. In all it is about 150 miles long. The river seems to flout nature's law, since it takes what looks like an uphill route to join the Tennessee River.

The Hiwassee drains an area of 2,700 square miles, part of which lies in Georgia, part in North Carolina, and part in Tennessee. The watershed is rectangular, about ninety miles long, and varies in width from about twenty-five miles near the middle to about fifty miles at each end. The drainage system includes, as tributary streams to the Hiwassee, the Nottely River, Valley River, and Toccoa-Ocoee River (called Toccoa in Georgia and Ocoee in Tennessee). These all flow northwestward from their headwaters on the Blue Ridge, which divides the Tennessee River Basin from the Gulf Coast and Atlantic Coast drainage. The portion of the watershed in Georgia, North Carolina, and parts of Tennessee is mountainous and about eighty-five percent in forest. Land along the upper rim is mostly 3,000 feet to 4,000 feet high.

Hiwassee, which has been spelled many ways, means "savannah" or "meadow." Tradition says that the name was given to the river by the famous Cherokee princess, Nancy Ward. The first indication of the white man's knowledge of the river is its appearance on Emanuel Bowen's "A New & Accurate Map of the Provinces of North & South Carolina," published in 1752.

Geologists believe the Hiwassee was part of the ancient Tennessee River system. This assumes that the first part of Tennessee land to rise above sea level at the time the Appalachians appeared was the highland region ancestral to today's Unaka Mountains of northeast Tennessee. The Hiwassee Dam in extreme western North Carolina and nearly all the reservoir it creates are in the Great Smoky Mountain formation of pre-Cambrian Age, further confirming this theory.

Today the Hiwassee, where not dammed or part of a reservoir, is for the most part a rapid, mountainous stream in the Cherokee National Forest, winding through a picturesque maze of woodlands, ravines, and rocky gorges. It has a total fall of over 900 feet in sixty miles, 300 feet of which is concentrated in one ten-mile stretch known as the Gorge. The downstream third of the river is relatively flat, with a fall of only fifty feet in the first forty miles. Below the mouth of the Ocoee the Hiwassee averages a width of about 300 feet.

Anthropologists believe at least three tribes have lived in the vicinity of the Hiwassee River: the Early Woodland, 2,000 years ago; the Yuchi, 500 years ago; and the Cherokee, arriving in the sixteenth or seventeenth centuries. When the earliest Euro-Americans settled in East Tennessee, they found the major river valleys occupied by the Cherokee who built rectangular pole houses like the Mississippian Indians, sometimes erected their town houses on mounds, and decorated their pottery with stamped designs like the earlier Woodland Indians.

Hiwassee Old Town or Great Hiwassee was the most important Cherokee town located on the river. One of Tennesseean John Sevier's soldiers wrote that "four hundred warriors could be raised here with one war whoop." The settlement stretched for 2 to 3 miles along the north side of the river near the Indian trading town of Columbus and near where today the bridge of U.S. Highway 411 crosses the Hiwassee River between Benton and Etowah, Tennessee. European trade articles and Cherokee artifacts have been found in this area in recent years.

A claim that Welsh voyagers came into the Tennessee country at an early time is based largely on a letter written in 1816 by John Sevier, first governor of Tennessee, describing a conversation he had in 1782 with Oconostoa, the chief warrior of the Cherokees. When asked about some "traces of very ancient fortifications" which Sevier had observed on the banks of the Hiwassee River, Oconostota had said that there was a tradition in his tribe that the forts had been built by white people who called themselves Welsh.

There is much more convincing evidence that the Spaniards were the first white men to reach the Hiwassee River. On June 1, 1540, De Soto's expedition camped near the Indian town of Canasoga where a delegation of twenty villagers met his column each carrying a basket of mulberries. Following the settlement of the Ocoee District by whites, Spanish swords, knives, canteens, buttons, and a bridle-bit were found on a farm; and near Murphy, North Carolina, similar discoveries were made of Spanish pipes, lead balls, and silver buttons bearing a faint Spanish design. As late as 1784 the Spanish claimed territory to the south banks of the Hiwassee River though they never occupied it.

In 1757 the English founded Fort Loudon on the nearby Little Tennessee River and from that time on Indian traders knew of the region. To counter the English, the French may have been stationed temporarily on the Hiwassee and may have considered constructing a fort there.

By Calhoun's Treaty of 1819 the federal government acquired Cherokee land between the Little Tennessee and the Hiwassee River. When surveyed into townships and sections this region became known as the Hiwassee District. The Cherokee, meanwhile, had been forced to move south of the river into the so-called Ocoee District; this was the last remaining land owned by the Cherokee in Tennessee. On December 29, 1835, the Cherokee signed the Treaty of New Echota by which they ceded the Ocoee District; two years later they were forced to move west. General Winfield Scott rounded up those who refused to move, placed 17,000 Cherokee into twenty-nine or more military camps, and then escorted them west on what has been called the Trail of Tears. Before leaving Tennessee the Indians, under the leadership of John Ross, held a final dramatic farewell ceremony at Rattlesnake Springs; for several miles they followed the Hiwassee before leaving it for the west.

The signing of the above two treaties was the signal for rapid white settlement. The village of Charleston was located on the south bank of the Hiwassee; it began as a trading post. Return J. Meigs, the Cherokee agent, was receiving mail addressed to the Hiwassee Agency there as early as 1819. He often used the Hiwassee River to transport produce of the Cherokees to Chattanooga or Knoxville for sale, reimbursing the Indians with the proceeds. The towns of Calhoun and Columbus were other early settlements. Although Columbus has disappeared, it was near the Great Indian War Path and the Old Federal Road, which crossed the Hiwassee nearby.

From various points in East Tennessee keelboats were laboriously poled up the Hiwassee and Ocoee to Hildebrand's, a trading post, where they were loaded on horse-drawn vehicles and carried to McNair's boatyard on the Conasauga River. This route, by which vessels floated from the Conasauga to the Coosa and Alabama rivers to the Gulf, was very popular. It eliminated the time and expense of working west to the Mississippi. In 1821 a keelboat, the *Tennessee Patriot*, some fifty feet long, took this route successfully, reaching its destination on March 2 with a cargo of flour and whiskey.

After about 1850, when James Gamble purchased the steamboat *Union*, copper ore was transported via the Ocoee and Hiwassee to Charleston. After the Civil War a number of steamboats plied the Hiwassee and their activity continued until the turn of the century. As late as 1894 the steamer *Ocoee* left the mouth of the Ocoee every Monday at seven A.M. on a regular trip to Chattanooga.

The population of the Hiwassee Valley today is somewhat more than 156,000, sixty percent of whom live in the relatively flat lower third of the drainage basin. Another fifteen percent live in the valley of the tributary Ocoee River, and about half the remainder reside in the vicinity of Murphy, North Carolina, where the best agricultural land lies. More than seventy percent of the river basin lies within national forests, and lumbering provides employment for many residents. Copper sulphide is being mined and smelted on the Ocoee Valley near Ducktown and Copperhill. Sulphuric acid is an important product. The region also contains many other minerals, a few of which are being mined on a small scale. Industrial growth was greatly spurred by the coming of TVA. The Southern Railway and the Louisville and Nashville Railroad run through the valley.

The Hiwassee has always been subject to flooding. The first remembered by early white settlers appears to be the flood of 1840, but serious floods have occurred at least twenty-two times since them. In 1886, a few miles above its mouth, the Hiwassee was six miles wide, and in 1898 at Murphy the flood was said to be the highest since the one of 1840. With the construction of dams, the Tennessee Valley Authority has greatly reduced the flooding danger. Of its fifty-one dams, the Authority now operates eight hydroelectric power plants on the Hiwassee and its tributaries in conjunction with flood control and navigational installations.

The U.S. Forest Service controls 150,870 acres just within the boundaries of Polk County in the Hiwassee River valley. This area serves today as a valuable recreation center. The river is one of the nation's outstanding scenic, trout, canoe, and float streams. As many as 50,000 white-water rafters use the river every year.

Sixty-nine species of fish inhabit the Hiwassee and of these, nineteen are game fish. Fish traps constructed by the Cherokee can still be seen today. Studies also indicate that 2,000 or more snail darters exist today in the Hiwassee River. (The idea that this species could only live in the Tellico River halted the construction of TVA's Tellico dam for several years.) The Hiwassee appears to be on its way toward becoming one of the better trout streams in the eastern United States. It has been designated a State Scenic River.

FURTHER READING: Thomas M. Lewis and Madeline Kneberg, *Tribes that Slumber* (1966). Roy G. Lillard, ed., *The History of Bradley County, Tennessee* (1976).

Roy G. Lillard

~~~~~~

The Holston River

Source: Merger of South Fork and North Fork of the Holston at Kingsport, Tennessee
Length: 140 miles
Tributaries: None of importance
Mouth: Merges with French Broad to form the Tennessee at Knoxville
Agricultural Products: Dairying, vegetables, fruits
Industries: Chemicals, textiles, innumerable products

The Holston, one of the major tributaries of the Tennessee River, consists of three forks all rising in the Appalachian ridges of southwestern Virginia. The Middle Fork first joins the South Fork Holston, then the North Fork merges with the South Fork at Kingsport, Tennessee, to form the Holston proper. It then flows 140 miles through

East Tennessee until it merges with the French Broad to form the Tennessee, at Knoxville.

Although the Indians referred to the upper reaches of the river as the Hogohegee, early Anglo explorers called it the Holston after the pioneer Stephen Holston. In 1746 he built a cabin along the banks of the South Fork somewhere near its confluence with the Watauga River, explored the areas, and traded with the Cherokees.

Other explorers-hunters-traders soon traveled through the Holston River region. In 1760 Daniel Boone crossed the Blue Ridge Mountains for the first time and hunted and trapped in the Holston and Watauga river valleys. That same year Virginians, on their way to relieve Fort Loudon on the Little Tennessee, built Fort Robinson on the Holston's Long Island. In 1761 a party of twenty hunters led by Elisha Walden traveled along the Holston before going through Cumberland Gap into Kentucky; the trail they followed, the Warrior's Path, crossed the Holston at Long Island.

In 1770 John Carter and William Parker established a trading post below the Long Island (near present Church Hill, Tennessee) to supply emigrants and traders canoeing down the Holston. Others followed, their farms dotting Carter's Valley between today's Kingsport and Rogersville, Tennessee. In 1772 surveyors completed the Lochaber Treaty line which disclosed that three of the four early settlements in East Tennessee were clearly outside the territory granted by the Cherokees to the British government. Since Carter's Valley was the furthest of the illegal settlements, John and his neighbors decided to join temporarily the Wataugans who were ready to defy anyone who threatened their illegal land holdings.

The only legal settlement, the North Holston, began about the same time as Carter's. Evan Shelby and his son, Isaac, established a store at Sapling Grove (Bristol, Tennessee-Virginia) located north of the South Fork Holston.

During the years of the Written Articles of Association (a temporary squatter's agreement), the North Holston area grew rapidly at the expense of the illegal Watauga settlements. Not only was the area clearly within Virginia, but also the forks of the Holston served restless pioneers as a natural, easily accessible highway. By 1773 North Holston had passed beyond the primitive stage, and the settlers had begun two roads to facilitate commerce with the east and west—the Island Road and the Watauga Road.

As a result of the activities of the North Holston area, small settlements began to develop near Long Island. In 1774 James King built a gristmill at the mouth of Reedy Creek and the Holston to take advantage of river traffic on the main river and North Fork Holston. The settlement that grew up around King's Mill eventually became known as Kingsport.

In 1775 an event transpired at Sycamore Shoals which influenced future events along the Holston. On March 17, Judge Richard Henderson's Transylvania Company purchased Kentucky from the Cherokees. Two weeks before that date, Henderson had dispatched Daniel Boone and thirty axemen to build a road from Long Island on the Holston to the new proprietary colony of Transylvania. In a separate agreement known as the Path Deed, Henderson secured additional lands including Carter's Valley so that settlers would not have to travel through Cherokee-owned lands to reach Kentucky. In accordance with a prior arrangement, Henderson turned over the Path Deed lands to John Carter and his new partner, Robert Lucas, who began immediately selling tracts to incoming settlers.

During the American Revolution most settlers living in the Holston Valley joined the patriot cause. Those living north of the South Fork Holston, already considered a part of Fincastle County, Virginia, joined the Fincastle Committee of Safety. Those living in the new settlements near Long Island and Carter's Valley organized the Pendleton District and petitioned in January, 1776, to be "incorporated" into Virginia. The petitioners' request was granted and their settlements became a part of Fincastle County. Before the end of the year, the revolutionary Virginia government divided Fincastle County, and all the Holston settlements became a part of the newly created Washington County.

By that time the Holston settlers had successfully withstood several determined Indian raids. On July 20, 1776, one hundred seventy men from the Holston communities defeated a large Cherokee war party caught off guard at Island Flats and seriously wounded one of their leaders, Dragging Canoe. That fall the local militiamen received help from a large contingent of North and South Carolinians and Georgians. One large force marched to the Holston, scattered the Cherokees, and burned their villages and crops. The next year, by the Treaty of Long Island, the Cherokees had to relinquish large tracts of land.

In 1779 Virginia ceded the Holston settlements to North Carolina and the settlers established Sullivan County. Colonel Evan Shelby also formed the first river expedition to subdue the Cherokees on Chickamauga Creek. In April, with 500 men, he descended the Holston and Tennessee to Chickamauga Creek. The Indians, surprised by the attack, offered no organized resistance as the raiders pursued and killed, burned towns and crops, and confiscated cattle and British supplies.

During the same year (1779), Long Island on the Holston served as the initial staging area for settlers moving to the Cumberland Valley of Middle Tennessee. The migration followed two routes, one, led by James Robertson, by land and the other, led by John Donelson, by water. By early 1780 they had arrived at their goal and established Fort Nashboro; it is present Nashville.

During the turbulent years following the Revolution, the settlers of East Tennessee, including those in the Holston communities, were involved with the abortive State of Franklin. The Franklin years were marked by land schemes, total disregard for the Indians, expansion, foreign intrigue, and projected river trade with the Spanish. Only after the legislature of North Carolina for a second time ceded its western lands to the new United States Government operating under the provisions of the Constitution did the people completely forget their independent state. Their region became the United States Territory South of the River Ohio; ex-Franklinites could await statehood according to prescribed procedures.

The new governor of the Southwest Territory, William Blount, chose sites near the Holston for his territorial capitals. He set up his first headquarters at Rocky Mount, the home of William Cobb, located between the forks of the Holston and the Watauga. In the summer of 1791, Governor Blount met a Cherokee delegation at White's Fort located four miles above the confluence of the Holston and French Broad rivers and signed the Treaty of the Holston. The Fort was ideally situated on the Holston River and was nearer than Rocky Mount to Nashboro. White designated it the new capital and changed its name to Knoxville in honor of Henry Knox, President Washington's Secretary of War.

Although most Tennesseans today know that Knoxville is located on the banks of the Tennessee River and not the Holston, such was not the case until the 1880s. Until then the name Holston applied from its headwaters to the junction with the Little Tennessee approximately thirty miles below Knoxville. The primary reason the river's name was changed between the French Broad and Little Tennessee was to secure federal appropriations for improvement of navigation on the Tennessee River.

The upper Holston, beginning at Long Island, was an important highway during the years of the Southwest Territory and throughout the nineteenth century. Many newcomers came into the region via the Holston. Kingsport became the head for water transportation to Knoxville; it was close to the first industry in East Tennessee, iron smelting. An iron furnace had been established on the North Fork Holston during the 1780s, and other furnaces were soon begun on the South Fork. The produce made from the iron was nails—a most important commodity on the frontier. Nails and agricultural products were floated down the Holston to Knoxville; from Knoxville the boats returned with dry goods and staples.

Steamboats further opened up potentials for the river's trade. In 1828 the *Atlas* ascended the Tennessee and Holston to the confluence with the French Broad. Beginning in 1835, steamboats plied regularly between Knoxville and Decatur, Alabama, during the high water season. But not until the 1850s did an infrequent steam vessel hazard the journey to Kingsport.

The completion of the East Tennessee and Virginia Railroad in 1858 between Bristol and Knoxville lessened for a time the importance of the Holston River as a trade route. But during the years after the Civil War, new salt industries in Virginia and East Tennessee revived the river's importance.

During the Civil War, the Holston and its tributary the French Broad played a significant role in lifting the siege of Knoxville. Arriving late in September to drive Union General Ambrose E. Burnside from the town, General James Longstreet realized that his force was outnumbered and instead of attacking decided to lay siege to the Union Army and starve it out. His strategy was sound but his battle map showed that the French Broad joined the Holston below Knoxville instead of four miles above the city, and he would not believe East Tennessee Confederate sympathizers who knew better. Longstreet therefore left the confluence of the two rivers unguarded. As a result people in the

French Broad and Holston valleys who were mainly Unionist floated badly needed provisions downriver to Burnside's army. On November 29, the Confederates unsuccessfully assaulted the Union positions and then retreated into Virginia. The Battle of Knoxville removed Confederate forces from East Tennessee and gave the Union full control of the navigable portions of the Tennessee River system.

People living along the river have always made effective use of it. They have also learned to respect it, for the river has been prone to catastrophic flooding. Its greatest and most unprecedented flood occurred in 1867. Mills, homes, barns, and stables thought to be out of the reach of high waters were all carried away by the rushing torrent. Other notable high water records along the river occurred in 1790, 1851, 1928, 1929, 1940, and 1944.

With the coming of the Tennessee Valley Authority the river was tamed. Cherokee Dam several miles upstream from the confluence of the Holston and French Broad rivers was completed December 5, 1941. Construction of one of the major dams in the TVA system, South Holston, was completed in 1950. Boone and Patrick Henry dams on the South Fork Holston were completed in 1953. Not only did these dams prevent major flooding, but their generating plants provide electricity for the people of the upper Tennessee Valley.

These government projects changed the entire complexion of the Holston River, which now feeds four man-made lakes: Cherokee, South Holston, Boone, and Patrick Henry. Together these reservoirs consist of over 700 miles of shoreline and provide sportspeople with long days of pleasure. Stretches of the river itself also provide exciting opportunities for fishermen and hunters alike.

Today the Holston, like too many rivers in this country, is polluted by industrial wastes. The entire North Fork Holston is contaminated by mercury, while the South Fork Holston and Holston are contaminated by other chemicals discharged by industries interested only in profit. Communities along their banks also must assume responsibility for the contamination; their sewage treatment plants are totally inadequate. And the people too are responsible. Not only do some of them discard garbage along the river's banks and creeks, but also —and more important—they do not demand that the federal, state, and local governments enforce regulations. Until they do, the river's pollution will remain.

FURTHER READING: Samuel C. Williams, *Dawn of Tennessee Valley and Tennessee History* (1937). Philip H. Hamer, (ed.), *Tennessee, 1673–1932*, 4 vols. (1933).

Emmett Essin

The Illinois River

Source: Convergence of Des Plaines and Kankakee Rivers forty-five miles southwest of Chicago
Length: 273 miles
Tributaries: Fox, Vermilion, Mackinaw, Spoon, Sangamon rivers
Agricultural Products: Grain, porks, beef, vegetables
Industries: Coal, steel products, petroleum refining, and transportation of products along the river

The Illinois River is formed by the convergence of the Des Plaines and Kankakee rivers some 45 miles southwest of Chicago and it flows diagonally across the Prairie State for 273 miles to empty into the Mississippi about 50 miles above St. Louis. Swelled by the Fox, Vermilion, Mackinaw, Spoon, Sangamon, and other streams, it drains 25,000 square miles of land and is second only to the Ohio River among the westward-flowing tributaries of the "Father of Waters."

For the first 63 miles, the Illinois runs westward through a deep, narrow valley carved thousands of years ago by glaciers; then it makes a great bend to the south and the valley broadens and the river drops so slightly that there is hardly any current. Sloughs and marshes border the stream and there is extensive woodland on its banks which once teemed with wild game. The surrounding valley contains some of the best farmland in the nation, extensive deposits of coal, clay, and limestone, and bustling cities and towns.

Throughout most of its course, the Illinois is one-quarter of a mile or less wide, but during the first part of its journey southward it reaches a broad basin called Peoria Lake. Actually a wide and deep place in the river, the "lake" is almost one and a half miles across. The valley adjacent to the river also varies in width from two to five miles in most places to fifteen miles above the mouth of the Sangamon.

Prehistoric people appeared along the Illinois at least 10,000 years ago, not very long after the last glacier receded. Known as Paleo-Indians and probably Eurasian in background, they lived on edible plants and mastodonic animals. In time, however, they began to cultivate seeds, make ceramic pottery and woven baskets, settle in villages, and bury their dead in earthen mounds. Labeled the "Hopewell" culture by anthropologists, it and the Indians who created it disappeared, for reasons which are not clear, sometime after 500 A.D.

A new group known as the "Middle Mississipians" next occupied the region. These Indians also raised grain, traded goods, and built mounds for burial purposes. In addition, they piled up other mounds on which they erected temples. None of the latter mounds exist along the Illinois today, but a state museum at Dickson Mounds near the river does mark a major burial site of these people. Again, for reasons as yet unknown, the Middle Mississipians and their culture vanished at about the time Columbus made his first voyage to the New World.

When the French arrived along the Illinois in the late seventeenth century, they found another, less sophisticated people living there. These were the Illiniwek, part of the Algonquin Nation and a federation of a number of tribes, most important of which were the Peoria, Kaskaskia, Cahokia, Michiganea, and Tamoroa. The French called these rather primitive and semi-nomadic Indians the "Illinois" and the name has remained.

Constant warfare with the fierce Iroquois and the invasion of their hunting grounds by white men took a heavy toll of the Illinois Indians, and by 1832 when the United States government placed them on a reservation in what is now Kansas, there were only slightly more than 100 of them left. Today, there are no known descendents of the Illinois Indians.

The first white men to travel over the Illinois and note its valley were the Frenchmen Father Jacques Marquette and Louis Jolliet who, in 1673, ascended the river from the Mississippi which they had been exploring. Seven years later, Robert Cavelier, Sieur de La Salle, came down the river as far as Peoria Lake where he built Fort Crevecoeur. During the next eighty years the French constructed several forts along the river and planted a few scattered Jesuit missions and trading posts on its banks.

France ceded the area to Great Britain in 1763 by the Treaty of Paris which ended the Seven Years' War, and the British held it until Americans under George Rogers Clark seized control from them in 1778 during the American Revolution. With the cessation of hostilities in 1782, the region was given to the Americans who began to move into what is now the state of Illinois from the southeast. It was not until the second quarter of the nineteenth century, however, that sizable numbers of Americans settled along the Illinois. At that time, Irish immigrants also came to work on canals and railroads and numerous Germans came in 1848 after unsuccessful revolutions in their homelands.

As settlement and commerce increased along the Illinois, a plan was formulated for a canal to connect Lake Michigan and the river. The idea was not a new one—Jolliet, La Salle, and others had recommended a canal to link the Chicago River which flowed into the lake with the Des Plaines to make a continuous water route from Lake Michigan. Efforts to get such a canal began as early as 1810, but political wrangling over physical aspects of the canal and financing problems delayed construction until 1836. The onset of economic depression in the following year held up actual completion of the canal until 1848.

The finished canal greatly enhanced the economic welfare of Illinois River towns and aided Chicago in its struggle to outstrip St. Louis since crops from the central Illinois prairies then poured into the lake city rather than the Mississippi port. However, competition of railroads in the late nineteenth century reduced the canal's importance and in 1935 it was converted to recreational use.

A wider and deeper canal was built during the last decade of the nineteenth century as part of the Great Lakes-to-Gulf system, and it has largely restored the important place the Illinois held in the prosperity of the river valley. Called the Chicago Sanitary and Ship Canal, it served the twin purposes of commerce and carrying Chicago's treated sewage out of Lake Michigan which provided the city's water supply and was becoming polluted. To accomplish this, engineers permanently reversed the flow of the Chicago River so that it became an outlet for the lake rather than an inlet; it was the first such engineering feat ever performed.

Between 1919 and 1933, the channel from Lockport on the Des Plaines to near Starved Rock on the Illinois was deepened, and dams and locks were constructed at various places on the river to improve navigation and control flooding. With the completion of the project, the Illinois Waterway, as the new system was named, permitted Great Lakes-to-Gulf traffic by vessels with as much as a 9-foot draft. Plans are currently projected to broaden and deepen the waterway still more so that larger oceangoing ships may use it and thus create an inland Atlantic-to-Gulf route via the St. Lawrence Seaway.

Steamboats first appeared on the Illinois about 1827, although there is some dispute as to the exact date. Early steamboats operated only near the mouth of the river, but by 1829 some were traveling as far north as Peoria and as new towns were platted upstream from Peoria during the 1830s and 1840s, steamboats made their way still farther northward. By mid-century, upper river ports were counting as many as 1,200 steamboat arrivals during a season. However, the advent of railway systems which provided faster and more efficient service caused steamboat enterprises to decline.

When the Illinois-Lake Michigan Canal was constructed in the last century, the Illinois was navigable by commercial vessels only to LaSalle, but today, with the deeper channel dredged during the 1920s, Morris, Seneca, Marseilles, and Ottawa, which are upstream from LaSalle, are properly called river cities. Morris

was formerly an important grain shipping center, and recent excavations there indicate it is located on a site occupied by prehistoric Indians. Seneca was a small river town until 1942 when the DuPont Corporation located an explosives plant there. Marseilles lies athwart two miles of rapids which have required the building of a dam and lock to get shipping past. Ottawa, built on both sides of the river, is located near the junction of the Fox River and was the site of the first Lincoln-Douglas debate in 1858. Between Ottawa and LaSalle are rugged sandstone cliffs, best known of which is Starved Rock where the explorer La Salle built Fort St. Louis in 1683 and where legend states that a band of Illinois Indians died of starvation while under seige.

Beyond Starved Rock on the north bank of the river are the sister cities of LaSalle and Peru which were established about 1830. LaSalle was the terminus of the Illinois-Lake Michigan Canal and benefited greatly from its location during the heyday of steamboating on the river. Peru has shared some of the benefits of location with LaSalle.

A little farther downstream are Spring Valley and Hennepin which are located on either side of the Great Bend of the Illinois. The former was a coal mining area until recently, while the latter, named for Father Louis Hennepin who accompanied La Salle on his exploration in 1679–1680, was at one time the terminus of a canal which connected the Illinois with the Mississippi at Rock Island. The Hennepin Canal, as it was generally called, was completed in 1907, but it failed to pay its way commercially and was abandoned in 1951. Today, like the Illinois-Lake Michigan Canal, it is a recreation area and a reminder of a bygone era.

As the Illinois flows southward to Peoria Lake it passes Henry, Sparland, Lacon, Chillicothe, and Rome, all of which were once thriving centers of commercial activity when steamboats plied the river. The revival of river traffic in more recent times has affected these towns only indirectly, and today they either languish or have turned to pursuits not dependent upon the river. Extensive hunting areas have been preserved on both sides of the river near these towns.

Many people, both in the past and at present,

consider Peoria the most beautiful city on the Illinois because of the deep, broad lake there and the neat city built on terraces up the bluffs. First settled by Americans in 1819, but with accumulating evidence that there was continuous French presence on the site between 1691 and 1819, Peoria is one of the oldest, if not the oldest, settled areas west of the Appalachian Mountains. Among the famous individuals who have lived there are Robert G. Ingersoll, the nineteenth-century agnostic orator-politician, and Jim Jordan, who played Fibber McGee during the golden days of radio. Among Peoria's industries are the Caterpillar Tractor Company which is the world's leading producer of earth-moving equipment. Today, Peoria and East Peoria across the river make up Illinois' second largest industrial and population center.

A few miles to the south of Peoria is Pekin which is situated on the east bank of the river. Founded in 1824, it is the oldest settlement in Tazewell County and was the home of David Davis, United States Supreme Court Justice and friend of Lincoln, and Everett M. Dirksen, United States Senator from 1950 to 1969.

Beyond Pekin are the river valley towns of Liverpool, Havana, and Beardstown. Liverpool was an early river port which turned to coal mining when the steamboat era passed. Havana is located near the junction of the Spoon River which was the setting of Edgar Lee Masters' famous *Spoon River Anthology*. Lewistown, where Masters lived, is on the Spoon not far from Havana. Beardstown was founded by Thomas Beard in 1827 and was a frequent stop of Lincoln when he was a circuit-riding lawyer. Indeed, it was the setting of the famous "almanac trial" in 1857 where Lincoln disproved a witness's testimony that he saw a crime committed by moonlight by using an almanac to show that the moon had already set at the time the crime was alleged to have happened. Beardstown was also the scene of some of the worst flooding along the Illinois. An especially severe

rose to over 23 feet and inundated Beardstown and a surrounding 18-mile-wide area. flood occurred in 1922 when the river waters

Between Havana and Beardstown a large island called "Grand Island" divides the river. Located on the east fork is the town of Bath which Lincoln once surveyed, while below Grand Island is the confluence of the Sangamon River which flows past New Salem where Lincoln spent a part of his early manhood.

Downstream from Beardstown are Meredosia and Naples. Meredosia was the terminus of the first railroad built to the Illinois in 1838 and an important shipping center during the steamboat period. Naples is located a few miles south of Meredosia and was at one time a leading grain shipping port. Even before steamboating began in earnest on the Illinois, a steamboat named the *Olitippa* was reported to have been built at Naples and operated on the river in that vicinity.

In its last sixty miles downstream, the Illinois broadens as it flows by such romantic places of the steamboating past as Florence, Montezuma, Bedford, Pearl, Kampsville, Hardin, and Grafton. Hardin is the last town actually on the Illinois and is situated on a ridge of land between it and the Mississippi; Grafton is on the Illinois shore at the point where the river and the "Father of Waters" meet. In earlier days the Illinois was so free of pollution when it reached Grafton that its clear waters did not immediately combine with the muddier waters of the Mississippi and the two streams flowed side by side for a mile or so.

Today, the Illinois River continues to be an important commercial highway whose historical associations are among the richest of all the traveled water routes in the nation.

FOR FURTHER READING: James Gray, *The Illinois*. A volume of "The Rivers of America" series. Edited by Stephen Vincent Benet and Carl Carmer. New York: Farrar and Rinehart, Inc., 1940. Harry Hansen, ed. *Illinois; A Descriptive and Historical Guide*. Revised edition. New York: Hastings House, 1974.

William L. Bowers

The Kanawha River

Source: Merging of New and Gauley rivers in south-central West Virginia
Length: 97 miles
Tributaries: Elk, Coal, and Pocatalico rivers
Mouth: Ohio River at Point Pleasant, West Virginia
Agricultural Products: Dairying, vegetables, fruit
Industries: Coal, salt, lumber, chemicals

The Kanawha, named for the Conoys, an Indian tribe of Algonquin linguistic stock, is formed by the merging of the New and Gauley rivers in south central West Virginia. It is West Virginia's largest inland waterway, averaging about 600 feet wide on its ninety-seven-mile course to the Ohio which it joins at Point Pleasant. Major tributaries include the Elk River entering at Charleston, the Coal River entering at Saint Albans and the Pocatalico River entering at Poca.

The discovery of the Kanawha is usually attributed to Thomas Batts and Robert Fallam, members of a party that left Appomattox, Virginia, on September 1, 1671, to explore across the western mountains. Approximately seventeen days later they came to the banks of a stream that flowed in a westerly direction and named the newly discovered stream Woods River, in honor of their patron, General Abraham Wood. Fallam kept a detailed daily journal of the trip that shows quite clearly that they had reached Peter's Falls, near the present Virginia-West Virginia border.

The name Kanawha was first used about 1760 for that portion of the stream below where the Greenbrier River joins the present New River. It was several years before the name was restricted still more to that portion of the stream below where the Gauley and New rivers merge. There are no records indicating why these changes were made.

The Kanawha is both an old and a new stream. It is old because it began in late Cretaceous time, perhaps 100 million years ago. Then, just a few million years ago, part of the land was uplifted and this gave the stream enough gradient to cut a deep channel. The steep, canyon-like walls indicate that part of it is a newly rejuvenated stream.

Just a few thousand years ago much of the Kanawha flowed along an entirely different course, as part of the ancient Teays River. The Teays was the greatest of the many rivers that helped wear down the Appalachians. During the last Ice Age it was blocked by glaciers near what is now Chillicothe, Ohio, and was generally replaced by the Ohio after the ice melted. The result of the damming was a great lake extending nearly 200 miles from the ice gorge to just above where the Gauley and New rivers merge to form the Kanawha. After the lake was filled, it overflowed near present Portsmouth, Ohio, and initiated a new channel to establish the present course of the Kanawha from Nitro to Point Pleasant where it enters the Ohio.

The earliest known inhabitants of the Kanawha River valley were the Paleo-Indians, nomadic big game hunters who occupied the area at least 14,000 years ago. Several other cultures followed these early immigrants, but the record is not extensive until the Adena Indians began to build their complex burial mounds along the Kanawha about 1000 B.C. They continued to occupy the area until about 1 A.D.

During 1883 to 1885, scientists from the Smithsonian Institution excavated some of the mounds. All of those investigated contained skeletons which had been buried in elaborate bark tombs along with exotic grave goods such as copper, mica, flint, shells, and shell beads. The artifacts recovered are in the Museum of Natural History in Washington, D.C.

The Armstrong Culture of 1 A.D. to 500 A.D. apparently represented a peaceful replacement of the Adenas. The main characteristic of this culture is their thin, orange-yellow pottery. Soon after 1000 A.D., stockaded villages were built in the valley by a people who cultivated corn, beans, and squash. These were permanent villages and had sizeable populations.

The first report by a white person of an Indian village along the Kanawha is probably that of Gabriel Arthur who, in 1674, was captured and taken to a village which he later described. Historians agree that the villagers were Shawnee and that the settlement was located along the Kanawha near the present town of Buffalo.

By about 1700 the valley was apparently empty of all but transient Indians. There is no assigned reason for the abandonment of the valley, but the finding of European trade goods from this time period is thought to indicate that European diseases, for which the Indians had no immunity, caused their demise. The powerful Iroquois nation controlled the region, but did not actively occupy it. However, in return for hunting rights granted by the Iroquois, the Shawnee kept white settlers from moving into the area until the late eighteenth century.

The end of Indian dominance opened the Kanawha Valley for travel and settlement. The first cabin was one built in 1771 by Simon Kenton and partners near where the Elk River enters the Kanawha, but it stood alone for several years. In 1788 the first settlement that can in any way be called permanent was established by George Clendenin at the mouth of the Elk River on the site of present Charleston. It was called Fort Lee, after Governor Henry Lee of Virginia, and in 1789, when Kanawha County was established, it had thirty inhabitants. It continued to attract population and was chartered as Charles Town by the Virginia Assembly on December 4, 1794. The name was later changed to Charleston by general agreement to avoid postal problems with a town of the same name in the eastern part of the state. Settlements were being made all along the river by this time, although the valley was still wild. The last passenger pigeon known in the area was killed near Winfield in 1895.

There are no records of transportation on the Kanawha until General Andrew Lewis, in 1774, constructed canoes at the mouth of the Elk to use in freighting his men and supplies to the mouth of the river for the upcoming battle with the Shawnee Chief Cornstalk. The Shawnee defeat at Point Pleasant greatly helped open the western territories for settlement.

By 1808 log rafts held together with hickory poles and loaded with salt were floated down the Kanawha to the western territories. But the Kanawha was a placid stream made up of long pools, from eight to twenty feet deep, separated by shoals over which only two to three feet of water flowed except during times of flooding. These shoals prevented the river from being used extensively except for about eight months of the year. It was not until January, 1821, during a flood, that the *Andrew Donnally* became the first steam boat to reach Charleston.

The making of salt was a constantly increasing activity when the Virginia Assembly of 1820–1821 authorized improvement of the river to a minimum three foot depth throughout the year. As the salt works continued to flourish, flatboats were constructed, loaded with salt and floated to Cincinnati where both the barge and the salt were sold. As the river was improved, the flatboats were made larger until some were 160 feet long by 50 feet wide. These larger barges could carry up to 2,000 barrels of salt weighing from 280 to 350 pounds each or a load of approximately 300 tons per barge. The building of barges soon became a second very profitable enterprise in the Charleston area. In 1829, 300 flatboats were constructed for about $400 each and 200 coopers were kept busy making thousands of barrels.

In 1837 the passenger steamboat *Tuckahoe* began regularly scheduled runs between Charleston and Cincinnati. In 1845 packets between Charleston and Gallipolis began daily service that continued until the Civil War. After the war West Virginia, as a new state, created a Kanawha River Board which operated two dredges and collected tolls. Additional improvements were not undertaken until the federal government, after listening to pleas from the salt and coal producers along the river, appropriated $25,000 in 1872 for developing a reservoir and sluice system for the river. It did not work.

In March, 1875, it was decided to construct eleven locks and dams to provide a channel with a minimum six-foot depth. Construction of the system was started in September, 1875. On June 4, 1881, the Board of Public Works for the state of West Virginia surrendered full control of the Kanawha to the United States. The entire series of dams and locks was completed in 1898. In that year the river carried more than a million tons of coal and 50,000 tons of merchandise and farm products. Dams 4 and 5, completed in 1880, were the first moveable dams for slack water improvement to be built in America. By the 1930s the government had created a minimum nine-foot channel on the Ohio, and many industrialists felt that the Kanawha should be similarly upgraded.

Congressional approval was forthcoming, and by January, 1938, the river level had been raised to accommodate a nine-foot channel. The Kanawha now carries about 14 million tons of freight annually, though rail and highway shipping still dominate the valley's transportation network as they have since the first railroad was completed through the area in January, 1873.

The first reference to industry along the Kanawha was by Mary Ingles, a Shawnee captive, who, after escaping, reported being taken to a salt seep where salt was being made by the Indians. This was in July, 1755, and was near the Burning Spring at Malden, a salt seep where natural gas escaped in quantity and which could be ignited at any time. George Washington once owned the spring and wrote about it in his journal.

The salt industry in the valley actually started, however, when Elisha Brooks set up a furnace near the mouth of Campbell's Creek in 1797. His production averaged about 150 pounds per day and he sold it for ten cents a pound.

The techniques used to make salt were not changed until Joseph Ruffner's sons, in obedience to their father's dying wish, entered the business. After rejecting several plans, they decided to search for more concentrated brine by digging a deep well, a completely new approach. They deepened a hole to bedrock and then drilled a hole in the rock with a hammer and steel drill. Upon reaching the limits of this technique, they attached a long iron drill fitted with a steel chisel bit to a spring pole and drilled even deeper by bouncing the spring pole up and down. After eighteen months, the first salt well ever drilled in the United States and probably the first drilled well in the world was in operation.

Horse mills were soon developed for pumping brine, but by 1827 horsepower had given way to steam power. Tinsmiths soon replaced the crude string-wrapped wooden pipes with tin ones and later, in turn, used copper, iron, and finally steel. A production of more than two million bushels was maintained for twenty years, with a peak production in excess of three million bushels in 1846.

It was in 1817 that John Turner opened the first coal mine along the Kanawha near Burning Springs and began to sell it for fuel to the salt works. By this time, the surrounding hills had been totally denuded of trees, all having been cut as fuel for the furnaces.

Drilling for salt also produced the first natural gas well in the world when gas was struck in Charleston in 1815. It was not, however, until 1841, when William Tompkins hit gas while drilling for brine, that it was piped and used as fuel for the evaporators and pumps.

In 1836 Colonel Aaron Stockton shipped coal on the Kanawha from Cannelton to Cincinnati. By 1855 the barging of coal was a regular thing. Today, when shipments aggregate about 14 million tons, the number one item is coal, followed in second place by chemicals and then by sand and gravel. Another industry which sprang up along the river in the middle nineteenth century was the production of "coal" oil. One factory at Cannelton, in operation from 1848 to 1861, extracted 1,500 gallons of oil each day from canneloid coal (a bituminous coal that burns with a bright flame), getting up to sixty gallons per ton of coal. The product cost fifteen cents per gallon to produce and sold for eighty-five cents. The cannel oil market vanished after the drilling for petroleum using tools developed to drill for salt proved successful in 1859.

The salt industry led to other chemical industries in the valley. In 1914 a major company established a chemical plant at South Charleston to manufacture bromine and magnesium chloride from salt. In the 1930s the manufacture of chlorine began. Another chemical process of note began on the lower Elk River when the first petrochemical plant was built in 1920. A still newer industry along the river is that of generating power from coal mined nearby.

The Kanawha has been of inestimable value to West Virginia since the earliest settlers arrived. The banks were lined with the finest of hardwood forests from which they could construct their homes and the waters teemed with bass, musky, walleye, brook trout, and catfish. The bottomland soils were good for agriculture, the adjacent hills contained coal deposits, and the river provided transportation for the numerous products produced by the state's citizens. The world-famous chemical industry, based upon the salt deposits under the valley, is the most important manufacturing industry. When everything is considered, it is impossible to imagine that a single river and valley could do any more

for a state than has the Kanawha over the years for West Virginia.

FURTHER READING: James Morton Callaghan, *Semi-Centennial History of West Virginia* (1913). V. B. Harris, *Great Kanawha* (1974).

William H. Gillespie

The Kankakee River

Source: A wet, boggy basin near South Bend, Indiana
Length: 225 miles
Tributaries: Iroquois River
Mouth: Joins Des Plaines River to form the Illinois near Joliet
Agricultural Products: Livestock, grain
Industries: Furniture, food processing

Descriptions of the Kankakee River by the early French explorers remind us of how much modern life has transformed the terrain of the Middle West. Father Louis Hennepin, paddling downriver in 1679 with the Sieur de La Salle and Henry de Tonty, described the Kankakee—called by Hennepin the Seignelay and by the Indians the Theakiki—as rising "in a plain in the midst of much boggy land, over which it is not easy to walk. . . . The River Seignelay is navigable for canoes to within a hundred paces of its source, and it increases to such an extent in a short time that it is almost as broad and deep as the Marne. It takes its course through vast marshes, where it winds about so, though its current is pretty strong, that after sailing on it for a whole day we sometimes found that we had not advanced more than two leagues in a straight line." As far as they could see, Hennepin added, "nothing was to be seen but marshes full of flags and alders." Today the marshes have been drained and the river straightened and farms have replaced the wilderness. But not without cost: wildlife has disappeared and flooding is a constant problem.

The Kankakee rises near South Bend, Indiana, in wet, boggy ground amidst which are three defined basins or small pools. The river flows 225 miles southwest and then west, finally joining the Des Plaines River near Joliet to form the Illinois.

Its strange name is an adaptation of the Indian word Theakiki, corrupted by the French Canadians to Kiakiki. That word meant "wolf," but according to the Frenchman Pierre Charlevoix, writing in 1721, this may have referred to an Indian tribe called the Mahingans who were also called Wolves. One authority has counted at least seventeen spellings of Kankakee and as many origins and meanings, from "wolf" to "swampy place" to "wonderful land." Kankakeeans prefer fur trader Gordon Hubbard's definition: "Ti - yar - ack - nauk: wonderful homeland."

There are 5,300 miles in the Kankakee Basin of which 3,140 are in northern Indiana. From the river's source to the Indiana-Illinois line is about seventy-five miles if measured in a straight line, but before the dredging programs got under way the river twisted and turned for a total of 240 miles in reaching that point. The reason for this swampy expanse of land through which the river meandered was a limestone arch near the state line above the town of Momence, Illinois. Until it was broken with the digging of the Williams ditch this limestone prevented the wearing down of the river bed, thus interfering with drainage and resulting in the vast, swampy region that constitutes the Indiana portion of the Kankakee system.

After the river passes by Momence it falls another twenty-five feet before receiving the waters of its tributary, the Iroquois, which flows in from the south at Aroma Park. From there, until it converges with the Des Plaines, it falls another 103 feet. The rapids near Altorf and Wilmington cause a sudden descent as the Kankakee drains its broad valley into the Illinois and thence into the Mississippi.

The Kankakee Valley was formed during the prehistoric ice ages when, with each retreat of the great ice sheets, moraines (long rounded ridges of soil, rocks, and sand) were formed. A series of these moraines crossed present northeastern Illinois in long arc-shapes and acted as dams, trapping great amounts of water from the melting ice. Weak spots in the moraines gave way, letting water form new paths. As the centuries passed much of the water drained away leaving long stretches of sand alternating with rich, black loam in which the lush prairie grass thrived.

Anthropologists believe the region has been occupied almost continuously from Paleolithic times, when primitive man speared mastodons there, until the present. When the whites arrived the Indians considering the Kankakee Valley their home were the Pottawatomis. They are believed to have settled in the valley sometime after 1700.

It is probable that the first whites on the stream were Father Jacques Marquette and his party who, in the spring of 1675, left Kaskaskia on the Mississippi for the St. Ignace Mission on the north side of the Straits of Michilimackinac (now better known as Mackinac). The party paddled up the Mississippi to the Illinois, up that river to the Kaskaskia, and up it to its source. Then Father Marquette's party trekked across a short portage, well known to the Indians, northeastward until they reached the St. Joseph River. Here they launched their canoes and paddled upstream to the river's mouth on the southeast shore of Lake Michigan.

In the autumn of 1833, in a treaty signed at Chicago, the Indians signed away their claim to the Kankakee country. However, its swampy terrain and the river's treacherousness curtailed settlement. Pioneers from the northeast ad-

vanced via the Great Lakes and northern Ohio and settled north of the Kankakee, while homeseekers from southern Indiana, Virginia, and Kentucky, settled south of the river valley. The few who first settled in the region were half hunters and half farmers. Especially did they avoid the area between Momence, Illinois, and Shelby, Indiana, which was known as the Beaver Lake region or as the Great Kankakee Marsh. There was simply too much grassy prairieland, too much swampland, for settlers accustomed to living in timbered country to accept. Wood was essential to the pioneers for fuel, for building homes and furniture and fences. Early pioneers believed that the prairie drinking water was no good. Prairie sod was hard to turn; the grass and roots were tough. Yet, after the Black Hawk War (1832) settlers began moving into the country.

Because it was a treacherous river the dozen or so fords across the Kankakee were heavily used and frequently resulted in forts, pioneer settlements, and finally towns growing at their sites. In LaPorte County, Indiana (the county next west from the city of South Bend), was the Pottawatomi Ford; in 1848 a toll bridge was built just above the ford, and when it burned, ferry service replaced it. The ford at Momence, Illinois, was used heavily by people driving their livestock, hogs and even turkeys, to the Chicago market. In 1834 the Illinois legislature approved funds for a road from Vincennes to Chicago which crossed the Kankakee above Momence. At various times that ford was known as the Upper Crossing, Westport, Hills Ford, and Lorain. Other fords were Sho-bar Crossing and Kaler Ford.

Commercial boat traffic on the Kankakee was of relatively short duration. In 1853, shortly after the Illinois Central reached the town of Kankakee (about thirty miles south of Joliet), a power boat (a flat-bottomed stern-wheeler whose power was supplied by two horses on a treadmill) was put into commission between Kankakee and the village of Aroma; it carried both passengers and freight. By the 1870s boats were coming from Chicago to Hanford's Landing, twelve miles below Kankakee. A charter was granted to the Illinois and Michigan Canal Company to open up the Kankakee. Locks and an aqueduct which crossed the Des Plaines River carried Kankakee waters into the canal system and made navigation from one river to the other possible. When ice carried away a dam at Wilmington in the winter of 1883 commercial navigation on the Kankakee halted and, with the competition of the railroads, it was never revived. Pleasure barges and some excursion steamboats still operated on the river into the 1890s. In winter skating parties ranged from Kankakee to Aroma and horse-drawn sleighs raced on the ice.

The tragedy of the Kankakee is what unthinking civilized man did to the tens of thousands of acres of swamps and bayous extending from Momence, Illinois, eastward, spreading over a wide expanse of northern Indiana. Here were stretches of open water, oak crowned islands, marshes thick with cattails, wild rice, and rushes. Millions of migratory birds nested in the region. The Miamis, Wyandottes, Illinois, Pottawotamis, and Kankakees hunted there but never upset the ecological balance. Especially abundant with game was the Beaver Lake country and the Black Marsh northeast of it, in Newton County, south of the Kankakee and hugging the Illinois border.

Then came white "sportsmen" who slaughtered the wild fowl and deer. Counterfeiters, horse thieves, and murderers hid out on Little Bogus and Big Bogus islands. Finally in the early 1900s, a Chicago furniture manufacturer bought all the available standing timber in the region, but only a few of the thousands of trees that were cut ever reached market; most were left to rot along the river.

As early as 1853 the state of Indiana undertook to reclaim a portion of the swamp by digging a drainage ditch, but it was not considered successful. Plans continued, however, and in a piecemeal way, the lakes and marshes were drained. Beaver Lake was drained in 1902. By 1917 the river was well on the way to being straightened and much of what had been marshland had become farmland. As for the wildlife that had used the region, its food, the wild rice, celery, duck potatoes, and other grasses and weeds were gone. The sandhill cranes, herons, ducks, and geese now fly over the region without stopping. And the thoughtless drainage left other problems.

A study completed in 1976 emphasized that the difficulties of flooding, soil erosion, and the need for adequate drainage for about 439,000 acres of existing cropland had not yet been solved. Solutions range from blowing out the rock ledge near Momence and rechanneling about 340 miles of the river and its tributaries, to restoring about 13,000 acres of what was once the flood plain. Yet opposition is so great that no plan is likely to be approved.

Something needs to be done, however, and eventually measures will be taken to undo what man has done. The "Grand Marsh," once a mecca for hunters and the hunted, has been destroyed; the call of the loon is but an echo in the wind. Nature's sponge, which had absorbed water slowly during the wet seasons and slowly relinquished it during the dry, keeping the Kankakee at a more uniform level, is now periodically flooded as the river attempts to return to its old path. Indiana farmers want to remove flood water quickly so they can plant their crops, while Illinois residents do not want to be flooded; environmentalists in both states want the Kankakee restored to its more or less natural state as a clean river that can have many recreational uses.

FURTHER READING: Fay Folsom Nichols, *The Kankakee* (1965). Burt E. Burroughs, *Tales of an Old "Border Town" and Along the Kankakee* (1925).

Ann Ferris

The Kentucky River

Source: Southeast Kentucky where North and Middle forks join near St. Helens
Length: 259 miles
Tributaries: South Fork, Dix, Red, and Elkhorn rivers
Mouth: Into Ohio at Carrolton, midway between Cincinnati and Louisville
Agricultural Products: Burley tobacco, hay, pork, grain
Industries: Coal, lumber, race horses, bourbon distilling

The Kentucky River originates in the mountains near the Kentucky-Virginia border, cuts a deep channel as it flows northwest through the Bluegrass, flows by the graves of Daniel and Rebecca Boone at Frankfort, the state capital, and empties into the Ohio at Carrollton, midway between Cincinnati and Louisville. Compared to the other major rivers which flow through or around the state—the Cumberland, the Tennessee, the Ohio and the Mississippi—the Kentucky is neither as large nor as famous. It flows from its sources to its mouth relatively uninhibited by modern technology much as it did when the area was a wilderness battleground for warring tribes from Tennessee and Ohio.

The three forks which form the upper reaches of the Kentucky spring up in the Cumberland Mountains in the southeast part of the state. The North Fork begins near the town of McRoberts, the Middle and the South forks on the western base of Pine Mountain. A lacework of branches, creeks and smaller rivers with names as picturesque as the mountaineers who live along them feed the three forks. Big Laurel, Greasy Creek, Troublesome, Red Bird, Cutshin, Upper and Lower Devil, Hell-for-Certain—these are the names which serve the mountain people much as street signs do city dwellers. Willie Sandlin, who won the Congressional Medal of Honor in World War I for bayoneting two dozen German machine gunners at Blois-des-Forges, brought glory and honor to Devel-Jump Branch on Hell-for-Certain Creek on the Middle Fork.

Along these mountain reaches of the Kentucky, violence is a way of life. With the powerful moonshine whiskey stirred into an already explosive mixture of Celtic, German, and Viking blood, the mountaineer has a tendency to settle all personal grievances with a deadly vengeance. The Middle Fork which flows through an almost inaccessible, sparsely settled countryside, has been relatively peaceful. But the waters of both the North and South forks have reverberated again and again to the sound of gunfire as mountaineers fought to the death in feuds, moonshine wars, and union battles.

The feuds, which raged for generations along the North and South forks of the Kentucky, were the legacy of the divisions caused by the Civil War. They began soon after Appomattox and lasted well into the twentieth century. The area around Troublesome Creek, which joins the North Fork in Breathitt County, became known nationally as "Bloody Breathitt." On the upper Troublesome, most of the population enlisted behind either "Cap" Hays, an ex-Confederate cavalryman, or Clabe Jones, a former Union guerrilla leader, to fight what became known as the "Knott County War." During this bloody continuation of the Civil War, six men died in a single exchange of gunfire at what is now Hindman, the county seat of Knott County. As late as 1921 at Clayhole in Bloody Breathitt, the right of a woman to vote in a local school board election was challenged, and in the ensuing gunfight nine men were shot to death and six badly wounded. Along the South Fork and its tributaries, Goose Creek and the Red Bird, and in the dusty streets of tiny Manchester, the county seat of Clay County, men died year after year in what was known as the "White-Baker War."

The moonshine wars began after the passage of the Volstead Act in 1919. The Kentucky River has always been associated with whiskey making. On the lower river the whiskey makers are licensed distillers responsible for such famous brands of bourbon as Bond and Lillard; they were closed during prohibition. But on the upper Kentucky where the three forks reach like bony fingers into the heart of the mountains, the whiskey makers have always been moonshiners. Some make straight corn liquor, but most make what is known as "sugar-top." When national prohibition came, they armed themselves with heavy-caliber pistols, high-powered rifles, and repeating shotguns loaded with buckshot, and prepared to defend their livelihood. The war between the mountaineers and law enforcement officials was savage. One small group of federal agents alone destroyed 365 stills in 1921 in eastern Kentucky. But the price was fearsome. Thirty-five federal agents died in these wars, and among local police who tried to enforce the law, the toll was higher. During the four-year term of one Letcher County sheriff, sixteen deputies were shot to death. Yet, despite the physical force of the federal and state governments and the moral force of the Fundamentalist Drys who preach against whiskey as the root of all evil, the moonshiner still flourishes along the upper Kentucky.

The union wars are a modern phenomenon which grew out of the ruthless economic exploitation of the mountains. During the first decades of the twentieth century, the mountain people along the upper Kentucky lived much as they had a century ago. But all around them, in the enormous stands of virgin timber which cloaked their stills and in the huge seams of coal beneath the ground over which they waged their feuds, was a wealth defying the imagination. Exploitation of the fantastic timber resources (one surviving giant felled in 1937 measured over eleven feet in diameter) began shortly after the Civil War but caused no drastic change in either the mountain people or the river; indeed, the latter played a major role until after the turn of the century. Outsiders, ranging from individual speculators to mammoth corporations based in Pittsburgh and Detroit, bought up for a pittance the timber rights and sometimes the mineral rights from the illiterate mountain folk. The timber was cut, the logs branded on their butt with the owner's mark and collected in booms. When the river rose sufficiently, the logs were locked together in rafts a hundred feet long and floated downriver to Frankfort and other mill sites. On a good freshet as many as 15,000 logs an hour might rush by Beattyville where the final juncture of the forks occurs. Like his cowhand counterparts who trailed the great herds along the western cattle trails, the mountaineer logger on the Kentucky became a legend. He

braved the natural and sometimes formidable hazards of the river, fought off thieves and other enemies, drank and brawled his way through the red light districts of Frankfort and other mill towns and, if he survived all this, began the long trek home to begin all over again.

On the eve of World War I, the railroads arrived in the mountains. The tracks followed the natural routes, the major rivers of the area. As everything else in the mountains of the upper Kentucky, the railroads brought with them their own particular brand of violence. Most of the contractors were from the deep South and used gangs of Negroes to lay the rails. Mountaineers who had sided with the Union but had never seen a Negro now worked side by side with the blacks. Under these conditions, violence inevitably attended every weekend. Black killed black and local officials ignored the homicides; whites killed blacks with virtual impunity. One contractor was famous for having killed a black on almost every Monday morning.

In the first half of the twentieth century the mountaineers were reduced to a status of bondage. The railroads made possible the ravaging of the mountains. The timber went quickly; coal was to be king. The coal owners owned the countryside. Railway tracks lined one bank or the other of the streams feeding the Kentucky; towns grew up overnight. Through booms and busts of a capricious economic system that hurt the poor most, the mountaineer was chained beneath the land he had always thought his own.

During the New Deal phase of the Great Depression, John L. Lewis and the United Mine Workers of America began the drive to organize miners along the upper reaches of the Kentucky. Harlan County, the westernmost part of which drains into the South and Middle forks of the Kentucky River, now earned the title of "Bloody Harlan." In the Battle of Evarts in 1931, three company policemen and one miner died. The companies submitted finally—at least, legally—but the union conflicts go on. When they rage, high-power rifles and dynamite prevail. The stranger must be wary.

The cheap coal which fueled the nation destroyed the upper reaches of the Kentucky. The three forks have been turned into sewers carrying coal dust and eroded soil. The mountaineers living along these reaches, the proud men John Fox, Jr., described in romantic fiction such as *Little Shepherd of Kingdom Come* and *Trail of the Lonesome Pine*, have been changed into the stereotype hillbilly living on welfare and useless to the modern world.

Before leaving the mountains, the three forks join, the North and Middle forks at St. Helens, the South a few miles downstream at Beattyville. The last major mountain tributary, the Red River, joins at the point where Estill, Clark, and Madison counties meet. The Kentucky is now ready for its run through the Bluegrass, a region contrasting as vividly with the Highlands as a color photograph with a black and white print. The "great Kentucky prairie" some called the rolling sea of grass which in its advanced stage of pollination causes a bluish haze to hang over it. Here, the Kentucky and its major tributary, the Dix River (originally spelled Dick's) cut magnificent gorges deep into the limestone to create the renowned Palisades. Just before entering the knobby, hilly area along the Ohio, the Elkhorn River, the last major tributary, joins the Kentucky.

The permanent settlement of Kentucky began on the eve of the Revolutionary War in the Bluegrass, and the Kentucky River played a central role. A bitter rivalry for the area existed between Virginians and North Carolinians. The former, led by James Harrod and George Rogers Clark, planted the first settlement, Harrodsburg, on the upper reaches of the Salt River near the Kentucky in 1774. But a year later, Judge Richard Henderson and a group of North Carolinians formed the Transylvania Land Company and for ten thousand dollars' worth of gewgaws and trade goods bought the Kentucky region from the Cherokees at Sycamore Shoals on the Watauga River at what is now Elizabethton, Tennessee. With Boone leading the vanguard, Henderson established Boonesborough on the Kentucky in 1775 not far from where the spectacular Clays Ferry Bridges, reputed to be the highest in the United States east of the Mississippi, carry Interstate 75 over the Kentucky River gorge. While Henderson and his Transylvania Company failed, Boonesboro survived.

Meanwhile the storm of the revolution burst over the little settlements of "Kentuck." During the negotiations at Sycamore Shoals, the young Cherokee chieftain Dragging Canoe warned the whites that Kentucky was a "dark and bloody ground." Events in the early years of settlement were to prove him a prophet, for violence between Indians and whites was almost a daily occurrence. Happy endings were few, such as Boone's rescue from the Indians of his daughter and the Callaway sisters, for the war in the West was a grim one. In 1778 Boone was captured and adopted by the Shawnee chief, Black Fish, but escaped and successfully led the defense of Boonesborough in the seige that followed. In the same year George Rogers Clark disrupted English-Indian activities north of the Ohio. Thereafter, the war moved northward. After the war the influx of settlers into the homelands of the northern and southern tribes reduced them to fighting for their very existence. Once the no-man's land reserved for fighting and hunting, Kentucky was left in peace.

From earliest times the lands of the middle and upper Kentucky were famous for their rich soil. Settlers poured in after the Revolution and farming flourished. Until the railroad era, the river system provided the main avenue of trade; for the farmers of the central part of the state, the Kentucky was the vital link by which they transported their hams, flour, whiskey, and other produce to New Orleans. Curd's, Scotts, and Shrylock's Ferries, and Frankfort became river ports. From there, keelboats floated down the Ohio, braved the treacherous falls at what is now Louisville and the droves of pirates that infested the river, then made the long, one-way run down the Mississippi.

Steamboats replaced keelboats shortly after the War of 1812. For almost half a century, a fleet of steamboats plied the river, loaded with produce for the growing mercantile centers of Cincinnati and Louisville and carrying famous Kentuckians and equally famous racehorses.

Since the Civil War, the region has become known for its burley tobacco—thin-leafed and light-colored—and its thoroughbred racehorses. America's growing addiction to cigarette smoking provided the impetus for the first industry; the horse, Lexington, foaled in 1850 on Dr. Elisha Warfield's farm on the Elkhorn Creek tributary of the Kentucky, marked the beginning of the second. At the time Dr. Warfield, who was primarily a breeder, sold the colt to a sportsman, the deep South had a monopoly on thoroughbred racing. Haughty challenges were sent upstarts. Lexington's new owner accepted and took the horse to New Orleans. In seven famous races the Kentucky horse vanquished the best horses the Old South could produce, losing only once but then, in the rematch, beating his former victor so decisively that no challengers were left. Lexington's progeny continued to build Kentucky's fame as a thoroughbred state. By 1880 Lexington-sired colts had earned nearly a million and a quarter dollars.

The Kentucky River drains the two most famous regions in the state—the Highlands and the Bluegrass—and a certain aura of romance still lingers over it. But the future of the river is not bright. Even before strip mining had begun to rip apart the ground cover of its watershed in the eastern mountains, the Kentucky at times—as any other river in the natural order of things—had been dangerous. A flood in 1937 destroyed portions of Frankfort. In 1939, Frozen

Creek, which feeds the North Fork in Breathitt County, rose so rapidly that an entire village and fifty-one of its inhabitants were swept to destruction. By our order, ruthless exploitation—in Harry Caudill's phrase, "the rape of the Cumberlands"—still prevails on the headwaters of the Kentucky. The results can only be disastrous. "Democracies favor expediency over form," Alexis de Toqueville wrote of America in the 1830s when the Kentucky's waters were pure enough to distill whiskey and the watershed was dense, virgin forest. A century and a half later, the upper reaches of the river are polluted with coal dust and laden with silt; the run-off area is stripped naked. Today, the Kentucky River is paying the price for flowing through a democracy.

FURTHER READING: Leland D. Baldwin, *The Keelboat Age on Western Waters* (1941). Harry M. Caudill, *Night Comes to the Cumberlands* (1962).

Ronnie Day

The Kiskiminetas-Conemaugh River

Sources: Conemaugh rises near Cresson, Pennsylvania; Kiskiminetas formed by convergence of Conemaugh and Loyalhanna rivers at Saltsburg, Pennsylvania
Length: Conemaugh c. 82 miles; Kiskiminetas, c. 26 miles
Tributaries: Little Conemaugh, South Fork, Stoney Creek; Loyalhanna for the Conemaugh; Blacklegs Creek and Beaver Run for the Kiskiminetas
Mouth: Kiskiminetas into the Allegheny River opposite Freeport
Agricultural Products: Vegetables, livestock
Industries: Coal mining, steel mills, timber

Although the Kiskiminetas-Conemaugh River of south-western Pennsylvania is just 108 miles long, it is rich in history. It served as an early highway to the American West and one of its floods caused the second largest disaster in American history.

Its principal artery, the Little Conemaugh,

rises on the western slope of the Alleghenies near their summit. Less than sixty yards from its source are the headwaters of the east-flowing West Branch of the Susquehanna. The Little Conemaugh flows west and south, is joined by the South Fork, and finally merges with Stoney Creek at Johnstown, where it becomes simply the Conemaugh. Flowing westward past Blairsville it joins Loyalhanna Creek at Saltsburg, at this point becoming the Kiskiminetas (an Indian name possibly meaning "cut spirit" or perhaps "make daylight"). For twenty-six miles (of a total of 108) the Kiski, as it is called locally, continues, northwest past Apollo and Leechburg and finally entering the Allegheny at Freeport. The Kiski's principal tributaries are Blacklegs Creek from the north and Beaver Run from the south.

Before 10,000 B.C. forests along the stream provided shelter for the Paleo-Indian culture and its successors, the Monongahela people. By 1656 the Iroquois had taken over and had made all of western Pennsylvania their hunting ground. In the 1700s the Delaware and Shawnee, pushed westward by white encroachment, lived there by permission of the Iroquois.

Fur traders found luxurious vegetation along the river, including wild blueberries, blackberries, and intertwining strawberries. They found also deciduous forests, predominantly oak, with hickory, poplar, chestnut, and walnut interspersed. Sugar maples provided sugar and syrup upon which the tribesmen and early settlers depended as a commodity of trade.

Certainly one of the first white men to enter the region was Christopher Gist, who on November 14, 1750 came to Loyalhannon, a Delaware town in an area which today is Ligonier. From the valley of the Loyalhanna he followed the river to its confluence with the Conemaugh which, as the Kiskiminetas, he then followed to the Allegheny. A few years later (1758) General John Forbes built a military road from Carlisle to Pittsburgh, and on this road at Ligonier he built a fort.

The earliest white settlers were mostly German, Scotch-Irish, English and Welsh. Robert Hanna, an Irishman, founded Hannas Town near Crabtree Creek, a Loyalhanna tributary. A year before the Declaration of Independence, on May 16, 1775, the settlers under the leadership of General Arthur St. Clair drew up the Hannas Town Resolves to resist British tyranny. On July 13, 1782, the town was attacked by a group of Senecas and British Regulars—one of the last border raids during the Revolution. Except for the courthouse-tavern, the fort, and one other dwelling, the entire town was burned.

Nearby where the river cuts its way through Laurel Hill and Chestnut Ridge is Packsaddle Gap, the deepest gorge in the Alleghenies. It still harbors a legendary ghost which seems to tarry in the mist at certain times of the night. When rival gangs of Irish and Scotch-Irish workers built a section of the Pennsylvania Railroad across the pass, tempers flared and erupted into fistfights resulting in no reported fatalities but in many a "broken head." The first road bridge on the Conemaugh was built in 1829 but lasted just one day, falling of its own weight overnight.

The first keelboat on the river was built by

Isaac Proctor in 1816 on the banks of Stoney Creek. The first steamboat to travel on the Kiski, the *New Castle*, ascended the river from Freeport to Leechburg in 1838, demonstrating that the stream was navigable for such craft.

Between 1826 and 1834 the state constructed the Pennsylvania Main Line Canal which extended to Pittsburgh from the Susquehanna at Columbia (with a rail connection to Philadelphia). The westward portion of this link followed the upper reaches of the Conemaugh on a "beautiful stone aqueduct," the piers of which were later incorporated in a Pennsylvania Railroad bridge.

At Tunnelton, east of Saltsburg, a tunnel carried the canal through a hill cutting out a loop of the Conemaugh. On the west side an aqueduct 412 feet in length spanned the Conemaugh with five stone arches. Proceeding downriver the canal reached Freeport, a depot for eastern goods being shipped to northwestern Pennsylvania. Here it crossed the Allegheny River on a large aqueduct.

Canalboats were built at Leechburg. Apollo was an important shipping center at the time of the canal. A feeder for the artery known as the Western Reservoir was begun in 1838 at South Fork above Johnstown; it took fifteen years to complete. Constructed to supply the canal during dry seasons, it contained 430 million cubic feet of water. The reservoir embankment was 931 feet long and 72 feet high—one of the largest earthen dams in the world at that time.

The Pennsylvania Railroad, completed to Pittsburgh in 1851, rendered the canal obsolete. Descending the western slope of the mountains by the Conemaugh Valley into Johnstown, the railroad continues across a seven-arched stone bridge and follows the river to Blairsville, an early canal town.

Even before the canal era the Conemaugh Valley had become an industrial area. Lumbering was carried on at Conemaugh Borough, Conemaugh Station, and Nineveh. Bundles of staves were shipped to the West Indies to be made into casks for rum to be sent back to America. Lumbering reached its peak in 1861. In addition to sawmills, the valley provided water, and hemlock bark for tanneries; power for grist and woolen mills; and salt from wells drilled in the Kiski Valley around 1800. By 1828 there were thirty wells at the Great Conemaugh Salt Works, a village two miles east of Saltsburg.

The valley possessed vast deposits of iron ore, coal, and limestone—all the ingredients for making iron and steel. In very early days charcoal furnaces were constructed near the streams since waterpower was needed to work the bellows and produce the air blast. Slag banks still bear witness to this industry.

The first iron forge at Johnstown was built in 1809. George S. King, known as the father of the iron industry in this area, organized the Cambria Iron Works there in 1852. During the Civil War iron plate and other munitions were made at this mill, and the first thirty-foot Bessemer steel rails in America were produced here in 1867. Cambria Iron was the largest producer in the country (perhaps in the world) by 1873, though by 1876 the J. Edgar Thompson works at Braddock had passed steel production at Johnstown. A subsidiary of the Cambria factory, Gautier Steel barbed wire works, was built above

1889 Johnstown Flood. Views of destruction and debris at and near Stone Railroad Bridge at confluence of Conemaugh River and Stony Creek at Johnstown. (Credit: Carnegie Library, Pittsburgh.)

Johnstown. Down the left bank of the Kiski, Vandergrift, a model industrial town, was founded in the early 1900s by Colonel Jacob J. Vandergrift, a wealthy steamship owner, clergyman, and industrialist.

A history of the river would not be complete without including its disasters. The first recorded flood in the area was in 1808. Another in 1811 washed out the Cambria forge. There were numerous "pumpkin floods" between 1816 and 1820 when thousands of these vegetables bobbed downstream to Johnstown from upland farms when the river overflowed.

For years residents had shuddered to think what would happen if the South Fork Dam should break during a deluge. The dam, about sixteen miles above Johnstown, contained the old Western Reservoir of canal days, enlarged and later called Conemaugh Lake. Although the dam, which held back 20 million tons of water, was in disrepair, some believed that it was impregnable. But May 30 and 31, 1889—two "memorial days"—proved otherwise.

First there was an extreme rain storm—the worst in the history of western Pennsylvania. Johnstown was already inundated from one end to the other, with water ten feet deep in places. Then, around 3:00 P.M. on May 31, just as a Johnstown newspaper editor was writing:

> It is idle to speculate what would be the result if this tremendous body of water ... should be thrown into the already submerged valley of the Conemaugh ...

the fishing lake behind the old South Fork Dam was making its way to Johnstown, the dam having given way. When the water, filled with debris from towns on the flats above, hit Johnstown it almost wiped the community out of existence. The load came to a stop at the stone railroad bridge while the water rushed on down the valley, through Pack Saddle Gap, and on to the Allegheny. (Floating materials were discovered as far away as the Mississippi River.) The flood was the greatest news since Lincoln's assassination.

It was as if all the history of the valley came down at once upon Johnstown: wood and furnishings from shattered houses, railroad cars, locomotives and tracks, mills, trees, boulders, corpses, animals and thousands of feet of wire from the Gautier works that bound the mass into gigantic packages. Adding to the horror, a tremendous fire broke out in the debris piled high at the bridge, all of which had to be dynamited for removal.

Among the real heroines was Clara Barton, who brought in her newly formed Red Cross and stayed five months to help. The flood, which became a household word all over America, caused over 2,200 deaths with $17 million in property damage. Second to the Galveston tidal wave, it was the worst national disaster in American history.

During the ensuing year less dramatic floods occurred in the valley while more and more pressure was put on the government to act. Then on St. Patrick's Day in March, 1936, came the second most devastating flood in the area—also inundating Pittsburgh fifty-eight miles away. Although fewer than twenty-five deaths resulted, property damage was worse—estimated at $41 million.

Finally Congress passed Flood Control Acts in 1936 and 1938 which resulted in enlarging the river channel, protecting the banks with concrete, and relocating tracks and highways. The gigantic Loyalhanna (1942) and Conemaugh (1953) reservoirs below Johnstown were designed principally to control the flow of the river and protect Pittsburgh.

Yet the drama repeated itself again in July, 1977. The flood caused more than eighty deaths and untold millions of property damage; the water level was the highest ever. May such historical events never again occur in the Kiski-Conemaugh Valley.

FURTHER READING: Thomas J. Chapman, *The Valley of the Conemaugh* (1965). David G. McCullough, *The Johnstown Flood* (1968).

Helene Smith

The Little Tennessee River

Source: Mountains of northeastern Georgia
Length: 134 miles
Tributaries: Cullasaja, Nantahala, Tuckaseegee, Cheoah, and Tellico rivers
Mouth: Joins Tennessee near Fort Loudon Dam, Lenoir City, Tennessee
Agricultural Products: Vegetables as truck crops
Industries: Tourism

The valley of the Little Tennessee River still is largely a wild green world and the river itself, though many times yoked with dams, never has been tamed completely. For 134 miles northwest from the tip of Georgia through North Carolina and Tennessee it bounds over rocky ledges and gurgles along mossy rockbeds in its more shallow runs. Its waters are clear and sparkling, home to the trout and muskellunge, the darter and salamander, some species unknown elsewhere. It meets the larger Tennessee River near Fort Loudon Dam at Lenoir City in lower East Tennessee.

Of the 2,650 square miles this river drains, more than half is forest-covered with pockets untouched by saw or axe and largely unchanged in thirty million years. Some of the highest mountains in eastern America, among the oldest in the world, are here. For long stretches they tower more than a mile high. One long crest has seventeen peaks above 6,000 feet. The high country is home to the deer and black bear, the squirrel, the turkey, the beaver, and the raven.

This wilderness was saved by an unusual pattern of land ownership. In the river valley lie parts of three national forests (Chattahoochee, Nantahala, and Cherokee); roughly half the Great Smoky Mountains National Park; and sizeable reservations surrounding eighteen dams of the Aluminum Company of America and the Tennessee Valley Authority.

This is a land of small winding roads, often unpaved, and of isolated hamlets and small villages. Only one town, Madisonville, Tennessee, near the river's mouth, is large enough to be officially classified as urban by the Post Office Department. The area's population is overwhelmingly white and Anglo-Saxon. Though four-lane highways have come to some sections in the last two decades, the longest continuous thoroughfare within the valley is not a highway but a footpath—some 130 miles of the famed Appalachian Trail.

The Little Tennessee reaches into high country with tributaries that have beautiful names given them by Cherokee Indians, who first lived along them. Cullasaja, Nantahala, Tuckaseegee, Oconaluftee, Cheoah, and Tellico are the major streams. The Indians make the words roll like music when they speak them. The Little Tennessee became known to the whites as the "River of the Cherokees" because they had many towns along it. Here stood Chota, their sacred town, a place of refuge and safety in war.

During the white-Indian wars the English built palisaded Fort Loudon on the lower river as protection for their Cherokee allies against the French. Fort Loudon's four-year history (1756–1760) was one of government bungling and bloody intrigue. The Indians finally laid seige to it and, apparently in reprisal for white betrayals, massacred the garrison as they marched away under truce.

Indian legends abound along the Little Tennessee. They tell of a monster in the river; a huge bird, hovering over the mountains; a giant who left unintelligible writings on stone; a great rabbit who lived on Gregory Bald. But no legends are more dramatic than the true story of how these people befriended the whites, were used as pawns in white conflicts, gradually were divested of their lands, and finally in the 1830s were driven west by forced march, the "Trail of Tears."

In one story the Indians won. It involves Tsali, the Cherokee martyr who surrendered to a white firing squad so a remnant band of his people could remain in their mountains. Tsali, his wife, two sons, and a brother were marching under guard when a soldier prodded Tsali's wife with a bayonet. Tsali and his kinsmen killed the soldier, routed the others and fled to a holdout Indian band hiding in the hills. There, though facing starvation, the Indians held out until an offer came from General Winfield Scott. It promised a chance for the hunted Indians to remain in the hills if Tsali and his sons and brother surrendered to die. Standing in fresh-dug graves, unblindfolded, they faced their executioners. At the last minute the younger son, Washington, was spared; the band of a thousand Indians clung to their hills and to many Indian ways. Today in Cherokee, North Carolina, at a tribal owned theater, the Tsali story is told each summer in "Unto These Hills," one of the earliest and best of regional outdoor dramas.

In an unusual arrangement with the government, the Cherokee, numbering more than 6,000, still controls property on these lands along the Oconaluftee and Tuckaseegee rivers (tributaries of the Little Tennessee), and in the Snowbird Mountains. They foster the old arts of wood-carving, basket-making, blow-gun shooting, and the game of stickball—much rougher than football—and played with bodies bare except for a breech cloth. Though they speak English, the soft, musical Cherokee language is still spoken and Cherokee songs and dances are used at a big Indian Fair in October of each year.

In the little townships much Indianness is preserved. Indians bake bean bread. Some homes use the "kanonah," an ancient long-handled pestle, to pound corn grains into the right consistency. They drop corn in lye water and wash it in a basket sieve for hominy. The "last born medicine man," Amoneta Sequoyah, claimed his secrets were handed down by Tsali's surviving son, Washington. He had a steady practice until his death in 1981.

The terrain of the Little Tennessee is largely high country and the whites who first conquered it were a sturdy breed, resourceful and independent. They were the adventurers who were willing to risk mountain journeys with a mule or ox and a few belongings pulled on a wooden sled, usually made from bent trunks of the sourwood tree. No wagon could penetrate those early trails. A man's riches were a few iron tools and utensils to build a cabin, till soil and cook food. His woman worked beside him, in house and field. She bore his children and reared them, usually without seeing a doctor. So complete was the isolation that some women, once settled in their cabins, never again left the homestead area, even for a visit to parents. Game and fish were supplemented with corn from an angular plot hung on a hillside.

Many of these early homesteads were on land which became a part of the Great Smoky Mountains National Park in the 1930s. The Park Service has preserved some of the buildings in sites at Oconaluftee and Cades Cove for the benefit of moderns who find such spartan living hard to picture. Recently the Service returned to the first-settler custom of using sleds with wooden runners. It found them more suitable than modern equipment for trail maintenance in the wilderness.

Nowhere was the War Between the States more bitterly fought than in this Tennessee-North Carolina mountain country. Loyalties on both sides were strong. They cut through family and church ties, separating and dividing. Though the states officially were Confederate, sympathies in the mountains more often were with the Union. The most vicious type of guerrilla fighting raged. After the war the healing was slow. Isolation remained; there was little technological progress. The oxen behind a simple plow remained well into the twentieth century. Travel was mainly by boat or horse and the river crossings by ferry and ford.

The only exception to this primitive way of life, both before and after the war, was along the lower thirty miles of the river. This was like deep-south plantation country, cultivated by slaves prior to the War, and owned largely by those with early roots in South Carolina and Virginia. They had access to New Orleans through rafts that could reach the main riverway on a high freshet. Once in New Orleans, crews sold the plantation produce and broke up the rafts. Then they bought finery for house and family, and hauled it overland by ox-cart. Later steamboats could make the round trip.

Living here was enlivened by week-long house parties, horse racing, hunting, cockfighting, music making and dancing. Tutors taught the children. Among several prominent families there also was fierce feuding which lasted for decades causing death, heartache, and bitterness. The river remained the thoroughfare for all this culture. Not a single highway bridge crossed the forty miles until 1929. Ferries, one every few miles, operated until the 1960s.

Though there is little large-scale industry in the Little Tennessee Valley proper, its wild waters create hydroelectric power for the world's largest aluminum complex at Alcoa, Tennessee, just outside the watershed boundary. Starting in 1916 the Aluminum Company of America cut a railroad into this wild area to build Cheoah Dam, first of a series to harness the water riches of the Little Tennessee Valley. These include not only sheer drops that increase power obtainable from water flow, but also an annual rainfall of sixty inches, more than any area in the United States except that near Puget Sound. Alcoa continued to extend its dam network even into the smaller creeks. During the Second World War the Tennessee Valley Authority built Fontana, the highest dam east of the Rocky Mountains; its first power went out in 1945 to ease the critical needs at Oak Ridge, Tennessee, birthplace of the atomic bomb.

Waters of Fontana Lake covered what had been profitably mined copper deposits at two sites, Hazel and Eagle Creeks. Mica was another mineral which was mined extensively in north Georgia and western North Carolina until after World War II. Cheaper imported material caused the industry to all but disappear. In the earliest days the preparation of sheet mica, used as "isinglass" in such items as oil stove windows and button-on automobile curtains, was a cottage industry. Families sat around the fireside in hillside cabins using sharp knives to separate mica into thin layers. Later it was in demand for electronics and weaponry. Some gold, silver, rubies, and emeralds have also been found in the region.

Private lumber companies came nearest to conquering the wildness of the valley. In the half-century between 1890 and 1940 they cut over much of the virgin forest in the highest mountains above the river, taking giant poplars more than twenty-five feet in circumference. Sure-footed men waited for spring freshets along the mountain waterways, rode the logs down to the main river towns, swapped them for cash, celebrated big, and headed back to the woods.

But the lumbermen did not get quite all the forest and a large part of what remains is drained by the Little Tennessee. Two things saved it: the passage of the Weeks Act in 1911 which allowed land-buying for National Forests, and establishment in the 1930s of Great Smoky Mountains National Park.

Strangely enough the major environmental fight on the Little Tennessee involved not a forest but a three-inch fish, the snail darter, against a $116 million concrete and earth dam. TVA swung the dam from a bluff at the mouth of the river and named it for the nearest river tributary, Tellico. Though nearly completed, environmentalists managed to halt construction for nearly a decade, but finally the snail darter was found to live in other places, the Cherokees lost a suit against inundation of their burial grounds, and construction was continued. The gates finally were closed at the dam in November 1979 and the new Tellico Lake was formed.

Fortunately this turmoil had little effect on the basic wilderness of the region. Most of the Little Tennessee Valley remains a green and rugged oasis in a too-crowded world, offering the luxury of silent woods, the solace of murmuring streams, and the majesty of misty mountains.

FURTHER READING: Alberta and Carson Brewer, *Valley So Wild* (1975). James Mooney, *Myths of the Cherokees* (1900).

Alberta Trulock Brewer

The Maumee River

Source: Confluence of St. Joseph and St. Mary's rivers at Fort Wayne
Length: 130 miles
Tributaries: Auglaize River; Tiffin River
Mouth: Into Lake Erie at Toledo, Ohio
Agricultural Products: Truck farming
Industries: Food processing, automotive industries, electrical manufacturing

One of the short but historically significant rivers in the Old Northwest is the Maumee. Along its 130-mile course from the center of Fort Wayne, Indiana, to its juncture with Lake Erie at Toledo, Ohio, this broad river flows northeasterly from one commercial-industrial center to another. It crosses productive agricultural lands that once constituted the forested hunting lands of the Miami, Ottawa, Potawatomi, Delaware, and Shawnee Indians.

Early French traders named the river the "Maumee," an English corruption of the French pronunciation of the Omee and Aumiami branches of the Miami Indian confederation. On occasion the river was also called the "Grand Rapids" and, more often, the "Miami-of-the-Lake" or "Miami-of-the-North" to distinguish it from the Miami River which flows south across southern Ohio.

Physically, the Maumee is the product of ancestral Glacial Lake Maumee of the last glacial age, between twenty-two and thirteen thousand years ago. The southwestern edge of the last Erie Lobe Glacier stretched across present Lake Erie and the Maumee Valley to the headwaters of the present river. As the bulk retreated to the northeast, a gigantic glacial lake was trapped between the receding glacier and its earlier western moraines. Meltwater drainage depressions became the major tributaries of the Maumee River and were located in parallel saucer-like curves around the borders of the old glacier. Such were the headwater origins of the St. Joseph's River drainage from Michigan and the St. Mary's River draining from southwestern Ohio to meet at the confluence of the Three Rivers (Fort Wayne) to form the Maumee. At an intermediate point midway to its present location in Lake Erie, the glacier drainage produced the Auglaize and Tiffin rivers draining northwestern Ohio.

For thousands of years the abandoned lake bed filled with vegetation, marked by towering forests of hardwoods. Wildlife flourished along the streams and marshes making the region attractive to the Indian mound builders and the historically better known Algonquian-speaking tribes. Native Americans established semi-permanent villages at strategic locations on the Maumee—at its Three Rivers origin, at the confluence of the Auglaize and Tiffin rivers, at its Grand Rapids, and on Maumee Bay at Lake Erie. At these sites the river provided fish and mollusks in abundance, flood plains for growing corn, and a water supply that not only attracted game, but also made possible a feasible mode of travel. The Miamis at the Three Rivers village of Kekionga were also able to prosper by charging a toll for use of the portage from the head of the Maumee to the Little Wabash River to the southwest. This portage enabled other tribes, and eventually the French and the British, to forge a transportation system between the Great Lakes and the Mississippi River valley.

Important white contact with the Native American population on the Maumee dates from the Iroquois Wars of the 1640s. The confederation of militant New York tribes, linked commercially to the British, seized control of the southern Great Lakes region to gain the profits from the fur-producing wildlife of the region. Miamis, Potawatomis, and Ottawas were driven from the area. They did not return until the late seventeenth century with the retreat of the Iroquois and new trade support from the French, who in the early 1700s established posts along the Maumee near major Indian villages.

George Croghan, an English trader, moved into the valley in the 1740s. French resistance from Detroit soon followed, and by the mid-1750s the British and French were once again at war in the interior of North America. Most of the Algonquian tribes of the Maumee area sided with the French, who lost, as the sacking of St. Phillipe (Fort Wayne) in 1760 demonstrated. Although peace came in 1763, Potawatomis, Ottawas, and Miamis temporarily surged back into control of the region under the leadership of Pontiac with nearly all British outposts being overthrown. Croghan talked Pontiac out of further rebellion, however, and the chief went into brief exile on Indianola Island on the Maumee. Britain then worked to consolidate her control of the fur trade and to maintain the territory as a buffer against colonial American agricultural expansion into the Ohio country.

During the American Revolution most Indians of the Maumee Valley fought for their new British trade partners against the more land-acquisitive Americans. Secure in their villages on the Maumee, the Indians made devastating raids upon outposts in Kentucky and along the Ohio River. While the Maumee Indians easily held their own during the Revolution, they had again backed the losing side. The 1783 Treaty of Paris gave to the United States Britain's claim to land south of the Great Lakes, but the Indians of that land had not been consulted and they believed that they were in control of the land at least as far south as the Ohio. To defend this land from new movements of Americans along the Ohio, Shawnee, and Miami, warriors continued their raiding in the Ohio Valley.

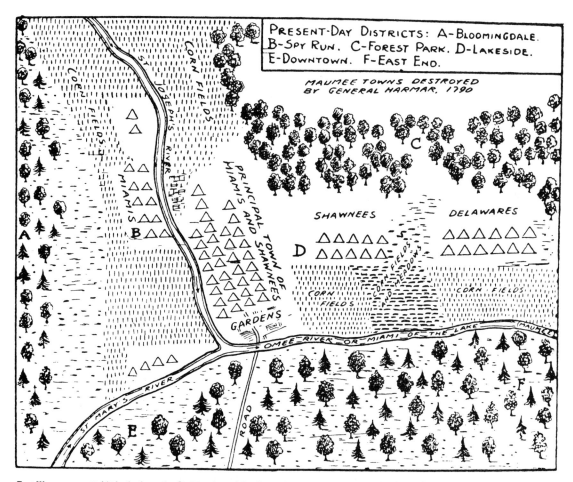

Fort Wayne was established where the St. Mary's and St. Joseph's Rivers meet to form the Maumee. This map of 1790 shows the positions of Indian settlements. (Courtesy Indiana Historical Society.)

By terms of the Confederation Congress's Land Ordinances of 1785 and 1787, Ohio was organized as a territory, and the new federal government felt obliged to protect American settlers and the nation's land claim from both the Indians and the British still on the Great Lakes. Efforts to affect treaties with the Miamis in 1788 failed, so the Ohio territorial governor, Arthur St. Clair, ordered General Josiah Harmar with 1,500 troops to move overland from Fort Washington (Cincinnati) to the main villages of the Miamis located at the Three Rivers. The plan was to sack Kekionga, destroy corn fields and stored foodstuffs, inflict military casualties on the villages from which Chief Little Turtle recruited troops, and thus take the pressure off southern Ohio and Kentucky. Harmar's 1790 expedition was a fiasco resulting in the death of nearly 200 Americans. The next year, with twice as many troops as his predecessor, St. Clair's army was defeated with over 600 killed. Now the Indians had become bolder and more arrogant than ever, while the British garrisoned a new fort on American soil near the foot of the Maumee rapids. But Washington's third choice, General Anthony Wayne, had learned from the disasters of the previous two. In 1794 he moved slowly north from Fort Washington, fortifying each section of his journey to the Maumee. At a site where a recent tornado had strewn fallen timbers about, the Indians on August 20, 1794, waited behind their natural fortifications. Wayne ordered his disciplined infantry into a bayonet charge and used his cavalry to flank the Indian retreat. Fleeing to the protection of Fort Miami, the routed Indians were shocked to find that the British were neither willing to fight nor to give them protection.

Wayne followed up his modest victory—about 100 Indians killed to thirty-one Americans—by reinforcing his chain of forts and heading up the Maumee to the Three Rivers junction where his troops constructed Fort Wayne. Along with Fort Defiance (where the Auglaize joins the Maumee) the Americans were now in control of most of the Northwest. The British evacuated Fort Miami the next year, while Wayne called for treaty negotiations at Fort Greenville south of the Maumee.

There, in August, 1795, the Northwest tribes, now referring to Wayne as "The Whirlwind,"

ceded southern Ohio to the whites and granted American control around each of the new forts on the Maumee. In subsequent treaties the Indians surrendered more Ohio and Indiana land, although the Maumee remained outside American settlement. French Canadians moved in to small settlements along the river. Fort Wayne continued as a small army garrison and government trading factory to wean Indian trade away from a continuing British presence.

By 1810 control of the strategic Maumee Valley had become a crucial concern once again for Americans. The Shawnee leader Tecumseh raised his voice against the treaties negotiated by his American opponent, William Henry Harrison. His plans were aided by the increasing tension between Great Britain and the United States. Battles with Tecumseh's forces, most notably at Tippecanoe Creek, were fought months before the United States declared war on Britain in the summer of 1812. Harrison was made commander of American forces in the Northwest and spent the next year and a half securing the Maumee Valley from the renewed threat of Indian-British control. Generals Harrison and James Winchester rushed to lift an Indian seige of Fort Wayne and then moved to rebuild Fort Defiance, now called Fort Winchester, on the west bank of the Auglaize.

The high price of controlling the Maumee Valley was paid in part early in 1813 when over 600 of Winchester's men were killed in an effort to counter British success at Detroit. In the wake of this disaster on the River Raisin, Harrison threw up hasty fortifications across the river from the old Fort Miami about ten miles south of present Toledo. Named Fort Meigs, in honor of Ohio's governor, Harrison was able to withstand seige by British and Indians under General Henry Proctor and Tecumseh and thus turn back the Indian-British drive into the Northwest. The seige of Fort Meigs was finally lifted by the arrival of fresh Kentucky troops who, while blunting the enemy's drive, tragically lost nearly 700 men.

Securing the river and benefiting from Commodore Oliver Hazard Perry's naval victory at Put-in-Bay on Lake Erie, Harrison by early October was able to pursue Proctor into Canada. At the Battle of the Thames, Harrison's reinforced troops trounced their enemy, killing Tecumseh and ending the last hope for unified Indian action in the region. It had been a closer contest than most Americans would remember, however, since Fort Dearborn (Chicago) and Detroit had both fallen: only Fort Meigs and Fort Wayne on either end of the Maumee held back the Indian-British alliance. Between 1790 and 1814 nearly 2,200 American soldiers had been killed fighting on or near the Maumee River in their effort to gain control of the Old Northwest.

The history of the Maumee Valley was peaceful following the War of 1812. Indian removal from the river that bore their name was hastened as land and canal speculation necessitated private control of Indian lands. By the early 1840s the Indians were gone.

Men at either end of the river in the 1820s promoted a canal to parallel the Maumee and Wabash rivers to the Ohio. Fort Wayne entrepreneurs needed new sources of commerce following the 1819 closure of the military fort and the subsequent removal of the Indian agency. Near the mouth of the Maumee, larger Lake Erie vessels began to put in at the small villages of Port Lawrence and Vistula, which merged in 1833 to form Toledo. The small community was boomed by Buffalo speculators interested in a canal and port facility there. The Indiana and Ohio governments cooperated with investment credits.

While both states nearly went bankrupt subsidizing the Wabash and Erie Canal from Toledo to Fort Wayne and eventually to Terre Haute, commerce at both ends of the Maumee picked up considerably. The influx of Irish and German emigrants for canal labor later provided workers to develop both agriculture and commerce in the valley. The coming of the railroads in the late 1850s, using in part the flat valley land for a roadbed, further advanced business and manufacturing.

By the 1870s the basic pattern of agricultural growth along the river valley and commercial-manufacturing developments at Fort Wayne and Toledo was clear. Fort Wayne expanded on the basis of commerce, food and lumber processing, railroad manufacturing, and eventual electrical and automotive industries. Toledo gained from Edward Drummond Libbey's introduction of glass manufacture in the 1880s.

Yet, ironically, by the 1950s the very success of the valley's agricultural and industrial development had brought problems to the Maumee. For years the runoff of chemical, petroleum, industrial, and human wastes had been allowed to flow into the Maumee until it had the near status of a drainage ditch between Fort Wayne and Toledo. A river that for centuries provided recreation and food was by the 1960s posted with lurid signs prohibiting swimming and fishing because of human health hazards. Civil and regional organizations to redeem the Maumee were organized by the early 1970s, but the twentieth-century fate of the Maumee would challenge the intelligence and courage of area residents, just as Indian troubles had challenged its inhabitants hundreds of years before.

FURTHER READING: Paul Woehrmann, *At the Headwaters of the Maumee* (1971). Nevin O. Winter, *A History of Northwest Ohio* (1917).

Clifford H. Scott

The Great and Little Miami Rivers

Sources: Miami: Indian Lake in southwest Ohio; Little Miami: rises in Clark County in west-central Ohio
Length: Miami, 160 miles; Little Miami, 95 miles
Tributaries: Miami: Stillwater, Mad, and Whitewater rivers; Little Miami: East Fork, Todd Fork
Mouths: Miami: Ohio River at southwest extremity; Little Miami: Ohio River at Cincinnati
Agricultural Products: Grain, hogs, dairy products, applies, grapes
Industries: Machine tools, furniture, some textiles

The Great and Little Miami rivers form what Ohioans call the Miami Valley. It constitutes much of southwestern Ohio and extends northeast about 150 miles from the Ohio River. The Miami is the more westerly of the two rivers, flowing into the Ohio in extreme southwest Ohio and originating about 160 miles to the northeast; the Little Miami flows into the Ohio just east of Cincinnati and rises about 140 miles northward. Both rivers are tumbling waterways interspersed with rapids and chutes and often flowing down narrow channels paved with small boulders. Products of the prehistoric Wisconsin Glacier, the two rivers and their watersheds cover 5,703 square miles, or approximately one-eighth of the State of Ohio.

The Valley possesses fertile soil and a salubrious climate. It has played a prominent role in the economic development of the state of Ohio. The fourteen counties comprising its watershed dominated the agricultural and industrial life of the state until the end of the nineteenth century. It served as the foundation for Ohio's reputation as a leading agricultural and industrial center of the United States.

Civilization in this lush valley dates back to approximately 1000 B.C. The Adena people, and later the Hopewell and Fort Ancient people, settled throughout the Miami country. Highly organized, sedentary societies with relatively stabilized economies, these prehistoric Indians had flourishing societies attested to by the artifacts found in the earthwork structures that dot the Miami country landscape. By the beginning of the seventeenth century, however, the prehistoric Indians had disappeared and new Indian tribes were moving into the land between the Miami rivers.

After a considerable period of instability, movement, and regrouping among the Indians of the vast lake, river, and forest country known as the Old Northwest, one of these groups, the Miamis, settled into the area between the Great and Little Miami rivers; they had previously lived in the area of present Wisconsin. They practiced a semi-agricultural economy and soon entered into trade relations with the French and the English.

While not the strongest of the Indian tribes in Ohio during this period, the Miamis furnished important leadership in the Indian defense against white encroachment on Indian lands during the second half of the eighteenth century. And it was the Miamis' intransigence that was responsible, in part, for making the Miami country the scene of the struggle between the French and the English for the control of the land beyond the Appalachians.

From the founding of Quebec in 1608, Frenchmen in Canada concentrated upon penetrating the interior of North America. By the early eighteenth century the French had set up fur-trading relations with the Ohio Indians and had established a chain of forts stretching from Canada through Ohio and on down to the French holdings in Louisiana. By the 1740s, however, the English, France's main rival on the North American continent, had also established fur trading ties with the Indians. Pickawillany (present Piqua), a Miami settlement on the Great Miami River, emerged as the center of English influence in the Ohio country when the Miami Chief, La Demoiselle, broke away from the French and openly courted the English traders.

The French retaliated against La Demoiselle's encouraging the English traders by sending an expeditionary force through the Ohio Country. French authorities hoped that this gesture would overawe the Indians and scare the English traders away from all territory claimed by the French. This force, under the direction of Celoron de Blainville, left Montreal in 1749.

Celoron and his men traveled down the Allegheny to the Ohio and then followed that river westward. At the mouth of each tributary along the way, Celoron buried a lead plate to emphasize French possession of the Ohio Country. When the force reached the mouth of the Great Miami River, which Celoron called *Rivière à la Roche* (Rocky River), he and his men turned northward and traveled upriver to Pickawillany. At the Miami town Celoron smoked a peace pipe with the Miami chiefs and urged them to return to the French fold. But the chiefs equivocated, and Celoron, upon his return to Canada, reported that the expedition had failed.

English interest in the Miami country continued to grow. Virginia, in particular, regarded this territory as its own private property. During the late 1740s a number of prominent Virginia planters joined together and organized the Ohio Company to trade with the Miami Indians, help counteract French influence, and encourage land speculation. In 1750 the Company sent Christopher Gist to explore the Ohio country. In 1751 he reached the Miami Valley, visited numerous Indian settlements, and established trade relations with the Miami Indians. After his departure, the French, enraged by the continued English interest, decided to punish both the Miamis and the English. French settlers and their Indian allies smashed the English trading post at Pickawillany and killed La Demoiselle. But the number of English traders in the Miami country continued to grow.

The struggle between the French and the English in the Miami country became part of the European Seven Years War (1754–1763). During this war, known in America as the French and Indian War, the battles between the French and the English continued at a heightened pace. At first the French held the advantage; but in 1757, when William Pitt became Prime Minister of England, the tide turned. Pitt, unlike his predecessor, focused attention on the war in America. He wanted not only to reduce French influence but to drive the French from North America. Soon the English and colonial forces halted the French, and, by the terms of the Peace of Paris in 1763, England ruled the Ohio country. Shortly thereafter settlers began moving into the land between the Great and the Little Miami rivers.

Despite the termination of French rule, and

later the expulsion of the British from the American colonies, the Indians in the Ohio country continued to threaten those settling in the newly won transmontane west. In the Miami country especially, skirmishes between the settlers and the Indians multiplied, and the Miami country became the focal point for the attempts of the new American government to secure the land beyond the Appalachian Mountains.

First the Americans attempted to conclude treaties with the various Ohio Indian tribes. One of the earliest of these treaties was signed with the Shawnee in 1786 at the mouth of the Great Miami River. But repeated Indian raids threatened the fragile alliances and in 1790 the Indians declared war on the settlers moving into the Miami country. The American government responded to the Indian challenge by sending General Josiah Harmer into the Miami Valley. The Indians quickly routed Harmer's forces and Harmer and his men fled to Cincinnati. In 1791 General St. Clair launched a campaign against the Indians and also met with defeat. Finally, in 1792 General Anthony Wayne took command of the American forces. Wayne moved his army from Cincinnati to Fort Greenville, the site of St. Clair's defeat, and drilled them intensively. At long last, in 1794 Wayne and his men defeated the Indian forces at the Battle of Fallen Timbers. The signing of the Greenville Treaty in 1795 virtually ended the Indian problem in the Miami country.

With the signing of the treaty, settlement in the region resumed. Those settlements which predated the outbreak of the Indian Wars in 1790 began to grow. Following the end of the Revolutionary War towns began to grow up along the Ohio River between the Great and the Little Miami rivers. Those early settlements were part of the Miami Purchase. In 1783 Judge John Cleves Symmes of New Jersey traveled down the Ohio River to select an appropriate site for a settlement. Taken with the beauty of the Miami country, he requested a two million acre land grant from Congress. Although Congress refused to grant such a large request, it eventually sold Symmes 311,682 acres of land. This tract, known as the Miami Purchase, lay between the Great and the Little Miami rivers. Between 1788 and 1790 three settlements were established, and with the removal of the In   n threat, the tiny settlements began to grow. And soon settlers started to establish new towns as they left the towns in the Miami Purchase and traveled up the waterways of the Miami country.

The years between 1795 and 1850 were a period of town building and farm clearing. Travel on the Great and the Little Miami rivers brought settlers into the heart of the fertile Miami country. They cleared the land, plowed the fields, and harvested bumper corn and wheat crops in the rich Miami bottoms. By 1820 the Miami country was the hog-raising center of the state. And despite concentration upon the production of grain and hogs, Miami country farmers also supported large dairy operations, orchards, and vineyards. Miami farmers quickly accumulated surpluses which they sold in the towns that dotted the Great and the Little Miami rivers.

As the small settlements grew into bustling market towns, businessmen became interested in finding ways to facilitate travel between Cincinnati and the towns along the Great Miami River. Only during the spring and autumnal floods could boats laden with goods manipulate it. Businessmen in the Miami country, as a result, became ardent supporters of Ohio's canal program. In 1825 work began on a canal to connect Cincinnati with Dayton. By 1848 the Miami and Erie Canal linked Lake Erie with the Ohio River. Commerce flourished, and by 1850 Miami Valley towns possessed over half the capital invested in manufacturing in the entire state of Ohio. Carding and fulling mills, paper mills, and flour mills dotted the Great Miami River and the canal. Cincinnati, the region's premier city, grew into a major candle and soap center and the pork-packing capital of the country. The towns in the Miami country also supported the production of woolen and cotton goods, beer, boots and shoes, steamboats, machine tools, and furniture. By 1850 the Miami country landscape had changed from a lush but untamed wilderness to the agro-industrial center of the state of Ohio.

Throughout the nineteenth century the Miami Valley led Ohio in industrial and agricultural output. But by the beginning of the twentieth century the Miami country's leadership began to falter. The spread of railway lines within the state supplanted the canal as the major avenue of commerce. The completion of the transcontinental railroad and the growth of Great Lakes navigation forced Ohio grain and livestock farmers to compete with the produce from the rich farmlands further west. While established manufacturing interests remained in the Miami country, new establishments located elsewhere in the state. But despite its lack of leadership in current agricultural and industrial affairs, the land nestled between the Great and the Little Miami rivers continues to contribute greatly to the health and welfare of the state of Ohio.

FURTHER READING: Havighurst, Walter. *River to the West: Three Centuries of the Ohio.* New York: G. P. Putnam's Sons, 1970. Smith, William E. *History of Southwestern Ohio: The Miami Valleys.* New York: Lewis Historical Publishing Co., 1964.

Patricia Mooney Melvin

The Monongahela River

Source: Confluence of West Fork and Tygart rivers at Fairmont, in northern West Virginia
Length: 128 miles
Tributaries: Cheat, Youghiogheny rivers
Mouth: Joins Allegheny to form Ohio River at Pittsburgh, Pennsylvania
Agricultural Products: Truck farming
Industries: Coal mining, petroleum refining, limestone mining

The Monongahela River is formed by the confluence of the West Fork River and the Tygart River, at Fairmont, in northern West Virginia. The Monongahela is only 128 miles long, joining with the Allegheny at Pittsburgh to form the Ohio. It is navigable for its full length, falling just a little over 150 feet—from 857 to 697 feet above sea level—in that distance. Some of its tributaries, the Cheat and Youghiogheny being most important, have their origins high in the Appalachians. The Monongahela's total drainage area is 7,340 square miles.

The name, like that of many other American rivers, is of Indian origin. For many years there was no agreement on how it should be spelled. A Trader's Map dated 1752, in the Library of Congress, spells it Mohungela, while a map appearing in a 1754 issue of the *London Magazine* spells it Mononguhela. The Ohio Company's instructions to land surveyor Christopher Gist in 1751 spelled it Mo-hon-gey-e-la, while Gist himself spelled it Mo-hon-ga-ly. All were attempts to spell what the Indians were saying. As to the meaning, there is fairly general agreement that

The Monongahela (from the right) joins the Allegheny at Pittsburgh's Golden Triangle to form the Ohio, flowing off at the left. (Photo courtesy The Gateway Clipper, Inc.)

the Indians were describing the river as having "many landslides" or "high banks or bluffs, breaking off and falling down at places." As railroad and highway builders were fated to discover, this is an apt description.

It was the uplifting that created the Appalachians in late Paleozoic times, about 500–600 million years ago, that brought about the Monongahela drainage system. Prior to that time the river had flowed north to Lake Erie. Then during the glacial period (600,000–12,000 years ago), the river was barred by a glacier-made dam at the present site of Beaver, Pennsylvania, north-northwest of Pittsburgh. It created huge prehistoric Lake Monongahela. When the lake was breached, the channel of the rushing stream cut southwestward through what became the Ohio Valley, and as a result of these and subsequent geologic events the waters of the Monongahela flow north to Pittsburgh, join the Allegheny, and flow southwestward as the Ohio River.

Evidence of the existence of Lake Monongahela consists of a line of terrace deposits at an elevation of approximately 1,100 feet above sea level, composed of sand and clay, often finely stratified and containing many plant fossils. These deposits, seventy feet thick at some places, were of value to the pioneers and their descendants in establishing a pottery industry.

Nor did it take the pioneers long to discover that the slopes along the banks of the rivers held outcroppings of valuable minerals. Iron ore, for example, spurred the construction of numerous furnaces, built of stone, and filled most of the needs of the settlers for iron tools for nearly a century.

Even before the American Revolution the richness of the Monongahela Valley had led frontiersmen to take up "tomahawk claims"—claims the boundaries of which were marked on trees with slashes from a tomahawk—and to settle there. It was illegal and dangerous, but neither of these deterred the settlers. The great, slow-moving river also provided an easy medium for travel. The Indians had used it for centuries, paddling their canoes on various missions, hunting game, on tribal business, or to attack their enemies.

An early settlement was at Redstone Old Fort

(—present Brownsville, Pennsylvania) where Nemacolin's Path, heavily used by the whites, came in from the southeast. From there the pioneers often set off downriver on flatboats. After the Revolution, although Indian depredations continued, there was no stopping the American pioneer, and the Monongahela Valley settled rapidly.

Those early pioneers soon discovered that they had a good cash crop: rye whiskey. One out of every ten farmers had a still. A horse could carry four bushels of rye, but if the farmer turned it into whiskey the same animals could carry the equivalent of twenty-four bushels. "Monongahela rye" soon became widely known, not only on the eastern seaboard, but also downstream as far away as New Orleans.

When Congress on March 3, 1791, passed an excise law imposing a tax of four pence a gallon on all distilled spirits the people of the Monongahela rose in protest. The discontent swelled into the Whiskey Rebellion of 1794. Although there was much marching and counter-marching, the rebellion collapsed upon a show of force by the federal government.

The produce of the Monongahela Valley prompted the development of better vessels for transporting it downriver to markets. With better woodworking facilities the palefaces improved the Indian dugout and called it a pirogue. Because it was clumsy and heavy to propel, this vessel was soon abandoned in favor of the bateau, a flat bottomed boat constructed of planks and propelled by both poles and oars. The final stage of early boat building was the flatboat, somewhat like a bateau, but larger, from fifteen to fifty feet in length.

Any craft used on the Monongahela had to be flat bottom or expansive in form, so as not to sink very deeply in the water. The river had a long series of natural pools, some of them several feet deep, but connecting the pools were shoals, or "riffles," as they were called, where the water flowed down over gently inclined slopes.

Flatboats were put together in boatyards at Morgantown, Brownsville, and elsewhere. Too heavy and cumbersome to handle against a current, they were sold, dismantled and sometimes used for lumber for the pioneers' first crude shelters after they reached their destination.

Then came the keelboat, built to travel upstream as well as downstream. In its construction a keel was laid along the middle, from stem to stern, with curved ribs outwards and upwards. A deck of planks was laid and a cabin was built in the hull, called the cargo-box, extending nearly the entire length but leaving above deck a narrow walkway on each side along which the boatmen walked in propelling the craft. This operation was accomplished by the men walking from prow to stern, each pushing a pole pressed against his padded shoulder.

Passage upstream was a slow and laborious process, especially at the riffles, but by the early nineteenth century keelboats were plying up and down the river with some regularity, running between Brownsville and Pittsburgh and occasionally working upstream as far as Morgantown. They carried passengers and the products of field and forest: iron in various forms, glass, flour, whiskey, lime, bear's oil and peltry. Mail (packets of letters) was often carried, and these boats, operating on regular schedules, came to be called packet boats.

On March 17, 1811, the hull of the first steamboat on the "western waters" was launched on the Monongahela River at Pittsburgh. This boat, the *New Orleans*, was designed to run as a regular packet boat between New Orleans and Natchez. As for the Monongahela River, steamboating was at first impractical because of its fluctuating water level except at certain seasons. Nevertheless attempts were made. The first steamboat to ranch Morgantown, the *Reindeer*, arrived on April 29, 1826.

In 1837 a Pennsylvania corporation, the Monongahela Navigation Company, was organized to survey the river and determine what needed to be done to improve it for navigation. Its experts decided that a system of locks and dams would have to be constructed, similar to those that had been used in Europe since the fifteenth century and which had more recently been used on the Erie Canal. These structures for the Monongahela, being in a river rather than a canal, would have to be much more sturdily built because of damage likely to be sustained from frequent heavy floods sweeping downstream carrying driftwood and ice. The dammed up water, more uniform in depth and with a somewhat reduced current, was called slackwater.

By 1844 the company, building upriver from Pittsburgh, had built four dams at a cost of $418,000, a tremendous sum at that time. This made the river navigable for regularly scheduled boats from Pittsburgh to Brownsville, a river port on the National Road, where connections were made with stagecoaches and wagons. From 1844 to 1852 the company carried more than 745,000 passengers between those two points, yielding a revenue of more than $126,000.

Spurred by the success of the Pennsylvania corporation, the Virginia General Assembly chartered a similar company to accomplish the same goal from the state line south to Morgantown and Fairmont. For years this company held discussions, but the magnitude of the task and the relative sparcity of the population prevented any actual progress being made. Meanwhile, between 1854 and 1865, locks and dams numbers five and six were completed in Pennsylvania with the slackwater reaching as far upriver as New Geneva. Stagecoaches were run from Fairmont and Morgantown, at first to Brownsville, then to New Geneva, to connect with the steamboats.

Only when the federal government entered the picture after the Civil War was progress made south of the Mason-Dixon line. A survey was made of the river from New Geneva to Morgantown in 1871, and slowly through the years additional locks and dams were constructed. Finally, in November, 1889, two large steamboats, the *James G. Blaine* and the *Adam Jacobs*, arrived at Morgantown from Pittsburgh, each carrying a brass band and a full contingent of passengers.

Completion of locks and dams ten through fifteen between Morgantown and Fairmont did not come until 1904, and even then did not result in regularly scheduled packet boat service. Within a few years railroads and automobile highways would make obsolescent the slackwater system the people had worked for over three-quarters of a century to achieve. But the river, the first in the United States to be improved for navigation, continued to bear an ever-increasing burden of freight, mostly coal in barges, but also petroleum products, limestone, and many other commodities. Recreational boating remains to this day a steadily increasing activity.

Through the years the Army Corps of Engineers has carried on a program of replacement of the original locks and dams with more modern facilities, sometimes eliminating an installation entirely, so that the old numbering system is no longer meaningful. Navigation is now rarely suspended because of floods or ice.

All of this was not without cost to the environment. Industrial development of the river valley through many decades has resulted in pollution of the stream that killed off the once rich fish population and the accumulation of debris that mars the loveliness of the scenic river banks.

But efforts during the past two decades to improve the environment have paid off in remarkable results that led U.S. Bureau of Outdoor Recreation officials to exclaim that there is "life again along the Monongahela River!" Industry is still there, but the pollution is under control and there is even fishing again in the river after a lapse of three-quarters of a century. The river is recuperating, and no one can predict what turn developments will take as we near the twenty-first century.

Today a journey upriver offers glimpses of twentieth-century heavy industry (the first thirty miles near Pittsburgh), Point Park and the riverside park upriver which prove that we can produce beautiful as well as ugly landscapes, an Aquatorium at Monongahela City, historical lore and Indian trails, petroglyphs, remnants of the early glass and pottery industry, Secretary of the Treasury Albert Gallatin's home, the Monon River Museum at Greenboro, a park at Point Marion where the Cheat River, the Monongahela's principal tributary, flows in, Morgantown, with West Virginia University's campus and the seventy-five acre Core Arboretum facing the river, and Prickett's Fort at Fairmont. Indeed, people along the Monongahela have much of which to be proud.

FURTHER READING: Richard Bissell, *The Monongahela* (1949). Earl L. Core, *The Monongalia Story*, 4 vols. (1974, 1976, 1979, 1982).

Earl L. Core

The Muskingum River

> *Source:* Confluence of Walhonding and Tuscarawas rivers at Coshocton, in east-central Ohio
> *Length:* 112.4 miles
> *Tributary:* Licking River
> *Mouth:* Into Ohio River at Marietta, Ohio
> *Agricultural Products:* Dairying, fruits, grain
> *Industries:* Recreation, coal, limestone, some manufacturing

The Muskingum River is the largest stream lying wholly within the state of Ohio. It is formed by the confluence of the Walhonding and Tuscarawas rivers at Coshocton, in the east-central part of the state. With all its branches the Muskingum drains 8,051 square miles, or nearly one-fifth of Ohio. Its drainage basin includes all of five counties—Holmes, Coshocton, Muskingum, Tuscarawas, and Wayne—and parts of twenty-two others. It flows southward to its confluence with the Ohio at Marietta, sixty miles away as the crow flies. The Muskingum does not flow in a straight line, however, but zigzags east and west several times as it winds its crooked 112.4 mile course. Its headwaters originate near Akron, Ohio, at an elevation of 738 feet; it has an average fall of 1.3 feet per mile, and drops to 585 feet above sea level at its mouth. Its principal tributary is the Licking, which flows in from the east at Zanesville. The Muskingum's average depth is five feet, and it is the only river in the state that is navigable for as long a distance as ninety miles.

The river was formed in prehistoric times by the melting of the ice sheet inching down from Canada, forming a vast lake among the hills. The lake eventually overflowed, washing away a section of the ridge, thus carving the Muskingum Valley, rich with forests and endowed with a moderate climate. A quiet, gently flowing stream, the Indian name of Muskingum—"elk eye river"—somehow seems appropriate.

The Muskingum has a long, romantic history involving the Indians. The prehistoric Indian cultures—Adena, Hopewell, and Middle Mississipian —existed there from 1000 B.C. to the mid-seventeenth century. The Adena and Hopewell were the Mound Builders leaving traces of their burial mounds and ceremonies in nearly 400 mound sites, one of which is presently included in the Mound Cemetery in Marietta, Ohio.

When the whites arrived on the scene the upper valley was occupied primarily by the Delawares. At the time of Columbus they had occupied the lands along the Delaware River and Bay and called themselves the Lenni Lenape or "real men." Due to persecution by the Iroquois and the coming of white settlers, the Delawares migrated west of the Muskingum and Tuscarawas valleys. One of their important towns belonging to the Turtle Tribe was Coshocton, of "Gos-choch-gung" as the Delawares called it.

Both the French and the English laid claim to the fur-rich Ohio Valley and its tributaries. In 1749 the Ohio Land Company, formed by Virginians, promoted western settlement thus increasing rivalries in the western country. After the French defeat in the French and Indian War (1755–1763) and the loss of the Mississippi Valley an Indian rebellion led by an Ottawa named Pontiac swept the back country. Peace followed after the accomplishments of Colonel Henry Bouquet in chasing the Indians.

However, no white person's scalp was safe in the Muskingum country until after the American Revolution, and in the brutal warfare that was carried on, the Indians were hardly safer from the whites. In the early war years the Americans, with the aid of Colonel George Morgan, the Indian agent, had maintained a precarious peace with the Delawares. Then in 1778 John Heckwelder, a trusted missionary, persuaded the Indians to come to Fort Pitt for a conference with the Americans. This meeting, held in September, resulted in a treaty that was totally misunderstood by the Delawares. In accordance with treaty provisions the Americans under General Lachlan McIntosh marched into Delaware country as if they owned it. Yet McIntosh's troops were ill-equipped, ill-fed, and ill-disciplined, and even though he succeeded in building Fort Laurens near Coshocton and Fort McIntosh to the east of it, his display of American "strength" disgusted the Delawares. McIntosh undid all the good that Colonel Morgan had achieved in past years. Almost immediately Fort Laurens fell under siege, and was only saved by a relief expedition sent there in the spring of 1779; in July it was abandoned.

Yet in that same year Delaware lands along the Muskingum were invaded by white squatters. When American authorities allowed them to remain, the Indians decided to make war. Knowing that the Delawares had turned hostile, Colonel Daniel Brodhead in the spring of 1781 marched out of Fort Pitt upon their villages and destroyed their central town, Coshocton; the Indians he captured were brutally murdered.

In March, 1782, following a wave of Indian depredations in the northern Ohio country, frontier ruffians led by Colonel David Williamson captured ninety-six Christian Delawares (sometimes called Moravian Indians) at Salem and Gnadenhutten on the Tuscawara and massacred them in cold blood. Although the Delawares had moved west to be with the Wyandots, they now pillaged far and wide. Colonel William Crawford led an army against them but his army was routed. Crawford was captured and tortured to death at the stake.

After the War settlers came west to seek new fortunes in the fertile Ohio countryside. To help protect them Colonel Josiah Harmar built Fort Harmar at the mouth of the Muskingum, and in 1785 and 1786 Congress signed treaties with the Indians and gave them a reservation in northern Ohio. On April 7, 1788, the Ohio Company's advance party, led by General Rufus Putnam, arrived at the confluence of the Muskingum and Ohio rivers and founded the first organized permanent American settlement in the Northwest Territory, Marietta, named in honor of

Queen Marie Antoinette. The settlers built their first homes in a fortified square called Campus Martius as protection against Indian hostilities.

And indeed Indian hostilities did occur. The "Big Bottom Massacre" of thirteen men, women, and children was the worst. It took place in January, 1791, about forty miles up the Muskingum; it was so-called for its location. Governor Arthur St. Clair and General Josiah Harmar both failed to chastise the Wyandot and Chippewa Indians responsible. This was finally accomplished by General Anthony Wayne at the Battle of Fallen Timbers in August, 1794. Subsequently the Treaty of Greenville (1795) cleared the Muskingum country of Indian lands.

Even as settlers were establishing themselves up and down the valley, others were migrating westward. To frontiersman Ebenezer Zane there was little sense in following the Ohio River down its long course from Wheeling, Virginia (now West Virginia), to Limestone (now Maysville), Kentucky. He built a trace (path) across land between those two points that cut off many miles; at the Muskingum crossing he established himself, and from that small beginning grew the city of Zanesville.

From the early 1800s upper Muskingum merchants and farmers transported their wares and produce down the river by flatboat to Marietta. The freight was then transferred to larger vessels bound for New Orleans. Marietta became a leading producer of sailing vessels and was a port of entry.

The *Rufus Putnam* was the first steamboat to run on Muskingum waters. Later the *Hope* and the *Mary Ann* were run on the stream during flood stage, but except at that time the river was too shallow. However, in March, 1863, the legislature provided for the construction of dams and locks so that steamers could run upriver to Zanesville. Such vessels as the *Julia Dean, Lorena, Buckeye Belle,* and *Jenny Lind* carried freight and passengers in the years when steamboating was as its height. Several vessels hit snags and sank while the *Buckeye Belle* exploded in 1852 and killed twenty-four persons. There is a memorial in the Beverly Cemetery to the unidentified dead of this accident. But railroads came and the steamboat became obsolete. The *W. P. Snyder, Jr.* was the last steampowered sternwheeled towboat to operate in America. It is still docked on the Muskingum at Marietta.

In 1886 the federal government took over the operation of the Muskingum navigational system. Nearly a quarter century later, in 1958, the state of Ohio's Department of Natural Resources reassumed responsibility for the locks and dams and has rehabilitated the entire system. Pleasure craft can now navigate the full length of the river. The Ohio Division of Parks and Recreation now operates the ten sets of locks encompassing 113 acres and controlling ninety-three miles of scenic waterways from Marietta north to Dresden, Ohio. All the locks are operated manually, many still containing the original wooden doors constructed in the 1840s. Many small country towns dot the shoreline, while new marinas are springing up each year.

The northern part of the Muskingum River Basin consists of moderately rolling till plains with a predominance of farmland, and urban development interspersed by small scattered wooded areas. The southern part of the basin is more rugged, consisting of steep forested slopes noted for their beautiful autumn foliage and green pines in winter. The basin is rich in recreational resources, with 312,872 acres devoted to those purposes. Vacationers find opportunities for boating, camping, hunting, and fishing.

They enjoy the serenity and charm of the Muskingum as it winds its way through the rolling hills and valleys of the beautiful Ohio countryside. Their feelings may best the felt in the words of the Reverend Harry E. Porter when he wrote:

> When God laid out Ohio
>   And chiseled out her hills,
> Laid high her stately ridges
>   And traced her winding rills,
> To crown that grand creation,
>   And leave it at its best,
> He carved the Blue Muskingum
>   The Hudson of the West.*

FURTHER READING: Clyde K. Swift, *The Muskingum Years* (1971), Thomas W. Lewis, *History of Southeast Ohio and the Muskingum Valley* (1928).
*From Norris F. Schneider, *The Muskingum River: A History and Guide.*

Barbara Haines Cowell

The New River

Source: Near Blowing Rock, Watauga County, North Carolina
Length: 320 miles
Tributaries: Greenbrier, Bluestone rivers
Mouth: Merges with Gauley River to form Kanawha (or Great Kanawha) at Gauley Ridge, West Virginia
Agricultural Products: Truck farming
Industries: Tourism; coal mining

New River originates at an elevation of nearly 4,000 feet on the west flank of the Blue Ridge, near Blowing Rock, North Carolina. It is one of the oldest rivers in the United States, following much the same course as the ancient Teays, a major river prior to its western portion being obliterated by Ice Age glaciers. Flowing generally north and occasionally west, the New cuts across two physiographic regions, the Valley and Ridge and then the Allegheny Plateau, thus severing the spine of the Alleghenies. On its way from North Carolina through Virginia and into West Virginia, it cuts through sandstones, shales, and limestones, finally carving the New River Gorge—often called the Grand Canyon of the East—through the plateau of West Virginia. For a total of 320 miles its course continues amid forested mountains and a patchwork of farms and towns before it sinks into the solemn depths of the gorge to emerge at Gauley Bridge, West Virginia, where it unites with the Gauley River to form the Great Kanawha.

In about 1650 rumors were circulating in colonial Virginia that a westward flowing river might provide a convenient route to the Pacific Ocean and the riches of the Orient. For many years it was called Wood's River in honor of Abraham Wood, a man of some prominence in colonial affairs, and only later did it become known as New River. It may have acquired its familiar name simply from the fact that it flowed in a "new" direction—westward—unlike the known rivers draining into the Atlantic.

On orders of Virginia's Governor Berkeley, Abraham Wood sent out an exploring party in September, 1671, led by Thomas Batts and Robert Fallam, "for the finding out the ebbing and flowing of the Waters on the other side of the Mountaines in order to the discovery of the South Sea . . . ." They spent over two weeks traveling west and toiling over the mountains until they "had a sight of a curious River . . . but [that] had a fall that made a great noise" on September 16. After claiming the land for King Charles II of England they returned east, falsely convinced that the movement of the tide could be detected in the river.

Even though the farthest point they reached remains uncertain, it may have been one of the falls of New River in Summers County, West Virginia, such as Bull Falls, Brooks Falls, or perhaps even Sandstone Falls. Near the falls an area was found where Indians had once lived and Fallam noted, "it being a piece of very rich ground, whereon ye Mohetons had formerly lived and grown up with weeds." In 1948 Ralph Solecki of the Smithsonian Institution recovered artifacts in the area prior to its being inundated by the lake created by Bluestone Dam at Hinton. At least three village sites were found near Bull Falls, and perhaps one of these was the place visited by Batts and Fallam over three centuries ago.

Fur traders and land agents were soon passing through the New River area. In fact, in 1671 Batts and Fallam had found trees blazed with lettering indicating that someone had already passed that way. In June 1750 while returning home to Virginia after discovering the Cumberland Gap, Dr. Thomas Walker's party camped on New River at the mouth of the "Green Bryer." Christopher Gist, an agent for the Ohio Company, crossed the river in May 1751 after spending the winter in the west with the Indians.

The French and Indian war (1754–1763) brought to an end the freedom to roam the wilderness without fear of the Indians. One of the most amazing tales of human survival was acted out at this time when Mary Ingles and others were taken prisoners by the Shawnees following an attack on the Draper's Meadow settlement near present Blacksburg, Virginia, in July 1755. She was forced to travel as far down the Ohio River as Big Bone Lick near Cincinnati where she was put to work making salt.

Mary Ingles decided that possible death in the wilderness was better than life as an Indian's slave. Joined by an older woman, she made a break for freedom, traveling up the Ohio, Kanawha and through the New River Gorge as winter was fast approaching. The two women trudged on day after weary day, eating anything that would offer some nourishment and sleeping in hollow logs for a little warmth until, late in November, they reached their destination at Draper's Meadows. Mary Ingles lived to an old age and related her ordeal many times.

During the mid-eighteenth century a tide of Scotch-Irish emigrants flowed south along the Shenandoah Valley, soon reaching the headwaters of the New. The area was settled essentially from Virginia in spite of the Blue Ridge posing a formidable barrier to settlement from the Piedmont to the east. The pioneer stock that settled in the mountain fastness often held in contempt the aristocracy of the lowlands, and it is little wonder that a century later many were Union sympathizers during the Civil War.

Chief Justice John Marshall headed a party that made a journey, largely by boat, in 1812 down the Greenbrier and New River to assess conditions for building a canal through the mountains. Little came of the scheme, and it remained for the steam locomotive to provide a means of rapid transportation along the New. Collis P. Huntington, determined to see construction to the Ohio River, assumed leadership of the Chesapeake and Ohio Railway following the Civil War. Construction crews from the east and west met near Hawk's Nest, West Virginia, where the last spike was driven in late January 1873.

It was during the construction of the railroad that John Henry's feat immortalized him in song and legend. To save distance in laying track where Greenbrier River meanders in a long loop a few miles from its confluence with the New, a long tunnel was cut through nearby Big Bend Mountains. Wagers were made that John Henry could beat the steam drill at cutting holes for the placing of explosives and he won only to collapse soon after and die from exhaustion and perhaps a cerebral hemorrhage. The real John Henry has been obscured with the passage of time and the growth of a legend, but the ballad speaks the truth with the line, "Dis hammer gonna be the death of me, Lawd, Lawd."

Unexpectedly the completion of the railroad stimulated the use of wide-keeled, flat-bottomed craft along portions of the river where the channel was suitable for their use. Such barges, often called bateaux from the French, were used to haul timber, tobacco and farm products to loading points for shipment by rail. A colorful era of life on the river grew up among the crews who poled the boats with tireless, grueling labor before the advent of the gasoline outboard motor.

With the construction of the railroad rich coal and timber resources became readily accessible. Coal camps grew up almost overnight when a seam was opened, only to be abandoned when the coal was exhausted. Men lived much of their lives in darkness and many died from mining accidents. Towns such as Beury, Red Ash, Fire Creek, Caperton, and Kaymoor once dotted the gorge country, but have long since passed into oblivion. They are fading memories to those still living who once lived, loved, and grieved there.

The lustiest town of all was Thurmond. The railroad was not only the town's blood, it was also its main street. Through Thurmond passed coal and timber for shipment by rail as well as gamblers from far and wide drawn by the reputation of the rather infamous Dunglen Hotel and its casino. It is claimed that a poker game there was kept underway without interruption for over a decade! The hotel and all the shady activity there was frowned upon by the "respectable" citizens of Thurmond, and they felt prayers had been answered when it burned to the ground in 1930.

Prosperity finally bid farewell to Thurmond and the gorge country and today, at many places, the only sign that civilization ever passed through the gorge is the railroad snaking along the river. The New now attracts a new breed of adventurers and is gaining popularity with whitewater canoeing and rafting enthusiasts. For many miles the only sign of human endeavor is the New River Gorge Bridge near Fayetteville creating a vast rainbow of steel nearly 900 feet above the river. The sense of wilderness at many places, both visually as well as in feeling, is the reason that federal legislation may soon protect a sizable corridor through the gorge.

For countless ages the river has offered a convenient avenue for the northward movement of plants that are essentially southern in distribution. The silverbell emerges from obscurity among the trees with its drooping, bell blossoms in April and its distribution in West Virginia closely parallels the course of the river. The rosebay rhododendron is found not much farther north than Grandview State Park near Beckley, West Virginia, where it presents a showy display along the gorge rim. Core's mallow, named for botanist Earl L. Core who discovered it, with rosy pink flowers and the appearance of a small hollyhock, was long known to grow only on a mountain slope at Narrows, Virginia.

The river has created a nursery for the evolution of a number of small fish which are restricted entirely to the New River drainage. Among these species that grow to only a few inches in length are the rather nondescript and even comically named Kanawha darter, tonguetied and suckermouth minnows, and the silvery Kanawha shiner. The angler will find excellent warm water game fishing along many stretches of the river where he may land trophy-size walleye, smallmouth bass, white bass, striped bass, and crappie.

New River has been spared the growth of vast metropolitan areas and industrial complexes and the way of life along its course changes slowly. Plans by an electric power company to build two huge dams at Galax, Virginia, were seen not only as a threat to the river that had remained wild along many stretches of its course, but also to a way of life that has changed little since the time of settlement. Even though 3,000 people would have been forced to move and at least one small North Carolina town flooded into oblivion, the power company insisted the dams were necessary to meet growing demands for electricity. After various maneuvers in the courts and elsewhere by those for as well as those against the dams, the project received its death blow in 1976 when President Ford signed into law a bill giving protection to twenty-six miles of the New River in North Carolina under provisions of the Wild and Scenic Rivers Act.

A new day had dawned for the New River. Appreciated and protected, it rolls on, speaking of things timeless to those who listen.

FURTHER READING: Kyle McCormick, *The New–Kanawha River and the Mine War of West Virginia* (1959). James R. Adkins, *New River Basin* (1976).

J. Lawrence Smith

The Nolichucky River

Source: Merger of the Toe and Cane rivers near Huntdale, North Carolina
Length: 150 miles
Tributaries: None of consequence
Mouth: Flows into French Broad River eleven miles north of Newport, Tennessee
Agricultural Products: Truck farming
Industries: Hydroelectric power; nuclear power; mica mining, asbestos

The Nolichucky River of east Tennessee and western North Carolina is one the main tributaries of the French Broad River, and that river is the largest tributary of the Tennessee. Stretching from near the Virginia-North Carolina border in the north to near the North Carolina-South Carolina border in the south, the French Broad River basin drains an area of 5,124 square miles, of which the Nolichucky represents 1,756 square miles; it is about 150 miles long.

Draining the northern portion of that river basin, the headwaters of the Nolichucky rise high in the Appalachian ridges of Avery, Mitchell, and Yancey Counties in western North Carolina. In that area the Toe and Cane rivers join near Huntdale, North Carolina, to form the Nolichucky, which then cuts through the Unaka

Mountains to emerge in Tennessee. The river, known as the Nonachunkeh by the Cherokees, eventually winds its way west and south to the French Broad and the Tennessee Valley Authority's Douglas Lake, a major TVA reservoir near Dandridge, Tennessee.

In 1673 James Needham, along with Gabriel Arthur, an indentured servant, and a party of Indians, made the first recorded English explorations over the Appalachians to southwest Virginia and into Nolichucky territory. Hoping to find a water route to India, silver, or gold, Abraham Wood, a Virginia trader, had financed Needham's trip into Eastern Tennessee. The expedition not only failed to fulfill Wood's objectives for the mission but even worse, their Indian guide, Indian John, killed Needham in a moment of rage. Gabriel Arthur barely escaped to tell of the trip; but because of rugged terrain, the lack of a strong economic motive, and fear of the Indians, only an occasional trapper or trader risked a trip into the Nolichucky country after Needham's story became known.

Unfortunately for the Cherokees, the isolation that they had enjoyed for nearly a century since

James Needham's trip ceased in 1763. By that date the long colonial struggle between France and Britain had ended in a British triumph. John Stuart, British superintendent of the southern tribes, and the colonial governors of Virginia, North Carolina, South Carolina, and Georgia informed the chiefs that France had relinquished to Britain the western territories. No longer able to play off the Europeans against each other, the Indian's control of his hunting grounds rapidly began to erode. This was the situation in spite of the Royal Proclamation of 1763 by which British authorities attempted to check the flow of white settlers across the Appalachians, but it was already too late for the Cherokee hunting grounds along the Nolichucky and other areas in east Tennessee.

The Needham party of 1673 had not discovered the Northwest Passage to India or precious metals, but Gabriel Arthur did return to Virginia with stories of rich bottom land, virgin forests, and many rivers. The real wealth of east Tennessee was its land; white settlers after 1763 recognized this and began to establish settlements along the Holston, Watauga, and Noli-

Nolichucky River. (Photo: Emmett Essin.)

chucky Rivers. In the areas of white settlement there were no major Indian towns, but the Cherokees considered the territory vital because it was part of their larger hunting ground that stretched from the Tennessee to the Ohio River. In time trouble between the Indians and the white settlers who increasingly encroached upon Indian land had to develop, but for a short interval after 1763 William Bean, John Carter, and Jacob Brown launched new settlements in east Tennessee in defiance of the Royal Proclamation of 1763.

Jacob Brown first came to the Nolichucky with a small party from the Carolinas in 1771. The land they had settled clearly was south of the Virginia-North Carolina border, but that caused them little concern at the time. When Alexander Cameron, a British agent, warned them that they must relinquish all Cherokee land south of the colonial border, the Nolichucky settlers complied with the order to leave. For a few months Brown and his group moved to the Watauga settlement, but they soon returned to their homes with a new plan to defeat the intent of the Proclamation of 1763. If they could not purchase their land from the Cherokees, they would lease it on a long-term basis, for Brown correctly believed that time was on the side of the white man. For the moment a troubling problem had been solved, but new land problems and war would soon cloud the future of the Nolichucky settlement.

In the meantime, land speculators looked toward the land beyond the Appalachians with eyes fixed upon the potential fortunes to be made there. In east Tennessee, Richard Henderson of North Carolina and his Transylvania Company made history with their enormous purchase in 1775. The Treaty of Sycamore Shoals gave Henderson and his colleagues title to some twenty million acres in Kentucky and Tennessee for ten thousand pounds in goods. The Watauga and Nolichucky settlers witnessed this purchase and decided to act while the Indians were assembled. Both groups made land purchase agreements with the Cherokees. Jacob Brown of Nolichucky purchased two tracts of land on March 25, 1775, that included most of the present Tennessee counties of Unicoi, Washington, and Greene.

As it turned out, the land purchases marked the beginning of trouble with the Indians and not the end. British agents recognized none of the land deals and maintained that the purchases were illegal under the terms of the Proclamation of 1763. Moreover, the struggle between the colonials and Britain that became the American Revolution had begun, and that changed even more the situation on the frontier. British agents now supplied the Indians with powder and guns and encouraged them to drive the white men from their lands.

Settlers along the Holston, Watauga, and Nolichucky braced to defend themselves against Indian attacks. Near the mouth of Big Limestone Creek and the Nolichucky, Jacob Brown's group built Fort Lee, the most western of the colonial forts in east Tennessee. But the fort was abandoned as many Nolichucky settlers fled to the Watauga settlement at Sycamore Shoals. Tradition has it that Nancy Ward, the Cherokee "Beloved Woman," warned the settlers of the proposed Indian campaign and their strategy.

When the Indians attacked in the summer of 1776, they destroyed the now abandoned Fort Lee and pressed their attack against the Holston and Watauga settlements. Chiefs Dragging Canoe and The Raven attacked the Holston settlements, and Old Abram assaulted Fort Caswell on the Watauga, which protected both the Watauga and Nolichucky settlers. The Indian raids failed to dislodge the colonials from either the Holston or Watauga settlements, and the next year the Nolichucky group returned to their homes on that river and constructed Fort Williams under the command of John Sevier.

"Nolichucky Jack," as John Sevier was known by friend and foe alike, became one of Tennessee's most famous sons. As a soldier he distinguished himself in the Indian wars and the Revolutionary War. Against the Indians "Nolichucky Jack" fought thirty-five battles and won thirty-five victories. After the war, Sevier increasingly turned to politics. He was the only governor of the "Lost State of Franklin," governor of Tennessee for six terms, and served four terms in the Congress of the United States. His military background, combined with his personal interests in land speculation, especially at the expense of Indians, made "Nolichucky Jack" a popular leader among his Tennessee constituents.

When Jacob Brown died in 1785 and John Sevier moved to the Knoxville area in 1790, the focus of attention shifted from the Nolichucky, Holston, and Watauga settlements to the west and the establishment of the state of Tennessee. Although Andrew Jackson, Davy Crockett, and Andrew Johnson all had roamed the banks of the Nolichucky in their youth, their reputations were national and not identified with any significant developments within the Nolichucky region. East Tennessee drifted into isolation and political impotence.

That remained true until the Civil War, which caused sharp divisions between counties, between neighbors, and between brothers in Tennessee, especially in upper east Tennessee. Most small farmers in the region supported the Union and a strong central government, but the people in the towns and the big farmers in the broad bottom lands of the river valleys joined the Confederacy. With the state of Tennessee in the Confederacy, many people in east Tennessee tried to separate again—this time from Tennessee.

Some east Tennesseans supported the old idea of the State of Franklin. There was, however, no chance that the "Lost State of Franklin" would be revived because the Confederacy maintained vital transportation and communication links with Virginia through east Tennessee. If the Unionists in east Tennessee served no other purpose for their cause during the conflict, they pinned down several thousand Confederate troops in the region to protect those links. Early in the war the east Tennessee Unionists had demonstrated their potential for destruction when some of them burned several key railroad bridges. Confederate retribution that followed left wounds in this region that lasted well into the twentieth century.

The modern Nolichucky River valley is a prosperous part of the Tennessee Valley Authority system. The earliest effort to harness the Nolichucky's power began in 1913, when the East Tennessee Power and Light Company constructed a dam to generate electricity. The Nolichucky Dam, some forty-six miles down river from its beginning, forms a reservoir (Lake Davy Crockett) eight miles long; it is located some eight miles south of Greeneville, Tennessee. The esti-

mated cost of the dam was under two million dollars. Though it is an impressive structure, TVA classifies the dam and its reservoir as a minor operation. When it acquired the Nolichucky Dam from the East Tennessee Power and Light Company in 1945, and in 1972, TVA removed the generators from the dam and now uses the reservoir as a wildlife preserve. Power requirements and flood control have been shifted from the Nolichucky Dam to Douglas Dam on the French Broad.

Since the construction of Douglas Dam in 1943, major flooding along the Nolichucky has not been a significant problem. That was not always the case. The Nolichucky's greatest documented disasters include the floods of March, 1867; May, 1901; and August, 1940. An even greater deluge than any recorded may have occurred in 1791, but there is very little documentation to support the magnitude of the flooding. Davy Crockett, however, thought it to be "the second epistle of Noah's fresh [a new flood]." Undoubtedly the biggest recorded flood of the Nolichucky took place in 1901, doing property damage estimated at $500,000.

The real danger from the Nolichucky River is not its high waters but what is in its water. In 1978 the TVA declared that the Nolichucky River has "critical pollution problems." The affected area includes all of the river down to the Nolichucky Dam. TVA stated that the problem is with "high level suspended solids coming from mica mining operations near Spruce Pine, North Carolina." Second, there is an even more serious threat to the river. Questions have been raised concerning a nuclear plant in Erwin, Tennessee, that may have leaked hazardous waste materials into the Nolichucky. Finally TVA suspects still another problem, the possibility of pollution from the mining of asbestos, which has been listed as a carcinogen. If these problems are not resolved quickly, the many chapters of the long and exciting history of the Nolichucky River valley may soon end; but if these problems are solvable, the valley's future is as bright as its past was glorious.

FURTHER READING: Wilma Dykeman, *The French Broad.* (1955). Stanley J. Folmsbee, Robert E. Corlew, and Enoch L. Mitchell, *Tennessee: A Short History.* (1969).

J. E. Wade

The Ohio River

Source: Confluence of Allegheny and Monongahela rivers at Pittsburgh, Pennsylvania
Length: 981 miles
Tributaries: (from the North) Muskingum, Hocking, Scioto, Miami, Wabash; (from the South) Kanawha, Big Sandy, Licking, Kentucky, Cumberland
Mouth: Into Mississippi River at Cairo, Illinois
Agricultural Products: Diversified
Industries: Diversified

The Ohio River, the principal eastern tributary of the Mississippi, drains the western slope of the Allegheny Mountains. It is 981 miles long, being formed in the heart of modern Pittsburgh by the confluence of the Allegheny and Monongahela rivers. It flows first northwest but then southwest to its meeting with the north-south main stem of the Mississippi at Cairo, in extreme southern Illinois. Its channel was carved during the Ice Age; generally much of the river flows at the southernmost edge of the great glaciers. The Ohio drains 203,900 square miles. Helping it accomplish this are its numerous tributaries. These include, from the north, the Muskingum, Hocking, Scioto, Miami, and Wabash, and from the south, the Kanawha, Big Sandy, Licking, Kentucky, Cumberland, and Tennessee.

At its source the Ohio is 710 feet above sea level. It falls to 250 feet where it meets the Mississippi, a drop of 460 feet. The gradient is fairly even except in its first ninety miles in which it falls eighty-seven feet. This geographical fact was of considerable significance to navigation before the earliest locks were built. The former prominence of Wheeling, West Virginia,

The City of Louisville, built in 1894, ran between Louisville and Cincinnati three times a week until May, 1917. She was possibly the fastest steamboat on the western rivers. (Photo courtesy C. W. Stoll, "Rock Hill Steamboats." Credit: Rare Book Department, Cincinnati Public Library.)

was due to that city's location which was the head of navigation for much of each year. Likewise the so-called Falls of the Ohio, actually rapids extending a little less than three miles along the river and dropping about twenty-six feet, formed an effective barrier. For more than half the year the "Falls" halted river passage and led to the founding of the cities of Louisville, Kentucky, and Jeffersonville and New Albany, Indiana. The Ohio is one of the few rivers of the Mississippi system which, even in its natural, pre-improvement state could sustain some degree of year-round navigation. Only the Mississippi below St. Louis and the Tennessee River, a tributary of the Ohio, can do likewise. Ice closes the upper Mississippi and the Missouri each winter.

Ohio, which is an Iroquoian word meaning fine (or large) river, was used as a highway by the Indians long before the coming of the Europeans. Sieur Robert Cavelier de La Salle probably reached the Ohio in 1669, and French coureurs de bois (roving fur traders) were probably aware of the river well before the eighteenth century; they called it La Belle Riviere. It was in the 1740s, however, that British colonial and French interests began to clash in the Ohio Valley. In 1749 the French took steps to secure their vast inland empire, sending Celoron de Blainville with 200 soldiers into the Ohio Valley where he buried lead plates proclaiming French sovereignty of the region. At almost the same time the Ohio Company out of Virginia, a speculative land company, was granted 200,000 acres on the east bank of the Ohio between the Monongahela and the Kanawha rivers.

The rivals clashed at the Forks of the Ohio—modern Pittsburgh. When the British set out to establish a fort there, they discovered that the French had beaten them to the site and were already constructing Fort Duquesne. George Washington's subsequent battle at Great Meadows, south-southeast of Pittsburgh, was the first action of the French and Indian War; Washington was defeated but returned to Virginia with most of his men. Not until 1758 did the English under Colonel John Forbes take the stronghold and rename it Fort Pitt.

In spite of British attempts to prevent pioneers from crossing the mountains, settlers trekked over Forbes's Road—essentially present

U.S. Highway 40—and then down the Ohio. The Indian menance was great, however, and there was much bitter warfare during the American Revolution. In 1778 George Rogers Clark started down the Ohio on a campaign to destroy British and Indian power in the region bounded by the Ohio, the Mississippi, and the Great Lakes. He made camp on now-disappeared Corn Island at the head of the rapids. It was a safe haven from Indian attack but even so, before the winter rains set in Clark moved his troops to the Kentucky mainland; there the settlement which became Louisville began. Soon he floated on down the Ohio to the abandoned French Fort Massac, not quite fifty miles above the mouth of the Ohio. From there he marched overland, captured Kaskaskia and Cahokia on the Mississippi, and, later, Vincennes on the Wabash. Clark's success curtailed Indian raids across the Ohio into Kentucky and may have contributed to the English decision in the Treaty of Paris (1783) to allow the new American nation to have the country west to the Mississippi.

Although Indian depredations continued into the early 1880s, settlers entered the Ohio Valley in increasing numbers after Clark took Vincennes in 1778. The pioneers came by many routes: via the Kittanning Path to the Allegheny River and down it to the Forks of the Ohio or beyond; via Forbes's Road; or, coming up the Potomac to Cumberland, Maryland, and thence over the mountains via Braddock's Road to Redstone Old Fort on the Monongahela, thence downriver to the Forks; today much of this is U.S. 40. Many carried with them Revolutionary War land warrants, an easy way for the new states to pay their veterans.

When the pioneers reached the river, be it the Monongahela, Allegheny, or Ohio, they gave business to flatboat builders who had come before them and found a lucrative way to make a living. So heavy was traffic and so dangerous the hazards of the river in its unimproved state that Zadoc Cramer, an enterprising Pittsburgh publisher, in 1801 issued a guidebook, *The Navigator*, which helped the emigrants on their hazardous journey. This little book, which went through twelve editions, included crude strip maps of the river and instructions as to which side of the islands to head, the sites of sand bars and other dangers.

Along with the pioneers on flatboats were professional flatboatmen, keelboatmen, and rivermen, using every conceivable variation of these boats. A whole society grew up along the river. Flatboatmen and keelboatmen did not get along. Their fights in the river towns along with the exploits of the semi-legendary hero, Mike Fink, are part of the legacy of that age and society. Flatboats served as freight carriers, general stores, floating medicine shows, moveable houses of prostitution, and even carried preachers who put in at riverside settlements and preached, using the deck for their church. The keelboats, which went upriver as well as down, carried mail and passengers, often on scheduled trips, as well as frontier freight of all kinds: honey, beeswax, "Monongahela rye" whiskey, iron implements from Pittsburgh, pelts, bear's oil, and "rock oil"—petroleum—used for medicinal purposes.

Then came the steamboat. New Yorker Nicholas Roosevelt, with his partners Robert Fulton and Robert R. Livingston, proposed to operate steamboats on the Ohio and Mississippi rivers. They scouted the route, purchased coal lands near the Ohio in southern Indiana as a source of fuel, and at Pittsburgh commenced construction of the steamboat *New Orleans*. It was designed like an ocean-going vessel, with a rounded hull, but no one today knows whether it was a sidewheeler or a stern wheeler. In October, 1811, Roosevelt navigated the boat down to Louisville, announcing its midnight arrival by blowing the whistle and awakening a surprised populace. Leaving his wife there to have a baby, he steamed upstream to Cincinnati to prove it could be done. Then, pausing to take aboard his wife and baby, the *New Orleans* ran the Falls of the Ohio and proceeded down the river, headed for the Mississippi at Cairo, Illinois, and on downstream to New Orleans.

The boat ran successfully through a flooded, debris-ridden deluge, the result of the great New Madrid earthquake of 1811. The steamboat reached New Orleans and then ran regularly between there and Natchez until it struck a stump and sank in 1817.

Aboard the *New Orleans* on that first trip was a quiet, studious, observant young man named Henry Miller Shreve. Upon his return to the Ohio he set about building a riverboat according

to his own ideas. At Wheeling, Virginia, he built a flatboat-type hull, but with a pointed bow like a keelboat. He then decked the hull and placed the machinery on it rather than in the hull. In 1815 he launched his new boat, christened the *Washington*. As someone observed, it floated *on* rather than *in* the water. Literally, a flatboat with an engine, paddlewheel, and superstructure, this was the first of the true river steamboats. The vessel drew very little water, had adequate power, and the hull remained buoyed up even under a load of freight. Shreve's idea was an instant success. By the 1830s steamboats were busy carrying the vast westering migration down the Ohio from whence they spread to populate America's midlands.

The Ohio River steamboat became the standard of the industry. The center of construction was in the Ohio Valley, with flourishing boatyards from above Pittsburgh on the Allegheny to twenty miles below the city: at Marietta, Wheeling, Cincinnati, and the so-called Falls cities— Louisville, Kentucky, and Jeffersonville, Indiana. Jeffboat, Inc., is today the oldest continuously operated shipyard in the United States. Steamboats built from before the Civil War until the twentieth century were to be found in service all over the world, and a few of them are still puffing along on remote Third World rivers.

At about the same time that steamboating was reaching its zenith, the canal boat era blossomed in the Ohio Valley. In the 1820s and 1830s seven canals were dug which affected Ohio River commerce. Of these, the Ohio and Erie Canal, which connected the Ohio at Portsmouth with Lake Erie at Cleveland, and the Miami and Erie, which connected Erie at Toledo with the Ohio at Cincinnati, were perhaps the most important. The canals were expensive to dig and costly to maintain, and the railroads soon threw them out of business.

The discovery of abundant coal deposits in the Ohio Valley and up Ohio River tributaries greatly increased the uses of the river as a transportation artery. When the water level—or "tides" as they were called locally—was high enough, coal barges were floated down the Monongahela, Kanawha, and other rivers to the Ohio. There the barges were put together in groups of ten, twelve or more, and towed to their destination, either downriver or perhaps upriver to feed the expanding iron furnaces of Pittsburgh. Towing had an unusual meaning here: in Europe it meant pulling the barges while here it meant pushing them. In reality—at least downstream—the towboat acted mostly as a giant rudder and guiding sweep to keep the tow off the banks and maneuver it around the numerous sharp bends. Upstream the towboat had to be powerful in order to push the barges against the current. From Civil War times to the present the towing of barges has been a part of the life of the river. Today immense tonnages of coal are transported both up and down the Ohio.

The coming of the railroads did not bring the demise of Ohio steamboating. At first the railroads ran simply to the river, where passengers and freight were transferred to steamboats. The Baltimore and Ohio reached Wheeling in 1851 and in 1852 the Pennsylvania reached Pittsburgh. In 1871 Guyandot (now Huntington, West Virginia) was founded as the western terminus of the Chesapeake and Ohio Railroad, whose eastern terminus was Hampton Roads, Virginia.

To accommodate these railroads packet companies came into existence. There was a fine line of packets—steamboats running on regular schedules—which ran from Cincinnati to connect with the Pennsylvania Railroad at Pittsburgh. To accommodate the B.&O. a new "Southern Line" ran from Wheeling to Louisville, while Collis Huntington's Chesapeake and Ohio backed the "White Collar Line" which ran the 160 miles from Huntington to Cincinnati. All the railroads eventually crossed the Ohio, and put an end to the packets, although the "White Collar Line" continued in business under different ownership until the mid-1930s. Steamboats of all kinds continued to operate until the coming of the automobile and hard-surfaced roads. These freed the farmers and merchants from the steamboat, and ended its period of dominance.

The steamboat age on the Ohio was a pleasant one. The Ohio Valley possesses extraordinarily beautiful scenery, high rugged hills, a narrow, winding stream studded with islands which widens out into many broad, expansive reaches below the mouth of the Great Kanawha. It is populated with bustling, thriving cities and picturesque hamlets. The population, whether An-

glo-Saxon agriculturalists or German, Czech, or Polish industrial workers, or the French at Gallipolis and the Swiss at Vevay, Indiana, all came to have affection for their beautiful river.

It was their link with neighboring river towns and with the larger cities of Cincinnati, Evansville, Louisville, Wheeling, or Pittsburgh. Even after the railroads came, luxurious steamboats running regular schedules carried the upper classes from place to place in luxury such as no passenger train could offer. Other, smaller packets ran schedules as frequently as every day to once or twice a week over shorter distances, often as little as thirty miles. A very close relationship grew up between the captains of such boats and their passengers; often, like local buses today, they stopped at farms fronting the river to pick up and discharge passengers and freight. Every steamboat was recognized by its whistle, which was slightly different from any other. The era, which lasted until the coming of the motor car, was a slower, pleasanter chapter in Ohio River life.

Because Americans used the Ohio for transportation, they began almost immediately to suggest ways of improving the river for that purpose. In 1830 a private company opened a two-mile-long canal on the Kentucky side at Louisville which, with a three-step lock, carried vessels around the Falls to a placid point downstream. For fifty years this company charged tolls before the federal government took over. During this period maintenance for transportation on the river consisted of removing snags and wrecks, some dredging, and the raising of a few dikes.

Although the Ohio was a year-round stream, there were times of low water when only specially built low-water boats could navigate the shallow places. A channel deep enough to support barges year-round was needed for the industrial development along the river. To this end, in 1885 the Davis Island Dam which formed a "pool" into the mouth of the Monongahela and Allegheny was opened. The dam was built in moveable sections called wickets. In the "up" position the dam gave an additional four, five, or more feet of water over troublesome sand bars and shoals. When the water flow increased, the sections of the dam could be lowered, one by one, and the river was open again until the flow diminished and the wickets were again raised to form a dam.

Congress then approved a project for fifty-four locks and dams over the 981-mile stretch to create a channel with a minimum depth of nine feet year around. An economic survey projected that such a project would generate 13,000,000 tons of freight with a favorable cost-savings ratio. In 1929 the grand plan was completed and the river was carrying 21,000,000 tons of shipping. (In the final design just fifty locks were found necessary.)

Predictions proved to be on the conservative side. Although the plan started slowly due to the Great Depression, its value was proved during the Second World War. More and more industrial plants moved into the Ohio Valley. Today all manner of commodities float up and down the Ohio. They range from liquid anhydrous ammonia for fertilizer, moved in vacuum-controlled tank barges at temperatures of −200°F, to molten sulphur and asphalt shipped in heated barges at temperatures approximating plus 300°F.

The river has served increasing tonnages that have made the 1929 Lock and Dam system hopelessly obsolete, for by now the tonnage on the Ohio exceeds 150,000,000. Today a new lock system with twenty-one high dams replacing the original fifty is nearing completion. The demands of modern times for electrical energy and the coal that powers most power plants have made the Ohio River and its carrying capacity a vital element in twentieth-century energy supply.

But what of the river itself? Despite industrialization there remain long stretches which take the observer back to pioneer days. Weekend vacationers use the Ohio for recreational purposes and attempts to clean up the river have in many cases succeeded. Game fish are again biting along the Ohio. Some stern-wheel steamboats still ply the waters, giving passengers a glimpse into a bygone era. The Ohio remains a beautiful river, but one that nevertheless serves a bustling, modern civilization. Its colorful foliage, life-bearing current, and individual mystique have always intrigued men and women and filled their souls with confidence and serenity.

FURTHER READING: Garnett Laidlaw Eskew, *Pageant of the Packets* (1929). Louis C. Hunter, *Steamboats on the Western Waters* (1949, 1980).

C. W. Stoll

The St. Louis River of Minnesota

Source: Seven Beaver Lake in Saint Louis County in northeast Minnesota
Length: About 160 miles
Tributaries: Whiteface, Cloquet, White Pine, and Midway rivers
Mouth: Into Lake Superior at Duluth, Minnesota
Agricultural Products: Negligible
Industries: Pulp paper mills; lumbering

The headwaters of the St. Louis River flow out of Seven Beaver Lake which lies approximately fifty miles north and twenty miles east of the estuary where the river empties into Lake Superior. From its source the St. Louis begins its flow to the southwest following the northern border of ancient Glacial Lake Upham. Minnesota's great Iron Range forms the northern rim of the drainage basin where six streams, the Partridge, the Embarrass, the East and West Two Rivers, and the East and West Swan Rivers, flow south to join the St. Louis. A major tributary, the Whiteface River, takes its headwaters from an impounded reservoir and flows across the old lake plain from the south and empties into the St. Louis just before the latter makes an abrupt turn to the southeast at the town of Floodwood.

Twenty miles downstream the Cloquet River, second largest tributary to the St. Louis, joins the river as do two other minor streams, the White Pine River and the Midway. After passing the city of Cloquet the St. Louis plunges down the rocky gorge at Jay Cooke Park before it widens out into a fifteen-mile estuary that begins at Fond du Lac. From here the river flows past the iron ore and commercial docks, the grain elevators, and the piers of the two cities which flank its mouth, Duluth, Minnesota, and Superior, Wisconsin. From source to mouth the river drops 1,100 feet, with approximately half of this descent between Cloquet and Fond du Lac. The St. Louis discharges an average of 2,000 cubic feet per second, although in times of high water this figure has reached a maximum of nearly 38,000 cubic feet per second.

First called the "Fond du Lac River," the St. Louis appeared on a Jesuit map drawn from the field notes of Father Claude Allouex who showed it as a short stream identified as the, "R. pour aller aux Nadoussi a 60 lieue vers le couchant," or the "river leading to the Sioux, 60 leagues to the West." About 1740 the St. Louis River appears on several maps as the "Fond du Lac River or St. Louis River." The name "St. Louis" was given to the river by the early French explorer, Pierre Gaultier de Varennes, Sieur de la Verendrye, who with his four sons and Indian guide, Ochagach, passed along its lower course in search of a passageway to the western sea. The name is derived from Louis IX, King of France, who in 1749 bestowed on La Verendrye the Cross of St. Louis in honor of his services to the monarch.

Long before (and after) la Verendrye the St. Louis afforded a route from Lake Superior to the interior. Travelers coming from the lake journeyed twenty miles upriver by canoe as far as the impassable falls and rapids at Fond du Lac. Here passengers disembarked and walked the first of two portages, Woman's Portage, about a half mile in length, while the canoes, still loaded, were pushed and pulled through the rapids. The second portage, the Grand Portage (not to be confused with the Grand Portage which connects the Pigeon River with Lake Superior) began immediately, and canoes, goods, and passengers began a seven mile detour around the

rapids. The canoemen, or voyageurs, transported everything to the top of the gorge. To make travel easier and to provide a means of protection the portage was divided into resting places or "pauses," each one a third to a half mile apart depending upon the difficulty of travel. The St. Louis River Grand Portage was seven miles long and had nineteen pauses. Canoe freight was carried in bales weighing from seventy-five to ninety pounds, and these were referred to as "pieces." Each voyageur would carry a load of two pieces (sometimes three or more) to the next pause, then return for more until the entire cargo had been transported the length of the portage. Travelers who used the Grand Portage marveled at the great strength and endurance of the French Canadian voyageurs who carried the heavy loads under the most difficult conditions and in all kinds of weather. One observer recorded in his journal an account of a voyageur who carried a load consisting of 350 pounds. Another traveler describes a half-Negro, half-Indian voyageur who carried six pieces, 450 pounds at a minimum, across the Grand portage.

Once across the Grand Portage travelers continued on up the St. Louis to Knife Portage where a mile-long bypass took them around still another falls. From here the travelers chose a variety of routes depending upon their destination. Those parties bound for the Mississippi River could leave the St. Louis River and follow the Old Portage or Prairie Portage to Prairie Lake and on down the Prairie River to Sandy Lake and the Mississippi. This route was favored by Indians and those persons with light canoe loads. A better-known route, and one which would accommodate more easily the heavier packs of the fur traders, was located on up the St. Louis. At the mouth of the East Savanna River travelers turned their canoes upstream to the headwaters where they crossed the six-mile Savanna Portage (often wading through swamp and mud to their knees), then down the West Savanna River to Sandy Lake and on to the Mississippi. After 1800, the Prairie Portage was seldom used and the Savanna Portage carried the most traffic. Travelers bound for the northern lakes continued up the St. Louis to the Embarrass River, on up that stream through a series of lakes and portages, over the height of land (the Laurentian Divide) to their final destination by way of the northward flowing streams.

The first white man to see the St. Louis River and to cross the Grand Portage was Daniel Greysolon, Sieur Du Lhut, a Frenchman from Montreal who was on the lower part of the river in the early summer of 1679. The purpose of his expedition was to arrange a peace between the Sioux and the Ojibwa, and, always mindful of his duty to the French crown, he lay claim to the area for that nation. The peace which he negotiated was short lived, but from this date forward for almost a century, the empire of New France controlled the western Great Lakes region.

The French and Indian War, the last in a series of wars for empire between England and France, removed the French from the continent. With its victory in 1763, England gained control over the vast wilderness area previously dominated by France, and the St. Louis River watershed passed into new hands. But subsequent events were to transfer possession of the western Great Lakes region to a third party. One of the primary objectives of the American Revolution was to establish the new nation's control over the lands to the west. The diplomats who gathered in Paris in 1783 negotiated a peace which gave the United States a northern boundary that extended through the middle of Lakes Ontario, Erie, and Huron, split the middle of the channel at Sault Ste. Marie, and proceeded through Lake Superior north of Isles Royale and Phelipeaux (the latter did not exist!), and from there "thence to the Long Lake . . . through the middle of said Long Lake, and the water communication between it and the Lake of the Woods . . . ." A most fateful decision for the St. Louis River! The peace commissioners were using a map drawn by John Mitchell, an Englishman who though born and educated in England had lived in the American colonies for almost half a century. Following his return to England in 1748, Mitchell published a map of the colonies and the interior of the continent in 1755. The errors on the Mitchell map were to directly effect the St. Louis River.

Four years prior to the Paris negotiations a group of Montreal fur traders formed a partnership which was to eventually control the fur trade from the St. Lawrence to the Pacific. The organization which they created was the Northwest Company. For the next several years this company would dominate the Great Lakes country and with it the St. Louis River artery of trade.

In 1792, a Northwest Company expedition under the command of Jean Baptiste Cadotte investigated the St. Louis River area with regard to its fur-producing potential. His optimistic report resulted in the creation of the Department of Fond du Lac and the construction of Fort St. Louis at the mouth of the river. A year later, Jean Baptiste Perrault, another employee of the Northwest Company, was employed to construct the buildings at the Fort St. Louis site. Despite the fact that the Peace of Paris (1783) established American sovereignty over the area, the Northwest Company by their sheer presence continued to dominate the St. Louis River for the next several years.

Shortly after the turn of the century a new rival appeared in the fur trade. The American Fur Company under the control of John Jacob Astor was chartered under the laws of the state of New York and rapidly spread its posts and influence into the Great Lakes country. In 1811 several of the more prominent men of the Northwest Company formed a five-year partnership with Astor under the name of the Southwest Company and began to operate the posts that lay on American soil, including Fort St. Louis.

The War of 1812 forced a separation, and Astor bought out his former partners. In addition, Congress passed legislation prohibiting the licensing of non-citizens as fur traders on the American side of the line. This left Astor in control of the St. Louis River basin. The location of Fort St. Louis at the mouth of the river had always posed some problems with regard to the transfer of cargoes since the whole process had to be repeated at the beginning of the Grand Portage. In a move to improve the operation of the fort, Astor decided to move the post some twenty miles upstream to a location just below the rapids at the present site of Fond du Lac.

The treaty of peace that closed the War of 1812 resolved some questions but opened still others. For one, the boundary between Lake Superior and Lake of the Woods had never been identified with any certainty. The commissioners who met at Ghent provided for settlement of this line by arbitration, a process begun in 1822 with Peter B. Porter representing the United States and Anthony Barclay representing the British. The tentative boundary which ran from Grand Portage (on the north shore of Lake Superior) north and west along the chain of border lakes was surveyed and both sides considered the matter settled. The British commissioner, however, ordered a second survey from Lake Superior to Rainy Lake by way of the St. Louis River under the assumption that the estuary of the river constituted the "Long Lake" named in the treaty of 1783. In return, Porter ordered a survey of the Kaministiquia River which empties into Lake Superior at some distance up the shore beyond Grand Portage. With his survey completed, Barclay argued that the true international boundary ran through the main channel of the St. Louis River to the mouth of the Embarrass, up that river to the head of navigation, across the portage to the Pike River and down that stream to Lake Vermillion, then through the lake and waters that connect to Rainy Lake and Lake of the Woods. Barclay pressed the undeniable fact that his survey followed an ancient commercial route to the north, that it had fewer portages and was therefore more navigable, that the St. Louis River was the largest tributary of Lake Superior, and (on less firm ground) that the old name of the St. Louis River was the "Lake River" and consequently the one referred to in the treaty. Barclay also persisted that since the boundary ran north of Isle Royale the framers of the treaty intended for the line to go south to the long lake since it would have been unnecessary to identify the island if the boundary were to continue north to either the Kaministiquia or Pigeon Rivers.

The American commissioner countered the British position by admitting that while the St. Louis River was a commercial route at one time, the preferred thoroughfare at the date of the treaty began at the Pigeon and followed the well-known "voyageur's highway" along the northern lakes to Rainy Lake and Lake of the Woods. The discussions dragged on until 1827 when the British commissioner agreed to give up his claim to the St. Louis River if the Americans would relinquish their claim to the ten-

mile strip of land between the Pigeon River and the village of Grand Portage. Still neither side would give in, and with the fate of this small insignificant strip of land unresolved the boundary remained unsettled until 1842 when the Webster-Ashburton treaty fixed the dividing line at the Pigeon River.

About 1830 the fur trade began to decline noticeably, and by 1850 fur no longer held first place in the Minnesota economy. The lake region was yielding to its second largest resource. Lumber became the dominant industry. When the forests of New England had been cut and marketed, the lumbermen moved to the Great Lakes states of Michigan, Wisconsin, and Minnesota. The lumber companies and their logging crews began to harvest the richest timberland in America. A variety of trees grew here, but the king of the timber industry was the white pine. It was a magnificent tree, a lumberman's dream, standing anywhere from 120 to 200 feet high with a diameter of thirty inches to five feet. The lumber was strong, light in weight, it seasoned well, and resisted both weather and time. The rivers of the lake states provided the transportation to bring logs to the mills. In Minnesota the St. Louis River and its tributaries became the arteries of the lumber traffic. The St. Louis, the Cloquet, the Embarrass, and the Whiteface were easy log-driving streams, while at several points, the St. Louis itself had water power sites that made sawmills possible. Cloquet, a small community located above the rapids and falls at the St. Louis River's Grand Portage was a natural gateway to thousands of acres of white pine and became known as the "White Pine Capital." In 1878, the first mills began operation in that area with logs carried by the St. Louis River. The site had such possibilities that Frederick Weyerhaeuser, one of the lumber kings of the upper midwest, established a mill at Cloquet. Between 1880 and 1883 eleven sawmills lined the shores of St. Louis Bay, the lower part of the river's estuary. Some of the logs were brought down the river while others were rafted in from Lake Superior. In 1902 the Duluth district (the central part of which was the St. Louis River basin) cut 1,031,775,000 board feet of lumber, a record never again equalled. By the turn of the century the lumber frontier was rapidly diminishing, and in a few years the lumbermen and their crews would once again move on, this time to the states of the Pacific Northwest. The Cloquet mill, for example, converted from lumber to pulp and paper.

The St. Louis River has enjoyed a rich and colorful history, but it has not been without cost. The towns and industries that have grown up along its banks have used the river for waste disposal. The waters of the St. Louis River, especially the lower part, have become polluted. The prospects, however, for a restored river look promising.

In the fall of 1978 the St. Louis River, estuary, and harbor received a new lease on life. The Western Lake Superior Sanitary District waste treatment plant, one of the most technologically advanced of its kind in the world, began operation. This facility promises to return the water to a condition more pristine than the Environmental Protection Agency's standards for fishing, swimming, and other uses. The treatment procedure used by the WLSSD involves moving polluted water from several points upstream through massive aqueducts to the processing station at Duluth. Once at the plant the large debris is removed and a "grit chamber" allows the sand to settle. Then, bacteria is added to the water to digest all potentially harmful organic matter. After passing through several chemical treatment reservoirs the last step is to replace the lost oxygen. Solid wastes removed by the plant are incinerated to provide steam which supplies some of the plant's energy demand. The costs are high, but the benefits will more than offset them. Once again the St. Louis River will run as clear and pure as the days when the Indian and the voyageur paddled their birchbark canoes along its course.

FURTHER READING: John Fritzen, *The History of Fond du Lac and Jay Cooke Park* (1978). Thomas F. Waters, *The Streams and Rivers of Minnesota* (1977).

Roy Hoover

The Tennessee River

Source: Junction of French Broad and Holston rivers above Knoxville, Tennessee
Length: 652 miles
Tributaries: Hiwassee, Little Tennessee, Clinch, Flint, Elk, Duck, Big Sandy, and Clarks rivers
Mouth: Into Ohio River at Paducah, Kentucky
Agricultural Products: Tobacco, cotton, vegetables
Industries: Electric power, recreation, aluminum, diversified manufactures

The Tennessee is really two rivers: today's man-made river (post-TVA), which is "less a river than a chain of lakes," and, buried beneath the lakes's stairsteps, an older river, decisive in America's history.

The older river was contrary. Insteady of taking the apparently more direct route eastward to the Atlantic, its headwaters traveled westward across the Unaka Mountains, eventually emptying into the Ohio River, then the Mississippi. Because the continental divide lay to the east, in the Blue Ridge Mountains, these streams had to work their way seaward by the much longer route, forming the fifth largest river in America.

The French Broad and the Holston met above Knoxville to become the Tennessee. It was not always known as such, however: not until the late nineteenth century and the prospect of Federal aid to "the Tennessee" did that name apply to the river between the mouth of the French Broad and the mouth of the Little Tennessee at Lenoir City. To the Indians, the Little Tennessee was *the* Tennessee, and the larger river was the Hogohegee.

As the Tennessee cut through Walden's Ridge below Chattanooga's Moccasin Bend, it arced back to the northwest through the steep gorges of "The Narrows." Here churned the perilous "Suck," "Boiling Pot," and "Skillet." At the center of the Great Bend, the river flowed southward once more, then near Guntersville, Al-bama, turned again to the northwest, passing over Muscle Shoals, the most formidable obstacle of all, near the tri-cities of Florence, Sheffield, and Tuscumbia.

The Muscle Shoals was a terrifying whitewater passage thirty-seven miles long. Little wonder that the river was divided into upper and lower Tennessee at this point! Below the Shoals the river flowed northward uneventfully for 200 miles, briefly becoming the border of Tennessee and Kentucky; above Paducah in the latter state, the Tennessee joined the Ohio.

The Tennessee was made up of three earlier rivers, "stuck together," says geologist Edward T. Luther, "like parts of some Rube Goldberg contraption designed to move water from one place to another in the most unlikely way possible." The oldest segment (the uppermost third) ran toward the Gulf as long ago as 285 million years. The middle segment appeared 75 million years ago, emptying at first into the Mississippi, then shifting its mouth toward Alabama. The last segment once flowed southward towards Alabama's Tombigbee River (and today's Tennessee-Tombigbee Waterway is a restoration of the Tennessee's ancient course). In the Pleistocene Ice Age (about 600,000 years ago) as the Mississippi and Ohio were scoured deeply enough to capture its drainage, this river reversed itself to flow northward.

Four successive Indian cultures existed in the Tennessee country in the prehistoric period. First were the Paleo-Indians who hunted large game; then (about 8000 B.C.) the Archaic Indians; then between 1000 B.C. and 700 A.D., the Woodland Indians flourished. Finally came the Mississippians, who built flat-topped pyramidal temple mounds with ramps, reflecting Meso-American influences.

In recorded times, Europeans found the Tennessee country peopled by several tribes, the most influential and largest being the Cherokee. From their town of Tanasi, Tanase, or Tenese—to mention only a few of the spellings—comes the name of the river and the state. The Cherokee, occupying eighty-towns, plied the Tennessee in dugout canoes, sometimes forty feet in length.

The Spanish under Hernando de Soto (1540) and Juan Pardo (1566–1567) were the first to traverse the Tennessee. For a century thereafter some trading with the Spanish took place and European diseases decreased the Indian population. Then came the English, the first ones into the Tennessee country being James Needham and an illiterate, probably indentured youth, Gabriel Arthur, who set out from the Virginia colony in 1673. Arthur barely missed death at the stake, was adopted by the Cherokee and eventually escaped; Needham also got back to Virginia.

The English colony most successful at linking the isolated upper Tennessee to the eastern seaboard was South Carolina. Part of each year Carolina traders lived in the back country, hunting and trading. In one exceptionally abundant year South Carolina exported 121,355 deerskins. For a time there was also a brisk trade in people: in 1708, one-third of the slave population of Charleston was Indian.

During the contest between the British and French for the Ohio Valley (1754–1763) the colonists promised to build a fort to protect the Overhill Cherokee from tribes siding with the French. This westernmost British redoubt was built on the Little Tennessee River near its entrance into the Tennessee. It was 1757 before the military commander, Raymond Demeré, could complete Fort Loudoun, named after the British commander-in-chief. For a time tensions with the Cherokee eased; soldiers sent for their wives and children were born at the fort.

But events elsewhere along the frontier brought on the Cherokee War of 1760–1761. In August, 1761, Demeré surrendered to Chief Oconostota. The fort's occupants marched out to be escorted to South Carolina but instead were massacred from ambush. Yet in spite of the capture of Fort Loudoun by the Cherokee, the British won the war against the French elsewhere, and in the course of their stand against the British the Cherokee lost half their warriors.

In the second half of the eighteenth century the Indians of the Tennessee country were involved also in the American Revolution. Again the Indians were the losers. By the last year of the War (1783) their displacement by white settlers seemed a foregone conclusion: many Revolutionary War soldiers had been paid in western land and this hastened the settlement of the Tennessee country.

Even before the Revolution the valleys of what

would become East Tennessee had begun to fill with settlers. In the next decades negotiations and armed force secured still more land. In the winter of 1779–1780 John Donelson led a party of 200 (including his teen-age daughter Rachel, Andrew Jackson's future wife) downriver from Fort Patrick Henry on the Holston toward the French Lick on the Cumberland—presently Nashville.

In the previous year a force under Colonel Evan Shelby had devastated eleven Chickamauga towns along the Tennessee River. Now the Chickamaugas had reoccupied their villages and were little disposed to welcome settlers. Below Lookout Mountain, near present Chattanooga, the Indians fired upon the flotilla and captured the last boat in the line, which had been quarantined with smallpox. According to tradition, the death or capture of its twenty-eight occupants was grimly avenged by the disease. Once past Muscle Shoals the party made good time and on April 24, 1780, approached the French Lick after a water journey of 1,000 miles.

With colonies becoming states, confusion about western land titles followed. Hopes for a state of Franklin ended when North Carolina ceded its western land to the Federal government. In 1790 the Territory of the United States South of the River Ohio was created with its capital at a new settlement just below the juncture of the French Broad with the Holston. Originally named White's Fort, it was renamed Knoxville in honor of Washington's Secretary of War.

Bulky exports from the Tennessee country had to be shipped out by flatboat, a cumbersome box perhaps twenty by one hundred feet steered from the stern and steadied by sweeps called "broadhorns." An Alabama variant was the highsided "cotton box." Once downriver, a flatboat was sold for lumber while the boatmen trudged home along the dangerous wilderness trails. The much narrower, pointed keelboat, sometimes with a sail, could travel either way on the Tennessee, provided it had a stalwart crew. Where poles could not touch bottom, the boat was pulled against the current by cordelling (using a towline along the bank), warping (using upstream skiffs and towlines) or bushwhacking (grabbing overhanging tree branches).

The steamboat age on the Tennessee began in 1821 with the arrival of the *Osage* at Florence, Alabama. In the 1830s the state of Tennessee improved the upper river enough to permit fairly regular service between Knoxville and Decatur, Alabama—six or seven months a year.

After Andrew Jackson and Isaac Shelby persuaded the Chickasaws to cede what would become West Tennessee and western Kentucky, the Cherokee were the only Indians left holding title along the Tennessee. They owned what would become several counties in Tennessee and Alabama and a sizeable third of Georgia. They had adapted many of the white people's ways. However, after Jackson was elected President, Georgia began to sell off Cherokee-owned land by lottery, unrestrained by the federal government. Tennessee soon joined in. In an 1835 case a Tennessee judge called Indians "mere wandering savages" who possibly "deserved to be exterminated as savage and pernicious beasts." All but a few hundred Cherokee were forced to leave. An immediate result of removal was the growth of [Chief John] Ross's Landing, strategically located as a potential rail and water terminus. Incorporated in 1839 as Chattanooga, within a few years it became the rail link between Nashville and Atlanta, a fact of fateful consequence during the Civil War.

The Union made far better use of the Tennessee which was planned as the avenue of Union advance. Confederate Fort Henry, just south of the Kentucky-Tennessee line, fell quickly, to be followed shortly by the fall of Fort Donelson on the Cumberland, just eleven miles away. Two months later at Shiloh Church, near Pittsburg Landing on the lower Tennessee south of Savannah (Tennessee), Confederates launched an attack on Federal troops massing there. Fighting began on April 6, 1862, and continued through the next day. In those two days each side lost about one-fourth its strength; no side could claim victory, but with the Confederate withdrawal of troops the lower Tennessee came under Federal control. To defend its supply lines, the Union built light-draft "tinclads" and assembled a marine brigade to pursue snipers. Muscle Shoals became a Confederate asset, blocking upriver travel by Union gunboats.

Not until Federal forces worked their way through Middle Tennessee following the rail line toward Atlanta did another large battle take place along the Tennessee. This was the Battle of Chickamauga, which led to Union forces being besieged in Chattanooga in the fall of 1863. With no steamboats above the Shoals, the Union sent in the first supplies on what was little more than a flatboat equipped with a steam engine and stern wheel. Quickly named the "Chicken Thief" by Confederates, it was the first in a fleet known as the Cracker Line; it managed to prevent a Union surrender. Grant, now commanding all Union forces in the west, led the lifting of the siege on November 23–25, 1863. After the "Battle Above the Clouds," the way was open to Atlanta and Sherman's March to the Sea.

Wartime destruction of railroads resulted in a postwar boon to steamboat traffic on the Tennessee. These were the days of refitted Union boats, local "store boats" carrying groceries, log rafts coming downstream with the spring freshet, occasional flatboats, new light-draft boats built to run the upper river or Muscle Shoals, and—by the turn of the century—towboats pushing their barges. In the period 1875–1900 the army engineers built or rebuilt canals, aqueducts, railroad towpaths, and docks, deepened the channel, and made other improvements to facilitate the transportation of people and goods along the river.

The first power proposal involving Muscle Shoals was introduced in Congress in 1898 by Joseph Wheeler, the ex-Confederate cavalryman, and from then until enactment of TVA in 1933 no session of Congress was without a bill to develop Muscle Shoals. Mobilizing for World War I, the Federal government authorized ni-

trate plants powered by a hydroelectric complex at the Shoals, but at war's end the massive Wilson Dam of that project was still unfinished. Not until the New Deal's Hundred Days did Senator George Norris of Nebraska, a consistent advocate of TVA, succeed in pushing through the legislation. Plans were made for expensive high dams to provide flood control and electric power. It would take twenty-five years and $2 billion to complete the project. Then in 1935 Congress provided for navigation by the maintenance of a nine-foot channel to Knoxville. This took ten years to achieve, but, once completed, dramatically increased tonnage on the river.

By the second half of this century TVA had become what historian Thomas K. McCraw calls "a successful but unrepeated experiment." Change in the region was dramatic: income rose 502% in TVA's first quarter century compared to a 321% increase nationally. Yet conflicts continue. Each removal and inundation of land for a new dam and lake has brought protest. Strip-mined coal, sulfurous emissions, and nuclear energy are newer controversies. "In retrospect, the real wonder is that a single TVA ever materialized," concludes McCraw.

Still TVA flourishes. And if the Tennessee is now more a succession of dams and lakes than a free-flowing stream, the region remains beautiful, abundant in all good things, and populated by a vigorous, hard-working people.

FURTHER READINGS: Donald Davidson, *The Tennessee* (1946–1948). Gilbert E. Govan and James W. Livingood, *The Chattanooga Country, 1540–1976: From Tomahawks to TVA* (1977).

Anne Dempster Taylor

The Wabash River

Source: Grand Lake in west-central Ohio
Length: 475 miles
Tributaries: Tippecanoe, Salomonie, Vermillion, Embarras, White, Little Wabash rivers, and others
Mouth: Flows into Ohio River at Ohio-Indiana Boundary
Agricultural Products: corn, hogs, cattle
Industries: Sand and gravel, hydroelectric power, diversified manufacturing

Wah-bah-shik-ki meant "white" or "shining water" to the Miami Indians inhabiting much of Indiana. The river, before muddying soil erosion, was said to be glistening silver in the summer sun—particularly in the upper reaches where the river bed was limestone. Early French travelers, using their own phonic system to spell difficult Indian words, shortened the spelling to Ouabachi and later to Oubache which for the English became as it remains, Wabash. Immortalized by Paul Dresser who composed "On the Banks of the Wabash," Indiana's official state song, the river has had a rich and colorful history.

From its source in Grand Lake in west-central Ohio the Wabash flows northwestward into Indiana to the Little River, thence west and southwest to the Tippecanoe, receiving on the way the waters of the Salomonie, Mississinewa, and Eel. Below Lafayette it turns southward and is enlarged by the Vermillion, Sugar, Raccoon, Busseron, Embarras, White, Patoka, and Little Wabash rivers before entering the Ohio at the extreme southwest corner of the state. The Wabash, along its 475-mile length, falls in a gradual slope gradient from an altitude of 1,285 feet to 313 feet. It drains a basin of 33,000 square miles which includes two-thirds of Indiana, has an annual discharge of over 28,000 cubic feet per water per second, and is the second largest tributary of the Ohio River system. From Terre Haute south to its mouth, the Wabash forms the boundary between Illinois and Indiana.

Prehistoric Mound Builders were the first known inhabitants of the Wabash River area. Dating from about 10,000 B.C., these diversified peoples left a rich archaeological record. Historic Indian occupants, not linked to the prehistoric natives, appeared in the latter part of the seventeenth century. During the heyday of Indian activity, as many as 5,000 warriors, all of Algonquin stock, lived along the Wabash which, according to Indian tradition, was their sacred river.

The Miami, the strongest of the Indian tribes in Indiana, moved to the upper reaches of the Wabash Valley late in the seventeenth century. The Wea or Quiatanon came with the Miami and settled near the mouth of the Tippecanoe. The Piankashaw, accompanying the Miami and Wea, centered near the Vermillion and further south along the Wabash near Vincennes. These three tribes, who occupied the Wabash-Maumee valley, were in part responsible for the later use of this trade route by the French.

Other tribes making the Wabash Valley their home were the Potawatomi, the Kickapoo, the Shockeys, and the Vermillion. In the late eighteenth century a few Shawnee arrived, including Tecumseh and The Prophet, both of whom figured prominently on the Wabash frontier.

Spain was the first world power to establish claim to the area, but she did not exploit or settle it. It was not until 1608 that France launched a century and a half of North American expansion which culminated in the creation of New France. At its zenith French possessions extended from the mouth of the St. Lawrence to the Mississippi and included sparse settlement throughout the vast area. Keystone to this arching, slowly developing and far-flung new world empire was the Maumee-Wabash route which connected the Great Lakes with the Ohio and Mississippi river systems.

However, English traders from east of the Appalachians slowly but persistently intruded. The French reacted with strategically located posts and missions. By the 1750s they had built Post Quiatanon on the Wabash eighteen miles below the mouth of the Tippecanoe, Post Miami, at present-day Fort Wayne, and Post Vincennes, eighty miles upriver from the junction of the

Ohio and Wabash rivers. These three posts, with their forts and small garrisons, served as a strategic line of communication within an empire beset by a dwindling supply of fur, by unsettling Indian relations, and by the increasing challenge of British competition.

The fate of the posts along the Wabash was decided after England's declaration of war against France in 1756. The British occupied Fort Miami and Quiatanon in 1760 and 1761 but did not take possession of Vincennes until 1777. By the Treaty of Paris (1763) France ceded to England all of her possessions east of the Mississippi. Save for place names the French people, customs, and institutions along the Wabash left no pervading influence.

The years of British control were full of confusion and conflict. Indians under Chief Pontiac, with French encouragement, rebelled against Britain's policies—no rum, higher prices for goods, and few presents. From Detroit the furor spread north and west, east as far as Fort Pitt and into the Wabash Valley. The garrison at Fort Miami surrendered; the stockade at Quiatanon likewise capitulated. When peace was restored within two years these forts and Vincennes remained unoccupied by British troops.

For governmental purposes the British added the territory north of the Ohio River, including the Wabash Valley, to the newly established colony of Quebec. Land speculators and Colonial and Spanish traders vied for friendship with the Indians and control of the valued trade. Save for about one year (1777–1778) the Wabash country was left without official British presence and protection.

Meanwhile Britain and her colonies went to war. In the West, Indians with British encouragement renewed their attacks on frontier posts. A young Virginian, George Rogers Clark, led a small force to take the French villages on the Mississippi and Wabash rivers: in 1778 he took Kaskaskia and Cahokia on the Mississippi and Vincennes on the Wabash. This spurred Lieutenant Governor Henry Hamilton in Detroit to organize a small army of 350 regulars, militia, and Indians to march southeast to the Wabash and Vincennes, which he retook with virtually no resistance. He held Vincennes for three months and one week. Early in February, 1779, Clark, with 170 men, left Kaskaskia for the fort

on the Wabash, 180 miles away. Through miles of icy, flooded river bottoms the little band struggled without adequate food and unable to build warming and drying fires for fear of detection. Within two days after arriving at the village, the town and nearby Fort Sackville surrendered. Clark's plans to proceed up the Wabash and thence to Detroit failed for want of sufficient forces.

Peace between Britain and the colonies was signed in September, 1783. The Wabash country, still inhabited by Indians, some English, numerous French and many adventurous Americans, now belonged to a new nation. It was now part of the United States though three European countries—Spain, France, and England—continued to look longingly upon the West while the Indians were in actual possesion of the land.

The years to the turn of the century (1800) were tense and experimental for the Wabash country. Until 1795 the Indian question was the territorial governor's most serious problem. With the Treaty of Greenville (1795) which followed the Battle of Fallen Timbers, fought along the Maumee, Indian disaffection was temporarily assuaged.

When the states relinquished their western claims, thus creating a public domain, the Confederation Congress passed the Ordinance of 1785, setting up a system of land survey, and the Northwest Ordinance of 1787, setting up a system whereby a territory could become a state. The possibility of stability came to the Wabash country. In May, 1800, Indiana (that part of the Old Northwest Territory except Ohio) became Indiana Territory, with its capital at Vincennes on the Wabash. William Henry Harrison was the territorial governor. Of the myriad of problems confronting him, Harrison was most sensitive to the smoldering Indian-white conflict.

On numerous occasions he met with representatives of the many Indian tribes. The Prophet, a one-eyed Shawnee leader, inveighed against white encroachment while threatening violent retaliation. Tecumseh, his brother, was an Indian statesman and a more effective Indian leader. He endeavored to establish an Indian confederacy binding together the Indians in the Old Northwest and Old Southwest to form a barrier against the advancing frontier.

In response to these Indian activities Governor Harrison, with 1,125 men, marched in the fall of 1811 toward Prophetstown near the junction of the Tippecanoe and Wabash rivers. At this camp near the Indian village was fought, on November 7, 1811, the Battle of Tippecanoe. From this "victory" over the Indians (for it was a close decision) the remnants of Harrison's army destroyed Prophetstown and returned to Vincennes. But Indian depredations continued, even to within seven miles of Vincennes, the Territorial capital. Then came the War of 1812 and again the Wabash-Maumee frontier rang with the clash of arms. Not until the Battle of the Thames (in Canada) where Tecumseh was killed did peace come to the Wabash country.

Statehood came for Indiana in 1816. The Wabash village of Vincennes was no longer the center of political and military activity, but its leadership continued in cultural affairs, and its population continued proportionate to the growth of the valley. In 1829 it was reported that 6,000 persons weekly were passing through Indianapolis for the Wabash country. By 1840 the territory from the Ohio River to Lafayette numbered from eighteen to forty-five persons per square mile.

Flatboats, as many as 300 each year during the 1820s and 1830s, left the Wabash for southern ports laden with produce. Keelboats, too, helped carry cereal grains, whiskey, beeswax, lard and beans, ginseng and fruit. Coal, live oxen, hogs and chickens, with packed pork from Terre Haute, swelled the Wabash trade. Pole boats of three to four tons' burden traveled upriver from Lafayette to Peru at eight to ten miles per day. Steamboats first reached Vincennes in 1823 and Lafayette in 1827, and with difficulty, Delphi and Logansport.

Along the banks of the Wabash was established in 1814–1815 the Rappite town of Harmonie where for a decade this prosperous religious community of skilled workers practiced celibacy and lived in peace and harmony. In 1824 they sold out to Robert Owen of Scotland, who called the town New Harmony. Here was initiated a community of equality which, though not long lived, remains noted for some of its many experiments and innovations in social living.

Construction of the Wabash and Erie Canal began at Fort Wayne in 1832. The waterway, which joined Lake Erie and the Ohio River by way of the Wabash-Maumee route, was 468 miles long—the longest canal built in America. For approximately half of its 380 Indiana miles it paralleled the Wabash. The sound of the Indian was replaced by the shouts of Irish laborers who worked on and stayed to live near the canal and whose presence helped alter the character of the Wabash Valley.

Along the valley, too, for years prior to the Civil War, the Underground Railroad operated one of its most successful systems. From Evansville upriver to Terre Haute, to Bloomingdale and north to Lafayette, slaves were secreted to some destination in Canada after leaving the Wabash at its confluence with the Tippecanoe.

Since 1960 the Wabash Valley Interstate Commission has planned for the development, utilization, control, and conservation of the resources of the Wabash Basin. Rechannelization and improved navigation, the Commission asserts, will facilitate marketing of the regions' coal, petroleum, sand, gravel, agricultural products and manufactured goods. Plans, too, have been proposed to restore the Wabash as a recreational facility and to preserve its fish and wildlife.

In book, song, folklore and tall tales, in restored sites and archaeological digs, the dramatic history of the Wabash speaks to our generation. What the future holds we leave to others. But the mood of the river remains perpetuated in Hoosier memory by the strains of "On the Banks of the Wabash, Far Away."

FURTHER READINGS: John D. Barnhart and Donald Carmony, *Indiana From Frontier to Industrial Commonwealth*, 4 vols. (1954). William E. Wilson, *The Wabash* (1940).

Herbert J. Rissler and
Donald B. Sheick

The Watauga River

Source: Slopes of Blue Ridge Mountains of western North Carolina near Grandfather Mountain
Length: 60 miles
Tributaries: None of significance
Mouth: Into South Fork of Holston at Boone Dam, southeast of Kingsport, Tennessee
Agricultural Products: Truck farming
Industries: Hydroelectric power, diversified industries

The Watauga River, meaning "beautiful river" in the language of the Cherokee Indians, is an important tributary of the South Fork Holston River. Rising on the slopes of the Blue Ridge of Western North Carolina near Grandfather Mountain, it alternately rushes and meanders for sixty miles through Johnson, Carter, Washington, and Sullivan counties in Tennessee before emerging into the South Fork Holston at Boone Lake. Few other rivers in the eastern part of the United States make as rapid a descent as does this river which flows precipitously by way of a series of gorges and valleys cut through the ridges of the Unaka mountains until the terrain flattens out near Elizabethton, Tennessee.

The river's name adequately describes it. Before the building of the Tennessee Valley Authority dams, it was a beautiful but dangerous river, without warning overflowing its banks to cause severe damage to farm lands and towns alike. After the completion of the TVA dams, it is still a beautiful river—now somewhat tamed—and provides its water for three man-made lakes—Watauga, Wilbur, and Boone.

Explorers began penetrating the Watauga River country during the seventeenth century, but not until the eighteenth century did trappers and hunters make any significant inroads. In 1746 Stephen Holston built a cabin along the bank of the river which now bears his name, explored the region of the Watauga Basin, and traded with the Cherokees. In 1748 he left the area, traveling by canoe down the Holston and Tennessee and by way of the Ohio and Mississippi rivers to Natchez, Mississippi. Dr. Thomas Walker, discoverer of the Cumberland Gap, no doubt traversed the Watauga country. In 1760

Daniel Boone crossed the Blue Ridge Mountain for the first time exploring and hunting in the Watauga and Holston valleys. Along a tributary of the Watauga, now named Boone's Creek, he paused to carve a message on a beech tree—"D. Boone Cilled A. Bar on tree in the year 1760." Just how much of the river he explored is unknown, but he did establish a camp near a deserted cabin somewhere along its banks and for a brief time he was accompanied by an elderly slave named Burrell. By 1765–1766 Indian traders were leading packhorses through the forested Watauga hills.

As in other frontier areas pioneers rapidly followed the paths blazed by the hunters and traders. In 1768 William Bean who had hunted with Boone in the area several years before, built a cabin and cleared land near the confluence of Boone's Creek and the Watauga River. The next year he led a party of his Pittsylvania County, Virginia, neighbors into the area, and others followed, their cabins dotting the banks of the river and its tributaries. In 1770 James Robertson from Orange County, North Carolina, visited the area and staked claim to land near the Sycamore Shoals of the Watauga. Here (near present-day Elizabethton, Tennessee) was a fertile valley suitable for farming with much of the timberland already cleared by the Cherokees. The next spring he led his family and a few others to this promising site. By that time other pioneers had established three other communities close to the Wataugans—North-of-Holston, Carter's Valley, and Nolichucky.

That the land around the Watauga was quickly being settled (about 100 families by the end of 1771) was natural because of ideal location and political friction especially with North Carolina. Virginians floated or followed along the banks of a natural and easily accessible highway, the Holston River. North Carolinians followed the Watauga even though its descent was not as easily traversed; some preferred a more indirect route and traveled across country where the terrain was not as rough until they found the Holston and then followed it to the Watauga

Basin. Former Regulators from North Carolina—rebels from the Tidewater government—also augmented the population. After the Battle of Alamance which occured in May, 1771, hundreds left their homes for a more hospitable, less authoritarian-governed region.

The initial years of settlement along the banks of the river were busy but peaceful ones. For the time being the Wataugans did not need to worry about the Cherokee, for in 1769 the Cherokee fought a bloody war with the Chickasaws. They lost the war and over one half their warriors. In 1772, however, the mood of the Wataugans changed; the existence of their settlements was threatened not by the Indians but the British. That year surveyors completed the Lochaber Treaty line with all its modifications along the southern boundary of Virginia. This survey disclosed that only the North-of-Holston settlement lay within lands the Cherokee had ceded to the British Government. The settlements of Watauga, Carter's Valley, and Nolichucky were all in Indian territory. When the news reached the Wataugans, they decided to defy royal authority and anyone else who tried to force them off the river. The settlers of Carter's Valley and Nolichucky temporarily left their homesteads and joined the Wataugans.

To protect themselves, the Wataugans needed a land agreement with the Cherokee and an orderly form of government. They realized that neither the North Carolina nor Virginia royal governors nor their assemblies would render any positive assistance. They also realized that under the provisions of the Proclamation of 1763 no one could legally purchase land from the Indians. The Proclamation, however, was vague about leasing Indian lands, and after hurried negotiations the Wataugans signed a ten-year lease for two tracts embracing the Watauga Basin and the Nolichucky settlement. They were gambling that within ten years they would be able to obtain a clear title to this land.

The next step for the settlers along the Watauga and Nolichucky rivers was to form a united front against royal and state authorities and to provide law and order for their frontier community. In May, 1772, they met at Sycamore Shoals and agreed to "Written Articles of Association." Although this document has been lost, it is not difficult to determine many of its provisions.

Many of the signers later moved to the Cumberland settlement (present Nashville) and signed the Cumberland Compact or migrated to Kentucky and signed the Boonesborough Resolution of 1775. Surely the Articles of 1772 set a precedent for these later agreements and perhaps also the first draft of the constitution for the state of Franklin. The Articles were designed as a temporary expedient to meet an emergency—a squatter's rights agreement for the people to abide by the rights of the majority until permanent provisions could be made to protect illegally held lands.

During the next two years the people along the river prospered under the provisions of the Articles, and other families joined them. But by 1774 they were growing apprehensive over Indian unrest. Since the land lease had made no provision for others moving to the settlements, the Cherokee complained to the British Indian agent who in turn ordered the Wataugans to leave. This order was ignored.

In the spring of 1774 Indian hostilities seemed imminent over the Billie affair. On the flats of Sycamore Shoals a Cherokee named Billie was killed while attending a horse race. A renegade from one of the Virginia settlements had deliberately shot him without warning. The other Cherokees there made threats and then left. The Billie incident was only partially settled to the satisfaction of the Indians, and the Wataugans began to consider building a fort.

After the conclusion of Lord Dunmore's War in 1774, an event transpired the next year at Sycamore Shoals which greatly influenced the western movement. The treaty ending the war eliminated the Shawnee's claim to Kentucky. The Cherokee was now the only tribe with any valid claim to the region. Quickly forming the Transylvania Company, Judge Richard Henderson of North Carolina and his associates purchased £10,000 worth of trade goods, and in December, 1774, proceeded to Sycamore Shoals. Henderson's grandiose scheme succeeded: he purchased Kentucky from the Cherokee in March, 1775, and established a proprietary colony embracing most of Kentucky for £2,000 and £8,000 worth of goods.

The misnamed Treaty of Sycamore Shoals gave the Wataugans the chance to change their ten-year lease into a purchase agreement. On

March 19, the Cherokee sold to them not only the acreage that they had previously leased but also additional lands. For £2,000 worth of goods, the Wataugans received all land on the Watauga "waters," below the South Holston, and the boundary of Virginia—some 2,000 square miles.

During the American Revolution events along the river helped further to solidify the Watauga communities. In 1775 the Wataugans formed a committee of safety, asked for assistance and recognition from Virginia and North Carolina, and in May, 1776, began to build Fort Watauga near the Sycamore Shoals one-half mile northeast of the mouth of Gap Creek. The fortress was completed in time to meet the expected Cherokee attack in July. For three weeks, 150 to 200 people were loosely besieged by the Indians. That fall the Wataugans joined with troops from Virginia, North Carolina, and as far away as Georgia to crush the Cherokee towns and effectively negate the Indian influence in East Tennessee. In 1777 North Carolina's revolutionary government accepted the Watauga communities as well as most of the present state of Tennessee as Washington District and invited the Wataugans to send representatives to Halifax, at that time the capital. The Wataugan's land holdings were then finally recognized. During the war men from the river communities served in campaigns throughout the South including Kings Mountain, against the Indians in the West, and on the Ohio frontier.

With the conclusion of the Revolutionary War, the people living along the Watauga along with their neighbors toward the north and west quickly became disgusted with the policies of North Carolina. The legislature had permitted eastern speculators to grab huge sections of land and had failed to create either a local superior court or a separate military district; and the governor had the audacity to warn the Wataugans to stop further squatting on Indian land.

The Wataugans were therefore happy when the legislature passed in June, 1784, an Act of Cession, turning over to the Congress of the Confederation all lands west of the mountains. The East Tennesseans met three times at Jonesboro, formed the state of Franklin, and sent representatives to the Congress seeking recognition as the fourteenth state of the Union. In the

meantime, however, the North Carolina legislature repealed the Act of Cession and established needed reforms for Washington District.

The State of Franklin was doomed from the beginning. The people split into factions over land, local disputes, and the nature of the government. Nor would the Congress of the Confederation recognize the state unless North Carolina did so. The final event which made the Wataugans forget their independent state was that the legislature of North Carolina once again ceded their western lands to the new government operating under the provisions of the United States Constitution. Now Wataugans could await separate statehood under prescribed procedures.

The Watauga River continued to play a role in the history of the region, but its years of dominance were over with the end of the state of Franklin. New communities grew up along its banks and tributaries, and during the early years of the nineteenth century some lumber was floated down it. During the Civil War, Union sympathizers burned several bridges crossing the river. In fact most families along the Watauga remained loyal to the United States after Tennessee seceded.

The river has treated the people living along it in an arbitrary manner. Usually it served the people's needs providing water and the needed force to generate electric power; at other times its flooded waters destroyed everything within its reach. The worst floods occurred in March, 1867, May, 1901, and August, 1940.

Beginning in 1912, the Watauga was used to generate electricity for the people of East Tennessee. In 1907 the Doe River Light and Power Company began purchasing land on the river five miles east of Elizabethton. Three years later the newly formed Watauga Power Company took over the construction. Known as Horseshoe Dam and later as Wilbur Dam, the 368-foot structure was built of cyclopean concrete and completed in 1912. After 1926 when an additional generator was added, the river-powered plant generated 3,700 kilowatts. In the following years the power complex changed ownership several times, culminating in the 1945 purchase by TVA.

Now, the appearance of the Watauga changed drastically. Construction on Watauga Dam located about two miles above Wilbur Dam began in February, 1942, but due to World War II was halted eight months later. In June, 1946, construction resumed, and the $32,370,000 project was completed in August, 1949. This impressive earth and rock-filled structure is some 900 feet long at the top and 318 feet high. Its powerhouse has a capacity of 50,000 kilowatts in two units. Man-made Lake Watauga extends 16.7 miles above the dam, covers 6,430 acres, and has over one hundred miles of shore line. One and a half miles below the mouth of the Watauga on the South Fork Holston River the TVA built Boone Dam which created Boone Lake. This two-pronged, man-made reservoir extends 17.3 miles up the South Fork Holston and 15.3 miles up the Watauga River.

TVA tamed the Watauga River making it more enjoyable not only for the majority of people of the region but also for the thousands of vacationers who yearly visit the area. The river and its lakes teem with fish; both Watauga and Boone lakes offer attractive settings for boat enthusiasts, water skiers, and campers.

How long will the Watauga River live up to its Indian name—beautiful river? It will depend on the river's level of pollution and the people's awareness. Despite federal regulations, semi-raw sewage and industrial waste is still dumped into the river and its tributaries. Along its banks people still discard junked car bodies and dump garbage. It was once a beautiful river; it still is—and it must remain—the beautiful river.

FURTHER READING: Samuel C. Williams, *Dawn of Tennessee Valley and Tennessee History* (1937), Philip H. Hamer, ed., *Tennessee, A History, 1673–1932*, 4 vols. (1933).

Emmett Essin

The Wisconsin River

Source: Lac Vieux Desert, on the Wisconsin-Michigan border
Length: 430 miles
Tributaries: Rib, Eau Pleine, Lemonweir, Plover, Baraboo, and Yellow rivers
Mouth: Into Mississippi below Prairie du Chien
Agricultural Products: Dairy products, diversified grains and vegetables
Industries: Food processing, diversified manufacturing

The Wisconsin River, at 430 miles the longest river in the state, has played a significant part in the lives of the region's inhabitants from prehistoric times to the present. The river, its name probably an adaptation of the Chippewa Indian word meaning "gathering of the water," rises out of Lac Vieux Desert, a large, shallow body of water straddling the Wisconsin-Michigan border. The river, adding water from such tributary streams as the Rib, Eau Pleine, Lemonweir, Plover, Baraboo, and Yellow rivers, flows generally south of the lake-strewn Laurentian Shield. It cuts through the sandstone plain in the south-

central part of the state, thus creating the scenic Wisconsin Dells region, now a state park. Below Portage it bends westward, but at that point, coming within one and one-half miles of the Fox River, a Portage Canal connects it with the eastflowing stream. Thus, from earliest times (with a portage prior to the digging of the canal) the Wisconsin was part of a system of waterways from Green Bay on the west coast of Lake Michigan to the Mississippi River, for the Wisconsin from Portage flows west-southwest to the Mississippi which it joins just below the city of Prairie du Chien.

Sometime after the last glacial period, between 7000 and 4500 B.C., Stone Age people of the Aqua-Plano culture inhabited the Great Lakes region including Wisconsin. Then came two other groups, the Boreal Archaic and the Old Copper, who worked the copper found in the region. The Boreal culture gradually changed to the Early Woodland, which had pottery. About 100 B.C. people of the Hopewell culture worked up the river valleys into Wisconsin north as far as their corn could grow. Finally came the Later Woodland period whose people built effigy mounds. They are believed to be the ancestors of the principal Wisconsin tribes of our own historic period: the Menominee, Sauks, Foxes, and Miamis, all using the Algonquian language. The Winnebago, another Wisconsin tribe, were a Siouan people.

It was the fur trade, religion, and the dynamics of international rivalries in North America that brought the first Europeans into Wisconsin. As the powerful Iroquois Confederacy threatened the wilderness trails, portages, and waterways south and southwest of the St. Lawrence, French traders forged new routes to the north across the Great Lakes. Eastern tribes, being pushed west to escape from Iroquois attacks, likewise settled in Wisconsin and French Jesuits, Recollects, and Sulpicians followed them, vying for control over the religious lives of the Indians. So, hugging the west shores of Lake Michigan from the Straits of Mackinac, French traders and missionaries came into the waters of Green Bay. Here their Indian guides directed them in canoes up the Fox River to a portage marked in La Salle's time (for he and his lieutenant Henry de Tonti were among the explorers) by the carving of two canoes on a tree. By this short portage west these curious Frenchmen came upon a clear, wide, sand-bottomed stream running south and then bending west. It was dotted with islands as it passed through a country that in spring, summer, and fall was characterized by magnificent pine forests broken by lush meadows giving way to rolling hills. Deer and elk grazed unmolested along its banks and the river abounded with fish. About sixty miles downriver the Wisconsin entered the Father of Waters, the Mississippi. South of the river they discovered the presence of lead, which in future years would be heavily mined and be the cause of considerable settlement.

Until 1763 Frenchmen held exclusive knowledge among whites of the Wisconsin region. Their information began with Jean Nicollet's report of that fur traders's trip to within a day's journey of the Wisconsin in 1634. In 1659 two other traders, Radisson and Groseilliers (memorized by Canadian school children as "Radishes and Galoshes") were on the Wisconsin to its

mouth. In 1660 a Jesuit, Father René Menard, may have advanced upriver to Lac Vieux Desert. In 1673 Pere Marquette and Louis Joliet floated down the Wisconsin to the Mississippi. And finally, in 1766, after the French had lost North America by the Treaty of Paris (1763) a Yankee, Jonathan Carver, explored the Fox-Wisconsin waterway and later wrote about it. Then came the American Revolution and subsequent ownership.

White settlement along the river was first at Indian towns where the fur trade was centered. Prairie du Chien—Chien (French for dog) being the name of an Indian chief—was of first importance. Both the Americans and the British built forts there which changed hands down through the War of 1812. The final fort was American Fort Crawford. Until the 1830s Prairie du Chien was the prime trading post in the Old Northwest, with lead miners and even local farmers looking upon it as the regional trade center as well as a place for protection should the Sauk, Fox, and Winnebago cause trouble.

In 1827 there was a Winnebago uprising led by their Chief Red Bird. The conflict was settled by Red Bird's surrender: it also provided a reason for the army's building Fort Winnebago at the portage. Red Bird meanwhile died in jail while awaiting trial, which upset his people. All the while whites were squatting on Winnebago lead lands south of the river, which made the Indians even more agitated. Yet, as always, they lost, in 1829 giving up those lands; subsequently the regional Indians gave up nearly eight million acres. Indeed the Sioux, Fox, Sauk, and Winnebagos were on the road to disappearance.

In 1832 the Sauk Chief Black Hawk attempted to return his people to the west side of the Mississippi by way of marching west from Lake Koshkonong in southern Wisconsin, across the Sauk Prairie to the Wisconsin, down and then across that river to the Mississippi above Prairie du Chien. The whites caught up with them before they reached the Wisconsin but in the Battle of Wisconsin Heights the Sauk held up the white advance and got away. The Indians placed elderly, women and children on a hastily constructed raft to float down the Wisconsin and across the Mississippi, but they were fired upon and literally massacred by the brave whites on shore. Up the Mississippi a few miles near the mouth of the Bad Axe River Black Hawk's remaining people were likewise slaughtered as they crossed the Mississippi or landed on the west bank, only there to be set upon by their enemies, the Sioux. Perhaps 100 survived out of the 1,000 who had begun the troubles a few weeks before.

By this time (1832) farming settlement was rapidly taking place south of the Wisconsin-Fox river waterway. German and other European liberals, hounded out of their homelands because of their revolutionary ideas, were cast as neighbors with Yankees possessed with the "western itch." Such a person was Connecticut-born Dr. William Beaumont. While an army doctor at Fort Crawford he persuaded a young Canadian trapper, whom he had treated some years before for a gunshot wound in the stomach, to come live with him. The young man had recovered, but the wound had never healed completely. Obligingly, the young man stayed with Dr. Beaumont, allowing the doctor to study the digestive system through the wound. In 1833 Dr. Beaumont published his observations. They were a landmark in the understanding of the digestive process.

These farmers, while in the main self-sustaining as were most farmers in the nineteenth century, nevertheless raised an important cash crop, wheat. By the mid-1850s Wisconsin had become the second largest producing state in the Union, shipping over 28,000,000 bushels. To get their product to market the citizens supported river improvements and construction of the Portage Canal, which was completed in 1856. Wisconsin remains to this day an important agricultural state though dairy products far outrank wheat in production.

The number one industry well into the twentieth century was, however, lumbering. As early as 1837 lumber interests had surveyed along the upper Wisconsin as far as Wasau. By 1848, when Wisconsin became a state, the entire upper valley was being settled, and the whack of the woodsman's axe and the rasping buzz of the bandsaw were familiar sounds on both sides of the river. Great rafts of lumber were assembled on the lower Wisconsin and rafted all the way

down the Wisconsin and Mississippi to St. Louis. It was a hasty, wasteful rape of the virgin forest, virtually ended by the 1920s. But glaring reality does not deter from the romance of Wisconsin lumbering, with its dittys, carousing, and Paul Bunyonesque tall tales.

With the expansion of industry, especially lumbering and paper making, enterprising men scanned the hundreds of rapids for possible waterpower sites. By 1870 some 1,288 waterwheels were furnishing more than 30,000 horsepower for Wisconsin industry. Gradually hydroelectric power assumed greatest importance and today there are more than fifty hydroelectric power installations along the Wisconsin. Intrinsic in their construction are large reservoirs, for the deforestation of the nineteenth century eliminated the steady flow of the Wisconsin's waters; the reservoirs attempt to accomplish what nature did before. So too have campaigns been launched, partially successful, to eliminate from the river industrial pollution, especially from pulp and paper mills.

Sometimes a river valley gains notoriety simply because that is where someone lived when he or she had an idea that met its time. In the southern Wisconsin river town of Roscobel in September, 1898, three lonely traveling salesmen—John H. Nicholson, Samuel E. Hill, and W. J. Knights—founded the Gideons, responsible for the Bibles in America's hotels and motels. At Portage a lad grew up in the 1870s and 1880s fascinated with the history of the American frontier, which he saw disappearing before his eyes. His name was Frederick Jackson Turner. As Professor Turner he published "The Significance of the Frontier in American History," an essay that had profound influence upon American history writing for two generations. In a lighter vein, five brothers who grew up along the Baraboo River, a Wisconsin tributary, became famous for their circus: their name was Ringling.

Today people have a new respect for rivers. For the pastoral Wisconsin, which has served humanity for thousands of years with transportation and waterpower, while outward from its banks the land has provided furs, timber, meadows for healthy dairy herds and fields growing nutritious grains, the future looks good. Canoeists paddle her waters enjoying the quiet, rural scenes; tourists view the Dells, relaxing from the cacophony of life in St. Louis, Chicago, and Milwaukee. And thinkers and innovators are probably right now at work along the river, their enterprises due to make changes in the national psyche, or the way of doing things, in the years ahead.

FURTHER READING: August Derleth, *The Wisconsin* (1942). James W. Nesbit, *Wisconsin: A History* (1973). Peter Lawrence Scanlan, *Prairie Du Chien: French, British, American* (1937).

Richard A. Bartlett

Rivers of the Northwest Mississippi Valley

In the Northwest Mississippi Valley we include the Mississippi and its greatest tributary, the impetuous, muddy Missouri. These two rivers receive the waters of hundreds of other streams. The character of the land through which the rivers flow changes drastically as they extend farther and farther west, some of them originating in the Rocky Mountains.

It was the French again who first pushed westward onto the northern Great Plains. They discovered such rivers as the Belle Fourche, Cheyenne, James, Kansas, Bighorn, and Powder which, like huge green serpents, twisted across the dry, treeless land. The inhabitants they encountered, unlike the Woodlands Indians to the east, were mounted and lived by the buffalo hunt. Bringing these nomads under control proved a formidable task, but white traders were able to deal with them from posts along the rivers, such as Fort Pierre on the Missouri and Fort Union at the mouth of the Yellowstone. The Army endeavored to place them on reservations— and tried to keep them there.

Then came the buffalo harvest of the 1870s followed first by a cattleman's frontier and finally by farming settlement. Great flood control, irrigation, and hydroelectric developments were launched to help make of the treeless land the nation's breadbasket. Some of the rivers are paltry when compared with the swollen streams in the more humid East, but because water is so needed in that parched land, they assume an importance out of all proportion to their size; nearly every drop of their precious moisture is accounted for.

This sampling of history of some Northwest Mississippi Valley rivers takes us all the way to the crest of the Rockies and south to the plains of Kansas. Only one of the streams, the Red River of the North, fails to give its waters to the Mississippi. Following the bed of ancient Lake Agassiz, it runs north into Canada and Lake Winnipeg.

Richard A. Bartlett

The Belle Fourche River of South Dakota

Source: **Rises in Campbell County in northeastern Wyoming**
Length: **About 290 miles**
Tributaries: **Redwater River, Owl Creek, Whitewood Creek**
Mouth: **Into Cheyenne River in south-central Meade County, South Dakota**
Agricultural Products: **Alfalfa, sugarbeets, corn, hay**
Industries: **Gold mining on tributaries**

The Belle Fourche River is the main tributary of the Cheyenne River system of South Dakota. Rising in northeastern Wyoming, it flows east skirting the northern foothills of the Black Hills and eventually joins the Cheyenne approximately halfway between the South Dakota border and the Missouri River. Over its course of some 300 miles, the Belle Fourche is fed by several significant tributaries of its own including Redwater River and Whitewood Creek, two streams that head in the heart of the Black Hills and flow north. Another tributary, Owl Creek, flows south into the main stream and is the site of the large Belle Fourche Reservoir. The gradient of the main stream varies from six to ten feet per mile making the river quite rapid. Tests have shown that in the spring the Belle Fourche can reach a discharge rate of over 5,000 cubic feet of water per second.

Early French explorers named the river Belle (beautiful) Fourche (fork) no doubt to contrast it from the more barren and treeless lower Cheyenne. Perhaps the La Verendrye brothers, apparent visitors to the Black Hills in 1452, offered this distinction since they supposedly identified the stream as the "Belle Reviere" in their journal. Other fur traders that followed left little on record regarding the river. The discovery of gold in the Black Hills in the 1870s, however, soon created a rush which challenged Indian claims to the region.

Although efforts had been made to explore the Black Hills prior to the discovery of gold, they had been relatively unsuccessful due to Indian resistance. One such party, led by Colonel Nelson Cole, did succeed in ascending part of the lower Belle Fourche in 1865 and even discovered what appeared to be traces of silver. Ten years later General George Armstrong Custer's well-supplied army was ordered to check out rumors of gold in the Black Hills. He left Fort Abraham Lincoln near Bismarck in July and marched southwesterly until striking the Belle Fourche near the mouth of the Redwater. The expedition then proceeded up the Redwater to the center of mining activity near French Creek, a tributary of the Cheyenne. Custer was impressed with the Redwater Valley, with its wide valley and high tree-covered ridges. His party, however, found little gold on the banks of the Redwater or those of the Belle Fourche.

After the geography of the entire Black Hills region became better known to miners, several soon prospected on the headwaters of all the Belle Fourche tributaries. Three experienced California argonauts, Moses and Fred Manuel and Hank Harney, struck it rich on Whitewood Creek in April 1876. They quickly consolidated their claims into the Homestake Gold Mine located some thirty miles from the confluence of the Whitewood and the Belle Fourche. The mine offered the most productive gold vein ever opened in the West. Unfortunately for the owners, they had little capital with which to develop it and sold out to a syndicate under the direction of George Hearst for $115,000. The Hearst conglomerate brought in the first stamping mills in July 1878. The wealth produced from this mine as well as another purchase in Montana called the Anaconda Copper Mine became the basis for the famous Hearst fortune.

The Homestake Mine near present Lead,

South Dakota, grew quite rapidly. Approximately twenty years after the first mill began, the mine's capitalization had reached $21 million. It employed a sophisticated method of gold extraction called the "batch process." First the ore was crushed in the stamp mill and then fed onto amalgamation plates that used mercury, cyanide, and other toxic chemicals to separate the precious metals. The process required large amounts of water, and the mine management fought constantly to maintain control of the water rights to Whitewood Creek. In addition, huge amounts of sludge discarded from the process were discharged directly into the Whitewood and quickly reached the Belle Fourche River thirty miles downstream.

Prospectors found little gold northwest of Whitewood Creek and this region attracted settlers intent on supplying the agricultural needs of the miners. "Buckskin Johnny" Spaulding first staked a claim for a ranch on the lower Redwater in 1876. Spaulding constructed his ranch house about four miles from the forks of the Creek. Half-a-dozen pioneers soon joined him on the grassy valley floor. The group included Eramus and John Deffebach, brothers who began another large cattle outfit just below the junction of the Belle Fourche and Redwater in 1878.

At the same time that Spaulding and the Deffebach brothers introduced cattle into the Redwater Valley, other newcomers formed a water district in order to divert the stream for irrigation. A private corporation soon constructed a main canal over thirty miles in length. It began a few miles above the forks on the east side of Redwater River, ran parallel to the river until reaching the forks, thence turned south and ran parallel to the Belle Fourche. The two streams were well suited for irrigation and the early projects brought approximately 5,000 new acres into production. This was one of the largest privately owned ditch companies in the United States.

The early settlers of the Redwater Valley laid out their first town called Minnesela in 1881. The townsite received its name from the Indian word for "Redwater" which early white men corrupted into "Minneshala." The name referred to the peculiar tint of the river water when it overflowed the banks, a common occur-

rence. The 1882 flood washed out much of the valley and ruined prospects for a crop. Cattlemen along the river valleys could drive their herds to high ground during floods but the irrigators suffered severe losses.

The inclement weather of 1886–87 injured both cattlemen and farmers on the Redwater and Belle Fourche rivers. During the summer the region suffered uncommon droughts which finally made it impossible to keep the wild range cattle away from irrigated crops. Much of the land in the river bottoms was overrun by thirsty cattle. The harsh blizzards of the following winter killed upwards of 80% of the cattle. Many had been driven into the northern hills from Texas only a year or two before.

The federal government recognized by the turn of the century that the Belle Fourche Valley was an ideal location for irrigation as well as flood control projects. Under the 1902 Newlands Act, Congress financed the construction of Belle Fourche Dam completed six years later. This earthen structure of over 6,000 feet in length actually extends across Owl Creek, a tributary of the Belle Fourche. A diversion canal from the Belle Fourche feeds the reservoir, and two other irrigation channels, both approximately 45 miles in length, bring water to the bottom lands below the project. The reservoir has a storage capacity of 192,000 acre-feet and can irrigate 57,000 acres. Farmers grow alfalfa, sugarbeets, corn, small grain, and hay on the artificially watered ground.

Studies conducted in the 1930s determined that another dam farther up the Belle Fourche would further enhance water control, assist in wildlife conservation, and provide for recreational use. The federal government finally completed the Keyhole Project in 1951 some 146 river-miles upstream into Wyoming from the Belle Fourche Project. Keyhole Dam is an earthen structure of 3,420 feet in length. It allows for a limited amount of irrigation at the same time that it fulfills a primary function of water storage for the Belle Fourche Project downriver. The dam has a capacity of 200,000 acre-feet, slightly more than its parent reservoir on Owl Creek.

Studies of the depression years brought to light another significant problem that the federal government unfortunately did nothing about. The WPA's Guidebook for the State of South

Dakota noted that a significant amount of pollution could be found in the Belle Fourche River system. The authors traced the problem to mining activity, especially the practice of the Homestake Mine of dumping its "tailings," or mine wastes, into the water. According to the men who undertook the writing project for South Dakota, Whitewood Creek had become a "dirty, leaden color, literally a flow of liquid mud."

For some years following the Depression both the federal and state governments still failed to do anything about the tailing problem. The State Health Department reported in 1959 that the extent of each daily dump had reached 2,400 tons of suspended solids. This had increased to 2,700 tons twelve years later. Finally in 1970 the Food and Drug Administration found dangerous levels of mercury in fish from the Belle Fourche and Cheyenne River systems. Whitewood Creek was so polluted that specimens could not be found in it for testing.

Further investigation brought to light some rather shocking statistics. Due to the need to use toxic materials in the gold amalgamation process, the tailings that were daily dumped into the creek contained an estimated 40 lbs. of mercury, 312 lbs. of cyanide, 240 lbs. of zinc, 72 lbs. of copper, and 9.5 tons of arsenic in the form of arsenopyrite. The arsenopyrite oxidized when it reached the Cheyenne River resulting in arsenic levels four times greater than Public Health Service guidelines for drinking water. The toxic materials had destroyed all aquatic life along Whitewood Creek from the mine downriver thirty miles to the Belle Fourche. Fish with high concentrations of mercury could be found as far downstream as the Missouri River.

When confronted with the findings, the Homestake Mine management stopped using mercury in its amalgamation process. However, other toxic materials were still being dumped along with huge amounts of tailings into Whitewood Creek as late as 1975. Current estimates suggest that 65 million tons of tailings have been discharged into the Whitewood-Belle Fourche system over the years. The muddy bottoms of the rivers contain large amounts of mercury and other toxic materials that never disappear. The construction of the Oahe Dam on the Missouri River further hinders the natural purification of the river system.

In 1971 the city of Lead and the Homestake Mine agreed to construct a sewage pond complex to handle future discharge. Unfortunately, local citizen groups opposed the idea on the grounds that toxic materials may seep from the ponds and pollute ground water. During public hearings held in December 1973, alternative plans were proposed. Some plan will no doubt soon be implemented if one has not already been completed. Nevertheless, much ecological damage has already been done on the lower Belle Fourche River which will not easily be repaired.

FURTHER READING: Joe Koller, "Minnesela Days," *South Dakota Historical Collections*, Vol. 24 (1949). *Pollution Affecting Water Quality of the Cheyenne River System of Western South Dakota* (1971).

Gary Clayton Anderson

The Bighorn/Wind River

Source: Confluence of Popo Agie and Wind Rivers at Riverton, Wyoming

Length: 336 miles

Tributaries: Shoshone, Greybull, Little Wind, Nowood rivers

Mouth: Flows into Yellowstone in south-central Montana

Agricultural Products: Hay, sugar beets, beans

Industries: Cattle ranching, oil, gas, and coal production

Before there were any Rocky Mountains the Bighorn (spelled Big Horn by the natives) River country was a huge, brackish, shark-infested lake, a sub-tropical habitat shaded by fig trees and magnolias. But mountains of granite thrusting upwards through the debris of a hundred million years were to produce a different climate, flora and fauna. By the time human folk arrived in the area—a scant 12,000 years ago—they found great wooly mammoths grazing in tall grass, grass soon to grow shorter and sparser as the mountain glaciers shrank away and precipitation decreased to its present four to ten inches. The sharks and magnolias, wooly mammoths and fig trees, were buried but provided, milleniums later, the fossil fuel that today so identifies the region.

Sharing headwaters with the Green, Snake, and Yellowstone rivers, the stream rises as the Wind River in the southern Absaroka Mountains just south of Yellowstone Park, at an elevation of 9,700 feet. It changes its course from east to north, then sculpts a cross section of the geologic timetable through the Owl Creek Mountains; then, as the Bighorn, scours a thousand-foot-deep trench between the Bighorn Mountains and the Pryors to the north, and joins the Yellowstone at 2,700-foot elevation. (While most references report the river's change of name at the confluence of the Wind River and the Popo Agie, official United States Geological Survey maps show it at the point the stream exits the Wind River Canyon, and a U.S. Geodetic Survey monument there, bearing the words THE WEDDING OF THE WATERS, heralds the change.)

The Bighorn is 336 miles long. Surrounded by four mountain ranges, its 23,000 square miles drainage contains some of the wettest and driest lands found in any river basin in the United States. Huge mountain snow packs deliver over thirty-two inches of water per year—mostly in early summer runoff—while annual precipitation in the basin delivers about one-tenth of an inch. To control the consequent extreme variations in flow and to provide water for the fertile but dry basin lands, dams and diversions have been constructed on both the upper canyon (Wind River) and lower canyon (Bighorn), at the same time dramatizing the segmented character of its human occupancy; *downstream, upstream,* and *midstream,* in that order.

While the white man's approach to the Bighorn was tentative and episodic, the Indian related to it continuously. From the mid-eighteenth century until the Fort Laramie Treaty of 1868, various Indian tribes fought over its hunting grounds, from the Yellowstone River all the way south to the northern end of the Laramie Range, from the Absarokas east across the Bighorns. The area was commonly called "Crow Country," however, so fiercely had that tribe defended it against Blackfoot, Arapaho, Cheyenne, and Sioux. Notwithstanding considerable fur trapping by the whites on its tributaries, the Bighorn region withstood all attempts to make the river a thoroughfare for the mountain man. The fur trade was just one brief episode in the river's long history.

Francois Antoine Laroque, an employee of the British Northwest Company, was the first white man to explore the Bighorn. The Crow warned him that he would be eaten by werewolves if he ventured further up than the lower canyon. Having been rejected by Lewis and Clark, he went instead up the Yellowstone to the Bighorn in 1805. He explored the lower reaches and part of the basin, entering from the western slope of the Bighorn Mountains. A year later, in 1806, William Clark's Yellowstone detachment, returning from the Pacific, noted that basin also.

Lewis and Clark inadvertently provided for the first extensive white exploration by giving John Colter, an expedition member, his military discharge at the Mandan villages (near present Bismarck, North Dakota) so that he might return to the Yellowstone with a pair of fur seekers named Dixon and Hancock. After a disappointing winter, Colter again set out for home only to encounter at the mouth of the Platte a second and more attractive opportunity to get back to the mountains.

His new employer, Manuel Lisa, sought to monopolize the fur trade of the Missouri River drainage. His trading post, Fort Raymond, was purposely located in friendly Crow lands, well away from the hostile Blackfeet but within trading distance of the Sioux and Cheyenne. It was to this haven on the Bighorn that Colter ran naked 220 miles from the Blackfeet who, after stripping him, invited him to run for his life. It was also from Fort Raymond that Colter made his epic exploration of the Bighorn Basin, the Grand Tetons, and, possibly, Yellowstone Park.

Dispatched by Lisa to contact Indians for trade, Colter, in 1807, with a thirty-pound pack, his gun and ammunition, crossed the Pryors to the Bighorn's major tributary, the Shoshone, which the Crow called "Stinking Water" for its sulphur thermal springs. Proceeding up the South Fork of the Shoshone, he may have worked his way to the headwaters of another tributary, the Greybull, and into the Wind River Range. In the course of this walk he also discovered the wonders of Jackson Hole. His description of the thermal springs near present Cody, Wyoming, was perhaps misconstrued as a description of the geysers of the Yellowstone, hence for some time the upper Yellowstone country bore the appellation "Colter's Hell."

The Bighorn offered an almost all-water route from the heart of the beaver country clear to St. Louis. Its tributaries, the Popo Agie, Little Wind, Greybull, Nowood, and Shoshone offered attractive trapping, but the hazards of the lower canyon forced a portage of such inconvenience that the river as a means of transportation was abandoned for the South Pass route. This overland trail made possible the rendezvous system which vastly increased the number of independent white trappers and resulted in a decline of company control over the Indian trade.

The second episodic gesture by the white man to the Bighorn (the first being the fur trade) had to do with major interests elsewhere, remote from the river basin itself. A route had to be found to the gold fields of Montana and Idaho and first choice was the Bozeman Trail from Fort Laramie into Montana. Although the Crow had been granted much of this land by the Fort Laramie Treaty Conference of 1851, the Sioux began infringing upon their Bighorn hunting lands at the same time that the whites began marching through there. These two developments doomed the Crow country.

The federal government had manifested little interest in the Bighorn country until the Raynolds-Maynadier Expedition of 1859–1860 which carried orders to explore the Bighorn and Yellowstone rivers. They were to determine the most direct and feasible routes from Fort Laramie to the Yellowstone, from the Yellowstone down to South Pass, and, in addition, to estimate the practicability of a route from the source of the Wind River to Three Forks in present Montana. It was the Raynolds-Maynadier Expedition that recommended the latter route, and that became the Bozeman Trail. Included was Maynadier's description of the midstream area which led Raynolds to doubt the value of the Bighorn Basin for human habitation. By 1865 the Sioux had forced the Crow into the northern reaches of the Bighorn. Increasingly strident demands from gold-seeking emigrants for protection from the Sioux led to the next episodes: the establishment of military escorts and permanent forts along the Bozeman Trail. For two years, 1866–1868, American soldiers were engaged in battles with Sioux Chief Red Cloud's warriors in an effort to keep the trail open. Finally the United States sought a negotiated peace. Of the several forts and engagements, only one of each related strictly to the river: Fort C. F. Smith and the "Hayfield Fight."

Fort C. F. Smith was located not far from the mouth of the lower canyon and for a time it was a sort of haven for the Crow who were intimidated by the Sioux. Reports of the Fetterman Massacre at Fort Phil Kearny, December 21, 1866, in which a detachment of eighty-one soldiers was decoyed into an ambush by Chief Crazy Horse, suggested to the Crow that Red Cloud would prevail. Leaving behind several braves to act as couriers for the Fort Smith command, on January 4, 1867 the Crow took down their lodges and headed south to the Wind River Valley. Sixteen months later their fears of Sioux victory were confirmed by the Fort Laramie Treaty of 1868, at which in exchange for military abandonment of the Bozeman Trail and indemnities, each tribe agreed to reside on strictly defined, white-administered reservations, with the Powder River country to be open exclusively to Indian hunting but not Indian occupancy.

What of the Crow? A separate treaty gave them a vastly reduced reservation beginning roughly at the midlower canyon (present Montana state line) and extending downstream to the Yellowstone. The eastern boundary included the drainage of the Little Bighorn (eight years later the scene of "Custer's Last Stand"), the western, that of Pryor Creek. A policy of domestication was thus begun. Even had the Crow not been so confined, the same Council that corralled them had created another reservation for their hereditary enemies, the Shoshone, on the upper end of the river, in the mountains and valley of Wind River. Shoshone Chief Washakie, traditional friend of the white man, had often challenged the Crow claim to the Bighorn; indeed, he duelled a Crow chief atop what is known today as Crowheart Butte, and had purportedly cut out and eaten his enemy's heart. His reservation included all the river through the upper canyon to the Hot Springs at present Thermopolis, Wyoming. Although both reservations were to be reduced by treaty or Congressional fiat, they still exist: Crow Indian *downstream*, Shoshone *upstream*. Washakie was prevailed upon to accept the Arapaho as temporary residents; they remain today on the Wind River Reservation.

The Bighorn's mining history is episodic, but it coincided closely enough with cattle raising to not disrupt the continued white man's occupancy of the river system. The first cattle came in at the Wind River end, but this time moved around the upper canyon to *midstream*, that part of the basin now between the two Indian reservations. From the arrival of Charles Carter's cattle at the junction of the North and South Forks of the Shoshone in 1879, until into the twentieth century, the Bighorn Basin was cattle country, or, more appropriately, "livestock" country because the basin had wars between cattle and sheep men.

This was the era of the "open range." Big operators announced their range claims, usually in association with a tributary stream: Nowood, Greybull, Paint Rock Creek, Shell Creek, North Fork of Stinking Water, South Fork of Stinking Water, Grass Creek, Gooseberry Creek, Owl Creek, Wood River. By legal and illegal means the barons engrossed huge areas of the basin upon which to graze their herds. Always water was the key, for who controlled the streams controlled the range around for as far as a cow could walk. Each cow required about forty acres of grazing land. Since Carter's arrival in 1879, water rights (appropriations) have been recorded and Wyoming water law increasingly codified to establish various uses under its doctrine of "beneficiality," as well as "priority" recording. Every tributary has its claimants, even the mainstream itself. Each claimant is identified by where, when, and specific amount of water, but none earlier than 1880.

Small settlements began appearing in the basin in the late 1880s along with modest small farming development. When the federal government launched a program to "reclaim" these arid regions by building water storage dams to supply water for irrigation districts, farming became a second major industry. The first such project was on the major tributary of the Bighorn, the Shoshone, it being the only significant tributary between the two canyons. Similar dams were built at the upper and lower canyons also. First came the Boysen Dam, where the river enters the Wind River Canyon; then the Yellowtail (for the Crow Chief), where it exits from the lower canyon. The Bighorn was tamed. Now there were irrigation projects and hydro-electric plants. Boating and fishing on the lakes added a tourist attraction to add revenue to the businesses of the basin towns.

Meanwhile large deposits of oil and gas were discovered and the basin's economy profited from this additional source of revenue. Even with the three dams, irrigation, hydroelectric power, tourists, and oil and gas, however, the basin has never supported more than 80,000 people, less than three per square mile. Only four towns in the basin have populations over 5,000: Riverton, Lander, Worland, and Cody.

With the energy crisis upon the nation, industrialists looked at the low-grade coal that lay under much of the basin. Major industrial concerns began buying farms and ranches in the Powder River country, around the Green River and even on the Laramie River, because coal-fired steam generating plants demand large amounts of water. With the land came water rights. Today the water rights in the Bighorn Basin are under judicial scrutiny, and the outcome of the litigation will decide the future occupations of some 25,000 claimants including the Indians on the Wind River Reservation. As for the *downstream* Crow, their million-acre reservation sits astride coal!

FURTHER READING: Edwin C. Bears, *Big Horn Canyon National Recreation Area: Montana-Wyoming, Historic Basic Data*, 2 vols. (1970). U.S. Department of Agriculture, *Wind-Bighorn-Clarks Fork River Basin*, Type IV Survey, Wyoming-Montana Supplement, 2 vols. (1974).

John T. Hinckley

The Cheyenne River of South Dakota

Source: Rises just east of Black Hills of Eastern Wyoming
Length: About 527 miles
Tributaries: Belle Fourche River; French, Spring, and Rapid creeks
Mouth: Joins Missouri River in central South Dakota
Agricultural Products: Alfalfa, hay, corn
Industries: Cattle ranching

The Cheyenne River System of South Dakota heads just east of the Black Hills in Wyoming. It drains 25,500 square miles of surface area, most of it in South Dakota, before emptying into the Missouri River over 300 miles downstream from its source. Along the river's main course, there is an average gradient of about seven feet per mile. This creates a rapid current, especially during the spring runoff. Conversely, the river becomes sluggish and shallow during the late summer or periods of drought. Although the discharge of the Cheyenne River was once calculated as high as 10,960 cubic feet per second, the construction of reservoirs in recent years in the Black Hills and on the Missouri River has limited the unpredictable nature of this scenic and rugged stream.

The Cheyenne and its major tributary the Belle Fourche (covered in a separate article), nearly encircle the majestic Black Hills of western South Dakota. The main channel skirts the southern and eastern foothills of this vacation land and is fed by numerous creeks. Most of these small streams have rapid, sustained, yearly flows interrupted only by the outer rim of the hills called the Limestone Outcrop. Many of them are noted for their excellent trout fishing and other recreational advantages. Although early mining activity and a few irrigation dams disrupted the natural flow of several of the tributaries, they still remain relatively free of obstructions as well as pollution. Only occasional floods or high runoffs alter these conditions by breaking down small amounts of mercury, a residue from mining, and other pollutants which briefly enter the streams and are soon washed downriver.

From the Black Hills eastward beyond the Limestone Outcrop, the Cheyenne River flows through near desolate country nominally called the Missouri Plateau. This treeless region is dotted with rugged badlands and scenic sandstone buttes. The river valley lies some two or three hundred feet below the surrounding plains, cut into the plateau by constant erosion. The runoffs have removed much of the topsoil from the plateau leaving in its place soft sands, shale, and clay or gumbo. Unfortunately, the Cheyenne's main tributary, the Belle Fourche, drains a mining district that adds considerable amounts of zinc, arsenic, mercury, and cyanide to the main stream which already has a high mineral content. Thus, once out of the hills, the water quality of the Cheyenne River is generally poor.

The early European explorers of South Dakota seldom reached the Black Hills and remained mostly in the more accessible Missouri River Valley. Consequently, much early information regarding the Cheyenne system came from Indians. Early white travelers apparently named the river after the Cheyenne people, a nomadic tribe that frequented its banks at the turn of the 19th century. One of the first accounts of the region left by Charles La Raye in 1802, also notes that such tribes as the Crow, Omaha, and Kiowa Apache inhabited the headwaters of the stream. A short time later, the aggressive Sioux expanded into the valley and eventually came to dominate the entire Black Hills.

Since most early French and American explorers found the lower Cheyenne River poorly suited for boat traffic, they generally avoided it. Lewis and Clark, for example, found "little water" flowing from the river's mouth while on their historic journey of exploration in October 1804. Spring thaws often brought swift currents and whirlpools, dangerous traps for canoes laden with valuable cargo. Accordingly, the lower Cheyenne played less of a role in the early fur trade than its excellent geographic location might have warranted.

Even with such disadvantages, the American Fur Company established at least two important trade posts on the banks of the Cheyenne during the 1830s. Company men constructed one at the mouth of Cherry Creek, halfway between the hills and the Missouri River. Another was built where the Belle Fourche joins the Cheyenne. A temporary establishment at the stream's mouth on the Missouri River was overshadowed by American Fur's main stockade thirty miles below at Fort Pierre. The Cheyenne River posts were obviously intended to capture the fur trade of the Black Hills. Many of the supplies destined for the posts as well as some of their returning peltry were shipped overland from Fort Pierre. This prevented the type of mishap recorded at the fort in April 1830: "Mr. Chardon unfortunately lost a canoe with 400 [buffalo] robes in descending the Cheyenne River."

Government personnel explored the periphery of the Black Hills and portions of the lower Cheyenne Valley in the 1850s. Because of the difficulties in traveling on the river, these parties frequently used land routes recommended by the traders. The main one struck due west across the plains from Fort Pierre, crossed over the Cheyenne to its northern bank at Cherry Creek, thence continued along the tablelands of the Missouri Plateau until reaching Bear Butte on the edge of the hills. American explorers generally concluded that the Cheyenne Valley was of little value and should be avoided.

Notwithstanding a treaty that guaranteed Indian ownership of the Black Hills forever, the discovery of gold in 1875 prompted a rush to the region that brought the eventual extinguishment of Indian title. By June, about fifteen miners had settled in the hills on French Creek, a tributary of the Cheyenne, and constructed small dams to divert the water for washing the gold out of the creek's sandy banks. The unpredictable nature of the water flow in French Creek made such endeavors dangerous and difficult. Many miners quickly looked elsewhere for placers, or surface mines, with a constant supply of water.

Other tributaries of the Cheyenne River were organized into ad hoc "mining districts" by fall. These regulated the filing of claims and brought a semblance of order. Spring and Rapid Creeks received considerable attention as well as a tributary of the latter called Castle Creek. Although the army temporarily removed most white intruders in a belated attempt to pacify hostile Indians, miners returned for good in 1876. The dramatic defeat of General George Armstrong Custer by the allied Sioux and Cheyenne at the Battle of the Little Bighorn that summer caused considerable consternation in most mining communities. Nevertheless, few prospectors abandoned their claims along the Cheyenne River tributaries.

Most of the mining towns that sprung up along the streams of the Black Hills had a precarious existence. One day they boomed as new speculators and miners rushed to the region, while the next could spell doom if placers suddenly played out. Miners were a restless breed with little loyalty to a prospective boom town. Occasionally a defunct community received a second chance however. Such was the case with Hill City located near Spring Creek, and Custer on French Creek. Hard rock mining companies gambled on bringing in machinery to pry loose the elusive gold and silver and temporarily revived the fledgling economies of both communities.

More often than not, mining left in its wake economic stagnation and ghost towns. The vast majority of miners failed to obtain a "grub stake," and most creek valleys were left with but one legacy from mining—ecological damage. Studies have recently concluded that during periods of high runoff, small amounts of mercury and other toxic substances still leach from the debris left behind by placer and hard rock mining. Fortunately, the amounts of toxic substances seldom exceed guidelines established by the Food and Drug Administration and disappear when the Cheyenne River tributaries return to normal flow.

The streams that flow from the Black Hills, especially those that flow south offered natural transportation avenues for early settlement. Stage and freight lines established routes along them into the mining districts within a year of the gold strike. Early travelers usually found these passages dangerous. One disillusioned miner left a warning to all who dared continue the trip up Red Canyon which led to the mine fields near Custer: "Look to your rifles well. For this is the Canyon of Hell." Several unsuspecting parties were laylaid along this route by bandits and Indians. The stage companies soon constructed way stations at crucial points on the Cheyenne River for protection. In some locales the steepness of the river's banks had forced stages to slow down making them vulnerable to highwaymen. The early stage and freighting routes west from the steamboat landing at Fort Pierre generally avoided the Cheyenne River as had earlier fur traders and travelers.

While miners were the first whites to explore many of the Cheyenne River tributaries in the Black Hills, cattlemen soon recognized that the creek valleys provided water and natural protection for large herds. One of the first ranch outfits in the region was established on Rapid Creek as early as 1878. Quickly, cattlemen stocked other valleys in the Hills as well as along the Cheyenne proper. By 1883, one observer estimated that

over 200,000 cows were driven from Texas north to the Hills annually. Cattlemen extended claims to much of the lower Cheyenne Valley by the early 1890s. Markets on Indian reservation and mining camps continued to stimulate the growth of the cattle industry despite the tragic winter of 1886–87 when severe storms breached even the protective valleys of the Black Hills. The heavy snows and winds forced cattle into gullies and up canyons where they perished by the thousands. Some ranchers placed their losses as high as eighty-five percent of their herd.

Many early Black Hills settlers turned to irrigated farming along the valley bottom lands rather than ranching. One of the earliest canals was constructed in the 1880s along the upper Cheyenne River near the Wyoming border. It reached fourteen miles in length and opened a large new section of farmland. Other frontiersmen followed by building half-a-dozen small ditches along Rapid Creek in the central hills. Ultimately, canals of varying length and width were opened along Beaver, Elk, Bear, Butte, Box Elder, Alkalai, French, Spring, and Battle Creeks. Most ditches were simple gravity diversions to lower benchlands built with pick and shovel. According to one estimate, over 26,000 acres of land were irrigated in the Black Hills region by 1906 (this included land in the Belle Fourche River Valley).

In order to better define water rights, the state of South Dakota passed a law in 1905 which gave state engineers the opportunity to help legitimatize water claims. Previous to this, claims often exceeded the ability of the stream to provide the necessary water. After the turn of the century, federally financed irrigation systems led to more government supervision and fairer distribution of water resources. The Newlands Act, passed by Congress in June 1902, allowed money collected from the sale of western lands to be applied to the construction of irrigation and flood control projects. Although several were funded immediately for the Belle Fourche River system, the Cheyenne tributaries did not receive attention until after the chronic water shortages of the 1930s indicated a need for storage reservoirs in the central and southern Black Hills.

Congress appropriated money for the first

major project in Rapid Creek Valley in 1942. Deerfield Dam was completed four years later with the assistance of the Farm Security and Works Progress Administrations. This earthen structure reaches a height of 133 feet and has a crest length of 825 feet. The federal government completed an extension of the Deerfield Project in 1956 when Pactola Dam went into operation several miles down Rapid Creek. Pactola Reservoir provides supplemental water for both Rapid City and Ellsworth Air Force Base. It also allows for the irrigation of nearly 9,000 acres of farm land. The Dam has a capacity of 90,000 acre-feet of water and a crest length of 1,255 feet. It is the mainstay of the irrigation system in the Rapid Valley.

The government completed construction on a second major irrigation and flood control project in southwestern South Dakota on the upper Cheyenne River in 1956. Angostura Dam is a concrete structure with earth-embankments on both wings. It stands 193 feet high and has a crest length of 2,030 feet. The reservoir allows for the irrigation of 12,100 acres of land from its 31-mile main channel. Working concurrently with the Dam is a 1,200 kilowatt hydroelectric plant located 500 feet down river. Overall, as of 1964, both private and governmental irrigation ditches deliver water to well over 20,000 acres of land in the Cheyenne River proper. On the Cheyenne tributaries, private and public investments account for another 13,000 acres.

Although irrigation has provided the principal motivation for most Black Hills water projects, flood control has rated a close second. The region is prone to flash floods because of its rugged terrain. Rapid Creek Valley, for example, has experienced ten flash floods in the last one hundred years. The most recent and by far the most tragic occurred on the evening of June 9, 1972. In the course of a few hours, an estimated 109 metric tons of water fell on the eastern Black Hills. A small earthen dam located just north of Rapid City soon filled with water and gave way. It had been built in 1932 for water storage and recreational uses. Experts now believe that the extreme volume of water that fell that day had more to do with the destructive results than the collapse of this small dam. Regardless, a wall of water eventually rumbled down Rapid Valley and passed through the center of Rapid City. It washed away virtually everything in its path including 5,000 homes and some 250 business establishments. The death toll reached well over 230 people.

It would be an understatement to suggest that the Rapid City flood renewed interest in water use in western South Dakota. Rapid City alone has invested $64 million in a new floodway through the center of the city. It also has turned the flood plain west of town into a park. The money for this project came from federal urban renewal funds and is indicative of continued governmental concern over water use in the region.

Unfortunately not all Black Hills communities remain as conscious of the dangers of flood waters. A 1975 governmental report completed by the U.S. Geological Survey notes that several communities continue to encourage or allow housing development on lands clearly susceptible to flash flooding. In other words, the tragedy of 1972 could easily occur sometime in the future. The report also urged a much closer inspection of dams, many of which are privately owned, since poorly located or maintained structures do more harm than good. It can only be hoped that in the future the example set by Rapid City will be followed by other communities.

The rivers and creeks of the Cheyenne system are clearly an asset to western South Dakota. They provide water for irrigated farms and ranches as well as rapidly growing urban areas like Rapid City. In addition, they offer recreational use to literally millions of vacationers that visit the Black Hills annually and support the economy of the area. Fortunately, with the proper planning and protection all of these uses can work concurrently for the benefit of tourists and South Dakotans alike.

FURTHER READING: Watson Parker, *Gold in the Black Hills* (1966); *South Dakota Flood Disaster* (1972).

Gary Clayton Anderson

The James River (South Dakota)

Source: Central North Dakota
Length: 710 miles
Tributaries: None of significance
Mouth: Missouri River south of Yankton, S.D.
Principal Cities: Aberdeen, Huron, and Mitchell
Agricultural Products: Wheat, corn
Industry: Cattle ranching

The James River rises in central North Dakota and enters South Dakota thirty-five miles northeast of Aberdeen and flows southeastwardly across the state until it empties into the Missouri just south of Yankton. This prairie stream, which virtually parallels the Missouri River in South Dakota, wanders aimlessly over low flatland for 710 miles to cover a straight line distance of 250 miles. So level is it—the James has an average gradient of four inches per mile—that it takes water in it three weeks to travel the length of the state. In 1970, *U.S. News and World Report* called it one of the most polluted streams in the United States, primarily because of the long periods in which there is no flow and water stands in pools, subject to contamination by rotting vegetal material and wastes from a variety of sources, including municipalities, farms, and wildlife refuges. Still, the James River is the only major stream in the area and is an important part of the environment.

An aerial view emphasizes the montonous flat landscape, rich in fertile soils, with the James River as a predominant natural physical feature. Previous channels of the mainstream have formed numerous oxbows throughout the area. These are easily identifiable during the late summer and early autumn because of the type of vegetative cover. Elm, cottonwood, ash, and boxelder trees flourish near the river's main stream channel. These wooded areas furnish one of the few habitats for wildlife in the region. Whitetail deer, waterfowl, pheasants, and fur-bearing animals thrive by its banks.

The Indians called the river Chan-san-san, meaning white or yellowish wood. In 1794, Jean Trudeau, a French trader, named it "Riviere aux Jackques," and it has since been known by this name in its Anglicized form. Even a Congressional act of 1861 officially changing the name to the Dakota River failed to change the people's minds. This law is still in existence, but James River persists and popularly the stream is known as "the Jim."

Although the James is reputed to be the longest unnavigable river in the world, the James River Navigation Company operated a steamship line on the northern portion of the stream during the late nineteenth century. An 1884 advertisements notified passengers that the "steamers 'NETTIE BALDWIN' and 'FANNIE L. PECK' will leave Columbia daily, weather permitting, for Pectoria, Eaton, Port Emma and other points." After sailing on the James for two days a passenger remarked that the scenery along the banks of the river was "not very interesting except for the many fine farms and houses."

Because of the moderate success of the private steamboat companies, enterprising newspapers in the region appealed to the federal government to study the possibility of making the James a commerical highway. They claimed that with a moderate expenditure an ample channel could be provided to float steamboats between Yankton and Jamestown—a distance of 400 miles. This would allow the farmers in the James River valley to transport their surplus products to market at one-half the expense of railway carriage. In 1886 an army engineer surveyed the stream. His final report was so unfavorable that the project was dropped.

Three of the state's larger cities are located along the James. Aberdeen, the third largest city in South Dakota, is situated on the site of glacial Lake Dakota. Charles H. Prior, immigration agent for the Milwaukee Railroad, chose the spot in 1880 because the Chicago, Milwaukee, St. Paul and Pacific Railway was to cross the Chicago and North Western tracks there. The city grew to be a major distributor of manufactured goods for the region.

Ninety miles south, on the west bank, is Huron. Marvin Hughitt, general manager of the Chicago and North Western Railroad, selected the site in 1879. Huron is dependent largely on the livestock industry and in addition to hosting the State Fair boasts of being "pheasant capital of the United States." Further south is Mitchell, its location also decided with the railroad in mind. Situated in a diversified farming region, the city is an important trade center, not to mention having the world's only Corn Palace.

Historically the Sioux occupied the James River area, moving willfully across the prairie in search of game. Gradually they ceded more land to the federal government until most of their reservations were located west of the Missouri River. There was one area along the James, however, that would cause friction between the white settlers and the Indians.

South of Aberdeen, near the Jim River crossing (so-called because early itinerant Indian traders crossed there), the Indians in the later 1870s built several dirt lodges. Military personnel stationed in nearby forts reported that this so-called Dirt Lodge Village was a rendezvous for hostile Indians seeking refuge from their patrols. One band of the Yanktonnais Sioux tribe, which was supposed to be living on the Crow Creek Reservation seventy-five miles west, was known to have taken up residence at the village and refused to yield to white homesteaders.

Mada-bo-das (Drifting Goose) and 250 of his followers held that when the Yanktons ceded the land in 1859, the Yanktonnais Tribe did not agree to the treaty; therefore, the land still belonged to the Indians. Drifting Goose was denied his claims because the Indians failed to meet the government's criteria for homesteading of "settlement, improvement, and cultivation." The band was removed, under protest, to the Crow Creek Reservation.

Then on June 27, 1879, Rutherford B. Hayes issued a presidential edict that townships 119, 120, and 121 of Dakota Territory, including Dirt Lodge Village, be "set apart as a reservation for the use of Mada-bo-das or Drifting Goose's band of Yanktonnais Indians." Upon his return to the Jim, Drifting Goose demanded that all whites be expelled.

With this 65,000 acres of choice land now designated as an Indian reservation, the white homesteaders wanted a hearing. The Indians were subsequently told that the whites had moved into the region, and in good faith had improved the land by cultivation, and for the Indians to retain their lands, they must do the same. Drifting Goose refused to comply with the ruling that his followers must make improvements like the whites. In 1880, federal troops escorted the Yanktonnais band to their permanent residence on the Crow Creek Reservation.

In the nineteenth century the Indians seemed to present the greatest obstacle to white settlement and progress along the James River; in the twentieth century it has been water. Because of its flat gradient and low banks the James cannot provide the water resource needs of the valley. Thus, the citizens of the region look to the Missouri River for supplemental water.

The most sophisticated plan undertaken by the federal government so far has been the Oahe Unit, which was part of the Missouri River Basin Project authorized by Congress in the Flood Control Act of 1944. The proposal calls for diversion of water from the Oahe Reservoir on the Missouri River to the James River Basin for the irrigation of 190,000 acres of land, for municipal and industrial use in seventeen towns and cities, for fish and wildlife development at eighteen locations, and for recreational developments. Other features include flood control, drainage of non-irrigable land, and lessening of river pollution.

In 1964 the Bureau of Reclamation completed the James Diversion Dam as an advance feature of the Oahe Unit. Located north of Huron, the structure consists primarily of a fifty-foot-long concrete overflow weir and a gated sluiceway. An auxiliary spillway, 1900' × 150', serves to protect the dam as a bypass for major floodflows. This dam supplies the city of Huron with a supplemental water supply.

Construction of the Oahe Unit started one of the most challenging phases of the Missouri River Basin development in South Dakota. But the project, which was estimated to cost over $300 million, was dealt a stunning blow in 1977 when President Carter stated that the federal government would withdraw funds from the

Oahe Unit. Water was the major issue during the 1978 South Dakota gubernatorial race. Moreover, all political candidates in the James River Basin must declare themselves either "pro-Oahe" or "anti-Oahe." Today it is still unclear if the residents of the area will have enough water for the production of irrigated crops, so necessary to meet the food needs of the nation.

FURTHER READING: Herbert S. Schell, *History of South Dakota* (1961). John Milton, *The Literature of South Dakota* (1976).

Roger Bromert

The Kansas, or Kaw River

Source: Junction of Republican and Smoky Hill rivers at Junction City, Kansas
Length: 185 miles
Tributaries: Big Blue, Delaware, and Wakarusa rivers
Mouth: Into Missouri River at Kansas City
Agricultural Products: Corn, wheat, livestock
Industries: Food processing, electronics

On a map of modern Kansas the river bearing the same name does not appear to be very long. It only appears to flow through the eastern quarter of the state from Junction City to Kansas City where it joins the Missouri River. The distance is about 130 miles as the crow flies or about 185 miles as the river flows.

If one looks more closely at the map, however, the river's beginnings can be traced as far west as modern Colorado. Actually, five major rivers—the Solomon, Saline, Smoky Hill, Republican and Big Blue—and many smaller streams feed the Kansas, or Kaw River, as Kansans sometimes call their wide and generally shallow stream.

The Solomon River and its south fork originate in northwest Kansas southwest of Colby. The two forks flow eastward across the rolling plains to west of Beloit in Mitchell County where they join together as one—the Solomon River. The river then moves southeast to near Abilene, where it empties into the Smoky Hill River.

Several miles west of Abilene another stream empties into the Smoky Hill. It is the Saline River, and like the Solomon it has its beginnings southwest of Colby in northwest Kansas. The Smoky Hill, unlike the Solomon and Saline

rivers, begins farther west on the eastern plains of Colorado. As it flows eastward it carries the waters from the Solomon and Saline eastward to Junction City. There the Republican River, which begins in south central Nebraska perhaps 200 miles to the northwest, flows into the Smoky Hill. At that spot close to Junction City the Kansas River is formed.

The Big Blue River, which like the Republican River begins in southern Nebraska, is the next major river to empty into the east-flowing Kansas. It does this just east of Manhattan, and between Manhattan and Kansas City, two other smaller rivers—the Delaware and Wakarusa—also flow into the Kansas before it empties into the Missouri River at Kansas City.

Just when the Kansa Indians first arrived in the region is unknown, but scholars believe they descended from Indians speaking a Siouan dialect. In the 1600s, these Siouan Indians moved from east of the Mississippi and followed the Missouri River west. In time they broke into smaller groups. One segment moved westward to the point where the Kansas River joins the Missouri. They became known as Kansa Indians.

The spelling of their name and in turn the spelling of the river, state and town names has gone through perhaps more changes than any other historic name in American history. Between 1650 and 1854, when Kansas Territory was established, more than eighty variations of the name appeared on maps, in books, and on the pages of journals and diaries kept by early explorers.

Most historians agree that the state derived its

name from the Kansas River, which in turn received its name from the tribe of Indians that lived along its banks.

Before the arrival of the white man, the Kansa Indians probably navigated the Kansas River in boats made of buffalo skins stretched over a light framework of wood. The seams were sewn with sinews. These water tight "bull boats" were very buoyant and capable of carrying a heavy cargo of pelts and furs.

At the junction of the Kansas and Missouri rivers, perhaps late in the 1600s, the Kansa Indians first met the "Big Knives," as their legends refer to white men. These first white men probably were French. Kansa legends say the French brought gifts and convinced the Kansa to establish trade.

Just who was the first white man to navigate the Kansas River is unknown, although in 1724 Etienne de Bourgmont crossed the river as he traveled to the headwaters of the Smoky Hill to establish trade with the Comanche Indians.

After the Louisiana Purchase President Thomas Jefferson sent Lewis and Clark to explore the region. Their party arrived at the mouth of the Kansas River on June 26, 1804. They camped in several locations nearby while spending several days gathering geographical data and gaining information on French trade with the Kansa Indians.

Government records tell how in 1827 keelboats were used to carry supplies from the mouth of the Kansas River westward to the mouth of what became known as Stonehouse Creek, about ten miles northwest of modern Lawrence, Kansas. There, Daniel Morgan Boone, son of Daniel Boone, worked as a government farmer among the Kansa Indians.

The following year, 1828, Frederick Chouteau used a keelboat to take goods up the river to a point about fifteen miles west of modern Topeka, Kansas, where a trading post had been established. In 1880, Chouteau, then an old man, recalled, "We would take a boat up with goods in August, and keep it there til the next spring, when we would bring it down loaded with peltries. At the mouth of the Kaw we shipped on steamboat to St. Louis."

By Chouteau's time the Kansas River was shown on maps of the region that Zebulon M. Pike and Stephen H. Long had crossed and labeled the "Great American Desert." Compared to the rich woodlands of the East, the Kansas River Valley and all of that which is today eastern Kansas was different. It is prairie land, but it was not a desert. Isaac McCoy, the missionary, wrote the Secretary of War in 1831 that what is today eastern Kansas was anything but "poor land." He described the soil as "almost invariably rich."

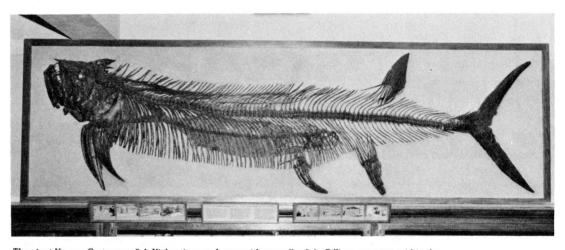

The giant Kansas Cretaceous fish Xiphactinus molossus *with a smaller fish,* Gillicus arcuatus, *within the abdominal cavity, is exhibited in the Sternberg Memorial Museum. It was found in the Smoky Hill chalk beds. (Photo by E. C. Almquist. Print courtesy Sternberg Memorial Museum, Fort Hays State University, Hays, Kansas.)*

That same year, 1831, "Peck's Guide to Emigrants" published at Boston, described the Kansas River as a "large, bold, navigable river, although its fickle channel and numerous snags must forever endanger commerce."

Many steamboat captains found the "fickle channel" when, in 1854, Kansas Territory was organized and the vast area from the Missouri River westward to the summit of the Rocky Mountains was up for grabs. It was then the center of a national controversy. Was it to be free or a slave state? Northerners, especially New Englanders, wanted to populate the region in hopes of making Kansas a free state. But pro-slavery forces from Missouri and other areas in the South had the same goal in mind. The Kansas River became interwoven with the events that followed as steamboats flocked to the Missouri River from all the rivers of the Mississippi Valley "like white winged-gulls to their banquet on the generous table of the sea." The steamboats were bringing settlers to Kansas Territory.

The first steamboat to ascend the Kansas River any distance was *Excel*, in the spring of 1854. A newspaper story in the Worcester (Mass.) *Spy* of March that year reported:

> The steamer Excel his been bought for a packet in the Kansas river trade, which will be the pioneer steamer of the territory, to ply between Kansas City at the mouth and 'as high as she can get.'

The 79-ton sternwheeler with a draft of two feet, loaded with 1,100 barrels of flour, started upstream in April 1854. One passenger, H. D. Meekin, later recalled, "We were two days on the trip. . . and found more difficulty in navigating the Kansas than we did the Missouri."

In October of that year the *Excel* made a short exploratory trip up the Smoky Hill River with little difficulty. Word of the successful navigation spread like a prairie fire and more and more steamboats began to ply the Kansas River, but it soon became obvious that only boats with a very shallow draft could do so successfully.

The distance, by river, from Kansas City to Fort Riley was about 178 miles. The successful navigation convinced some New Mexican traders that freight could be carried up the Kansas River to Fort Riley where it could be transferred to wagons heading southwest over the Santa Fe Trail. That trail began at Kansas City. These traders saw a savings in land carriage and a shorter journey to Santa Fe by perhaps 200 miles.

Between 1854 and 1864 at least thirty-three steamboats with names like *Bee*, *New Lucy*, *Lizzie*, *Hartford*, *Perry*, *Morning Star*, *Far West*, *Jacob Sass* and *Kate Swinney* plied the Kansas River at one time or another. Most of the early settlements in Kansas were along the Kansas River; cities like Lawrence, Lecompton, Topeka, Manhattan and Junction City. Many settlers arrived by boat.

In 1859 the *Silver Lake* took the first load of Kansas corn downriver to Kansas City and other steamboats carried the first wheat to eastern markets. Kansas is today known as the "wheat state." When gold was discovered in 1858 in far western Kansas Territory—now Colorado—a Pittsburgh (Pa.) newspaper reported that the steamboat *Col. Gus Linn* would go up the Kaw within 150 miles of Pikes Peak. Obviously this was false. It was more than 500 miles from Kansas City to Cherry Creek (Denver) and steamboat travel was pretty much limited to about 200 miles west of Kansas City.

Steamboating on the Kansas River came to an abrupt end soon after February, 1864, when the Kansas legislature, swayed by powerful railroad interests, declared the Kansas, Republican, Smoky Hill, Solomon and Big Blue rivers not navigable and authorized the railroads to build bridges across these streams.

Albert R. Greene, who became Kansas railroad commissioner in 1887, later wrote that the railroads wanted the Kansas River "lawfully obstructed by bridges and destroyed as a competitor." Ironically, in the spring of 1866 a flood carried away the Kansas Pacific Railroad bridge at the mouth of the Kansas River. The railroad chartered the *Alexander Majors*, a big sidewheeler, to carry passengers as far as Lawrence until the bridge could be rebuilt. The *Alexander Majors* was the last steamboat to ply the Kansas River.

In 1879 the U. S. Army Engineers undertook a survey to determine whether the Kansas River could be made navigable. To make it so, they reported, "would probably be of much benefit to the people living along the stream." Their report said that if dams or dykes were built, if bridges were provided with draws, a short canal with a lock built around the dam at Lawrence and the snags in the river removed, small steamers could navigate the stream at all but the lowest stages of water. The cost, aside from remodeling bridges and building the canal, was estimated at $450,000. The railroads, however, not wanting to remodel their bridges nor encourage competition, appear to have influenced the final decision against improving the Kansas River for navigation.

Since then the Kansas River has contributed little to commerce in Kansas. Annual spring flooding—massive floods occurred in some years like 1903, 1908, and 1951—brought about the construction of dams and reservoirs by the Corp of Army Engineers on all of its major tributaries. Today the river rarely floods except in very low areas close to the stream.

The Kansas, or Kaw River remains a beautiful stream. Countless trees line its banks along its gently winding route through eastern Kansas. Fishermen still find many catfish and other varieties in its muddy waters. But gone are those magic days when a whistle blast signaled a steamboat around the bend on the Kansas River.

FURTHER READING: Floyd Benjamin Streeter, *The Kaw: Heart of a Nation* (1941; 1975). Kenneth Sidney Davis, *River on The Rampage* (1953).

David Dary

The Loup River

Source: Merger of North, Middle, and South Loup rivers in south-central Nebraska
Length: 68 miles
Tributaries: Cedar River
Mouth: Into Platte River at Columbus, Nebraska
Agricultural Products: Livestock, corn, wheat, alfalfa
Industries: Food processing

The Loup River is formed by the North, Middle, and South Loup rivers which merge in south-central Nebraska; it then flows sixty-eight miles east to the Platte River at Columbus. This tells little about a river system which drains the extensive Sandhills region of northwestern Nebraska. The rivers appear to cradle the Sandhills on the south and east with tentacles running into the vast interior of this grass-covered desert. Together the Loup rivers collect water from some 15,000 square miles of drainage area within and outside the Sandhills region. Starting as clear flowing streams, they flow out of the Sandhills through rolling to rough uplands and rich farmlands before reaching the Platte.

Over the huge Sandhills region the rainfall percolates into the sand and gradually moves through the ground into North and Middle Loup rivers which act as huge drains. Their flows remain practically constant throughout each year and are not subject to the cyclic variations common to most streams. The Middle Loup, the principal tributary, rises in the Sandhill region near the village of King. It flows southeasterly to Boelus and then northeasterly to St. Paul, a distance of about 221 miles. The major tributary of the Middle Loup is the Dismal River which joins it at Dunning. The Dismal is the site of the fabled ranch home of the legendary Febold Feboldson, a Paul Bunyon-like Swedish pioneer on the Great Plains who cut and sold frozen postholes. The South Loup River enters the Middle Loup about twelve miles below Rockville and is about 152 miles long; with its tributaries it drains 2,400 miles of rolling to rough upland.

The North Loup River also rises in the Sandhills close to the headwaters of the Middle Loup. It flows generally parallel to the Middle Loup and after flowing some 212 miles joins it near St. Paul. The Calamus River is its only tributary of significance and it joins the North Loup near Burwell. The Calamus River is one of the most stable streams in the world due to the percolating ground waters. Further downstream, where the silty soils absorb only a small part of the heavier rainfall, there is a much larger runoff. Over a period of years this has created a flat, fertile valley that varies from one to three miles in width.

As the Loup River flows eastward from its formation by the junction of the North and Middle Loups it receives practically no additional flow from the south, but another major tributary, the Cedar, flows nearly parallel to the North Loup. This river rises on the eastern edge of the Sandhills and extends southeast to its junction with the Loup near Fullerton. The Cedar produces a steady flow in its upper reaches, but the uplands of the lower portion of the stream are of less absorbent soils and heavier runoffs follow summer rains in this section.

Except for its lower regions the Loup area was among the last parts of the state to be occupied by the whites, yet it was first explored more than 250 years ago. A Spanish expedition commanded by General Don Pedro de Villasur made the journey from Santa Fe, starting June 16, 1720. Although some question it, he probably reached the river near present Columbus on August 10, 1720. In the early morning hours of the next day the Spanish and their Indian allies were attacked by local Indians. The Spanish force was wiped out and its Indian allies fled the scene.

A much better documented account of whites in the Loup River area is that of James Mackay's expedition of 1796. Mackay was a Scot employed by the Spanish to make an exploration of the upper Missouri. His notes are all in French (his name is sometimes spelled Jacques Machey) and have suffered some in translation. He seems to have traveled northwest from his starting point near Homer (today a small town west and south of Sioux City on the Nebraska side of the Missouri), entering the Sandhills from the north. Then he moved down through the lake region of the upper North Loup and Calamus rivers. From there he traveled east to his starting point. One thing about him that the experts do agree upon is his account of the Sandhills near the head of the North Loup. On his map he refers to the "Grand Desert of moving sand where are neither wood, nor soil, nor stone, nor water, nor animals except some little tortoises of various colors." This may be an early contribution to the myth of the Great American Desert.

Prior to the white man's arrival in the Loup Valley, Indians had occupied the region for many years. Examination of a number of ancient dwelling sites indicates the presence of the Woodlands culture. When the white people first came in contact with native American residents of the Valley, the Pawnee were living on the lower reaches of the Loup and were using the Sandhill region for hunting. Contrary to Mackay, the region was noted for its large numbers of buffalo, deer, elk and antelope. In June, 1820, Major Stephen H. Long on his official exploring expedition spent some time with these Pawnee. The Major was impressed by the wealth of their villages. For miles up and down the river large herds of horses were grazing. Patches of maize, tomatoes, pumpkins and squash dotted the landscape. The Pawnee were certainly a force to be reckoned with by other tribes or the occasional trader venturing into their hunting grounds.

But in 1831 smallpox struck the tribe. Their agent, John Dougherty, estimated that one-half of them had died. When a treaty between the government and the Pawnee was signed on October 9, 1834, the survivors living on the south side of the Platte vacated their land and reassembled with their brethren along the Loup and westward along the Platte.

But now a new scourge threatened. The Sioux swept down the North Loup and Cedar and raided the Pawnee villages. The federal government, although having treaties with the Pawnee, did little to check these raids. In 1849 another dread disease, cholera, struck the Pawnee. Thus weakened and harassed by their enemies, the tribe in September of 1857 ceded all its original territory except a strip thirty miles long and fifteen miles wide along the lower Loup River. This area was known as the Nance County Reservation and continued to be their home until the remnants of the tribe were removed to Indian Territory (present Oklahoma) in 1876. During the Plains Indian wars of the 1870s the world learned of the remarkable tracking abilities of Colonel North's Pawnee scouts who were glad to help the white soldiers chastise the Sioux.

Both cattlemen and sodbusters were slow to

move into the Sandhill region, but by the early 1870s both had discovered the good grazing in the hills and the tillable soils in the valleys. Since the valleys of the Loup formed natural routes into central Nebraska the bottom lands along the watercourses were soon settled and it began to look as though the great herds of cattle would be excluded from their watering places.

The resulting conflict between the cattlemen and the "nesters" (as cattlemen called the settlers) was probably nowhere more dramatic than in the valleys of the Loup. Cattlemen anxious to defend their rights to watering places let their cattle overrun crops with little consideration for the farmers. Settlers, on the other hand, having bona fide homesteads and a claim to their land, struck back in the only ways they knew how, by fencing off their acreages, driving off the cattle, or adopting herd laws that restricted cattle movement. Cattlemen were victims of rustling which was hardly unexpected since the cattle were frequently beyond their owner's reach. Since the real culprits could not be apprehended in the act of rustling and the cattlemen were already prejudiced against the settlers, they blamed all of them. The climax to this struggle was the Olive-Mitchell-Ketchum case of 1878.

I. P. Olive, a Texas cattleman, established his headquarters in the southeastern Sandhills. He was accompanied to Nebraska by his brother, Robert Olive, who had assumed the name of Bob Stevens. Luther M. Mitchell and Ami Ketchum were homesteaders on Clear Creek, a stream which parallels the Middle Loup but is in the South Loup's watershed. Between Ketchum and Robert Olive, alias Bob Stevens, there was "bad blood." Stevens had accused Ketchum of stealing cattle and on several occasions had threatened to kill him.

Stevens finally got himself deputized and obtained a warrant for Ketchum's arrest. Gunfire ensued when he approached Ketchum's place. Stevens received a mortal wound and Ketchum was in turn wounded before the posse rode off. Mitchell and Ketchum then packed up their few household goods and left for Merrick County to the southeast, fearing for their lives if they stayed where they were.

After Ketchum's wounds were dressed the two

men gave themselves up to stand trial for the attack on Stevens. But a sheriff handed them over to the Olive group. The following day they were found dead, Ketchum hanging with his legs badly burned and Mitchell lying on the ground with one arm drawn up to Ketchum's by handcuffs; his other arm was burned off to the shoulder. Olive was tried for the crime and sentenced, but was released from the penitentiary in a year on a technicality. The incident, even though it is not typical, does demonstrate the intensity of the struggle between cattlemen and settlers in the Loup Valley.

There were still other hardships. The Sioux sometimes moved down the valley to attack the Pawnee and on their return frequently stole cattle, horses, and any available food. The continuing Sioux raids resulted in substantial material losses but on only one occasion did it result in loss of life. Nevertheless the settlers in the valley requested military protection and a company was sent from Fort Omaha for their protection. On June 16, 1874, Congress authorized a fort just in time to avert a mass exodus from the Loup Valley. Completion of the first building of Fort Hartsuft, northwest of Grand Island, in December, 1874, was celebrated with a grand ball to which the entire countryside was invited.

The Indians no longer raid up and down the valleys and the cattlemen and farmers have learned to live in harmony. From time to time, however, other tensions have disturbed the people in the Loup valleys. Depression and drought in the 1890s converted many farmers of the region to Populism, while similar circumstances in the 1930s brought participation in the Farmer's Holiday Movement. Fist fights broke out at a rally in Loup City addressed by "Mother" Ella Reeve Bloor, a seventy-two year old agitator for the American Communist Party. "Mother" Bloor subsequently served a thirty-day jail sentence for inciting a riot.

General prosperity has resulted from the development of a mixed agricultural economy along the valleys of the Loup. The North and Middle Loup Power and Irrigation Projects developed in the 1930s have done much to stabilize the area's economy. More recently there have been extensive developments of center pivot irrigation in the river basins. The heavy drain which this latest development has placed on the groundwater supply and its apparent affect on stream flow are a cause of concern today. The close relationship of agriculture to the Loup River will continue to shape the future of the area as it has in the past.

FURTHER READING: James C. Olson, *History of Nebraska* (1966). George E. Hyde, *The Pawnee Indians* (1951).

Philip S. Holmgren

The Minnesota River

> *Source:* **Big Stone Lake on northeast South Dakota, west-central Minnesota boundary**
> *Length:* **332 miles**
> *Tributaries:* **Blue Earth River**
> *Mouth:* **Into Mississippi at St. Paul**
> *Agricultural Products:* **Corn, soy beans, peas, oats, wheat, alfalfa, sugar beets**
> *Industries:* **Food processing, quarrying of granite, limestone, and dolomite, farm implements, and diversified manufacturing**

The Minnesota River flows from Big Stone Lake, a long, narrow body of water in northeast South Dakota and western Minnesota, first southeast and then northeast 332 miles across Minnesota to its junction with the Mississippi at St. Paul. Its descent is gentle, from 960 feet above sea level at its place of origin to 690 feet at its mouth. Only at Granite Falls do two drops occur sufficient to erect hydro-electric installations using the river to drive the turbines.

The Minnesota River valley, through which the river meanders today, was ground out by glacial melt-water containing silt, sand, pebbles, and gravels constituting a liquid abrasive that carved away everything before it. The waters originated in prehistoric Lake Agassiz which stretched from Big Stone Lake 700 miles northward into Canada. When, eventually, the upper ice wall broke and the lake water could flow in the more natural direction of north, the great river to the south was reduced to the Minnesota River of today, and the gorge became the Minnesota River valley.

During the first half of its journey from Big Stone Lake across Minnesota, the stream flows over very old igneous rocks worn smooth by glacial ice and waters. These granites and gneisses are about three and one-half billion years old, among the oldest rocks known. Continuing its downward journey, the Minnesota glides slowly over a variety of sedimentary rocks—quartzites, dolomites, limestones, sandstones, and conglomerates. All the rocky outcroppings divert the stream's flow, add to the variety of landscapes, and provide material for commercially produced tombstones, architectural stone, cement, crushed rock, and sand.

Ancient human skeletal remains indicate that prehistoric man lived along the shores of Glacial Lake Agassiz and Glacial River Warren (the name geologists have given to the prehistoric river). From then on there is evidence of continual occupation of the valley. Nomadic peoples tarried there before continuing their wandering, usually in a westerly direction. Along the highest part of the valley walls, often on a point with a magnificent view of the river and valley below, ancient peoples erected thousands of earthen mounds. These earthworks, more numerous in the lower half of the valley, give mute evidence of early burial customs. Some of them still exist; easily accessible are those in the City Park at Chaska. In historic times the Iowa, Oto, and Sioux (or Lakota) are known to have lived in or near the valley.

It was the Sioux who told the explorers, fur traders, and missionaries that the river was called the "Minne-sota." Minne meant "water" and sota meant "somewhat clouded." At least, this is the interpretation of the Reverand Gideon

Pond, who lived and worked with the Sioux for many years. Others have translated the word somewhat differently.

Siouxan people occupied a large part of what is now Minnesota until the Chippewas to the north and east began trading with the white man. Armed with firearms, the Chippewas inflicted disastrous losses on the Sioux, who still used stone-age weapons. The Sioux were forced to leave their homes in central Minnesota; many moved to sites along the Minnesota River. Some tribes moved west onto the prairies, becoming, in a relatively short time, the colorful, fighting prairie horsemen, symbolic today of the American Indian.

The first white visitors to the Minnesota River valley found there the M'dewakanton, Sissitons, Wahpetons, and Wapekute tribes, known collectively as the Santee Sioux. Hunting, fishing, wild plants—in particular wild rice—and some agricultural products provided them with varied food supply. Habitations of animal skins or tree bark provided adequate protection from the extreme variations in temperature. It was a rich region from which the Sioux obtained food, tools, shelter, and enough free time to develop fairly complex social and religious customs.

Into this Sioux country in 1700 paddled a small group of white men led by Pierre Charles LeSueur, seeking copper. LeSueur named the river the St. Pierre, or St. Peters, and for 150 years it retained the name. In 1849, by petition of the territorial legislature, Congress decided to use the old aboriginal name Minnesota. A short distance up the tributary stream now called the Blue Earth River, the group halted and built the first known fort in the valley. They hunted buffalo, mined the green-tinted clay they assumed was copper ore, and left written records of their activities. One hundred and thirty-five years later, when scientist George W. Featherstonaugh in 1835 entered the valley, he found no trace of LeSueur's fort. The bluish-green ore he identified as a silicate of iron.

Today the city of LeSueur, a few miles downstream in the Minnesota Valley, is the home of the world's largest canning company; it uses the trade name Green Giant for its products. Green peas in cans lined with copper-colored coating are shipped to France—not quite the export Pierre LeSueur anticipated!

In 1805 Lieutenant Zebulon Pike, leading an expedition up the Mississippi to secure and explore that part of the Louisiana Purchase for the United States, pitched camp on a low island at the mouth of the Minnesota. On Pike Island (as it has ever since been known) he concluded with the Sioux the first land treaty in what became Minnesota. The land acquired became the base for most of the important events of the valley and even of the state of Minnesota for the next century. There, for many years, was the center of federal power in Indian territory. Today it has been engulfed by the tentacles of Minneapolis-St. Paul, and their suburbs. The center of government, financial power, entertainment and education has shifted only a few miles from Pike's Island.

Warfare between the Sioux and other tribes including the Chippewa was a part of Siouxan life by the 1800s. Into this situation came the United States Army which in 1820 began construction of a fort on the top of a steep bluff at the junction of the Minnesota and Mississippi. Fort Snelling was built of limestone and designed to withstand attack by any conceivable number of Indian warriors. The high walls, thick stone construction, and displays of garrison strength impressed the Indians; the Fort was never attacked.

The lure of furs pulled white men into the valley. From the first visits in the late 1600s to the final days of the fur business in the 1850s the trader was a vital factor in life along the Minnesota. At its height the region from Big Stone Lake to the Mississippi was dotted with fur posts run by men with names such as Renville, LaFramboise, Faribault, and Mooers. Some disappeared into obscurity while others adapted to changing times and became important in politics and business. Counties and communities felt honored in assuming their names. The life experiences of these colorful characters is a remarkable account of the history of the Minnesota Valley. One of the most noteworthy of these men was Henry H. Sibley, who arrived in the valley in 1834 as representative of the American Fur Company. His life at Mendota, across from Fort Snelling, his travels and adventures in the valley, and his performance as Minnesota's first governor all make him an important personage of the fur trade era.

By 1851 the Sioux were feeling the increasing pressure of white civilization. In treaties at Traverse des Sioux and Mendota the government purchased from them most of southern Minnesota, some thirty million acres in all. Soon the Sioux residing in the Minnesota and Mississippi valleys were removed to a reservation, a strip of land ten miles wide that paralleled the upper Minnesota River on the south side. Extending from Big Stone Lake southeast to a line just west of present New Ulm, it seemed to the whites that the Indians had been given adequate territory. The upper agency, near the Yellow Medicine River, and the lower agency, near the Redwood River, were the centers of Sioux population.

Because Fort Snelling was many miles away, in 1853 a new fort was erected northwest of New Ulm on the north side of the Minnesota. This site, named Fort Ridgely, was the training ground for many Civil War soldiers who achieved fame in the struggle. The few professionals remaining in 1862 combined with civilian forces to hold off some of the most well-planned Indian attacks in American history. Plans are under way to reconstruct the fort; at present the site is a state park with a fine interpretive center.

The long blast of a steam whistle in 1850 created consternation among the Indians and signaled a change in the lives of all inhabitants. The first steamboat to travel on the Minnesota, the *Anthony Wayne*, chugged upstream from the Mississippi. For the next two decades steamers plied the crooked Minnesota whenever water levels and absence of ice permitted. Specially designed shallow draft boats reached New Ulm, Fort Ridgely, and even further upriver. Boats with names such as *Time and Tide*, *Frank Steele*, and *Favorite* became famous throughout the valley. The unusual men who captained these steamers seemed undaunted by explosions, ice, snags, and cutthroat competition. They provided necessary transportation until the railroads appeared in the 1870s.

The steamboats served an increasing population and a plethora of towns as a result of the Sioux treaties of 1851. Among them New Ulm was unique. German immigrants led by Frederich Beinhorn formed a colonization association in Chicago, formulated plans, collected funds, sent out search parties, and finally selected a site on the Minnesota near Big Cottonwood River. Here rich farmland, a navigable river, a forest upstream, and freedom from persecution beckoned the colonists. Plans were drawn, streets, blocks, and all town plans determined before the first building was erected. When another group, the Turner Society under the leadership of William Pfaender, combined with the Beinhorn group, the future of New Ulm was assured.

Not in their plans, however, was the devastating Sioux uprising of 1862. The Indians pillaged the upper Minnesota Valley. If measured by lives lost, this was the worst Indian outbreak in American history with a loss of 450 to 800 whites and an undetermined number of Indian casualties. The Sioux were at first successful, but the defense of Fort Ridgely and New Ulm changed the direction of their attacks and they were soon in retreat.

For a time New Ulm was deserted. After the second attack the inhabitants fled in a caravan of mounted men, wagons loaded with women and children and the sick and wounded. Most of the town's 220 structures had gone up in smoke while thirty barricaded buildings in the town's center now stood abandoned. Most of the white defenders survived, and when the hostilities were over, New Ulm revived.

Raw troops under the command of Henry W. Sibley pursued the Indians. The Battle of Wood Lake was a clear victory for his troops. Soon the Indians were in disarray, being captured, and their white captives being released. As punishment the Indians lost the valley, which was opened for white settlement. Small groups of Sioux returned, however, and their descendants still call the Minnesota Valley their home.

The Minnesota River flows quietly and slowly. Valley soils produce heavy yields of farm products. Canoes, small boats, cabin cruisers and barges move about on the river. Efforts continue to improve the quality of the water, the air, and the soil. The inhabitants have pride in their ancestors and confidence in their future, and are proud to live along the "Sky-tinted Water" that is the Minnesota River.

FURTHER READING: Evan Jones, *The Minnesota, Forgotten River* (1962). George Schwartz and George Thiel, *Minnesota's Rocks and Waters* (1954).

Paul W. Klammer

The Mississippi River

Source: Lake Itasca in northwestern Minnesota
Length: 2,348 miles
Tributaries: Ohio, Missouri (sometimes considered a part of the main river), and many, many other rivers
Mouth: Below New Orleans, Louisiana, into Gulf of Mexico
Agricultural Products: Diversified
Industries: Diversified

The Mississippi River is the backbone of America. It rises in Lake Itasca in northwestern Minnesota and flows about 2,348 miles south to the Gulf of Mexico, draining 1,234,700 square miles. Its major tributaries, and their tributaries in turn, drain virtually all the land from the Rocky Mountains in the West to the Appalachians in the East. Mighty rivers like the Missouri, the Ohio, the Arkansas, the Red, and in a sense the upper Mississippi itself, all flow into the main stem of the Mississippi, which begins at St. Louis and empties into the Gulf 100 miles south of New Orleans. (If the Missouri is considered part of the Mississippi, and it sometimes is, then the Mississippi is 3,892 miles long.) Until the coming of the railroads, control of the lower Mississippi was the key to control of the land between the mountains. The river was the only satisfactory outlet by which the region's wealth could be extracted. Its strategic position and its importance as a trade route made it a bone of contention between warring empires from the mid-sixteenth century through the early years of the nineteenth century; it was the key to Union victory in the American Civil War.

On the eve of the coming of the Europeans to the Mississippi, there was little to indicate that it would become the focal point of such a struggle. Peaceful Indians, members of various larger "nations" but for the most part concerned only with neighboring villages, occupied the banks of the river from north to south. They were agriculturalists living for the most part in permanent settlements typical of primitive farming cultures. Because of the efficiency of their farming techniques, the population was dense compared to other Native American cultures. They were descendants of an earlier and far more elaborate culture which built the huge mounds found up and down the Mississippi Valley. Only the Natchez retained much of that earlier culture. Their chiefs fancied themselves descendants of the sun, and human sacrifices were regularly practiced at their temple, the seat of their power. The Natchez were among the most bellicose natives along the river and would create problems for successive white explorers.

The first Europeans to encounter the Mississippi did so with a sense of disappointment rather than of joy. Hernando De Soto landed in Florida in May of 1539 with an army of over 600 men. He burned and pillaged his way through Georgia, the Carolinas, Tennessee, Alabama, and Mississippi, and finally arrived on the banks of the Mississippi River in April of 1541. The river vexed the impatient conquistador. It was almost a mile across, the current was strong and deep, and the water was muddy and continually charged with floating trees. He set his men to work building rafts to cross the river and waited anxiously to resume his search for gold. While encamped on the river bank, a party of several hundred Indians in canoes, "with their bows and arrows, painted and decorated with feathers of various colors, and defended with shields made from skins of bisons . . .", approached his army. As was his usual practice he greeted the delegation with a hail of crossbow bolts, killing five or six. Failing to recognize the importance of the river he discovered, De Soto crossed it and resumed his quest, killing as he went.

His search for gold was fruitless, and after a year of marching and counter-marching, he returned to the Mississippi. On May 21, 1542, De Soto died on the banks of the river he had discovered. In order to conceal his death from the natives, Luis Moscoso, his second in command, had him secretly buried in the river. The macabre scene must have been one of the strangest events in the Mississippi's long history. After much fumbling about, Moscoso used the river trail to lead the De Soto party to the Gulf and Spanish Mexico and safety in 1543. Of the more than 600 men who began the expedition, only 311 survived. They had found no mineral wealth, and displayed a complete lack of interest in developing other aspects of the Mississippi basin. It would be more than 100 years before Europeans would return to the Mississippi.

In the seventeenth century, however, a number of events occurred which would affect the great river. First, France built the foundations of a New World Empire in the St. Lawrence Valley. Since efforts to establish agricultural enterprises met with little success the economic cornerstone of New France became the fur trade. Second, England planted colonies along the Atlantic coast of North America. Their rapid growth and the scarcity of land east of the Appalachians eventually brought first fur traders and then pioneer farmers into the Mississippi Valley. Third, Spain's power was diminished and her hold on her American empire became more tenuous. Fourth, the growing European presence in North America had a profound effect on the peaceful Indians of the Mississippi Valley. The Europeans introduced diseases for which the natives had no immunity. Those Indians of the Mississippi basin living in densely populated permanent villages were most susceptible to epidemics. Smallpox, and cholera particularly, decimated the population. The Europeans drove many of the eastern tribes out of their traditional lands. The eastern Indians, more warlike in nature, fought to gain new territories in the West. The wars, too, added to the destruction of the Indians of the Mississippi Valley. By the time of the second European visitation to the great river, the native population was greatly reduced and significantly more hostile.

Impetus for French expansion into the Mississippi Valley came from Jean Talon, the "Great Intendant," who elevated New France to a thriving colony. His efforts to expand French control into the interior of North America relied upon the efforts of licensed fur traders hungry for profit, and Jesuit missionaries hungry for new souls to save. Just such a team was Louis Jolliet and Father Jacques Marquette. Talon directed the two men to undertake an expedition to the "Great River," and so they did, reaching the Mississippi on June 17, 1673. Continuing downstream, the two intrepid adventurers reached the juncture of the Missouri, which Marquette

hypothesized could eventually lead one to the Pacific. On downriver they made their way, rescued on several occasions from hostile Indians by displaying their calumet or peacepipe, the universal sign that the bearer came in peace. They traveled as far south as the Arkansas, and there were convinced that the Mississippi must certainly flow into the Gulf of Mexico. If they continued south they feared they would be captured by the Spanish, whom they believed occupied the mouth of the river. They turned back with the news of their discovery.

Even as Marquette and Joliet were departing for the wilderness, a new Intendant, Louis Count de Frontenac, became governor of New France on Talon's recall in 1672. Frontenac chose Robert Cavelier, Seur de La Salle, to develop the Mississippi for France. La Salle, a dreamer and visionary, was given grants to develop the fur trade in the Mississippi Valley and along the Great Lakes. Years of preparation followed; finally in January, 1680, La Salle and his lieutenant, Henri de Tonty, built Fort Crevecoeur overlooking Lake Peoria near the Illinois River. La Salle hoped to launch his conquest of the Mississippi from this base. Once Crevecoeur was secure, La Salle dispatched Father Louis Hennepin to explore the upper Mississippi.

Father Hennepin's exploration of the upper portion of the river greatly added to the knowledge of that part of North America. He discovered and named the Falls of St. Anthony (at the present site of St. Paul-Minneapolis) and kept a detailed account of the geography and ethnology of the region. Father Hennepin's accounts of his travels and sufferings were widely read in Europe and spread much knowledge of the upper Mississippi. Those who remained at Ft. Crevecoeur found themselves caught up in the Iroquois invasion of the Illinois country and fled for their lives. When La Salle returned in the fall of 1680, he found his fort in ruins. Not until June, 1681, did he find his lieutenant, Tonty. They rebuilt their fort near present day Ottawa, Illinois, and in early 1682 finally began their long-awaited journey down the Mississippi.

The trip itself was uneventful and on April 9, 1682 they arrived at the mouth of the Mississippi. As was the custom of the day, they claimed the whole of the Mississippi basin for the King of France. La Salle named the territory Louisiana in honor of his king. He knew, however, that in order to control this river system he would have to establish a post at the mouth of this mightiest of rivers. Unfortunately, La Salle's patron, Frontenac, was replaced that same year, 1682, by de la Barre, and it was necessary for La Salle to return to France to retain his position as developer of the Mississippi. He succeeded in court but failed in his efforts to establish a French post at the mouth of the Mississippi. His expedition was blown off course and landed on the coast of Texas in 1684. Attempting to return to French territory, he was killed by his men when they mutinied against his leadership. Even as La Salle was failing in his efforts to consolidate French control of the Mississippi, English colonists from the other side of the Appalachians were challenging the French claim.

English fur traders, operating from Virginia and the Carolinas, were already into the interior when La Salle made his voyage down the Mississippi. One of La Salle's own men, Jean Couture, became a leader of the Carolina traders and centered his operations at Arkansas Post near the juncture of the Arkansas and Mississippi. The French and English continued the battle for Indian loyalty, but the British had lost control of most of the tribes by 1717. A key to that control was a series of permanent settlements built by the French under the direction of Antoine Crozat. Most important was the establishment of New Orleans by Jean Baptiste Le Moyne Bienville in 1718. By this time the development of Louisiana had been entrusted to the Western Company under the direction of John Law, a Scottish banker. After years of financial disappointments, the Natchez war in which the French lost heavily forced the colony to return to royal control in 1731.

The Treaty of Paris of 1763 ended the Seven Years' War and France's hope for an empire in North America. In order to secure their ally Spain's acceptance of a peace settlement, they ceded all of Louisiana west of the Mississippi to that country in 1762. In negotiations with the British the next year they were able to obtain for Spain the city of New Orleans as well. While Britain received all of the territory east of the river, including Spanish Florida, France left a great legacy to the region. Most of the population was either of French or French-Canadian

extraction. The institutions and customs of the region were conspicuously French as well.

Before the English could exploit their newly won empire, they found themselves embroiled in a conflict with their North American colonists who were anxious to press out beyond the mountains to establish farms and permanent settlements. Such a presence would have led directly to Indian war. British policy, however, envisioned a continuation of the fur trade which, in turn, depended upon continued good relations with the Indians. Adding to British western problems was Spain's control of the lower Mississippi and New Orleans.

Spain dominated the lower Mississippi for the next thirty-seven years until 1800. While the British fought a losing battle with their colonies on the east coast, the Spanish tried with varying success to bring the lower Mississippi under control. French resentment and Spanish ineptitude got them off to a poor start, which resulted in a rebellion against Spanish authority in 1768; Spain regained control the next year. During the American Revolution, New Orleans became a supply center for American forces operating in the west. The principal actions along the Mississippi during the Revolution were initiated by George Rogers Clark. Clark relied upon support of French settlers along the Mississippi and with their cooperation captured Kaskaskia and shortly thereafter Cahokia, the two principal British strongholds on the river. The French alliance had brought both France and Spain into the war and that meant that all the lower Mississippi was either administered or occupied by people friendly to the Americans.

After the Treaty of Paris of 1783, the United States was in control of all of the east bank of the Mississippi with an important exception. In order to get Spanish agreement to the peace settlement, Britain ceded the Floridas back to Spain. As a result, Spain controlled both sides of the Mississippi from the line 31° latitude south. To make matters worse, Spain and the new United States found themselves in a dispute over the United States-Florida boundary, the Spanish insisting on the 32°30' line. Louisiana was of principal importance to Spain as a buffer between the United States and Spain's rich holdings in Mexico. For the next fifteen years the Spanish would strive to prevent American expansion across the Appalachians through their control of the mouth of the Mississippi. Western Americans became increasingly angered by Spanish control over their destiny and hostility between the two nations grew, with the lower Mississippi as the focal point. The Spanish thought they had won a victory when John Jay, in negotiations with Don Diego de Gardoqui, agreed to relinquish the right to navigate on the Mississippi for thirty years in exchange for commercial concessions on the part of Spain. Spain's hopes were dashed, however, when western interests blocked ratification of the treaty.

Western anger over this episode led to the Spanish Conspiracy. The plan would have detached the west from the United States and resulted in its union with Spanish Louisiana. This intrigue failed, partly because Spain, due to European considerations, entered into Pinckney's Treaty, or the Treaty of San Lorenzo, signed on October 17, 1795. This instrument granted the United States free navigation of the Mississippi, with the right of deposit at New Orleans for three years and later at some other convenient spot. It also fixed Florida's boundary at 31°. In many ways this treaty ended Spain's hopes for Louisiana.

In 1800 Spain transferred Louisiana to France and Napoleon Bonaparte. By that time there were significant settled areas around New Orleans and Natchez. Sugar cane cultivation provided a new economic activity for the inhabitants of the lower Mississippi. Nonetheless, the settlements further upriver such as Arkansas Post (actually on the Arkansas), Fort Prudhomme at Chickasaw Bluffs (present Memphis, Tennessee), Kaskaskia, and St. Louis-Cahokia were still primarily fur-trading centers with a little supplementary farming. Defeat in Haiti and war in Europe soon altered Napoleon's dreams for a new French empire in North America. Meanwhile, the United States, alarmed by what appeared to be the French revocation of the right of deposit at New Orleans on October 16, 1802, had undertaken negotiations to gain control of the lower Mississippi from France by purchase.

President Jefferson dispatched James Monroe to aid the American Minister in Paris, Robert R. Livingston. Monroe's instructions authorized

him to offer ten million dollars for the Isle (city) of New Orleans and the Floridas, which in fact France did not possess at the time. The actual negotiations are masked behind legends, but a treaty was signed on April 30, 1803, in which the United States received the Isle of Orleans and the rest of Louisiana for the equivalent of fifteen million dollars. On November 30, 1803, Spain turned the administration of Louisiana over to the French, who in turn presented it to William C. Claiborne and General James Wilkinson, the American representatives, on December 20. At long last the struggle over the Mississippi seemed to be over. By the terms of the treaty, admittedly somewhat vague, the United States held legal title to the entire basin drained by the Mississippi.

In the years between the end of the American Revolution and the outbreak of the War of 1812, the nature of Mississippi usage was changing. For more than a hundred years it had served as a practically deserted highway connecting a string of trading posts. As American farmers flooded into the Ohio River Valley, they too made use of the river. New Orleans became the great southern terminus for first flatboats and then keelboats carrying produce and passengers from the Ohio Valley. Traffic picked up on the Mississippi, and as the importance of the fur trade diminished along the river itself, many of the communities adjusted their services to meet the needs of these new and more numerous river people.

The keelboatmen and the flatboatmen were romantic figures. Tied only to the river, they drank and fought amongst themselves and with the townspeople along its banks. For the most part they were only farmers off on a summer spree, but a few truly rough customers emerged like the legendary Mike Fink. Some of those who found the life of the river more attractive than farming became river robbers or sharpers. Mark Twain's writings are full of these characters, such as the Duke of Bilgewater and the Dauphin. Pirates roamed the river from the Ohio to Natchez. While the flatboats and keelboats and their colorful crews were eventually driven off the river by competition from the steamboat, they continued to be a part of river life for many years.

The years 1811 and 1812 were turning points

in Mississippi River history. A series of three major earthquakes and a number of smaller tremors completely changed the face of the river. The first quake hit in December of 1811 and by the time the earth had stabilized, new islands had been formed, old ones had disappeared, the famous Chickasaw Bluffs were destroyed, numerous communities damaged, and an abortive religious revival was started. Over one million square miles of land felt the earth's shifting. The first steamboat to travel on the river, the *New Orleans*, was caught in the upheaval but successfully reached the city of the same name. Not until 1816 did Henry Shreve build a truly satisfactory river steamboat, the *Washington*: it was basically a flatboat with a super-structure, an engine and a paddle wheel. By 1820 there were more than seventy-five such boats operating on the Mississippi. In 1812 Louisiana became a state; the same year marked the outbreak of the War of 1812.

The importance of the Mississippi was so great to the United States that perhaps the most famous battle of the War of 1812 was fought for its control. The attack on New Orleans was part of a British plan which, if successful, might well have crippled the young nation. The British knew that if they could seize control of New Orleans and the lower Mississippi, they could destroy the economy of the Mississippi basin. They no doubt hoped that the polyglot population of Louisiana could then be convinced to give their allegiance to Britain, who still maintained strong interests in the fur trade of the southeast and the upper Mississippi Valley. Andrew Jackson won total victory at New Orleans and emerged as a national hero. The story of that battle, fought on January 8, 1815, after peace had been signed (December 24, 1814, at Ghent, Belgium), is one of the most remarkable tales in American history. The Mississippi River would now enter a forty-five-year period during which it would serve as the principal outlet for agricultural goods produced all along its tributaries.

Naturalist Thomas Nuttall made a journey down the Mississippi in early 1819 and spent the summer and fall exploring its western tributaries. He still found the river relatively devoid of population, ". . . truly magnificent though generally bordered by the most gloomy solitudes, in which there are no visible traces of the abode of man." In spite of Nuttall's description of the Mississippi as devoid of significant population, there were by 1820 some settlements such as Cape Girardeau and St. Louis on the upper river which were taking on importance. Nuttall's description of the lower river, on the other hand, gives an entirely different picture. He was impressed by what he called, "the opulent town of Natchez" and by the prosperous plantations at Port Coupee, but disapproved of the slavery which made them possible.

Just as the Mississippi reached its zenith as an artery for trade and commerce in the decades before the American Civil War, events taking place elsewhere would eventually end the reign of the river as a dominant force in the life of the Midwest and South. Americans first viewed the railroad as a curiosity, but by 1860 it had begun to alter the nature of trade on the Mississippi. In the years following the Civil War the river would continue to serve as a conduit for cotton, sugar, and tobacco, but as railroads were built across the south the river grew less and less important in the life of the people. Nonetheless, the river became a key to the conquest of the South in the Civil War.

Curiously enough, the South failed to recognize the river's importance to their cause. The lower Mississippi and its tributaries were the scene of a Union campaign of a very unique nature. The principal battle in that campaign was the siege of Vicksburg. New Orleans had fallen to Union forces in April of 1862, and the way lay open to Northern domination of the Mississippi providing Vicksburg, the only defendable point on the river, could be taken. Until May, 1862, that town was ignored by Southern defenders. Through the efforts of General Mansfield Lovell, however, defenses were finally prepared, and just in time. On June 28, 1862, several squat, ugly gunboats in Admiral James Farragut's river squadron steamed up river. With great effort they were able to get through the batteries at Vicksburg and spent several weeks above the city before returning to New Orleans. It was clear that the Union could control the river only if Vicksburg was captured, and that could only be accomplished by a combined land-river assault.

Ulysses S. Grant began his campaign to open

the Mississippi in December of 1862. By this time General J. C. Pemberton commanded the Confederate forces protecting the city. Grant's efforts to approach the place from his base at Memphis failed because of difficult terrain to the north of the city. In desperation he abandoned Memphis and crossed to the west side of the river, moved to a point below Vicksburg and there recrossed the river. Approaching from the east, he soon had the defenders trapped. Supported by the river fleet, Grant tried to capture the city in three bloody attacks on May 22. He failed, and settled back to starve the defenders out. He did not have a long wait. Vicksburg fell on July 4, 1863. Five days later Port Hudson, north of Baton Rouge, the last Confederate base on the river, surrendered and the Union controlled the Mississippi. Denied access to the men and supplies of the West, the rest of the South eventually suffered the same fate as Vicksburg.

In the years following the war, the great steamboats would continue to ply the Mississippi, but most of the river people who had grown up in the days before the war knew it was not the same. Twain's treatment of the river in fiction and non-fiction dominates the popular view of the river's history. Mention the Mississippi and certain images invariably come to mind: the *Robert E. Lee* racing up river on a moonlit night;

riverboat gamblers in top hats or fancy lace shirts; the minstrel shows with banjo players and blackface comedians; and, of course, Mark Twain himself in a crumpled white suit and a string tie.

But this was only a very small part of that river's grand story. The true drama was in the clash of empires that dominated the Mississippi's history for the two and one-half centuries from its discovery in 1542 by De Soto to the battle of New Orleans in January of 1815. In a way, all that followed was anticlimax.

But this only means that the Mississippi's stirring, romantic past has been replaced with continuing but unromantic service to a busy world. It is navigable to St. Paul-Minneapolis, with huge, long barges carrying everything from coal to automobiles for delivery to a voracious world. To protect their lands from flooding, people along the lower reaches have built levees so high that in some places the river runs like a gigantic aquaduct *above* the surrounding countryside. The Mississippi remains a great natural resource which is being studied and protected even as it is subject to ever greater usage.

FURTHER READING: Hodding Carter, *Lower Mississippi* (1942). Walter Havighurst, *Voices on the River: The Story of the Mississippi Waterways* (1964).

Robert Smith

The Missouri River

Source: Confluence of Jefferson, Madison, and Gallatin rivers in southwestern Montana
Length: 2,714 miles
Tributaries: Teton, Marias, Judith, Musselshell, Yellowstone, Little Missouri, Cheyenne, Niobrara, Platte, James, Kansas, and still other rivers
Mouth: Into Mississippi River just north of Saint Louis, Missouri
Agricultural Products: Cattle, wheat, corn
Industries: Food processing, hydroelectric power

The Missouri is the longest and one of the largest rivers in the United States. It flows 2,714 miles along an irregular course from its headwaters in the Rocky Mountains to its confluence with the

Mississippi seventeen miles upstream from St. Louis, and it drains 580,000 square miles of land. Except for an accident of history that brought early wayfarers in contact with the upper Mississippi before they reached the eastern shore of the Missouri, it might have been designated the main stem of the water system that has drained the interior parts of North America into the Gulf of Mexico since the Pleistocene Age.

Since glacial action altered the physical geography of the continent, it has transported water, soil and debris from several physiographic regions in enormous quantities. The Missouri has received run-off from the Rocky Mountains through the upper tributaries Jefferson, Madison and Gallatin where they merge near present Three Forks, Montana. It has cut a deep gorge called "Gates of the Mountains" below Helena, cascaded 500 feet down over a series of waterfalls near the base of the mountains, and flowed eastward through the Montana plains to gather drainage from the Teton, Marias, Judith, Musselshell, Milk, and Yellowstone Rivers before angling down across the Dakota plains. Below the bend near Williston, North Dakota it has swelled rapidly from discharges out of the Little Missouri, Heart, Cannonball, Grand, Moreau, Cheyenne, White, and Niobrara Rivers, then meandered in a southeasterly direction through the semiarid prairies, where it has drained the James, Big Sioux, Platte, Kansas, Osage, and Gasconade Rivers before making its descent across the alluvial basin to the Mississippi. Until

its waters were impounded by earthen dams in the 20th century, the Missouri discharged as few as 13,000 cubic feet per second in periods of drought and as many as 800,000 cubic feet per second at floodtime, and carried some 550,000,000 tons of earth to the Mississippi each year.

Because of its size and central location, the Missouri has had a human history even more varied and interesting than the land it has drained. From prehistoric times to the 18th century, twelve groups of Indians camped near its shores. Missouris, Osages, and Kaw (Kansas) occupied the lower reaches as far up as the mouth of the Platte. Omahas and Poncas lived between the Platte and the White. Arikaras, Mandans, Hidatsas, and Gros Ventres maintained villages from the White to the vicinity of the Heart. Assiniboines held the open ranges between the Heart and the Milk. Crows defended

North of Helena, Montana, the Missouri squeezes through the Big Belt Mountains in a gorge named by Captain Lewis (of the Lewis and Clark Expedition) "The Gates of the Rocky Mountains." (Courtesy Montana Historical Society.)

territories surrounding the lower Yellowstone, and Blackfeet claimed the area from the Milk River to the Rockies.

In the 18th century, Sioux people muscled in along the middle Missouri basin after they were driven from the woodlands of Minnesota and Wisconsin. Yanktons chased the Omahas and Poncas across the river and settled on the east bank between the Platte and the Moreau. Tetons drove the Arikaras northward and occupied the spacious Black Hills region from the west bank of the Missouri in Dakota country to the high plains of eastern Montana and Wyoming.

By that time, non-Indians had also entered the scene. French colonials Jacques Marquette and Louis Jolliet were first to sight the Missouri in 1673 when they crossed its mouth, and assigned it the name of the tribe camped nearby. Sieur de la Verendrye reached the upper basin when he trekked down from Fort LaReine southwest of Lake Manitoba to barter with Mandans in 1739. Others appeared on similar expeditions during the ensuing years, and because of their activities French leaders were able to claim imperial rights to the region surrounding the Missouri, which they called "Upper Louisiana," until they signed their trans-Mississippi holdings over to the Spanish at the settlement of San Ildefonso in 1762. Subsequently the Spanish administered Upper Louisiana until they turned it back to the French in the Second Treaty of San Ildefonso in 1800, whereupon French leaders again asserted imperial rights until they sold the region to the United States as part of the Louisiana Purchase in 1803.

Like Frenchmen before them, Spaniards put far more effort into the development of Lower than Upper Louisiana through the period 1762–1800, yet they increased non-Indian operations along the Missouri considerably. They founded St. Louis near the mouth of the river in the 1760s and dispatched traders as far north as the Platte in the 1770s and 1780s. To enlarge trading revenues as well as to stave off competition from British Canadians, they encouraged expeditions farther upstream during the waning years of the 18th century. With official sanction, Juan Munier trekked up to the mouth of the Niobrara in 1789. Jacques D'Eglise penetrated Mandan country the following year. St. Louis merchants organized the Missouri Company and supported

trade as far up as the Montana plains a short time later.

After the acquisition of Upper Louisiana by the United States, Missouri valley commerce continued to grow. Manuel Lisa organized the St. Louis Fur Company and dominated trade to the edge of the Rockies until his death in 1820. When Lisa's enterprise faltered under poor management a few years later, the Rocky Mountain Company and the Western Department of the American Fur Company moved out to take its place. Led by the dynamic William Ashley and Pierre Choteau, Jr., respectively, these two commercial giants and several smaller companies used the Missouri and its basin as an arterial waterway and a source of furs and robes until their business went into decline just before mid-century.

Close behind trading parties came several important military expeditions. First and foremost was that led by Meriwether Lewis and William Clark, who traveled the course of the Missouri full length in the years 1804–06. Next was the expedition of Henry Atkinson, who under orders from Secretary of War John C. Calhoun founded Camp Missouri (Fort Atkinson) near the mouth of the Platte for the purposes of maintaining peace between Indian tribes and discouraging further intrusions by Canadian merchants. After Atkinson came Colonel Henry Leavenworth and Indian Agent Benjamin O'Fallon on a punitive expedition to avenge an attack upon Ashley's traders by the Arikaras.

Once U.S. military forces established federal authority in the Missouri Valley region, they withdrew as treaty-makers settled issues with the Indians that had required the military presence. Federal forces finally returned in the 1850s, however, as race relations deteriorated. Mormon and gentile overlanders cut across the southern edge of Sioux country en route to the Interior Basin and the Pacific Slope. Town founders and land speculators settled along the Missouri as far up as the James. After the massacre of Lt. James L. Grattan's column near Fort Laramie in 1854, General William S. Harney stationed troops at Forts Lookout and Randall on the middle Missouri basin to prevent further Indian resistance. And from the founding of Fort Randall in 1856 to the end of the 19th century, the Missouri Valley bristled with guns as federal forces battled to establish military superiority over the Sioux and their allies in a succession of wars: The Minnesota Sioux War of 1862–63, Red Cloud's War of the late 1860s, the Great Sioux War of 1876–77, and the confrontation on the Great Sioux Reservation that culminated in the assassination of Sitting Bull and the Massacre at Wounded Knee. Only after the Sioux gave up the fight in the 1890s, and accepted confinement to small reserves, did U.S. military forces again withdraw from the region.

On their early travels up the Missouri, traders and soldiers both relied upon such man-powered craft as dugouts, bullboats, keelboats, and mackinaw boats, but as their transportation needs increased both groups transferred to steamboats. As early as 1819, traders transported cargo on the *Independence* and soldiers rode the *Western Engineer* between St. Louis and the mouth of the Platte. In 1831 Pierre Choteau, Jr. initiated regular steamboat service on the lower Missouri when he took the *Yellowstone* to Fort Tecumseh (which he later named Fort Pierre after himself), and in 1832 he extended service to Fort Union on the upper Missouri. By 1859 steamboats reached their highest point of navigation at Fort Benton. In 1862 they became vital links in a chain of transcontinental carriers, due to the completion of the Mullen Road between the Missouri and Columbia Rivers. After that they transported more than 1,000,000 tons of cargo on the Missouri each year until they were replaced by railroads.

Important as steamboats were to commerce, transporting passengers and cargo for military stations, Indian agencies, mining communities, agricultural settlements and commercial centers, they also sustained a "Steamboat Civilization" from St. Louis to Fort Benton. Some members of this peculiar society manned docking facilities at the river's edge, and some operated wood stations at regular intervals up and down the river to sell fuel to boat captains. Some managed commercial depots that connected steamboat lines with cross-country wagoners, and some ran livery barns, blacksmith shops, postal stations, and banks. Others operated stores, lodging places, and saloons which dealt in goods and services that ranged from household utensils, food and clothing to games of chance, spirituous beverages and feminine companionship.

The vice along the river is better remembered than the legitimate business. Often functioning under the guise of stage stations, general stores, or terminals for freighting companies, these liquor, gambling, and prostitution dens catered to the rough river society, soldiers, and Indians on the nearby reservations. Almost legendary places such as William Shakel's Honolulu Ranch, Harney City, Oacoma, and Fort Pierre thrived along the Missouri.

By the 1880s the river culture was already in decline, and by the end of the 19th century it had all but disappeared, due to the coming of the railroads. Each time a new track reached the east bank of the Missouri, steamboat operators lost business. By 1887, many steamboat operators had already gone out of business, and the few who survived sent their last commercial expeditions to Fort Benton in the spring of 1890. After that, their cargos were the goods they hauled between docking places on the lower Missouri, and their principal fares were persons they carried upstream to catch glimpses of steamboats and valley culture before both became antiquarian curiosities.

These tourists scanned places where distinguished people had traveled frequently during the previous century. Romanticist George Catlin and landscapist Karl Bodmer had ridden steamboats to paint wilderness scenes and Indian habits that would soon be desecrated by non-Indian civilization. John James Audubon had taken notes for his survey of bird life on the North American continent. Edwin Denig had prepared manuscript for his invaluable memoirs while trading along the Missouri in the company of an Assiniboine wife. Father Pierre-Jean DeSmet had traveled upstream as "envoy extraordinary of the Government" to negotiate peace with Sitting Bull, and the Hunkpapa leader later had gone downstream by steamboat to suffer imprisonment at Fort Randall. Chief Joseph had failed to make good his escape into Canada when he was trapped north of the Missouri.

The days of eminent figures such as these were nearly over by the 1890s, and the era of pragmatic developers was about to begin. Until the outset of the 20th century, the only group that had worked to change the Missouri had been the U.S. Army Corps of Engineers. With authorization from an appropriations act of 1832, Corps personnel had initiated efforts to improve the river's navigability by launching snagboats to remove obstacles from the channel and to cut down overhanging trees in 1838. Their responsibilities had been enlarged somewhat after the establishment of the Missouri River Commission in the 1880s, under whose supervision they were ordered to begin work on channelization. But as river towns grew into diversified commercial centers and as whole new settlements were born in the surrounding countryside with needs for water, power, and transportation service, plans for multiple-use development in the Missouri basin came under discussion.

Congressmen led the way with the Reclamation Act of 1902 (the Newlands Act), which authorized federal expenditures to support projects along western rivers. Foremost among those was need for water from the river for irrigation. Settlers had suffered sufficiently from climatic cycles to place high priority on future agricultural stability through dry farming techniques and crop watering. Another principal need was the development of some method of flood control. The Great Flood of 1881, which had uprooted Indian communities, leveled the buildings at Fort Pierre, and sent residents of other river towns scurrying for higher ground, had been only an extreme example of a problem that caused hardship almost every year. Spring rains and melting snow from the low country brought the Missouri over its banks in April, and melting snow from the Rockies inundated crops almost every June. Still other interests wanted hydroelectric power and the construction of dams or bridges to carry traffic across the Missouri on principal roads.

Through the next four decades two schools of thought arose. One, which had support among people on the lower reaches of the Missouri, favored small dams to contain floods and to release a continuous flow of water for commercial navigation as far up as Sioux City. The other, which was championed mainly by people who lived upstream from Sioux City, espoused the building of large dams to hold back water for irrigation, to generate electrical power, and to accommodate arterial highways.

When major floods in 1942 and 1943 convinced advocates of both schools that it was to their mutual benefit to find common ground, they compromised with the Pick-Sloan Plan. The basis for the Flood Control Act of 1944, passed by Congress, it incorporated some of the aims of both sides, and portions of the plans of General Lewis Pick of the Army Engineers and W. Glenn Sloan of the Bureau of Reclamation.

By then, one mainstem facility, the Fort Peck Dam, was almost finished between the Milk and Musselshell rivers. A massive structure two miles long and half a mile wide, it had the capacity to satisfy all of the needs that had been expressed by the people it was constructed to serve; it blocked early summer flood water from the Rockies, stored 6,000,000,000 gallons of water for irrigation and municipal use, produced electrical power, and made a crossing over the Missouri on Montana Highway 24. The Flood Control Act and subsequent legislation supported the construction of five more dams downstream with similar capabilities, and all were completed within two decades.

Most non-Indians have viewed the completion of the six mainstem dams across the Missouri as a salutary accomplishment. The dams have solved the flood problem, stabilized the river channel for barge navigation downstream from Sioux City, and served as crossings on arterial roads. They have produced power for consumption by municipalities, rural cooperatives, and private companies at reasonable rates. They have created lakes teeming with fish whose shorelines have become useful for both recreation and wildlife habitat, and they have established huge reservoirs that have afforded farmers and ranchers in the region an opportunity to stabilize agricultural production through extensive reclamation.

Such a massive plan, involving immense public works, the removal of people and farms for lake bottoms, the management of water for too many purposes, so that some interest or some section is certain to feel discriminated against, has had its detractors. Indians who had taken up land allotments close to the Missouri because of the abundance there of wood, water, fish, game, herbs, berries, wild vegetables, and protection against the harsh winters have been more critical of the government's plan and its treatment of those it has forced to move elsewhere. Some non-Indians, on the other hand, insist that the Indians have been treated with great consideration and equity.

Rehabilitation funds were spent to satisfy Indian needs. Some went into farm and livestock programs, land purchases, and industrial developments. Some were spent on community centers, educational costs, and new homes. Some paid bills for health care, established special assistance programs for needy families, met administration costs, and so forth.

Whether non-Indians gave up the most by the loss of taxable land and agricultural production, or Indians suffered most for their intangible losses, has become a moot question. Seventy-five years of discussion and labor have placed the Missouri and its basin under human control, and to one degree or another every resident of the region is the better for it. Only two issues remain for future settlement. One is reclamation. In the mid-1970s small farmers and ecologists forced the suspension of construction on major irrigation works by the Bureau of Reclamation, leaving determination of the extent of crop watering to the future. The other issue is permanency. The failure of developers to construct small dams on Missouri River tributaries has already caused severe siltation. Lewis and Clark Lake at the mouth of the Niobrara, for example, and Oahe at the mouth of the Moreau have already been damaged by huge deposits of silt. Some observers have predicted that unless many small dams are constructed on the tributaries, the Missouri valley could eventually turn into a grotesque series of mud flats and waterfalls.

FURTHER READING: Hiram Martin Chittenden, *History of Early Steamboat Navigation on the Missouri River*, 2 vols. (1903) Stanley Vestal, *The Missouri* (1945).

Herbert T. Hoover

The Niobrara River

Source: Rises in high plains of eastern Wyoming
Length: 430 miles
Tributaries: Snake, Minnechaduza, Keya Paha, Ponca, and other rivers
Mouth: Into Missouri at northeast border of Nebraska
Agricultural Products: Wheat, beef (cattle ranching)
Industries: None of significance

Rising in the High Plains in eastern Wyoming, the Niobrara River ripples across northern Nebraska for 430 miles, eventually spilling into the Missouri river on the northeastern border of Nebraska. The clear, fast-flowing waters have so intrigued men who have known the river that no matter who named it, in whatever language, it was known as Running Water. Long-ago French fur trappers called it L'Eau Qui Court, the French translation of the Siouan Indian name *Niobrara*; both of them meant Running Water, the English name which a few others called it. The river has been known as the Niobrara since the early 20th century. It is pronounced Nigh-O-Brer-A.

The Niobrara is fed by scores of tributaries that rise out of a vast underground sea, ranging from such rivulets as the Barngrover, Whistle, Pebble, and Pepper Creeks in the far west, to larger streams as the Snake and Minnechaduza in its central reaches, and the Keya Paha and the Ponca further eastward. The river that bubbles and churns through land that is now ranch country and farmland was important to native Americans a hundred years and more ago.

During the 1800s, three different tribal groups of Plains Indians lived near the Niobrara river: the nomadic Sioux in the western reaches who plunged down across the canyons of the river to follow the buffalo which provided them the necessities of life; the semi-sedentary Pawnee who crossed the broader, more placid Niobrara in the central area in their twice-a-year buffalo hunts; and the agricultural Ponca in the eastern area who cultivated their small farm plots of corn, beans, and squash in the rich bottom land that adjoined the river.

From the quieter waters feeding into the Niobrara, men trapped beaver, muskrat, mink, and other small fur-bearing animals, though the waters of the Niobrara itself are too fast-moving for trapping. The French fur traders used the river as their highway back to the fur centers in St. Louis. Onto their canoes they piled bales of dried pelts and then paddled downstream on the fast current, following the Niobrara into the Missouri and floating down the muddy Missouri a thousand miles to St. Louis. One fur-trading post from bygone days still exists; it is the Museum of the Fur Trade, on Bordeaux Creek, near Chadron, Nebraska, thirty-five miles of twisting waterway from the Niobrara.

Although the Niobrara itself was never the scene of Indian battles, the massacre at Wounded Knee in 1890 took place only thirty-five miles north of the river. The Brule and Oglala Sioux, penned up in reservations a few miles away in South Dakota, began to prepare for the Ghost Dance, a ritualistic form of worship which hopefully would bring back the buffalo and the way of living for the by then displaced Plains Indians. Frightened white settlers in the area called in the military, and by the end of the day on December 29, the Sioux at Wounded Knee Creek were dead, men, women, and children.

In its westernmost reaches, as a new little river, the Niobrara trickles past Agate, where the Fossil Beds National Monument contains a rich deposit of Miocene mammal fossils. From there, the stream wanders through ranch country. About thirty miles east of Agate, the Box Butte dam, completed in 1946, impounds water for the Mirage (pronounced mere-age) Flats irrigation project which irrigates 35,000 acres (or 14,160 hectares) of land.

Among the homesteads in the westernmost part of the Niobrara watershed was that of Old Jules, whose daughter, author Mari Sandoz, has written extensively of the area.

For the next sixty to seventy miles, the tributaries that flow into the Niobrara are larger: the Snake, for instance, whose waters roar across a broad, deep waterfall on their way to the junction with the Niobrara, and the Minnechaduza, which flows into the larger river near Valentine. From Sand Hills springs, near Valentine, other waters bubble out of the ground and eventually flow into the Niobrara, including those which form two deep waterfalls, Fort Falls and Smith Falls, before they spill into the canyon that contains the Niobrara.

During the 120-mile portion across Cherry County, the Niobrara winds through steep bluffs and canyons, most of them wooded. For seven miles, the river flows through Fort Niobrara National Wildlife Refuge, built on the site of old Fort Niobrara, established in 1880 and operated for twenty-six years as a buffer against the Dakota Sioux. The wildlife refuge contains herds of buffalo, long-horned cattle, antelope, prairie dog towns, and stands of grasses native to the region. This part of the river is considered the most scenic and is open to canoeing and float trips setting out from Valentine.

After the river leaves the canyons and bluffs of Cherry County, it flattens out into wider, more tranquil waters flowing through pasturelands and farms. Two small dams—Cornell, not far east out of Valentine, and Spencer, about ninety-five miles eastward—impound some water from time to time for irrigation, and construction of another dam, a larger one at Norden, is under discussion in federal circles. By the time the Niobrara reaches its destination, it is a combination of many streams; Redbird, Eagle, Turkey, Spring, Big Sandy, Bone, Long Pine, Keya Paha, Ponca, and many other creeks which have mingled their waters into one.

Many of those streams cut their way through rugged butte country, creating caves and remote rocky formations which provided hiding places a generation ago for men evading the law. The Long Pine, for instance, courses through the area now known as Hidden Paradise but for many years acknowledged unofficially as Bad Man's Hangout, where men from time to time cooled off and rested, while others searched for them. For much of the length of the Niobrara, the terrain is rough enough to provide cover for numbers of men and horses; for several decades at the turn of the century, "Gone to the Niobrara" meant escaping the law. Kid Wade, Doc Middleton, other men of lesser repute spent enough time in the 300-mile hideout area of the Niobrara to become well-acquainted with it.

With its ranches and farmlands, northern Nebraska is sparsely populated, and in all the 430-mile length of the Niobrara, the river flows past only two towns. The larger of these is Valentine, county seat of Cherry County, mid-point on the river. The town came into being in the late 1880s, about the time that Fort Niobrara was established, and it supplied the fort with goods and services that the government agency could not. The town was named for the Honorable Edward Kimball Valentine, the Nebraska representative in Congress from 1879 to 1885. It is a thriving commercial center of about 2,600 persons who supply goods and services to ranchers for a radius of perhaps a hundred miles. The town provides banking, legal and medical services, a library, museum, courthouse and post office, churches and schools and a hospital, and stores and shops for provisions and equipment to ranchers, some of whom live in areas so remote they can come to town only spasmodically.

The town is not far from the Pine Ridge reservation in South Dakota, and on the Saturday of Annuity Day, when Indians are paid their subsistence by the federal government, the wide main street of Valentine is especially busy serving the Sioux who come to town to buy supplies. One of the favorite recreations of all Sand Hillers is a rodeo, horsemanship at its best, and in the late summer and early fall, there are rodeos in Valentine when riders can display their skill and speed at riding, roping, and generally handling spirited horses.

During the winter months, the town grows in size somewhat when high school-aged children of ranchers move to town to go to school. Sometimes the mother will accompany the children and will set up housekeeping for them in a house in town, going home to the menfolk on the ranch only on weekends during the winter; in other instances, the children will live with family friends or in boarding houses in Valentine during the week, to return home to the ranch on weekends whenever the roads are passable. Valentine is a ranch town, completely different in

functions, philosophy and attitudes from similar-sized communities in other parts of the country.

The other town along the Niobrara river is the village of Niobrara, more than two hundred miles down-stream in a farming area. Niobrara sits near the confluence of the Niobrara and Missouri rivers, and is one of the oldest yet newest settlements in Nebraska. It has been in three different locations, represented two different cultures, and has been burned down and flooded out. Its most recent relocation was in 1976.

The first white men to consider the area as a homesite were Mormons who, in 1845, could see possibilities in the location but were discouraged by the presence of the Ponca Indians who were already established there, living in villages and tilling their garden plots near the river's edge. But eleven years later, in 1856, two years after Nebraska became a territory, a group of businessmen ignored prior claims to land ownership and established the L'Eau Qui Court Town Company, staking out 3,000 acres of prime bottomland for their community. The Ponca who watched the goings-on were not happy; this had been the site of a tribal village for many years. During the winter they burned some of the white men's town. By spring, however, the two groups had reached agreement and lived together in relative peace and harmony, owning the land jointly.

On March 29, 1881, the Niobrara overflowed its banks, flooding out the town, and the village of Niobrara moved upland to a plateau twenty feet higher in elevation. Even in its new location, however, the town never became a thriving business center; other than the ferry which carried passengers across the Missouri river, below the confluence of the two rivers, it was not unlike many other similar villages established about that same time. The population was never as large as 1,000 people.

But activities farther downstream on the Missouri river were to make a drastic change in the town of Niobrara. Part of the Missouri River Basin flood-control project, started in the late 1940s, was the damming of waters to create the Lewis and Clark Lake, twenty miles downstream. When the Gavins Point dam was completed and the lake began to fill, residents of

Niobrara noticed their basements were flooding; the soil acted as a wick, raising the water table. In the early 1970s, it was evident that the town would have to move again. By 1976, the homes, churches, businesses, and even the parks of Niobrara, had been moved again to even higher, drier land, and the 600 residents were settled in a new location.

Although the Niobrara River is not commercial—no freight traverses its shallow, sometimes rock-ridden waters, no great catches of fish come from its fast current. It is considered the state's most scenic river, and its history helps keep alive the stories of Nebraska's lusty past.

FURTHER READING: Mari Sandoz, *Love Song to the Plains* (1961; 1966). Dorothy Weyer Creigh, *Nebraska: A History* (1977).

Dorothy Weyer Creigh

The Platte-South Platte-North Platte rivers

Sources: South Platte near Fairplay in central Colorado Rockies; North Platte in North Park, Colorado; Platte, by convergence of South and North Platte at North Platte, Nebraska
Length: South Platte, 450 miles; North Platte, 600 miles; Platte, 310 miles
Tributaries: South Platte: Clear Creek, Boulder Creek, the Big Thompson River, St. Vrain and Cache La Poudre Rivers; North Platte: Sweetwater, Medicine Bow, and Laramie rivers; Platte: Loup and Elkhorn rivers
Mouths: North Platte and South Platte join at North Platte, Nebraska, to form Platte River; Platte enters Missouri River at Plattsmouth, Nebraska
Agricultural Products: South Platte: Sugar beets, wheat, other grains; North Platte: Sugar beets, beans, potatoes, corn; Platte: Sugar beets, alfalfa, wheat, corn.
Industries: Food processing, especially sugar beets and alfalfa dehydrating

The Platte River and the North and South Platte which join to form it constitute an important segment of the central high plains. Their drainage extends from the inner parks of the Colorado Rockies eastward to the Missouri River. So similar is the climate, flora and fauna of the rivers (save for the mountain segment which is not shared by the Platte) and so vital are all three rivers to the land and habitation through which they flow, that they are treated here each as a separate and important entity.

High in the snow-covered Rocky Mountains, the tiny streams that become the South Platte River gather in a marshy meadow near Fairplay in central Colorado. By the time the river joins

the North Platte in Nebraska, 450 miles downstream, to form the Platte, it has tumbled through narrow canyons in the San Isabel National Forest and meandered over much of central Colorado. It has changed directions many times, flowing south, then north, and finally east before it spreads out across the broad plains of eastern Colorado and western Nebraska. It provides water for two million people on its journey, irrigates vast acres of farmland, and supplies hydroelectric power for homes and industries in two states.

Its principal tributaries are Clear Creek, Boulder Creek, the Big Thompson, St. Vrain and Cache la Poudre rivers. Although the South Platte is a rushing torrent at snowmelt time as it plunges through the mountains, by the time it rolls onto the prairie it is wide and shallow. This befits its name, which means "flat," given it by early French trappers and explorers.

As a mountain stream it was important to trappers seeking beaver pelts. In the mid-nineteenth century gold and silver miners used the cold, clear mountain waters for their placers. Downriver in the flatlands the South Platte was long a hunting ground for Plains Indians who followed the buffalo. Major Stephen H. Long in 1819 reported being with Pawnee Indians along the South Platte, and William H. Ashley, a fur trader, spent four days with Pawnees in an 1825 buffalo surround (a form of round-up) in the South Platte country. By the time of the Californians and Oregonians the Oglala and Brule

Sioux were the predominant Indians along the downstream part of the river.

The clash of cultures, which had begun with the California gold rush of 1849, continued as an estimated 350,000 used the Platte River trail on their way to Oregon or Utah. They brought with them disease, trampled the grass, and slaughtered the buffalo. Their presence was certain to result in bloodshed. The big outbreak came on August 7, 1864, when Cheyennes, Arapahoes, and Brules attacked emigrant trains and stage stations between Julesburg and Fort Kearny in a massive attack on the "Holy Road," as the Indians called the Overland Trail. Fortunately not many lives were lost before the U.S. Army sent troops to escort further traffic along the Oregon Trail. In October the soldiers set a huge prairie fire from Julesburg to Fort Kearney, a distance of 170 miles, to drive the Indians from the area.

Although a few souls homesteaded along the South Platte as a result of the Pike's Peak rush of 1859, settlement on the plains did not begin significantly until the 1870s with the completion of the Union Pacific Railroad. The range cattle industry was heavily involved. From 1875 until 1885, Ogallala, Nebraska, was the end of the Texas Trail, a rip-roaring, wide-open town of dusty cowboys who had trailed longhorn cattle up from Texas to the railyards for shipment to eastern markets. Many of the early settlers along the South Platte were ranchers. The passage of the Nebraska herd law in 1887 (which required cattlemen to fence in their stock) and the "Big Die-Up" in the winter of that year, when thousands of cattle succumbed to the intense cold, ended this first, speculative wave of ranching.

Now homesteaders came in to farm along the river and its tributaries. By 1899 almost 150,000 acres in Nebraska were under irrigation, most of it in the South and North Platte valleys. In 1902 the Reclamation Act provided for federal financing of irrigation construction; since then 95 percent of South Platte water has been used for irrigation purposes and, later, also for hydroelectric power. Meanwhile Denver, Boulder, Fort Collins, Loveland, Greeley, Fort Morgan, and Sterling began depending in whole or in part on South Platte water for municipal uses.

Downstream, the South Platte became fertile farmland, much of it concentrated in the production of sugar beets but some also in wheat and other grains. Between the municipalities and the agriculturalists, most of the South Platte's average flow of 230,000 acre-feet per year is put to good use.

Rising in Colorado's North Park, 200 miles or so north of the South Platte's origin, is the North Platte River. It flows north into Wyoming, where it makes a great bend eastward across the plains of central Nebraska. It flows 600 miles as a broad, shallow, rapidly moving stream before it joins the South Platte at the town of North Platte, Nebraska, to form the Platte River. In its long course the snow-fed river provides water for irrigation, the generation of electric power, and for recreation.

The first European to write about the North Platte was Robert Stuart, who traveled the area in 1813. The first men to travel by wagon along the North Platte were Jedediah Smith, David Jackson, and William Sublette, fur traders, in 1830. Because South Pass was an easy mountain crossing of the Rocky Mountains and the route led up the North Platte and then up its tributary, the Sweetwater, the river assumed great importance. For twenty-five years, from 1841 to 1866, the North Platte valley beyond the Platte was covered with wagon trains fumbling along either side of the river. The Pony Express and telegraph also followed the North Platte.

The land then was the home of nomadic Sioux, Cheyenne, and Arapahoe. In the cottonwood breaks along the North Platte they hunted antelope and gamebirds which augmented their regular diet of bison or buffalo. In 1849 the U.S. Army purchased Fort William, a fur trading post on the North Platte near the present Nebraska-Wyoming boundary, renamed it Fort Laramie, and prepared to protect travelers on the Overland Trail. There in 1851 the nomadic Plains Indians signed a treaty which established reservation boundaries. In August, 1854, the Grattan Massacre occurred in which, as a result of controversy involving a Mormon's cow, Lieutenant John Grattan and his force of twenty-nine men were massacred. The next year General William S. Harney chastised the Brule Indians (a segment of the Sioux) at Ash Hollow; 136 tribal members were killed. In 1868 another Indian treaty was signed at Fort Laramie, and after that most Indian troubles occurred outside of the North Platte valley.

One of the first bridges over the North Platte was Henry T. Clark's toll bridge, built in 1876 west of present Bridgeport, Nebraska. It catered to gold miners headed for the Black Hills of Dakota. In the 1880s a few ranchers settled along the North Platte, and as early as 1889 farmers were irrigating, using North Platte water. In 1910 the Pathfinder Reservoir was completed southwest of Casper, Wyoming; in 1928 a regulatory reservoir was completed at Guernsey, Wyoming, and later such reservoirs were constructed at Lake Alice and Lake Minitare in Nebraska. Since the 1930s dams have been constructed on the North Platte for the generation of hydroelectricity, with some of the water being used for irrigation. These include the George W. Kingsley Dam near Ogallala, the second largest hydraulic fill dam in the world, and the Kendrick Project that impounds water behind Seminoe, Kortes, and Alcova dams south of Casper. The Grayrocks Dam near Wheatland, Wyoming, is located on the Laramie River, a major North Platte tributary. Its waters cool a coal-fired power plant. Irrigation and hydroelectric projects use up most of the North Platte's water.

Through the years the shallow, sandy-bottomed North Platte has changed its appearance, its sandy islands forming a braided pattern, its rising and falling water levels changing the river's course. Through much of the valley the river flows at almost the same level as the surrounding farmland. Because of the many dams, however, flooding is a rarity.

North Platte River towns include Scottsbluff, Nebraska, and Torrington, Douglas, Casper, and Saratoga, Wyoming. The lakes formed by the dams are now recreational centers for water sports; sailing regattas provide an astonishing sight in this most interior part of the United States.

Wyoming, now booming with oil, gas, and coal, would like more of the North Platte's water, but Nebraska has the legal claim to most of it. A majority of that state's million acres of farmland that is irrigated with surface water obtains that water directly or indirectly from the North Platte. Though Nebraskans' claims

have legality behind them, the damming of so much of the river has resulted in a restricted downstream flow. Conservationists want to protect all of the river, for it is one of the great flyways of Sandhills cranes, Canadian geese, ducks of all kinds, and whooping cranes.

By the time the North Platte joins the South Platte to form the Platte River, the tributary streams have already served mankind well. Now, as a single river, the Platte, like a broad flat ribbon, stretches across the breadth of Nebraska, glistening in the sunlight of spring and early summer, sandy and dry in late fall. It is 310 miles from its point of origin to its mouth at Plattsmouth, where it joins the Missouri. The water ripples over stretches of quicksand as well as the fine sandy bottom that gives it its clarity. It is the largest river in Nebraska.

The Platte was derided by travelers who termed it the mile-wide, inch-deep river. Washington Irving called it the most magnificent and useless of rivers; Mark Twain said that if it were laid on end, it would make a respectable river. To early settlers it was a barrier dividing the state north and south. It was, they said, "too shallow to be ferried, too broad to be forded, and the people were too poor to bridge it."

The river, whose name means "flat," was named by French fur traders who skimmed its shallow waters in round bullboats made of animal skins; earlier the Indians in the area had called the stream Nibraskier, their term carrying the same meaning. They used the valley as their east-west highway following animal trails along its banks.

But for the California, Oregon, and Utah-bound emigrants, its broad valley was the best highway in the world. It was also a route for the first transcontinental telegraph, erected in 1861, which in turn replaced the Pony Express. Today it is the route of the Union Pacific Railroad and Interstate Highway 80.

Two Indian uprisings in the Platte Valley took place on August 7, 1864, part of a concerted attack planned by Cheyennes, Brules, and Arapahoes, on stage coaches, emigrant trains, freight trains, stations, and ranches in the valley. There was loss of life at Plum Creek (now Lexington), where a wagon train was attacked, and at Fort McPherson, near present Crawford, Nebraska, but a telegrapher at Plum Creek was able to send warnings to other settlements so that other white men in the area fled.

That part of the Platte lying between Lexington and Grand Island, a seventy-mile stretch in central Nebraska, is on an enormous flyway, and each spring hundreds of thousands of birds, especially Sandhills cranes and other large-sized birds, stop for six weeks or more to feed and to rest from their long flights from South America to the Arctic Circle. In the nearby fields they feed from grains, and on spits of land forming islands in the braided river they mate. At dawn and at dusk during the spring migrating season the sky is dark with the fluttering birds, and the air is filled with the sounds of their throaty calls and the flapping of their powerful wings. Their fall sojourn on their southbound flight is not so long. Wildlife conservancy groups are establishing refuges along the Platte.

It was here, in the broad valley of this shallow river, that the sod house, barbed wire, and windmill culture of the late nineteenth century in the Great Plains evolved. By 1900 the Platte Valley was covered with tens of thousands of windmills, creaking in the wind, pumping water from shallow wells onto the farmland. They have now been replaced by center-pivot irrigation systems. In the eastern part of the valley the fields are planted to corn and sorghums; in the central and western parts, to alfalfa, a forage crop. Dozens of alfalfa dehydration plants process the pungent alfalfa.

Although it was too shallow to be navigable, the river for centuries spilled over its banks as the North and South Platte, swollen with snow-water, joined to form the one big river. By late May much of the river was dry. Although there are no dams on the Platte, there are many on its tributary streams and the two rivers that create it. When Interstate 80 was being constructed, highway engineers dredged landfill in such a way that a series of lakes was formed; today there are thirty-one man-made lakes fed by underground water from the Platte system.

Unimpressive though it was to early sightseers, the Platte River and valley was the first part of Nebraska settled, and such towns as Gothenburg, Lexington, Kearney, Grand Island, Central City, Columbus, Fremont, and Plattsmouth attest to its continuing fertility. And in spite of its unimpressiveness, three and a half million acre-feet of water, on the average, flows from the Platte each year into the Missouri.

FURTHER READING: Dorothy Weyer Creigh, *Nebraska: A History* (1977). James C. Olson, *History of Nebraska* (1955; 1966).

Dorothy Weyer Creigh

The Powder River

Source: Confluence of several branches in foothills of Bighorn Mountains in central Wyoming, including North, Middle, and South Forks, Dry Fork, and Salt Creek
Length: About 375 miles
Tributaries: Little Powder River, Crazy Woman Creek, Clear Creek, and Piney Creek
Mouth: Into Yellowstone in eastern Montana
Agricultural Products: Hay
Industries: Cattle ranching; oil and coal

Powder River drains much of the great trough that lies between the Big Horn Mountains of Wyoming and the Black Hills of South Dakota, and a broad strip of the High Plains. Its North and Middle Forks drain the secluded desert basin known as the Hole-in-the-Wall. South Fork, Dry Fork, and Salt Creek drain a high saddle that separates the Powder Basin from that of the North Platte River.

All those tributaries come together within a few miles of one another in north central Wyoming. Running east a short distance, the main stream suddenly makes a sharp bend to the left, and for the rest of its course runs north-northeast to join the Yellowstone more than 200 miles away in Montana. This makes it one of the longest northward-flowing streams in the American West. With its bends and turns, it is estimated as being 375 miles long.

Other streams capture the run-off from the

periphery of the Black Hills, so Powder River gets most of its water from the eastern slope of the Big Horns. The headwaters of Crazy Woman Creek, Clear Fork, and Piney Creek, all lie in mountain passes with an elevation above 9,000 feet, fed by snowmelt from peaks that range up to the 13,165-foot top of Cloud's Peak, visible for more than a hundred miles in all directions. Once these creeks exit from the foothills, they quickly lose their troutstream characteristics and become slow, meandering waterways winding along the floor of deeply entrenched valleys that they have been carving for millions of years.

Around the southern rim of the Powder Basin, erosion dissected the ancient land surface into rough hills and great, free-standing buttes. The highest ridges catch just enough moisture to support pine trees on their upper, north slopes. Lower ridges have a scanty growth of juniper. Above 5,000 feet, the Big Horns are covered with pine. At the foot of these mountains lies a belt of rolling hill country where a turf of hardy grasses makes one of the world's finest pastures. Elsewhere in the Powder Basin, sagebrush is constantly visible intermixed with short bunch grasses and an occasional yucca and prickly pear.

The region has played host to man for at least 13,000 years. For the first half of that time, the residents were small bands of highly specialized big-game hunters. They were followed for a period of several thousand years by other cultures better adapted to survival during a long, dry period, through their skills at desert foraging. Then the climate began to change to today's conditions, and toward the end of prehistoric times we find other hunter/forager cultures stalking the antelope and deer, driving the buffalo over convenient cliffs and making many uses of the plants of the region.

To all this long procession of men in prehistoric times, the Powder itself formed a barrier, for in the spring furious spring floods swept down its narrow trench. But in times of drought in late summer, it held a lifegiving though purgative supply of water when many tributaries went dry. Such a stream was destined always for the role of water source or obstacle, and never as a highway!

In historic times, Pierre and Louis Joseph de la Verendrye may have seen Powder River on their fruitless quest for an easy route to the "Western Sea" in 1742–43. Their record has confused generations of historians. Elusive journalist Charles le Raye crossed the Powder in southern Montana in 1802 but did not tarry long. Scholarly fur trader Francois Antoine Larocque in 1805 made a systematic exploration of much of the middle course of Powder River, and was certainly the first white man of record to ascend Piney Creek.

Larocque found the country firmly in the hands of the Crow Indians. Recent comers, they had in a little more than a generation deserted farms and homes on the bottomlands of the Missouri River to take up wholeheartedly the equestrian way of life. Equipped with guns and steel-edged weapons, they swept into the Powder Basin in the years after the Verendrye's time, and made it for a hundred years their own country.

In the year 1811, Wilson Price Hunt led a force of John Jacob Astor's American Fur Company men across the Powder Basin. Other mountain men figured prominently in the history of the Powder Basin. Jedediah Smith led some of William Henry Ashley's men past the Pumpkin Buttes to Powder River in 1823. That same year another Ashley party under William Weber trapped on the tributaries of the Powder. For the next twenty years and more, only the fur company men and the free-trappers frequented the region.

In 1851, Father Pierre Jean DeSmet brought a colorful cavalcade of Indians up through the Powder River country en route to treaty negotiations near Fort Laramie. British sportsman Sir St. George Gore hunted down the Powder in 1855, guided by old mountain man Jim Bridger.

Conflict with the Sioux aroused military interest in the Powder River country in the late 1850s. The Army sent out Captain William F. Raynolds and Lieutenant Henry Maynadier of the Corps of Topographical Engineers to map the region. The maps Raynolds's men prepared were the first good maps ever made of the Powder Basin.

Four years later, a Montana promoter, John Bozeman, set out to popularize a route to the town that soon bore his name in the Gallatin Valley of Montana. The Bozeman Trail entered the Powder Basin from the southeast and veered steadily northwest to the Yellowstone River.

In the four years that separated Raynolds' expedition from Bozeman's, the powerful Sioux, with their Cheyenne and Arapaho allies, pushed the Crows west of the Big Horn River and into the mountains, and constituted a barrier to white advancement. Because a military presence in the Powder Basin would draw away the hostiles from the Union Pacific, then under construction, Brigadier General Patrick E. Connor in the summer of 1865 started diversionary operations with a three-pronged sweep through the Powder River Country. One footsore column, led by Colonel Nelson Cole, fought one of the largest engagements of the Indian Wars on Powder River, just six miles downstream from present Broadus, Montana. Skillful use of artillery by his Civil War combat veterans minimized army casualties, so the action is less well known than many Army defeats.

Conner left two companies of "Galvanized Yankees," (former Confederates, recruited for Indian fighting) and a company of friendly Winnebago Indians at a new post called Fort Connor on Powder River, just three miles below the mouth of Dry Fork. The next year these men were replaced by units of the 18th U.S. Infantry under command of Colonel Henry B. Carrington. Garrisoning the post now called Fort Reno, other units went on to build Fort Phil Kearny on Piney Creek, as well as another post (Fort C. F. Smith) far off on the Big Horn. One of Carrington's fiery subordinates, Captain William J. Fetterman fell into an Indian ambush on December 21, 1866 and died along with eighty-one men.

The disaster was unparalleled in the history of the West to that date. Soon taciturn Colonel John E. Smith, a brilliant Civil War combat leader, took over the reins and kept the Indians occupied with minimum losses to the soldiers until the summer of 1868. Then, with the railroad safely past hostile country, the Army closed down the holding action and abandoned the Powder River Country.

Eight years later tension between the Sioux on the one hand and the whites with their Crow allies on the other built to the breaking point. With the government and the Crows enraged by Sioux depredations in Montana, and the Sioux furious over white prospectors's invasion of the Black Hills, war came to the intervening Powder River Country.

Brigadier General George Crook launched a fast strike into the Powder country in March of 1876. His main force under Colonel Joseph J. Reynolds fought an all-day battle with a Northern Cheyenne camp on Powder River just north of the Montana line, thus drawing that tribe into the war.

Crook took another column north in the spring, but crossed the Powder Basin without incident to fight his campaign's major battle on the Rosebud. A week later, the Custer column that had crossed lower Powder River not long before ran into disaster on the Little Big Horn.

In the fall of 1876, with the main concentrations of hostiles on the run, Crook scoured the upper Powder Country and his second in command, R. S. Mackenzie, defeated the Cheyennes in an epic battle on Red Fork in November. When the expedition withdrew, it left a major base camp, Cantonment Reno, on Powder River at the mouth of Dry Fork. Then in 1878, the Army built a fine new post, Fort McKinney, on Clear Fork at the foot of the Big Horns. Army spending for supplies and construction materials at the fort drew in farmers, small ranchers, and contractors, who soon founded the village of Buffalo nearby.

By 1878, buffalo hunters had cleaned out the remnants of the once great buffalo herds. Now, in the spring of 1879, cattlemen from southern Wyoming pushed their longhorns into the Powder Basin. Speculation by foreign investors, poor management, and overstocking all laid the groundwork for disaster when one of those hard winters the Powder Basin gets every twenty years or so swept down in 1886–87. Major cattle companies collapsed. Surviving open-range outfits contested for the use of the range with an influx of small ranchers who brought with them barbed wire and the irrigation shovel.

Again tension built to the breaking point between the forces battling for the Powder Basin. The climax came when corporate cattle interests launched the "Johnson County Invasion," that climaxed at the T.A. Ranch when hundreds of men besieged the cattlemen and their hired guns until the army could take the invaders into custody.

But other ranchers found more creative solutions to the problems of effective range management. They found that irrigated hay ground formed the best base of operations. Steadily they bought up more and more of the choice portions of the land until by World War I, little public land lay within the Basin.

For the most part, Powder River country is range land of low productivity, requiring thirty-five to forty acres to support one cow. Cattlemen had the country to themselves until the years just before World War I. Then oil men found the great Salt Creek field in the southern part of the Basin. It has been active constantly since 1915. Other fields were opened in and around the Powder Basin in the 1940s and the 1960s. The oil business brought wealth to many ranchers, but it did not disturb the ranch country much, once development work was complete.

A new energy crisis in the early 1970s brought another period of change, perhaps greater than any of those described above. Vast deposits of low-grade, low-sulfur coal lie buried within the Powder Basin. Much of this coal can be obtained by low-cost shallow strip mining. As a result, in ten years, the population of the Powder Basin has doubled, and the end of development is not yet in sight.

But much of the new development lies around the rim of the Basin. The Powder continues to flow undisturbed down the center, one of the few rivers of America to have along its course only two towns, Kaycee, Wyoming and Broadus, Montana, with a total population of less than 3,000. In between them the muddy, alkaline waters of Powder River wend their way amidst scenery not greatly different from that the first explorers saw.

FURTHER READING: Helena Huntington Smith, *War on Powder River*, (1967). Harold D. Roberts, *Salt Creek, Wyoming: The Story of a Great Oil Field*, (1956).

Robert A. Murray

The Red River of the North

Source: Joining of Bois de Sioux and Otter Tail rivers at Breckenridge, Minnesota
Length: 350 miles
Tributaries: Sheyenne, Red Lake, and Pembina rivers (U.S.) and Assiniboine River (Manitoba, Canada)
Mouth: Into Lake Winnipeg, Manitoba
Agricultural Products: Wheat
Industries: Agribusiness

The Red River of the North courses its way 350 miles through the midsection of the Red River Valley, a pancake-flat basin running along the Minnesota-North Dakota border and on into southern Manitoba. Its principal tributaries are the Sheyenne and Red Lake rivers in the U.S. and the Assiniboine in Canada. Now known as a premier agricultural region, the Red River Valley initially evolved as a result of a leveling glacial action during the latter stages of the ice age. As the glaciers retreated northward, they blocked a hugh body of water which 19th century scholars later labeled Lake Agassiz.

The glacial lake, which at its greatest stage covered much of south-central Canada as well as the U.S. portion of the Red River Valley, slipped northward as the glaciers continued to melt. Left behind from the glaciers and the lake was the flat Red River plain, covered with thick layers of glacial till. Running through the midst of the level lake bed, in its lowest section, was a broad river. Through the centuries, this river decreased in size, simultaneously depositing layers of a silt-like sediment on top of the original glacial till. The ultimate result was a rich, fertile soil which by the late 19th century would form the base for a world-famous agricultural system.

The Red River itself came to be quite narrow and shallow along its southern portion, becoming wider and deeper while proceeding northward. Formed by the fusion of the Bois de Sioux and Otter Tail rivers at what is now Brecken-ridge, Minnesota, the Red twists and threads its way into Canada, finally emptying into Manitoba's Lake Winnipeg. The river's winding route is a major identifying characteristic. Though no point is more than a few miles from a hypothetical median line, the Red River is so crooked that the distance by water between any two riverside locations is approximately twice that of a direct land route connecting the points.

Level and treeless, in its natural state the Red River Valley was blanketed by mile upon mile of thick prairie grass, broken only by occasional sloughs and the thin strands of timber lining the Red River and its tributaries. The valley was home to a wide variety of wildlife, the most noteworthy being the great herds of buffalo which once roamed its landscape. The animals, fish and fowl in and near the Red River attracted Indian tribes, especially during the 17th and 18th centuries. The initial modes of human transport on the Red were the Indians' canoes, ranging from large birchbark vessels to small, solid timber dugouts.

French and English fur traders were present along the Red River's northern reaches by the mid-1700s. The junction of the Red and Assiniboine rivers (site of present-day Winnipeg) and the junction of the Red and Pembina rivers (at the current international boundary line) were key trading post centers. Their populations consisted of traders, Indians, and the Métis race of mixed bloods resulting from French-Indian marriages.

The first permanent white settlement along the Red River was established in 1811–12 near modern-day Winnipeg by a group of Scottish immigrants. These Selkirkers, named after the colony's promoter, Lord Selkirk, were intent upon carving out a New World agricultural enterprise. Three large (about 40′ by 8′) Mackinaw boats, which carried a group of Selkirk colonists and their cargo of seed back from southeastern Wisconsin, up the Mississippi, Minnesota, and Red rivers to their home in the spring of 1820, were the first non-Indian conveyances on the Red River.

Little use was made of the Red River during the next four decades. Trade between the northern Red River Valley and the present-day St. Paul, Minnesota, area began to develop significantly during the 1840s. Commerce at that stage moved principally via trains of ox or horse-drawn two-wheeled wooden carts that squeaked

hideously. Mechanized transportation in the Red River Valley finally made its appearance in the late 1850s.

By 1858 trade between the St. Paul merchants and the people of the Fort Garry (Winnipeg) area had reached substantial proportions. Carried north on the carts were agricultural implements, household goods, and a wide variety of day-to-day necessities. St. Paul, in return, received huge quantities of animal furs and buffalo robes from the valley region.

Influenced by the establishment of Fort Abercrombie (between present Wahpeton and Fargo) on the upper portion of the Red River and the permission granted the Hudson's Bay Company to transport goods of English origin in bond via St. Paul, that city's merchants decided to support a steamboat upon the Red River of the North. In early 1859 St. Paul businessmen offered a monetary bonus to anyone who could successfully place a steamboat in operation. The money went to Anson Northup, a St. Paul contractor. He dismantled a boat he owned on the upper Mississippi, sawed a quantity of lumber, and with a crew of men and horses hauled the machinery and lumber overland during the winter to the banks of the Red River.

The Red's first steamboat, named after its owner, was constructed in the spring of 1859, a few miles north of the modern-day twin cities of Fargo, N.D., and Moorhead, Minnesota. The boat, about ninety feet in length and powered by a 100-horsepower engine, was functional if not fancy; one traveler on it referred to the *Anson Northup* as "that tub of a boat." Low water during the late summer severely hampered the vessel's usefulness, as it would that of all steamers which were to eventually travel the shallow, twisting Red.

The *Anson Northup*, renamed the *Pioneer*, sank the following winter north of Fort Garry, but a new and larger steamboat, the *International*, was launched at Georgetown (just north of Moorhead, Minnesota) in the spring of 1862. The vessel was 136 feet long, with a gross tonnage capacity of 172 tons—a very large boat for the small, winding Red. The *International*'s size created immediate problems, as navigating the river's sharp bends with their overhanging trees soon resulted in damage to funnels, the pilot house, and the paddle wheel. Low water at

Goose Rapids, the perennial trouble spot midway between the modern cities of Fargo and Grand Forks, N.D., caused problems later in the summer. Then, in August and September, the famous Sioux Uprising of 1862 put a final damper on that season's navigation.

For steamboating the rest of the 1860s were lethargic. The Hudson's Bay Company now retained sole possession of the *International* and only carried Company freight. This restrictiveness, coupled with the Red's almost annual low-water syndrome, resulted in a resurgence of the cart trains, while the steamboat, for the most part, sat idle.

In 1869 Canada's fertile upper Red River Valley, in and about Fort Garry, was the scene of a bitter revolt against Canadian authority. The region was until 1869 under Hudson's Bay Company jurisdiction, and its few inhabitants, the half-blood Métis, lived virtually without government on land never surveyed or owned by them. Resenting Canadian authority and fearful of losing their lands, they rebelled under Louis Riel. As first they were successful, taking Fort Garry, but they incurred the wrath of Canadians in the eastern provinces when they executed a young Canadian as a traitor. When an armed force marched upon them Riel fled and the Red River Rebellion collapsed. Canada subsequently (1870) created the Province of Manitoba and set aside a vast acreage for the Métis, though many chose not to stay.

The next decade witnessed the heyday of Red River steam navigation. James J. Hill was a transportation agent in St. Paul at this time. He astutely perceived that the moment was ripe for increased commerical activity in the Red River Valley, and in the summer of 1870 began hauling freight to the Red River, where it was loaded on flatboats for the trip downstream. In 1871, along with two partners, Hill constructed the *Selkirk*, a 110-foot sternwheeler. The *Selkirk* and the Hudson's Bay Company's *International* were soon in lively competition for freight and passengers, with a number of flatboats also carrying a substantial amount of cargo.

To legally operate a vessel in American waters, the Hudson's Bay Company, a foreign firm, had transferred title of their steamboat to their American agent, Norman Kittson. But in 1872, Kittson and Hill, who were old friends, merged

their interests to form what was called the Red River Transportation Line. Business grew rapidly as settlement in the valley increased, and by the time the two men, along with other minor partners, officially incorporated the Red River Transportation Company in 1874, there were five steamboats and their accompanying barges operating on the Red River.

Manitobans were queasy about having their commercial lifeline tightly controlled by Americans. It was not until 1874 that they finally took action. In that year a group of Winnipeg merchants, along with a few disenchanted Minnesotans, formed the Merchants International Steamboat Line. By the spring of 1875 they had two fine steamboats, the *Minnesota* and the *Manitoba*, on the river in a direct challenge to the Red River Transportation Company. Rate cuts soon followed as the Red River Transportation Company strove to defeat its competition. This in itself strained the new company's resources. Then, in June 1875, a collision between the *International* and the *Manitoba* sank the latter. Though the *Manitoba* was later raised and put back in service, by fall it was obvious that the Merchants Line would fail.

Canadians resigned themselves to the American company's monopoly until the arrival of a north-south railroad line between Winnipeg and St. Paul. And the railroad was not long in coming. The new southern valley twin cities of Fargo and Moorhead already had both steamboat and railroad serivce, and it was only a matter of time before the east-west rail lines would begin reaching north.

In the meantime, the Red River Transportation Company enjoyed a boom. The amount of freight and passengers reached record highs during the late 1870s as farms and towns sprouted up across both the Canadian and American portions of the valley. The riverside cities of Fargo-Moorhead, Grand Forks and Winnipeg were growing rapidly, while further out on the Red River plain acre after acre of virgin sod felt the farmer's plow. This was the period of the great bonanza wheat farms, huge commercial enterprises owning thousands of acres. They used many men, horses, and machines on each farm unit. Oliver Dalrymple was a leader in the operation of these early forms of agribusiness.

While much of the Red River Transportation

Company's freight during the late 1870s consisted of supplies for the region's growing agricultural economy, a significant amount also consisted of railroad construction supplies. The Canadians were building the Canadian Pacific Railroad, with a branch extending south to the American border. Simultaneously, Jim Hill, who had always viewed the Red River steamboat era as simply a transitional phase in the region's commercial development, had procured the St. Paul and Pacific Railroad and was laying its line northward. By the end of the year 1878, the Winnipeg-St. Paul rail connection was a reality. The golden age of Red River steam navigation had, in essence, come to an end.

As Jim Hill correctly perceived, the riverboat was a transitional mode of transportation—the integral cog between the cart and the railroad. The steamboat was a definite improvement over the cart, but was still confined to the seasonal whims of the twisting Red River. The paddle wheeler in turn was no match for the iron horse, which could roam over the flat prairie year-round and do it at a much faster pace.

Only small pleasure craft have trod the placid surface of the American portion of the Red in the years since the demise of the steamboat. Tourist vessels and other limited commercial traffic do operate in the Winnipeg vicinity, but generally speaking, the Red's importance as a navigational waterway has been minimal during the past few decades.

Now, the usually sluggish, muddy Red gains most of its notoriety from the flooding which often occurs along its banks. This phenomenon is far from new. Historical accounts make frequent note of widespread flooding of the land near the Red River. Since the rivers of the Red River Basin do drain northward, the possibility and degree of spring flooding usually depends to a large extent upon the amount of snowfall the region receives.

The floods that do occur often affect much of the Red River Valley floor, the bed of ancient Lake Agassiz. There may be two types of flooding: (1) that resulting from stream bank overflow, and (2) that caused by runoff from snowmelt or heavy rainfall. Historically, the larger floods have resulted primarily from spring snowmelt, with water at times covering areas of farmland several miles wide. The northern part of the valley's American sector usually suffers more than its southern counterpart on account of the increased flow as the river proceeds toward Lake Winnipeg. The Winnipeg metropolitan area has been aided by construction of a floodway which diverts rising water around the city, while American river communities are protected to a degree by permanent earthen dikes.

FURTHER READING: Hiram M. Drache, *The Challenge of the Prairie: Life and Times of the Red River Pioneers* (1970). Elwyn B. Robinson, *History of North Dakota* (1966)

Don Lillehoe

The Republican River

Source: Junction of North Fork and Arikaree rivers near Haigler, in southwestern Nebraska; a few miles east, the South Fork joins near Benkelman
Length: 420 miles
Tributaries: Frenchman Creek, Red Willow and Medicine Creek, Horse Creek, and many others.
Mouth: Joins Smoky Hill River forming Kansas River at Junction City, Kansas
Agricultural Products: Wheat
Industries: Hydroelectric power; recreation

Named in jest, the 420-mile Republican River was for years a capricious body of water as she flowed across southern Nebraska and into central Kansas, flooding the countryside spasmodically. With the installation of flood control dams she has settled into predictable activity, and her manufactured lakes provide water for irrigation and for recreation.

According to legend, the Republican was named by Spanish explorers at about the time of the American Revolution. Ordinarily the Spanish gave religious names to geographic areas, but when they saw this river, their sense of humor took over. A band of independent Pawnees had refused to leave the riverbank to move with other tribesmen to another location; the amused Spaniards saw similarities between this situation and that of the colonists in New England who were then fighting to establish the Republic. So they named the river La Nacion de la Republica, and it has been called the Republican ever since.

The river is formed by the junction of the North Fork and the Arikaree rivers, and a few miles further east, at Benkelman, the South Fork joins. As the river flows eastward across rolling grasslands, other tributaries roll into it: Frenchman Creek, Red Willow and Medicine Creek, Horse Creek, Blackwood, Driftwood, Beaver, Sappa, Turkey, and scores of others. The Republican itself is broad and shallow; most of the small creeks that feed it are clear and sparkling, some of them flowing rapidly over a sandy bed, then disappearing into the sand to reappear farther downstream with as great a volume as before, the underground current retaining its force as it filters through the sand. The Republican River valley is from 4 to 8 miles wide, and each of the tributaries has a similar valley, the broad, flat areas interspersed among the canyons and bluffs of southern Nebraska.

The river flows in a fairly straight east-west pattern through Nebraska until it reaches the town of Superior, two-thirds of the way across the state; there it turns abruptly southward, flowing in a southeasterly direction for more than 50 miles until it joins the Smoky Hill to form the Kansas River at Junction City.

For hundreds of years, the Republican valley was the feeding ground for millions of bison, called buffalo, who sought the rich native grasses that grew there. The Republican herd, one of the four great herds that covered the central part of the United States, grazed in large circles, perhaps as large as 300 miles in diameter, wintering along the Republican River. Other game was in the area too—antelope, deer, and all kinds of small game and birds—but it was the buffalo that drew the Indians there for their great hunts, twice a year for whole communities of Pawnee, in the eastern part of the watershed, and Dakota Sioux, in the western part. The buffalo provided almost all the sustenance for the Indians—food, shelter, clothing, fuel—and much of the religious pattern and philosophic beliefs; the lives of the Plains Indians were related to the buffalo.

The earliest white men to live in the area were trappers who sought the pelts of small animals, especially beaver. They generally lived in dugouts or rough shacks near the river, leading solitary lives and not considering themselves to be permanent settlers. Other, even more itinerant hunters were the buffalo men who during the 1860s and early 1870s slaughtered buffalo in wholesale quantities for their hides, leaving the carcasses to rot. Within a 15-year span, the concentrated commercial hunting by the white men destroyed the buffalo herds, even those great numbers along the Republican River.

The native Americans had lost the animals which provided their sustenance. In addition, they lost their land. After 1854, when Nebraska became a territory, various tribes were forced to cede lands to the government, piece by piece. The semi-nomadic Pawnee were finally left with only a small hunting area adjoining the Republican, where they were hemmed in by the whites and harassed by their hereditary enemies, the Sioux. In 1873, a hunting party of 700 Pawnee under Sky Chief was attached by Oglala and Teton Sioux near the Republican river in an area now known as Massacre Canyon. The surviving Pawnee moved shortly thereafter to Indian Territory, Oklahoma.

White homesteaders began to settle in the Republican valley in the early 1870s, part of the population boom that exploded across the Great Plains generally, Nebraska particularly. The ten Nebraska counties through which the Republican flows had a total population of 87 persons in 1870; ten years later, in 1880, their population was 10,148! The phenomenal increase was caused by the availability of free or inexpensive lands, some of them homestead lands supplied by the United States government, some of them railroad lands which the government had given the railroad companies in return for their building rails into the area. The Republican Valley branch of the Burlington Railroad was completed in 1882, bringing goods and people into the area and intensifying the already frantic settlement process.

Whereas farmlands were generally taken up by individual families, the villages were organized by land companies; they established villages at the confluences of creeks and the Republican River, where water provided power for mills. The town of Red Cloud, the setting for some of author Willa Cather's books, was founded in 1870, and in rapid succession, towns sprang up farther west along the river: Guide Rock and Inavale, Riverton, Franklin, Bloomington and Naponee, Republican City, Alma, Orleans, Stanford, Beaver City (on Beaver Creek, leading into the Republican), Arapahoe, Holbrook, Cambridge, Bartley, Indianola, McCook, Trenton, Stratton, and Benkelman. The fertile land along the Republican attracted thousands of enthusiastic newcomers, those in the eastern reaches intent on farming the croplands, and those in the western area raising livestock on the ranchlands. During World War I, when wheat

reached an unheard-of 2 dollars a bushel, farmers discovered that their land, which they had previously considered suitable only for raising livestock, was capable of growing crops; since then, much of the Republican River valley has been turned over to wheat production, mile after mile of golden grain ripening in the early summer sunlight.

For years, the Republican River had a tradition of too little or too much, drying up in times of drought or flooding in times of heavy rainfall. During the Dust Bowl years of the 1930s, when much of the Great Plains dried up under the unrelenting sun, the Republican and its tributaries became mere trickles, and what water was left in them was not usable for no irrigation facilities had been developed. Then came the rains and the run-off of water from the winter snows. But instead of being life-giving, the water was life-destroying, creating widespread havoc. The devastating flood of late May, 1935, drowned more than 100 persons between Oxford and Trenton, damaged or washed away hundreds of homes, and inundated thousands of acres of farmlands. Another flood, of lesser intensity, caused the drowning of 13 persons near Cambridge in mid-June, 1947; ironically, work had already begun by then on the Harlan county dam for flood control, and high waters destroyed much of the work that had already taken place on the dam itself. By that time, the Republican River had been included in the Missouri River basin project under the Federal Flood Control Act of December, 1944.

Among the dams and reservoirs that have since been built for flood control, irrigation, and power generation are the Bonny Dam on South Fork in Colorado; the Trenton Dam, which creates Swanson Lake on the South Fork near Trenton; the Enders dam and reservoir on Frenchman Creek near Wauneta; Medicine Creek dam which forms Henry Strunk Lake on Medicine Creek near Cambridge; and the Red Willow dam on Red Willow creek which forms Hugh Butler Lake near McCook, all of them Bureau of Reclamation projects. The Harlan County dam, which forms the Harlan County reservoir on the Republican near Alma, was constructed by Army Engineers. Further downstream the Bureau of Reclamation has constructed the Superior-Courtland dam at Guide

Rock, and in Kansas, the Love-well Reservoir on a branch of the Republican. Near the mouth of the river are Milford Dam and its lake, near Clay Center.

By the time the Harlan county dam was completed in 1952, the old village of Republican City had been evacuated and moved to a new location for its original site was about to be under water. Houses and other buildings which were salvageable were moved; those which were not reusable were abandoned and new ones built in the new location, where new utilities were installed. It took 5 years, until 1957, for the lake to reach its normal level; in the meantime, there had been some releases of water from it for irrigation purposes. Since 1957, the lake has been fully operational.

In addition to impounding waters to provide flood control, irrigation water and power generation, the dammed up streams provide recreational facilities. The Harlan county reservoir contains 350,000 acre-feet of water in its normal level, and has facilities for an additional 150,000 acre feet of water for flood control storage. At its normal level, it has 13,600 surface acres of water with a 75-mile shoreline. Resorts and communities of cabins for fishermen, boaters, water-skiers, and other water enthusiasts have been developed around each of the newly created lakes. Milford Lake, between Clay Center and Junction City, Kansas, is the largest of the Republican River reservoirs; it contains 16,189 surface acres of water at normal level and has a shoreline of 163 miles, making it the largest lake in Kansas. The dam was built between 1962 and 1964 at a cost of nearly 49 million dollars.

Water is usually stored in the reservoirs or lakes from September through May, and released for the irrigation season during June, July, and August. Flows in the river during much of the year are small unless excessive rain or snow-melt prematurely fill the reservoirs.

The Nebraska Game and Parks Commission has designated a 55-mile stretch of the Republican from the Harlan county reservoir east to the Guide Rock diversion dam as a canoeing area. This segment contains several scenic islands, and most of the area is heavily wooded on both banks, primarily with willows and cottonwood.

The Republican, a pretty river, has been tamed for useful purposes. Its waters have always been too shallow and too unpredictable for use in freighting, but they are disciplined now so that they provide irrigation for crop production and water for power production. In addition, they provide pleasure for thousands of sportsmen in Nebraska and Kansas.

ADDITIONAL READING: A. T. Andreas, *History of Nebraska* (1882; 1975). James C. Olson, *History of Nebraska* (1955, 1966).

Dorothy Weyer Creigh

The Smoky Hill River

Source: Junction of two Forks in Logan County in western Kansas
Length: 550 miles
Tributaries: Ladder, Hackberry, Big, and Chapman creeks, and Saline and Solomon rivers
Mouth: Joins Republican River northeast of Junction City, Kansas, to form the Kansas or Kaw River
Agricultural Products: Dryland wheat farming
Industries: Petroleum, limestone quarrying, cattle feeding

The Smoky Hill River, a shallow, meandering prairie stream about 550 miles long, rises in two forks in eastern Colorado. The two forks join in western Kansas. The river is over 4,000 feet high at its headwaters and about 1,000 feet high where it merges with the Republican River northeast of Junction City, Kansas, forming the Kansas River. It flows through the High Plains, the Blue Hills Uplands, the Smoky Hills Uplands, and into the Flint Hills. Major tributaries of the Smoky are Ladder, Hackberry, Big, and Chapman Creeks, and the Saline and Solomon Rivers.

The Smoky is characterized by a flat valley several miles wide in some places. Trees and shrubs grow only in narrow paths along the river bed and its tributaries. The ground cover is northern grama-buffalo prairie grass in the western and Blue Stem grama-prairie grass in the eastern part of the drainage area. A large oil field is located in the central area, and new discoveries are still being made. Postrock limestone, used for fence posts and for building materials by the early settlers on the treeless plains, cuts across the central drainage of the Smoky.

The river cuts into the chalk beds of an ancient sea of the Cretaceous period and, in western Kansas, the results were the Smoky Hill Badlands. The chalk beds in Trego, Gove, and Logan counties provide some of the best Cretaceous fossils in the world. Othniel Marsh, Edward D. Cope, Benjamin Mudge, and Charles H. Sternberg and his son George collected from the Dakota formation near Ellsworth and Kanapolis and the Niobrara formation to the west. One of the most dramatic fossils found in the Smoky Hill chalk beds was the internationally famous fish within a fish (*Gillicus arcuatus* swallowed by a *Xiphactinus molossus*), collected in Gove County in 1952.

Many Indian archeological sites are found along the Smoky drainage. These include the El Quartelejo (Apache) Pueblo ruins on Beaver Creek in Scott County, paleo-Indian sites, and petroglyphs in Ellsworth and Russell counties. Among the major Indian groups that crossed the Smoky during their annual migrations or hunts were the Cheyennes, Arapahoes, Comanches, Apaches, Kiowas, Wichitas (Quiviras), and Pawnees.

The Smoky Hill Valley was traversed by a number of early explorers. There is evidence that in 1541 Francisco Vasquez de Coronado was at Indian villages just south of the river. Members of the Leyva-Humaña expedition of 1593–1594 probably observed the river. Over a hundred years later the expedition of Pedro de Villasur crossed the river in 1720 in search of Pawnee villages along the Platte. Four years later members of the expedition of Etienne Veniard de Bourgmont traveled west on the river. The Pedro Vial party was on the Smoky near present Abilene, Kansas, in late 1793.

Americans also explored the river. Zebulon Pike crossed the Smoky in 1806, George C. Sibley in mid-1811, and Sylvester Pattie in 1824. Jedediah Smith led a group out of St. Louis in 1825 which traveled to the junction of the Smoky and Republican rivers before turning north to the Platte. John C. Frémont led an expedition to the same junction in 1843 and explored west along the Smoky to the Solomon. The following summer, on his return from California, Frémont reached the headwaters of the Smoky in Colorado. The following year he wrote from Bent's Fort that the valley of the Kansas and the Smoky Hill rivers constituted the best and most direct route to the Rocky Mountains. Military needs prompted further exploration of the river. Brevet Captain John Pope explored along the Smoky in 1851 in search of a less arid route to replace the Santa Fe Trail. Late in 1852 an army group from Fort Leavenworth selected a site for a military post near the junction of the Republican and the Smoky. Originally called Camp Centre, it was established the following year as Fort Riley.

Three permanent military outposts were built along the Smoky Hill to protect railroad workers and, later, settlers: Fort Harker, Fort Hays, originally Fort Fletcher before a devastating flood and subsequent relocation; and Fort Wallace. These posts suffered heavy casualties during the cholera plague of 1867. There were also temporary military posts created between 1867 and 1869 during Indian uprisings.

Several attempts were made to navigate the Smoky. The first steamboat on it was the *Excel*, which made a short trip up the Smoky from Fort Riley in June, 1854. The *Belle of Salina* was placed on the river in 1876, and in 1877 a small boat with a steam engine was on Big Creek near Fort Hays.

Abilene was staked out in 1861, and five years later Ellsworth was founded about sixty miles to the west at the Smoky Hill Crossing, where the military road cut south across the river to Fort Zarah and the Santa Fe Trail at the great bend of the Arkansas River. Both towns were cattle shipping centers and experienced the violence and vice associated with trail's end.

Gold in the Rockies spurred the development of a route west via the Smoky. David A. Butterfield successfully opened the Smoky Hill Trail to the mountains in 1865. The following spring Butterfield sold out to his rival, Ben Holladay of the Holladay Overland and Express Company, and soon Wells, Fargo and Company acquired the Overland. Indian attacks hampered travel on the trail and reduced profits, and the coming of the railroad put an end to the business, although settlers followed the trail west for many more years.

The Kansas Pacific Railroad (Union Pacific Railroad, Eastern Division), which built through Kansas in the late 1860s, ran along the north bank of the Smoky Hill and followed the river into Colorado Territory where it picked up the Big Sandy and continued towards Denver.

Many towns sprang up along the railroad and the Smoky, and some soon became ghost towns. One such town was Phil Sheridan, built at rail's end in 1868. It was for a brief time a typical end-of-track town with gambling, prostitution, and shootings, but its population by 1870 had departed for the town Kit Carson in Colorado. It was at this site that William F. "Buffalo Bill" Cody made his reputation for shooting buffalo. Other "wild west" towns, such as Hays City, gained permanency.

Indians, especially the Cheyennes, were a problem along the Smoky during early settlement. Stage stations were attacked, railroad workers were killed, and the garrisons at the western Kansas posts were constantly in the field. The last Indian raids along the Smoky were in 1878 when a band of Northern Cheyenne, led by Dull Knife and Little Wolf, fled from reservation life at Fort Reno in Indian Territory. The band crossed the Smoky south of Buffalo Park as the group headed north. This "Last Indian Raid in Kansas" took the lives of about forty settlers.

Pioneers along the Smoky were tillers of the soil who survived Indian raids, grasshopper plagues, droughts, blizzards, and prairie fires. Those who acquired lands in western Kansas and eastern Colorado turned increasingly from wheat and corn to cattle and sheep. The semi-arid lands forced three adjustments in agriculture—dryland farming, irrigation, and commercial cattle feedlots. The Fort Hays Experiment Station is the world's largest dryland experiment station.

In the central region of the Smoky Hill Valley, water from a number of reservoirs built by the Army Engineers and the Bureau of Reclamation protect the fertile bottomlands from periodic flooding and also provide water for irrigation. The major pollution is from water erosion which is silting up the streams and reservoirs.

Early settlers along the Smoky tended to come from the Midwest, but as the line of settlement moved westward after the Civil War, European immigrants established a number of communities. A large group of Swedes settled on Kansas Pacific and government lands near the Smoky in the late 1860s. This *framtidslandet*, land of the future, in the Smoky Hill Valley became the center of Swedish Lutheranism in Kansas. To the west a large group of immigrants from Bohemia, or Czechoslovakia, settled in the 1870s.

Protestant Germans from Russia settled along and near the river in the 1870s, but the largest group of Germans from Russia to settle along the Smoky were Roman Catholics who arrived in 1876 and 1877. They lived in villages rather than on individual farms, and their life centered around their churches.

English immigrants came to Kansas as individuals or as families, so only two colonies of Englishmen were established in Kansas. One of these was the Victoria Colony, set up in 1873 along the Smoky and its Big Creek and North Fork tributaries. The founder, George Grant, established minimum estates of 640 acres for his English aristocrat colonists and their herdsmen and servants. He introduced Angus cattle to the United States and experimented with blooded sheep, cattle, and horses on the harsh plains before the speculative venture collapsed in 1878.

Many small ethnic and religious colonies were established in the region. There was a small colony of Irishmen in Saline County in 1859. Austrians, Hungarians, Czechs, and Swedes established colonies in the western drainage area of the Smoky. A French colony and several Dutch colonies settled along the Solomon. A black community, composed primarily of former slaves, was established at Nicodemus on the South Fork of the Solomon River. A number of River Brethren and Church of the Brethren groups settled in western Kansas, and there were Dunkard colonies in the eastern drainage area of the Smoky.

Most of the large immigrant colonies that

were established in Kansas were located in the Smoky Hill valley, and here the native customs and cultures have survived for over a century. Kansas has been enriched by them, for they were thrifty, industrious, honest people, seeking the best education possible for their children. The Smoky passes near the campuses of Fort Hays State University in Hays, Bethany College in Lindsborg, and Kansas Wesleyan University and Marymount College in Salina. One of the most famous churches in the valley is St. Fidelis in Victoria, named "The Cathedral of the Plains" by William Jennings Bryan. It was built of native limestone by Volga Germans who had settled along the Smoky and its tributaries.

There was extensive military activity along the river during World War II. The Smoky Hill Army Air Field, later Schilling Air Force Base, was established at Salina, as was Camp Phillips, and the Smoky Hill Bombing Range. Walker Army Air Field was established to train B-29 crews for raids on Japan. Schilling remained open until the 1960s, and today the air field is used for local air traffic and by major commercial airlines for training crews for large commercial jets.

The land is sparsely populated along the drainage of the Smoky Hill except in Junction City, Abilene, Salina, and Hays. All the counties along the river and its tributaries except two have lost population. Three counties, Cloud, Mitchell, and Ottawa, had their maximum population at the time of the 1890 census, and six others had theirs when the 1910 census was taken.

The region has produced its share of important people. President Dwight D. Eisenhower grew up in Abilene. Auto manufacturer Walter P. Chrysler spent his boyhood in Ellis, just north of the Smoky, and Dr. Gerald W. Tomanek, internationally known grasslands expert, resides in Ellis County.

The Smoky Hill is paralleled by Interstate 70, a major artery across the nation's heartland. The valley provides good recreation. The many reservoirs provide fishing, boating, and camping. There is good pheasant and quail hunting, with some dove and turkey. Deer are available again along the river and its tributaries, and antelope herds are found in several areas along the river.

FURTHER READING: Robert W. Richmond, *Kansas a Land of Contrasts* (1980). Robert R. Dykstra, *The Cattle Towns* (1968).

James L. Forsythe

The Sweetwater River

Source: Southern slopes of Wind River Mountains in west-central Wyoming
Length: 175 miles
Tributaries: None of significance
Mouth: Into Pathfinder Reservoir of the North Platte, southwest of Casper, Wyoming
Agricultural Products: Hay
Industries: Cattle ranching, uranium mining

Rivers do not have to be long to have historical importance. The Sweetwater River of Wyoming is only 175 miles long, but without its clean, fresh waters the emigrants on the Oregon, California, and Mormon trails would have suffered terribly from lack of water.

The Sweetwater, a tributary of the North Platte, heads in west central Wyoming on the southern slopes of the snow-capped Wind River Mountains. It flows south along the east edge of the Continental Divide for twenty miles, then (in South Pass) turns eastward, and meanders in that direction for 150 miles until it empties into Pathfinder Reservoir, southwest of Casper. Before 1911, when the Bureau of Reclamation completed Pathfinder Dam on the North Platte, the Sweetwater had maintained its separate identity for fifteen more miles. The dam backs up the Sweetwater as well as the North Platte.

In most places the Sweetwater is no more than forty feet wide and two or three feet deep. It drops from an elevation of 7,500 feet in South Pass to about 6,000 feet at Pathfinder Reservoir. After leaving South Pass it descends rapidly through a beautiful canyon, then flows slowly through a narrow valley no more than ten miles wide. It carries considerably less water in the twentieth century than in the nineteenth because its flow has been much reduced by diversions for irrigation of hay meadows.

Trails traced along the river by wild game and Indians (Shoshonis, Crows, Arapahoes, and Cheyennes), antedated the arrival of the white men. Robert Stuart and six companions (eastbound after helping establish John Jacob Astor's fur-trading post, Astoria, at the mouth of the Columbia River) followed the lower Sweetwater in October, 1812, finding many bison. In March, 1824, some of William H. Ashley's mountain men—Jedediah Smith, Thomas Fitzpatrick, William L. Sublette, James Clyman, James Bridger, and six others—no doubt saw the upper waters on their way westward through South Pass. Thereafter many mountain men en route between St. Louis and the fur trade rendezvous became well acquainted with the Sweetwater. Ashley's trappers gave the river its name because it was much more potable than the other streams and the alkalai lakes in the vicinity.

In the quarter century between 1841 and 1866 the Oregon, Mormon, and California trails brought more than 300,000 emigrants along the river on their way through Wyoming. Hundreds of diaries give details of experiences on the trails. During the years 1849–1853 when the trails were most crowded, the emigrants found little fuel except cow chips and sagebrush, and few game animals. In July and August little grass remained within a mile of the trails. Sand blew in the emigrant's faces most of the time. A freighter in 1858 reported that human graves and ox carcasses lined the trails, making the valley "a vast charnel house."

Each year many emigrants celebrated the Fourth of July at Independence Rock, a mound of gray granite which covered twenty-five acres of the north bank of the stream. Thousands of emigrants painted or chiseled their names on the sides of the Rock. Sad to say, all but a few of the 19th century names have been removed by weathering and exfoliation.

Because the river sometimes flows beside high rocks as it meanders from one side of the valley to the other, many of the emigrants forded the Sweetwater a total of nine times. At one of these crossings in 1859 Horace Greeley's trunk fell off a stagecoach and disappeared in a deep pool. The famous New York publisher mourned the loss of several white suits.

Indians rarely interfered with the emigrants along the Sweetwater part of the trail. As a precaution, however, small military garrisons were stationed at several stations in the 1860s. The worst tragedy occurred in October and November, 1856, when more than 100 Mormons in several handcart companies froze to death.

Cattlemen began settling in the valley in the 1870s, to be joined later by sheepmen. Under various land laws the stockmen acquired title to small acreages on which they established their headquarters. For free pasturage they occupied adjacent public land. Almost all of the valley has been devoted to livestock grazing from 1880 to the present time. In the 1880s, small settlers who sought to share use of the public lands received short shrift from the large operators. This "war" between the big ranchers and the "nesters" was especially serious around the Sweetwater and the northeast of there, around Casper. In 1889 James Averell and Ella Watson ("Cattle Kate"), who tried to homestead on the river, were lynched, allegedly because they possessed stolen stock. In 1892 came the "Johnson County War" involving hired gunmen and, eventually, United States troops called in to keep order.

Except for a few temporary gold-rush communities which flourished briefly in South Pass, 1867–1869, no settlements of any size appeared near the Sweetwater until the late 1950s when uranium mining and processing brought Jeffrey City into being fifty miles east of South Pass. However, at the tiny settlement of South Pass City, a few miles northeast of the Sweetwater, lived William H. Bright who brought about the passage of woman suffrage by the Wyoming Territorial Legislature in 1869.

An asphalt-paved highway (U.S. 287) carries heavy tourist traffic through the valley to Grand Teton and Yellowstone National Parks every summer. From the highway and Jeffrey City the valley looks much as it did a century ago, for few people live on the land. Ruts left by emigrants of the nineteenth-century migration are still visible. The ranches are still very large. Best known is the Sun Ranch at Devil's Gate, five miles west of Independence Rock. It was founded by Tom Sun, a Frenchman, in the 1870s.

Antelope (pronghorn) graze with the domestic livestock. Small herds of moose emerge from the Wind River Mountains to winter in willow stands in South Pass. Brook and rainbow trout and a few cutthroats attract fishermen to the upper river. The lower river has rainbows and browns that are neither numerous nor endangered. Poor flows, poor habitat, warm, slow-moving water, and inhospitable ranchers restrict fishing. Attempts by the Game and Fish Department to purchase easements for public fishing have failed.

As a Bicentennial project, Wyoming acquired title to Independence Rock in the 1970s. As more people visit the famous landmark, they will become better acquainted with the historic Sweetwater River, which flows within 100 feet of the south end of the rock.

FURTHER READING: T.A. Larson, *History of Wyoming* (1965; 1978). Wyoming Writer's Project, *Wyoming, A Guide to the History, Highways and People* (1941).

T.A. Larson

The White River of South Dakota

Source: Rises in northwestern Nebraska
Length: About 325 miles
Tributaries: Little White River; White Clay, Wounded Knee, Medicine Root, Bear in the Lodge, and Pipe Black creeks
Mouth: Flows into Missouri River in southeastern Lyma County, South Dakota
Agricultural Products: Hay, wheat
Industries: Cattle ranching

The White River of the southern Missouri Plateau is unique because of its varied geography. The stream rises in northwestern Nebraska and flows north into South Dakota through a broad and fertile valley. Approximately eighty percent of the river basin's 10,200 square miles are in South Dakota, however, and shortly after crossing the border the stream gradually turns east and enters a section of the South Dakota Badlands. After flowing through terrain dominated by high cliffs and sandstone for seventy miles, the White is joined from the south by its major tributary, the Little White. The remaining thirty miles from the forks of these rivers to the Missouri is again characterized by sloping banks covered with a mixture of shrubs, glassland, and clusters of trees.

The Indians called the White River the "Makizita-wakpa," or literally translated "earth that makes a yellow water." Europeans thought the river looked more white than yellow and named the stream accordingly. The source of the discoloration is erosion which occurs principally after the White enters the Badlands. Runoffs from rains pick up a considerable amount of clay and minerals, especially silica, a by-product of sandstone that dominates the landscape. The relatively high altitude of the badlands adds to the erosion problem. Thunderstorms often create flash floods that swirl down the denuded buttes carrying mineral-rich water to the main channel far below.

Near the headwaters of the White, the stream has a high gradient and before irrigation dams affected the river, it had a rapid flow similar to other Missouri Plateau streams. But once the White enters the Badlands (a National Monument), the gradient declines to less than four feet per mile. Here one can often find standing pools of water covered by a white scum formed from mineral deposits. Some areas of the river may even dry up during periods of drought. The unpredictable nature of the water flow in the Badland region made early travel on the White difficult at best.

Even though the river valley is occasionally dry, the Badlands section is characterized by spectacular scenery. Towering over the northern bank for about sixty miles is the so-called "Great Wall." Early travelers found these steep cliffs nearly impossible to pass through in order to reach the river below. Recently, engineers have cut grades in the wall in several places to allow modern highways to cross the river.

The region bordering the south bank of the White eventually merges with the Sand Hills of Nebraska. Much of this area is dotted with sandstone and shale buttes, yet it is less rugged in appearance than the north bank. Intermixed with the buttes are a number of small creeks that generally run north to the main stream. The most important are White Clay Creek on the west, followed to the east by the Wounded Knee, the Medicine Root, the Redwater, the Bear in the Lodge, and finally the Pipe Black. All these tributaries maintain a yearly flow of relatively clear water

Although the Sioux or Dakota Indians were late arrivals in the White River Valley, they had driven other tribes from the region when white men first appeared in substantial numbers on the Missouri River shortly after 1800. The abundant game in the valley soon attracted fur traders who followed the Sioux up the river basin. The traders built posts at the mouths of several tributaries including the Black Pipe and Wounded Knee Creeks, as well as the Little White River. The Dakota exchanged their furs for guns, knives, kettles, and other sundry household goods at the posts. Following a successful winter, the trader often built a "bull boat" to transport his furs downriver to the Missouri. Such boats were ingeniously made by covering a wood frame with buffalo hides, a contraption that probably worked well in the shallow, mud-filled White River.

The dominant Dakota tribes that regularly inhabited the White River included the Brulé subdivision of the Teton, and the Yankton. Black tail deer, big horn sheep, and bison provided a reliable food source for them, yet they also cultivated small vegetable gardens, mostly of corn. One early observer noted that the Brulé and the Yankton considered the valley "one of the choice spots on earth." When supplied with meat, the Indians could resort to one of the picturesque small, wooded creek valleys and spend their time on amusements and in celebration.

After the U.S. Army defeated the Sioux Nation in 1877, that portion of the White River Valley in South Dakota was divided into two large reservations. Pine Ridge Agency in the western section of the basin near White Clay Creek became the home of Red Cloud's Oglala Sioux Tribe. Its counterpart in the east, Rosebud Agency, was assigned to the followers of Spotted Tail's Brulé Dakota. The agents established cattle herds and attempted to induce the Sioux to farm. On both reservations, however, the Dakota defied governmental acculturation. With the religious, social, and political structure of the Western Dakota people still intact, relations between government personnel and the hostile segments of each tribe remained tense throughout the 1870s and 1880s.

Widespread dissatisfaction as well as a new native, religious revival that swept across the northern plains in 1890 soon brought turmoil to the White River reservations and disaster for a large body of Dakota people. The government quickly sent in troops to quell disturbances and stop the Ghost Dance, the main ritual of the religious revival. Many Sioux fled the agencies and gathered at the mouths of Medicine Root, Wounded Knee, and White Clay Creeks to practice their outlawed dancing. In November 1890, a large group moved northwest of the White River into the Badlands to a stronghold fortress named Cuny Table. Throughout the next thirty days the government negotiated with the ghost dancers to bring about their voluntary return to the reservation. Just as most gave in and began filing back to White Clay Creek, news of the death of Sitting Bull, leader of the Hunkpapa Sioux at Standing Rock Reservation, reached the people at Pine Ridge. The venerable old chief had been shot by Indian police sent by the agency to arrest him.

The death of Sitting Bull intensified the

dissatisfaction on Dakota reservations in South Dakota. This was especially so for the followers of Big Foot on the Cheyenne River Reservation north of Pine Ridge. Upon hearing the sad news, he led his people south towards Pine Ridge apparently intent on joining the hostile Oglala and Brulé factions. Cavalry troops went in hot pursuit hoping that the great wall along the north bank of White River would act as a barrier and prevent the union of the so-called hostile Indians. But by using pickaxes and shovels, the Miniconjou refugees, the majority of which were women and children, opened a passageway to the valley floor below (the pass is still called Big Foot Pass). Once there, Big Foot's people soon recognized the fruitlessness of their effort. A ghost dance uprising had not taken place on Pine Ridge. Cold, hungry, Big Foot himself unable to walk and probably dying, the band surrendered to about 500 troops of the Seventh Cavalry and bedded down for the night on the banks of Wounded Knee Creek, a western tributary of the White.

At dawn on the morning of December 9, 1890, the officers in charge ordered the Miniconjou warriors to surrender their arms. At no time prior to this had the Miniconjous as a group indicated any willingness to engage American troops in combat, and they were completely surrounded by cavalry. Nevertheless, the Indian leaders decided to give up the broken and old guns and keep the newer ones hidden. A subsequent search provoked an incident in which a rifle accidentally discharged and a violent slaughter ensued. Using Hotchkiss artillery guns, the Indian camp was quickly silenced with grapeshot. After a brief hand-to-hand struggle, the mismatched Dakota warriors were virtually destroyed. Women and children also fell under intense fire from the troops with tragic results. When the smoke cleared, at least 146 Miniconjou people lay dead. Estimates later placed the total Indian dead at close to 200. Casualties among Seventh Cavalry troopers numbered a mere 25, some no doubt killed by the crossfire of their own men. The tragedy at Wounded Knee remains one of the most significant historical events to occur along the White River.

In the aftermath of the Wounded Knee massacre, the Sioux returned to a reservation life that

offered little promise or opportunity. The White River Valley is not conducive to large-scale irrigation like other western South Dakota streams, and much of the basin today is good only for grazing. Only one irrigation project of any size has been constructed on the reservations. The Bureau of Indian Affairs built two earthen reservoirs on White Clay Creek in the 1930s to open new land to cultivation. The first dam is located a few hundred yards above the Nebraska state line. With a capacity of 1,500 acre-feet of water, it can irrigate from 200–400 acres of land. The second dam on White Clay Creek has a capacity of 7,200 acre-feet and is located nineteen miles downstream. It provides water for some 600 acres of farmland. Both projects are under the control of the reservation tribal council.

Elsewhere in the river basin, irrigation had been more successful. Settlers built private ditches along the headwaters of White River in Nebraska as early as the 1880s. The government completed a much larger project near Whitney in 1923 that also proved successful. North of the White River in Pennington County, South Dakota, the Interior Colony attempted to irrigate approximately 1,000 acres of land in scattered plots in 1910. Three years later, this private project failed. In all, about 6,000 acres of land are irrigated along the White River today.

The Bureau of Indian Affairs has considered the development of other irrigation projects. Two possible reservoir sites are on the main channel of the White and on the Little White River. The construction of the Slim Butte Dam, five miles north of the Nebraska line on the main stream would allow the irrigation of an added 6,940 acres of land and provide some flood control. The other location on the Little White is six miles south of where the forks join to create the main stream. Unfortunately, the geography of both sites places stringent limits on the amount of land that could be irrigated.

The completion of either project has been encouraged by the bureau as well as tribal officials because of the boost it would provide to the reservation economy. Congress has yet to fund construction of either project, however, since it is questionable whether the benefits outweigh the cost. There is little doubt that efforts to stimulate the economy on the reservations are necessary. The occupation of Wounded Knee, South Dakota, in 1972 by militant Indians demanding change is clearly indicative of the growing dissatisfaction and despair among Native Americans. The problem is simply that the White River Basin, while picturesque, is still one of the least productive regions in America. It lacks the water resources necessary to turn a desert region into productive farmland.

FURTHER READING: Robert M. Utley, *The Last Days of the Sioux Nation* (1963). Herbert S. Schell, *History of South Dakota* (1961).

Gary Clayton Anderson

The Yellowstone River

Source: Northeast side of Yount's Peak southeast of Yellowstone Park
Length: 671 miles
Tributaries: Lamar, Clarks Fork of the Yellowstone, Bighorn, Rosebud, Powder, and smaller streams
Mouth: Into Missouri at North Dakota-Montana boundary
Agricultural Products: wheat, sugar, alfalfa
Industries: Coal and oil extraction

Snowdrifts on the northwest side of Yount's Peak, a 12,165-foot-high landmark in the Absaroka Mountains of northwest Wyoming, spawn rivulets that coalesce into the Yellowstone River. The location is just a few miles southeast of Yellowstone National Park.

The river then flows north into the park along the Thorofare, a swampy valley. Moose, deer, elk, and bear are common in this out-of-the-way region where fishermen find the trout lively and plentiful. Soon, however, the river flows into the southeastern arm of Yellowstone Lake. (Many believe, incorrectly, that Yellowstone River rises out of the Lake.)

The river leaves at the Lake's northernmost point, Fishing Bridge, gliding placidly northward through Hayden Valley, Dragon's Mouth Spring and the Mud Volcano—signs of the region's volcanic past—and past the Nez Percés Ford where the tribe led by Chief Joseph and Looking Glass crossed the river in 1877. Shortly thereafter the current increases and, bending eastward, the river spills over the Upper Falls, 109 feet high; a very short distance later it flows over the spectacular Lower Falls, 308 feet high.

Now the river is at the Grand Canyon of the Yellowstone, known to geologists as the Fourth Canyon. It is twenty-four miles long, deep, precipitous, and of many colors with yellow predominating. Park officials consider this canyon as ending at Lamar Junction, where the Lamar River enters the Yellowstone from the east.

The river now curves west and, where Black Tail Deer Creek flows in, enters the seven-mile-long Third Canyon, deep, narrow, but not of beautiful colorations. Near the north boundary of the park the Yellowstone emerges from the canyon, crosses into Montana and flows generally north for the next fifty-six miles to the town of Livingston. On the way it passes through sublimely beautiful Paradise Valley and the Second and First canyons, both imposing but non-spectacular when compared with the two canyons above.

This Upper Yellowstone country has a history all its own. John Colter, who was with Lewis and Clark but returned to the mountain country before going back to civilization, may have observed some of Yellowstone's mud pots, hot springs, and geysers as early as 1807. (The exact site of "Colter's Hell" has never been determined.) By 1850 several trappers—Warren Ferris and Osborne Russell for certain, and others including Jim Bridger in all probability—had been in the region. With gold discoveries in Montana in the 1860s still others were in the area, though not all their names are known.

Reliable information about the Upper Yellowstone country had to await the Washburn-

Langford-Doane expedition of 1870. This group's discoveries so whetted curiosities that the following year (1871) the United States Geological and Geographical Survey of the Territories (the Hayden Survey) entered the region and returned with the first scientifically corroborated information about the Lake, the Grand Canyon, and the thermal phenomena. Officials of the Northern Pacific Railroad, which would pass close to the northern boundary, mounted a lobbying campaign to push through Congress a bill to create a national park embracing much of the Upper Yellowstone. On March 1, 1872, the Yellowstone National Park was created when President Grant signed the bill.

Fifty-six miles north of the park boundary, about 120 miles downstream from the Yellowstone's source, the river makes a great bend and flows thereafter east and then northeast 400–450 miles across the arid northern plains to its junction with the Missouri. This takes place just east of the Montana-North Dakota line. This

Lower Yellowstone country, often called the Yellowstone Basin, also has its own history.

It was high plains buffalo country to the Indians. To the north the river's tributary streams are rarely more than fifty miles long; to the south such rivers as the Clarks Fork (of the Yellowstone), Bighorn, Rosebud, Tongue, and Powder extend southward as much as 500 miles. People still refer occasionally to regions as the North Side and the South Side of the Yellowstone.

Indians, once they had horses, found the Yellowstone valley ideal for their nomadic life style. The Crows were there first, but tribes whose home grounds were on the fringes of the Basin entered it for hunting and to make war upon rival tribes. From the upper Missouri country came the Blackfeet (Piegans and Bloods), Assiniboines, and Gros Ventres. From the west came the Flatheads, Shoshones, and Nez Perces out of the mountains. The Sioux and Cheyennes entered from the south and east.

After the turmoil of its journey through the Park, the Yellowstone flows placidly down Paradise Valley below the Park. (Credit: Montana Historical Society, Helena.)

The first white man to see the Yellowstone was probably a Frenchman named Menard who claimed in the 1790s to have been to the Upper Yellowstone, or "La Roche Jaune"—river of the yellow rock—as he called it (thus the name: Yellowstone). Not until Lewis and Clark returned from the Pacific was the river really explored below the great bend. A contingent led by William Clark crossed Bozeman Pass, fashioned dugout canoes, and floated downriver to the Missouri. Clark paused at a rock formation to carve his name. This landmark later known as Pompey's Pillar is still in existence about fifty miles downriver from Billings.

Even as Lewis and Clark, reunited at the mouth of the Yellowstone, floated on down the Missouri, traders and trappers were already working into the upper Missouri and high plains region. John Colter returned a third time with St. Louis fur trader Manuel Lisa who in 1807 built a fort where the Bighorn enters the Yellowstone; Lisa traded there until 1811 when he abandoned the post. In 1821 Fort Benton was established there (not the Fort Benton on the upper Missouri) but was abandoned after a massacre there in 1823.

In 1827 Kenneth McKenzie, working for John Jacob Astor's American Fur Company, established Fort Union at the mouth of the Yellowstone. Significantly, the first steamboat ever to reach Fort Union (1832) was named the *Yellowstone*. In 1837 fur traders innocently brought smallpox into the high plains and upper Missouri country, decimating many of the tribes that lived in the Yellowstone Basin. Beaver hats went out of style, ending the search for beaver, and by the 1860s buffalo hides were the principal traffic remaining of the once vigorous fur trade.

By this time, however, gold had been discovered at Alder Gulch (Virginia City) and Last Chance Gulch (Helena) and in other remote places in western Montana and Idaho. In 1863 John Bozeman and John Jacobs blazed a shortcut from near present Casper on the Oregon Trail north along the east flank of the Bighorn Mountains to the Yellowstone River, which was then followed to near Bozeman Pass; from there the miners trekked overland to the mines. Because of Sioux and Cheyenne hostility this was a hazardous route, yet many took the risk.

The Federal government allowed the Indians to hunt south of the Yellowstone but not reside there, a reservation having been given them in Dakota. But these restrictions were resented. When the Northern Pacific began building up the Yellowstone Valley, the Sioux and Cheyenne harassed work crews and the army units protecting them. Road building ended temporarily with the Panic of 1873, but the Sioux, who were subsequently deprived of their hallowed Black Hills by the gold rush of 1875, continued to cause trouble. Finally orders were given to round up these Indians and herd them back onto their reservations.

Since the Indians did not obey, the Army stepped in to enforce the order. After an unsuccessful winter campaign the army planned a three-pronged entrapment, two of the prongs involving the Yellowstone (the third was to be from the south). General Gibbon advanced down the Yellowstone with 450 infantry and cavalrymen, and General Terry came west from Fort Abraham Lincoln (near present Bismarck). Colonel George Armstrong Custer was at first with Terry; when on his own he and his men were annihilated in the Battle of the Little Big Horn, June 25, 1876. In spite of this reverse the hostiles were cleared from the Yellowstone Basin by the summer of 1877. Two forts offered residents of the vast region some protection: Fort Custer at the mouth of the Little Bighorn, and, more important, Fort Keogh where the Tongue River flows into the Yellowstone; it is now Miles City, Montana.

Segregation of the Indians onto reservations coincided with the demise of the buffalo, opening the way for the open range cattle industry. Nelson Story herded Texas longhorns up the dangerous Bozeman Trail in 1866. From then on Montana Territory, including the great Yellowstone Basin, was occupied increasingly by big outfits, many of them owned by eastern or British investors. Billings, Miles City, and Glendive along the Yellowstone all prospered as cattle towns. Some sheep were also grazed in the river valley without causing violence with the cattlemen as occurred in other parts of the West.

A number of factors—the coming of the railroads, more strongly enforced land laws, the need for protected, blooded livestock, and the terrible winter of 1886–1887—contributed to the end of Montana's open range. On the lower

Yellowstone losses were as high as 90 percent of the herd. However, cattle ranching has remained as a way of life.

In 1883 the Northern Pacific was completed as a transcontinental railroad. The line through the years chalked up a miserable financial record but it nevertheless meant much to the settlement and prosperity of the Yellowstone Basin.

After 1900 farm settlement assumed importance along the Yellowstone. Minor irrigation schemes involving the river were the Huntley Project east of Billings and the lower Yellowstone Project near the river's mouth. Dry farming enthusiasts settled large expanses of the Yellowstone Basin, turning the earth, as the Indians said, upside down. Good weather and high prices of wheat during the First World War contributed to a misplaced optimism.

After the War farm prices declined precipitously and depression set in. Thousands of Montana farms were abandoned, mortgages were foreclosed, and the state had the dubious honor of being the only one of the forty-eight to lose population in the 1920s. Bad times continued with the depression of the 1930s, but with World War II farming bounded back aided by good prices and good weather. Today Montana farming is strictly agribusiness with larger farms and fewer farmers, larger and more specialized cattle ranches with fewer cowboys.

Energy began to assume importance in the Yellowstone Basin after the Second World War. Billings became the site of oil refineries and the eastern terminus of the Yellowstone Pipeline to Spokane, Washington. Discoveries of oil and gas were made throughout central and eastern Montana, around Glendive on the Yellowstone and along its tributary in Wyoming, the Powder River. Natural gas became more abundant.

But it is coal—sub-bituminous and lignite—that today arouses interest and concern in the Yellowstone Basin. Montana as a whole has thirteen percent of the nation's coal reserves, and much of that coal lies in the Basin. It has been mined along the Upper Yellowstone since the 1880s but production in that area declined after the First World War. South of Forsyth in the southern Yellowstone Basin, a hundred miles or so from Billings, is Colestrip, where several powerful companies are leasing land and stripping coal from beneath the soil. The fuel is then shipped to Billings, to Minnesota, Illinois, and other far off states.

As the energy crunch of the mid-1970s worsened, plans were released for construction of more than a score of huge coal-fired power plants needing 2.6 million acre-feet of water from the Yellowstone and its tributaries. Coal interests approached Crow and Cheyenne officials about the possibilities of working their reservation lands. Ranchers had to decide whether to lease their lands for coal-stripping operations or to fight the powerful interests. Montanans had to decide: should the state encourage mining or pass stringent environmental laws restricting the exploitation? Was Montana to become a National Sacrifice Area? And what about the Yellowstone's waters? Unlike nearly every other western river, the Yellowstone still runs relatively free. Now plans call for dams to retain water so as to maintain a steady supply as coal producers and utility giants express their needs for the resource.

At present the Yellowstone's future is uncertain. What happens to that noble river that flows through the fragile ecosystem of the semi-arid high northern plains will be an indication of just how sincere Americans are in their commitment to the land, the rivers, and the future quality of the American landscape.

FURTHER READING: Richard A. Bartlett, *Nature's Yellowstone* (1974). Mark H. Brown, *The Plainsmen of the Yellowstone* (1961). K. Ross Toole, *The Rape of the Plains* (1976).

Richard A. Bartlett

Rivers of the Southeast and Texas

Although it is difficult finding common characteristics for rivers of humid Florida and of west Texas, some similar traits are discernible. All of the rivers of this vast region in times of normal rainfall carry enormous quantities of rainfall to the Gulf. Most are sluggish, deep, and muddy. In times of heavy rainfall they can rise dramatically and cause flood damage. Originally most were navigable for some distance above their mouth. Many are still kept so today by modern dredging operations. Most have been subject to damming for flood control and hydroelectric power.

When Europeans reached these rivers they found Indians settled in villages along their banks. Creeks, Choctaws, Chickasaws, and (after about 1800) Seminoles were among the tribes flourishing east of the Mississippi and south of the Ohio. West of the Mississippi some tribes blended agriculture with buffalo hunting, which they did to the West on the Great Plains. There, along the Arkansas, Brazos, Pecos, and Rio Grande, they clashed with the nomadic Kiowa and Comanche.

Whites first traded with and then drove off the Indians. Because Americans desired safe river traffic to the South, they acquired the Floridas through which a number of rivers flowed before reaching the Gulf. The steamboat replaced the Indian war canoe on the southern waters and from the Suwannee to the Brazos a cotton plantation society developed. It flourished until the Civil War when lumbering and turpentining set in. Along the Rio Grande, Pecos, and Brazos, cattle ranching flourished. Today, as part of the "Sun Belt," all the rivers of the Southeast and Texas are in greater use than ever before.

This sampling of the history of these diverse waterways emphasizes the strategic role they have played in the lives of the people living along their banks.

Richard A. Bartlett

The Alabama River

Source: Confluence of Coos and Tallapoosa rivers in south-central Alabama, just north of Montgomery
Length: 318 miles
Tributaries: Cahaba, Tombigbee
Mouth: When joined by Tombigbee, becomes Mobile River which flows into Mobile Bay
Agricultural products: Cotton
Industries: Oil, fertilizer, wood products, pulpwood and papermaking

"There is perhaps no river so winding as the Alabama," wrote an admiring British traveler in 1858. From the deck of a steamer coming upriver from Mobile, the English gentleman marveled that the "boat's head is turned toward every point of the compass . . . often within the space of a few minutes." He was not the first nor the last to be impressed by the Alabama. William Darby, an American mapmaker, had written in 1817 that the stream was "the finest river to its length in all North America. . . ."

The Alabama (named for an early Indian tribe, the Alabamas), begins its confluence of the Coosa and Tallapoosa rivers near the geological demarcation known as the "fall line"; this point is in south-central Alabama. To the northeast lie the piedmont, hills, and mountainous regions where, historically, agriculture was on a small scale. More importantly, the river makes its languid way to the south and southwest. It drains the alluvial Black Belt that in the nineteenth century was the state's cotton kingdom and flows through the coastal "piney-woods" toward Mobile Bay and the Gulf of Mexico, 318 miles from the Alabama's source.

The warm brown waters flow gently to the Bay. There are no falls or rapids and no excessive currents at any of its sand bars and shoals. Along the way the river is fed by numerous smaller streams until it joins the Tombigbee River about forty-five miles north of Mobile. There the two waterways become the Mobile River which, with several divisions, flows into Mobile Bay.

The Alabama's history is intricately bound with that of the state with which it shares a common name. From early times Indians inhabited its banks, fished its waters, and used it as a highway. The Spanish conquistador Hernando De Soto and his 600 soldiers were the first white men to see the river. In 1540 the conquistador and Tuskaloosa, Black Warrior chief of the Maubillian tribes, met at a village in present Montgomery County. Taking Tuskaloosa prisoner, De Soto marched south to Maubilla, capital of the tribe (located near the banks of the Alabama or Tombigbee in lower Clarke County), and there fought a bloody battle in which 2,500 Indians were killed while Spanish losses were light. Bows and arrows and weapons of stone were no match for Spanish swords and muskets. From Maubilla De Soto gathered his intruders and moved west, ultimately to his death and into history.

More than a century and a half passed before white men came again to the Alabama. This time the motivation was economic gain. Early in the eighteenth century British, French, and Spanish traders bartered goods for furs. Mobile was founded by the French in 1711, and shortly afterwards Sieur de Bienville explored the river valley to the north making pacts of friendship with the resident Muscogees and Alabamas.

After the American Revolution the Americans greatly accelerated their western expansion. In the southwest their fiercest opponents were the Creeks, who occupied much of the Alabama. The most savage fighting took place beginning in

August, 1813, at Fort Mims, located near the lower reaches of the Alabama River. There Creek Indians staged a surprise attack and massacred over 250 whites—probably the worst Indian massacre of whites in American history. The Indians were led by the half-blood William Weatherford (Red Eagle).

Foremost among the American fighters in the ensuing frontier struggles was the intrepid Tennessean, Andrew Jackson. In 1814 he defeated Chief Menowa at the Battle of Horseshoe Bend on Alabama's Tallapoosa River. The victory was as important, although it is less well known, as was Jackson's defeat of the British at New Orleans in 1815. After their loss, the Creeks signed the Treaty of Fort Jackson and surrendered extensive tracts of land in Alabama and Georgia. The Alabama River valley was now thrown open for settlement.

Carved out of Mississippi when it became a state in 1817, the Territory of Alabama increased rapidly in population, and on December 4, 1819, was admitted into the Union as the twenty-second state. Important towns sprouted along the Alabama River and played significant roles in the state's history. Montgomery, founded in 1817, became the state capital in 1846. In 1861 the river city was the scene of the South's secession convention and the inauguration of Jefferson Davis as President of the Confederate States of America. It served as the capital of the embryonic nation from February 4 to May 21, 1861, and earned its nickname as the "Cradle of the Confederacy."

Other towns included Claiborne, originally a fort constructed during the War of 1812 on a bluff called Alabama Heights, and Cahaba, located southwest of Selma, where the Cahaba River flows into the Alabama. Cahaba became the first state capital and prospered until 1826 when unpredictable floods and highly predictable politics resulted in the capital's removal to Tuscaloosa. The town of Cahaba served as a prisoner of war camp in 1863, and was known as Castle Morgan to 2,151 Union soldiers. Another flood in 1865 resulted in the removal of the county seat from Cahaba to Selma. A final irony occurred at the turn of the century: a former slave bought and dismantled what remained of Cahaba and shipped the salvageable parts downriver to Mobile.

Selma, nestled on bluffs above the Alabama, was founded in 1819 and served as a major ordnance center for Confederate military and naval forces. It fell to General James H. Wilson on April 2, 1865, when his Union forces defeated General Nathan Bedford Forrest. A century later Selma was the center of national interest as a result of the civil rights struggle there led by the Reverend Martin Luther King, Jr. The black leader conducted a historic freedom march from Selma's Edmund Pettus Bridge that spanned the Alabama River to Montgomery some sixty miles away.

Alabama's population in 1820 was 127,901, but the opening of new lands attracted so many people that by 1840 the state had 590,756 residents. Much of this growth was made possible by the development of steamboats for commercial and passenger service. Previously the river had been populated by canoes, rafts, flatboats with their one-way cargo of cotton (once unloaded at Mobile they were disassembled and sold as lumber), and long, narrow keelboats that could be pulled, rowed, and poled.

As many as six weeks were required for a keelboat to go downstream from Montgomery to Mobile. Yet when the *Harriet* inaugurated steamboat service in 1821, the trip was made in just ten days. From then until the first decades of the twentieth century, steamboats regularly plied the Alabama between Mobile and Montgomery, with some making runs north to Wetumpka on the Coosa.

Since the packets were woodburners, they made occasional stops at woodyards manned by muscular blacks. Hissing steam, the sternwheelers and the larger side-wheelers—some were over 250 feet long and had three decks—moved downstream picking up cotton at various landings as they went. They often carried as many as 150 to 200 passengers. After discharging their cargoes—from 1,500 to 3,000 bales—the packets made the return trip. Bearing such euphonious names as the *Medora, Sara Spann, Nettie Quill,* and *Jenny Lind,* the steamboats were laden with finery and luxuries. Their cargoes ranged from wines to silks, from whiskey and liquors to opium that was used for medicinal purposes. More practical goods included "plantation supplies": iron, nails, lumber, and hardware.

In the Black Belt, towns were few but many planters had landings on the river where the steamers stopped and loaded cotton. One traveler in the 1850s complained that "considerable delay was caused by our stoppages to take in cargo—for we were laden, at length, almost to the very water's edge." Despite his irritation he was fascinated by the loading process involving black slaves. "The men keep the most perfect time by means of their songs," he wrote. "These ditties, though nearly meaningless, have music in them, and as all join in the perpetually recurring chorus, a rough harmony is produced, by no means unpleasing." Quickly the job was done.

Frederick Law Olmstead, who later designed New York City's Central Park, booked passage aboard the *Fashion* on a run from Montgomery to Mobile. He wrote of how shipping went on day and night, for there were over 200 landings between the two cities. Often, if the loading was at night, passengers dined and danced in the steamer's gilded saloon while the slaves carried out their work by pitch-pine torches.

Besides Olmstead, several celebrated personages traveled on the Alabama River. The French hero Lafayette and his entourage (including a special band of musicians sent from New Orleans) in 1825 boarded the *Anderson* and steamed in triumph downriver to Cahawba, Claiborne, and Mobile. Louis Kossuth, the Hungarian freedom fighter, stopped at Mobile in 1852, boarded the *Pratt* and steamed upriver to Montgomery for a round of rallies and speeches.

Snags in the river, burst boilers, collisions, sandbars, and storms all took their toll. Negligent dredging operations further reduced the Alabama to shallowdraft traffic. Even more devastating, the railroad boom in the post Civil War decades ended significant commercial operations on the river. Ribbons of steel criss-crossed the state, and the Alabama River lapsed into somnolence, no longer a pulsating artery. Its period of economic romanticism had ended.

Despite the decline, a few businessmen and politicians maintained an interest in the river's economic possibilities. As early as 1878 Congress appropriated a million dollars to keep the channel open. It was argued that not only should commercial traffic between Mobile and Montgomery be revitalized, but also that the Coosa River north of the capital should be navigable to Rome, Georgia. This would create a waterway over 600 miles long, draining 22,800 square miles, and extending from the Piedmont to the Gulf. The Coosa-Alabama River Improvement Association was formed in 1890, but despite its many efforts, little progress was made. New impetus came in 1922 with the establishment of the State Docks at the Port of Mobile. Then in 1934 the United States Army Corps of Engineers made an extensive report to Congress outlining a series of locks and dams on the Alabama-Coosa system that would provide a nine-foot channel from Mobile to Rome.

The Great Depression and World War II caused further delays, but the Rivers and Harbors Act of 1945 appropriated $60 million for the initial work. Navigation, the production of hydroelectric power, flood control, the development of recreational facilities, and commercial expansion were compelling reasons for pushing the project. Bureaucratic frustration followed, but by the mid-1950s the Coosa-Alabama River Improvement Association, with headquarters in Montgomery, pushed harder than ever. Finally, construction was begun in the 1960s by the Mobile District Office of the United States Army Corps of Engineers.

Between 1963 and 1979 three dam and lock projects on the Alabama were completed. A navigation dam and lock was constructed at Claiborne, eighty-six miles above the river's mouth in Monroe County. At Millers Ferry, 145 miles upriver in Wilcox County, a combination navigation lock and hydroelectric power dam was built. Jones Bluff, located in Lowndes and Autauga counties 250 miles to the north, was the location for the third project, a combination navigation lock and power dam.

The Coosa River development was modified by Congress in 1954. A series of dams and reservoirs had been constructed previously by the Alabama Power Company. The Company was authorized to improve and expand its facilities, and in partnership with this effort, the Army Engineers was to build federal locks at these dams. Future navigation on the Coosa seems assured.

In the meantime, commercial barge transportation on the Alabama became big business. The long, low barges and the steady hum of diesel engines became familiar sights and sounds. The Alabama State Docks constructed three public docks with waterside grain elevators on the river, and various private industries built docks for oil, fertilizer, wood products, and building material.

Lakes impounded above the dams provided over 35,000 acres of water recreation area, and hundreds of millions of kilowatt hours of electric energy are produced annually. The long-neglected Alabama River throbs with life and energy once more.

FURTHER READING: Mill Frazer, *Early History of Steamboats in Alabama* (1907). E. G. Brown, *Rivers of Alabama*.

William Warren Rogers
William Warren Rogers, Jr.

The Apalachicola, Flint, and Chattahoochee

The Chattahoochee:
Source: Blue Ridge Mountains of northeast Georgia
Length: 436 miles
Tributaries: None of significance
Mouth: Joins the Flint at Jim Woodruff Dam and Lake Seminole on Florida-Georgia border
The Flint:
Source: Rises just south of Atlanta, Georgia
Length: 265 miles
Tributaries: None of significance
Mouth: Joins the Chattahoochee at Jim Woodruff Dam and Lake Seminole on the Florida-Georgia border
The Apalachicola:
Source: Lake Seminole on Florida-Georgia border, where Flint and Chattahoochee rivers merge
Length: 90 miles
Tributaries: None of significance
Mouth: Into Apalachicola Bay on the Gulf of Mexico, at Apalachicola, Florida
Agricultural Products of the Three Rivers area: Cattle, soy beans, cotton, peanuts, pecans, truck vegetables
Industries of the Three Rivers area: Lumbering, paper making, textiles, diversified industries

The Chattahoochee River rises in the Blue Ridge Mountains of northeast Georgia and flows southwest for 200 miles past Atlanta before turning southward. For another 200 miles the river forms the boundary between Georgia and Alabama. The Flint River also rises in north Georgia—just south of present Atlanta—and flows in a gentle arc to join the Chattahoochee from the east at the southwest corner of the state. There, at Jim Woodruff Dam and Lake

Seminole, the two rivers form the Apalachicola which meanders through farm, swamp, and forest land for ninety miles toward the bay of the same name in the Gulf of Mexico. These streams drain a fertile area of more than 19,000 square miles; they flow through the very heart of Dixie.

The farmlands produce cattle, soy beans, cotton, peanuts, corn, peaches, pecans, and truck crops. Pine and hardwood forests provide building materials and paper products. Factories, many once powered by the waters of the Flint and Chattahoochee, turn raw materials into finished textiles and lumber products.

The poet Sidney Lanier in his "Song of the Chattahoochee" described in lyrical cadence that river's rushing waters as they flowed out of the Georgia counties of Habersham and Hall:

Out of the hills of Habersham,
Down the valleys of Hall,
I hurry amain to reach the plain,
Run the rapid and leap the fall,
Split at the rock and together again,
Accept my bed, or narrow or wide,
And flee from folly on every side
With a lover's pain to attain the plain
Far from the hills of Habersham,
Far from the valley of Hall.

But Lanier's vision is darkened by the long shadows of a history of conquest, bloodshed, and exploitation.

The earliest record of human contact in the three-river region was left in 1528 by the

Spanish explorer Panfilo Narvaez. Nearly a century later missionaries from St. Augustine, Florida, entered the region; however, it was not until British traders from South Carolina began trading with the Creek Indians that Spain developed a serious interest in the river system. From 1680 until the close of the French and Indian War (1763) France, Spain, and England battled for the region's rich fur trade. When the fighting was over Spain and France were defeated and England remained uncontested in the region.

For only twenty years did the British flag fly over the newly acquired territory. American independence gave the United States a claim to the Chattahoochee and Flint rivers. At the same time, England returned East and West Florida to Spain (their boundary being the Apalachicola). The growing United States and the declining Spanish Empire did not settle their territorial disputes until Spain ceded the Floridas to the United States in 1821.

Even after the long struggle between European empires was ended, two strong Indian nations remained in the region: the Cherokees and the Lower Creeks. The Lower Creeks lived principally along the Chattahoochee with some along the Flint, as well as along the upper reaches of the Apalachicola. The Cherokees occupied the mountainous headwater areas of the Chattahoochee and Flint in north Georgia. When Spain regained the Floridas in 1783 it granted the British trading firm of Panton, Leslie, and Company permission to trade with these and other tribes. The firm established a branch at Prospect Bluffs on the lower Apalachicola and having negotiated favorable trade relations with the Creeks through their chief, Alexander McGillivray, carried on a vigorous trade with that tribe. Long pack trains loaded with trade goods made their way to Creek towns along the rivers and returned with furs. But the tranquility did not last for long.

First came William Augustus Bowles, a soldier of fortune, who had served with both the British and the Spanish. Bowles was by marriage a chief of the Creek nation. He tried to unite the Seminoles, Creeks, Cherokees, and Choctaws into one mighty nation called Muskogee with himself at its head, but his efforts were doomed to failure. Opposing him was the trusted Ameri-

can Indian agent, Benjamin Hawkins, who had an outpost on the Chattahoochee. Hawkins arrested Bowles and turned him over to the Spanish, who incarcerated him in a Cuban prison, where he died in 1806. The State of Muskogee died with him. After more reversals, the Creeks, by the Treaty of Fort Jackson (March, 1814), ceded a vast tract of territory along the lower Chattahoochee River.

During these same years (1812–1815) the British, as part of their strategy to win the War of 1812, landed a detachment at the mouth of the Apalachicola and proceeded upriver, building an earthwork position near one of the stores belonging to Panton, Leslie, and Company. In addition to the military contingent, more than 300 slaves and several hundred Indians congregated at the position. The major British thrust took place at New Orleans, however, where Jackson defeated them in January, 1815. Evacuating the Apalachicola post, the British turned the fort and their weapons and supplies over to the Indians and former slaves.

Renamed Negro Fort, this post became one of the largest concentrations of blacks and Indians in the old Southwest. From this center they raided into south Georgia and Alabama Territory. Since Spain was unable to police the region, in 1816 General Edmund P. Gaines and Colonel Duncan Clinch led a small American army to the Chattahoochee River. It was joined by the Creek Chief, Chilly McIntosh, and his warriors. The military force moved down the Chattahoochee from Fort Mitchell (below the future Columbus, Georgia) toward Negro Fort. Meanwhile two gunboats commanded by Sailing Master J. Loomis entered the Apalachicola River. He warped the vessels upstream to Negro Fort and began firing hot shot. The first red hot ball entered the magazine, and Negro Fort exploded with a terrifying roar. The explosion killed 270 of the more than 300 occupants. Negro Fort ceased to exist, and American forces withdrew.

Within two years after destroying Negro Fort, Andrew Jackson and General Gaines led a second invasion into Spanish territory. Jackson not only captured and executed Alexander Arbuthnot and Robert Ambrister, British merchants who traded with the Indians, but also occupied

St. Marks and Pensacola. Meanwhile James Gadsden, serving on Jackson's staff, mapped the area and built Fort Gadsden at the site of the old Negro Fort. A small contingent remained at Fort Gadsden until Spain ceded Florida to the United States. Today it is a state park.

By 1819, the long period of war and filibustering had ended but the Indians were more hard-pressed than ever. The Creeks and Cherokees faced an increasing number of American settlers. Wave after wave of land-hungry farmers rushed into the Flint and Chattahoochee valleys. By 1819, the Creeks and Cherokees still retained only a small portion of their once vast empire on the Chattahoochee River. When gold was discovered on treaty lands in northeastern Georgia the gold seekers would not be stopped—not even by the Supreme Court of the United States. The Cherokees were driven from their lands on the upper Chattahoochee. Only the Creeks remained encamped along the lower river.

The influx of farmers after the War of 1812 so swelled Alabama's population that she achieved statehood in 1819. Her farmers, building the cotton kingdom on plantation slavery, demanded the Creek lands along the Chattahoochee. Unwilling to await an orderly implementation of Jackson's removal plan, rapacious Americans moved to the Creek lands. The Army was called in to keep out the settlers. When one was killed by the soldiers, a small "Intruder's War" threatened to break out at Irwinton (the future Eufaula), Alabama. Even as Francis Scott Key negotiated with Alabama officials, the Indians attacked.

During this Creek War (1836–1837) hundreds of settlers fled to Columbus, Georgia, or Fort Mitchell in Alabama for safety. Travelers reported that every steamboat was filled with refugees. The fighting subsided as bands of Creek warriors were either captured by soldiers, or escaped into Florida. The old men, women, and children were rounded up, concentrated in camps, and then forcefully transported to Indian Territory west of the Mississippi River. The proud Creek nation ceased to exist along the banks of the Chattahoochee.

Americans rapidly filled the Creek lands, slavery flourished, and cotton was king. Apalachicola became the major seaport for the river sys-

tem; Columbus, Georgia, used Chattahoochee waterpower to become the commercial and manufacturing center of the Chattahoochee Valley; and Albany, on the Flint River, served a rapidly expanding agricultural economy. Steamboats plying the Apalachicola, Chattahoochee, and Flint rivers to the head of navigation at Columbus and Albany transported bales of cotton to distant markets and returned loaded with foodstuffs and manufactured goods. During the quarter of a century from Indian removal to the outbreak of the Civil War, the lands along the rivers provided prosperity for some. Others found only the agony of slavery.

More than 125 steamboats served the rivers during the three decades from 1830 to the Civil War. Almost all of these boats were shallow draft sidewheel steamers. The *Edwin Forest* drew less than twenty-four inches when loaded. Another such boat, the *Ben Franklin*, was noted for making the trip between Eufaula and Apalachicola "so long as the bottom of the river was moist." Steamboat wrecks were common. Most accidents were due to snags or to grounding on sand bars. These were minor incidents when compared with the major problem of fire and explosion. In most of these the cargoes were saved and few passengers suffered injury.

When slavery was threatened by outside forces, the river valley reverberated with demands for secession. Citizens eagerly followed their state into the Confederacy. They risked all to preserve the "peculiar institution." Apalachicola was blockaded by the Union steamer *Montgomery* on June 11, 1861, but not until April 2, 1862, did a Union party enter Apalachicola without firing a shot. The troops withdrew a few days later and Apalachicola remained free but uneasy for the remainder of the war.

Further north, Confederates retained control of the Chattahoochee until they were challenged for the upper river in 1864. General Joseph E. Johnston slowed Sherman's drive toward Atlanta but could not stop him. Johnston's strong defensive position on the west bank of the Chattahoochee northwest of Atlanta was weakened when some of Sherman's troops on June 17, 1864 forded the Chattahoochee above the Confederate position. Johnston, his right outflanked, could only retreat again. The Battle of Peachtree

Creek and the fall of Atlanta followed within weeks.

Columbus became the focal point of contact during the last days of the war. The city at the falls of the Chattahoochee River was one of the major manufacturing centers of the Confederacy. Almost a week after General Lee surrendered at Appomattox, General James Wilson attacked the Confederate positions on the Alabama side of the Chattahoochee. In the confusion of the night attack, the Confederates quickly gave way. Wilson's men crossed the bridges and the next morning, Wilson was in Columbus. But the war was over. The skirmish on the west bank of the Chattahoochee River was the last battle of the Civil War fought east of the Mississippi River.

Four years of war left scars on the river system. Columbus' industries were destroyed. The river boats that once plied the Chattahoochee, Flint, and Apalachicola were either sunk or in a state of disrepair. The harbor at Apalachicola was filled with silt and debris. In addition to the wartime damages the social and economic structure of the river valleys were destroyed. Risking all, the Confederates lost all, and had to rebuild. The plantation economy was replaced by tenant farming which, in time, developed into the destructive crop lien system, known as sharecropping.

The once rich lands of the Chattahoochee and Flint valleys were robbed of their fertility by overplanting and wasteful farming methods. Not until the New Deal of the 1930s did agricultural and conservation programs slowly turn the gullies and barren farms into productive acres. Farmers in the Chattahoochee and Flint river valleys planted pine trees, adopted scientific farming methods and raised cover crops to check erosion. The research of a former slave, George Washington Carver, resulted in the new crops of peanuts and soybeans, which replaced cotton and helped restore agricultural prosperity to the Chattahoochee and Flint valleys.

The river fleet was not rebuilt after the Civil War. Although the Army Engineers began to clear the streams of sand bars, snags, and wartime debris in 1873, only a small number of boats plied the waters. By 1900, river boats had ceased to perform a significant function on the rivers.

After the Second World War the Army Engineers restored transportation possibilities to the river system by erecting a series of locks and dams. Lake Blackshear on the Flint River north of Albany was built for flood control and conservation. The Jim Woodruff Lock and Dam at Chattahoochee, Florida, impounded the waters of both rivers to create Lake Seminole; when the water flowed out of the lake, it was as the Apalachicola. Another lock and dam at Columbia, Alabama, on the Chattahoochee, extended a nine-foot channel to Fort Gaines, a small Georgia community. The Walter F. George Lock and Dam, completed there in the 1960s, extended the navigable channel to Columbus.

The rushing waters of the Chattahoochee and Flint rivers have been slowed by the system of locks and dams. Indian villages and frontier towns have grown into modern urban areas. Woodland trails have given way to railroads and highways. Steamboats have been replaced by diesel-powered towboats and barges. A century after the last battle of the Civil War was fought, the farmers of the devastated region have developed a productive agricultural society. A few Indian mounds remain as a reminder of the past. A Civil War gunboat is preserved at Columbus, and a few highway markers point out historic sites.

Yet changes may come. Alabama and Georgia want the Army Engineers to straighten the rivers, deepen the channels, and build more locks and dams so that larger barges can serve the upstream population. But the Apalachicola flows through swamp and forestland where tupelo honey is taken, and it flows into Apalachicola Bay, one of the richest sources of marine life in the world, and a virtually unpolluted one. The Bay would face destruction if the swamps were dried, the floods ended, and a through channel replaced the present meandering river. Production of tupelo honey would cease. The conflict is a bitter one, with Florida fighting to keep the system as it is, and Georgia and Alabama campaigning for the barges. So far, Florida has won.

FURTHER READING: Isaac J. Cox, *The West Florida Controversy* (1918). Kathryn Abbey Hanna, *Florida, Land of Change* (1941).

Harry P. Owens

The Arkansas River

Source: Rises near Leadville, in the central Colorado Rockies
Length: 1,450 miles
Tributaries: Salt Fork, Cimarron, Verdigris, Grand, Canadian, and others
Mouth: Into Mississippi River at Desha County, Arkansas
Agricultural products: Melons, especially cantaloupes, alfalfa, hay, wheat, cattle ranching and feeding
Industries: None of significance

Few people are aware that for twenty-six years, 1820–1846, the boundary of the United States with Mexico was the Arkansas River. With a length of 1,450 miles it is the longest tributary in the Missouri-Mississippi system. It is also a river possessing many characteristics. Rising near Leadville, in central Colorado, it flows southward as a mountain brook but gathers tributary waters rapidly. In its first 125 miles it has turned east, dropped 5,000 feet, and entered the spectacular Grand Canyon of the Arkansas. This chasm, sometimes known as the Royal Gorge, is crossed by a world-renowned suspension bridge 1,053 feet above the river. A cable railway carries visitors down to the canyon floor where run tracks of the Denver and Rio Grande Western Railroad, suspended from the nearly perpendicular walls by in intricately engineered system of supports.

The Arkansas soon leaves the ten-mile long canyon and continues flowing southeast by east. When it reaches the iron and steel manufacturing center of Pueblo, it is on the Great Plains, and the once fast-flowing torrent enters a phase of slower, more tranquil movement. Its waters create a green, serpentine line in the arid Great Plains. In the valley fruits, vegetables, and melons are grown. Rocky Ford melons, especially cantaloupes, are nationally renowned. On into southeastern Colorado flows the Arkansas, interrupted in its flow by the John Martin Dam and Reservoir between Las Animas and Lamar. The river then continues into Kansas, past Garden City and Dodge City, approximately where it passes into a more humid climate. It then bends

northeasterly past Larned and Great Bend where it again turns southeasterly. It flows past Hutchinson and Wichita and then heads nearly due southward into Oklahoma.

It is in that state where the Arkansas, which during much of the year is nearly dry because of irrigation diversion, receives the waters of the Salt Fork of the Arkansas, flowing in near Ponca City from the west, and the Cimarron, also coming in from the west at Tulsa. Southeast of that city it receives the waters of the Verdigris and Neosho (known in Oklahoma as the Grand) which flow south out of Kansas, and the Canadian, which flows in from the west at Robert S. Kerr Lake near Fort Smith, Arkansas.

The stream continues southeastward into its namesake state, passing through Little Rock and Pine Bluff, finally meandering through a swampy, island-and-bayou studded mouth into the Mississippi in Desha County, some thirty to forty miles north (and across the river) from Greenville, Mississippi.

Such a long river, traversing four states, draining 160,500 square miles, falling 11,400 feet from source to mouth, is certain to have a long and complex history. The Ute Indians inhabited its mountain regions, Kiowa, Arapahoes, Comanches, Cheyennes, Pawnees, and Prairie Apaches in the Great Plains segment, and more sedentary Indians, such as the Wichita (probably the Quiviras of Coronado's time) and the Quapaws inhabited the lower reaches of the stream.

By a coincidence not even known at the time to the participants, Indians at two separate locations along the Arkansas first saw white men in the year 1541. Spurred into exploring what the Spanish called "the northern mystery" in search of riches and the Seven Cities of Cibola, two expeditions, one led by Hernando de Soto and the other by Vasquez de Coronado, touched the Arkansas. De Soto approached from the east, spent part of the years 1541 and 1542 in what is now the state of Arkansas and was probably as far upstream as Little Rock. The conquistidor left Arkansas by way of the

The Royal Gorge Bridge over the upper Arkansas is more than 1,053 feet above the riverbed. Note the railroad tracks on the right of the river. (Courtesy The Royal Gorge Bridge Company.)

Mississippi, where he died and was buried; about half of his force eventually reached safety again near present Tampico, Mexico.

Coronado, meanwhile, had come up from west-central Mexico, wintered just north of present Albuquerque, and the following spring with a select party of about forty men, headed northeast for Quivera, a place rumored to be teeming with gold and precious gems. The conquistador probably reached the Arkansas near present Ford, Kansas, having crossed the river's two principal tributaries, the Canadian and the Cimarron. He explored the Quivira lands to the north and east, failed to find gold or gems, and returned to Mexico. At one time, historians have estimated, the Coronado and De Soto parties were within two or three days' riding distance of each other. Although the Spanish reached the Kansas section of the Arkansas several times in the next sixty years (to 1601), the more significant Spanish activity to influence Arkansas River history was the settling of the upper Rio Grande and the founding of Santa Fe in 1610. The inhabitants of the upper Rio Grande country, so far removed from all other Spanish (later Mexican) cities, were a potential market for American trade goods, and the Spanish had silver, furs, and mules to offer in exchange. The lure of the Santa Fe trade was of great significance in the history of the Arkansas.

The next Europeans to manifest an interest in the river were the French. In 1682 Robert Cavelier, Sieur de La Salle paused at the mouth to take possession of the Arkansas and in 1686 his lieutenant, Henri de Tonti, established Arkansas Post on high land near the mouth. (Today Arkansas Post National Memorial is near the site.) The oldest white settlement in the Mississippi Valley, it was later colonized by John Law's Company of the Indies (a French speculative scheme), and was the first capital of Arkansas Territory, 1819–1821. It was captured by Union troops during the Civil War and renamed Fort Hindman.

The French desired trade with the southwest Indians and with the Spanish in their remote settlements, and to this end a number of daring trade expeditions headed into the Arkansas Valley in the ensuing years after 1819. Their ultimate destination was Santa Fe. Peter and Paul Mallet reached the New Mexico capital in 1739 and returned via the Canadian and Arkansas rivers the next year. Some of the Frenchmen who followed were not welcomed in Santa Fe; they were thrown in jail. Spanish fear of the French, who were more successful at trading with, and commanding the loyalty of, the Plains Indians, prompted several Spanish expeditions north from Santa Fe into and north beyond the Arkansas Valley to intercept their French rivals. After 1763, when Spain won Louisiana west of the Mississippi, her interest in the Arkansas and the Great Plains declined.

Then the United States acquired Louisiana. The Spanish took a very restricted view of the extent of the territory acquired and contested any American assumptions of ownership west of the Mississippi. When in 1806 Lieutenant Zebulon Montgomery Pike headed southwest from Fort Bellefontaine (near St. Louis) into the Arkansas region, already a Spanish force led by Lt. Facundo Melgares had been sent to intercept him. Though the Melgares expedition failed to find Pike, it did explore what was considered by them New Spain's northeastern frontier, met with Comanche, Pawnee, and Kansa Indians, and followed the Arkansas up to the mountains before returning to Santa Fe. Pike, with twenty-three men, struck the Arkansas near present Larned, Kansas. There he sent a small contingent downstream in two canoes. It arrived safely at the Mississippi—the first official American exploration of the lower Arkansas. Pike meanwhile worked on up the valley, siting the peak that bears his name on November 6, 1806; subsequently he led his small force into the mountains, floated back down the Arkansas through the Royal Gorge, but at about that point left the river and struck southward to the headwaters of the Rio Grande. There he built a stockade (south of present Alamosa, Colorado) and there the Spanish took him prisoner. Later he was returned to the States. The Spanish continued to be serious about keeping Americans out of New Mexico. Between 1806 and 1819 they imprisoned a number of American traders, often confiscating valuable peltry, horses, and provisions in the process.

By the Adams-Onís, or Florida Treaty of 1819, the Arkansas, from a point due north of the Red River, up the Arkansas to its source was decreed a part of the boundary between New Spain and the United States. Then Mexico overthrew the Spanish and from 1820 until 1846 the Arkansas was the boundary between the United States and Mexico.

Trade still attracted Americans into the Arkansas country. In 1821 a Missourian, William Becknell, was warmly welcomed with his trade goods at Santa Fe. This launched the colorful era of the Santa Fe Trail, immortalized in Josiah Gregg's *Commerce of the Prairies*. Each spring as soon as the grass was green the traders assembled their outfits at Council Grove, about 150 miles southwest of Independence, Missouri, on the Neosho River. Southwestward the creaking wagons moved at twelve or fifteen miles a day. They reached the Arkansas near the Great Bend. The trail followed along the north bank all the way to Bent's Fort (near present La Junta, Colorado—it has been reconstructed by the National Park Service), swerved south through Raton Pass, and so on to Santa Fe.

Becknell also forged the trail via the Cimarron Cutoff, which reduced the 800-mile trip by about 100 miles. It was a popular but dangerous shortcut. Indians and a long stretch without water were the chief dangers; Jedediah Smith, the mountain man, was killed by Comanches while searching for water on the dry Cimarron River.

Even as the Santa Fe Trail was becoming ever busier in the years prior to the Civil War, other events were taking place on the lower Arkansas. The forced removal of the Five Civilized Tribes from their homes in the southeast, their trails west, and final settlement in Indian Territory (now Oklahoma) brought activity along the river. It was already filling with emigrants from Kentucky and Tennessee with settlement reaching Little Rock. On Arkansas's western borders Fort Smith and, in eastern Indian Territory, Fort Gibson were established to maintain peace and keep the whites out. It was to be for many years a wild, desperado-infested country. "Hanging Judge" Parker dealt out a stern justice from his court at Fort Smith. Gradually, however, a southern cotton-growing society was established along the lower Arkansas.

The upper Arkansas of Kansas and Colorado had much more history to be made along its banks before it would settle into a cattle-raising and agricultural economy. California gold seekers used the Santa Fe Trail on part of their journey. When the Pike's Peak Rush took place in 1858–1859, a number of argonauts used the Santa Fe Trail as far west as Pueblo.

In the period following the Civil War there was ceaseless activity along the upper Arkansas. Hide hunters began a massive slaughter of the great southern herd of buffalo, while the Santa Fe Railroad pushed upstream, reaching the Colorado line by late 1872. The fierce Kiowa, Arapaho, Cheyenne, and Comanche witnessed the killing of the buffalo and the coming of the iron horse with anger and the Indians fought back. From forts Leavenworth, Dodge, Larned, Atkinson, Harker, Hays, Wallace, and other lonely outposts the army fought a continuous, bitter, bloody battle for possession of the southern plains. Yet the defeat of the Indians was never in doubt. They could never overcome such men as those buffalo hunters who holed up at Adobe Walls near the Canadian River in 1874 and killed fifteen of the attacking braves before the Indians called off the attack.

Hardly were the buffalo killed off and the Indians on reservations before the Texas cattle drives brought new excitement to the Arkansas River towns of Wichita, Hutchinson, and Dodge City. When the great drives ended, large cattle companies which grazed their herds on the public domain without cost came into the Arkansas Valley. Later the railroad sold hundreds of thousands of acres to homesteaders, establishing the agricultural pattern of settlement along the valley which has remained to this day. Meanwhile the Santa Fe pushed on into New Mexico via Raton Pass while the Denver and Rio Grande inched up the Arkansas, into the mountains and through the Royal Gorge to Leadville.

Leadville! Nearly two miles high, that community has had more fluctuations than most mining camps. It was founded in 1860 as Oro City and within two months had a population of 5,000. The gold-bearing sands were soon exhausted and the community was almost abandoned. Then, in the mid-1870s, silver was discovered and in 1878 the mining camp was rechristened Leadville; at its height it had a population of 15,000. It was there that H.A.W. Tabor grubstaked two lucky German prospectors; Tabor parlayed his stake into a fortune worth $9–12 million, only to lose it all when silver declined in price. Later other metals were discovered in the Leadville region. Today molybdenum, mined at nearby Bartlett Mountain, is the source of much of Leadville's prosperity; another source is tourism.

Back onto the Great Plains, the Arkansas was considered a natural resource to be exploited. Private interests first organized dam and irrigation companies. Soon Kansas and Colorado were engaging in litigation over their riparian rights. An Arkansas River Compact, approved in 1949, provides for the allotment of waters between the two states; other compacts involving Arkansas watershed states have been or are being negotiated. The John Martin Dam and Reservoir in southeastern Colorado is one result of such compromises.

Finally, difficult as it may seem, the McClellan-Kerr Arkansas River Navigation System, completed in 1971 with seventeen locks in its 440 miles, has opened navigation to Catoosa, a Tulsa suburb, and made landlocked Tulsa a seaport!

Indeed, the Arkansas River, little known outside of the region it traverses, is one of the most historically and economically important rivers in America.

FURTHER READING: Clyde Brion Davis, *The Arkansas* (1940). W. Eugene Hollon, *The Southwest, Old and New* (1961).

Richard A. Bartlett

The Black Warrior River

Source: Joining of Mulberry Fork and Locust Fork twenty miles west of Birmingham
Length: 178 miles
Tributaries: Daniels Creek
Mouth: Juncture with Tombigbee River near Demopolis, Alabama
Agricultural products: Cattle raising, cotton, peanuts
Industries: Coal mining, lumbering, iron smelting

From rivulets and creeks of six northern Alabama counties, the Black Warrior River forms and grows into one of the South's most scenic and commercially important rivers. Two main tributaries, the Mulberry Fork and the Locust Fork, meet in the heart of the Black Warrior basin 20 miles west of the industrial city of Birmingham, and from this point southward, the Warrior is a series of deep, dark green pools formed by dams. From its mouth at the confluence with the Tombigbee River near Demopolis to its furthest limit of navigation upstream is about 178 meandering miles. Over half of the river's upstream course has a fall of five feet per mile. The region through which it flows is rich in coal, timber, and iron ore and has become heavily dependent upon the river.

Englishman Henry Popple's 1733 map of the Alabama area gives the river two names, "Tascaloosa," and "Pedoge." The spelling of the first name appears on later maps as Tuscaloosa, but the name Pedoge is lost to history. A Creek Indian chieftain named Tusca-loosa met the Spanish explorer Hernando DeSoto and 600 of his conquistadors in west-central Alabama in 1540 with tragic consequences for the Indians and for the Spaniards. The English translation of the chief's name—Black Warrior—is carried by the river today.

Beginning about 12,000 years ago during the last ice age, the Alabama region has been occupied by four prehistoric Indian groups: the Paleo, Archaic, Woodland, and Mound Builders. The latter group, apparently related to the Mayan culture, became established on the Warrior River near the present town of Moundville about A.D. 600. Early 19th century maps show most of the Black Warrior River basin as part of the Choctaw Indian territory, but the Warrior basin also included a region of common hunting ground for Creeks and Choctaws within the divide between the Warrior and the Tombigbee Rivers.

Over 150 years after DeSoto, the French established trading territories which included the Warrior River basin and surrounding region. Western operations for this territory were centered at Fort Tombecbee on the Tombigbee ("Bigbee") River west of the Warrior. The name of Chevalier Antoine de la Mothe Cadillac, one-time governor of this isolated territory, graces many a luxury automobile that today plies his old trading territory; but, in general, the early French influence on the region and on its people was slight. No French place names appear on the late 19th century or modern maps of the region. A great number of place names of today are, instead, Indian names.

British control of the Warrior River basin began in 1763 at the end of the French and Indian War. With American independence in 1783, the area became part of the State of Georgia, which in 1802 ceded the region to the United States Government. It was then designated as part of Mississippi Territory. The region became a part of Alabama Territory in 1817, and part of the State of Alabama in 1819.

The first permanent white settlers came into upper parts of the river basin area before 1820, after Andrew Jackson had established grounds for removal of all Indians to lands further west by defeating the powerful Creek Indians. The native Choctaws were generally friendly, and the Black Warrior basin was only sparsely occupied by these people.

Le Clerk Milfort, a Frenchman who lived among Alabama Indians in the 1770s, described the Choctaw Indians of the Warrior River region favorably, but noticed that they seldom bathed and that the smoke of their lightwood fires (probably long leaf pine) made their bodies assume a sooty color (another possibility for the origin of the name Black Warrior).

Coal lies under the hills of the Black Warrior basin—over forty separate beds—according to today's geologists. If one knows where to look in steep-sided coves and hollows, the earth can be scratched away to expose a coal bed that may be a few inches or several feet thick. Before the dams were built, and when the river and tributary streams were low and water ran sparsely over the river's shoals, one could look down through the clear water north of the town of Tuscaloosa and see coal beds exposed in the stream bottom. In 1850, state geologist Michael Toumey observed, ". . . the coal measures are made up of hard and soft beds, the latter are worn down or washed away whilst the former are left, and hence the bed of the river (above the town of Tuscaloosa) consists of a succession of level reaches and shoals. In the level portions, beds of coal are generally found."

In the shallow, flat reaches of the shoals, during late summer and fall, farmers who had laid by their crops, pried the coal loose from the enclosing shale and loaded it on flatboats strengthened with gunwales of solid timbers. The "first class" boats had a capacity of about 2,000 bushels of coal, drew twenty or thirty inches of water, and cost around seventy dollars. When the winter rains came and the river rose to roaring torrents over the shoals, the river men pushed their stout, heavily laden and mostly uncontrollable flatboats into the rushing stream, aiming their flight downstream at points where they knew the water was deepest and where submerged rocks were fewest. The success of three months' work plus the cost of the boat, not to mention the lives of those aboard, depended on how well the farmers-turned-rivermen knew the shoals and how skillfully they could wrestle the steering oar. They knew that success was not always possible—that many boats (about one in seven) were dashed to splinters or caught sideways on rocks and tumbled about until broken and until the hard-won coal was snatched away by the current.

After the wild trip past the town of Tuscaloosa, the successful rivermen suddenly found themselves in quieter but roily water, moving rapidly downstream. From that point to Demopolis, some 120 river miles, the only things they had to watch for were snags, overhanging vines and trees, logs and sandbars. After Demopolis, there were almost 220 river miles on the Tombigbee and Mobile Rivers before reaching Mobile. There, the coal could be sold for $1 to $1.50 a bushel (or barrel), the same price as coal imported from Liverpool, England. At Tuscaloosa, the coal would bring only ten to twelve cents per bushel. In August, September, and October of 1849, about 200 persons, mostly farmers, were engaged in the coal trade in Alabama. Most of them worked the beds in the Warrior, but some were engaged at the three underground mines along the river.

Indians lived beside the Warrior for thousands of years and left no evidence of any effort to change it. Civilized man, however, developed a dissatisfaction, if not disgust, with the Warrior and its upredictable ways. The Warrior's channel from its mouth at Demopolis to Tuscaloosa was originally obstructed to such an extent that navigation at low water was impossible, and was extremely hazardous at high water. At Tuscaloosa, where the gradient of the river abruptly changes, the river level could rise as much as fifty feet in a few hours, after heavy rains upstream. To the early settlers, it seemed most important to make the river a dependable route for commerce. Without it, comfortable survival in the Alabama wilderness was not possible. Early projects to improve navigation consisted of an individual or two hacking away at fallen timbers over a short stretch of the river.

Two different plans for river improvement were put forth before 1849. One consisted of the construction of jetties intended to turn the water into a narrower, and thus deeper channel. This plan appeared good, but its execution was a failure. Jetties not connected with the bank and not reaching above moderately high water became a menace rather than a help. The second plan was carried out with an intention of removing rocks and dead timber from prominent points. Keeping the river clear, however, became a continuing problem; nevertheless, inhabitants of the region soon developed a dependence on the river, on which shallow draft steamboats carried cotton, coal and farm goods downstream, and life's necessities and luxuries upstream.

Navigation of the river stopped at Tuscaloosa where shoals barred passage upstream. Up to the time of the Civil War, the river had allowed the region to become very productive and quite prosperous—so much so that the area became a target for federal invaders during the war.

Prior to 1879, little had been done toward making navigation possible upstream from Tuscaloosa. Some work by men with government contracts was accomplished in 1835 and 1850, but the results were disappointing. Then, on March 3, 1879, Congress approved an act providing for a survey of the river from Tuscaloosa to the junction of Mulberry and Sipsey Forks. The survey report presented sufficiently favorable evidence to warrant further study and for the next eight years, investigations and studies continued.

In 1887, a project was adopted for the extension of navigation to Daniels Creek, about fourteen miles above Tuscaloosa, by a slack-water system of five locks with fixed dams, the minimum navigable depth to be six feet. In the spring of 1888, construction of the first lock on the river, Lock No. 10 at Tuscaloosa, was begun, and by 1895, work on Lock Numbers 10, 11 and 12 had been completed. In November 1895, the locks were opened to traffic; and on January 12, 1896, the first tow of coal passed down the river, reaching tidewater at Mobile eighteen days later.

The success of the first improvement was very encouraging to advocates of river transportation, and, in a few years' time, projects were approved by Congress providing for year-round navigable depth of six feet over the river from its mouth to the coal fields on the upper reaches. By 1908 four locks and dams carrying navigation above Tuscaloosa had been completed, three were under construction, and plans were prepared for still another.

The Black Warrior-Warrior-Tombigbee project was authorized by a series of fourteen Congressional acts from 1884 to 1945 to provide a navigation channel nine feet deep and 200 feet wide, where practicable, from Mobile to points on the Mulberry, Sipsey, and Locust Forks a few miles above Port Birmingham. The original system of seventeen dams and eighteen locks was constructed between 1895 and 1915. In 1940, a new lock and dam was completed at Tuscaloosa to replace three of the original small low-lift structures, and in 1955, a second new lock and dam was substantially completed at Demopolis to replace four more of the original structures.

Not satisfied with making navigation possible past Tuscaloosa to Port Birmingham, various proposals toward extending navigation up the Sipsey Fork, a tributary to Mulberry Fork, were brought about by advocates of river development. This resulted in the raising of Lock and Dam Number seventeen (renamed the John Hollis Bankhead Lock and Dam in 1955) to extend navigation into the Sipsey Fork. In 1956, the Alabama Power Company filed application for a project to construct Lewis Smith Dam on the Sipsey Fork, a tributary to Locust Fork. This project also included development work on Bankhead Dam.

The shoals are now covered by deep water behind dams, tug boats move coal downstream and iron ore and other materials upstream, and to many, the river appears to have reached a balance between nature and man. However, in the late 1970s, surveys of water quality along major ports of the river showed some grave problems. Stretches of the river were contaminated by sewage and industrial waste, and some tributary streams were showing affects of siltation resulting from coal strip mining. Activ-

ities to correct this situation are underway, although much remains to be done to bring the water quality back to acceptable standards.

Forests of pine and hardwood cover much of the river basin, supporting a prosperous timber and paper industry. A great variety of fish and game make the region ideal for sportsmen. Today, the river is not the same as it once was along some of its course; but the present-day traveler-adventurer would do well to travel the Warrior River. There is still much that remains there of America's original beauty.

FURTHER READING: J. H. Foshee, *Alabama Canoe Rides and Float Trips* (1975). E. G. Brown, "Black Warrior River," in *Rivers of Alabama* (1968).

Everett Smith

The Brazos River

Source: Merger of Double Mountain Fork with Salt Fork in north-central Stonewall County, about 160 miles west of Fort Worth, Texas
Length: 870 miles
Tributaries: Clear Fork, Paluxy, Bosque, Little, Yegus, Little Brazos, and Navasota rivers
Mouth: Into Gulf of Mexico at Freeport, southwest of Galveston
Agricultural products: Corn, soybeans, grain sorghum, cotton, rice, pecans, cattle
Industries: Diversified

In its long journey to the Gulf the Brazos crosses most of Texas's physiographic regions—the dry High Plains, West Texas, the Lower Rolling Plains, the West Cross Timbers, the Grand Prairie Rolling Hills, and the humid Gulf Coastal Plain. It has played a major role in Texas history from Spanish times to the present. It slices across Texas history as it does across the map of the state. The Republic's first capital was on its bluffs near the coast, and settlement moved up its long valley. Most of early Anglo-American history was made along the banks of the Brazos or across her many fords.

Unlike other major Texas rivers it lies solely

within the state boundaries, although it might be argued that in wet years normally dry arroyos of eastern New Mexico send some flow into the Brazos. With its three forks rising high on the Llano Estacado near Muleshoe, and its waters flowing 870 miles to the Gulf of Mexico at Freeport and Velasco, it cuts through the geographic center of the state. It is the third longest river in Texas, behind the Rio Grande and the Red rivers, drains some 42,800 square miles, and ranks fifth among Texas rivers with a yearly discharge of 5,301,000 acre-feet of water. Also, the Brazos is one of the most difficult rivers in the state to control, depositing an estimated 104,250 tons of topsoil a year in its meandering lower course. During the twentieth century it has frequently been referred to as the "Muddy Brazos," but a female traveler crossing the middle Brazos in the summer of 1858 recorded: "Our other adventure was fording the Brazos River, a broad, swift-running stream, so limpid that the stones in the water were clearly visible." She goes on to describe one of the very real dangers to early travelers, quicksand along its banks.

The upper Brazos is formed by three main branches called forks. Double Mountain Fork is the longest branch of the river. It rises about sixty miles northwest of Lubbock, near Muleshoe, and sometimes even draws waters from eastern New Mexico. Its several branches flow about 165 miles in a generally southeastward direction until in north-central Stonewall County—about 160 miles west of Fort Worth—the Double Mountain Fork is joined by the Salt Fork to form the Brazos River proper.

After the Salt's confluence with the Double Mountain Fork, the river makes a northerly swing before turning southward. Northwest of Fort Worth the main river is joined by the Clear Fork near the town of South Bend. At this point the Brazos has become a large river, and it once more begins a southeastward angle through the center of the state, being dammed at Palo Pinto, where Possum Kingdom Lake is formed, and south of Fort Worth, where Lake Whitney is impounded. South of Waco the Great Falls of the Brazos occur, after which the river winds southwest to the Gulf which it enters at Freeport, southwest of Galveston. On its way the river has served as the boundary for a number of counties.

In the course of its journey the Brazos is augmented by a number of important tributaries. The Paluxy River, famous for the Cretaceous dinosaur tracks over 130 million years old exposed in the river bed near Glen Rose, joins the Brazos southwest of Fort Worth. The Bosque River, after it is dammed to form Lake Waco, enters the Brazos. Little River, formed by the confluence of the Leon and Lampasas rivers, combines with the Brazos southeast of Waco near the old steamboat town of Port Sullivan. Stream flow is further increased by the addition of three tributaries quite close together: the Yegus, after forming Lake Somerville, comes in west of Navasota; and the Little Brazos and the Navasota. At this point the Brazos ceases to be a western stream and becomes a deep, broad eastern river.

The Brazos is actually three rivers in one. On the High Plains it is a typical southwestern stream, really a rather broad, shallow, sandy, intermittent creek whose waters are laden with heavy amounts of gypsum and sodium. This is short grass country. In places the hills are al-most barren except for clumps of scrub and tangled cedar thickets. It is said that before the coming of the white man and his overgrazing, Indian brush fires kept the cedar confined to only very rough and broken terrain, and lush grass grew everywhere.

The Middle Brazos was the most unspoiled portion of the stream until a number of reservoirs were created in the last few decades. Along its banks are wooded sections, frequently containing great pecan and oak trees, interspersed with more open country, and then broad prairies covered with deep verdant grass and a myriad of wildflowers. During the middle of the nineteenth century this was the center of buffalo hunting, and the great bison herds were joined by numerous wild cattle and mustangs.

As the river drops down into the Gulf Coastal Plain it becomes a deep, broad, rolling southern river, flowing past leveed corn, soybean, grain sorghum, cotton, and rice fields as well as great pecan orchards and expansive cattle grazing lands. As one writer has described the Lower Brazos: "Down at the River's mouth the traveler meets with tangled wildwood, morass and forests with trees of giant size." Here is where Stephen F. Austin's settlements were made in 1820, and in ante-bellum times the rich soil and salubrious climate nurtured prosperous and productive sugar and cotton plantations along the banks and back from the river. Today a few of these fine plantation homes still survive, but most fell into decay and ruin long ago.

The first recorded European contact with the Brazos River was during the Alonzo de Piñeda mapping expedition of the Texas coast in 1519. About a decade later Cabeza de Vaca would have had to live along its banks and cross it several times during his sojourn on the coast. About 1541 Francisco Vásquez de Coronado was the first white man to see the upper reaches of the river when he located potable water at Double Mountain, and extracted much needed salt from the Salt Fork. Over a hundred years later Sieur de La Salle and others established the nature of the meandering lower course of the river.

Cartographic work on the upper reaches was begun by the Albert Pike expedition in 1832, at which time he mapped and named the Salt Fork. Randolph B. Marcy, the famous western military explorer, led many expeditions into the region beginning in 1847 and continuing after the Civil War. Marcy's activities, coupled with such expeditions as M.K. Kellogg's of 1872, fully revealed the upper drainage basin of the Brazos River.

Perusal of old maps reveals considerable confusion over the location of the real Brazos de Dios during the early days of Spanish suzerainty. Nueces and Trinidad were used by some cartographers as names for the present-day Brazos, and sometimes the Brazos and Colorado (of Texas) became reversed; however, well before the end of the eighteenth century the name Brazos was well established. The Frenchman La Salle in the late seventeenth century recorded the Caddo Indian name as Tokonohomo, and applied his own of Maligne.

The source of the present name is even more confusing than what river is really the original Brazos. One legend has it that the Coronado expedition was about to perish from thirst when an Indian guide led them to water at Double Mountain, and the Spanish named the stream El Rio de Los Brazos de Dios, because they had been saved from death by the Arms of God. Another story has it that a ship off the Texas coast ran out of drinking water, the crew was on the verge of death, when the ship crossed a streak of discolored brackish water, followed it to its source, which was the mouth of the Brazos, and in thankfulness to God named the river Brazos de Dios. One legend also adds to the buried treasure stories. A group of Spanish gold miners in the San Saba region was forced to abandon its mines due to the terrible drought of 1760. Indians told them of a village to the east, near modern Waco, on a river which never went dry. In desperate straits, they were forced to bury most of their gold bullion during the long march. Finally, after much hardship and death, they reached the river and named it Brazos. There are many other legends about individuals saved from thirst and hostile Indians and so naming it Brazos de Dios. Documentation is such that one can select the story one prefers without fear of serious challenge.

In 1831 Albert Pike was informed by knowledgeable people that until the great drought of the mid-eighteenth century, there was confusion about which was the Brazos and which was the Colorado. The Colorado ceased flowing and almost dried up, while the Brazos continued to flow, thus proving that the present Brazos was the original. This story seems to be confirmed by the data presented on the various maps of the period.

Spain showed little interest in the Brazos River except as to where the best fords were located. They were important in maintaining communications between the San Antonio settlements and those in East Texas. Modern Texas began in December, 1821, when the schooner *Lively* arrived off the mouth of the Brazos with the first of Stephen F. Austin's "Old Three Hundred," his first settlers. Josiah H. Bell moved up the Brazos a few miles and established a plantation near present East Columbia. The town of Velasco sprang up at the mouth of the river and it was where, in 1832, that the first shot of the Texas Revolution was fired. In 1823 San Felipe de Austin was founded at the Atascosito Crossing and soon became the center of the Austin colony. (Today it is west of Houston and just north of Interstate 10.) All of the early Texas governmental conventions were held at San Felipe and it was the provisional capital for several years. San Felipe was by-passed when the Convention of 1836 convened at Washington-on-the-Brazos, near Navasota, and when San Felipe was burned during the Texas Revolution it never recovered.

Early travel accounts all attested to the salubrious climate and the rich, fertile soil along the Brazos, and especially along the second bottoms not subject to annual overflow. It was a genuine flood plain soil, capable of producing great crops of cotton and sugar cane without threat of exhaustion. The ante-bellum cotton and sugar plantations established along the banks of the Brazos were among the finest in Texas, and were the homes of some of the wealthiest and most influential men in the state. Jared Groce had several plantations in the Hempstead region, and in the mid-1820s built the first cotton gin and shipped the first cotton out of Texas. One of the finest plantations was "Orozimbo," the home of Dr. James A. E. Phelps, which also served as the place of confinement for Santa Anna following his capture at San Jacinto.

Stephen F. Austin spent considerable time at his sister's plantation, "Peach Point," and was originally buried there.

Steam navigation reached the Brazos in 1830 when the *Ariel* began serving the plantations along the lower reaches of the river. In 1840 the Middle Brazos was opened to steam transportation by the *Mustang* which tied up at Port Sullivan near present Cameron. Although boats would eventually reach as far upriver as the Great Falls near present Marlin, practical navigation ended at Hidalgo Shoals just above Washington and 250 river miles from the Gulf. In fact, San Felipe, some 160 river miles from the mouth, marked the upstream limits of regular service. Everything above that point was seasonal high water navigation. Railroad development during the latter part of the nineteenth century drove the Brazos steamboats into oblivion.

Periodic flooding, with major inundations occurring in 1842, 1899, and 1913, cost the people of Texas great property losses and many lives. Several attempts to make the Brazos a navigable stream by a series of locks failed largely due to the flooding conditions every few years. The Brazos River Authority was created in 1929 for the primary purpose of flood control. While the river can still be awesome at flood stage, the many dams and reservoirs built since World War II prevent flooding on the scale of earlier times.

The Brazos River today is a major factor in Texas life just as it was in times past. In its long course it winds through or near a number of the state's leading metropolitan centers. Several leading universities stand on its banks. The many reservoirs in its valley serve as sources of power, water, and places of recreation for growing urban centers. And finally, even though the sugar cane and much of the cotton have disappeared, the Brazos Valley remains one of the richest agricultural regions in the State of Texas.

FURTHER READING: John Graves, *Goodbye to a River* (1960). Julien Hyer, *The Land of Beginning Again: The Romance of the Brazos* (1952). Nath Winfield and Pamela Puryear, *Sandbars and Sternwheelers: Steam Navigation on the Brazos* (1976).

Victor H. Treat

The Coosa River

Source: Juncture of Oostanaula and Etowa rivers at Rome, Georgia
Length: 286 miles
Tributaries: Chattooga River
Mouth: Merges with Tallapoosa River north of Montgomery, Alabama, to form Alabama River
Agricultural products: Tobacco, cotton, poultry
Industries: Cattle raising, textiles, rubber, steel, hydroelectric power

The Coosa River is formed in northwest Georgia within the limits of the city of Rome. Here two streams bearing the euphonious Cherokee names of Oostanaula and Etowah merge into the Coosa. The river flows west about twenty-five miles, crosses into Alabama, and then flows in a southwesterly direction, finally joining the Tallapoosa River just north of Montgomery to form the Alabama River. The Coosa is about 286 miles long.

From Rome, Georgia, down to Gadsden, Alabama, the Coosa is navigable for shallow-draft boats. Then the river breaks into rapids which increase in intensity as the Coosa approaches the coastal plain, falling 248 feet in one span of fifty miles.

The soils and topography of the Coosa Valley are a result of the geologic activity which folded the rocks at different angles. Deposits of iron ore, limestone, coal, clay, talc, marble, graphite, bauxite, and other minerals enrich the valley between the Georgia-Alabama border and the

Coosa's confluence with the Tallapoosa. The Valley also receives one of the heaviest concentrations of rainfall of any river in America.

The Indian heritage in the Coosa Valley is as varied and rich as its natural resources. "Coosha," an Indian word meaning reed, was the name of a Muskogean tribe, also known as Creeks, inhabiting high ground along the river. From the earliest white man's presence, Creeks and Cherokees shared the Coosa's waters although much of the time they were enemies. Their canoes plied the river in a lively trade both to the south and north of their territories.

The Sieur de Bienville dispatched troops up the Alabama River and established Fort Toulouse in 1714 at the sacred Creek site called Hickory Ground between the juncture of the Coosa and Tallapoosa. The Frenchman left Captain Marchand to command the fort; the captain subsequently married an Indian princess named Sehoy. Their daughter in turn married a Scot trader named Lachlan McGillivray. Their son, Alexander, though he had more white than Indian blood coursing through his veins, lived as a Creek and precipitated the most tragic epoch in the Coosa's history.

For a time Alexander McGillivray engaged in a flourishing trade with British commercial agents and Spanish officials in Florida, playing Spain and America against each other in an attempt to preserve Creek hegemony in the lower Coosa Valley. Later Charles Weatherford, another grandson of Marchand and Sehoy, reluctantly led the Creeks into battle in defense of their lands against American encroachment. The Fort Mims massacre in August, 1813, brought Andrew Jackson into the upper Coosa Valley in pursuit of the Creeks. After establishing Fort Strother at Ten Islands, near present Pell City, Jackson met the Creeks at Horseshoe Bend on the Tallapoosa and defeated them (March 1814). Later that year he forced them to sign away 23 million acres of land as part of the Treaty of Fort Jackson. Most of the land was west of the Coosa River.

With the Indians cowed, white settlers now entered the Coosa country. To many of them the Coosa was their water road to the outside world, and some were soon earning their living on the river. Such a man was John Lay who construct-

ed a cabin near the village of Gadsden in the early 1800s. His flatboats transported tobacco, cotton, corn, honey, whiskey, cattle, and poultry to the Gulf. His son, Cummins Lay, became the most reputable steamboat navigator on the upper Coosa, making history during the Civil War by piloting the *Laura Moore* all the way from Rome across the rapids down to near Montgomery. Hiding along the banks from federal troops, he waited until flood season swelled the river and then steamed to his destination.

At the height of the steamboat era, just prior to the Civil War, as many as eight steamers plied the upper Coosa. Such graceful boats as the *Magnolia*, *Coosa*, *Gadsden*, and *Laura Moore*, drawing only three feet of water, carried an ever-increasing cargo of cotton down river. The coming of the railroads together with the depressed period following the Civil War brought an end to vigorous steamboat transportation in the late nineteenth century, although the *Annie M.* remained a Coosa River landmark until she sank in 1933.

The first proposals for harnessing the Coosa were adopted by the federal government about 1872 and consisted of plans for thirty-one new low-lift locks and dams. Four locks were built on the upper end of the rapids before work was abandoned in 1890. This initial program for river development changed drastically when John Lay's grandson, William Patrick Lay, built a hydroelectric plant on Will's Creek, a Coosa tributary near Gadsden. In 1906 he organized the Alabama Power Company with capital stock of $5,000 and became its first president.

Lay also established the Coosa-Alabama River Improvement Association and served as its first president. When the first survey to determine the Coosa's potential for hydroelectric power and barge traffic was unsatisfactory, a more favorable survey was conducted under Colonel H. B. Ferguson of the United States Army Engineers. Ferguson's report went along with Lay's own concept of a multipurpose project involving dams and locks for electric power, flood control, and navigation; there would also be reservoirs constructed on the Etowah and the Tallapoosa, Coosa tributaries, which would be used for the production of electric power.

Implementation of the plan was soon under

way. The first major dam, built with private capital and appropriately named Lay Dam, was completed in 1914. In 1923 Mitchell Dam at Duncan's Riffle was finished, and in 1928 Jordan Dam a few miles from Wetumpka went into operation. Meanwhile, Martin Dam on the Tallapoosa had created one of the largest manmade reservoirs in the world. Locks 1–5 also were constructed between Gadsden and Talladega, and lock 12 opened at Alexander City.

In 1954 the Alabama Power Company announced a second major phase of Coosa construction. The $194 million program, one of the largest ever undertaken using private capital, was scheduled for completion by 1968. By the late 1960s the Coosa, which had been called the "second greatest undeveloped waterway in America" fifteen years earlier, boasted four new dams: Weiss at Centre, H. Neely Henry near Ragland, Logan Martin near Pell City, and Walter Bouldin, connected by canal to Jordan at Wetumpka. The Coosa dams could generate two million kilowatts, and the four new dams ended the disastrous river floods by impounding 635,000 acres of water.

All of this contributed little to navigation. In 1945 Congress proposed the construction of a navigable waterway from Rome, Georgia, to Montgomery, but dredging of the nine-foot navigation channel bogged down for lack of funds. The Coosa-Alabama River Improvement Association and new industries in the valley lobbied during the 1960s and 1970s for further navigational development. Gadsden, a Coosa River industrial town hard hit by slumps in the textile, rubber, and steel industries, experienced unemployment as high as twelve percent in the 1970s. Beginning in the fall of 1978, Congress authorized the Corps of Engineers to begin designing the Coosa-Alabama Waterway, the first step toward construction of the project anticipated for the 1980s. The major beneficiary would be Gadsden's Republic Steel Company which imports its iron ore from South America.

The proposed waterway brought objections from environmentalists who pointed to the reduction of water quality as a result of inevitable spills and increased barge traffic. Their objections highlighted a historical change in the nature of the river during the twentieth century: the dams, locks, and hydroelectric machinery

had changed the Coosa's aquatic environment. This has brought about the extinction of many species of unionid mollusks (a family of mussels).

Alabama rivers, in general, contained a greater diversity of these fresh water invertebrates than any other state. In the 1800s E. R. Schowalter, a physician living in Uniontown, Alabama, collected mollusks on the Coosa and sent some of them to Isaac Lea who used them to define new species; other specimens ended up in the Alabama Museum of Natural History. From this collection, Calvin Goodrich produced a number of papers on the aquatic mollusks of Alabama which established that the Coosa River had more endemic species than any other river in North America.

In a 1944 publication, Goodrich described the huge original colonies, before concluding sadly that many of the exotic types collected first by Schowalter were now extinct. Dams had backed water over the shoals where they thrived and created silt-accumulating lakes; at least fifty endemic species had perished. Collectors in 1959 could find no specimens of several endemic genera collected earlier, and the impoundment of the Coosa by Logan Martin Dam destroyed additional species on the Choccolocco Creek, a tributary near Anniston. The Lock 3 dam inundated all the remaining rapids known historically as Ten Island Shoals and destroyed additional species on Big Canoe Creek. Although some Coosa tributaries still contained relict populations of the endemic species above their flooded mouths, even these were disappearing rapidly.

Industrial pollution of the river resulted in a conference on Coosa problems in August, 1963, which proposed cleaning up the worst industrial polluters near Rome. Such efforts did not reverse the trend, and in the early 1970s mercury accumulations in fish became so hazardous that a fishing ban was declared for portions of the river.

Citizens of the Coosa Valley share America's ambivalence over the fate of her great rivers. The proposed Coosa Waterway will create 1,000 jobs for ten years and will encourage new industries and open dormant mines. Such projects are welcomed by many valley residents, but others disagree.

One passionate Coosa defender was Tom

Sims, the son of a Coosa steamboat captain and creator of "Popeye the Sailor" and "Wimpy." Another was the late Kelly Fitzpatrick, a Wetumpka river artist and historian who joined ecologists and sportsmen who demanded that the river be preserved against the relentless and destructive demands for "progress." Nothing less than the future of the historic Coosa River is at stake in these debates.

FURTHER READING: Hughes Reynolds, *The Coosa River Valley: From DeSoto to Hydroelectric Power* (1977).

Wayne Flynt

The Neches River

Source: Rises about sixty miles east of Dallas, Texas
Length: 260 miles
Tributaries: None of significance
Mouth: Gulf of Mexico below Beaumont, Texas
Agricultural products: Rice
Industry: Petrochemicals

To the casual traveler passing through Beaumont, Texas, the muddy brown Neches River appears as a deep, sluggish workhorse of a waterway. Few clues exist which hint at the romance of its former beauty. This once rustic and picturesque river now serves as the maritime Main Street of a petrochemical and industrial complex stretching dozens of miles along its banks. The river forms the transportation backbone of a region rich in lumber, rice, oil, gas, and chemical production. Refineries, chemical plants, docks for oceangoing freighters and tankers, shipyards, and warehouses line the banks near its mouth. Groves of pecan, cypress, and oak which once shaded its tranquil waters as they flowed into Sabine Lake and on to the Gulf of Mexico, have long since disappeared. The river has fulfilled its destiny as a vital natural resource for a growing coastal region dependent upon commerce, industry, and transportation.

The historical destiny of the Neches, like all rivers, has been determined by its geography. A map of east Texas confirms the river's significant location. It makes a leisurely transition along its course from a meandering stream to a major industrial waterway. Rising in the blacklands approximately sixty miles east of Dallas, the river flows gently to the southeast for 260 miles, where its waters pass into Sabine Lake on the Texas-Louisiana border. The waters of Sabine Lake flow through Sabine Pass, a deepwater channel, into the Gulf of Mexico: geographers consider the Neches as flowing into the Gulf. Along its journey the Neches forms the boundary between thirteen Texas counties and, although Beaumont is the only major city on its banks, the river passes near the inland towns of Tyler, Palestine, Lufkin, and Jasper. Traversing the eastern coastal plain of Texas, the Neches has a drainage area of approximately 10,000 square miles. Several dams on its lower reaches store water for irrigation uses and water supply for nearby cities.

The river takes its name from the Neche Indians who called it the Snow River and lived along its banks. The Neche seems to have been a peaceful, sedentary tribe. They raised corn, beans, sunflowers, melons, and a strain of harsh tobacco. They also hunted the deer, turkey, and other small game which abounded along the rivers of east Texas. Like other tribes of the Hasinai group of which they were a part, the Neche had a relatively sophisticated social organization. Each village had its hereditary chief. The various villages formed a loose confederation with a head chief and a head priest, who maintained a central fire in a temple somewhere to the east of the river.

Much of what is known about the Neche Indians must be based upon conjecture since they did not fare well with the Europeans. La Salle and his French explorers visited the Neche in 1687, ending their peaceful existence. With the French as their allies, the Neche took advantage of the military power of their visitors to attack a neighboring tribe with whom they had long had a rivalry. Although temporarily a dominant force, the local power of the Neche ended with the Spanish arrival. Friars from New Spain came to the river in the early 1700s, bestowing upon it the name which it carries to this day. They subdued the Neche and at a site west of the present Alto, Texas, founded the mission of San Francisco de los Neches in 1716. Although it failed in the late 1720s, European dominance of the region continued.

By the middle 1700s Spaniards and Frenchmen were regular visitors to the Neches River. The Neche Indians began to lose their identity as all of the tribes of the region blended together in response to increasing European contact. Cattle raising fostered by the Spanish depended upon the rich grasslands found along the upper portions of the river. The French, operating out of Natchitoches and the Louisiana settlements, were also known to camp along the Neches. The closing years of the eighteenth century marked the final years of rustic tranquility along the river. Henceforth, the Neches River would play a major role in the sweep of history across the Texas frontier.

The role began at a diplomat's bargaining table far from the lush river valleys of east Texas. In 1819, American Secretary of State John Quincy Adams negotiated the Adams-Onis Treaty with Spain which, among other things, set the western boundary of the Louisiana Purchase at the Sabine River. This failed to please many Americans who wanted to claim parts of Spanish Texas for the United States. These expansionists argued that the Neches, farther to the west, and not the Sabine, was the true western boundary of Louisiana mentioned in the treaty. They noted that the document stipulated that the river serving as the boundary had cypress growing along its coastal reaches. The Neches had such cypress growths, while the Sabine River did not. Although these claims seemed tenuous to many at the time, from 1819 onwards many Americans claimed the area between the two rivers as United States territory. The Neches Boundary Dispute, as this claim was known, became a moot question in 1836 with the establishment of the Republic of Texas.

The Texas Revolution began a new chapter in the history of the Neches River. American immigrants came into the region by the hundreds in the 1820s and 1830s. Mexico, after winning her own independence from Spain early in the 1800s, suddenly realized the threat which an expanding United States presented to her northern territories. Many Americans, especially southerners, advocated taking Mexican territory by force. In an effort to forestall this, Mexico offered land to Americans who would take a loyalty oath to the Mexican government and settle in east Texas. Stephen Austin led the influx of Americans into the area in 1824. Hundreds followed during the next decade, with the result that Anglo-Americans began to populate the river valleys of east Texas.

The Neches River also added new Indian inhabitants at about the same time the Americans arrived. The discovery of gold in Georgia coupled with President Andrew Jackson's Indian removal policy forced some of the southeastern Cherokee westward into Texas. Many settled in the Neches River area, especially along the northern parts in the blacklands belt. Led by Chief Bowles, they made their primary settlement near present-day Dallas.

Friction soon developed between the Cherokee, other Indians, and the American settlers as each group sought to control the rich river bottom lands of the region. These pressures erupted into open warfare after the Anglo-American victory over Mexico and the foundation of the Republic of Texas. Texans felt that the Cherokee were being influenced by Mexican agents who, anxious to regain Texas for Mexico, assisted the Indians in maintaining opposition to the Republic. In late 1838, Thomas Jefferson Rusk and his men attacked an Indian village in an effort to capture a Mexican agent supposedly hiding there. The Cherokee responded by initiating a series of raids on Anglo settlements.

By the summer of 1839, the Cherokee War was a reality. A Texan force of 500 men, raised especially for dealing a decisive blow to the Cherokee, attacked the Indians at their main village. A substantial group of warriors including Chief Bowles escaped and made their way to the banks of the Neches, where they made their final stand on the river several miles from present-day Tyler. There, on July 15 and 16, occurred the Battle of the Neches. The Indians were defeated, Chief Bowles met his death on the battlefield, and the surviving Cherokee warriors fled.

The end of the Cherokee menace guaranteed the peaceful settlement of the Neches River valley by small farmers and stockmen. Tyler, the major town near the upper reaches of the river, was organized in 1847. It soon became the center of a fertile agricultural region with cotton and corn as the principal crops. A flourishing lumber industry developed down river in the rich timber lands. The growth of the entire Neches region was assisted by the increasing prosperity of Beaumont at the river's mouth.

Beaumont had been founded in 1838. The town soon became a trade center of the Gulf coast. Cattlemen, lumbermen, farmers, and cotton planters all along the Neches came to look upon Beaumont as their outlet to world markets. River captains sailed up the Neches as far as possible, thereby adding to the region's prosperity. A bar at the mouth of the river and several shallow sand bars, however, made river navigation difficult. Nevertheless, the Neches River had become a major area of cotton farming and timber harvesting by the end of the 1800s. The lower reaches of the river were well on their way to becoming a transportation resource.

The opening days of the twentieth century guaranteed the river's modern destiny. By 1900 the search for new oil fields had extended to the Texas Gulf coast. In that year Anthony F. Lucas began drilling a test well at Spindletop near Beaumont. On the morning of January 10, 1901, one of the most legendary events in the history of the oil industry occurred at the Lucas well.

About 10:30 that morning, as the drilling crew busily lowered a new bit into the well casing, intense pressure from below blew the pipe casing, swivels, and rotary tackle upwards through the top of the derrick. As surprised workmen scrambled for safety, the well rocked with an intense explosion. The earth rumbled. Oil, gas, drilling mud, rocks, and pieces of machinery shot hundreds of feet into the air with a roar that was heard for miles. A black gusher of crude oil shot into the air high above what remained of the derrick.

For the next six days a majestic, rich geyser of oil spewed 75,000 barrels of crude a day into a huge black lake which had formed around the well. The modern Texas petroleum industry had been born, and the Neches River was its first home. The areas around the river provided many men with their fortunes. Land in the Spindletop field was soon selling for as much as $200,000 an acre while new oil companies such as Gulf and Texaco were organized to pump the rich deposits.

Oil brought to the Neches River and Beaumont a prosperity previously unimagined. It caused a major population influx into the coastal area as oil companies built collecting facilities, docks, and refineries. This economic boom also provided the incentive for making the lower reaches of the Neches into a deep water port for oceangoing vessels. In the 1890s Arthur E. Stilwell, founder of the town of Port Arthur, dreamed of a deep-dredged system of channels along the Neches and Sabine rivers which would link them to the Gulf of Mexico through Sabine Pass. The production at Spindletop Oil Field demanded that Stilwell's dream become a reality.

By 1912 the network of deep-dredged channels was virtually complete. The Sabine-Neches waterway begins with a deep channel across the bar of Sabine Pass at the Gulf of Mexico and extends up Sabine Lake, where it splits into two arms. One provides deep-water access for Beaumont, while the other extends seventeen miles to the town of Orange.

By the 1930s this waterway had become one of the major industrial centers of Texas. The depression decade also completed petroleum's domination of the Neches River when, in 1930, a major oil field was discovered near Tyler on its upper portions. This new field, known as the East Texas, quickly became the largest and richest in the world. From 1931 to 1944, its production was double that of any other oil field in the world. Not until the discovery of the Middle Eastern deposits did the East Texas field cease to be the globe's largest. Hence, by the middle of the twentieth century, the Neches River had completed its transition from an Indian hunting ground to the River of Black Gold.

FURTHER READING: Walter P. Webb, Ed., *The Handbook of Texas* (2 vols., 1952); Walter Rundell, Jr., *Early Texas Oil* (1977).

Light Townsend Cummins

The Neosho-Grand River

Source: Rises in Morris County, in east-central Kansas

Length: About 460 miles

Tributaries: None of significance

Mouth: Becomes Grand River at Kansas-Oklahoma border and as the Grand flows into Arkansas River at Muskogee, Oklahoma

Agricultural products: Corn, wheat

Industries: Petroleum, cement, ceramic materials (clay), coal, lead

The Neosho River originates in Morris County, Kansas. The Neosho Unit or valley is an elongated area of about 6,300 square miles. The river itself flows south-southeastward down the eastern third of Kansas and Oklahoma and joins the Arkansas River near Muskogee, Oklahoma. The total length of the river is between 450–500 miles. After the river flows into Oklahoma it is known as the Grand. The principal tributary of the Neosho in Kansas is the Cottonwood River, which originates in Morris County and joins the Neosho in Lyon County east of Emporia. At their junction, the Cottonwood has several times the drainage area of the parent stream. From this junction to the Oklahoma state line, a distance of approximately 100 miles, the valley averages about 25 miles in width and includes all or parts of 19 counties in Kansas. The Neosho is the largest tributary of the Arkansas River on the north, and under federal law is considered a navigable stream.

The Neosho Unit comprises about eight percent of the area of Kansas and nearly the same percent of the state-wide population. Economic activities are varied, including pasture and farm land, some mineral production, and in the southern portion of the state miscellaneous, small manufacturing concerns. The Unit is well served by railroads, state and federal highways, and local farm-to-market roads. While some of the valleys of the numerous tributaries are quite narrow, the land is hilly to rolling, with much of the upland still in native grass.

On approximately the upper fourth of the Neosho, the stream slopes exceed ten feet per mile, but decrease to less than 2 feet per mile for the remainder of the distance in the state. The flood plain of the Neosho River has a maximum width of five miles near Burlington, Iola, and Humboldt, Kansas, and narrows to approximately three-fourths of a mile.

The Unit has a greater variety of minerals than any other area in Kansas. Currently, nine minerals of economic importance are found: oil, gas, cement, ceramic materials (clay), coal, lead, zinc, stone, sand, and gravel. Oil and gas are economically of importance. Gas was first discovered in 1893 near Iola, enabling the city to become an important industrial center, with zinc smelters, iron and brass casting foundries, brick and tile plants, and cement all taking advantage of the free fuel supplied by the city. At the peak of gas production in 1907, the 300 gas wells in the Iola field were producing 750 million cubic feet per day. In a brief period of three years the extravagant use of gas, including a tremendous amount of waste, depleted the gas to the point where supplies were insufficient to meet the demands of industry, and the boom collapsed. Today gas production is still found in many parts of the Unit, but production is relatively modest.

Three cement plants are located in the Unit. No data are available on their production, but presumably it would be nearly great enough to supply state demands. Cement is made from limestone and clay of the Pennsylvanian Age. The reserves of these materials are virtually inexhaustible.

Coal mining in the Neosho Unit at one time was a major industry but has steadily decreased to the point where today it is of minor importance. Coal mining dates back to the territorial days of Kansas and vast reserves still remain. It is possible that, with the energy crisis, coal production will once again become important.

The Neosho River marks the approximate western limits of pioneering practices which had been followed across the eastern part of the United States for nearly 250 years. For the first time in the pioneer experience the settlers found a shortage of lumber and a shortage of surface water. These shortages became more apparent as the frontier moved west from the Neosho, and the pioneers were faced with a totally new pioneer experience.

The river has been known by several different names. Early hunters referred to it as Six Bulls River. Stephen Long in the account of his expedition of 1819–20 refers to the Neosho or the Grand. Today the name Neosho is used in Kansas and it is called the Grand in Oklahoma. Neosho is spelled several different ways by different traders and trappers. The word Neosho apparently comes from the Osage Indians and there is a disagreement as to its definition. One authority says Neosho means "Ne"—water and "osho"—means clear—hence, clear water. Another authority disagrees saying the word means "Ne"—water and "osho"—muddy, hence, muddy water. Strangely, both are correct. Diaries and letters of early settlers along the river refer to the schools of fish that may be seen in the deep holes and describe it as a beautiful crystal clear stream. However, as settlement increased along the river, and its tributaries, the land was plowed and erosion from the fields washed into the river and gave the stream a murky appearance.

It is difficult to determine when the river was discovered by the white man, but perhaps it was French Lieutenant Charles DuTisne, who refers to the Neosho or Grand River on his exploration of what is now Kansas and Oklahoma about 1719.

Kansas is basically a prairie state which implies an absence of trees. The early settlers in Kansas estimated that no more than two percent of the area of the state was covered with timber. This estimate was made in the eastern portion where the trees are most numerous. The banks of the Neosho, however, were lined with a heavy growth of timber. Many species of elm, hackberry, Cottonwood, mulberry, oak, sycamore, ash, hickory, walnut, pecan, locust, to name but a few, were found in abundance. Probably the most valuable species from an economic point of view is the black walnut. Kansas black walnut was in great demand for gun stocks in both World War I and World War II. An early settler on the Neosho, who wanted timber to build his house, tells of being given permission to clear the dead timber from a

quarter section of land belonging to a friend. When looking over the timber he found a perfect mass of ancient dead black walnut trees overlapping each other with young trees so dense it was almost impossible to penetrate. Many of these trees were four feet in diameter. These were cut into two inch planks and the settler remarked that it was the most beautiful timber he had ever seen. Timber on the Neosho was in great demand by early settlers and most of it was cut for lumber, fuel and fences, with numerous saw mills found along its banks. As other sources of energy—coal, gas, and oil—were found, however, the demand for timber declined and once again there is a heavy growth of trees. Some of the best stands of timber in Kansas may be found along the Neosho River. In spite of over a hundred years of cutting there are more trees in Kansas today than when the white man first came to the state.

Many varieties of game were found along the Unit. Early settlers reported finding deer, wildcat, fox, elk, antelope, and buffalo. In addition, there were rabbits, squirrels, raccoons, opossum, beaver, mink, otter, and muskrats. Game birds most frequently reported include turkeys, prairie chickens, quail, ducks, geese and pheasants. The river had a large variety of game and rough fish. From all indications Kansas was a hunters' paradise. Lieutenant Zebulon M. Pike, who in 1806 marched from St. Louis to what is now known as the Cottonwood River valley, reported he had never seen such an abundance and variety of game. He mentions riding through a herd of buffalo for most of a day and reported that game was killed only for food. He reports game was never killed early in the day because it was so abundant he was confident game could be found whenever it was needed.

Probably the most historic town on the Neosho is Council Grove, Kansas. It provided the last opportunity to purchase provisions on the Santa Fe Trail between Independence, Missouri and Santa Fe, New Mexico. Here was found a large stand of oak timber, estimated to be over 200 years old, which made up the largest natural growth of timber from this point to the Rocky Mountains. Since this was the last timber crossing from here to Santa Fe, oak, hickory and ash logs were cut and lashed beneath the wagons to be used as spare parts in case the wagons broke down. At this grove of timber, parties assembled, organized their caravans of wagons and pack animals, and elected their trail bosses to conduct their wagon trains to Santa Fe.

The American Forest Association has placed several trees in Council Grove in the Hall of Fame for trees. Among them is Council Oak, where in August of 1825 U.S. Commissioners made a treaty with the Great and Little Osage Nations for the right of way across their lands to Santa Fe. It was after the signing of this treaty that Council Grove acquired its name. General George A. Custer camped under a large elm which bears his name. A cache of stone was located by a large oak in which passing caravans left letters. This tree is still standing and became known as Post Office Oak.

A territorial governor of Kansas, Andrew H. Reeder, with other officials visited Council Grove in 1854 with the intention of making it the territorial capital of the state, but learned no treaty could be made with the Indians for the land, and the plan was dropped. On the Neosho's west bank in Council Grove in 1850, the Kansas Methodist Mission , better known as the Kaw Mission, was established as a school for the Kansas or Kaw Indians. This building is still standing today and is in excellent condition. The Kansas Indians were removed to a reservation in 1847 on the Neosho River near Council Grove. It contained nearly 400 square miles. The government built over 100 stone houses for the Indians, but they refused to live in them because they were so strange. Some of these houses are still standing and the foundations of others may still be seen. The Indians left this reservation in 1873. Part of Council Grove is now classified as a National Historical Landmark District.

In addition to the Kaw Mission many other missions were established on the banks of the Neosho River. Probably the first Indian mission and school in what is now Kansas was Mission Neosho which was started in September, 1824 by the Reverend Benton Pixley and his wife on the west bank of the Neosho not far from present Shaw, Kansas, in Neosho County. By the end of the year the Mission opened a Protestant school for Osage children. The mission and school were both closed in 1829, largely due to the opposition of the Osage traders and subagents. The

reason for this opposition is not clear. In March of 1830 the Boudinot Mission, successor to Mission Neosho, was founded for the Osage Indians by the Reverend Nathanial P. Dodge and his wife on the east bank of the Neosho about 10 miles south of Mission Neosho and 2 1/2 miles north of present St. Paul in Neosho County.

Later the emphasis of the Mission schools was shifted to trade schools when in 1847 the Osage Catholic Manual Labor School was founded near St. Paul, Kansas. This school was successful and became known as the "cradle of civilization in the Neosho Valley." During the first few years attendance was limited to Osage Indian students. In 1853 other tribes were admitted. The enrollment grew from a total of 35 students the first year to a total of 190 in 1861.

Numerous other missions were established on the Neosho with varying degrees of success. Even though most failed, they were important in the history of the Neosho River Unit. They represent the early attempts on the part of the whites to convert the Indians to their way of life.

The history of the Neosho Unit is one of too much or too little rainfall. The unit has experienced many destructive floods and many disastrous droughts. This pattern is a natural part of the weather conditions of the area and will continue as long as present climatic conditions exist. Both droughts and floods play havoc with the economy and cause much human suffering.

One of the most serious droughts to hit the Neosho was the drought of June 19, 1859 to November 1860. Not a shower of rain fell at any one time to wet the earth more than 2 inches. The ground broke open in great cracks; there was little food produced. The searing winds of July and August devastated everything before it. Fall wheat came up but withered and died. Most counties did not harvest a bushel. Prairie grass grew until July and perished. Rivers, springs, and wells dried up. The bed of the Neosho in the southern part of Kansas was so dry it was used as a road. During the summer the temperature reached 112–114 degrees in the shade, and with scorching wind it kept at these figures for weeks. Stories are recorded of eggs roasting in the sand at mid-day. A committee of the legislature estimated that one-third of the territory's population was dependent for subsistence on outside sources. The Kansas relief committee was established and various groups from across the nation contributed over eight million pounds of food, clothing, medicine, and seeds to the territory. President James Buchanan is said to have contributed the first 100 dollars to the relief funds. Other droughts have occurred at regular intervals, causing great hardships, but relief measures of today have lessened much of the suffering.

Nearly twenty disastrous floods have occurred, bringing a great measure of destruction in the Neosho Unit. The first major flood most frequently mentioned occurred in 1844, and the last, and perhaps the worst, was in 1951. Floods are a natural consequence of surface runoff temporarily exceeding the capacity of the stream channels. This would cause little concern except that residents have found the flood plain a desirable location for towns, farms, factories and transportation facilities.

Records of the gauging station on the Cottonwood River at Cottonwood Falls, Kansas, provide a good example of the magnitude of the overflow on the Neosho which is more or less typical of the stream flow in the Neosho Valley Unit. The average annual runoff at this station is 311,000 acre-feet. However, the annual runoff in 1956 was only 7,590 acre-feet, as compared with the flood year of 1951 when the annual runoff was 1,735,000 acre feet. As a point of interest, runoff at Cottonwood Falls in the single month of July, 1951 exceeded the annual runoff in each year of record except 1941 and 1951. Further, the July, 1951 runoff volume at Cottonwood Falls was 27 percent greater than all the flow which passed the gauging station during the six-year period from October 1, 1951 to September 20, 1957. Such extremes of drought and flood have caused millions of dollars of damage to the Unit. Many small communities which were flooded in 1951 have never been rebuilt and today remain only as name places or ghost towns.

In order to lessen the devastation caused by

the floods, the Army Corps of Engineers has constructed three large reservoirs on the Neosho in Kansas: Marion reservoir on the headwaters of the Cottonwood river; the Council Grove reservoir near Council Grove, and John Redmond reservoir near Burlington. Near the Redmond Reservoir the Wolf Creek Nuclear Power plant is under construction. In Oklahoma three major reservoirs are found on the Grand. Two of these, the Grand Lake of the Cherokees and Lake Hudson, are operated by the Grand River Dam authority of Oklahoma and only during periods of flood control are they under the jurisdiction of the Corps of Engineers. Lake Fort Gibson is a federal project under the control of the Corps of Engineers. In addition to flood control, these reservoirs furnish many water-related recreational activities which have become increasingly important pastimes in this country. Fort Gibson is one of the ten most heavily visited lakes in the nation. The Grand Lake of the Cherokees has one of the longest shorelines of any lake in America—it is 1,300 miles long. It is interesting to note the airline distance from Kansas City to Los Angeles is 1,356 miles.

Fort Gibson, on the junction of the Grand and Arkansas Rivers, has played an important role in the early history of the midwest. The fort was established in the early 1800s and was the base of operations for Washington Irving on his trips to the West. General Zachary Taylor, later to become President of the United States, was in command at Fort Gibson before the Mexican War. Lieutenant Jefferson Davis, later President of the Confederacy, married Taylor's daughter. The Grand (Neosho) River in Oklahoma, once the land of the Cherokee Nation, today is nearly one continuous lake from the time it enters the state until it flows into the Arkansas River at Muskogee.

FURTHER READINGS: John D. Bright, ed., *Kansas: The First Century* (4 vols., 1956). Nyle H. Miller *et. al.*, *Kansas: A Pictorial History* (1961).

Walt Butcher

The Pascagoula River

Source: Confluence of Leaf and Chickasawhay rivers in George County, southeastern Mississippi
Length: 81 miles
Tributaries: Red and Black creeks
Mouth: Into Mississippi Sound and Gulf of Mexico near Pascagoula, Mississippi
Agricultural products: Insignificant
Industries: Extractive: sand, clay, limestone, bauxite, bentonite; pine and hardwood lumbering; commercial fishing and shipbuilding

The Pascagoula River, which is formed by the confluence of the Leaf and Chickasawhay rivers in present-day George County in southeastern Mississippi, drains an area of 3,100 square miles on its eighty-one mile route to the Mississippi Sound (Gulf of Mexico). Throughout its course, the width of the river varies from 300 to 800 feet, and its banks vary rather uniformly from approximately fifteen feet at the river's headwaters to submergence level at its mouth. Because it empties into the Mississippi Sound, the Pascagoula is a tidal river, and tidal effects at low water are apparent for a distance of forty-two miles, where Red and Black creeks join the Pascagoula to form Dead Lake.

Physiographically, the Pascagoula lies within the Coastal Pine Meadows and the Long Leaf Pine Hills, which are both characterized by the existence of strata formed during the late geologic ages by deposition of sediments in and along inland seas. Natural resources along the river include sand, clay, limestone, marl, pine and hardwood forests, petroleum, salt, sandstone, bauxite, and bentonite. Fish and wildlife in and along the river include several species of commercial and sport fisheries, whitetail deer, rabbit, squirrel, raccoon, fox, dove, quail, duck, and other native and migratory birdlife.

As is characteristic of most rivers in Mississippi, the Pascagoula has undergone drastic changes since the earliest historic period, primarily because of an overabundance of sedimentation. The geological factors contributing to this problem have been abetted by silt and driftwood following the cutting of virgin forests in the late nineteenth century. Geologists assume that the Pascagoula is an old river because its valley is wide in proportion to its length. A myriad of bayous, sloughs, and half-moon lakes, some of which are miles in length, offers further evidence of the changing course of the river. Interestingly, as if tired of changing its course, the river forks about twelve miles north of its mouth to form two separate streams, one flowing on the east side of the valley and the other on the west to the Gulf. Still, the East Pascagoula and the West Pascagoula are connected by a series of slow-moving bayous, the names of which are colloquial expressions of their geography, their uses, or their dominant characteristics: Alligator, Swift, Crooked, Log Boom, Longview, and Haulover, just to name a few.

Despite the fact that the river even today winds seemingly without direction to the Gulf, the Pascagoula is navigable on its lower courses. The state of Mississippi and the federal government moved to improve the lower reaches of the river as early as 1818. In that year the Mississippi legislature established a commission to raise $3,000 by means of a lottery for improving the navigability of the Pascagoula, Leaf, and Chickasawhay rivers. In 1828 Congress turned over to the state legislature $8,000 it had earlier appropriated to improve the East Fork of the lower Pascagoula. By 1890 the channel of that branch had been dredged sufficient to accommodate a ship of 2,000 tons and an overall length of 270 feet. With the lumber boom of the late nineteenth century, private corporations moved in to further develop the channel, a trend continued to the present day.

It is not known with certainty when man first inhabited the banks of the Pascagoula and its tributaries. Archaeological evidence is scarce. Extremely difficult terrain, extensive vegetation, and lack of Indian mounds and other conspicuous remnants of prehistoric culture have thwarted archaeologists. The evidence which does exist (primarily prehistoric small villages or camp sites) might indicate an association with cultural stages from Tchefuncte through Troyville occupations (500 B.C. to 800 A.D.). Much more is known about settlement in early historic times. Hernando DeSoto was possibly the first European to encounter native Americans along the Pascagoula. While his exact route remains obscure, a 1687 map pinpoints the expedition's crossing of the Pascagoula in 1540, a few miles below the confluence of the Leaf and Chickasawhay, an area near the location of the "Grand Village of the Pascagoula" on a 1721 map.

It was left to the French to first document contact between European and Indian civilizations along the Pascagoula. While the colonial powers of Spain, England, and France maneu-

vered for dominance in the New World, Pierre Le Moyne, Sieur d'Iberville, began preparations for an expedition to colonize Louisiana. After exploring several coastal islands along the northern shore of the Gulf, Iberville landed near the Pascagoula River in February, 1699. The French explorer was favorably impressed, and constructed Fort Maurepas near present-day Ocean Springs that summer. In August Iberville's younger brother, Jean-Baptiste Le Moyne, ascended the Pascagoula River, possibly as far north as the confluence of the Leaf and Chickasawhay, and for the first time met the Indians

The Ingalls Shipyards at the mouth of the Pascagoula River are among the nation's largest. (Photo courtesy Ingalls Shipyards.)

from whom the river received its name. The name Pascagoula was given to the Indians by their northern neighbors, the Choctaw. Literally, the name is derived from two Choctaw words: paska, which means "bread," and okla, which means "people." Thus, the Pascagoula were the "bread people" or "nation of bread" to the Choctaw, a fact substantiated by the French who noted the Pascagoula's adeptness at making bread from flour derived from the persimmon.

In addition to the Pascagoula, the Biloxi, Moctobi, and Capinan(s) lived along the river. Their origins are subjects of debate, but it appears likely that the Biloxi were of Siouan stock, while the Pascagoula were Muskhogeans. Less is known of the Moctobi and Capinan(s), and it is generally assumed that they were either subdivisions of the two larger tribes or the names by which the Biloxi and Pascagoula were known to each other.

Whatever the case, the Biloxi lived along the Pascagoula from its mouth northward for twenty-five to forty miles, while the main villages of the Pascagoulas were located from sixty miles upriver to near its headwaters. Both tribes were small: the Biloxi numbered 420 and the Pascagoula 455 at the time of European contact. They fell easy prey to the white man's diseases and by 1720 their populations were reduced by fifty percent. After the Treaty of Paris in 1763, which transferred French lands east of the Mississippi to England, the Indians migrated further westward into Texas, and by 1910 the Pascagoula and Biloxi were virtually extinct.

Perhaps the most interesting legends associated with the Pascagoula River are rooted in Indian folklore. The stream is known by many even today as the "Singing River," and it is a fact that a strange "music" has emanated from the river on still nights, historically, though the noises wrought by industrialization and urbanization along the river's banks have made it difficult to discern in recent years. Actually, the music, which was noted by Iberville in 1699, was a humming or murmuring sound which rose and fell in a regular manner. Several Indian legends and scientific hypotheses have been suggested for the mysterious sounds. One theory has the sounds coming from a species of fish which travels up river to spawn. Another attributes the humming to the grating of sand along

the river's slate bottom, and another insists it is currents whistling past underwater caves, while still another attributes the sounds to natural gas escaping from sand beds in the river. Whatever the case, the causes of the mysterious music of the Pascagoula have been memorialized in written and oral history, in prose, and even in song.

White settlement along the Pascagoula in the century after European contact was sporadic. Notable among the French concessionaires in the area were Joseph Simon La Pointe, Hugo Ernestus Krebs, and Antoine de Chaumont. The improperly named Old Spanish Fort, which was likely a carpenter shop on the 1715 La Pointe concession, stands today as the oldest extant structure in the lower Mississippi Valley. Krebs, a German from Alsace-Lorraine, migrated to an area near the La Pointe concession in 1730. In 1772 Bernard Romans, an English adventurer and botanist, visited the Krebs plantation and was shown a contraption invented by Krebs to gin cotton at the rate of eighty pounds a day. Of course, Krebs failed to take full advantage of his invention, and twenty years later northerner Eli Whitney marched into history with a machine capable of ginning only fifty pounds a day. But, the most significant concession was that of Chaumont, whose activities were a product of John Law's infamous "Mississippi Bubble," an early eighteenth century get-rich-quick scheme. Chaumont's 1,700 shares in the West Indian Company resulted in an extensive concession in 1719, which comprised a greater portion of the land between what are now Martin's Bluff and Vancleve. A number of French colonists settled there in the 1720s. Law's scheme, however, depended on the belief that there was an abundance of precious metals in Louisiana. When a scarcity of metals resulted, the bubble burst, and colonization along the Pascagoula River suffered accordingly.

Most of the French settlers along the Pascagoula remained even after France lost her territory east of the Mississippi by the Treaty of Paris (1763), but by the end of the American Revolution the Spanish had gained control of West Florida and the settlements along the Pascagoula. It is from this period that the previously mentioned Old Spanish Fort received its name. Spain allowed the settlers to retain their land in return for an oath of allegiance to its king and to the Roman Catholic Church. Thus, the area remained largely French in origin, though American settlers of English background began to trickle in from the eastern seaboard.

After the Louisiana Purchase in 1803, the territory which included the Pascagoula was the subject of more controversy. Spain claimed that Napoleon had had no right to sell West Florida to the United States and continued to exercise control over it. A subsequent rebellion in 1810 resulted in the establishment of the Republic of West Florida which applied for admission to the Union. In 1811 the Pascagoula area was organized into a parish of Mississippi Territory, and the following year it was officially annexed to Mississippi Territory as Jackson County. In the War of 1812, able-bodied settlers along the river joined Andrew Jackson as he crossed the river in November, 1814, enroute to the Battle of New Orleans.

Life along the slow-moving, southern stream returned to normal, with slow growth, after the War of 1812. In 1849, however, Colonel George W. White, who had distinguished himself during the Mexican War, gathered 550 soldiers of fortune on Round Island, three miles south of the mouth of the Pascagoula, to launch an expedition whose hope it was to capture Cuba. The Round Island expedition failed when President Zachary Taylor ordered it halted. But, because of the expansionist mentality in the South before the Civil War, the President was vilified in the southern pass.

The Pascagoula River became industrially important after the Civil War with the establishment of thriving lumber and shipbuilding industries. Along the river were large stands of long leaf pine, pitch pine, live oak, Spanish oak, cypress, and magnolia. To be sure, there were a few small sawmills along the river as early as the 1850s, and harvesting timber (particularly yellow pine and cypress), burning charcoal, and turpentine farming were industries before the Civil War. It was not until a railroad linking the river with New Orleans and Mobile was completed in 1870 and the channel of Pascagoula Bay was deepened in the 1880s, however, that the race for lumber was on. After the timber was milled, it was shipped throughout the world. The boom continued until the 1920s, by which time the forests were virtually stripped. Reforestation and selective cutting in recent years have revived the forests, and the lumber industry continues even today.

Shipbuilding is today even more important to life along the Pascagoula than the lumber industry. While the former existed there as early as the 1770s and a full-scale shipyard was in operation by 1838, it was not until World War I that the industry reached a fever pitch. The need for the famous "liberty ships" to aid the Allied cause in Europe was the impetus needed to turn the Pascagoula area into one of the great shipbuilding centers of the world. Its reputation was continued in 1938, when Ingalls Iron Works opened its shipyard on the banks of the river. The yard produced about 100 vessels during World War II, and later contributions by Ingalls, later known as Litton Industries, included some of the country's first nuclear submarines and automated cargo liners; today the shipyard rivals tourism as the most important economic factor in the Gulf Coast counties.

The Pascagoula's outlook for the future is bright. In 1976, the Mississippi legislature authorized the Mississippi Wildlife Heritage Committee to purchase from private ownership a 32,000 acre tract of land in the heart of the Pascagoula River basin. The land is unquestionably the finest and most unaltered natural area left in the State. Included are thirty-eight miles fronting the Pascagoula, fifteen miles fronting on Black Creek, over fifty natural oxbow lakes and dead river runs, 180 million board feet of timber, and an abundance of wildlife. Remnant populations of several rare and endangered species, including panther, black bear, Mississippi swallowtail kite, and Atlantic sturgeon, may inhabit the area. The acquisition of this land assures that future generations will know nature in its purest form. Perhaps the lessons taught to past generations by the Pascagoula will not be lost on future generations; hopefully, too, the Pascagoula will ebb and flow interminably in more than the great haze of memory.

FURTHER READING: Cyril Edward Cain, *Four Centuries on the Pascagoula, Country,* 2 vols. (1953–1962). Dunbar Rowland, *History of Mississippi, the Heart of the South,* 4 vols. (1925).

Robert J. Bailey

The Pearl River

Source: Rises in Winston, Attala, and Neshoba counties in east-central Mississippi
Length: 490 miles
Tributaries: None of significance
Mouth: Divides fifty miles from mouth into East Pearl, which flows into Lake Borgne, and the West Pearl, which flows into Rigolets River, the main outlet of Lake Pontchartrain
Agricultural products: Cotton, cattle
Industries: None of significance

The Pearl River, or the Mighty Pearl as it is affectionately known to Mississippians, rises in the east-central part of Mississippi, in the counties of Winston, Attala, and Neshoba. This places its headwaters near the mother mound of the Choctaw Indians, Nanih Waiya. It was around

Snagboat on the Pearl River between Jackson and Carthage, 1910. Note: that the name of boat, legible in picture, is Pearl. (Mississippi Dept. of Archives and History.)

this mound that this branch of the Muskogean Indians ended their wanderings and founded their home after a long journey from their original dwelling place, which is thought to have been somewhere in the western United States. Legends foretelling their extinction if they strayed too far from the mound forbade them to move again. As they multiplied, their villages grew in number and spread to outlying lands, all still in the general region of Nanih Waiya.

The Pearl flows in a southwesterly direction for 172 miles to Jackson, Mississippi, then turns southeasterly for 313 miles to the mouth: in all it is 490 miles long. Fifty miles from its mouth the river divides into two streams, the East Pearl River and the West Pearl River. The East Pearl flows into Lake Borgne and forms the boundary line between Mississippi and Louisiana. The West Pearl moves into the state of Louisiana and flows into the Rigolets, the main outlet of Lake Pontchartrain.

Legend has fostered the story that the Pearl, the second most important river in the state of Mississippi, was named by the French explorer Bienville. In October, 1698, he with his older brother Iberville set out with 200 colonists to establish the first permanent white settlement in the lower Mississippi Valley. The town was established near present Ocean Springs, Mississippi, and was named Biloxi in honor of the Indians of that area. On one exploring expedition from there Bienville led a party that traversed the coastal area around the mouth of a river that emptied into the Gulf of Mexico. Here he discovered an Indian gathering ground where pirogues were made and repaired. Among the debris scattered on the shoreline he found pearls, which supposedly had come from shells which the Indians used to scrape the interior of their canoes. He christened the river La Rivière aux Perles.

The legend persists, but history does not corroborate the existence of pearl-bearing mollusks in the Pearl River. Nevertheless the river has borne its name ever since, while the region wherein it flows was known first as Florida and later—and for a much longer period—as Louisiana. A map by Johann Baptist Homann, bearing the date 1687 in the cartouche, shows a "R. aux Perles," as does the DeLisle map of 1718 and John Senex's copy of that map in 1721.

Long before the white man came the native Americans of the region, the Choctaws, had their own name for the river. They first called it *Ecfinatcha* but later changed the name to *Talcatcha*; this they later shortened to *Hacha*, their word for river. They had villages up and down its banks, and used the river for fishing and occasionally for transportation. However, these people were primarily agrarian and were not fleet swimmers, as were their brother tribesmen, the Chickasaws. Choctaws of today attribute this lack of fondness for water among their people to legends concerning man-devouring monsters that inhabited the river. They likened these creatures to giant crayfish and similar biting, clawing inhabitants of the water. Fact probably is at the foundation of this legend in the form of alligators and gars, which still inhabit the southern swamps of the river. The Chickasaws lived farther north and thus were not exposed to such creatures.

The earliest known survey of the river is an extremely detailed account by a French officer named Régis du Roullet between July 14 and August 8, 1732. It is a navigator's survey, noting compass readings, soundings, width of the river, and landmarks. The narration is accompanied by several excellent maps, one of which follows Roullet's trip by land up to the Indian village of Boukfouka, where he enlisted the aid of the inhabitants for his trip down the Pearl. Villages and landmarks are carefully noted. On the map the Pearl is very detailed, with all tributaries and bayous carefully noted. The underlying reason for this survey was to study not only the navigability of the river, but also to establish an amicable relationship with the Choctaws, whom the French hoped to make their allies.

The river, especially the upper part, is a tortuous one: it twists and turns at sharp angles. The lower path is markedly straighter. In the upper part it is shallow, with a depth ranging from inches to several feet during normal, nonflood periods. The lower parts of the river are considerably deeper, which made navigation possible during the eighteenth and nineteenth centuries.

During the twentieth century the river was still partially navigable. In the many sharp bends on the upper river, the normally slow-moving, muddy water develops a turbulence that increases the depth and flow speed to such a degree that boating and swimming become hazardous. The many cave-ins, with the accompanying trees and vegetation, tend to obstruct the river and form another danger. The beautiful white sandbars are inviting to picnickers and nature lovers, but venturing into the unstable river water can be dangerous.

The river was not always of this nature. An engineer recalled in 1879 that when the Pearl was first settled it was a clear stream, "practically free from obstructions, with very tortuous channels and stable banks." But when white men cleared the lands and made cut-offs to eliminate bends, the river increased in velocity, forming new cave-ins and new bends. Brush and trees from the caving banks choked the river, resulting in a flood plain cut by traces of old and new channels, and a stream full of snags and bars. From Edinburg to Jackson, such a situation prevails—an area of about 500 square miles.

The width of flooded land can vary from one to five miles. Towns most prone to be affected by the flooding are Edinburg, Monticello, Columbia, Bogalusa, and Pearl River, Louisiana; and, unfortunately, the whole area around Mississippi's capital city of Jackson. Despite the everpresent threat of flooding, Jackson was chosen in 1821 to replace Natchez, which was not centrally located. The site of the future capital was then known as LeFleur's Bluff, so named because a French-Canadian, Louis LeFleur, had a thriving trading post there. In 1822 Peter Aaron Van Dorn laid out precise plans for the capital, thus making Jackson a planned city. It bears a checkerboard pattern, with alternate squares marked as parks or "greens"—an idea Van Dorn picked up from Thomas Jefferson. The city was named for Andrew Jackson. (The original map of this plan can be viewed at the Mississippi Department of Archives and History in Jackson.)

During the nineteenth century the Pearl was navigable as far up as Madisonville above Jackson. Cotton and other products were shipped downriver to New Orleans. Snag boats worked constantly up and down the river to keep the channel cleared. The pilot for any boat on this perverse waterway had to be skilled in the art of river navigation.

During the Civil War Federal troops which had occupied the lower part of the state set out to establish supply lines up the Pearl. A Captain Summers was the only competent pilot left around. He lived near Logtown, where the Federal soldiers went to find him. On the road to his house they passed a man and stopped to ask specific instructions. He directed them to a not-too-distant house under some large oak trees. Then he hid out in the Pearl River swamps, for the man was the sought-after Captain Summers.

Eventually the Union officers gave up the search and hired an inexperienced pilot. The outcome was a sunken Federal gunboat named the *Wabash*. Captain Summers watched the whole episode from a tall tree in the swamps! Ever since then the bayou flowing into the Pearl at that spot has been known as Wabash Bayou. For many years the boat was visible during low water.

Early in the nineteenth century large fortunes were made on the lower East Pearl River at a place called Honey Island. At the time pirates and brigands abounded in this area, their prey along the Gulf Coast and in New Orleans easily accessible, and a swift escape assured through the Pearl and its bayous and tributaries. They made their headquarters at Honey Island, where they could easily hide their caches of stolen goods. The King of Honey Island was Pierre Rameau. It was said that he came from a wealthy family in Scotland, but he chose to make his own name and fortune. Such was his success that he was able to maintain one of the finest homes in New Orleans under an assumed name and circulated in the best of the Crescent City's society.

The most successful business venture ever to use the Pearl River was the timber industry. Fortunes were made almost overnight in the lower portions of the East Pearl River during the latter part of the nineteenth and the early twentieth centuries. The mills were located in Logtown, Pearlington, and Gainesville. Timber was gathered from as far up as Columbia. The Pearl and its tributaries were an excellent means of transportation for the timber. The logs, once the trees were felled and prepared, were floated downriver to the sawmills. Pearlington, in the last quarter of the nineteenth century, reputedly had the world's largest sawmill.

Today there is little commerce or industry connected with Pearl River. However, the Pearl River Basin Development District is turning the Basin into a beautiful recreational area. The river is being cleaned up and dock areas with park facilities are being constructed. Young people—and many "older youngsters"—have found a healthy form of recreation by following the Agency's boatway maps on a float trip down the Pearl.

In Jackson, Mississippi, the Pearl River Valley Water Supply District has provided the Ross Barnett Reservoir, made possible by an act of the Mississippi Legislature in 1958. Its purpose was to supply water, but it has become the city's, and one of the state's, most beautiful recreational areas. Boating, fishing, and picnicking bring old and young alike to this reservoir. Also, an entirely new and attractively tranquil residential area has been created for the capital city.

FURTHER READING: Samuel Grady Thigpen, *Pearl River, Highway to Glory* (1965). John K. Buttersworth, *Mississippi Yesterday and Today* (1964).

Jo Ann Blissard Bomar

The Pecos River

Source: Rises in Mora County in the Sangre de Cristo Mountains in north-central New Mexico
Length: 735 Miles
Tributaries: Hondo, Gallinas, Felix
Mouth: Joins Rio Grande about 40 miles upstream from Del Rio, Texas
Agricultural Products: Cattle ranching, cotton, truck crops
Industries: Petroleum

The Pecos River starts in Mora County in north-central New Mexico. There, from high in the Sangre de Cristo Range, the river flows about 735 miles in a south and southeastern direction until it joins the Rio Grande about forty miles upstream from Del Rio, Texas. Throughout its course the river drops about 11,000 feet. After leaving the mountains it flows through a semi-arid and arid region that drains about 27,000 square miles. In southern New Mexico the river widens into a basin that leads to a broad shallow valley. This valley starts near the Texas-New Mexico border and extends to Girvin, Texas. Irrigation started here in 1877. Below Sheffield and on to its confluence with the Rio Grande, the river has cut a very deep gorge (in places over 1,000 feet deep) that extends for 125 miles. It is along here that the river has long acted as a barrier to movement and as a discouragement to irrigation efforts.

In 1541, while seeking Cabeza de Vaca's seven cities of Cibola, Francisco Vasquez de Coronado first bridged the river at Horsehead Crossing in the vicinity of Salt Lake. It was then called the Rio Cicuye, the name of an early Indian pueblo. Then, in 1583, Antonio de Espejo, while establishing a route between Mexico and the Pueblo region, called the river the Rio de las Vacas (because of the many herds of bison to be seen there). Seven years later, Gaspar Castano de Sousas traveled up the Pecos that he called Rio Salado because of the salty taste of the water. He was out to conquer pueblos in New Mexico. Then finally, in 1598, Juan de Oñate under contract to settle New Mexico, referred to the river in his reports as the Pecos. The word is said

to come from the Qq'ueres language of New Mexico Indians. One final name for the already over-named river was the Puerco. By this word the Mexicans along the shore described the river's dirty nature.

Towns on or near the Pecos are: Santa Rosa, Ft. Sumner, Roswell, and Carlsbad, all in New Mexico, and Pecos, Iraan, and Sheffield in Texas. Other points of interest are Captain Pope's Wells and several river crossings. John Pope was later to command the Union Army of Virginia and to be soundly defeated at the Second Battle of Bull Run. In the 1850s, as a member of the elite Topographical Engineers, he dug these wells while attempting to carry out a mission of providing a string of artesian water sources through the Llano Estacado, or Staked Plains of West Texas. This was all a part of Secretary of War Jefferson Davis' plan to popularize a Southern route to California that might influence the choice of the route for the first transcontinental railroad. In fact, to further this cause, Jefferson Davis also imported camels and had the army use them in the trans-Pecos region as proof that people could survive the desert-like conditions of the far Southwest.

Historically important river crossings in New Mexico were the Santa Fe Trail crossing in the upper reaches of the Pecos and the Lake Navajo crossing. In Texas there were the Emigrant crossing near where Toyah Creek joins the Pecos, Pope's crossing near his wells, the Old Y crossing in the alkali flats area, and Horsehead crossing near Salt Lake. Most noted of the crossings is Horsehead, so named because of the many horse and mule skeletons found lying there. This was because Horsehead was on the Comanche trail from Chihuahua, Mexico, and the last water hole was sixty miles away. Indians heading out of Mexico with stolen horses would let the thirst-crazed animals plunge into the Pecos and drink until they would sicken and die. In 1864, William A. Peril drove one of the first cattle herds across Horsehead crossing. Two years later, Charles Goodnight and Oliver Loving, key names in the history of the "long drives," used this crossing while taking a herd to Ft. Sumner, New Mexico, and Pueblo, Colorado. Eventually, some 250,000 cattle would follow their route. Horsehead was also used by the Butterfield Overland Express. With the exception of the relay stations and the home stations of the stagecoach company, those riding the line saw no man-made object for 400 miles heading out through west Texas to El Paso.

There were several forts at or near the river. In New Mexico, Ft. Sumner was established as a military stronghold in 1862. Its ruins are near the present town of that name. Nearby is the grave of Billy the Kid. In Texas, Ft. Stockton was built at the crossing of the Old San Antonio Road and the Comanche Trail, near Comanche Springs. Manned in early 1859, it was to serve as protection for the San Antonio-San Diego mail route. Abandoned during the Civil War, the station was re-occupied by troops for almost twenty years starting in 1867. Ft. Lancaster was opened in August of 1855. It was located less than one mile above the junction of Live Oak Creek with the Pecos, and was built to safeguard the military road linking San Antonio with El Paso. Vacated at the time of Texas secession, the fort was briefly used again in 1868.

Dams in New Mexico have created reservoirs at Alamogordo and Lake McMillan. In the Texas portion of the Pecos are Red Bluff Lake, Imperial Reservoir, and Zimmerman Reservoir. Main tributaries are the Hondo, Gallinas, Felix, Black, and Delaware rivers in New Mexico, and, in Texas, the intermittent Toyah, Comanche, and Live Oak creeks.

Due to light summer rainfall in the Pecos area, and heavy irrigation from the middle and upper parts of the river, it normally has a modest flow. However, a sudden cloudburst can always trigger a flash flood and a major flood can occur almost every year. One in 1954, for example, washed away a high bridge on the route between Del Rio and Langtry. As for pollution, it is mainly in the central area where agricultural and petroleum operations are most concentrated.

To the west of the Pecos River, and bounded by New Mexico to the north and Mexico to the southwest, is the Trans-Pecos region of Texas. About the size of the state of West Virginia, it is topographically extremely diverse and contains the only true mountains in the state. Historically speaking, it is a region that is unique when compared with the rest of Texas. It is both economically and psychologically a unit to itself, and the state was quite late in offering it aid in its development.

One individual who offered his own distinctive form of direction to the region was Judge Roy Bean—the "Law" West of the Pecos. Bean was born in Kentucky about 1825. As a young man, he and his brother formed a trading expedition to go to Chihuahua. Because of some undisclosed difficulties, the brothers left Mexico in a hurry. Later, Bean showed up in California escaping from jail where he had been placed for dueling. Then after running saloons in California and New Mexico, he drifted back to San Antonio. There, for twenty years, he held an assortment of jobs and became legendary because of his great talent at scheming to raise money, avoiding the payment of bills, and winning lawsuits.

Family and monetary problems caused him to leave San Antonio in 1882. He set up a tent saloon for railroad workers who were building a line westward toward the Pecos River. In August of that year, Captain T. L. Oglesby of the Texas Rangers appointed him justice of the peace with instructions to bring peace to that lawless region. By the end of the year he had established his combination saloon and courtroom at Langtry, just a few miles west of the Pecos River.

As judge, Bean's interpretations of the law were frequently unique. When marriages that he conducted did not work out well, he granted divorces under the guise that he was only correcting his own mistakes. At one time he acquitted the murderer of a Chinese railroad worker because in his law books he could find no provision that made it illegal to kill a Chinese. Another time, a Mexican worker for the Southern Pacific Railroad got drunk, tried to walk across a long trestle bridge, tripped, fell off the bridge, and broke his neck. Judge Bean was called in to investigate the matter. A search of the corpse's pockets revealed fifty-two dollars and a pistol. Bean had the body taken to his courtroom and, assuming that the dead man could not speak English, appointed a court interpreter. A trial was then conducted and the corpse was found guilty on three counts: public drunkenness, trespassing on railroad property, and carrying a concealed weapon. Bean then decreed that the court would confiscate the weapon and that the corpse would be fined fifty-two dollars for its crimes.

Despite his checkered background and many distinctive legal findings, Judge Roy Bean at least brought some order and some form of legal authority to a region of Texas that otherwise would have remained lawless.

Even more colorful than Judge Roy Bean was Pecos Bill, the mythical "Greatest Cowboy of All Times." Bill was the youngest of eighteen children in a family of Texas pioneers. He was lost when he fell out of a wagon that was crossing the Pecos River and, with all those children to keep track of, it was three or four days later when his parents detected his absence. In the meantime, the coyotes had found him, had adopted him, and would raise him. Later, when he returned to civilization as an adult and was finally convinced that he was human, he became a ranch hand and developed all sorts of new methods for solving ranching problems. He trained gophers to dig post holes, roped entire herds of cattle with one swing of his lariat, and killed snakes by feeding them mothballs that had been filled with nitroglycerin and chili powder. He thought up the branding iron to discourage rustling and created cowboy songs to calm the herds. He invented centipedes and tarantulas for pets. Rattlesnakes hid in the cacti when he approached them—they were afraid that he would bite them.

On the day that Bill was to be married, his girl friend, Slue-Foot Sue, wanted to see if she could ride Bill's horse, the Widow-Maker. However, the horse bucked Sue so high in the air that she almost hit her head on the moon. After she fell back down her steel-sprung bustle kept her bouncing up and down for four days until Bill had to shoot her to keep her from dying from starvation. There are several theories on the death of Bill. One was that he died from drinking fishhooks in his nitroglycerin and whiskey. The other was that he laughed himself to death at the greenhorns who came to call themselves cowboys.

Faced with so much hard work and the need for tremendous endurance, cowhands found that the tall tales of Pecos Bill lightened their drab lives and gave them a hero.

The Pecos, a remote but significant land feature of Texas, has witnessed many historical events: the actions of the Indians; the coming of Spanish and Anglo explorers and tradesmen; the camels; the Confederate invasion of New Mexico and its failure; the cattle drives; and the coming of ranchers, farmers, and oilmen. These are events that man knows about; however, we will never know of many other happenings that the river might have experienced in its long and colorful life.

FURTHER READING: Bill Leftwich, *Tracks Along the Pecos* (1957).

Allan C. Ashcraft

The Perdido River

Source: Rises in Escambia County in extreme south-
ern Alabama
Length: 60 miles
Tributaries: None of significance
Mouth: Perdido Bay, west of Pensacola, Florida
Agricultural products: Some corn, soybeans
Industries: Fishing, lumbering, paper making

Rising in Escambia County, Alabama, the Perdido River lazily cuts its way through the limestone and clay soils of northwest Florida and
eastern Alabama before spilling its spring-fed
waters into the Gulf of Mexico. A small river,
averaging a width fifty to seventy-five feet, and
relatively short, about sixty miles long, it forms
the most southern and western border between
Alabama and Florida.

In many ways the Perdido is typical of panhandle Florida and Gulf coast rivers. Its clear
waters placidly flow through most of the year,
but in the rainy season numerous tributaries
swell its more modest normal size and the Perdido overflows its banks. On the lower sections of
the river its broad flood plain averages one-
quarter mile in width. In the north, limestone
cliffs, often reaching twenty feet in height, keep
the river within its banks, but increase its rate of
flow considerably.

The area through which the Perdido flows is
rich in flora and fauna. Hardwoods, among
them Florida maple, live oaks, and sweetgum,
line the river banks, intermingling on the broad
flood plain with the thick underbrush, occasional evergreens, and native wild spruce. The Sabal
Palm, Florida's state tree (locally known as the
palmetto or cabbage palm) is also interspersed
through much of the region.

The hardwood stands on the lower end and
evergreens further north benefit significantly
from the rich soil deposits. A product of the
Mesozoic and Tertiary geologic eras, the Northern Highlands and Coastal Lowlands have rich
limestone and clay deposits interspersed with
sand, shell and gravel. In the Northern Highlands the rich ultisols make farming profitable

today as in the past. Grains, corn and soybeans
are major agricultural products grown in this
area.

The river fauna is equally extensive. Deer,
black bear, and the Florida panther once
roamed this area in substantial numbers. Today
deer are the only large animals remaining in
significant numbers, and for part of the Perdido's length hunting preserves stabilize the deer
population. Small game abounds, with opossum, rabbit, raccoon, and squirrels predominating.

In the river proper fish, turtles, snakes, crayfish, and numerous insects make this a rich
ecological area. Emptying into Perdido Bay, the
river waters mix with the Gulf waters forming
part of the rich northwest Florida estuary, home
to millions of shrimp, oysters, and other small
marine life.

As with the flora and fauna, the history of the
river in terms of New World exploration and
subsequent colonization is long and varied. The
first Europeans to see the Perdido were probably
members of the ill-fated Panfilo de Narváez
expedition of 1528. These Spanish conquistado-
res passed the mouth of the Perdido enroute to
their ultimate demise, for most of them it was at
the mouth of the Mississippi River.

Through the long era of colonial warfare between France, Spain, and England for the ultimate control of North America, the Perdido area
began to take on increased significance. Originally controlled and settled by the Spanish, the
Perdido's region became a focal point and major
settlements were established at Mobile, Alabama, and Pensacola, Florida. These towns provided the physical control for Spain's New
World province of West Florida, stretching from
the Apalachicola River in northcentral Florida
to the Mississippi River. Bordered on the north
by the thirty-first parallel, this area remained a
point of contention well into the American period, permanent United States control not being
established until 1821.

With the Louisiana purchase in 1803 control

and ownership of the Gulf coast region became more important to the Americans. Southern dependence on the extensive southeastern river system for the transportation and distribution of agricultural products almost demanded that Americans control West Florida. Equally important, while United States power was growing, Spain's power and authority in the Floridas was waning. Sentiment began to mount for American possession of the region.

In Paris, at the Louisiana Purchase negotiations, the United States representatives, principally Robert R. Livingston and James Monroe, tried to purchase West Florida as part of the purchase agreement. However, Napoleon, who now controlled the area by virtue of France's authority over Spain, refused to include it in the settlement. (England had controlled the region after the 1763 Peace of Paris Treaty, but Spanish sovereignty was reestablished in 1783. The region remained Spanish until 1821 except during the period the Spanish government was controlled by Napoleon.)

United States control of the Louisiana territory was secured, but West Florida remained an unsolved problem and tension in the region continued to build. In 1809 President James Madison advanced the claim put forth earlier by President Thomas Jefferson that West Florida should be considered part of the Louisiana Purchase, but this claim was not upheld. At this point, with government action not forthcoming, private individuals began to take matters into their own hands and they seized West Florida; thus was born in September, 1810 the short-lived Republic of West Florida. It embraced the area between the Mississippi and Pearl Rivers.

On October 27, 1810 President Madison validated this action by issuing a proclamation annexing the region *and* extending the boundary of the seized territory eastward to the Perdido River. This river then became the most southern and eastern boundary of the United States. When John Quincy Adams, United States Minister to Russia, embarrassedly explained this "acquisition" to the Czar, the Czar replied not to worry, "Everyone always grows a little in this world." The English were not as understanding. The London *Times* reported, "Mr. Madison's dirty swindling maneuvers in respect to Louisi-

ana and the Floridas remain to be punished." The Americans would remember this during the War of 1812.

With the outbreak of war in 1812 the United States recognized the need for controlled and defensible southern borders. On May 14, 1812, Congress formally annexed the West Florida region between the Pearl and Perdido Rivers. The next year, in April, 1813, the city of Mobile was taken from the Spanish. With hostilities concluded this area became the only permanent territory acquired by the United States during the War of 1812.

However, the conclusion of the war did not bring peace to the Florida region. Indian troubles, national disputes, and problems concerning the return of runaway slaves who sought sanctuary in Spanish Florida each contributed to the unrest. Also, southern cotton interests increasingly demanded the purchase or seizure of Spanish Florida. Many felt it only logical to expand to the south into Florida as had been done with the validated West Florida acquisition.

In April, 1818, American irregulars under the leadership of Andrew Jackson and with the unofficial approval of the United States government marched into Spanish Florida, seized the small Gulf coast port of St. Marks (San Marcos de Apalachee), and executed two British traders found there. In the next few weeks Jackson captured every major Spanish town in north and west Florida, with the exception of St. Augustine on the east coast. In addition he seized the Spanish treasury, deposed the Spanish governor, and declared American law to be in force. (He later expressed regrets that he did not hang the Spanish governor.)

Spain was infuriated. It appeared that all Spanish holdings east of the Perdido River would be acquired by the United States through legal or illegal means, whichever proved to be the more successful. Faced with an impending international crisis, President James Monroe's able Secretary of State, John Quincy Adams, in a bold maneuver, demanded satisfaction for American grievances against Spain over Florida, threatening the use of force to secure our goals. In effect, he told Spain to govern and control her North American possession on the eastern seaboard and Gulf coast or cede it to the United States. Troubles in Europe coupled with Spain's weak colonial position limited her options.

On February 22, 1819, the United States and Spain concluded the Adams-Oñis Treaty. By its provisions the United States acquired all of Spanish East Florida, received validation for the earlier West Florida seizure, assumed $5 million in claims by United States citizens against Spain, gave up its shadowy claim to Texas, and formalized the western boundary of the Louisiana purchase. Since Spain did not ratify the treaty within the original six months time period proscribed, Congress did not formally accept the treaty until February 19, 1821. Finally, in the third decade of the nineteenth century, both the east and west banks of the Perdido River became United States territory, almost three hundred years after its discovery.

During the treaty negotiation period Alabama was admitted to the United States as the 22d state, December 14, 1819, making the Perdido River a state border as well as a national one. Not until 26 years later did Florida become a state, on March 3, 1845, making the Perdido River the border between the two states, which it remains today. Alabama had orignally hoped to secure a more extensive Gulf coast border and looked to the newly acquired Florida territory with covetous eyes. This hope would not be realized. The new territory's borders remained static and Alabama was not able to expand further south or east.

In the Civil War period, of course, the Perdido River was the border for two of the Confederate states, making a total of five flags that have flown over its area. Today, Five Flag festivals are celebrated in Pensacola and other Gulf coast towns. After 1865 and the return to United States control, the Perdido region began to grow, but the contemporary river setting mirrors that of one hundred years ago. With the exception of the city of Pensacola, only agricultural and forest lands interspersed with a few small hamlets greet the modern visitor to the Perdido area.

Today, much of the river's length and the surrounding area serve two primary functions, one economic and one recreational. Lumbering has always been a major southern economic

activity and that remains true in the present. The St. Regis Paper Company and other large conglomerates own or lease much of this area for tree farming, the pine pulp being used in numerous paper products. There is some growing controversy about the ecological effect of industrial pollutants, but widespread pollution is not evident. Large stands of uniform pines, the physical plant, and the "paper mill odor" are the most visible evidence of this major economic activity.

In terms of farming the present Perdido area is more economically depressed. Farming continues, but on a smaller scale than in the past. As such, St. Regis and its competitors provide the major source of employment and income in this more isolated rural area. Additionally, fishing in the rich Perdido Bay estuary provides income for area residents, but many are forced to commute to Pensacola for more positive employment opportunities.

Recreation provides the other major activity for the Perdido region. Camping and hunting in managed areas, with extensive wildlife populations and undeveloped expanses, provides leisure activity for many. Private hunting clubs lease part of the pulp lands, bringing two-fold utilization to the land. Swimming, fresh water fishing, picnicking and bird watching are other leisure pursuits for area residents or visitors. The small town of Perdido, Alabama, takes its name from the river, but few outside the immediate area are aware of the history or present role of the river.

As with many of the nation's undeveloped rivers, the Perdido today is a river championed by diametrically opposed groups. Florida is one of the United States' fastest growing states. Only in northwest Florida does one find the "land of the past"—rolling hills, extensive forest growths (both managed and unmanaged) and clear untouched rivers. Environmentalists seek to preserve the natural scenic beauty of the river and its surroundings, but many, including sizable numbers of local residents, hope for future industrial development. Industry creates jobs and jobs generate income for those citizens already in the region or those who hope to move there. In many ways this problem is emblematic of the general United States situation, the forces of the present struggling with the problems of the future.

The Perdido is a clear, scenic, and natural river. It peacefully flows most of the year, slowly winding its way to the Gulf. What the future holds for the Perdido River is uncertain. Further and more extensive development is probable. It is to be hoped that the Perdido River can serve both those who seek to utilize its resources and those who seek to preserve them without destroying the beauty and character of the river. It deserves such a fate.

ADDITIONAL READINGS: Isaac J. Cox, *The West Florida Controversy, 1798–1813* (1967). Edward A. Fernald and Robert B. Marcus, *Florida, A Geographical Approach* (1975).

William H. Graves

The Red River of the South

Source: Confluence of North Fork and Prairie Dog Town creeks north of Vernon, Texas
Length: 1,300 miles
Tributaries: Washita, Wichita, Kiamichi, Grand, Cimarron, Canadian rivers
Mouth: part of the waters enter Atchafalaya River which flows south into the Gulf of Mexico; part flow into Mississippi as Old River, near Alexandria, Louisiana
Agricultural products: pecans, wheat, cotton
Industries: oil and gas, gypsum

The headwaters of the incredibly complex Red River are to be found in the New Mexico portion of the Llano Estacado (or Staked Plains). This level, arid section of the southwest, spawns headwater streams of the Canadian, Brazos, and Colorado rivers of Texas, as well as the Red.

The streams most important to the creation of Red River are Palo Duro and Tierra Blanca creeks, which merge southwest of Amarillo to form Prairie Dog Town Fork, a name that well conveys the nature of the country through which it flows. Just east of Canyon, Texas, the stream enters the rugged Palo Duro Canyon, now a state park. It continues southeast out of the canyon and at the southwest corner of Oklahoma begins its course as the Texas-Oklahoma boundary. The river continues until it leaves Oklahoma at the state's extreme southeast corner. Just north of Vernon, Texas, the North Fork of the Red joins Prairie Dog Town Creek; from then on the stream is known as the Red River. Although the North Fork carries less water than Prairie Dog Town Creek, the former was, until a Supreme Court decision in 1896, considered by Texas as that state's boundary with Oklahoma.

Just north of Denison, Texas, is the Denison Dam, completed in 1943. It creates Lake Texoma, one of the largest reservoirs in the United States, including, as its name implies, portions of both Texas and Oklahoma. As a boundary the Red continues southeast another 150 miles to Texarkana, though, strictly speaking, the river's south bank rather than the river or its channel forms the Texas-Oklahoma boundary. It is during the Oklahoma-Texas portion of its 1,300 mile journey that the Red receives the waters of most of its tributaries. The Washita, an Oklahoma stream, is remembered historically for General Custer's attack on the Cheyenne Indians in 1868 in which he killed 103 natives, of which just eleven were warriors.

The Wichita flows in from Texas above Wichita Falls and, coming down from southeastern Oklahoma, the Kiamichi adds to the Red's waters. Progressively the climate becomes more humid, and at least from Lake Texoma eastward the Red no longer flows through arid country. Upon leaving Oklahoma it flows eastward about thirty miles into Arkansas, forming the Texas-Arkansas boundary, then, at Fulton, Arkansas, the Red turns south-southeast, leaves Arkansas and enters the final state through which it flows, Louisiana. It now assumes all the aspects of a sluggish southern stream. Swamps, bayous, and hummocks abound. Steamboats and barges push up as far as Shreveport. The river continues in a southeasterly direction past Alexandria to about forty-five miles above Baton Rouge, where the low terrain proves too much for the torpid stream. Part of the Red's waters enter the Atchafalaya River which parallels the Mississippi on the west, flowing about 170 miles into Atchafalaya Bay of the Gulf of Mexico. The other part continues as Old River, flowing seven more miles southeast into the Mississippi.

At times the Red is a violent river. Its name is derived from the reddish color it receives from silt acquired from the red sandstone hills along its upper reaches. In 1843 and 1908 the Red flooded disastrously, cresting at as much as forty-three feet above low water and cutting new channels which left some river ports and trading posts high and dry.

Centuries before Europeans came to the region, Indians occupying the lower reaches of the Red had coped with the vexations of the Great Red River Raft. This was an unusual log jam completely covering the river and extending upstream 160 miles from Campti, a small community about half way between Alexandria and Shreveport. The Great Raft had existed for so long that trees ten inches in circumference grew above it, though amidst the dense insect and snake-infested shrubbery the gurgling waters underneath could be heard and often seen. When the Raft got too thick or the river rose in a freshet, the water sought an easier passage. The result was lakes, bayous, and islands along the length of the raft. Cane River Lake at Natchitoches was part of the main channel until 1832. Indians, early traders and trappers, and settlers searched along the watery jungle for a channel deep enough to carry their vessels, even shallow draft steamboats, past the Raft and on upriver to southeastern Oklahoma.

The humid reaches of the Red, even into southeastern Oklahoma, were inhabited by the Caddoan Indians at the time of white arrival. Several tribes including the Natchitoches and the Washitas, were united in a loose confederacy. Because the Red River was a natural highway into Texas, Oklahoma, and the Great Plains, these Indians were, from their meeting with De Soto in 1541, and by 1714 with the French, in a sort of no-man's-land in which the Spanish to the west and the French along the Mississippi vied for their loyalty. Fort St. Jean Baptiste,

present Natchitoches, was founded in 1714 by the French where at that time the Raft ended upstream; the town was also on El Camino Real, the Spanish trail between Mexico and the Mississippi.

Indian troubles continued after American occupation following the Louisiana Purchase in 1803. Finally, in 1835, the United States bought Caddo Indian lands for $80,000. When the Indians, as part of the agreement, moved into Texas, more trouble ensued. They finally moved north, settling along the Washita River in Indian Territory (Oklahoma) where titles to their homes were confirmed by the federal government in 1872.

Emigrants to the Red River first settled along its lower reaches. Mostly Southerners from Kentucky and Tennessee, they added to a polyglot population including the French and Spanish inhabitants of Alexandria and Pineville, which faced each other across the river. Cotton, timber products, and furs gave to these towns a sound economy and provided the incentive for upriver expansion. But hindering reliable steamboat service, so necessary to the valley's economy, was the Red River Raft.

The Federal government manifested an interest in eliminating the obstruction because it wanted steamboat service upriver at least to Fort Towson, near where the Kiamichi meets the Red in southeastern Oklahoma. With the resettlement of the Five Civilized Tribes into Indian Territory, the need for cheap and reliable transportation into Oklahoma was pressing.

The task of destroying the Great Raft was assigned to Henry Miller Shreve, a riverboatman who has been given credit (perhaps mistakenly) for building the first true steamboat. Beginning in 1833 at Campti, using battering-ram vessels of his own design, he cleared eighty miles the first year and in five more years destroyed the Raft.

Shreveport, named for this indomitable riverman, rapidly became a flourishing metropolis serving a cotton plantation economy. It was prosperous even during Reconstruction. When oil and gas were found in nearby areas, the city experienced even more good times. In 1967 the Army Engineers launched a project to create a nine-foot channel 294 miles long, including nine locks and dams, to further facilitate travel on the Red River. Shreveport's continued prosperity seems assured.

The portion of the Red River country consisting of prairies and plains has been of interest to Americans since the Louisiana Purchase. In 1806 a group labeled the "Exploring Expedition of Red River," but perhaps better known as the Freeman Expedition for its leader, Thomas Freeman, reached present southeastern Oklahoma where they were met by a Spanish force and turned back. In the same year (1806) Lieutenant Zebulon Montgomery Pike headed west. What Pike thought was the Red River was in reality the Rio Grande. He was taken prisoner by the Spanish and later released without having found the source of the Red. Stephen H. Long of the Topographical Engineers in 1820 believed he was floating down the Red, but was disappointed to discover that he was on the Canadian River instead.

In 1849 Colonel Randolph B. Marcy escorted 479 California-bound gold seekers westward to Santa Fe from Fort Smith, then returned, crossing the Red at present Preston, Texas, northwest of Denison. In 1852 he made a thorough exploration of the western Oklahoma-north Texas region—the Red River country—and was the first to ascertain that the Red has two main branches coming together near the 100th meridian. Marcy stated, and in 1896 the Supreme Court agreed, that the southern branch of the Red (Prairie Dog Town Creek) should be considered the main stream. However, Marcy's surveyor, Captain George B. McClellan, figured the 100th meridian fifty miles too far east, thus causing litigation for many years between Texas and Oklahoma over their common border.

Marcy commented also on the Cross Timbers, a belt of timber five to thirty miles wide, extending from Fort Worth, Texas, northeast to southern Kansas; the Red flowed through it above Denison. The Cross Timbers were a dreaded hindrance to emigrants and to cattlemen, for the Texas longhorns "spooked" at the sight of the woods and resisted being driven through them. Washington Irving, who had been at the Red River in 1832, commented in his journals about them.

By the time Marcy was making his explora-

tions, Indian Territory (Oklahoma) had been settled in part by the Five Civilized Tribes and other smaller Indian groups. Then came the Civil War. The field of operations was primarily on the lower Red River in Louisiana although the Five Civilized Tribes sided with the Confederacy, punishment for which decision consisted of their losing much of their land after the war. Union forces under the command of General Nathaniel P. Banks were ordered to invade the Red River Valley. Alexandria and Pineville fell peaceably. Then Banks had the Red River dammed, using railroad cars, houses, cotton gins, and anything else available, in order to raise the water level so that his steamboats could navigate upstream. Union forces pushed upriver to Natchitoches and Mansfield, where Bank's 25,000 men were defeated by a Confederate force of 12,000 led by Generals Kirby Smith and Dirk Taylor. The Union troops then retreated south to Pleasant Hill (also near Natchitoches) where they were again defeated. The Red River was freed of military activities for the remainder of the war. The valley recovered quickly and settlement continued. In 1873 Shreveport was linked by railroad with Dallas, a portent of the decline in river shipping that accelerated as railroads expanded.

But the peace and prosperity that settled over the lower reaches of the Red River did not extend onto the plains of the Red River country in Oklahoma and Texas. There the Southern tribes—Comanches, Kiowas, Southern Cheyennes, and Arapahoes especially—contested white settlements, the railroads, and above all the destruction of their principal sorce of food, the buffalo. Finally, in 1874-1875, the warfare became so fierce that it bears the name of the Red River War. When it ended, after innumerable skirmishes such as the Battle of Adobe Walls in 1875, the Indians were defeated, the bison gone, and the southern plains from central Kansas to central Texas open for white occupation.

Now the way was opened for the cattlemen's open range. Several of the great trails leading north out of Texas crossed the Red. Especially important were the Chisholm Trail, which crossed the Red north of Henrietta, Texas, and the Western Trail, which crossed the Red at Doan's Store, north of Vernon, Texas.

When the railroads came and the free range ended, the Red River Valley settled into the stability of civilized, settled country. Cotton and oil in the lower reaches, and oil, pecans, gypsum, wheat, and cotton in its upper portions continued to give to the valley a relatively stable, diversified though primarily agricultural economy. "The Red River Valley," writes historian Charles W. Harris, "is virtually a 'little America,' for within the borders of its states can be found practically all the ethnic and cultural varieties which exist within the country as a whole."

FURTHER READING: James L. Haley, *The Buffalo War: The History of the Red River Indian Uprising of 1874* (1976). Ludwell H. Johnson, *Red River Campaign* (1958). A. W. Neville, *The Red River Valley Then and Now* (1948). Carl Newton Tyson, *The Red River in Southwestern History* (1981).

Richard A. Bartlett

The Rio Grande

Source: Rises in San Juan Mountains of southwestern Colorado
Length: 1,800 miles
Tributaries: Rock, Alamosa, Trinchera creeks, Conejos, Red, Chama rivers, Galisteo Creek, Jemez River, Rio Puerco, Rio Salado, Rio Conchos, Pecos, Devil's River, Rio Salado, Rio San Juan
Mouth: Into Gulf of Mexico at Brownsville, Texas
Agricultural products: Cotton, wheat, cattle, truck vegetables
Industries: Diversified and growing

The Rio Grande, also called the Rio Bravo or Rio Bravo Del Norte, is the fifth longest river in North America. Starting in the San Juan Mountains of Colorado, it flows about 1,800 miles east and then south through New Mexico, then southeastward to form the border between Texas and the Mexican states of Chihuaha, Coahuila, Nuevo Leon, and Tamaulipas. The normally sluggish river drains over 170,000 square miles before it flows into the Gulf of Mexico. In its course the river drops from about two and a half miles to sea level. Main tributaries, some intermittent, are: Rock Creek, Alamosa Creek, Trinchera Creek, and the Conejos River in Colorado; the Red River, Chama River, Galisteo Creek, Jemez River, Rio Puerco, and Rio Salado in New Mexico, and Rio Conchos, Pecos, Devil's River, Rio Salado, and Rio San Juan in Texas and Mexico.

Spanish Captain Alonso Alvarrez de Pineda and his four ships sighted the river's mouth in the fall of 1519. They called the Rio Grande the "River of Palms" after the trees that lined the shores and were as tall as their ships's masts.

Unsuccessful expeditions were sent out in 1520 and 1523 to establish a Spanish presence, but both failed. When the four survivors of the ill-fated Narvaez expedition to Florida, including Alva Nunez Cabeza de Vaca, were rescued in 1536 near where the Conchos River flows into the Rio Grande, their stories of splendid cities and gold along the river sparked new explorations.

In 1540 Captain Francisco Vasquez de Coronado, in the course of his explorations, examined pueblos along the Rio Grande and its main tributary, the Pecos River of Texas. Although Coronado eventually reached southeastern Kansas, he never found gold; however, his expedition added greatly to Spanish knowledge of the Southwest.

Englishmen first sited the Rio Grande in 1568. Three survivors of a small naval engagement off the coast of Mexico landed about thirty miles north of Tampico. They crossed the Rio Grande and walked the incredible distance to safety in eastern Canada.

In 1598 Don Juan de Onate undertook an impressive colonizing adventure. With over 100 families and 300 single men he arrived at the Rio Grande near El Paso, formally taking possession of the river and establishing the town of San Juan in present New Mexico. Activity in the river valley for the next 100 years included religious expansion and the maintenance of supply routes. Then in the 1680s the Indians along the upper reaches of the river attacked the widely scattered, poorly defended missions; they also took the village of Santa Fe. In 1692 the Spanish returned to the upper Rio Grande, reasserted their dominance and punished the Indians.

Meanwhile Spanish attention had been diverted to the lower reaches of the river. In 1683 General Domingo Jironza Petriz de Cruzate became governor of the province and established his seat of government at El Paso. From there, church officials sent Franciscan priests to the east to fulfill requests from Texas tribes for Christian training. The Spanish had also shown concern over rumors of an approaching French menace.

With 300 men in four ships, Rene Robert Cavalier, Sieur de LaSalle, set out to establish a base at the mouth of the Mississippi, but his ships missed the mouth and eventually landed on the shores of Matagorda Bay. There LaSalle built several forts, possibly constructing an outpost as far west as the Rio Grande. Later he was killed by his own men as he tried to lead a small party to seek help from French-held areas to the north. The French menace resulted in considerable Spanish activity along the Rio Grande and into east Texas.

Meanwhile the Spanish settlement along the upper Rio Grande in New Mexico, despite Apache harassment, quickly recovered. Santa Fe was rebuilt, Albuquerque established, El Paso continued to exist, and more missions were erected. Along the lower river in the early 1700s a number of villages were developed, but as the century wore on Spain neglected her holdings. An uncertain bridge across the Rio Grande was minimally maintained at El Paso.

By the early 1800s Americans were moving into east Texas. An American explorer, Zebulon Pike, was captured along the upper Rio Grande, taken to Santa Fe and then Chihuahua, and finally released at the Spanish-Louisiana border. Later Pike removed the notes he had hidden in the barrels of his soldiers' weapons and pieced together a surprisingly comprehensive report about the area that he had seen.

A few years later, in 1810, a Mexican priest, Father Hidalgo, issued his Grito de Dolores (Cry of Dolores) and started a revolt against Spain. Father Hidalgo's uprising failed, but within a decade revolt had flamed anew and by 1821 Mexico had attained its freedom. By that time the Adams-Onís Treaty had settled differences between Spain and the United States, with the western boundary of the Louisiana Purchase being fixed at the Sabine River and thence northward and westward, ultimately to the Pacific.

Mexico's constant political unrest, the increasing number of Anglo-Americans coming into Texas, and many other factors all set the stage for the Texas Revolution. In 1835 irate Texans drove inept Mexican regulars south of the Rio Grande. Texans then declared their independence at Washington-on-the-Brazos.

Santa Anna, the Mexican dictator, took command of his field forces. On the Rio Grande, during his northward advance, he decided to rest his weary men. It was there that Texas intelligence agents discovered that border bakeries were working around the clock to prepare bread and tortillas for the Mexican army. This led Texas leaders to conclude that Santa Anna was preparing for a deep penetration into the rebellious region. There then followed the Mexican dictator's extremely expensive and thoroughly meaningless victory at the Alamo, his cold-blooded massacre of Texans at Goliad, and his coming to terms with a wisely deceptive Sam Houston at San Jacinto.

New Mexicans meanwhile realized that they had been suffering from the same ills that had upset the Texans. One year after San Jacinto, open revolt broke out in Santa Cruz. In rapid order the rebels scattered the small Mexican military force in New Mexico and took control of Santa Fe. About the same time, Indians killed the Mexican-appointed governor. Jose Gonzales then set up a rebel government, but was quickly replaced by a rival, Don Manuel Armigo.

In the following decade unrest continued in New Mexico as Texans undertook several military expeditions into that province. Also, the international scene changed as the United States finally came to favor Texas annexation while Texas adamantly laid claim to the disputed land between the Nueces River and the Rio Grande. Mexicans threatened war if Texas was annexed to the United States; nevertheless, annexation took place in late 1845.

Now United States troops under Zachary Taylor were moved to Corpus Christi where they set about preparing a supply base at Point Isabel, less than ten miles from the mouth of the Rio Grande, and a military stronghold dubbed Fort Texas (Brownsville). As Taylor's main force shifted back and forth to protect both of these key points, one of his scouting patrols was attacked by Mexican troops upriver from Fort Texas. The American commander promptly called for 5,000 volunteers and sent news of the clash to President James K. Polk. The President then had the excuse that he needed to secure a declaration of war on Mexico.

Taylor meanwhile made contact with the enemy near the water hole at Palo Alto. There, on May 8, 1846 (four days before Senate approval of Polk's war declaration), the Mexicans were repulsed. Taylor then forced the numerically superior enemy to the south bank of the river. A little over a week later the Mexicans pulled back from Matamoros towards Monterey. Taylor then occupied Matamoros, awaited reinforcements, and then pushed southward to Monterey which in late September fell to the Americans. The real climax in northern Mexico took place at Buena Vista in February, 1847. Taylor withstood massive enemy attacks until the Mexicans withdrew. Then his forces took up blocking positions while attention shifted to Vera Cruz and General Winfield Scott's campaign to Mexico City.

Negotiations resulted in the Treaty of Guadalupe Hidalgo. Mexico ceded all the present southwest quadrant of the United States (less the Gadsden Strip) to the North Americans. In exchange Mexico was paid $15,000,000 plus claims that its people held against Mexico. Far upriver during this war, General Stephen Watts Kearny took Santa Fe without resistance.

As the year 1850 drew near, old hatreds between Texans and New Mexicans centered on a boundary dispute. New Mexico claimed a sizable piece of land to the east of the Rio Grande which today constitutes the eastern half of the state. Texas claimed that it was their land and that they also owned a panhandle extending into present Wyoming. In the Compromise of 1850

the United States offered to pay Texas $10,000,000 if the state would accept her present boundary with New Mexico. Although most Texans scorned this offer, speculators holding Republic of Texas securities used their influence and the offer was accepted.

When the Civil War came, Texas, with strong ties to the South, joined the Confederacy; New Mexico stayed with the Union. This gave Lieutenant Colonel John R. Baylor a way to regain "unredeemed Texas" from New Mexico. Without authorization he called for volunteers to go "buffalo hunting" in New Mexico. Making their way past El Paso, these 300 irregulars worked their way up the Rio Grande, driving small Union garrisons before them. At Mesilla they established a Confederate government and, feeling that they had spread themselves too thin, called for reinforcements. The Confederate high command ordered General Henry H. Sibley to form a brigade in San Antonio and hasten to New Mexico to support the invaders. As for the Union, it amassed its retreating garrisons in northern New Mexico and rushed in reinforcements from California and Colorado (including one regiment under "Kit" Carson). Well above Santa Fe, the two forces clashed at Glorieta Pass. During the fighting a lucky Union patrol fell upon a weakly guarded Confederate supply train and destroyed it. The badly weakened and severely harassed Texans fell back to the western tip of Texas.

Texas's Rio Grande boundary was of significance to the Confederacy, for it marked the border of the only neutral country that touched it. Mexico could well serve as a market for Texas cotton and a source of supplies. However, during the Civil War period Mexico was subjected to French occupation. Northern Mexico was a no-man's-land of French forces, rebels following Juarez, local strongmen, and even bandits who controlled towns and portions of Mexican states. Despite these conditions and primitive transportation facilities, a sizable trade developed between Texas and Mexico.

From San Antonio huge ox-drawn wagons loaded with ten to twelve bales of cotton and carrying food and water for teamsters and oxen headed for Brownsville and Matamoros to sell the cotton and bring back badly needed goods to Texas. Because the Rio Grande was an international body of water, foreign ships picked up the cotton at Matamoros. This trade was disrupted, however, when Union invaders took the lower reaches of the river and Lincoln tied up a British ship over international legal questions. After this the cotton caravans had to be re-routed through Eagle Pass; from there the cotton was hauled to Bagdad, a boom town thirty miles above the mouth of the Rio Grande. There, scores of ships of all nations waited beyond the sandbars as lighters brought bales to them through shark-infested waters.

After Appomattox General Philip H. Sheridan brought 40,000 troops to the Rio Grande to enforce American demands that the French puppet regime leave Mexico. For the rest of the century the soldiers were busy subduing the Indians and clamping down on raiding bandits. Cattle drives became successful, mining was profitable near the river's headwaters, and such isolated parts of the river as the Big Bend of Texas were explored. After the Mexican Revolution of 1911 there was disorder in the region culminating in General Pershing's punitive expedition into northern Mexico in 1916.

Early in the twentieth century it was agreed that the Rio Grande would be closed to ship navigation. And a number of irrigation developments, such as the Armistad Reservoir near El Rio, have been constructed.

The river occasionally shifts the course of its lower bed. One such shift triggered the Chamizal border dispute involving land located between El Paso and Juarez. In 1963, about 100 years after the shift occurred, the matter was settled between the governments of Mexico and the United States.

Since the days of Cabeza de Vaca and Juan de Oñate the Rio Grande has figured in the lives of civilized people. There is no reason to believe that its days of glory have gone; on the contrary, with Mexico's industrializing it may just now be entering its most significant era.

FURTHER READING: Paul Horgan, *Great River: The Rio Grande in North American History* (1965). Laura Gilpin, *The Rio Grande, River of Destiny* (1949).

Allan C. Ashcraft

~~~~~~

The Sabine River

> **Source:** Near Greenville, northeast of Dallas, Texas, as the Cowleach Fork.
> **Length:** 380 miles
> **Tributaries:** Neches River flows into Lake Sabine
> **Mouth:** Into Gulf of Mexico at Sabine Pass
> **Industries:** Petroleum refineries, petro-chemicals, rice mills, shipyards, paper mills
> **Agricultural products:** Tree farms, cotton, rice, hay, potatoes, tomatoes, cattle, chickens, truck farming

The Sabine rises as the Cowleach Fork near the town of Greenville, northeast of Dallas. Beginning in an area with an average rainfall of thirty-seven inches annually, it flows 380 miles and drains 9,733 square miles before emptying into the Gulf of Mexico in an area with an average rainfall of fifty inches. The river flows southeast across Hunt and enters Rains and Van Zandt counties where it forms the county line. Here the river is dammed to form large, 36,700-acre Lake Tawakoni. It follows an eastward course across Gregg County and forms the county line between Harrison and Rusk and Harrison and Panola counties. Then it turns southward into Panola County, intersects the State of Louisiana boundary, and from that point on serves as the state line for 180 miles straight south to the Gulf of Mexico.

The river is dammed at a little more than half this distance forming a great lake, Toledo Bend Reservoir. This is the largest lake in Texas, impounding 186,500 acres, and is sixty-five miles long. On downstream in Orange County the river again widens into Lake Sabine where the center channel marks the eastern boundary of part of Orange and Jefferson counties and intersects the Gulf Intracoastal Waterway; the Neches River also flows into Lake Sabine. Below the lake the Sabine enters the Gulf via a narrow channel, Sabine Pass. The annual discharge at its mouth, 6,952,000 acre-feet, makes it in volume the largest river in Texas.

The Sabine River was named by the Spanish explorer Domingo Ramón in 1716 and translates into Cypress Tree River. American Indians occupied the Sabine drainage basin many thousands of years before the coming of the white man. It was roughly the western boundary of the highly developed eastern village-dwelling woodland people loosely referred to as the Temple or Mound Builders. They entered East Texas shortly after the time of Christ, and developed a high level of culture which still existed when the first incursions were made by Europeans into what is now Texas and Louisiana. Although it is too general and all-inclusive, the term Caddo is used to designate all of the agricultural-type Indians in East Texas. Indians of the Caddoan linguistic stock were concentrated along the Sabine, especially its middle and upper course. There were nine tribes loosely formed into the Hasinai Confederation. More than likely, the name of the state came from the Caddo word Tayshas, which meant "ally," or "friend." This was corrupted to Tejas by the Spanish and specifically given to one of the nine Hasinai tribes, but often used as a general term for all of the Caddo. It was further corrupted to the present-day Texas.

The first European to view the Sabine was the Spanish explorer and cartographer Alonso de Piñeda in 1519 when he mapped the coast; however, the first to actually touch the river was Cabeza de Vaca when he skirted the estuary in 1528. In 1543 the remains of the De Soto expedition, then under the leadership of Luis de Moscoso, made the first European contact with the Caddo and explored the upper reaches of the Sabine and adjoining areas. Later in 1687 the La Salle expedition made contact with the Hasanai, probably somewhat south of Moscoso's activities.

Due to the fear of another French attack the Spanish dispatched Alonso de Leon in 1690 to establish Mission San Francisco de los Tejas near present-day Weches. Continued French activity out of Louisiana confirmed Spanish fears of French duplicity and further settlements were authorized, but none survived more than a few years. In 1713 France established an outpost at Natchitoches, Louisiana, and French forces led by Louis de Saint Denis became a thorn in the side of Spain. The Spanish quickly responded with the founding of Nacogdoches in 1716 by Domingo Ramón, and Los Adaes in present Louisiana. Los Adaes, established to counter Natchitoches, served as the capital of Texas between 1721 and 1773. After Louisiana was acquired by Spain in 1763, Los Adaes was gradually abandoned.

The Sabine was considered as just one more river in the area until Spain was forced to cede Louisiana back to France in 1800. In fact, considerable confusion existed on what and where the Sabine was. The situation become explosive after France sold the territory to the United States in 1803. Neither the Spanish nor the French had ever attempted to demark the boundaries of Louisiana except on the east, and when the United States assumed sovereignty over the vast undefined region, no one was sure what it comprised. As might be expected, beginning with the Jefferson administration the United States claimed as much as possible. Jefferson dispatched an American force under the infamous General James Wilkinson to secure the western border of Louisiana in 1806. Wilkinson and General Simón Herrera, the Spanish commander in East Texas, prudently agreed not to push the border issue, and created a buffer or neutral zone between the Sabine and the Arroyo Hondo to the east. This "neutral ground," since it was not officially policed by either side, became a center of criminal activities frequented by pirates, smugglers, and an assortment of unsavory characters. These conditions continued until 1812 when Louisiana became a state, claiming the Sabine as her western boundary. Also, as Anglo-American settlers began to push westward into Texas the lawless element in the neutral zone declined in importance.

Thomas Jefferson's successors all made concerted efforts to enforce America's shadowy claim to Texas based on the Louisiana Purchase, claiming as far southwest as the Rio Grande, but Spain and later Mexico resisted all American pressures. Following the War of 1812, Spain was fully aware that the hold on her North American possessions was tenuous at best. After Jackson's invasion of Florida in 1818 forced a Spanish reassessment, Secretary of State John Quincy Adams and Spanish Minister Luis de Onís began negotiating on Florida. These negotiations culminated in the Adams-Onís Treaty of 1819, and passed ownership to the United States of all of Florida. In return, the United States, among other things, agreed to the demarcation of the Louisiana Purchase and Spain's northern provinces. Adams accepted, later with considerable regret, the Sabine River as the boundary to thirty-two degrees north latitude, which was where the Sabine began a westward swing into Texas, and then due north to the Red River. After the Adams-Onís Treaty went into effect in 1821, the United States, using some old maps, raised the question of whether the Neches was really the Sabine. Jackson later instructed American diplomats Anthony Butler and Joel R. Poinsett to push the issue with Mexico, but to no avail. After much acrimonious debate, the Sabine boundary was accepted in 1828 by the United States and Mexico.

During and following the Texas Revolution, Jackson and Van Buren kept large American forces stationed at nearby Fort Jessup, Louisiana, to control the Sabine line. One controversial theory on the Texas Revolution claims that Sam Houston was retreating eastward to the Sabine where he expected American troops to intervene, but the opportunity at San Jacinto negated the plan. There can be little doubt the United States violated both the spirit and letter of neutrality during the Texas Revolution. After Texas independence in 1836 when immediate annexation proved to be impossible due to the slavery issue, the Sabine River was accepted by both sides as the boundary. When Texas joined the Union in 1845, it became the official state line between Texas and Louisiana.

Laguna de Rio Sabinas, or Sabine Lake, and Sabine Pass played an important role in Confederate efforts to circumvent the Union blockade. It was relatively easy to bring goods down the Sabine and run them out at an opportune time to Europe. The bar on the Gulf side of the Pass, and extensive shoal water, provided ideal conditions for either departure or return through the gauntlet of blockading Union warships. Early in 1863 several Confederate cotton-clad steamers (steamers armored with cotton bales) attacked and captured two of the Union ships stationed at the mouth of the Pass. The Union high command in the middle of 1863 decided to chastise the rebels, and at the same time warn the French in Mexico to remain neutral. General Nathanial Prentiss Banks, Union commander at New Orleans, was ordered to "raise the flag in Texas." In compliance with this order, Banks dispatched an invasion force of 4,000 infantry and a large naval squadron under General William Buel Franklin to seize Sabine Pass.

Guarding the narrow entrance was an earthenwork fortification much run down called Fort Sabine. It was armed with six cannon and manned by forty-two men, mostly Irish Houstonians, under the command of Lieutenants N.H. Smith and Richard (Dick) Dowling. Ordered to abandon the position, they refused, and prepared to meet the Union attack. On September 8, 1863, three Union gunboats attacked the fort, and during the ensuing exchange of fire two of the attacking vessels, the *Sachem* and the *Clifton*, were disabled and captured. Franklin, with his support ships cut in half, afraid of Confederate cotton-clads among his transports, withdrew to New Orleans. The Battle of Sabine Pass, while a small insignificant Civil War battle by eastern standards, was still the most spectacular engagement in Texas, and did much to shore up Confederate morale. Today, just outside the Beaumont naval yard, the walking beam from the *Clifton*, dredged up from the lake, is on display.

From the very beginning of Texas statehood Louisiana has raised questions on the Sabine boundary. In recent years there has been serious litigation in the Federal courts in which Louisiana has claimed the western bank of the river to be her boundary. This is a highly controversial issue, not just because of the questions of sovereignty and pride, but because vast reserves of oil and gas are at stake.

Today the Sabine taps a rich agricultural hinterland where tree farming, logging for lumber and pulp, cotton, rice, hay, potatoes, tomatoes, cattle, chickens, hogs, and truck farming are major endeavors. Nearer the Gulf, petroleum refineries, chemical and petro-chemical plants, rice mills, shipyards, steel fabricating plants, food-packing industries, and paper mills dot the landscape. Through the years, efforts have been made to widen and deepen the Sabine, and jetties have been built to control the tides and erosion, allowing oceangoing vessels to safely enter the lake and the river. Thriving ports such as Beaumont, Orange, and Port Arthur give the area world-wide connections either from the sea or via the Intracoastal Canal. With the almost unlimited supply of water, the salubrious climate, and adequate fuel supplies, the "Golden Triangle," as the area is known, will continue to boom far into the future.

FURTHER READING: Herbert E. Bolton, *Texas in the Middle Eighteenth Century* (1915). Rupert Richardson, *Texas: The Lone Star State* (1970).

Victor H. Treat

The St. Francis River

Source: Hills of southeastern Missouri
Length: 475 miles
Tributaries: None of significance
Mouth: Into Mississippi north of Helena, Arkansas
Agricultural Products: Diversified
Industries: None of significance

The St. Francis River is one of the five major waterways draining the state of Arkansas. It drops rapidly from its source in the hills of southeastern Missouri, but as it moves into the flatlands it gradually slows its pace, taking on the sluggish, meandering character more typical of the river as it moves toward the Mississippi. As it passes present-day St. Francis, Arkansas, its channel becomes very ill-defined, creating a "spread" which continues for 100 miles. Then the river moves into the true alluvial valley of the Mississippi, eventually emptying into that river near the town of Helena, 475 miles from its source.

As with most rivers in America, the St. Francis has been looked upon primarily as a problem to be resolved. Here, as elsewhere, the advance of settlement brought in its train the inevitable urge to manipulate. "What can be done to render this extraordinary country a fit habitation for man?"—the question was first posed in 1836, and it has received, over the years, the desired answer: the river has now been cleared, ditched, channelled, dammed, and leveed so extensively that few stretches now resemble the wild state.

Ironically, the St. Francis had been a "fit habitation" for perhaps ten thousand years before plans were afoot to make it so. Furthermore, because it has generally been a docile stream, subject to few violent overflows, it has left the record of prehistoric culture in a remarkably good state of preservation. Its basin has become one of the most important centers of archaeological research in North America.

Excavations along the river began before the Civil War (with amateurs vastly outnumbering professional researchers), and the appearance in 1909–1910 of the large, well-funded expedition headed by Clarence B. Moore of the Academy of Natural Sciences marked the beginning of modern systematic analysis of the area. Moore had his problems: he was disappointed to find that pothunters had stripped away in decades what the river had preserved for centuries; then the expedition's float upriver was blocked by unreconstructed whites who threatened to murder every black aboard. Still, twenty-one sites were excavated, and Moore left satisfied that the area's reputation as a rich repository of aboriginal earthenware was justified.

Research efforts have accelerated since Moore's time. In the 1930s, J. D. Harrington of the University of Missouri, cooperating with the Missouri Archaeological Society, initiated an extensive program of site-plotting. Arkansas joined in these activities with the establishment of the Arkansas Archaeological Survey in 1967. Under the direction of Charles S. McGimsey, the Survey has since sponsored additional site-plotting projects as well as a series of digs. Much work remains to be done (over three thousand prehistoric sites have been identified to date), but a reasonably clear understanding of the long relationship between the St. Francis and the Amerindians has emerged.

The St. Francis River Basin may have been supporting a human population as early as 10,000 B.C. Although no site offering definitive proof of the existence of Paleo-Indian culture (10,000 B.C.–8500 B.C.) has yet been identified, scattered artifact finds indicate that the earliest aboriginal presence may be dated from that period. Certainly the food supply would have been adequate. Mastodon, giant beaver, ground sloth, and other megafauna all found the St. Francis to be a congenial environment.

The archaeological evidence is unequivocal for the Dalton stage (8500 B.C.–7000 B.C.). Nowhere in the southeastern United States has an equally heavy concentration in sites dating from the period appeared. The most carefully investigated at present is the Brand site, excavated by the Arkansas Archaeological Survey in the early 1970s. Evidence from this site suggests that small hunting bands roamed the area, often travelling by water in dugout canoe-like boats, stopping at Brand and other spots to butcher their kill and to store provisions.

For reasons unknown, these bands nearly disappeared in succeeding centuries. Little evidence of human activity during the Early or Middle Archaic periods (7000 B.C.–3000 B.C.) has yet surfaced. In the Late Archaic period (3000 B.C.–500 B.C.), however, the humans returned, and in large numbers: most of the sites in the St. Francis Basin date from that period.

Gradually the level of cultural sophistication increased, producing eventually the distinctive mound-building cultures which has had an enduring fascination for professionals and amateurs alike. The best-known of the mound-builder settlements is the Snodgrass site in Ripley and Butler counties, Missouri. Radiocarbon-dated to 1275–1350 A.D., this site reveals the presence of a very complex, and apparently very beleaguered community. Of the ninety structures erected at Snodgrass, thirty-eight were within a walled compound, and all were protected by an encircling moat. Why this and other relatively advanced groups in the St. Francis Basin found such elaborate protective measures necessary, and why they seem to have declined

before Europeans first penetrated the area, are questions anthropologists have not yet answered.

In any case, the measures would have been of little use against the new invaders. Moats and compounds were no defense against the European-based diseases accompanying the De Soto expedition as it moved toward the St. Francis in 1541. De Soto and his men were a bedraggled crew by this time, and probably managed to push no farther north than present-day Parkin, Arkansas (information that the residents of New Madrid, Missouri, consider the rankest sort of historical revisionism), but their viral companions continued upriver on a mission of destruction. By the time the French expedition under Marquette and Joliet re-established contact over a century later, the aboriginal population was but a shadow of that which De Soto had reported.

As control of the interior passed to Euroamericans, and then between varieties of the latter, interest in the St. Francis and the territory it drained began to focus vigorously upon its economic potential. Frenchmen had been exploiting the lead deposits on the upper St. Francis throughout the eighteenth century. Shortly after 1800, the citizens of the United States moved in, hoping that the mineral resources would produce quick fortunes (Moses Austin of Virginia encouraged his claim by calling it "Potosi"—an insufficient stimulus, as it turned out). With the acquisition of territorial status, the flow of population increased, and continued to do so despite the area's growing reputation for unhealthiness. Even the New Madrid earthquake of 1811–12, a catastrophic upheaval that produced an even greater abundance of swamplands, only temporarily interrupted the flood of settlers. With this influx, the days of the St. Francis as a free-flowing stream were numbered.

Residents began petitioning the United States government for improvements along the river in 1836, choosing as their champion Senator S. F. Linn of Missouri. In his talent for visionary bombast, the ex-country doctor may have had peers, but certainly no superiors: open this river, he declared, and iron mines to rival those of Sweden would swing into production; drain the swamps, and bring under cultivation "a million or two acres, surpassing in fertility the favored borders of the Nile"—this and more, and all for a mere thirty thousand dollars! The Senate Committee had long since learned, however, that translating frontier rhetoric into plain English often required the services of a surveyor, so it sent W. B. Guion of the Topographical Engineers out to investigate. Guion returned to report that Sweden and Egypt appeared safe, as the banks along a 111-mile stretch were too low to make navigation feasible; beyond removing the seven huge "rafts" below Greenville, Missouri (the same Greenville that the traveller George Featherstonhaugh would describe a few years later as "a poor wretched collection of four or five wooden cabins, where the miserable inhabitants die by inches of chills and fever"), the projected benefits of improvement would not match the outlay.

Despite repeated efforts by the Arkansas legislature to secure Congressional appropriations, few alterations were made until after the Civil War. Then a series of small projects did clear the river up to Greenville, and activity increased thereafter. By 1905, 200 miles of the river's course between New Madrid, Missouri, and Helena, Arkansas had been leveed. But these and other improvements did not transform the St. Francis into an important waterway. It did support some steamboat traffic, but that dwindled; when the steamboat *St. Francis*, the last Mississippi-style craft plying those waters, sank in 1875, serious navigation ended. Railroads and other forms of land transportation proved to be both cheaper and more convenient. For a time a lumbering industry exploited the forests of oak, hickory, and walnut, but that had played itself out by the 1920s. By the end of the decade, carriage was down to 135,000 tons.

Flood-control and drainage projects continued, however, and they did help to develop the agricultural base upon which the economy of the basin has depended in this century. In 1928, following the great Mississippi Flood of the previous year, the St. Francis Basin became part of the general Mississippi River flood-control project. Out of this came numerous major alterations, including the Wappapelo Reservoir on the upper part of the river. These alterations were capped by the completion in 1977 of the giant Huxtable pumping plant, touted by the U. S. Army Corps of Engineers as "the largest of its kind in the world." Built at a cost of $30 million, this plant has the capacity to pump interior drainage from approximately 2,000 square miles of the St. Francis River Basin over a levee during the high water stage of the Mississippi, and to do so at the rate of 5.4 million gallons a minute.

It is hardly necessary to add that all these projects are the stuff of nightmares for environmentalists. The impact has been tempered only slightly by the creation of the Big Lake Wildlife Refuge, which spans nearly 10,000 acres just south of the Missouri-Arkansas line. And, from that perspective, there are many sleepless nights to come, for the Corps has plenty of red-lined projections left on its map. It is a new environment now, and the St. Francis is a new river.

FURTHER READING: John G. Fletcher, *Arkansas* (1947). Iroquois Research Institute (Prepared for the Memphis District of the U.S. Army Engineers), *Predicting Cultural Resources in the St. Francis River Basin, A Research Design* (1978).

David Sloan

The Suwannee River

Source: Okefenokee Swamp in southeastern Georgia
Length: 250 miles
Tributaries: Alapaha, Withlacoochee, and Santa Fe rivers
Mouth: Gulf of Mexico twelve miles north of Cedar Key, in west-central Florida
Agricultural products: Negligible but some truck farming
Industries: None

To most Americans the Suwannee River is closely associated with Stephen Foster's famous song "Way Down Upon the Swanee River." As a result the Suwannee has become a river whose name is familiar to Americans, most of whom are not aware of its geography. Indeed, Foster himself did not use the name because he wanted to pay tribute to a famous southern river, but because he needed a two-syllable word for the line of a song he was writing. As far as we know Foster, a native of Pennsylvania, never saw the Suwannee and he apparently obtained the name from a map in his brother's office in Pittsburgh. He had considered using either the Yazoo in Mississippi or the Peedee in South Carolina, but he quickly settled upon the "Swanee" when it blended so nicely into the opening lines of his ballad.

The Suwannee is a rather small river extending just 250 miles from its source to mouth. It rises in the Okefenokee Swamp which encompasses a large section of southeastern Georgia. Cypress trees festooned with Spanish moss so shield the swamp from sunlight that the light which filters through appears green, adding to its mystery.

After flowing out of the great swamp the river moves through the sandy hills, limestone banks, and hardwood hammocks of northern Florida. Wider now, the stream moves westwardly turning and twisting through green valleys and picking up strength from the Alapaha, a rather long river (190 miles) coming down out of south-central Georgia; it joins the Suwannee a few miles southwest of the north Florida town of Jasper. Further along the river is joined by the Withlacoochee which enters from the north at Ellaville. The final important tributary is the Santa Fe which flows west out of central Florida into the Suwannee near Branford, Florida. As the river approaches the coastal lowlands it widens and flows through swamp marshes before entering the Gulf of Mexico some twelve miles above Cedar Key and twenty-two miles south of Cross City. Gulf tides sweep twenty-five miles up the Suwannee channel and the river has been dredged 135 miles, all the way to the mouth of the Withlacoochee.

The Suwannee's twisting, winding pattern prompted the Seminole Indians to speak of the stream as the "Winding River." Indeed, some authorities hold that the word "Suwannee" is derived from an Indian word meaning "Crooked Black Water," the blackness due to the decaying vegetation, or "River of Reeds." Others think the word was an Indian or Negro modification of the Spanish "San Juanita" or "Little St. Johns."

European presence in the Suwannee region antedates the American purchase of Florida by many decades. When the Spanish arrived they found most of the region embraced in the Indian province of Timucua. They established missions and converted many of the Timucuans to Christianity, but this once proud accomplishment of Spanish Florida came to a tragic end as a result of warfare between England and Spain during the late 17th and early 18th centuries. The Mission of Santa Catalina on the banks of the Itchetucknee, a tributary of the Santa Fe, was destroyed by a force of Carolinians and their Indian allies in 1685. By 1708 only St. Augustine was left.

From that time until the late 1700s the region of the Suwannee was virtually devoid of human occupancy. The bands of Creek Indians who moved into Florida in the latter part of the 18th century came to be known as "Seminoles." Some, such as the group led by Chief Alligator (Halpatter Tustenuggee) settled in the region of the Suwannee although most of the Seminoles preferred for their agricultural pursuits the Alachua prairie lands further south or the Tallahassee Red Hills to the west.

Some pirate craft were known to operate out of the lower reaches of the Suwannee during the latter part of the 18th century, preying on ships in the Gulf of Mexico. All in all, however, as of 1821 when the area became a part of the United States, there were few settlers in the region. If a traveler to the locale at that time encountered anyone, the likelihood would have been that it was a Seminole Indian, a runaway slave, a cattle rustler, or a smuggler. There were no roads in the area except the overgrown path of the Old Spanish Trail which ran from St. Augustine to St. Marks, a distance of about 200 miles.

Settlers, mainly from adjacent Georgia, started moving into the Suwannee environs during the 1820s. One was an Indian Agent named Reuben Charles who operated a ferry across the Suwannee at the point where the Old Spanish Trail crossed the river. Additional settlers moved in during the 1830s.

The Suwannee region was one of the centers of activity during the Second Seminole War (1835–1842), one of the longest and bloodiest Indian wars in American history. One of Chief Osceola's most effective battle leaders was Chief Alligator who had lived previously in the Suwannee region. The swampy areas at both ends of the river offered excellent cover for bands of Seminoles engaged in guerrilla warfare against the army and the settlers. One important army fort was built near the river at the site of present Suwannee Springs.

The first recorded use of steamboats on the Suwannee was in the winter of 1836–1837 when an army craft took supplies to this beleagured post. Fort White on the Santa Fe was also an important fort in the area.

The end of the Seminole War ushered in a period of growth and development. Although some fine plantations were built along the river the region was more characterized by small farms with few or no slaves. In ante-bellum Florida the Suwannee was the historic dividing line between East and Middle Florida (and before that it had been the boundary between East and West Florida). Most of the large plantations with many slaves were found in Middle Florida, the area west of the Suwannee. Among the rural folk of the region East Florida was the land of "hog and hominy" whereas Middle Florida was the land of "sowins and chicken." "Sowins" was

the local term for a dish of cornmeal made sour by baking it in the sun.

Life along the Suwannee was characterized more by frontier farms of log cabins with mud and stick chimneys. Hog killings were social events enlivened with hard liquor from the settlers' own stills. The people of the Suwannee were proud and independent frontier folk conditioned to hardship. Their children grew up with little formal education, learning only hunting, fishing, chopping, and hoeing. Even though they owned few slaves they defended the southern system with vigor. Yankees were hated almost as much as Indians.

The Suwannee country was not the scene of much military activity during the Civil War although blockade runners from Cuba did use the river to bring supplies to the Confederacy. In September, 1863, the steamboat *Madison* was deliberately sunk in the estuary by Confederate forces in order to deprive Union gunboats of the use of the river. The largest battle in Florida during the war took place in February, 1864, at Olustee, about twenty-five miles east of the Suwannee. It was a Confederate victory which checked a major Union thrust westward from Jacksonville.

After the war when there was some economic growth based upon cotton and lumber, river traffic on the Suwannee increased. The 1880s and 1890s marked the high point of steamboating on the Suwannee. *The Belle of the Suwannee* was the most famous boat plying its waters. It was severely damaged in a hurricane in 1896, but was rebuilt. A few years later it was wrecked on some shoals near Cedar Key. The *City of Hawksville*, which operated until 1923, was the last of the Suwannee's steamers.

During the 20th century the Suwannee did not play a major economic role in Florida's development. The boll weavil destroyed the cotton cultivation of the region during the 1920s and lumbering declined during the 1930s. Since the Second World War the primary use of the river has been for recreational purposes. Canoe trips in particular have become a popular pastime along the stream.

The most committed canoeists start their trip at Fargo, Georgia, on the southern edge of the Okefenokee Swamp. At that point the river is sluggish; swamp sawgrass abounds. As they

5

move downriver the current picks up although the only white water of significance is found at Suwannee Shoals a few miles above White Springs. This, the largest community on the upper reaches of the Suwannee, is also the site of the Stephen Foster Center which features a museum, displays, and carillon concerts in honor of the song writer who made the river famous. White Springs and Suwannee Springs, which is further down the river, were famous health spas in the 19th century. Presently only the foundations of once-elegant hotels remain as monuments to that era.

Near the confluence of the Withlacoochee River is the Suwannee State Park which offers camping and shower facilities. (Florida has two Withlacoochee Rivers; the northern one flows into the Suwannee while the one in Central Florida is not affiliated; it flows directly into the Gulf of Mexico). Altogether there are thirty-one recreational developments along the river. Many canoeists stop at Branford, about twelve miles above the confluence of the Santa Fe. Below there the river changes character as it nears the Gulf and canoeists find mosquitoes to be their greatest hardship. The town of Suwannee, once called Suwannee Old Town, is a small fishing village on the river delta. It stands as an oasis in an inhospitable area, although there was once a stately grove of live oak and water oak there; it was known as the "Old Town Hammock." Unless canoeists are intent on going into the Gulf they stop at this point.

The popularity of canoeing augmented by desires of conservationists prompted the Department of the Interior in 1974 to recommend that the Suwannee be included in the Wild and Scenic River System, but this proposal has not materialized. Conservationists, environmentalists, and canoeing enthusiasts see little immediate threat to the scenic river, but regard some type of protection as essential for the future. Although those who love the Suwannee differ as to methods of protection all agree that the river should remain unspoiled and continue to offer its magic to future Americans.

FURTHER READING: Dorothy Kaucher, *The Suwannee* (1972). Cecile H. Matschat, *Suwannee River: Strange Green Land* (1938).

Edward F. Keuchel

The Yazoo River

Source: Convergence of Tallahatchie and Yalobusha rivers at Greenwood, Mississippi
Length: 189 miles
Tributaries: Sunflower River, Steele Bayou
Mouth: Into Mississippi River at Vicksburg
Agricultural Products: Cotton, soybeans
Industries: Negligible

The Yazoo River System rises in the hill country of northeast Mississippi and flows southwestward to empty into the Mississippi River at Vicksburg. The total length including its numerous tributaries rank it second only to the Ohio River among the streams that flow from the east into the Mississippi. Never more than 100 yards wide when inside their tenuous banks, these rivers that make up the drainage system for one third of the state of Mississippi wander for a total of 1,420 miles, twisting and turning out of the hills and down through the Mississippi Delta, carrying alluvial soil deposited by millenia of flooding by the Mississippi and other, lesser rivers.

Once these streams come down out of the hill country in northeast Mississippi, they do not touch again the bluff hills that define with topographical absolutism the Delta area until they reach Yazoo City. This business center has existed since the late 1820s because of its location and the consequent permanent landing that was possible there. The Yazoo River Basin comprises 13,400 square miles and drains both hill lands and the broad alluvial valley. The oval-shaped floodplain is about 200 miles long and sixty-five miles wide.

The system begins with the Coldwater River,

which starts its flow south just below the Tennessee state line. It gathers in numerous streams and bayous and flows for 220 miles before it joins the Little Tallahatchie, a 190-mile stream, and the Yacona, already 130 miles long, to form the Tallahatchie River which, in turn, meets the Yalobusha River (165 miles long) at Greenwood, Mississippi, 111 miles south. As the Yazoo the stream runs to Vicksburg, 189 miles southwest. On the way it is joined first by the Sunflower River, which has flowed for 240 miles south entirely through Delta land, then by Steele Bayou, a 175-mile stream that has roughly paralleled the Sunflower for most of its channel.

Geographical origins of the rivers are shrouded in mystery. Wide crescent lakes and bayous in the Delta land were formed by some force not presently accounted for. Perhaps the Ohio River once used this area as its channel. To substantiate the possibility of such a major change in a river channel, the Mississippi River is known to have flowed through a channel far west of the present one, and the entrance of the Yazoo River into the Mississippi at Vicksburg has changed significantly since the Spanish settlers walked along its banks and described it in the 1600s. The rivers are alive, always growing and shrinking, turning back into themselves, eating away land and depositing silt, only partially controlled by man who constantly seeks to harness the power of the ever-moving water.

The name "Yazoo" has evoked a panorama of emotions. The Indian tribe that was the original namesake was known for its warlike nature. To Georgians involved in the land speculations of the 1790s the name created wild excitement over the possibility of outlandish profits. The meaning for "Yazoo" was most often given as "death." This name could have come from the many deaths caused by malaria in its swampy environs, or from the fact that the tribe "fought to its death." Other meanings with equally valid authenticity are "leaf," "hunting ground to go to," and "to blow on an instrument."

Since Indian times the history of the Yazoo River has been intimately tied into the economy of the region. The river was the cause of the settlement of the area in the early 1800s, as soon as the land was wrested from the various Indian tribes in a series of treaties engineered by Andrew Jackson. The infamous "trail of tears" over

which the Choctaws and Creeks passed on their way to Indian Territory (Oklahoma) follows the Yazoo River.

Cotton was then and still remains the primary export of the region. In 1857 there were 150 landings on the Yazoo between Vicksburg and Greenwood, just 100 miles upstream. These landings were rudimentary affairs, actually mud banks into which that strange, American-created vessel, the riverboat, could tie, take on cotton, and then shove off again. Dodging snags and driftwood and miraculously finding the channel which, due to the boat's design, needed to be only fourteen inches deep, the craft headed for still another landing.

Downstream-bound riverboats gathered cotton from the beginning of harvest time in late summer until long after Christmas. During the summer dry spells only the "mosquito fleet" could navigate. Such a boat as the *Yazoo Planter* was only 110 feet long and 26 feet in beam. In high water, boats of 200 tons were not unusual.

The trip downriver and transshipment onto ocean-going steamships at New Orleans was a worry in the early days. The riverboats were piled with cotton as high as the superstructure which was exposed to every rain. Boats frequently burned from overheated boilers. Farmers complained that cotton was stolen regularly in New Orleans so that when the shipment was weighed in Manchester or Liverpool, England, there was considerably less arriving than had left the plantation. Planters were further irritated when the city of New Orleans taxed every bale that landed on its wharf even though the cargo was transient.

To offset these problems, several farmers investigated making Vicksburg into an international harbor. The New Orleans agents reacted in fine, capitalistic style, offering to pay the city tax themselves and guaranteeing a "true weight" on the cotton. This left only the hazards of the river trip, which in no way could be totally avoided, and the movement died down.

In the post-Civil War era the river remained a center of activity, for railroads were slow to be built in the swampy, cypress-studded area. The most famous of Yazoo River steamboat lines, in its heyday in the 1880s, was the Parisot Line, known locally as the "P-Line." Sherman Parisot had begun his career in 1847 with the purchase of a tiny steamer, the *John Wesley*, which ran between Yazoo City and Vicksburg. By 1877–1878 he was advertising a total of eight steamers running the Yazoo, Tallahatchie, and Sunflower rivers.

River traffic continued until the early 1900s when railroads finally crisscrossed the Yazoo Delta, but river traffic revived in the 1960s when the cost of bulk shipments of cotton and soybeans (added in the post-World War II period) became less by barge than by train. Today there are several landings doing business along the river.

During the Civil War, the river played a significant role in the attempt by the Union forces to divide the Confederacy by controlling the Mississippi River. Union campaigns during the early stages of the war were all unsuccessful. The local people defended the river by such methods as tying chains across it to ensnare the Union gunboats. In 1863 a torpedo sank an ironclad, the *Baron DeKalb*, just south of Yazoo City. (In dry summer weather the remnants of the boat are still visible in the river just below Yazoo City.) Another Union ironclad sunk by an underwater device in the Yazoo was the *Cairo*. It has been raised, is currently being restored, and will be displayed permanently in the museum at Vicksburg.

The most important long-range contribution to the war effort was through the naval yard at Yazoo City where ironclads, the ships of the future, were constructed from 1862 to 1864. The most famous of these, the *Arkansas*, wreaked havoc on the Union concentration of boats above Vicksburg before succumbing to an old rival, the Union ship *Essex*, in the Mississippi River close to Baton Rouge.

From a purely tactical viewpoint, the occupation of Vicksburg was the focal point of the western campaign of the Union forces, for with Vicksburg under control, the Mississippi River split the Confederacy right down the middle. Ulysses S. Grant, in command of the western campaign, chose the Yazoo and its tributaries as the route through which to conquer Vicksburg. The campaign began in earnest in February, 1863. Grant planned to cut the levee that had been constructed in 1857 along the Mississippi to separate it from the Yazoo River System. Prior to the construction of this levee, in high floodwater boats could move from the Mississippi into the Coldwater River by way of Moon Lake, Yazoo Pass, and Cassidy's Bayou, and thence downstream into the Yazoo River and back into the Mississippi river at Vicksburg. It was the back door to the town.

The embankment was easily dynamited and Union gunboats began fighting their way through the bayous and streams to Vicksburg, 500 tortuous miles south. One method of defense used constantly by the southern home guard was to sink vessels in the rivers to block passage. Of course, this blocked their own boats also, but the far more numerous Union gunboats were hampered more than the few Confederate boats. Moreover, their commanders were frequently capable of by-passing the blocked area. The Union gunboats were ultimately superior, however, and by May, 1863, the Yazoo River System belonged to Grant. Vicksburg and the Confederacy's fate was sealed.

The Yazoo Delta area is peculiarly susceptible to floods. The floodplain, with almost no altitude change from Memphis to Vicksburg, is bounded by a continuous series of abrupt bluffs that rise 100 feet above the adjacent flatland. Within this oval-shaped area there is no natural barrier to the spring waters that cascade down the Mississippi River from Canada nor from the interlocking streams that form the Yazoo River System. Consequently, the entire area has been inundated with Nile-like regularity. In the early 1800s farmers built their houses on stilts above the flood level or farmed the Delta land when it dried out but lived in the hills over the bluff.

Floods remained a fact of life for the Delta people until the catastrophic event of 1927 when 23,000 square miles in the lower Mississippi alluvial valley flooded making roughly 700,000 people homeless. The Army Engineers then established a post at Vicksburg and built the Mississippi levees to record heights. The oxbow curves of the Yazoo River were straightened to speed the water southward into the Mississippi. Floods were so infrequent that thousands more acres of Delta land were cleared and drained and cultivated.

However, in 1973 another interesting aspect to water control appeared. The Mississippi River levees were so high that they carried with great efficiency a record number of gallons of water from Canadian snows and the Ohio system spring rains. When the waters passed the mouth of the Yazoo River, they found a lower water level and, therefore, backed up into the Yazoo Deltaland. Instead of a rush of flood water from broken levees as in 1927, the Yazoo Basin farmers watched the backwater creep inch by inch out of the drainage ditches, across the newly planted fields, into their houses. In May of 1973, 90 percent of the land area in Sharkey and Issaquena counties was under water.

Human ingenuity still had not conquered the river.

FURTHER READING: Harriet C. DeCell and JoAnne Prichard, *Yazoo: Its Legends and Legacies* (1976). Louis C. Hunter, *Steamboats on the Western Waters* (1949; 1969).

Harriet DeCell

Rivers of the Great Basin and Arizona

Early explorers and geographers believed there had to be, somewhere in the western desert, a river, named by them the San Buenaventura, that drained the Great Basin into the Pacific via a gorge through the Sierras. Eventually, however, they realized that the rivers were land-locked. Some flowed into lakes, such as the Bear into Great Salt Lake or the Sevier into Sevier Lake. Others, such as the Carson and Humboldt, simply dried up in a swampy "sink." Yet the rivers were of great importance. Humboldt water was crucial for survival to the California-bound forty-niners, and today many farms and some towns in the desert exist because of the waters from these rivers.

To the south was the Colorado River, the largest, longest, and most important of all Great Basin and Arizona rivers. Without Colorado River water and the electrical energy produced at its dams, large parts of Arizona and California would suffer from drought and energy shortages. So too are Arizonans dependent upon the Salt, Verde, and Gila rivers to slake their thirst and prevent crops from withering.

All the Great Basin and Arizona rivers have long, romantic histories. Some of Coronado's men first observed the Grand Canyon. Father Eusebio Kino journeyed along the Gila, and Fathers Dominguez and Escalante crossed the Colorado, Green, and Sevier. In the nineteenth century Mountain Men learned how to cross the arid wastes using the rivers.

Mormons settled at Salt Lake in 1847 and diverted water for irrigation from streams rushing down from the Wasatch Mountains.

Just because these rivers occasionally dry up and even when swollen to flood stage are small in comparison with the streams of more humid climes does not detract from their importance. In this sampling of Great Basin and Arizona rivers we become aware of their importance as well as of their colorful history.

Richard A. Bartlett

The Bear River

Source: Near Hayden Peak in Uinta Mountains of northern Utah.
Length: About 500 miles
Tributaries: Smith's Fork, Thomas Fork, Cub River, Malad River, Little Bear River
Mouth: Flows into Bear River Bay of Great Salt Lake
Agricultural Products: Sugar Beets, truck vegetables, ranching
Industries: Hydroelectric power

The Bear River is the largest tributary to the Great Salt Lake, running as much as 1.4 million acre-feet of water into the sterile inland sea. The Bear is also the largest stream in North America that does not reach the ocean. While it is a river virtually unknown to most people, for the residents of its 6,900-square mile drainage area it is of life-giving importance. At first a rushing, boulder-strewn young stream swelled by the melting snow water, it soon becomes a characteristically mature river, spending most of its 500 miles meandering through a flat, often arid land. In its course it makes a near loop, rising near Hayden Peak in the Uinta Mountains of northeastern Utah, flowing north into southwestern Wyoming, west into southeastern Idaho, then south back into Utah. Eventually it flows into Bear River Bay of the Great Salt Lake. This is just ninety miles west of the river's place of origin; in its journey it has crossed state boundaries five times.

Prior to the coming of the whites, Shoshone Indians were the principal beneficiaries of the Bear's waters and green valleys. Occasionally bands of Cheyenne, Blackfoot, and Crow Indians attacked them. When left alone the Shoshones lived simple lives that included some agriculture and much hunting. When the whites first arrived, the Indians willingly shared their meager surplus with them.

Directly or indirectly it was the quest for beaver peltry that brought the first white people into the Bear River region. On his return to the United States from Astoria in 1812 Robert Stuart and his party encountered some white men fishing along the Snake River. They described the Bear River country to the south so intriguingly to Stuart that he determined to cross from the Snake to the Portneuf and then over the divide to see the Bear River country. He probably first saw it in the vicinity of Soda Springs, Idaho, the northernmost point on the river. Stuart called it Miller's River in honor of his guide, Joseph Miller.

In 1824 fur trader William Sublette led a party from the upper valley of Green River to Soda Springs in southeast Idaho and into present Cache Valley, Utah. Jim Bridger, a member of his party, left the party on a bet to "discover" Great Salt Lake. His description is the first one recorded by EuroAmericans of the sterile body of water. So attractive were the stories told about the Bear River region that the trappers' rendezvous of 1825 and 1827 were held there. (The rendezvous were mountain fairs where Indians, trappers, and traders met to exchange goods and frolic for a few days.) It was from the Bear River rendezvous that Jedediah Smith began his odyssey southwest to California. In 1827 William Ashley brought a cannon mounted on a four-wheel carriage to the rendezvous, but there is no record of its being used.

Competition among fur traders was heated. Peter Skene Ogden represented the Hudson's Bay Company in the interior regions of the Northwest. His orders were to trap as many animals as possible so that Americans would not want to enter the territory. Even so, a few dauntless mountain men went in. Among them were Captain B.L.E. Bonneville, Zenos Leonard, and Black Harris, a black free trapper. In 1834,

Rivers in arid lands are heavily used. Utah's Bear River produces hydroelectric power as in this scene west of Cache Canyon; it also furnishes water for irrigation. (Courtesy A. J. Simmonds, Utah State University.)

near the end of the fur harvest, a number of missionaries passed through the Bear River region on their way to Oregon. Among them were Jason and Daniel Lee, Methodists who settled in the Willamette Valley; and Marcus Whitman, representing the American Board of Missions, who in 1836 settled with his wife Narcissa in central Idaho. A few years later the Jesuit missionary, Father Jean Paul De Smet, paused along the Bear River in his travels into the Northwest.

Indeed, in the 1830s and 1840s a parade of emigrants, traders and trappers, businessmen and missionaries enjoyed the water and grass of the Bear River country. After all, it constituted the water supply for 300 miles along the Oregon Trail. Nathaniel Wyeth, a Boston ice dealer, passed through in 1834. With the trapper Osborne Russell he helped build Fort Hall in southeastern Idaho. In 1841 the Bartleson-Bidwell party left the Oregon Trail at Bear River and headed due west; they were the first emigrants to successfully make it overland to California. In 1843 Captain John C. Fremont headed an expedition bound for the Columbia River. On August 21 he recorded that,

> An hour's travel this morning brought us into the fertile and picturesque valley of Bear River, the principal tributary of the Great Salt Lake. The stream is here 200 feet wide, fringed with willows and occasional groups of hawthorns. We were now entering a region which for us possessed a strange and extraordinary interest. We were upon the waters of the famous lake [Salt Lake] which forms a salient point among the remarkable geographical features of the country, and around which the vague and superstitious accounts of the trappers had thrown a delightful obscurity, which we anticipated pleasure in dispelling, but which, in the meantime, left a crowded field for the exercise of the imagination.

The Mormons, who were into the region in 1847, found in the valleys of the Bear River and the Great Salt Lake the resources necessary for successful agricultural settlement. Although they were discouraged by such mountain men as Black Harris and Jim Bridger, the Pioneer Band continued on and was camped at the mouth of Sulphur Creek on the Bear by July 10, 1847. By July 24 the Band had arrived at Great Salt Lake: that date is celebrated in Utah as Pioneer Day.

Soon the Mormons were busy exploring their new Zion. In the spring of 1848 a party set out down the Bear to survey the Great Salt Lake. Their craft, dubbed the *Mud Hen*, reached "Mud Bay" (Bear River Bay) on April 22 after hauling provisions through three miles of mud in search of water deep enough to launch their boat.

In 1849 Captain John W. Gunnison and Albert Carrington of the U.S. Topographical Engineers were caught on the mud flat and nearly perished in a snowstorm. Only by covering themselves with their boat sail were they saved from freezing to death. In the winter of 1854 an army supply force was quartered in Salt Lake City. Its passage through the Bear River Valley helped establish the trail along the River as a military road. Meanwhile, Indian depredations, committed especially by the Bannocks, took place from Bear River to the Humboldt River to the west.

During the Civil War Colonel Patrick Connor was stationed with his troops at Fort Douglas, out of Salt Lake City. Aware of the continued pillaging by the Bannocks of emigrant trains, Connor determined to chastise the Indians, who were encamped in Cache Valley on Bear River. In 1863 he took his troops north, attacked their winter quarters and killed perhaps 300 of them. Besides earning Connor his brigadier star, the battle brought peace to the valley.

The coming of the transcontinental railroad, although it runs east and west while the Bear runs north and south, nevertheless brought temporary prosperity to the Bear River country. The "hell-on-wheels" town that sprouted there was Corinne, dubbed by the Mormons "The Burg on the Bear." Although Brigham Young enticed the Union Pacific to establish its rail yards at Ogden and many Corinne establishments abandoned Corinne for Ogden, "the Burg" continued to thrive. It was the best transshipment point for the mines of Montana and Idaho to the north. It was also the point of departure for passengers taking the stage for Montana. Plans were even made for irrigation diversion of Bear River water, but nothing came of that in the 1870s.

For awhile, also, Corinne was the head of navigation for boats coming up the Bear from Great Salt Lake. However, the sand/mud bar at the mouth made navigation difficult, while after 1874 the lake level dropped perceptibly and left the natural harbors dry. Commerce shifted to Ogden and Salt Lake where population and demand was greatest. The railroad simply drove water transportation out of business.

The key to settlement in the Great Basin has always been water. Communities were established at several points along the Bear in the 1860s and in all cases the agricultural lands were irrigated with Bear water. Although the region, with elevations up to 5,900 feet, has a short growing season, not only hay and grass but potatoes and wheat also have been grown successfully.

As early as 1878 geologists John Wesley Powell and Grove Karl Gilbert recognized the river's importance to settlement and predicted controversy over water allotments among the territories (later states) of Utah, Wyoming, and Idaho. Interest was so great that one of the earliest stream-gauging stations in the country was established in 1889 near Collinston.

The demand for water by the farmers of Wyoming, Idaho, and Utah, coupled with needs of power companies for hydroelectric development, brought on many decades of controversy. Bear Lake, close by the river but not naturally a part of it, was connected to the river by inlet and outlet canals completed in 1918. The lake stores water and helps prevent floods. Other dams and fourteen hydroelectric facilities have since been built.

Between 1955 and 1958 the Bear River Compact, an agreement in which the rights, vis-à-vis the river, of Utah, Wyoming, Idaho, and the federal government were defined, was approved by Congress and the President, and by the three states involved. As the Compact states, it is "to remove the causes of present and future controversy over the distribution and use of the waters

of the Bear River." Today the Bear watershed, with its tributaries (of which only the Malad is of real significance) supplies water for nearly a half million acres. The Compact is an excellent example of intergovernmental cooperation for common good.

To the hard-working, isolated residents of the Bear River country the stream is as important as the Nile is to the Egyptians. It sustains their agriculture, provides them with hydroelectric power, helps maintain waterfowl refuges, and provides them with recreation facilities.

FURTHER READING: Brigham D. Madsen, *The Bannock of Idaho* (1958). Dale L. Morgan, *The Great Salt Lake* (1977).

Jay M. Haymond

The Carson River

Source: Juncture of East and West Forks of Carson River, near Genoa, Nevada
Length: 125 miles
Mouth: Carson Sink and Lahontan Reservoir
Industries: Gold, silver mining
Agriculture: Cattle grazing

Near Genoa, the oldest town in Nevada, the east and west forks of the Carson join to form the Carson River. It then flows northward about 125 miles past Carson City to the base of the once great Comstock mines and, since 1915, to the Lahontan Reservoir, a part of the Newlands Irrigation project. The river and its east and west forks stood astride the emigrant trails to California and the "Rush to Washoe"—the Comstock mines—in 1859. Its waters provided the impetus for the growth of population, agriculture, and industry. Here ranchers brought lands under irrigation as early as the 1850s, entrepreneurs constructed stamp mills to serve the Comstock, and early settlers pushed for independence from Mormon-dominated Utah Territory.

The Carson River is one of several streams flowing from the eastern side of the Sierras into the lake bed of ancient Lake Lahontan which covered much of western Nevada during the

close of the last Ice Age. All that remains of this ancient lake are dry sinks; Walker Lake, fed by the Walker River; and Pyramid Lake fed by the Truckee. Before the Lahontan Dam blocked its flow, the Carson River spent itself into the Carson Sink which sometimes extended to the Humboldt Sink. Its waters also found their way to the south along another branch of the sink called Carson Lake.

Before the coming of white men, waters of the Carson ran freely. From the Sierras in springtime, freshets from its two forks united into the slower moving valley river that then lost itself in the desert. Indians placed small dams and wiers in the river to trap fish, but no other utilization of its water resources for agricultural or mining uses occurred.

The early fur trade explorers, Joseph Reddeford Walker and Peter Skene Ogden, touched upon the Carson Sink but did not discover the Carson River or its forks. There is evidence that the Bidwell-Bartleson party of 1841, the first overland emigrant party to California, camped along the shores of Carson Lake before they proceeded south to the Walker River. After Captain John C. Fremont discovered Pyramid Lake and the Truckee River in January, 1844, his southward course brought him to the Carson Sink. In that year of high water it joined with the Humboldt and he wrote on January 17, 1844: "This stream joined with the open valley of another to the eastward; but which way the main water ran, it was impossible to tell." Fremont moved up the river, hauling his mountain howitzer with him, and camped near the future site of Fort Churchill. He soon left this river, which he named for Carson after his favorite guide, Kit Carson, and pushed south to the Walker River where he resolved to make a perilous winter crossing of the Sierra. In the following year, 1845, he crossed the Great Basin from the Salt Lake Desert. On this trip he again reached the banks of the Carson and then headed north from its waters over the mountains via the Truckee River route.

Increased migration to California in 1845 and 1846 brought many tired emigrants to the banks of the Carson after their hard journey across the Forty Mile Desert. Their point of encampment on the river came to be called Ragtown. The name was an appropriate description for the rags and other refuse discarded by overland travelers at this point on the river. With the opening of the Carson Pass road in 1848, the Carson River route became the main way west over the Sierras to California's gold country.

The route also offered opportunities for eager placer miners to try their luck in the small streams of adjacent mountains. One of these was in Gold Canyon along the reaches of the lower Carson Valley. Placer mining further up the canyon eventually led to the discovery of the fabulous Comstock Lode in 1859.

Meanwhile Mormon businessmen in 1850 and 1851 had established a trading post to serve the Carson Pass traffic; it was located where the two forks of the Carson join to form the main river. John Reese in 1851 established the first permanent white settlement at Mormon Station, later named Genoa, in the future territory and state of Nevada. Reese was an enterprising businessman, purchasing lands from the Indians, building the first toll bridge over the Carson, and employing Chinese labor to build a canal from the Carson to aid the placer mining in Gold Canyon.

With trading, mining, and agricultural settlement on its upper forks, the Carson River valley

presented a picture of a diverse pioneer community by the mid-1850s. There was, however, a growing resentment among the non-Mormons against being governed by Utah Territory. The arrival of 39 Mormons under the leadership of Orson Hyde in 1855 increased the tension. In 1857 unexpected events caused Mormon President Brigham Young to order the return of his followers to Salt Lake City to defend Zion against an approaching federal army. This opened the way for others to move quickly against Mormon rule in the valley.

The new squatter government established at Genoa in 1857 quickly demanded independence from Utah. Just two years later placer miners at the head of Gold Canyon uncovered an outcropping ledge of the rich Comstock Lode. The ensuing "Rush to Washoe"—"Washoe" being the name given to the range of Sierra foothills where the silver was found—brought thousands of miners seeking quick riches. But mining in the Comstock required more than a pan, shovel, and pickaxe, for the ore was embedded in hard quartz rock buried deep beneath the ground. Major capital investment was required to sink shafts, build transportation outlets, and construct processing plants for the ore. The Carson River was to play a vital role in serving the Comstock community because of its close proximity, the railroad that would be built along its banks, and because of the water power derived from it for turning stamp mills. In 1861 such mills for processing the ore were built on the Carson and in 1869 there were seventeen such mills standing on its banks from Empire to Dayton. The Carson River thus became Nevada's first industrial river. Its power operated the great crushers or stamps that reduced the quartz to powder and pebbles readying it for the extraction of gold and silver.

As the face of the peaceful valley communities changed under the impact of Comstock development, an Indian uprising broke out in May, 1860, at Pyramid Lake. This Paiute War prompted the military to build Fort Churchill on the lower reaches of the Carson between Virginia City and Pyramid Lake to the north. The fort also defended a new trail that had been opened across the Basin south of the Humboldt River route and through the Reese River country. The Pony Express followed this route, connecting with the Carson River at Fort Churchill before the swift ponies dashed down the Carson and disappeared over Carson Pass to Placerville and Sacramento. The telegraph, which replaced the Pony Express in the spring of 1861, also followed the Carson River.

Transportation into the Carson Valley attracted the attention of William Sharon, the Bank of California representative to the Comstock. He initiated the construction of one of the most profitable railroads in the nation, the Virginia and Truckee. It extended from Virginia City down Gold Canyon to the Carson River and then to Carson City. The river course of the railroad is significant because it transported ore from the mines of the Comstock to the mills along the river. The mines, the mills, and the railroad formed the triad of Nevada's industrial empire of 1870, and the river was an integral part of this system of industrial production.

Not only was waterpower available from the Carson, but also the forks were used to transport logs desperately needed to brace the underground tunneling in the mines and provide fuel for the steam power of locomotives and mining machinery. Log drives, a frequent occurrence on the river, were conducted by damming the rivers and then unleashing the water which then carried thousands of cords of lumber down from the Sierra into Nevada. This interstate transportation of logs on the forks of the river converted it to the status of a navigable stream. It is one of the few intrastate rivers under federal control because of the interstate nature of the commerce that has occurred on its east and west forks.

The Carson River was the subject of early water-law decisions by state courts. In adopting the common law doctrine of riparian rights, the courts ruled in favor of the milling interests and their use of water directly along the banks of the river. Such a doctrine supported by the courts was surprising for an arid state such as Nevada to employ, but it definitely protected the water level of the river for the mills in their down-

stream locations. Only in drought years did the river's waters come into dispute. Ranchers of the upper Carson tributaries demanded more from the downstream milling interests, but the mills, fortified by court decisions, felt justified in sending men into the upstream communities to tear out ranchers' diversion dams.

In the 1890s, however, the courts adopted prior appropriation for the state water doctrine, and since the ranchers were there before the mills, the ranchers won. This decision confirmed the decline of the Comstock industrial complex and the growing importance of agriculture.

The Newlands Act (1902) brought additional agricultural enterprise into the state and new demands on the waters of the lower Carson. One of the first irrigation projects undertaken by the Bureau of Reclamation was the Truckee and Carson project. In 1915 government engineers completed the Lahontan Dam on the lower Carson beyond the decaying mills that had largely been washed away in the great flood of 1907. The dam stored water and generated power. Henceforth water disputes on the Carson involved the large ranchers, the government-sponsored agricultural project, and more recently, the urban needs of a growing metropolitan area, Carson City.

In addition to the agricultural and industrial uses of the Carson's waters, urban growth demands in Carson City forced a building moratorium in 1977 because of a declared shortage of river and ground water. The planned Watasheamu project for a series of storage reservoirs on the East Carson River proposes to make the river a more efficient servant of the community of the future. In the past, however, the Carson River aided travelers, provided the cradle for the first settlement and political life in western Nevada, and was the scene of conflict among ranchers, millmen, and the federal government.

FURTHER READING: Grace Dangberg, *Conflict on the Carson* (1975). Russell R. Elliott, *History of Nevada* (1973).

William D. Rowley

The Colorado River

Source: Grand Lake in northwestern Colorado Rockies

Length: About 1,400 miles

Tributaries: Among many, Williams Fork, Roaring Fork, Dolores, and Gunnison rivers in Colorado; Green, Dirty Devil, and San Juan in Utah; Little Colorado, Virgin, and Gila rivers in Arizona

Mouth: Into Gulf of Lower California in extreme northwestern Mexico

Agricultural products: Vegetables of all kinds, citrus fruits, dates, cotton, sugar beets

Industries: Hydroelectric power, uranium mining and oil shale in tributary areas

One of the most extraordinary rivers in the world is the mighty Colorado. Although for most of its 1,400 miles it flows in deep canyons, including the world-renowned Grand Canyon, through rugged mountains, arid buttes and plateaus, it supplies water for millions of people and irrigation for hundreds of thousands of otherwise arid acres which by its waters have been turned into highly productive farm land. It accomplishes all this because the Colorado carries the only water available. Since the stream has had an annual flow in drought years of as little as five million acre-feet of water, and has carried as much as twenty-five million acre-feet in wet years, the problems it poses to hydraulic engineers, irrigation interests, hydroelectric authorities, and the representatives of millions of people who depend upon its water for drinking and other purposes are immense. In sum, the Colorado is a life-giving artery in an arid land.

It begins on the western slope of the Colorado Rockies at Grand Lake, about seventy airline miles northwest of Denver. The stream flows west-southwest past the cities of Glenwood Springs, Rifle, and Grand Junction—cities profiting in recent years from the oil shale and uranium in the region. As the river approaches the Utah line it passes through the Colorado National Monument, noted for its magnificent cliffs, a part of the geologic formation called the Uncompahgre scarp. Shortly thereafter the river crosses into Utah about midway between that state's north-south boundaries. The Colorado

then continues south-southwest, while to the northwest is another spectacular geologic phenomenon, the colorful red sandstone cut by wind and rain into the shapes that have given the area its name: Arches National Monument.

A few miles further downstream, within the boundaries of Canyonlands National Park, the Colorado joins its greatest tributary, the Green River. By this time, however, the Colorado (originally known as the Grand from Grand Lake to its junction with the Green) has been swollen by the convergence of a number of substantial streams. Among them are the Williams Fork and Roaring Fork, and the Muddy, Blue, Dolores, and Gunnison rivers. Taken together, they drain some of the most awe-inspiring mountain country in all North America.

Some authorities would like to consider the Colorado (Grand) as a tributary, and the Green as the real upper Colorado. If this was so the Colorado would be about 1,700 miles long. The Green flows south from central Wyoming where its head streams arise out of the Green River Lakes high in the Wind River Range. The river comes down out of the mountains, flows across sandy wastes punctuated by weird badland formations and then, below Green River, Wyoming, confronts the east-west running Uinta Mountains. Originally the Green picked up speed and flowed tumultuously through the Uintas by way of the deep, rugged Flaming Gorge, but construction of Flaming Gorge Dam and the deep, long reservoir behind it put an end there to the river's wild ways. (The area is now known as the Flaming Gorge Recreation Area.)

Below the dam the Green veers sharply to the east into Colorado, bends southward and then westward, crossing back into Utah. Straddling the boundary, including the river and spectacular cliffs, is the Dinosaur National Monument. Here, uncovered by the abrasive waters of the Colorado where in Jurassic times, about 140 million years ago, the carcasses had piled up as the result of a flood, lies the greatest deposit of dinosaur fossils known to man. The Monument includes Brown's Hole, a favorite rest and relaxation place for the beaver-trapping mountain men and, later, a hideout for desperadoes and cattle rustlers. Both the Canyon of Lodore and the canyon of an important Green tributary, the Yampa, are also embraced within the Dinosaur National Monument.

Back again in Utah, the Green flows southward through Desolation, Gray, and Labyrinth canyons to its junction with the Colorado within Canyonlands National Park. In its flow of 730 miles the Green has added the waters of Blacks Fork in Wyoming, of the Yampa in Colorado, and of the Duchesne, Price, and San Rafael rivers of Utah.

Now, swollen with the Green's waters, the Colorado veers west-southwest into Glen Canyon, today a 200-mile strip of deep reservoir named Lake Powell, backed up by the Glen Canyon Dam near Lee's Ferry. Glen Canyon National Recreation Area importunes sportsmen to float over some of the most beautiful grottoes and side canyons ever seen by man, but now inundated and lost forever. Population statistics of Utah, Arizona, and California probably attest to the need for the dam and resultant reservoir, but it was constructed at great aesthetic loss.

Below the dam the river flows wild and free for about 175 miles. Now well into Arizona, it enters Marble Canyon which extends to the mouth of the Little Colorado. A little below there the river swings prevailingly west and enters the world-famous Grand Canyon (a national park) where geologists can trace 280 million years of earth history.

The river continues its tortuous journey across western Arizona, its rapid flow slowed and finally ended as its waters constitute Lake Mead, the reservoir created by Boulder Dam across the Black Canyon. Southbound once again, the current is slowed by Lake Mohave, created by Davis Dam, and Lake Havasu, backed up by Parker Dam. Just north of the city of Needles, California, the river becomes the boundary between Arizona and California. Again and again its flow is slowed and the amount of water reduced as reservoir and dam after reservoir and dam control its passage. By the time the waters are impounded behind Imperial Dam, about eighteen miles above Yuma, little is left of the original waters, yet still enough to divert water

into the All American Canal System which brings life-giving water to California's fertile Imperial and Coachella valleys.

What is left of the Colorado's water is highly saline. It is this residue of a magnificent river that flows into Mexico after briefly serving as the international boundary. But the Colorado's contribution to civilization is not yet over: in Mexico water is diverted through Morelos Dam into the fertile Mexicali Valley. The Colorado has the most extensive delta in the world. It is not shaped like a triangle, "but ... as a widespread, overturned Y with its arms pointing to the northwest and to the south, with the great silt-laden river flowing in a southwesterly direction into the base of the Y near Yuma: from there it flows toward the Gulf of Lower California." For its last sixty miles it is known as the Hardy River. It has drained 244,000 square miles. The Green, San Juan, Little Colorado, Virgin, and Gila rivers have all helped as the Colorado's tributaries.

Such an overview hardly does justice to this wildest and most complicated of America's rivers. Yet the real romance of the Colorado involves man's approach to it, how civilization has used the river, and abused it. Pueblo Indians picked their way down to fertile shelves deep in the canyons where, safe from intruders, they could raise little plots of corn and beans and squash and live peaceful, protected lives. A few Indians still reside in the vast Colorado River world.

In 1539 the Spaniard Francisco de Ulloa first observed from the prow of his ship the dangerous tidal bores (waves) at the mouth of the Colorado, and suggested in his log that this must be indication of a river extending into the continent. The next year, in conjunction with Coronado's expedition in search of the fabled Seven Cities, Admiral Hernando de Alarcon sailed up the Gulf of California, entered the Colorado River channel, and navigated about 100 miles above the mouth of the Gila before turning back. At almost the same time one of Coronado's lieutenants, Melchior Diaz, reached the Colorado and even found letters buried where Alarcon had turned around to return downstream. More than sixty years later still other Spaniards, this time affiliated with Don Juan de Oñate, marched west from New Mexico and reached the Colorado where the Bill Williams Fork flows in (at present Parker Dam). As the seventeenth century advanced, various Black Robes traversed the arid southwest. In 1701 Father Eusebio Kino walked the banks of the Colorado. In 1776 Franciscan Father Francisco Garces skirted the Grand Canyon and lived to tell about it. In that same year, out of Santa Fe, an expedition led by Father Francisco Atanasio Dominguez and Father Francisco Silvestre Velez de Escalante searched for a land route between New Mexico and California. They never got there, but by the time they were back in Santa Fe they had seen the Green and Colorado rivers and had crossed the Colorado below present Lee's Ferry; that point, one of the few fords on the river, is known to this day as the Crossing of the Fathers.

But the days of Spanish dominance were numbered. Little more was heard from them concerning the Colorado River country, but their presence there is noted today by botanists who attribute to the Spanish the introduction into the canyons of the tamarisk, an exotic plant that has worked far upstream, pushing out all other flora as it has advanced.

Nearly fifty years passed after the Dominguez-Escalante and Garces explorations. Then, in 1824, an American fur trader, William H. Ashley, floated down the Green from where it cuts into the Uinta Range, just south of Green River, Wyoming, to the head of Desolation Canyon in northeastern Utah. Ashley kept a journal which has been published and lived to return East and recount his adventures.

From Ashley's explorations on, at least some part of the Colorado-Green River system rarely went more than four or five years without some curious mountain man, government official, or military man observing it. In 1826 an English naval lieutenant named Robert W. H. Hardy sailed a small schooner, the *Bruja*, upriver to the mouth of the Gila. Mountain man James Ohio Pattie probably traversed the rim of the Grand Canyon at about the same time and certainly trappers and traders unknown to us roamed the region in the 1820s, 1830s, and 1840s. Then came Brigham Young and Mormon settlement at Salt Lake. From 1855 on these energetic people explored and became familiar with the startlingly beautiful canyon and mesa country east and south of their first settlements.

By 1851 steamboating was being tried on the lower Colorado. In 1858 U.S. Army Lieutenant Joseph Christmas Ives guided his little steamboat, the *Explorer*, all the way to the foot of Black Canyon while an overland party sent out by him advanced along the floor of the Grand Canyon before climbing out and advancing east over the Colorado Plateau to Fort Defiance, New Mexico. In 1859 Captain John Macomb, U.S. Army, advancing overland from Santa Fe, reached the point in present Canyonlands National Park where the Green joins the Colorado. Still others—a civilian "Captain" Sam Adams and a mountain man named James White—were on the river in the 1860s.

The publicity that enlightened the world about the Colorado was a result of one-armed John Wesley Powell's two trips down the "unknown" Colorado from Green River, Wyoming, in 1869 and 1871. Powell was a brilliant scientist, a good publicity man, and a bureaucratic empire builder. In the post-Civil War period, when the nation turned its eyes west (and when, therefore, the Colorado-Green region would have rapidly become known under any circumstances) Powell's beautifully written reports, pictures provided by competent photographers, and paintings by accomplished artists, all made the public aware of the exotic Colorado. So well known did the region become that—hard to believe!—a railroad was contemplated down the canyon and in 1889–1890 Robert Brewster Stanton ran a survey for such a line.

In 1908 Grand Canyon National Park was created, the first of several national parks, monuments, and recreation areas to be established along the river. Yet traversing the Green and Colorado in boats did not become a popular outing until after the Second World War. Today it is a lucrative business; people get on waiting lists for the privilege of making these trips in boats or rafts. Conservationists are now asking if the Colorado's canyons, those not yet inundated because of dams, are "being loved to death." A continuing controversy involves how much civilization in the form of motorboats, elevators to the canyon floor, and airplanes carrying sightseers overhead, should be allowed.

The greatest controversies engendered over the Colorado River, however, have been those concerned with water usage—for irrigation, drinking, and other human purposes, for hydro-electric power, recreation, and even bird sanctuaries. The so-called Upper Basin States—Wyoming, Utah, Colorado, and New Mexico—have vied with the Lower Basin States—Nevada, Arizona, and California—for the available water. Arizona and California have eyed each other with jealousy and distrust. Across the international border, Mexico let it be known that it expected to receive its share of Colorado waters. Farmers throughout the seven-state region contemplated irrigation projects that would turn arid acres into fertile fields. Los Angeles and Phoenix thirsted for Colorado River water for their burgeoning populations. There was always the danger of a Colorado River flood such as the one that created the Salton Sea in California's northern Imperial Valley in 1905. Private and public power interests politicked for permits to build hydroelectric dams. By 1920 it was clear that the Colorado River carried the most sought after water in the United States.

Since prehistoric times inhabitants of the Colorado River Basin have used the river for irrigation. White settlers quickly grasped the potential, and by 1903 more than 300,000 acres were under irrigation with Colorado River water in the Imperial Valley. There followed the Palo Verde Project, bringing another 70,000 acres into irrigation upriver and spawning the town of Blythe, California. There was a Yuma Project and (involving tributaries to the Colorado) the Salt River Project with its Roosevelt Dam, bringing water to Phoenix. Far upriver was the Grand Valley Project near where the Gunnison joins the Colorado; the town of Grand Junction, Colorado, owes much to that development. And there were other isolated projects either operational or in the planning stage.

Clearly the time had come for overall planning. If projects were allowed to proliferate, engineers warned, the water would all be used and some areas would be left dry. In 1919 the governor of Utah called a conference. Three years later (in 1922) the mutual concerns of the seven Basin states resulted in the signing, by representatives of six of the seven, of the Colorado River Compact. This document divided the river waters at the head of the Grand Canyon and allotted percentages of the total flow to the states above and below. Unfortunately all had to agree if the Compact was to be valid, but Arizona refused to sign. At stake was the future of the Imperial Valley, Arizona's growth, the fight between public and private power interests, and even questions of the first dam's location—for the first of many steps in achieving the Compact's goals were plans for a dam.

What followed for eight years is one of the most complex studies of democracy at work in the annals of American history. Selfishness and magnanimity, plans and counterplans, arguments and counterarguments, lobbies opposing other lobbies, court decisions, newspapers defending and newspapers damning, public interest versus private interests; dedicated men who lost their health or even their lives through overwork, temporary victories, and heartbreaking defeats, all fill the tens of thousands of pages devoted to the controversy.

A pattern of success began to appear as early as December, 1928, when the Boulder Canyon Act passed Congress and was signed by President Hoover. It assured the validity of the Colorado River Compact without Arizona's signature. Less than two years later (1930) Arizona won a court case contesting the allottment of an enormous quantity of water to California; having won the case and gained a reasonable percentage of the water, Arizona complied with the Compact and the way was cleared for construction of Boulder Dam. Completed in 1936, it would be but the first of several dams built over the next thirty years, all according to plan. The Colorado River Aquaduct and All-American Canal were also on the drawing boards, and in time were also completed.

Today there are higher dams and wider ones, but none more awe-inspiring than Hoover Dam (as it has been known officially since 1947 although President Hoover opposed a dam at that place until he realized that it was going to become a reality). To view the flood-lit structure at night, hear the roar of water pouring through the turbines and the power surging through the high tension lines is to comprehend man's victory over nature. No other structure on earth seems so appropriate for the wild Colorado.

With its sister dams, reservoirs, aqueducts, canals, hydroelectric facilities, and recreation areas, the Colorado River Project has proved a success—for now. But the Colorado is a silt-swollen stream. In time the silt will cut down on the efficiency of the projects. There is increasing salinization. And time works on the river's side. In the 1980s the cost of Hoover Dam will have been amortized and Lake Mead will have achieved its ultimate dimensions. The silt continues to flow down the Colorado. In 200 years Lake Mead will be filled with it. That is a fraction of a fraction of the river's age.

For how long will man control the Colorado?

FURTHER READING: Frank Waters, *The Colorado* (1946). T. H. Watkins and Contributors, *The Grand Colorado* (1969).

Richard A. Bartlett

* Beverley BowenMoeller, *Phil Swing and Boulder Dam* (1971), p. 4.

The Gila River

> *Source:* Mogollon Mountains of southwest New Mexico
> *Length:* 650 miles
> *Tributaries:* San Francisco, San Pedro, Santa Cruz, Salt, and Agua Fria rivers
> *Mouth:* Into Colorado River at Yuma, Arizona
> *Agricultural Products:* Citrus fruits, winter vegetables
> *Industries:* Copper, gold, silver mining; tourism

From its watershed in the lofty Mogollon Mountains of southwestern New Mexico to its confluence nearly 650 miles away with the Colorado River near Yuma, Arizona, the Gila River cuts through some of the most arid land in America. Yet it has a long record of habitation. When the United States was founded in 1776 the Spanish had already been farming, mining, or exploring the Gila Valley for almost 250 years. The Apache and Navajo Indians had been there for 500 years, the ancient Anasazi Indians were there as early as 100 A.D., and prehistoric man was there 10,000 years ago. Geologic evidence indicates that the river is at least 200 million years old.

Today the Gila (a Spanish version of the Yuman word Hah-quah-sa-eel, meaning "running water which is salty") flows through a land of contrasts where cacti grow tall like trees and snakes move sideways on the ground. The native flora and fauna have uniquely evolved to meet the environmental conditions imposed upon them by the climate of that region. It is a land where the temperatures may rise higher than 120° F. in the summer and fall below zero in winter. It may not rain for six months at a time. Yet its panoramic scenery, spectacular sunsets, and generally mild winters attract both large numbers of tourists and permanent residents.

Mountain vistas, grasslands, and desert plains compose the Gila watershed and valley. The 10,000-foot elevations of the Mogollon Mountains give birth to the numerous small streams that flow together to form the main course of the Gila. At this altitude the climate is similar to the more northern Hudsonian and Canadian belts with Ponderosa pine and Douglas fir growing to majestic heights. As it flows from southwestern New Mexico into southeastern Arizona, the Gila quickly loses altitude. At Cliff, New Mexico, it is at an elevation of 4,800 feet, at Duncan, Arizona, at 3,500 feet, and by the time the Gila flows into the Colorado River it is at 141 feet, barely above sea level.

The New Mexico mountains quickly give way to grasslands which in turn give way to the great Sonoran-Chihuahuan Desert. In the grasslands pronghorn antelope, mule deer, and today, cattle predominate. At one time grizzly bear and desert bighorn sheep roamed the Gila, but today both have disappeared from this part of their native habitat.

It is, however, the desert that has produced the most specialized, most bizarre creatures in North America. One settler discussing the native flora and fauna stated that "If you touch it, it stings you; if you pet it, it bites you, and if you eat it, it kills you!" Giant centipedes, deadly scorpions, tarantulas, and the Gila Monster (America's only poisonous lizard) are well known examples of the lesser loved creatures of this harsh land.

The Gila Desert flora have also adjusted to the environment. Cacti predominate: there are several hundred species from tiny silver-dollar-sized ones to the giant saquero which can reach 100 feet in height. The fishhook, barrel, and prickly pear are more commonly known species. Other flora includes the tumbleweed (Russian thistle) and many species of sagebrush. The primrose, yellow daisy and poppy are common southwestern flowers that add fresh color to the desert during their blooming seasons.

In the Triassic Period of the Mesozoic Era, the Gila flowed west into a great sea where southern California is today. Fifty million years later, during the Jurassic Period, the land rose sharply on each side and the basin areas of the present Southwest were formed. The Gila was one vast primordial swamp and during the Cretaceous Era dinosaurs roamed the lush, hot land. But the climate began to change, and about 60,000,000 years ago the Age of Dinosaurs gave way to the Age of Mammals.

During the Cenozoic Era the land began to take on more modern characteristics. The Rockies and Sierras were formed. As the land dried the waters of the Gila River emerged. The land was stripped of its wetness but enriched in other ways. Deposits of gold, silver, uranium, and other precious metals now lay close to the surface.

Some authorities believe early man was in the Gila Valley 25,000 years ago. Pre-Columbian Indians left the first signs of extensive human habitation in the area. The Anasazi, Mogollon, and Hohokam cultures existed in the Gila region as early as 100 A.D. and by 1,000 A.D. these peoples had developed an extensive hunting, gathering, and farming culture.

However, by 1300, due to population pressures, climatic conditions, or soil exhaustion, these peoples began to disappear. The "Ancient Ones," as the Navahos called them, left behind extensive cliff dwellings and surface ruins. Montezuma Castle and Tuzigoot are striking exam-

ples of pre-Columbian culture in the Gila region. Both of these ruins have been preserved by the National Park Service and may be seen by the modern visitor to southern Arizona.

The next peoples to come into the Gila Valley were the Apaches and Navahoes, linguistic relatives from the north, who pushed into the Southwest between 1200 and 1400. There they encountered tribes already in the region, including the Pueblos, Zunis, and Pimas, with whom they evolved an extensive inter-cultural symbiosis. Most of these people were or became sedentary, with the exception of the Apaches who developed a life-style based on warfare, tribute, and plunder. First the Spanish, then the Mexicans, and finally the Americans tried to subdue the Apaches with little or no success. Not until the late nineteenth century did the technologically superior Americans triumph over these fierce desert fighters. Troops were stationed at Fort Apache as late as 1923.

The first non-native American to see the Gila was not a Spaniard or even a European, but an African named Estaban (or Estabanico), a slave belonging to an early conquistador. Esteban, followed by Fray Marcos de Niza, explored southern Arizona in 1539. Esteban was killed by the Zunis but Fray Marcos fled back to Mexico. The next year Coronado crossed the Gila in search of the mythical Seven Cities of Cibola.

The Spanish called the areas south of the Gila Primeria Alta and hoped to colonize it. Not until 1687, however, did a figure emerge who would be the first European colonizer in the American southwest. This was Eusebio Francisco Kino, known as the "Padre on Horseback." Between his first entrance to the region in 1687 and his death in 1711 Father Kino traveled widely and converted thousands of southwest Indians to Christianity. He founded three missions in the Gila watershed, probably the most famous of which is San Xavier del Bac, south of Tucson. It is still in use.

Distance, climate, the native population, financial shortages, and political machinations all hindered Spain's progress on her northern frontier. By 1800 only two small outposts along the Gila remained, one at Tucson and one at Tubac, when the young United States began to turn its attentions to the desert southwest.

In 1821 when Mexico secured her independence from Spain many Americans hoped for new trading concessions which could open up the Gila area for American economic penetration. The lure of beaver, precious metals, and trade brought the first American entrepreneurs into the region. They included the mountain men James and Ohio Pattie, Pauline Weaver, William Wolfskill, and Ewing Young. Then came the Mexican War, 1846–1848. By provisions of the Treaty of Guadaloupe Hidalgo the United States acquired all the southwest north of the Gila River. It was soon discovered, however, that all the major trails and a possible railroad route through the region lay south of the river. To rectify this error Congress in 1853 approved the Gadsden Purchase, buying a broad area south of the Gila and establishing the modern United States-Mexican border. This rounded out the continental boundaries of the United States.

During the second half of the nineteenth century the Southwest began to acquire many of the industries for which it is known today. Cattle, limited farming, and the dry, healthy climate attracted many, but the dream of gold and silver lured the greatest numbers. Copper was mined by Americans on the Gila prior to 1830, but not until the 1850s were substantial discoveries made of silver and gold. Mining camps were quickly founded and as quickly abandoned as new strikes were made or the ore played out. Today, only the names remain: the Gunsight mine, the Bib Bub, the Wandering Jew, and the two most famous mines of the Southwest, the Vulture and the Lost Dutchman. Modern prospectors and even tourists still comb the Superstition Mountains east of Phoenix to look for a trace of the lost motherlode.

This unique region had also been the scene of some unusual American experiments. In 1856, under the direction of Secretary of War Jefferson Davis, the Army experimented with camels as beasts of burden in the desert Southwest. Though successful, political, economic, and military pressures ended this unusual experiment, though there were verified sightings of camels in Arizona as late as 1909! In the 1850s the San Antonio and San Diego Stage Company used mules exclusively. This "Jackass Line" was eventually incorporated into the better known Butterfield Overland Mail Company.

In the American period, as with Spanish and Mexicans earlier, there was almost continual trouble with the Apaches. They refused to give up their traditional lifestyles for the white man's way. Not until the end of the nineteenth century was the United States able to pacify these tribes, overcoming their stone age technology with such modern devices as the railroad and telegraph. When the famous Apache leader Geronimo was finally captured in 1886 he was the last major Indian leader to be subdued in the United States. Due to the Indian problems and the international border the role of the military in the region was substantial. Fort Crittenden (later Fort Buchanan), Fort Grant, Fort Apache, and Fort Yuma are well-known names associated with the Gila area.

The Gila Valley today reflects its vast Indian, Spanish, Mexican, and American heritage. This is most evident in its architecture and the faces of its people. The area is part of the emerging sunbelt and its population continues to grow, placing new stresses on the fragile Southwestern ecosystem. Gold and silver mining continues. Water reclamation projects have made agriculture very profitable, with citrus and winter vegetables predominating. Industry, tourism, retirement villages, and excellent educational opportunities attract both visitors and permanent residents. It is one of the fastest growing areas in the nation.

In many ways the Gila and its Valley are typical of modern America. The area has a long and varied past, a prosperous present, but an uncertain future. New agricultural and industrial demands, plus population pressures, must be balanced against the environment and past experience. If the Southwest of the Gila is going to continue to prosper it must look for guidance to the long history of humankind in the region.

FURTHER READING: J. Frank Dobie, *Coronado's Children* (1934). Odie B. Faulk, *Destiny Road* (1973).

William H. Graves

The Humboldt River

Source: Ruby Mountains of northeast Nevada
Length: 300 miles
Tributaries: Mary River, North Fork, Little Humboldt River
Mouth: Flows into Humboldt Lake (or Sink)
Agricultural products: Some hay; cattle ranching
Industries: None of significance

Some 250 miles west of the Great Salt Lake and 150 miles south of the Snake River and the old Oregon Trail, the Humboldt River forms amidst the Ruby Mountains of northeast Nevada. It flows in a meandering course southwesterly to spend itself out in a "sink" of marshes in the western desert, at the base of the high Sierras. This most historically important river in the Great Basin twists and turns for nearly 500 miles across northern Nevada, but as the crow flies the distance is slightly under 300 miles. At its end it is a muddy, alkaline, stagnant excuse for a river. Yet it emerges from the mountains swollen with snow water that once offered hope to parched California-bound travelers crossing from the Great Salt Desert to the east or from the Oregon Trail to the north. Since it is the only east-west running stream between the Rockies and the Sierras, it was the lifeline for gold seekers crossing overland to California.

The first white people to use the Humboldt were the mountain men who discovered its beaver and also its significance to travelers. It was probably Peter Skene Ogden of the Hudson's Bay Company who in 1828 first trapped beaver on the Humboldt. In the following year he returned to this "Unknown River" and descended it to its sink. Some say that this intrepid trapper named it "Mary's River"; others insist he just called it the "Unknown." In any event Ogden discovered to his disappointment that it did not flow to the sea. He had hoped it would, that perhaps it was the San Buenaventura River of the mapmakers, flowing out of the central Sierras to the bay of San Francisco or the bay of Monterey. No such river exists.

Americans knew of the Humboldt only through rumors heard from the British company men. Even Jedediah Smith did not come upon it in his travels across the Basin in 1826 and 1827. Americans did not appear along the Humboldt until 1833 when Captain Benjamin Bonneville sent mountain man Joe Walker on a reconnaissance from the Rockies toward California. Walker's 1833–1834 expedition to California and return via the Humboldt revealed a feasible route along the banks of the desert river. Most importantly he discovered a route between the Oregon Trail in the Snake country to what would become the California trail along the banks of this Unknown River. Walker also fought Indians along the Humboldt and terrified them with his white man's weapons.

It would be several years, however, before emigrants left the Oregon Trail for the challenge of the relatively unknown California route. The Bidwell-Bartleson party separated from their Oregon-bound companions in 1841 and reached the Humboldt across the northern tip of the Salt Desert without utilizing Walker's route from the Oregon Trail. This group of bickering, quarrelsome emigrants succeeded with the help of the river, but lost all their wagons, animals, and possessions before they arrived safely over the mountains into California. They were the vanguard of a greater emigration that would turn off from the Oregon Trail and head for California. They had received only the instructions not to go too far south lest they perish in a sagebrush desert and not go too far north lest they end in a desert of great black rocks. They sought the Humboldt's fresh waters, knowing that without them they might perish. In 1842 and 1844 more emigrant parties passed along the California trail with women and children.

The unknown desert river was a poor excuse for the grandiose, mythical San Buenaventura. In the years of heavy travel the Humboldt became a cruel, taunting guide to the golden valleys of California. From a stream of fresh, potable water it dwindled gradually into a muddy, alkaline stream disgusting to animals and humans alike; finally it sank into the ground. Ahead lay the dreaded Forty Mile Desert with

The Humboldt River twists and turns like a snake in its death struggle. This is west of Elko, Nevada, looking east. Notice the road in the upper part of the picture. (Courtesy Nevada Historical Society.)

the next water sources at either the Carson or Truckee rivers. But before travelers departed from the Humboldt it provided them near its sink with a "Big Meadows" where they could rest and gather forage for their animals in preparation for the desert crossing.

The year 1844 brought John C. Fremont of the U.S. Topographical Engineers to the northern Great Basin from the Oregon country. He too was interested in the mythical San Buenaventura, but found only rivers that flowed east and west and never through the Sierras to the Pacific. He already knew of the existence of the "Unknown River" that ended in marshes, but such a river was of no interest to him. He returned to the settled East. The following year Fremont re-entered the Great Basin from the Great Salt Lake. By this time he had concluded that the area between the Rockies and the Sierras was a basin of interior drainage with no outlet to the sea. Part of his force came west by the route of the Unknown River, but Fremont stayed south of it. From this distance he named

it the Humboldt after the German scientist of worldwide fame, Alexander von Humboldt (1769–1859). He (Humboldt) never saw the river nor did Fremont ever travel along its banks.

The Pathfinder's reports were read avidly by many easterners and midwesterners who were ready to move to new lands, especially to California. Increasing numbers of them left the trail to Oregon to head south and southwest. In the spring of 1846 the Edwin Bryant group and the Donner party took the advice of a young writer-adventurer, Lansford W. Hastings. He advised them to leave the Oregon trail shortly after crossing South Pass in the Rockies, turning south toward the Salt Lake. From there they would cross the Salt Desert and after a short mountainous interlude they would reach the secure waters of the Humboldt that would take them almost to the Sierras. For the Donner party this advice would contribute to their disaster in the Sierras during the winter of 1846–1847. Along the banks of the Humboldt dissension arose in the party: one person was abandoned along the trail, another banished for murder, and one murdered for his money. The term "ill-fated Donner party" was well deserved even along the banks of the Humboldt. Eventually forty of the eighty-seven members who chose the Hastings Cut-off to the Humboldt met death, most of them in the mountains by starvation.

The Donner tragedy gave the Humboldt River route to California a bad name. It would not be until the gold rush of 1849 that fears inspired by the Donner tragedy would be overcome. The army of gold seekers moving along the Humboldt in '49 cluttered the route with abandoned excess baggage. The Indians (or the Diggers as they were called because they dug for roots, insects, and other sources of food in this desolate country) ransacked what was left behind. In 1850 travelers along the "golden trail" brought too few provisions with them and faced starvation and cholera on the Humboldt. Thousands of animals had destroyed most of the forage along the river, which was polluted with rotting carcasses. One Iowa traveler in 1850 described the river as the "meanest and muddiest, filthiest stream. Most cordially do I hate you," he wrote.

As the migration continued, Mormon businessmen in the newly settled Salt Lake City took notice of trade possibilities along the trail. They were intrigued especially by prospects of a trading post just west of the Humboldt Sink, at the base of the Sierras and along the banks of the Carson. In 1855 the Church directed nearly 500 Saints under apostle Orson Hyde to travel over the Humboldt trail to secure for the Mormons the lands east of California and especially those of the Carson Valley.

Apostle Hyde guided his Saints to the base of the Sierras, but he did not like the route, describing the Humboldt trail as "too monstrous for a Christian trail of wagons to traverse." They remained at their stations barely two years, returning in 1857, again via the Humboldt Valley.

Then came the discovery of the Comstock Lode in western Nevada, and the Civil War. The Humboldt served as the chief artery linking the new mining center with the East. South of the river a competitive route opened between Salt Lake City and the settlements of western Nevada through the Reese River country. The Pony Express and telegraph would follow it. Soon, however, the Humboldt would attain new importance as the Central Pacific laid its rails along the river. The highway of steel would finally link to the Union Pacific at Promontory Point, Utah, in May, 1869.

The railroad aided the growth of the cattle kingdom along the banks of the Humboldt and spurred the development of the river's two major towns, Elko and Winnemucca. No major mineral strikes occurred along its banks, but it served as a highway to the mining riches of California and western Nevada. Mining, cattle, and transportation activity flourished along its course. The cattle men saw to it that the water rights were so monopolized that small farmers could not get a start in this hostile country.

Large ranches flourished. Some smaller ones have held out largely by virtue of the Rye Patch Dam reclamation project of 1927. As a result, limited crops are raised in the Humboldt Sink and Big Meadows. The town of Lovelock serves these farmers and small ranchers. In the twentieth century the automobile has used the Humboldt route, Highway 40 (and later Interstate 80), the principal artery to northern California and San Francisco, just as the Central Pacific used it in the railway age. For today's automobile traveler the Humboldt River still points the way toward the setting sun, the Golden Gate, and the riches and mysteries of the Orient.

FURTHER READING: Dale L. Morgan, *The Humboldt: Highroad of the West* (1943). Samuel G. Houghton, *A Trace of Desert Waters: The Great Basin Story* (1976).

William D. Rowley

The Salt River

Source: Convergence of White and Black Rivers 40 miles northeast of Globe, Arizona
Length: 200 miles
Tributaries: Big Bonita, Cedar, Carrizo, Cibecue, Canyon, Cherry, Tonto, Fish, Pinto, and Pinal creeks, among many.
Mouth: Gila River 15 miles west of Phoenix
Agricultural Products: Cotton, citrus, truck vegetables
Industries: Electronic factories

Since the Salt is Arizona's most bountiful intra-state river, it seems not only appropriate but quite logical that Phoenix, the state's largest urban area, should be located on the Salt River—or rather, on what was at one time the Salt River. Near Phoenix today, except for occasional but severe and unpredictable flooding, the Salt's dry bed remains the only vestige of a once-abundant perennial stream. Four upstream dams now regulate the Salt's flow, while still another dam diverts water, on demand, to the extensive irrigation system which turns the Salt River valley into a sprawling, verdant oasis.

The Salt rises in a part of Arizona whose traits contradict the stereotypes associated with the state, for Arizona's White Mountains, 180 miles east of Phoenix, are of another world. Here one sees ferns and moss, fir trees and green meadows, rather than cholla and mesquite, saguaro and barren desert. Rippling cold, clear streams drain the region in contrast to the dry washes found elsewhere. This is the state's most productive rainfall area with precipitation varying from three to four times the eleven inches that fall annually on Phoenix.

It is on the sides of Mount Baldy, at 11,590 feet the highest point in the White Mountains, that two waterways, the White River and the Black River (sometimes called the Upper Salt) are formed. The region is associated with the northwest-southeast running Mogollon Rim, part of an oragraphic condition that increases precipitation and reduces evaporation in the vast region. By the time they have joined to form the Salt, about forty miles northeast of Globe, the two source streams have drained 380,000 acre-feet of water per year from 1,864 square miles.

The 6,232 square mile Salt River watershed lies within Arizona. Hydrologists divide this basin into three regions: (1) the upper sub-basin, which comprises thirty percent of the total watershed and extends from Baldy Peak 120 miles southwest and west to the confluence with the Black (Upper Salt) and White rivers; (2) the middle sub-basin, which extends southwestward approximately 70 miles from the two rivers' confluence to Roosevelt Dam, and (3) the lower sub-basin, which continues westward forty miles from Roosevelt Dam through three more dams until it meets the Verde River on the flood plain of the Salt River valley. The Salt's riverbed continues forty miles westward beyond the Verde's mouth through metropolitan Phoenix before it reaches its original mouth into the also-dry Gila River. The total length of the Salt is about 270 miles.

Land characteristics of the Salt River basin vary from rugged mountains to gently rolling hills and flatlands, from Alpine meadows to deep, rugged canyons carved by erosion cutting through down-faulted rims. Bounded by the Mazatzal Mountains on the west, the Mogollon Rim on the north, the White Mountains on the north and east, and the Usery, Superstition, Pinal, and Apache mountains on the south, the basin is a rugged and isolated area 144 miles long east to west and eighty-two miles wide north to south.

The Salt is served by many tributaries, almost all of which flow northeast to southwest or north to south as a consequence of the Mogollon Rim and the rainshadow condition. Big Bonita, Cedar, Carrizo, Cibecue, Canyon, Cherry, and Tonto creeks flow down the Rim to the Salt. A few small sources such as Fish, Pinto, and Pinal creeks flow from south to north. Like the lesser creeks and washes these tributaries are usually intermittent.

Human residents found the combination of warm weather and the Salt River's available surface water attractive enough to support a pre-Columbian agrarian culture which may have endured for more than 2,000 years. Ancient living sites, artifacts, and irrigation canals in the

Roosevelt Dam on Salt River. (Photo: Ray Manley Studio, Tucson, AZ.)

area where Phoenix now stands present evidence that what archeologists have designated as the "Hohokam culture" flourished during five archeological periods, the earliest going back as far as 300 B.C. Remains of these Hohokam people indicate they had a well-developed, elaborate, and intensive canal irrigation technology as well as substantial land-modification methods which enabled them to grow crops during the 225-day frost-free period which characterizes this area. Additional evidence demonstrates that the Hohokam people understood useful masonry construction techniques and farming implement design.

Ironically, it has not been the extreme aridity of the region which has caused the Salt River valley's residents—prehistoric and modern alike—their greatest discomfort. Rather it has

been the raging, uncontrollable flood waters rushing down the otherwise quiet Salt River bed, sweeping away diversion dams and dikes, destroying canals, buildings, fields, livestock, and human inhabitants of the flood plain. By the time Anglos arrived in the 1820s the Hohokam were gone. Archeologists today feel that the unpredictable floods more than any other influence drove the Indians away. For a time the area resisted modern development for the same reason.

Finally, nineteenth-century Arizona pioneers managed to "harness" the Salt River and "tame" its erratic habits. Today, four dams and a new elaborate canal system regulate and distribute the Salt's great gift. More than a million people remain dependent upon the river to provide boating and fishing, electric power and drinking water, and irrigation for farms and homes.

As early as 1539 the Spaniard Fray Marcos de Niza crossed the White Mountains and the headwaters of the Salt in his quest for the Seven Cities of Cibola. He called the Salt the Rio Azul (Blue River). A year later the Spanish explorer Francisco Vasquez de Coronado, accompanied by Fray Marcos, marched to the Colorado Plateau. To cross the Salt his men built rafts. Later reports referred to the river as the Rio de los Balsas, or the River of Rafts. Eighteenth century Spanish maps showed it as Rio de la Asuncion or Rio Asuncion, the River of Assumption. However, by that time other maps used Rio Salada or Salinas—Salt River. Some saline quality can be detected at the mouth of two of the river's lesser tributaries, Salt River Draw and Canyon Creek. Salt deposits at the mouths of these two creeks had served Indians for some time.

When Anglos came to trap the Salt River basin in the early nineteenth century, they found Apache Indians living there. This tribe was successful, for a time, in defending the region against white settlers. Mormons, coming in from Utah in the 1870s, settled along the upper Little Colorado River tributaries on the leeward side of the White Mountains. They made only one attempt to occupy land drained by the Salt River system. In 1877 Mormon Oscar Cluff discovered a small timbered valley with a number of springs which formed the head of Carrizo Creek, a Salt tributary. He called it Forest Dale. A year later, eighteen Mormon families moved into this idyllic site. But in 1881 the Apaches claimed Forest Dale as their rightful property, and the Anglos were forced to leave. The Mormons made no other attempts to settle in the Salt River basin.

Since the region appeared to be so inhospitable, little other Anglo settlement took place and the land was left to the Apaches. In 1871 the federal government established the Fort Apache Indian Reservation, to which in 1897 the San Carlos Indian Reservation was added. In 1905 President Theodore Roosevelt proclaimed the Tonto Forest Preserve; this was designated a National Forest in 1908. Two-thirds of the Tonto National Forest is located in the Salt River Basin.

In 1870 the federal government established a fort on the White River about twenty miles upstream from its confluence with the Black River. Although it carried several names in its early years, after 1879 it was known as Camp Apache. It was a focal point of the last Arizona Indian wars. On December 28, 1872, a fierce battle in the Salt River Canyon claimed the lives of seventy-five Indians. In September, 1881, the White Mountain Apaches attacked Fort Apache, one of the few times Arizona Indians staged a direct attack on an army post.

Other violence characterized the Salt River watershed in these early years. In Pleasant Valley on Cherry Creek cattlemen in the 1880s resisted the intrusion of sheepmen. A great six-year battle, the Graham-Tewksbury feud, erupted and cost the lives of twenty-nine men. Also known as the Pleasant Valley War, this feud rid the area of sheep, cost the life of every male member of the Graham family, and left only one Tewksbury survivor. Today the Pleasant Valley and its only town, Young, is distantly isolated and rustically bucolic and bears no trace of its bitter heritage.

Due to its remoteness and to federal management, the Salt River watershed still has an abundance of wildlife. The Salt's waters, particularly in the high mountain tributaries and in the man-made lakes, are fished for rainbow trout, large mouth, small mouth, and yellow bass, and other game fish. But the region is growing in human population and the present density outside of Globe-Miami of 1 to 2.5 persons per square mile is certain to rise rapidly. With the rise will end the primitive nature of the Salt River basin. The Forest Service has long-range plans for the region as a "retreat and recreation haven" for Phoenix and Tucson residents, while the Apaches want to develop their own lumbering, livestock, agricultural, and recreation economy.

At its lower levels the Salt River has seen the touch of human "management" for some time. A Confederate army deserter, Jack Swilling, was the first person to start a renewal of the ancient Hohokam irrigated agrarian economy. Excavating the ancient Indian canals, Swilling established a community which was producing crops by 1868. A small town, Pumpkinville, developed, but settlers changed the name to the more dignified Phoenix in 1870. Southeast of there, in 1877, a Mormon band formed the farming community of Mesa. By 1900 more than 180,000 acres were being farmed in the Salt River Valley, but the vagaries of weather forced these early Phoenicians (the name Phoenix and nearby residents gave themselves) to look to the federal government for help.

In 1905 construction began on a dam at the confluence of the Salt River with Tonto Creek. In 1911 Theodore Roosevelt, who was President at the time of passage of the Newlands Reclamation Act, dedicated the dam in his name. Roosevelt Dam was followed by three other Salt River dams downstream: Horse Mesa (1927); Mormon Flat (1926); and Stewart Mountain (1930); there are still other diversion dams and 138 miles of main canals. About 250,000 acres are irrigated.

Yet recent floods in the Phoenix area have prompted a search for still more control of the Salt's waters. The plans are embodied in the controversial Central Arizona Project to provide flood protection and also to store water brought to south-central Arizona from the Colorado River via an aquaduct. But a large dam at the confluence of the Salt and Verde has been cancelled and plans for the rest of the Project are advancing very slowly.

"God enriches," says the State of Arizona motto. But thanks to rivers like the Salt, Arizonans have enriched themselves through exploitation and management of the state's erratic and unruly water supply. The rivers and the desert have been conquered. For the time being, anyway. Experts predict that Arizona's population could grow to 5.8 million by the year 2000. Arizonans might do well if they would heed the words of an early American explorer of the Southwest, John Wesley Powell. He said, simply: "There is not sufficient water to supply these lands."

FURTHER READING: Arizona Department of Health Services, *Final Report, Water Quality Management Basin Plan, Salt River Basin, Arizona* (1977). Courtland L. Smith, *The Salt River Project* (1972).

James W. Byrkit

The Sevier River of Utah

Source: Convergence in southwest-central Utah of Panguitch and Assay creeks
Length: About 325 miles
Tributaries: San Pitch River and lesser streams
Mouth: Flows into Sevier Lake in west-central Utah
Agricultural products: Alfalfa, sugar beets, potatoes; some cattle, sheep, and poultry
Industries: Electric power

In central Utah two important geologic regions adjoin in a confusing maze of canyons and plateaus. One is the Great Basin, whose eastern boundary merges with the other region, known as the Colorado Plateau. The resultant mountains, valleys, and tablelands form the intricate watershed of the Sevier River. It is formed in southwest-central Utah where the Panguitch and Assay creeks converge; it then flows north about 240 miles, then bends and flows southwest for another eighty-five miles, eventually flowing into Sevier Lake. Although just fifteen to twenty percent of the Sevier's drainage is of mountainous country, most of its water comes from there. Indeed, for much of the remainder of its flow the river passes through arid, even desert terrain. Where the river turns to flow southwest it is joined by its principal tributary, the San Pitch. All told, the Sevier drains about 5,500 square miles.

At the time of white exploration the Indians along the Sevier were the Paiutes, Utes, and Goshutes. In 1776 an expedition searching for a route from Santa Fe to Monterey, California, under the leadership of Fathers Francisco Antanasio Dominguez and Silvestre Velez de Escalante came upon bands of Paiutes living along the Sevier. These primitive people were distinguished from other Indians by their beards and were said by the Padres to resemble the Spanish more than the typical Indians.

Don Bernardo de Miera, the expedition's military cartographer, named the now dry Sevier Lake for himself (Miera) and called the river Rio Buenaventura, perhaps believing it was the same river they had crossed in eastern Utah, now called the Green River. This misapplication was to confuse explorers for more than fifty years, but was dispelled in 1842 by John C. Fremont in his survey of the Great Basin. The name Sevier is thought to be derived from Rio Seviro, the name applied by the Spanish trappers Moricio Arce and Lagos Garcia, who came out of Taos in 1813 and traded with the Utes around Utah Lake. After an altercation, the trappers escaped south to the "Rio Sebero." Other trappers came into the region when they learned of its abundance of fur-bearing animals.

Fur trappers were numerous in the region until after 1830 when most of the beaver were trapped out. Probably the best known trapper into the region was Jedediah Smith. He started south from the Great Salt Lake Valley in September, 1826, hoping to return by the next summer's rendezvous. He and the seventeen men with him went up the Sevier from near where the Padres had crossed fifty years before. The party then left the river where it emerges from Marysvale Canyon at the south end of Sevier Valley and worked west and south, descending the Virgin and Colorado rivers and working up the Mojave. They spent an uncomfortable time in California because they were riding horses stolen from the rancheros by Mojave Indians. Smith was searching for a river flowing from the east along which he could return to Salt Lake. Finding none, the determined mountain man took two men, some horses and mules, and headed east over the Sierras in mid-May, 1827. Bucking snowdrifts up to eight feet high, they crossed the Sierras and what is now central Nevada and after great hardships—especially suffering from thirst—reached safety in the Salt Lake Valley. Smith made one other trip over a part of this route which included the Sevier section.

The Utes, who had horses, were more widespread and dominant in the region than the Paiutes. Utes controlled land from western Colorado to the eastern edge of the Great Basin, and were strong enough to build up a trade route between old Mexico through Santa Fe into Cali-

fornia. Sometimes called the Old Spanish Trail, this route encountered the Sevier River at several points. One was at Salina where the trail turned south and then west as it ran along the river to the point where the Sevier emerges from Marysvale Canyon. In 1830 a party of trappers headed by William Wolfskill headed for California along this Spanish Trail. Wolfskill's record of the journey includes descriptions of the Sevier country and the party's crossing of the river.

One well-known Ute chief who enjoyed a measure of control over the trade going up and down the Spanish Trail and who had his headquarters on the Sevier was Chief Wakara. He was well-suited to his times, able to see beyond his provincial world and to plan to accommodate the future. However, even he could not anticipate the enormity of the events that overcame his people. When settlers came after 1850 Wakara counseled his people to accept the whites, hoping they would teach his people their agricultural skills.

Troubles still arose, however, and in 1852 the alarmed natives chose war, since known as the Walker War for the corrupted name of Wakara. One of its casualties was Captain John W. Gunnison who was leading a government railroad survey team west. His party entered the Sevier Valley at Salina, close by the scene of an incident in which whites had slain three Indians. Gunnison continued along the river to its mouth at Sevier Lake where, on October 26, 1854, the vengeful Indians killed the Captain and four of his party.

Although Utah's core community was settled between 1847 and 1854, the incentive to colonize outside of what is known as the Wasatch front came about as a result of retrenchment brought on by the Utah War of 1858. This was a bloodless altercation between the people of Utah Territory and the United States government. Established settlements were abandoned in San Bernardino, California; Carson, Nevada; Moab, Utah; and Salmon, Idaho. Thus pressure was created to find places for these people within what became the borders of Utah. Water being essential for any such enterprise, the Sevier River near its mouth was settled and in 1859 irrigation began. The soil was suitable for farming.

Uncontrolled flooding caused the settlers to abandon their enterprise, however, and not until

1874 were they established there permanently. The river was not a wild river in the sense that it carried a huge volume of water all the time, but floodwaters made diversion near the mouth very difficult.

Meanwhile other communities were established upstream and along the Sevier's tributaries. Richfield, which became the seat of Sevier County in 1867, was settled in 1866, then abandoned due to Indian troubles, and reestablished in 1872. Communities along the San Pitch were settled as early as 1850 but barely survived until the end of Indian hostilities. Panguitch on the upper Sevier was settled in 1864 but failed until the end of hostilities in 1871.

Success in diverting Sevier waters near the river's mouth finally came in 1912 as a result of efforts involving the Mormon Church, Utah, and the federal government. With settlement, other diversions have taken place upriver and along the tributaries, but always the usage has been agricultural; no industries have prospered in the area although coal-fired steam generating plants in the region are a new possibility.

As soon as diversion plans became successful, conflicts arose over the portions of water that various sections or districts could use legitimately. By the so-called Higgins decree of 1900 the waters of the lower half of the Sevier were divided and a commission established to adjudicate the rights of dissatisfied users; the Vermil-

lion Dam was stipulated as a division point. This was only the beginning: other decisions and decrees followed until by 1926 all Sevier waters were being adjudicated. Difficulties continued as more winter runoff was stored, more settlement took place, and every drop of water began to count. On November 30, 1936, by the "Cox Decree" (for Judge LeRoy Cox who handed it down), final allotments of waters was achieved.

Indeed, the Sevier River is one of the most completely consumed rivers in the United States. Less than one percent or 44,840 acre-feet of the total precipitation in the drainage area, some 6.5 million acre-feet, is not consumed within the basin. Most of the time Sevier Lake is dry. Water consumption is about 1,103,540 acre-feet annually, with agriculture accounting for 99 percent of the usage. Nonconsumptive uses are also important. There is recreational boating and fishing, while the waters furnish an excellent water fowl habitat.

People of the Sevier drainage, most of them Mormons, have strived mightily to make their arid, isolated valleys bring forth the agricultural products needed by the rest of the nation. Through hard work and cooperative effort they have enjoyed considerable success.

FURTHER READING: J. C. Alter, *Utah, the Storied Domain*, 3 vols. (1932). S. George Ellsworth, *Utah's Heritage* (1972).

Jay M. Haymond

The Truckee River

> *Source:* North end of Lake Tahoe
> *Length:* About 120 miles
> *Tributaries:* None of significance
> *Mouth:* Flows into Pyramid Lake in western Nevada
> *Agricultural products:* Hay ranching
> *Industries:* Negligible

The Truckee River of northern California and western Nevada flows only a hundred miles. It begins at the north end of Lake Tahoe high in the Sierras and moves to a desert rendezvous with

the barren shores of Pyramid Lake in Nevada. The green, salty waters of the lake illustrate the dramatic changes in the countryside through which the river flows. For the weary, westbound traveler crossing the sage and sand of northern Nevada, the Truckee was the first sign of a better place ahead. Its sparkling, cool waters and the green growth along its banks promised a gateway to California through the spectacular Sierras.

As a source of water and the route through the

mountains to the Great Valley of California, the Truckee provided the natural conditions for urban and agricultural growth in the Reno area. Without the river making its way eastward from lakes Tahoe to Pyramid, the Truckee meadows would be merely another dry region along the eastern slope of the Sierras. However, the geologic action that formed the Great Basin and raised up the Sierras also created natural lake reservoirs such as Lake Tahoe which hold the moisture driven in by winds from the Pacific. The spring thaws release water gradually from the snow pack into the rivers that flow into the Great Basin. The Truckee is only one of several watercourses which flow from the Sierras to an evaporative end in the sands and sunlight of the Great Basin.

In addition to providing the basis for an urban trading and transportation center (Reno), the river has helped sustain an irrigated hay ranching economy in adjoining valleys and in the government reclamation project centered at Fallon, Nevada. The Truckee's swift waters and precipitous drop from the Sierras has also served from early years of the twentieth century to generate hydroelectric power. The waters, however, have been polluted from time to time by lumber-related industries. Sawmills and a pulp mill have choked its waters, killed the brook trout, and posed a threat to the health of downstream residents in Reno. With the recent growth of population in the Tahoe Basin and along the banks of the Truckee to Reno, the quality of the Truckee's water has become a vital question to the growth prospects of the entire area. Some of the earliest questions relating to the pollution of interstate streams involved the Truckee. Upstream users in California often showed indifference to the protests of downstream communities in Nevada until recent federal water standards forced a closer monitoring of the stream and stricter sewage treatment plants on the higher reaches of the river.

Although there are continuing problems related to the quality of the Truckee's water, the quantity of the stream's flow is also crucial. The urban and agricultural uses of the water over the years have helped reduce the flow into Pyramid Lake and accelerated the drop in the lake's surface. The Indians at Pyramid Lake Indian Reservation on which the lake and the mouth of the river is located have demanded a higher rate of flow in order to maintain the lake at acceptable levels and slow its salination. In the 1970s this question occasioned complicated water suits with the Department of the Interior representing the Pyramid Lake Indians against various state and local interests which insist they should have the water because they put it to a higher beneficial use than do the Indians.

Americans have known of the Truckee since the early 1840s. Captain John C. Fremont's expedition on its way home from Oregon first discovered the river on January 15, 1844. Fremont had proceeded south along the eastern side of the Cascades and the Sierras with every expectation of finding a river known to imaginative cartographers as the San Buenaventura. It was supposed to run from the central Rockies through the deserts to the west, finally flowing through the Sierras and so to the California coast. Its existence had been asserted by members of the Dominguez-Escalante expedition in 1776 when they failed to find a route from Santa Fe to Monterey and had turned back after reaching the Ute Indian country of Utah. Mapmakers accepted this river as real and gave it a name.

It was this non-existent river that Fremont hoped to find on his southward course from the interior of the Oregon country. After plodding through cold, snowy deserts, he suddenly came upon "a sheet of green water some twenty miles broad." Fremont, concluding that it was an unknown body of water, gave it the name Pyramid because the islands near the shore reminded him of the pyramids of Egypt. Local Indians told him there was a river at the other end of the lake. Reaching it, he wrote, "we found the inlet of a large fresh water stream, and all at once were satisfied that it was neither Mary's River (the Humboldt) nor the waters of the Sacramento. . . ."

The Pathfinder and his hungry men enjoyed a feast of "salmon trout" provided by the Indians. "On this 15th day of January, 1844, they [the Indians] made on the ground a drawing of the river," he wrote, "which they represented as issuing from another lake in the mountains three or four days distant, in a direction a little west of south." On January 16, Fremont noted, "we continued on our journey along this beautiful stream, which we naturally called the Salmon Trout River." He abandoned the river on

January 17 because, since it flowed in the wrong direction, it could not possibly be the mythical San Buenaventura.

In the early fall of the same year (1844), the California-bound Elisha Stevens party crossed the Sierras by way of the Truckee Pass. Far to the eastward, at the beginning of the Forty Mile Desert and the Humboldt Sink, they had faced the decision of whether to push directly west or strike out for another stream further to the south. A Paiute Indian whom they called Truckee urged them to take a more westerly course, saying that a river could be found in that direction. The Stevens party followed his advice and, finding the river just as he had said they would, named it for him.

Although the Stevens party in 1844 successfully crossed the Sierras via the Truckee, so difficult was the terrain that their mountain man guide, Caleb Greenwood, searched for a detour on his way east. He discovered the easier route via Dog Creek in a nearby valley. More emigrants came in 1845, while 1846 witnessed a large migration. After an exhausting struggle in the Forty Mile Desert, Edwin Bryant on August 20, 1846, described the Truckee in his monumental *What I Saw in California:* "We saw at the distance of abut two miles, the course of Truckee River, indicated by a line of willows, grass, and other green herbage, and a number of tall trees—the last a sight that has not saluted us for five hundred miles."

The Truckee route was the one followed by the Donner party, which bogged down in the snowy Sierras from November, 1846, to April, 1847. Some members camped at the then named "Truckee Lake," later renamed Donner Lake, and another group including the Donner family camped five miles back upon the trail on Alder Creek, a small tributary. Forty persons of the eighty-seven members in the Donner party perished, most of them in the snows of Truckee Pass. Cannibalism even took place during their terrible ordeal. News of the tragedy sharply curtailed travel over the Truckee route in the following years. Only the discovery of gold in California revived the use of the pass, though most gold seekers took the Carson Pass road, opened in 1848, to the heart of the gold country.

During the 1850s the Truckee route was rarely used, but in 1863 California railroad entrepreneurs indicated that the new Central Pacific would use the Donner Pass route. The news sufficed to prompt the building of a new wagon road over the pass to tap the trade arising from exploitation of the Comstock Lode at Virginia City, Nevada Territory. As the railhead advanced over the mountains, it followed the river and cut its way through the forbidding Truckee canyon, aided with nitroglycerin and the toil of 10,000 Chinese laborers. The railroad was responsible for the river towns of Truckee, Verdi, and Reno; it left the river just beyond the big bend at Wadsworth where the Truckee turns north toward Pyramid Lake.

The Truckee meant tragedy to the Pyramid Lake Indians. Close to the Truckee, on May 12, 1860, occurred the first bloody battle of the Pyramid Lake Indian War. It came about as follows. Tensions between whites and Indians had mounted during the winter of 1859–1860. A series of incidents set a locally raised militia marching against the Pyramid Lake Indians. On the river route to the lake the Indians ambushed the militia, killing seventy-six of the 105 volunteers. Within two weeks a force of over 700 whites marched down the Truckee to chastise the Indians. These same people with whom Fremont had feasted were driven from their homes on the lake into the deserts to the north. However, through the efforts of Indian agents, the Paiutes were restored to their homes at Pyramid Lake within the year, where they remain to this day as proprietors of the lake and the lands of the lower Truckee.

During the nineteenth century the river irrigated haylands in the Truckee meadows. Its waters carried logs to sawmills along its banks. With the National Reclamation Act making funding possible, the Truckee and Carson Irrigation Project began at Fallon, Nevada, in 1903. By 1907 the Derby diversion dam and canal was completed; this gave the project water sources from both the Carson and Truckee rivers.

In the twentieth century Reno became famous as the divorce capital of the nation. From its hotel windows disillusioned spouses tossed their wedding rings into the waters of the Truckee. Tourist industries associated with divorce, gambling, and winter sports at the Tahoe Basin and Truckee areas have stimulated a high growth rate all along the Truckee River from Tahoe to the old railroad town of Wadsworth.

Projected growth figures indicate the Truckee

meadows will eventually have a population of 388,000. How the Truckee will serve these people is one of the major environmental questions of the region. Occasional floods and the need for water storage had by 1930 prompted the building of dams along the river's tributaries. Recent court decisions have sustained the Orr ditch decree of 1944 which divided the waters of the river between urban, agricultural, and Indian needs in the area. A 1977 decision essentially endorsed the present trend toward growth and thwarted Indian attempts to have those water

rights redefined in favor of the Pyramid Lake Indians and their fisheries. The Truckee River remains an essential participant in the process of change and growth for the area. It is as important today as it was in the 1840s when pioneers had to have its life-giving waters or perish.

FURTHER READING: George R. Stewart, *The California Trail* (1962). Samuel G. Houghton, *A Trace of Desert Waters: The Great Basin Story* (1976).

William D. Rowley

The Verde River

Source: Del Rio Springs, 30 miles southeast of Seligman, Arizona
Length: 180 miles
Tributaries: Oak, Beaver, and Clear creeks; East Verde River
Mouth: Joins Salt River a few miles northeast of Phoenix, Arizona
Agricultural products: Citrus, cotton, truck vegetables
Industries: Copper mining

Most of Arizona is arid, with an annual rainfall of as little as three inches at Yuma, in the southwest corner of the state, and an overall average of seven inches. With so little water, Arizona in its natural state is, for the most part, a desert. Only in its central and northern high country are there mountains and forests that receive ample rainfall, if 23″ a year may be considered ample! It is this nearby source of water that is southern Arizona's real salvation. Without it Phoenix and Tucson could never have become the sprawling metropolises they are today, nor could millions of acres of desert land be made to produce cotton, citrus, and vegetables.

In such an arid state the drainage pattern is simple, for, there being relatively little water, there are relatively few rivers. With the exception of the Bill Williams and the Little Colorado, which flow directly into the Colorado, Arizona's rivers tend to flow into the west-running Gila

River, which also flows into the Colorado. The Gila's principal tributary is the Salt River, and in its turn, the Salt's principal tributary is the Verde. Yet in many ways the Verde has a more colorful history than the Salt.

Since 1945 the only Arizona river (not including the Colorado, Arizona's western boundary) that is a perennial waterway is the Verde, and even its water can be cut off by two flood-control dams. It drains more than 6,600 square miles of north central Arizona including much of the Colorado Plateau. For thousands of years its valley, a serpentine artery of verdant green across the barren desert landscape, has been a haven of sustenance for humans, animals, and birds.

The Verde rises at Del Rio Springs, about thirty miles southeast of Seligman, at an elevation of 4,348 feet. From this point snow-capped mountains can be seen in three directions, the obvious sources of the Verde's waters. The river flows in a southeasterly direction through the lush Verde Valley. This ends abruptly as the Verde enters a rugged chasm which separates the Upper Verde region from the Lower Verde. The Lower Verde remains mountainous until it reaches the desert floor a few miles from its junction with the Salt, into which it flows sluggishly, at an altitude of 2,340 feet. In all, the Verde is about 180 miles long.

Even before people arrived wild life teemed along the Verde. Birds from all over the Southwest came there, using its lush flora as a suitable haven from the desert in which to breed. The river remains to this day one of the most important breeding bird habitats in North America. Doves, quail, meadowlarks, hawks, owls, roadrunners, woodpeckers, swifts, swallows, wrens, ducks, herons, and geese abound. When the Spanish explorer Antonio de Espejo scouted the Verde Valley in 1583 he recorded seeing parrots there also. So, too, did mammals abound: deer, antelope, squirrel, beaver, muskrats, otter, porcupines, jack rabbits, skunks, raccoons, bats, chipmunks, mountain lions, bobcats, foxes, and badgers. Before overgrazing by ranchers and draining of marshy land, there were places along the Verde where a horse stood belly deep in grass.

The first Americans to visit the Verde appear to have been a segment of a trapper brigade which included the mountain men James Ohio Pattie and Ewing Young. While one contingent worked up the Salt, the other worked up the Verde to its headwaters, returning to its mouth at the Salt. Thereafter the Verde was frequented by mountain men seeking beaver and other wild life and a pleasant refuge from the desert. Kit Carson trapped the Verde in 1829.

The Treaty of Guadalupe Hidalgo, ending the Mexican War, made Arizona an American territory. Yet not until 1863 was a territorial government established for the region. The site chosen was at Del Rio Springs, headwaters of the Verde. (Four months later the capital was moved to Granite Creek, a tributary a few miles to the southwest.)

While trapping declined, mining increased. The greatest find along the Verde was copper, discovered along a 30-degree slope some 2,000 feet above the valley floor. At first the inaccessibility of the ore, and the long distance to market, discouraged development. Then the Montana copper king, William Andrews Clark, decided to develop the site which had been named "Jerome." He built a narrow-gauge railroad connecting the mine to the Santa Fe standard gauge line 26 miles to the west. Clark's railway, the United Verde and Pacific railroad, had 126 curves. People called it "the crookedest line in the world." It first ran in 1895 and was abandoned in 1920 after a standard gauge line along the Verde River to the mine had been completed.

While no great silver or gold discoveries have been made in recent times, the Spanish left behind a legend of a rich gold vein on the Upper Verde. Today lost-mine seekers search for it about ten miles east of Perkinsville, a tiny ranching community. Apaches are said to have discovered the vein in an arroyo which ran up from the Verde. The Spanish drove out the Indians and operated the mine themselves. Its ore was so rich that it was smelted easily. According to the legend, they stacked the bullion in the tunnel. When the Apaches attacked, only two Spaniards escaped, carrying with them or later drawing from memory a map of the location. To this day the mine has not been located.

About thirty-five miles downstream from Sullivan Lake (filled with the Verde's waters), is Sycamore Canyon—a wild, unspoiled region of 47,762 acres—designated by the Department of Agriculture as a wilderness area. It angles into the Verde from the north. At about this point the Verde turns south and enters the Verde Valley. Twenty-five miles across and forty miles long, the valley is a veritable oasis, a "sink" below the normal surface of the land, the result of two geologic faults. Unfortunately the sink enables a temperature inversion which traps polluted air in the Valley.

The most northerly town on the river is Clarkdale. It was established in 1912 as the site of William A. Clark's smelter for Jerome's copper ore. It finally closed in 1953 with few regrets, (although it brought ten years of depression to the Valley), for its noxious fumes burned everything—paint on houses, people's lungs, trees and gardens, while the forested slopes were denuded as fuel for the smelter. To this was added overgrazing by cattle. The destruction of this Eden in the desert was under way. However, early settlers successfully established farms with gardens and orchards along with privately owned irrigation systems.

After meandering along the valley floor the river leaves the Verde Valley via the Verde Chasm, down which the water rushes to the Lower Verde. The chasm remains wild, with deer, mountain lions, beaver, ducks, and cranes in abundance. By this time several tributaries have added their waters to the Verde, most notably Oak Creek, Beaver Creek, and Clear Creek. At Beaver Creek's confluence lie the remains of Fort Lincoln, built in 1866 as a base for soldiers stationed there to protect the first settlers in the valley from Indian attacks. Those settlers had come from Fort Whipple in 1865 to raise fruits and vegetables for miners and soldiers. Pauline Weaver, a famous mountain man, died here in his tent in 1867. (Later the fort moved a mile south and became known as Camp Verde.) In the 1870s captured Indians were held on a reservation nearby. Camp Verde was abandoned in 1891.

The Camp Verde area has figured prominently in the Central Arizona Project, a massive program to bring Colorado River water into Arizona's south-central desert. Plans formulated in 1944 provided for a 139-mile tunnel to spill 3,000 cubic feet of water per second into the Verde at a point near Camp Verde, thus making of the river a mere irrigation ditch. Additional dams along the Verde were planned to impound and regulate the discharge of the water. These plans have since been abandoned.

Below the chasm the Lower Verde is a more torpid stream. Still, southeast-northwest running mountains cut up the terrain. Nearby is the remains of Verde Hot Springs, a rustic lodge and spa, which burned in 1958. Fossil Springs, a few miles away, discharge 20,000 gallons of water a minute and have been used as the power source for an economically efficient hydro-electric operation that has existed since 1907.

Farther downstream the last important tributary, the East Verde, flows into the Verde. Its waters are controlled and the amount increased by an agreement between the Phelps Dodge Corporation (copper mining) and the Salt River Project. Water from the Little Colorado watershed is pumped over a divide and spilled into the East Verde.

Further downstream the Verde becomes Horseshoe Reservoir created by Horseshoe Dam, again built by Phelps Dodge under terms of another deal. Eighteen miles below is Bartlett Dam. It is part of the Salt River Project, was completed in 1939, and, with Horseshoe Dam, holds enough water to irrigate thousands of acres of once unproductive desert land.

Below Bartlett Dam, the Verde is out of the rugged transition zone of mountains that lie between Arizona's "Upper River Basin" and the arid southwest deserts. From Bartlett Dam to the confluence with the Salt, the river meanders across the flat desert plain.

Seven miles above its mouth is Fort McDowell, established September 7, 1865, to protect settlers. It was abandoned Septembr 18, 1890, but the area was included in the subsequent Fort McDowell Indian Reservation. Today about 300 members of the Mohave-Apache (Yavapai) tribe live in this four- by ten-mile parallelogram of cottonwood, cacti, and mesquite.

Even though the government had considered the land useless when it was given to the Indians, time and development made the little reservation of great strategic importance. The Central Arizona Project envisioned a dam at the confluence of the Verde with the Salt, a dam whose waters would inundate 60% of the McDowell Indian Reservation. So strong were the protests that in 1977 the plans for the dam were abandoned.

The future of the Verde is in doubt. Once it watered a serpentine Eden of flora and fauna flowing from the highlands through rugged, arid mountains onto the desert floor, where it joined the west-running Salt. Its banks teemed with deer, antelope, bear, mountain lions, muskrats, and beaver; catfish and fat bass filled the river, and birds by the tens of thousands nested along its banks.

Then came humans, lusting for minerals, anxious to establish farms, desiring the good life in a sterile, arid land which could be made delightful with water. Mine or mill tailings polluted the water, and dams and ditches depleted its flow. Now the need for water has grown until the channel itself is being cleared of cottonwood, sycamore, and willow because they consume the precious fluid. As marshes are drained and flora is destroyed, the fauna must disappear. Birds cannot nest nor animals hide nor fish survive. If the process is allowed to continue, then the Verde will become an ugly ditch, the valley a sterile habitat for people—and only for people.

FURTHER READING: University of Arizona Faculty, *Arizona: Its People and Resources* (1972). Rufus K. Wyllys, *Arizona—History of a Frontier State* (1950).

James W. Byrkit

The Walker River

Source: Convergence of East Walker and West Walk-
er rivers south of Yerington, in west-central Nevada
Length: 50 miles
Tributaries: None of consequence
Mouth: Into Walker Lake, in western Nevada
Agricultural products: Cattle ranching, dairying, hay,
grain, potatoes, onions
Industries: Copper, gold, and silver mining

Water is a precious natural resource in Nevada, the center of the arid Great Basin. The state receives an average of only nine inches of precipitation annually, and its land area of 110,540 square miles has a mere 752 square miles of water surface. Consequently, western Nevada, which receives as little as four inches of precipitation, depends greatly on three rivers and their tributaries fed mainly by snowpack in the towering Sierra Nevadas of California to support its agriculture, livestock, mining and urban development.

These rivers, the Truckee, Carson, and Walker, have supported life for thousands of years. Originally they fed giant prehistoric Lake Lahontan, which in the late Pleistocene stretched some 200 miles from present-day Hawthorne, Nevada, almost to the Oregon border and extended from near Battle Mountain, Nevada, some 175 miles to Honey Lake, California. After the Ice Age the lake disappeared, and the rivers flowed into smaller lakes or terminated in sinks.

The Walker, the least important of the three in volume of water flow, is formed principally by two forks. One, the East Walker, heads near Bridgeport, California, and flows north about twenty-five miles before entering Nevada. It continues in a northerly direction for forty miles to Mason Valley. The other and more important fork, the West Walker, heads about twenty miles west of Bridgeport, flows north about thirty-five miles through Antelope Valley and enters Nevada. It continues for about another twenty-five miles through Smith and Mason Valleys where it merges with the East Walker to form the Walker River. From the southern end of Mason Valley the river moves north, then makes a wide

turn to the southeast through the Walker River Indian Reservation and terminates in Walker Lake; it is about fifty miles long. The river basin contains about 2.7 million acres, of which 2.1 million are in Nevada. It includes part of Mono County, California, and Lyon, Douglas, and Mineral counties in Nevada.

The Walker basin, with highly mineralized mountains, narrow valleys and several large desert oases, has been described as a "wild, lonely and beautiful land." In its natural state, before the advent of crops and grazing, it was covered at lower elevations with sagebrush (Artemisia tridentata), shadscale (Atriplex confertifolia) and perennial grasses that produced a natural hay. At elevations above 6,000 feet piñon and juniper trees dominate. At elevations between 8,000 and 10,000 feet the sagebrush and grass replace the trees, giving a barren appearance to these high mountainous areas. The basin enjoys relatively mild weather, but only about four months of the year are frost-free.

Although explorers who visited the basin in the 19th century considered the land practically worthless, the Paiutes and Washoes who lived close to the river saw it as relatively lush. The lake and river, which they called Agai Hoop (Trout River), provided an abundance of fish, and they found the mountains and valleys rich in deer, antelope, mountain sheep and jackrabbits which they hunted with bows and arrows. They also gathered pine nuts and other seeds and made baskets from the grass, which sometimes grew as high as a horse. But with the arrival of outsiders, particularly cattlemen and farmers, the Indians' world changed; the newcomers, in ever greater numbers, found new uses for the land.

The first explorers to be on or near the Walker were probably trappers Jedediah Smith in 1827 and Peter Skene Ogden in 1829. Both were in search of beaver, but their exact routes are unknown. The man who became best acquainted with the area was Joseph Reddeford Walker, an expert trapper-explorer, for whom a later explorer, John C. Fremont, named the river and lake. In 1834 Walker led a party of fifty-two men through the Walker River country on his trip from California to Salt Lake. The Bidwell-Bartleson party, the first emigrant group to cross the Great Basin, arrived at the West Walker in 1841 on their way through the Sierras to California after following the Humboldt to its sink and traveling southward. Fremont, when he circled the Great Basin two years later, wrote that the Walker River "ran through broad bottoms, having a fine meadow-like appearance." Again in 1845 another Fremont expedition, with Walker as guide, was in the area, as were about 250 emigrants on their way to California. With the Gold Rush the numbers increased, with wagon trains moving regularly westward to the Mother Lode. The Walker appealed to emigrants as it did to explorers because of the fish and other food the Indians provided.

The first settlers brought mining and agriculture, and these are still the major local industries. Beginning in 1859 California cattlemen brought their herds to the two largest Walker valleys to graze on the plentiful sagebrush and bunch grass, partly because of drought in California. A party of four or five men, most of whom were named Smith, settled in what became known as Smith Valley, and Nathaniel H.A. "Hock" Mason, also a cattleman, was the pioneer settler in the valley named for him. In 1861 the Smith party planted barley and vegetables and found the land good for cultivation. With the rise of mining in the Walker basin in 1860 there developed a brisk demand for farm products. Other settlers took up land, irrigation ditches were dug diverting the river water, and hay, grain, and vegetables supplemented livestock production.

Gold had been discovered in the Mono Lake area in 1852, and when Nevada's Comstock rush began prospectors combed nearby mountains to duplicate that discovery. This led to important gold and silver strikes in the Walker basin that brought thousands of people to camps such as Aurora, Coryville, and Granite, Nevada, and Bodie, California. Within a decade Aurora produced $29,000,000 from surface bonanzas. Its population, which for a time included Sam Clemens, approached 10,000 and then went into decline in the late 1870s. Like Aurora, Bodie was another Cinderella town. The rush for gold and

silver there began in 1861, and within two decades that roaring camp had equalled Aurora's production and population. Today both are ghost towns.

Intensive searches led to other gold and silver discoveries near the Walker and its tributaries at Pine Grove, Rockland, Cambridge and the opening of copper mines in the Singatse Mountains. By 1881 the Carson and Colorado railroad provided transport service from Reno to the lower Walker River and Walker Lake area and mining camps west of Hawthorne. Although mining went into decline in the 1880s, it revived in the period 1910–1920 and declined again. In 1952 Anaconda Copper Corporation began an open-pit operation near Yerington, the principal town of the Walker basin. After producing as much as 5,000,000 pounds of copper per month, the company closed down in 1978 due to falling copper prices and nearly exhausted ore deposits at that location. But the basin is still rich in minerals, and it is expected that mining, particularly of extensive iron ore deposits, will be a major future contributor to the area's economy.

The trend toward consolidation of ranch and farm lands in the Far West in the late 19th century appeared here with two giant firms buying out a number of smaller holdings. The Pacific Livestock Company, owned by Miller and Lux, formed the Walker River Ranch, which included the 20,000 acres belonging to "Hock" Mason. The Rickey ranches in Antelope, Slinkard, and Bridgeport valleys were part of a 200,000-acre holding that also included land in the Owens Valley of California. Also at this time new settlers, many of them Portuguese and Italian immigrants, took up farming in Mason and Smith valleys. They specialized in row crops, such as potatoes and onions, and dairying, which continue to the present. The immigrants are credited with modernizing and diversifying the agriculture and in bringing new lands under cultivation. The Miller, Lux, and Rickey ranches were sold off in smaller parcels in the 1920s.

By the turn of the century it was apparent that a limit would soon be reached on land under irrigation unless facilities were increased and water flow controlled. Only 40,000 of the available 175,000 acres of lowland area was irrigated. But the demand for foodstuffs for the Tonopah and Goldfield mining districts was increasing, as were land filings and water rights granted. However, wide fluctuations in the Sierra precipitation plagued settlers with high water in the late spring and early summer and low water in fall and winter. Especially hurt by heavy upstream use was the Walker River Indian Reservation, created in 1859 for the Paiutes and consisting of 300,000 acres. It originally included the lake and thirty miles of the river to the north. Much of its cropland was either washed out by floods or starved by drought. Mason Valley ranchers coveted its lands, while most of the 500 reservation Indians were forced to find work on more prosperous white ranches and farms. The reservation was reduced in size as a result of the Dawes Severalty Act and opened in 1906 to outside (non-Indian) miners. However, in 1936 it was restored to approximately its original size.

Increasing competition for the available water, drastically short in drought years, led to creation in 1919 of the privately owned and financed Walker River Irrigation District. It included all irrigated areas in Nevada on the Walker and its branches, except for the Indian reservation. The organization's principal accomplishment was construction of Topaz Reservoir on the West Walker, completed in 1922, and Bridgeport Reservoir on the East Walker, completed two years later. A third and smaller project, Weber Reservoir, constructed by the federal government for the reservation, was completed in 1937.

The reservoirs led to increased irrigation—to a maximum of 126,000 acres at one point in the 1920s—but fluctuations in river flow have restricted it to a norm of about 80,000 acres. There simply is not enough water to meet demand. In some drought years farmers have had to drill wells to save their crops. For most of this century Walker Lake has receded at a rate of two feet per year. This and creation of Weber Reservoir have prevented the trout from swimming upstream to spawn. Consequently, the lake must be stocked artificially. Also, the lake has grown increasingly saline as less and less fresh water mixes with dissolved solids. It is predicted that by 1995 the lake will be uninhabitable for the native fish species. Efforts are being made to introduce other fish, possibly from Africa or Russia, that will be able to live and reproduce.

Today the Walker basin has a population of about 20,000. The principal town, Yerington, has 2,300 residents and is the county seat of Lyon County. Hawthorne, at the south end of Walker Lake, has a population of about 3,500 and is the site of a military ammunition depot established in 1926.

What does the future hold for the Walker basin? Some basic decisions must be made. Maintaining a low-population, pastoral-recreational environment would require the withdrawal of some water rights and a reduction in land irrigated. This would help to maintain Walker Lake, or at least part of it, and encourage sports fishing and recreation upstream, as well as a desirable environmental quality. Conversely, increased agriculture, mining, urban development and some industrialization—also considered desirable—would require construction of several new reservoirs and probably the sacrifice of Walker Lake. It is not likely that much new land could be put under irrigation, but serious flooding in Antelope and Mason valleys from spring snowmelt could be controlled. Whatever alternative is selected, it is clear that no new water is available for the Walker and its branches.

The Walker River's history mirrors much of the West's development. The Indians' idyllic life was disturbed by outsiders who used the river first as an aid to emigration. Later they exploited the minerals and utilized the land for agriculture and a larger population. The Indians were granted reservation lands and water that the whites coveted and managed to obtain. Although the reservation and the Indians' water were later restored, the Indians have lived on the fringes of the dominant society, providing a needed labor base for the white man's prosperous farms and ranches. However, all that has been accomplished here has been built with a limited and unpredictable water supply, and this creates a dilemma for future development of this ruggedly beautiful land.

FURTHER READING: Russell R. Elliott, *History of Nevada* (1973). Edward C. Johnson, *Walker River Paiutes: A Tribal History* (1975).

Robert W. Davenport

Rivers of the Pacific Coast and Alaska

Most Pacific Coast rivers are relatively short, tumbling rapidly out of the Sierras or Cascades toward the nearby Pacific. A few run their course from mountains of origin north across arid prairies to the Columbia. And the mighty Columbia is an exception to the rule of shortness, rising in British Columbia and flowing 1,200 miles south into Washington State and west to the Pacific.

Such California rivers as the American, Feather, Sacramento, and San Joaquin loom large in the story of the California gold rush. It was along a tributary of the American River that James Marshall discovered gold in 1848. The resulting stampede changed the peaceful flow of the rivers. Hillsides were denuded of timber. Aquaducts diverted high-country water to points at which it was forced out of nozzles called monitors, washing away entire hillsides and filling the rivers with silt. Steamboating ended because of sandbars while fertile farmlands were inundated by floods. And subsequent population growth necessitated a more systematic control over the rivers. Yet some of them, especially the coastal streams of northern California, still flow free. Such stretches of water as the lower Klamath offer thrills to canoeists and raftsmen, as does the Rogue River of southern Oregon.

On northward, the Columbia, dammed at Grand Coulee, beckons the adventurer into the interior. Its principal tributary, the Snake, twists out of southern Yellowstone Park and flows south, around, and then northwest of the Grand Tetons. The Salmon, Clearwater, Owyhee, John Day, and Willamette likewise swell the waters of the Columbia by the time it reaches the Pacific. Taken as a whole the Pacific Coast rivers drain one of the finest areas for human habitation on earth.

North to Alaska still other rivers attract our attention. The Yukon and Copper rivers remind us that Alaska is still a largely untapped resource for the future.

Richard A. Bartlett

The American River

Source: Rises in three separate forks in the high Sierras
Length: 100 miles along any of the three forks. The Middle Fork joins the South Fork near Auburn; 18 miles on downstream the South Fork and North Fork converge; for 30 miles the river flows as a single entity.
Tributaries: None of significance beyond the three forks
Mouth: Into Sacramento River at Sacramento
Agricultural products: Little of significance
Industries: Hydroelectric power; tourism

The American River rises in the Sierra Nevada, on the watershed west of Lake Tahoe. Its three forks drop 6,000 feet through deep gorges and narrow valleys in their first fifty miles, joining to form the main stream below the foothill town of Auburn. It joins the Sacramento in the city of the same name. Measured along any of its three branches, the American can be said to be about a hundred miles long; its drainage basin is about 2,000 square miles between the Bear River to the north and the Consumnas to the south.

The wooded canyons of the American were the undisturbed hunting grounds of the Maidu Indians until the arrival of a party of American fur trappers led by Jedediah Smith. In May, 1827, Smith and his party, with 1,500 pounds of beaver and otter pelts, tried unsuccessfully to cross the Sierras south of Lake Tahoe. Defeated by the still unmelted snow, Smith retreated and three weeks later conquered the Sierras by way of the Stanislaus River and Ebbetts Pass.

Twelve years later John Sutter founded his agricultural empire of New Helvetia on the banks of the American within the present limits of Sacramento. Sutter's Fort, with its adobe walls and brass canon, its flour mill, tannery, distillery, and other primitive manufactories became the goal of American immigrants who crossed the plains in the wake of the Bartleson-Bidwell party of 1841.

It was the hope of reaching Sutter's Fort in time to send back supplies to his starving expeditionary force that sustained John C. Fremont as he and Kit Carson led an advance party down the American River in the winter of 1844. As they neared the confluence of the American and Sacramento rivers they were greeted by a well-dressed and mounted Indian, one of Captain Sutter's vaqueros, who told them in Spanish that they were upon the Rio de los Americanos. Sutter welcomed the hungry men with "good beef, excellent bread, and delicious salmon," and sent provisions and horses back to their stranded companions.

In Fremont's official report is his cartographer's map of the American River. It is shown rising in Lake Tahoe, a mistake that does not appear in his journal, and flowing past Sutter's Fort. This report, published in both London and New York in 1846, stirred an already strong interest in the wonders of California; there can be no doubt that it greatly reinforced America's drive to the Pacific shore.

Soon a greater incentive appeared to persuade people to emigrate to California. On January 24, 1848—the year California fell into American hands—James Marshall, who with the help of some newly arrived Mormon immigrants was building a sawmill up the American River from New Helvetia, noticed some glittering specks at the bottom of the newly dug tailrace. He picked up one flake, then another, and another. That evening he is reported to have said, "Boys, I believe I have found a gold mine."

Sutter did what he could to keep it secret while rushing the sawmill to completion. But secrets involving gold cannot be kept, and rumors began to fly. By the summer of 1848 even the most respected citizens could talk of nothing but their finds. John Sinclair, a settler who owned Rancho del Paso on the American River, organized a party of fifty Indians who took out

Sutter's Mill on the American River where James Marshall discovered gold. (Credit: Wells Fargo Bank History Room.)

$16,000 in gold using Indian willow baskets. Thomas Larkin, who served as United States Consul at Monterey, wrote, "I have had in my hands several pieces of gold about twenty-three carats fine, weighing from one to two pounds. Indeed, I have heard of one specimen that weighed twenty-five pounds."

News of this nature, from people of such prominence, was quick to travel as ships reached the Sandwich Islands, Oregon, Mexico, and New Orleans. Skeptical eastern newspapers threw caution to the winds after a tea caddy of gold arrived and President Polk's State of the Union message of December, 1848, described the gold finds in California in sufficient detail to inflame the imagination of even the most prudent.

So it was "Ho for California!" for an estimated 39,000 immigrants who arrived by sea and 42,000 more who made the trek by land in 1849. The newcomers centered their attentions on the American River because not only was it famous for Marshall's discovery but also because the mines along the river and its forks continued to be among the richest in California.

The richest deposits of gold were found in gravel bars that the river currents piled up on the convex sides of the bends in the streams. Some bars developed into towns, others were uprooted and then abandoned, but the exuberant story of the gold rush can be told by their very names: Sailor Claim, Mammoth Bar, Texas Bar, Buckeye, Yankee Bar, Sardine, Drunkard's Bar, Horseshoe, Rattlesnake, Milk Punch, Deadman Bar, and Ruby Point Slide. Some scenes of extravagant finds are recalled from a miner's song:

> I heard of gold at Sutter's Mill
> At Michigan Bluff and Iowa Hill
> But never thought it was rich until,
> I started off to prospect.
> At Yankee Jim's I bought a purse,
> Inquired for Iowa Hill, of course,
> And traveled on, but what was worse,
> Fetched up in Shirt-tail Canyon.

Michigan Bluff is 2,000 feet above the gorge of the Middle and North Forks of the American River. The diggings at Iowa Hill, on the North Fork of the American, were so rich that by 1880 they had produced over $20,000,000. Yankee Jim is said to be named for a shrewd young Irishman who discovered a valuable pocket of gold in the ridges away from the river banks. He was able to keep the secret to himself until his gold bags bulged so that swarms of miners left the river and took to the hills after him. The story of Shirt-tail Canyon starts on a hot day in the summer of 1849 as two Oregon prospectors made their way into a wooded canyon. Hearing no sound save that of their own voices, they were astonished to find a solitary miner, naked except for a short shirt, busily picking gold from a rock with a knife. "Where the devil is this place?" they asked. The miner took a look at this own attire and replied, "Don't yet know its name. Let's call it Shirt-tail Canyon." Shirt-tail Canyon and its branches, Grizzly Canyon, Refuge Canyon, and Devil's Canyon, are little more than names, but North Fork Dry Diggings turned into the respectable town of Auburn.

By 1849 Auburn was famous as the place where a man could make $1,000 a day, but the camp might have gone the way of other mining towns had it not been the center of a network of wagon trails. The miners were already tunneling into the rocky walls of the steep gorges near Auburn and roads were blasted and hacked out of the mountains to serve their needs. Stage coaches fanned out in all directions to serve the occupants of hundreds of mining camps in the Sierra foothills. The tribulations of the stage-coach passengers are celebrated in this gold rush song:

> There's no respect for youth or age
> On board a California stage,
> But pull and haul about for seats
> As bedbugs do about the sheets.

> The ladies are compelled to sit
> With dresses in tobacco spit;
> The gentlemen don't seem to care,
> But talk on politics and swear.
> The dust is deep in summer time,
> The mountains very hard to climb;
> And drivers often stop and yell,
> "Get out, all hands, and push—*up hill!*"
> They promise when your fare you pay,
> "You'll have to walk but half the way";
> Then add aside, with cunning laugh,
> "You'll push and pull the other half!"

By 1856 California's first railroad ran twenty-two miles from Sacramento to the American River town of Folsom. This short line was sufficient to convince Californians that the answer to their problem of isolation was a transcontinental railroad. For many years they campaigned for it; in 1869 the "great transcontinental" became a reality. By then the fever of the gold rush was over, but the promise of a new life in golden California was just as appealing as ever and a lot easier to reach.

Two important developments had far-reaching effects on the lives of people living along the American River: mining became less important than farming, and the nature of mining changed as hydraulic mining companies devastated the river landscape. By 1870 there were 36,340 miners in the region while 47,900 people were employed there in agricultural pursuits. The central river valleys of the Sacramento and San Joaquin were producing millions of tons of wheat that when milled was called "California White Velvet."

The wheat empires were threatened with spring floods on the Sacramento caused by winter rains and the melting Sierra snowpack as the American, the Feather, and the Yuba added tons of mud "slikens" from hydraulic mining to their normal load of silt and rocks. The story of the farmers' struggles to stop hydraulic mining and to harness the rivers for both flood control and irrigation purposes may be found in the history of the Sacramento and San Joaquin. By 1969 the annual value of agricultural production in California exceeded the total value of all the gold mined there since 1848, and the agricultural productivity of the American River region contributed a respectable share of the total.

To prevent flood damage, aid in irrigation, and produce hydroelectric power on the American River, the Army Engineers backed up over one million acre-feet of water in Folsom Dam and further upstream impounded 26 million cubic feet of northern water behind the North Fork Dam. In addition to the levees and dams built by the Engineers and the Bureau of Reclamation, the river was further harnessed for hydroelectric power by private companies. Pacific Gas and Electric built the first electric power project on the American at Folsom in 1895. It is now maintained as a historic site.

Today the American River functions mainly as a source for hydroelectric power. Its branches, in the rocky foothills country, are dotted with historical markers that tell the story of the river bars of the gold rush. Tourists are still encouraged, by local hardware stores, to buy a pan and try their luck.

FURTHER READING: Rodman W. Paul, *The California Gold Discovery* (1966). Margaret Sanborn, *The American, River of El Dorado* (1974).

The Clark Fork and Flathead rivers

Source: Rises near Butte, Montana
Length: About 300 miles
Tributaries: Flathead and Bitterroot rivers
Mouth: Flows into Lake Pend Oreille in northern Idaho
Agricultural products: Sugar beets, potatoes, cherries
Industries: Copper, silver and gold mining, aluminum manufacturing, hydroelectric power

Flowing off mountains of granite and limestone, the streams carrying the runoff of the western slope of Montana's Rocky Mountains are clear and clean. They thunder through gorges and over rapids with enough power to set huge water turbines spinning. But in other stretches the same streams are deep and placid, inviting first the traffic of Indian canoes and later the steamboats and motor launches of the whites.

The principal river carrying these waters is the Clark Fork. It is about 300 miles long from its place of origin near Butte, Montana, northwest into Idaho's sylvan Lake Pend Oreille. It carries with it the waters of many tributaries, of which the Flathead and the Bitterroot are the most important.

The present scene of twisting gorges and tortuous mountains was not always so. Toward the end of the most recent Ice Age (about 10,000 years ago) the melted ice waters were restrained by a dam of ice and debris located near where Clark Fork enters Idaho. The result was a massive lake that inundated valleys and covered mountains. (At Missoula the lake is estimated to have been 1,000 feet deep!) As the climate warmed and the water rose, the soggy debris dam washed out releasing water measured in the hundreds of cubic miles. That portion of the earth's surface was altered forever. Mountains reappeared and streams resumed their ancient courses. In the passing of centuries forests reappeared. By Lewis's and Clark's time little remained to tell the story of this cataclysm. Only in recent years have earth scientists felt sure that it happened at all.

When Lewis and Clark ventured westward in the early 1800s they traveled briefly northward down the valley of the Bitterroot. Information from the local Indians made it clear that the Bitterroot flowed into a different river system than the Salmon-Snake, and Lewis designated this northern system as Clark's River. On the way home the next year he saw the stream that joins the Bitterroot near Missoula, and called it the East Fork of Clark's River; today it is simply known as the Clark Fork.

As explorers the Captains had the privilege of naming geographical features but, since their maps were not available to those who followed them, many of the names they designated faded into obscurity. The Clark Fork and the Flathead did not achieve permanence without competition. The Flathead, a beautiful river and lake, originates in Canada, flows south into Flathead Lake, and out of it south and west to its junction

The destructiveness of hydraulic mining is clearly shown here. (Credit: History Division of Los Angeles Museum of Natural History.)

with the Clark Fork; it is about 245 miles long. Sometimes it was called the Pend Oreille. As for the Clark Fork, it has been called the Hell Gate for Hell Gate Canyon through which it flows, the Missoula, for the town of the same name, and the Deer Lodge, the Indian name for its upper reaches. Below the mouth of the Flathead it has also been designated the Pend Oreille.

Although early maps carried grim warning of ambush and slaughter in the Flathead-Clark Fork region, there were never any bloody confrontations to mar its history. Prior to 1810 Indians did carry on tribal warfare around Hell Gate Canyon and indeed, the white man's arrival increased tribal warfare. But no major clashes occurred and the peacefulness of the region was only marred by the usual bloodletting of whites against whites in the frontier society.

Not until 1855 did Governor Isaac I. Stevens of Washington Territory negotiate agreements among the residents of the area. Whites could occupy the Clark Fork drainage and wars were ended between the Blackfeet and other tribes. The pacts proved generally durable and effective, although ironically the Flathead Treaty has since 1970 been a source of contention between Indians and resident whites, with the waters of the Flathead and Clark Fork prominent in the litigation.

The 1855 agreement turned over to the Flatheads and their allies the land from the Jocko Valley, north of Missoula, to a line bisecting

Flathead Lake, and this discouraged white intrusion. Also, since the Flathead Valley was not on the direct road to anywhere, and there were no recognized treasures in gold, lumber, fertile soil or water power, the whites settled elsewhere. (These treasures were there, but were more easily accessible elsewhere.) So the scene of action shifted after 1855 to the Clark Fork from its sources along the Continental Divide to its confluence with the Flathead.

Following Governor Stevens's transcontinental exploring party in 1853 came a road building crew under Lieutenant John Mullan. While his men were hacking out the military trail known as the Mullan Road, James and Granville Stuart checked a rumor that placer gold existed in the side-creeks of the Clark Fork between Deer Lodge and Missoula. By 1860 the existence of "color" was confirmed and soon the clear waters of the Hell Gate (as they called Clark Fork) were muddied by mining operations, especially from activity up a tributary called Gold Creek. Although no real bonanza developed, the word of the discoveries spread through the mountains and lured enough people into the country to staff the real gold rush which was soon to erupt on the Missouri headwaters at Bannack, not far away.

This rich discovery nearly drained the population from the Gold Creek camps, but a few stayed on and turned their attention to farming and stock raising. One settler was Johnny Grant, a young trader-turned-cattleman, whose range between Deer Lodge and Garrison is today marked as the pioneer cattle ranching venture in Montana.

In January, 1864, a small posse rode across the Divide and down Clark Fork in pursuit of some desperadoes from Henry Plummer's shattered gang. Four of these "road agents" were lynched at the Hell Gate settlement, another at nearby Frenchtown, and a sixth at Fort Owen in the Bitterroot Valley. It may be noted that the camp at Gold Creek had achieved already the distinction of being the scene of Montana's first hanging, performed in 1862 by an Idaho posse that pounced on three horse thieves and executed one of the two who survived the shoot-out.

In the mid-1870s the rich ores of Butte, at the headwaters of Clark Fork, added silver and especially copper to Montana's treasures. Butte, with its "Richest Hill on Earth," quickly grew into Montana's first urban area. A notable citizen who moved there from Deer Lodge was William Andrews Clark, whose rise to wealth and prominence progressed with Butte's notoriety.

The opening of the Butte mines led to the next assault on the resources of the upper Clark Fork as the demand for wood sent gangs of woodcutters into the evergreen forests. Competing gangs clashed occasionally; the Cramer Gulch war, upriver from Missoula, was one such episode. Origins of the "War of the Copper Kings," involving Clark and Marcus Daly, also can be traced to the reckless cutting of the forests, some of them on restricted federal lands.

Exploitation of the Butte copper depoits was hampered by the absence of a railroad. In 1881 the narrow guage Utah Northern came in from the south. Then in 1883 the Northern Pacific was completed. Although it did not yet serve Butte directly, it brought changes to the canyons of the Clark Fork. Crossing Mullan Pass west of Helena, the road followed the Little Blackfoot to its junction with Clark Fork at Garrison and stayed with the major stream for some seventy miles to Missoula. Then the builders ran into trouble.

Where Mullan had been able to avoid bridge building and heavy earth moving by running his trail over adjacent hillsides, the rails, which could not follow such contours, competed with the river for possession of the canyon, in places even for the stream bed itself. The terrain was worst below Missoula, so the surveyors turned northward to the northwest running Jocko, a tributary of the Flathead, and there awaited the building crews working from the west.

Meanwhile the crews from Spokane had swung northward to cross above Lake Pend Oreille and place themselves on the water grade of the Clark Fork for the run across Idaho's panhandle into Montana. Even then it was not easy going. Since there was no road to bring in the iron and steel, prefabricated boats were assembled on the river where it was navigable; these little steamboats proved satisfactory. One or two tough little craft fought their way to the Thompson Falls area of Montana. The best known was the *Katie Hallett*, which helped to assure the arrival of the railroad near the mouth of the Flathead River before she grounded on a rocky bar.

Building this stretch along the Clark Fork and

Flathead rivers took a heavy cost in human life. Accidents were frequent although off-work violence seems to have caused the greater number of deaths. A newsman reported of the construction camp of Rock Island that it had "a vast need for a lynching society. . . . Twenty men are reported missing," the writer added, "and twelve of them have been found floating in the river with their skulls broken." Some said that over 1,000 Chinese had met death on the Northern Pacific. Clearly Northern Pacific construction was no place for delicate types.

The Flathead-Jocko route avoided canyon terrain but replaced it with a steep grade down into Missoula, or a tough one going out of the town. To this engineering difficulty was added sociological trouble, for the railroad traversed the southern fringe of the Flathead Indian Reservation. The Indians reported that the trains were killing their prized horses. Dissatisfied with the compensation offered by the railroad, the Native Americans took to throwing rocks at passenger car windows and otherwise damaging railroad property. A visit by U.S. Deputy Marshall J.X. Biedler, still glorying in his role as executioner for the 1864 vigilantes, soon put a stop to these depredations.

While the Northern Pacific ran south of Flathead country, transportation to the north of there remained primitive until recent times. Steep slopes and dense timber around the lake made road building difficult. The immediate answer was boats. In place of fragile Indian canoes came sailboats and then steamers, from squat little tugs for pushing logs to stately passenger vessels such as the *Klondike*. From 1910 until 1924 this stately queen of the lake ran from Polson to Kalispell during the ice-free season. Steamers were also tried on the lower Flathead from Dixon to Polson, but the fast, shallow current was too much for them. The Northern Pacific finally built a spur to Polson, thus putting an end to steamboating endeavors on the lower Flathead.

The cataracts which hindered navigation drew the attention of electric power interests. In 1916 an investor-owned utility built a power plant at Thompson Falls; later facilities were constructed at Noxon Rapids below Thompson Falls and at Cabinet Gorge in Idaho. The upper reaches of Clark Fork flow mostly unimpeded by dams, a minor exception being at Milltown.

There a tiny plant with a few acres of shallow reservoir behind the dam has been in continuous operation since William Clark built it in 1907 for his lumber operations.

The Flathead River, and even its forks, are big enough to yield hydroelectric power. Just below the lake the Flathead enters a narrow gorge suited for installation. Work began on the project in 1930 and was completed as the Kerr Dam in 1938. On the Flathead's South Fork, near Glacier National Park, is the stream's only government-owned plant, at Hungry Horse. Availability of its power led quickly to the placement of an aluminum plant at nearby Columbia Falls.

The arrival of this industry, like the building of the Great Northern Railroad in 1889, marked the invasion of one of the country's last wildernesses. The region has been protected by its remoteness, by Indian lands on two sides, by the lake, and by the ramparts of the Continental Divide. Passing through equally primitive land to its source in southeastern British Columbia, the Flathead continues to shelter wolves, moose, caribou, wolverines and grizzly bears. The isolation has also helped to keep streams uncontaminated, even before Glacier Park was set aside to preserve the pristine conditions. Except for airborne pollution from the aluminum plant, the region still qualifies as unspoiled. This has been underlined by the establishment in 1978 of the Great Bear Wilderness, expanding already protected areas at the head of the South Fork of the Flathead. Below the lake, in a semiwild reserve near Dixon, the federal government maintains a herd of American bison.

Flathead Lake has proved hospitable for exotic game fish. Salmon have thrived and lake trout have done well in the deep, cold water that is their habitat. Another of the lake's residents is a "monster" which surfaces every few years, revealing an appearance similar to its counterpart in Loch Ness. Scoffers declare it is either a sturgeon, strayed in from the Columbia, or perhaps a seal, even farther from home.

Although this is a land with irrigated agriculture, the Flathead-Clark Fork system is lightly drawn upon for such use. Some diversion occurs along the main channels, but most of the developments are on tributaries, as is the case in the substantial project along the Flathead below the lake. Here the snowy Mission Range feeds several big creeks whose waters are stored in reservoirs to support a thriving mixed agriculture. Only minor irrigation appears along the main Clark Fork, partly due to an abundance of more easily managed sidestreams, and to the moderate need for water in an area that receives much of its rainfall at optimum times during the growing season.

When the waters of the Clark Fork finally reach the Columbia, they are little the worse for their long journey, considering that they have been dammed, harnessed, swum in, boated upon, and used for commercial and domestic purposes. Perhaps the waters are somewhat tainted with mine runoff and flavored with sawdust, but the torrent remains fit for the added demands it will meet on its way to the western sea.

FURTHER READING: Merrill Burlingame and K. Ross Toole, *A History of Montana* (1957). Michael P. Malone and Richard B. Roeder, *Montana: A History of Two Centuries* (1977).

Stanley R. Davison

The Columbia River

Source: Columbia Lake in southwest British Columbia
Length: 1,210 miles
Mouth: Pacific Ocean at Oregon-Washington boundary
Tributaries: Snake, Kootenai, Pend Oreille, Spokane, Willamette, John Day, Deschutes, and Cowlitz Rivers
Cities: Portland, Vancouver
Agricultural Products: Wheat, fruits
Industries: Aluminum, salmon fisheries

If the Mississippi is the Father of Waters, surely the Columbia is the eldest daughter, for she discharges from her mammoth basin 160 million acre-feet of water annually—more than any other river in the United States except the Mississippi. She originates at an altitude of 2,650 feet in Columbia Lake in southeast British Columbia, flows north around the Selkirk Mountains and then south to the Washington border, having flowed 465 miles in Canada. The Columbia then makes a great sweep west and finally forms the Oregon-Washington boundary until the river empties into the Pacific. In all, the river is 1,210 miles long.

Within the Columbia Basin are four distinct physical sectors: the Rocky Mountains, the basaltic Snake River plain and the Columbia Plateau; the Cascade Range; and the Puget Trough—a lowland area between the Cascade and the Coastal ranges which includes the Cowlitz River in Washington and the Willamette in Oregon. All told, the Columbia Basin embraces 259,000 square miles of which 220,000 lie in the United States. It is an area larger than France.

Besides the Snake, which drains forty-nine percent of the Columbia system, the Columbia receives the waters of the Kootenai, Pend Oreille, Clark Fork, Spokane, Willamette, John Day, and Deschutes rivers. Many other streams, some quite large, also swell the Columbia's waters.

Discovery of the Columbia is credited to the American Captain Robert Gray, who sailed through the breakers in his ship *Columbia* on May 11, 1792, and anchored ten miles from the mouth. He named the river in honor of his ship. Just a few months later (October) British Captain George Vancouver, in North Pacific waters with several ships, dispatched Lieutenant William Robert Broughton in the brig *Chatham*, to explore the Columbia. Lieutenant Broughton crossed the treacherous sandbar and then rowed in a small boat upstream about a hundred miles; he gave Mount Hood its name.

More than a dozen years later (in 1805) Lewis and Clark floated down the Columbia after their long journey from near St. Louis. Some of their elation as they approached their goal comes through in Lewis' Journal: "The fog suddenly clearing away, we were at last presented with the glorious sight of the ocean—that ocean, the object of all our labors, the reward of all our anxieties. . . ." The explorers erected Fort Clat-

The broad Columbia River winds its way past the city of The Dalles, Oregon (lower left), past industrial plants and westward through the Cascade Range to the Pacific Ocean. This aerial view, looking northwestward, shows typical rugged high plateau area along the Columbia in central and eastern Oregon and Washington. Mt. Adams and the tip of Mt. Rainier in Washington are in the background. (Oregon State Highway Department Photo.)

sop on the south side of the river and there spent the winter of 1805–1806.

The first explorer to map the Columbia from source to mouth was a scientific-minded employee of the British North West Company, David Thompson. He approached the river by crossing the Canadian Rockies at Athabasca Pass in present Alberta. Not until July, 1811, did Thompson follow the Columbia to its mouth. There he discovered that John Jacob Astor's

Pacific Fur Company had already established Astoria to siphon off the fur trade of the lower Columbia. (Astoria would be sold to the North West Company in 1812 and returned to American hands in 1818. A commemorative column at Astoria recalls the achievement.)

When the whites arrived in the Pacific Northwest they found relatively heavy Indian settlement along the coast and up the estuaries. Altogether, 125 tribes have been counted in the region. Along the Columbia or nearby its waters were the Chinooks, Clatsops, Willamettes, and Tillamooks. In the early decades of the nineteenth century their numbers were sharply reduced by the white man's "ague and fever."

Alexander Ross of the 1811 Astor party which came to the Columbia on the ill-fated ship *Tonquin* characterized the lower Columbia tribes as being "commercial rather than a warlike people." Of special interest was the lower Columbia Chinook culture which centered on the great river. The Chinooks had developed a traditional oral mythology. They counted themselves wealthy, practiced polygamy, and owned slaves traded from the interior. Here, too, was the potlatch custom, an expression of generosity in which a wealthy tribesman feasted his neighbors and gave away his material possessions.

In 1824 Fort Vancouver was established by the Hudson's Bay Company near the present site of Vancouver, Washington. It was headquarters of the Columbia District which extended to the Rockies. In this huge area French Canadians and Highland Scots carried on a highly efficient enterprise led by the Chief Factor, Dr. John McLoughlin.

Each year the fur brigades made their way from Fort Vancouver up the Columbia, carrying in the large batteaux bales of furs gathered in the previous year. Each vessel, manned by voyageurs, traveled eighteen hours a day until it attained its destination, York Factory on the shores of Hudson's Bay.

Portages had to be made twice in the first 200 miles upriver. The first navigational obstruction, 160–165 miles from the mouth, was the Cascades, now called Cascade Locks. These were a series of rapids so violent that between 1877 and 1896 a series of locks were installed to overcome the danger.

The second and more serious obstruction lay upstream another 35–40 miles. Here the mighty river surged through narrow basaltic channels two and one-half miles long. The turbulent, constricted water could seldom be navigated, requiring first a portage and later a by-pass canal system. The Dalles (French for "stones" or "slabs") of the Columbia, as the area was named by French traders, ended upriver at the horseshoe falls called by the Indian name "Celilo." Here natives took salmon by the hundreds of thousands during the spawning season.

The earliest travelers tried to run the Dalles. For some the experience ended in tragedy and for all it was a frightful chapter in their journey. Narcissa Whitman, wife of the missionary Marcus Whitman, found the Dalles "a terrific sight, and a frightful place to be in. . . ." Peter Skene Ogden, a leading trader, lost a boat, some men, and his company journals trying to run the same rapids.

Here on both sides of the Columbia lived tribes speaking the Chinook and Sahaptin languages. By virtue of their permanent residence along the narrows, the Indians exacted tolls from travelers and became middlemen exchanging the goods of the lower-river Indian culture with those of the upriver Indian horse culture. Neither Lewis and Clark nor Wilson Price Hunt and the Astorians had pleasant experiences with these Indians.

Besides these obstructions, the mid- and lower Columbia have several important islands. Below the Dalles are several Memaloose islands—Memaloose being an Indian word for "death" or "the dead." As Indian burial grounds these islands were curiosities to early travelers who could view the skeletons on racks and mats, surrounded by baskets and other cherished possessions.

West of the mouth of the Willamette lies the Columbia's largest island, Wap-pa-to (the Indian name for the herb "arrowhead" or "sagittaria"). Still another important island is Sauvie, named for Laurent Sauve, a French Canadian. Some of the earliest Oregon pioneers settled on Sauvie, where farms and orchards have flourished.

The Columbia and its great drainage region had become politically significant by the early nineteenth century. Diplomacy kept the disputants short of war, but American pressure was constant. No little part in applying this force was played by the pioneers who came into Oregon in rising numbers. The Hudson's Bay Company, perhaps foreseeing difficulties, in 1825 retreated to north of the river, leaving the south bank to the Americans. By the Transcontinental Treaty, also known as the Florida Treaty (1821), Spain relinquished all claims to the Oregon country and accepted the 42nd parallel (the present boundary of California and Oregon) as the northern limit of her domain. By a treaty with Russia in 1824 that country agreed that the southern boundary of Russian Alaska would be 54° 40′. This left the United States and England with claims to Oregon country. By the Convention of 1818 they had agreed to a joint occupation.

Americans had been aware of the Columbia country since the visitations of Captain Gray in 1792, Lewis and Clark in 1805–06, and the Astorians in 1811, but the young nation was too preoccupied with other problems in these years to show much interest. In the early 1820s a Congressman from Virginia, John Floyd, tried to alert people to Oregon's potential and by 1831 a New England businessman, Nathaniel Wyeth, was prepared to go there. He arrived at Fort Vancouver in 1832, having followed the route that became the Oregon Trail. In 1833 he returned East but was back again in 1834. On this journey he brought with him two Methodist missionaries, Jason and Daniel Lee. Wyeth finally returned to New England, but Daniel Lee established a mission at the Dalles while Jason settled in the Willamette Valley.

This was just the beginning of missionary activity. By 1836 Presbyterians, of whom Marcus and Narcissa Whitman are best known, had established four missions on the Columbia's tributaries. Meanwhile Catholics had arrived in the Columbia country. Probably the best known was Jesuit Father Pierre Jean de Smet from St. Louis. All these religious endeavors helped spread the news of Oregon's salubrious climate and fertile soil to religious adherents back East, leading to a swelling of farmer migration to Oregon that grew each year after 1841.

The Oregon Trail ended at the Dalles until 1846. Those weary pioneers who reached there had to cut pines and build large rafts to transport them on the last stages of the journey; livestock were driven along the rough trail on the south bank while families launched themselves upon the broad, roily waters. Over thirty miles downriver the Cascades required landing and portage before the watery journey could continue. After 1846 an extension of the Oregon Trail, the Barlow Road, led wagons around the south edge of Mount Hood and down difficult terrain to the Sandy River, a Columbia tributary.

Punishment of the Cayuse nation for the Whitman massacre in 1847 opened the way for settlement of the region north of the Columbia. General Indian wars in 1855 and 1856, followed by General Sheridan's chastisement of the Yakima Indians after the Civil War, ended all Indian resistance by 1868.

Meanwhile steamboats had arrived on the Columbia. In the early 1860s gold discoveries in British Columbia and in Idaho Territory lured thousands of miners from all over the world. Steamboat companies earned huge profits carrying passengers and freight to the fields and bullion downriver towards its eventual destination, the San Francisco mint. When, in the 1870s, gold production declined, steamers began taking cargoes of grain from the new wheatlands in the upper Columbia country. Wool, hides, lumber, and farm produce also appeared on steamboat invoices. Then came railroads running up both sides of the Columbia, and steamboating declined drastically.

Meanwhile the annual salmon runs endured. These powerful fish came annually by the millions to the spawning grounds of the upper Columbia basin. Canneries took an increasing toll. The first salmon cannery on the Columbia in 1866 processed 4,000 cases of fish. In 1911 some 772,668 cases—over five million dollars worth—were obtained in what an Oregon historian called an orgy of "unrestrained greed and shortsighted policy." Even the Indians' reliance on the salmon as a principal food source was drawing to a close by the early twentieth century.

More detrimental than the taking of the salmon was the search for energy. The possibilities of harnessing the Columbia for massive electrical power development was early realized, and it was not long before the river ceased to flow freely to the sea. With dams came canneries, paper mills, and aluminum plants; flooding was ended, and irrigation helped turn thousands of acres of desert land into productive farmland. The dams also marked the virtual extinction of the great fish runs.

The Columbia Basin Project, a child of the Reclamation Act of 1902, required the impoundment of the waters of the middle Columbia. The key dam in the project was Grand Coulee, 550 feet high and more than 4,000 feet wide. In spring surges the water runs over the spillway creating a waterfall half as wide and twice as high as Niagara Falls. The project was completed in 1942, just in time for its power to be used

The ancient Columbia River fishing grounds at Celilo Falls along U.S. Highway 30 in Oregon were a favorite for Indians. Each year tribesmen turned out in great numbers to catch their year's supply of fish. Using long poles and special nets and standing on special platforms built out over the rapids the fishermen scooped in thousands of salmon during the season's run. Here is shown the once familiar fishing scene at the falls. (Oregon State Highway Commission Photo.)

for war industries. Today (1982) nearly a dozen dams control the river.

While they are of extreme importance in an energy-short age, the construction of these dams has not been without loss. Cumulative mortalities of small salmon trying to fight their way to the life-giving sea is between 73 and 94 percent. The Hanford atomic plant raises temperatures of the river by one degree, and the cumulative effects of all the dams has been to raise the average water temperature five degrees. The resultant temperatures are far above the optimum ranges for the survival of the salmon. Clearly these noble fish are in a precarious situation.

Today only the Columbia between its mouth and Bonneville Dam retains some semblance of its appearance as it was first observed by Lewis and Clark. But its awesome size is not wholly masked by man's concrete and steel girdles, and its rich history continues. Cross the river on the bridge between Astoria on the Oregon side, and Megler, Washington, and drink in the vast expanse of the mighty Columbia as it joins the sea. No one can say that it is a river without a future, regardless of its past.

FURTHER READING: Charles Gates and Dorothy O. Johansen, *Empire of the Columbia* (1967). William D. Lyman, *Columbia River* (1963). Oscar Winther, *The Great Northwest* (1960).

Keith Clark

The Copper River (Alaska)

Source: North Slope of Wrangell Mountains on Alaska-Canadian border in south-central Alaska
Length: 300 miles
Tributaries: Bremner, Chistochina, Chitina, Gakona, Gulkana, Klutina, Siana, Tasnuna, Tazlina, Tiekel, and Tonsina rivers
Mouth: Flows into Gulf of Alaska
Agricultural products: None of significance
Industries: Salmon fishing, copper, gold, and silver mining

The Copper River, its name taken from the copper found along its tributaries, forms on the north slope of the Wrangell Mountains which rise on the Alaska-Canada border in south-central Alaska. Sweeping around the foothills of those peaks and then flowing south, the Copper enters the Gulf of Alaska about twenty-one miles northwest of the now-abandoned town of Katalla and twenty-seven miles southwest of the fishing village of Cordova.

That discharge point is reached after the river winds its way nearly three hundred miles and drains an area of 24,000 square miles, making it the principal waterway of the fourth largest river system in the state of Alaska. Major tributaries include the Bremner, Chistochina, Chitina, Gakona, Gulkana, Klutina, Slana, Tasnuna, Tazlina, Tiekel, and Tonsina rivers, all glacier fed.

Overall, the river valley climate is mild for an area in which ice and snow cover some of the mountains all year round. Summers are warm, with temperatures reaching eighty degrees-plus Farenheit, while winters are cold to very cold. At times, thermometers in the river drainage area register as much as fifty-five degrees below zero. Precipitation throughout the basin ranges from five to fifteen inches annually, with snow accumulations of thirty to eighty inches having been recorded in a year.

These climatic conditions occur over the length of a corridor that was once heavily glaciated and still has active glaciers over a substantial part of its area. Ice Age glaciers retreated to leave a large portion of the Copper River Plateau, which forms the northwestern boundary of the Copper River basin, and terraces along the

major tributaries. The middle portion of the river has now cut deeply into this sedimentary accumulation and is characterized by high and steep cliff-like banks. South of the small community of Chitina, after rushing through Wood Canyon, the Copper cuts through the Chugach Mountains and is partially obstructed by three glaciers before meandering across a broad delta to reach the Gulf of Alaska and the North Pacific.

While glaciers still feed and in some measure block the flow of the Copper River, one radiocarbon date supports a general retreat of glaciers some 9,000 years ago and an almost immediate run of salmon.

Salmon, with a catch that has reached as high as 1,298,294 fish annually in recent years, may have been the attraction that drew prehistoric man to the Copper River.

Very little archaeological evidence has been found to reveal prehistoric man's life along the river. Oral tradition does indicate that north of Wood Canyon, about sixty miles from the river's mouth, was the territory of the Ahtna, a branch of the interior Athapascan Indians, while the river delta was the habitat of the Eyak, a culturally distinct coastal native group. The Eyak did not ascend the river above Miles and Childs glaciers, and the region between those locations and Wood Canyon was an aboriginal no-man's land.

South of that no-man's land, Eyak territory extended between what is now Cordova on the west and Cape Martin on the east. The villages of Eyak, a few miles outside Cordova, and Alaganik, about twenty miles to the southeast, were the two most important Eyak settlements. Middlemen in trade between Chugach Eskimos and the Ahtna, the Eyak also heavily used the marine resources of the area, taking salmon with dipnets and spears, hooking halibut in ocean waters, and clamming along the shores. Late in the 1800s, Eyak became the site of a cannery and then later, in the early 1900s, location of a naval radio station. Alaganik consisted, just before the turn of the century, of twelve houses. Shortly after 1900, during construction of the Copper River and Northwestern Railway, machine

Drawing titled "Start from Alaganik," artist unknown, taken from "Military Reconnoissance (sic) in Alaska" by Lt. Henry T. Allen, Second U.S. Cavalry, (1885), published in Compilation Narratives of Exploration in Alaska, Washington USGPO: 1900. According to Allen's text, the expedition which was to leave Alaganik in late March 1885 to ascend the Copper River consisted of five canoes, himself, Sgt. Cady Robertson, 2nd U.S. Cavalry, civilian Peder Johnson, 5 coast natives, and 2 Midnooskies. (From: Explorations in Alaska, 1869–1900, U.S. Government Printing Office, 1900.)

shops and a quarry were established on the site. Now only graves remain, and survivors from the Eyak are few, with only one or two people knowing anything of the Eyak language.

Far from the Eyak to the north, above Wood Canyon, the Ahtna Indians occupied semi-permanent villages which tended to be located at confluences of major tributaries and the Copper River. Each settlement consisted of anywhere from one to several families, each with a chief or headman. Houses, which were semi-subterranean and are evidenced today by structural remains which can be found along the banks of the Copper, varied in size from eight by ten to twenty-four by thirty-six feet. Some had two

rooms, one of which may have been used for a sweat bath.

Salmon provided the major source of food for the families of twenty to thirty Ahtna, who may have occupied one or several houses. Taken with traps, weirs, dip nets, and some spears in clear tributaries of the silty Copper River, the salmon were sun dried. Both Upper River Ahtna, in the area around Tazlina and Gulkana, and Lower River people, near Copper Center and Chitina, also hunted for moose and caribou and other land mammals, using the meat themselves and trading hides and furs, along with copper, to the coastal Eyak and Eskimo.

In 1783, sailing offshore from these coastal

natives, Russian explorer Leyontiy Nagaev reported that he had discovered a large river the natives called the Atna.

Successive Russian attempts to ascend and explore the waterway (Tarachanov in 1796, Samoylov also in 1796, Partichken or Lastochkin in 1798, Boyanov in 1803, Klimoffsky in 1819, Gregorieff in 1843–44, Malakov in 1844, and Serebrennikof in 1847–48) resulted in murder of at least two of the explorers by native inhabitants and were generally unsuccessful. There is some indication that Klimoffsky did, in 1819, reach the Chitina and possibly the Gulkana Rivers, and established a small trading post at the mouth of the Chitina. This did not survive long, but in 1858 a small Russian settlement, Mednovsky Odinochka ("one-man post") was established just south of the juncture of the Chitina and Copper Rivers. It was the last Russian-American Company enclave to be established in what later was to become known as Alaska.

Little interest was shown immediately in the Copper River area after American purchase of Russian America in 1867. G.C. Holt, an Alaska Commercial Company trader, did, in 1882, investigate the feasibility of a mercantile venture at the old site of Mednovsky Odinochka but recommended against it (a few years later Holt, falling prey to the same dangers as his Russian predecessors, was murdered by Copper River natives).

Government exploration, beginning with W.R. Abercrombie of the U.S. Army in 1884, intervened between the first commercial interest represented by Holt and ultimate exploration of the Copper River area. Other Army and U.S. Geological Survey investigators (Lt. Henry T. Allen, Lt. Frederick Schwatka, Oscar Rohn, F.C. Schrader, and Walter C. Mendenhall) during the years 1885–1900 expanded the initial data collected by Abercrombie.

Outside government, prospectors trickled into the region and, in 1899, the first commercial prospect was located in the valley of the Chitina. The following year discovery of the Bonanza Mine, near the confluence of the Kennicott and Chitina Rivers some sixty miles to the east of the Copper, resulted in a dramatic change in the history of the region.

That copper location (later named for the 1860s explorer of Alaska Robert B. Kennicott

but misspelled as Kennecott), coupled with gold finds on other streams flowing into the Copper River, intensified demands for a means to market for mineral production.

The Copper River and Northwestern Railway resulted. Backed by well-financed Guggenheim interests, it began in Cordova, then headed east to the Copper River delta. From there, the rail line started north, winding its way along the banks of the Copper to Chitina where it again struck east, this time for the Kennecott Mines. The first spike for the road was driven on August 26, 1906, at Cordova.

Years of difficult construction followed. In the interim, a small fleet of steamboats carried construction supplies on the Copper and its tributaries and also moved some of the copper ore produced at Kennecott from mine to railhead. The *Chitina*, launched on July 4, 1907, was the first of these boats, its components having been carried and sledded over mountain passes to the meeting of the Tasnuna and Copper Rivers before being assembled. As rails extended north, the *Chitina* and her sisters were broken up for parts or used for worker housing. Today, they are gone, although some reports say that sunken hulks can be seen underwater in the lake at the terminus of Miles Glacier.

The last spike on the railway was driven on March 29, 1911. Ninety-five of the total 195 miles of track were laid on bridges and trestles. In the section from Cordova to Chitina alone, 129 bridges were used.

Shipments, made from the copper mines at Kennecott, were sent south once or twice a week. Between 1911 and 1938 (when railway service was discontinued), 591,535 tons of copper and 9,000,000 ounces of silver valued at over $200,000,000 were shipped to the coast. Other activity was stimulated by the large-scale copper mining of the Guggenheim interests (sometimes known as the Alaska Syndicate) and by 1916 some thirty placer mines and eight hydraulic operations along the Copper's tributaries were producing gold.

This gradually decreased as prices for copper and gold diminished in the 1920s. In 1932 even the rich Kennecott Mines were closed although a small caretaker staff remained until 1938. The shutdown was a death blow for the Copper River and Northwestern Railway. It ceased operations in October of 1938 and was abandoned that same year.

In 1945 the railway right-of-way was transferred to the United States, and in 1953 Congress appropriated $550,000 for conversion of the railbed to a highway. This project, completed to Mile 49 outside Cordova, was halted by Alaska's Good Friday earthquake of 1964 and has since been stymied by environmental concerns.

Today, the Copper River remains much as it must have been before European civilization disrupted the lives of the Eyak and Ahtna, a silt-laden stream of great beauty, rich in resources and dangerous to the unwary traveler.

FURTHER READING: Lone E. Jansen, *The Copper Spike*, (1975). Sepp Weber, *Wild Rivers of Alaska* (1976).

William S. Hanable

The Deschutes River

Source: Little Lava Lake in south-central Oregon
Length: 250 miles
Tributaries: Metolus River; Crooked River
Mouth: Columbia River 10 miles above The Dalles
Agricultural products: Wheat, fruits
Industries: Lumbering, ranching

The Deschutes has been described as one of America's strangest rivers. It has a remarkably even flow because rain and snow waters are trapped in a giant lava sponge that releases the water at a steady rate. It is a stream that has maintained its right of way against flooding lava; it is a river fed by many springs. The state of Oregon has designated it a state scenic waterway.

The Deschutes rises at Little Lava Lake in the high eastern slopes of the Cascade Range in south-central Oregon. Close by is the larger Elk Lake, and both have a northwestern backdrop of the 10,000-foot Three Sisters Peaks. From Bend, the principal city along the Deschutes, these three peaks dominate the Cascade skyline to the west.

The river flows first south, but leaves Wickiup Reservoir flowing east and shortly bends north, flowing about 250 miles before it enters the Columbia about ten miles east of The Dalles. It drains much of the great Columbia Plateau, a region of rolling hills, black obsidian buttes, level, sage-covered valleys, and uplands ideal for cattle grazing.

Geologically the entire region is of volcanic origin. The upper Deschutes flows gently and has challenged such trout fishermen as Herbert Hoover, while the lower river has cut chasms 1,000 to 1,500 feet deep into the plateau, producing spectacular scenery and challenging whitewater boatmen and raftsmen. So spectacular are the volcanic formations of the lower Deschutes that a Lavalands Visitor Center has been established south of Bend close to 6,000-year-old Lava Butte.

Long before the first white fur trappers arrived, Indians occupied the Deschutes River drainage. Camps at the Fort Rock caves in the upper Deschutes country have yielded artifacts left by hunters of 13,000 years ago. Some of their camps have been found also under the dust left when Mount Mazama, in southern Oregon, erupted violently some 6,500 years ago. Yet time has erased virtually all other signs of primitive man even as time and the elements have opened geologic history by cutting the deep Deschutes gorge north of the little town of Maupin, exposing strata that tell the story of geologic upheavals.

The first white men to pay attention to the Deschutes was a party led by the Hudson's Bay Company leader, Peter Skene Ogden. On December 1, 1825, he and his trapper brigade, including French Canadians with their families and some friendly Indians, camped on the east bank of a swift stream that flowed from the south into

The Deschutes River cuts through the sun-soaked, arid terrain of central Oregon as it enters Lake Billy Chinook, a reservoir which also catches the flow of the Metolius and Crooked River. Lake Chinook is the feature attraction of Cove Palisades State Park which offers facilities for boating, overnight camping, picnicking and swimming. (Oregon Department of Transportation Photo 7715.)

the Columbia. The Frenchmen called the stream Rivière des Chutes—the River of Falls—though the falls were in the nearby Columbia three miles below the mouth. Soon Rivière was dropped and Deschutes became the permanent name. (The next morning, minus a few horses stolen by skulking Indians, Ogden continued his exploration of central Oregon.)

Other explorers followed. One of them was Nathaniel J. Wyeth, a New England business-man. In the cold December of 1834 he led a trapping party into the headwaters of the Des-chutes. He was also in pursuit of some Hawaiian employees (whom he called Kanackas) who had stolen horses and provisions from camp and fled. Wyeth's party traded with the Indians in the Deschutes area, obtaining plenty of dogs for food. Deer, elk, bear, and wolves were observed. Wyeth finally had the opportunity to trap for beaver. Although he did not take many because Hudson's Bay trappers had been there before, he did take one huge old fellow weighing sixty-five pounds and another of seventy pounds, the larg-est beaver he had ever seen.

Wyeth and his men suffered terribly from the cold and occasional hunger as they explored the headwaters of the Deschutes. Storms were vio-lent. "The cracking of the falling trees and the howling of the blast was more grand than com-fortable," he commented. From the upper Des-chutes country the brigade floated downstream in log canoes they had hacked out of towering pines. Later these canoes had to be abandoned as the men made their way on foot down the Deschute chasms to the Columbia, and on down that river to Fort Vancouver.

Eight years later John C. Fremont entered the region. With 104 horses and mules and a moun-tain howitzer, Fremont's party started up the Deschutes in November, 1843, and arrived at Klamath Lake early in December. His adven-tures and observations of this section of his second expedition were subsequently related in his Report, which was widely read.

Then came the Pacific Railroad Surveys—a federal project to determine the most feasible routes to the West—and in conjunction with the surveys, the search for a route from California north to Oregon. The task of leading a survey party north from the Sacramento River valley

fell to Lieutenant Henry L. Abbot. His party avoided conflict with the Klamath and Pit River Indians and forged through the wild eastern Cascade foothills to a Deschutes tributary, the Metolius River, and so north via the Deschutes to the Columbia. The high cliffs, steep canyons, and remoteness of the Deschutes drainage prompted Lieutenant Abbot to file a negative Report. No railroad, he said, could be built through such a rugged wilderness area.

But some good came from the Pacific Railroad Survey of the Deschutes region. Accompanying the party was a brilliant scientist, Dr. John A. Newberry. Like Fremont before him, Newberry had observed the deep pumiceous dust and the volcanically shattered, heavily glaciated moun-tains that constituted the Cascade skyline. In-deed, Newberry wrote that "something had hap-pened in those timbered hills," but he failed to notice the evidence of the explosion of Mount Mazama on the Cascade divide just west of the survey party trail. (A nearby mountain *is* named in his honor.)

The major, spectacular discovery which Fre-mont and Newberry missed had been made on June 12, 1853, not far from Deschutes headwa-ters. A group of gold seekers headed by John W. Hillman discovered Crater Lake, and the peak upon which it rests still bears Hillman's name.

By the 1850s cattlemen were aware of the fine range offered by the Columbia plateau. Soon they were pushing their herds deeper and deeper into the Deschutes drainage, sometimes follow-ing trails made by an Indian chief named Pau-lina. He was killed in 1857 in an attack led by a pioneer rancher, Howard Maupin, on Trout Creek, a small Deschutes tributary. Although the Indians continued to make raids on stockmen, miners, and hunters, no major battle ever took place between the Indians and whites on the Deschutes River. And although the region was heavily prospected, the closest gold rush took place along the John Day River drainage to the east.

Lieutenant Abbot had rejected the idea of a railroad between California and the Columbia via the Deschutes, but Jim Hill, the "Empire Builder" of the Great Northern, ignored Lieu-tenant Abbot's recommendations. He purchased the charter of the Oregon Trunk, which was a railroad on paper only, and in 1909 announced that he would connect Bend, 165 miles up the Deschutes, with the Great Northern, which ran along the Columbia's northern bank. Quietly his agents began purchasing rights of way; survey and track-laying crews were not far behind.

But E.H. Harriman of the Union Pacific knew that Jim Hill sought a bigger goal—no less than a railroad from the Columbia to San Francisco, which at the time was served exclusively by Harriman's lines. This meant war! Soon Harriman's survey and track-laying crews were vying for every mile of feasible right-of-way. At mile seventy-five Harriman won. A rancher over whose land the tracks must be laid—for there was no place else they could go—had sold out to Harriman. The Great Northern agreed to halt at Bend while Harriman built through to lines coming up from San Francisco. Later the Great Northern did push south to join the east-west running Western Pacific.

Bend, the principal city along the Deschutes, was founded in 1900 by Alexander M. Drake, a "developer" from the Midwest. He saw agricultural possibilities in the region, while his wife fell in love with the snowy Cascade skyline to the west. Today Bend is a thriving city of more than 16,000, a center for agricultural, ranching, and lumbering activities.

In 1900 the Deschutes raced unfettered to the Columbia, but the potentialities for irrigation and hydroelectric power were soon recognized. Today the Deschutes loses its identity many times. Just a few miles after it has emerged as a stream it loses itself in the man-dammed Crane Prairie Reservoir. Downstream a few more miles it is again trapped in the big Wickiup Reservoir. The stream now dashes north over Pringle Falls and Benham Falls, past Lava Island, and then lingers for a time in Bend's Mirror Pond, one of the beauty spots of western America.

But at Bend the rolling river takes on a new character. Missing are the riverside meadows and wandering streams. Although much of its flow has by now been diverted by irrigation canals, the remaining waters plunge into a rocky gorge, deeper and deeper, until finally the flow of the Deschutes and its tributaries, the Metolius and Crooked River, are captured in the scenic Cove region. Here, where the gorges of the converging rivers are over 400 feet deep, the Pelton Dam and Round Butte Dam back up deep, cold waters in Lake Simtustus and Lake Billy Chinook Reservoirs, and two giant hydroelectric installations hum incessantly. Due west of them is the Warm Springs Indian Reservation.

It is a land still looking to a future "great day coming," yet the white-water raftsmen can observe twenty million years of geologic history rush before their eyes as they run the Deschutes canyons. Astronauts visited Mount Newberry because its sterility reminded scientists of a moonscape—a sure lesson in using the past to prepare for the future. And withal its geologic history, the Deschutes country is beautiful. When Hill and Harriman laid the golden spike in Bend, October 5, 1911, the spike subsequently disappeared. Some said that Jim Hill gave it to Bill Hanley, a local cattle king and friend of the railroad tycoon.

"I built the road so I could come and visit you, Bill," Hill reportedly said. Even the "Empire Builder" was captured by the Deschutes country.

FURTHER READING: Stewart H. Holbrook, *The Columbia* (1956).

Phil F. Brogan

The Feather River

Source: Junction of South, Middle, and North forks
near Oroville, California
Length: 100 miles (250 miles if any of the forks are
included, as they sometimes are)
Tributaries: Yuba and Bear rivers
Mouth: Flows into Sacramento River at Verona, Cali-
fornia
Agricultural products: None of significance
Industries: Tourism, some mining, hydroelectric

To Californians the Feather River is synony-
mous with gold, heartbreak, and some of the
most grandiose promotional schemes the world
has seen. It is a fickle river, opening her treasure
to some miners but perversely bursting the bubbles of schemers who tried to "get it all in one
getting."

The Feather's watershed rises high in the
Sierras of north-central California and its three
main branches—north, middle, and south—
tumble down through rocky gorges and forested
mountain slopes to the Sacramento Valley floor.
All told, the three forks flow about 250 miles
before joining the Sacramento.

The River was named in 1817 when Captain
Luis Arguello, later a governor of Mexican California, led an exploring party into the depths of
the Feather River canyon. It was spring, and the
river's surface was yellow with willow catkins
which, to the Captain, appeared to be feathers
floating downstream. He dubbed it "El Rio de
las Plumas," a name perpetuated in California's
Plumas (feathers) County, through which much
of the river flows. Had Arguello only known, the
yellow-colored waters were an omen of activities that, a half century later, would gain for the
River the accolade of "the golden Feather."

It was on the Fourth of July, 1848, that John
Bidwell, one of the first Americans to enter
California overland, discovered gold at what
was immediately known as Bidwell Bar on the
Feather. The strike brought a trickle of gold
miners into the northern Sierra foothills that
soon burgeoned into a flood of prospecting humanity. By the mid-1850s the Feather had yielded some $10 million in gold, $3 million taken
from Rich Bar alone. Bidwell himself once
brought out "as much gold as two pack mules
could carry."

By the mid-1850s the placers had given out.
Later miners had pooled their resources to build
wing dams—temporary rock and earth structures that angled down stream allowing water
to be pumped out of the pockets in order to work
the dry stream beds. Such dams were primitive,
short-lived, and dangerous. They leaked and
often collapsed, releasing a rush of water that
sent workers bowling end over end like jack-
straws. Yet the handsome returns were deemed
worth the risk.

For example, the Cape Claim Dam above Oroville recovered a cool million in the forty-two
days before it fell apart while nearby the Greek
Claim Dam yielded $250,000 in the few days it
lasted. By the time Major Frank McLaughlin
arrived in 1878, the length of the Feather was
crisscrossed and honeycombed with these haphazardly constructed, risky dams.

McLaughlin was a bombastic, colorful promoter, sort of a cross between Buffalo Bill, P.T.
Barnum, and Mack the Knife. Nobody knew
much about him except that he claimed to be a
bosom friend of Bat Masterson, and to have once
backed down Wyatt Earp in a near gunfight. He
burst onto the streets of Oroville, principal city
and supply point for the Feather River mines,
and excited everyone with his fancy talk and
promises of gold "still to be had."

Instead of those makeshift dams, he argued,
why not divert the River and work the former
bed at leisure? At Big Bend, fourteen miles
upriver, such a diversion could be engineered
provided money was obtained for blasting
through the base of a mountain. Not to be
deterred, McLaughlin headed East and there
found his "angel." He was R.V. Pierce, whose Dr.
Pierce's Golden Medical Discovery had swept
the nation and made him a fortune. Armed with
the Doctor's money, McLaughlin set out to drive
a 12,000-foot tunnel through solid rock. He did,

and then, finding the tunnel too small, went back and tapped the Doctor for still more money.

The tunnel was finally completed and the mighty Feather roared through the mountain into a different channel. Fourteen miles of the old river bed lay bare. Miners set to work extracting the gold—and found none. The gradient, they realized, was too steep. The River had raced by too fast to lay down deposits.

Determined to prove that he was right, McLaughlin hired a crew to dig far down from the surface. At twenty feet it struck something— a Chinese wheelbarrow and other artifacts left from the days of '49! Only then did McLaughlin learn that the Big Bend had been worked out years before. Subsequently hydraulic mining upstream, which released millions of tons of silt, had raised the river bed to its present height. Dr. Pierce was $150,000 sadder and wiser while McLaughlin, a perennial optimist, sat back to figure other ways of extracting gold from the Feather River.

Another immense undertaking along the Feather was the Spring Valley Mining and Irrigation Company, organized in 1870 with eastern capital. The plan was to bring water for hydraulic mining at the dry diggings at the base of Table Mountain, a mesa cut off from the surrounding foothills by one of the Feather's perverse bends.

The water was obtained by impounding the run-off from the high mountain watershed of the North Fork. By an ingenious series of dams, ditches, siphons, and pipes it was carried fifty-three miles and finally impounded in a reservoir on the top of Table Mountain. From there it rushed downhill under great pressure to operate the hydraulic monitors—cannon-shaped nozzles that shot water onto hillsides with such pressure that whole mountains gave way to their force. At one time the company was extracting $70,000 in gold a month.

The Spring Valley Company was the largest, most elaborate mining operation in the world at the time, and naturally it drew Major Frank McLaughlin's attention. One of his "clients" back East was Thomas A. Edison, who was looking for a source of platinum to use as filaments for his new incandescent light bulbs. And

the Spring Valley Company was a large producer of platinum-bearing black sand—which miners ignored in their search for gold.

McLaughlin finagled himself into control of the Company and persuaded Edison to invest in platinum-extracting equipment. But the equipment failed to extract the platinum satisfactorily, Edison retreated from the venture, and McLaughlin made a fast buck by turning over the Company and moving on to grander schemes.

At the Big Bend he had diverted just a section; now he proposed diverting the entire Feather River in order to work the whole bed. Among his backers was William H. Vanderbilt. McLaughlin built a dam from whence he proposed to divert the water into canals and flumes. It took ten miles of roads, five miles of iron pipe, forty miles of telephone wire, 7,000 workers and 10,000 mules and horses to do the job.

All that remains today of McLaughlin's biggest fiasco is the aquaduct consisting of a solid mass of rock 6,000 feet long, 20 feet high and 12 feet thick. Because the gold, if any was there, was lodged under gigantic boulders embedded like concrete in the stream bed, virtually none was obtained. McLaughlin finally gave up on the Feather and took himself and his schemes elsewhere. He left the stage for another promoter just as high flying and enigmatic.

This was M. J. Cooney, who came to Oroville in 1907 in pursuit of a will-o'-the-wisp rumor of a diamond deposit at the Spring Valley mining site. From the earliest years of the gold rush in the Feather River country, miners had been troubled with "little white pebbles" that clogged their Long Toms (sluice boxes) along with a sticky blue clay that made doubly troublesome the recovery of gold dust. On a hunch someone sent one of the "pebbles" to New York for appaisal. It was pronounced a diamond "gem of the first water."

Cooney formed the United States Diamond Mining Company, carried on extensive prospecting, and finally announced that he had found a "pipe" of kimberlite (blue clay), the true matrix of diamonds. He and his mining superintendent drilled 200 feet deep into the pipe, set off a charge of dynamite and recovered what Cooney exuberantly proclaimed were diamonds.

Within days of his diamond find a contingent representing a South African diamond cartel arrived in Oroville. The strangers conferred with Cooney, who almost immediately retracted his statements about diamonds, avowing that he had been mistaken. The diamonds, he said, were only phenacytes, a beryllium silicate of small value. Then he closed his mine, obliterated all traces of its location and with his superintendent left town by night, leaving his investors in the lurch.

Were diamonds found in the Feather River country? No one knows, but there are members of the area's pioneering mining families who are still wearing inherited sparklers of from two to five carats, appraised as genuine diamonds, that they swear were mined nearby. Olive growers around Oroville pass winter evenings speculating over how many diamonds may be in the sixty or so feet thick tailings carried downriver at the time of hydraulicking operations and over which their groves are flourishing.

The mining boom has long since ended, but other industries had other uses for the waters of the Feather. The Pacific Gas and Electric Company enlarged the Spring Valley dam at Big Meadows to create Lake Almanor, the source of water for nine of the biggest and most important powerhouses along the Feather. At Oroville the California Water Plan has constructed the highest (730 feet) and costliest ($450 million) earth fill dam in the world. It impounds 3.5 million acre-feet of water that backs up for fifteen miles in all three forks.

Yet, in spite of all the thoughtless—and occasionally thoughtful—changes wrought upon the Feather, it is still a beautiful stream. Today it is sports fishermen who tread its banks. And there is a lot of stream to fish: it is estimated that the three forks and their tributaries add up to about 800 miles of trout streams. Most of them are in the largest primeval forest in California, the 2 million acres of the Plumas National Forest.

FURTHER READING: Jim Martin, *Guidebook to the Feather River Country* (1972.)

Vivienne L. George

The John Day River

Source: Rises in Strawberry Mountains of east-central Oregon
Length: 280 miles
Tributaries: North, South, and Middle forks; many smaller streams
Mouth: Flows into Columbia River at John Day Dam
Agricultural products: Alfalfa, wheat
Industries: Stock raising, lumbering, recreation

John Day was a restless Virginian who roved the Pacific shore and explored remote river basins in search of furs. Two rivers bear his name: one in Clatsop County in the extreme northwest corner of Oregon, and the other, the subject of this essay, which flows through eleven counties embracing much of central Oregon before discharging into the Columbia. Through part of its course the John Day runs in a deep canyon more than seventy miles long that is reminiscent of the canyons of the Snake and the Colorado.

The river is about 280 miles long, but its three forks—North, South, and Middle—drain 7,840 square miles. In places swift and beautiful, the stream has an annual discharge of 1,460,000 acre-feet and carries off 198 tons of material per square mile. This results in more than 750,000 tons of sediment delivered into the Columbia River annually, far more than the amount carried by any other river in the state.

John Day was one of the Astorians who in 1810–1811 made the perilous overland crossing from Missouri to Oregon with Wilson Price Hunt. He and a companion, Ramsay Crooks, separated from the rest of the party and were rescued in starving condition by others from Fort Astoria near the river that bears Day's name. His mind was affected temporarily but eventually his sanity returned. He remained a trapper in the Northwest until his death in 1820.

After the Astorians came the Hudson's Bay Company's Peter Skene Ogden who, in his 1825–26 Snake Expedition, traveled east from the Crooked River valley near present Prineville, in central Oregon, to cross the divide and strike the John Day River near Picture Gorge. John Work succeeded Ogden as leader of the Snake River fur expeditions and in 1830–31 trapped the John Day; again in 1833 Work's expedition traveled up the John Day from its mouth.

Stephen H. L. Meek, who had been with Benjamin Bonneville in 1834, also traveled a part of the river, trapping and hunting. In 1845 he led an emigrant party from Fort Boise across eastern and central Oregon along what proved to be a disastrously difficult route. However, some of the survivors had found gold nuggets along the way, and this spurred prospecting parties into central Oregon. In 1861 gold was found up Canyon Creek, a John Day tributary. By 1864 Canyon City was a thriving mining center and county seat of Grant County, which embraced 14,664 square miles.

Wagons carrying nuggets, dust, and gold ore moved along a road to the Dalles, later termed the Dalles-Canyon City Military Road. Over that route, too, came livestock to supply the mining camps and military forces that guarded them against Snake Indian raids. At its zenith Canyon City had a population of 10,000 including hundreds of Chinese who worked the mine tailings. One of the early day residents was Cincinnatus Hiner (poet Joaquin Miller) who served as a county judge. Ultimately more than $26,000,000 was taken from the Canyon City strike. Other mining communities sprouted on John Day tributaries. The towns bore such names as Susanville and Granite.

To the John Day Valley came settlers who raised cattle, built log cabins and established the communities of Prairie City, John Day, Mount Vernon, and Dayville. Later, flocks of sheep came in, herded by Basques, Scots, and Irish. With time there was intense competition for grass. Some bands of as many as 10,000 sheep were trailed to eastern markets before rail connections crept closer. The John Day country has also produced fine horses.

Two military installations were established in 1864–65 to protect the miners and guard against designs by Confederate raiders, for many miners had Southern antecedents. (One early mining camp was named "Dixie.") Camp Logan was near present Prairie City; Camp Watson was west of Dayville. Both posts were manned originally by Oregon volunteers but garrisons were replaced by regulars after 1865.

Army detachments patrolled the road which paralleled the John Day River in the upper valley. Patrols traveled south as well, to the northern edges of Harney Valley. A typical report reveals that these patrols involved physical hardship and danger. The officer in charge was Lt. Charles Brugure Western:

> Hd. Qtrs. Camp Logan, Oregon, May 5, 1867.
> Sir:— . . . I left Camp, April 20th, 1867, with a detachment of 1 sergeant, 2 corporals and 10 privates of Co. F, 8th Cavalry, to pursue, and if possible to punish, a band of Snake Indians who had been committing depredations on the Canyon City road. . . .
> April 26th, crossed the mountains toward Harney Lake and camped after dark in a canyon, having traveled 40 miles. It was almost impossible to get the horses over the mountains, the mud and snow being from one to four feet deep. . . . The next morning (27th) shortly after daylight, I came up to the Indians. . . . I at once attacked them, attempting to cross the river mounted, but finding that was impossible, from the river being filled with driftwood, dismounted, left three men to hold the horses and crossed afoot, the water being neck deep. The Indians, numbering 40 or 50, of whom 21 or 22 were warriors . . . fled in every direction. The pursuit was continued until the perfectly exhausted condition of the men compelled its cessation.
> . . . . The next morning, April 28th, I started on my return to Camp Logan. . . . For a day and a half before reaching the Canyon City road the men were without anything to eat. . . .*

Today, of the 5,126,000 acres in the basin, about 550,000 are classified as cropland, and 2,260,000 are forested. Farmers and ranchers in the upper John Day Valley pasture stock in natural meadows and, with irrigation, grow alfalfa. The forests still provide timber for small local mills. The economy is based on lumbering and stockraising, although recreation uses are increasing. Population density (1970) was about

Portland Oregonian, May 21, 1867.

1.5 persons per square mile compared with the state average of 20.5. A relatively large deer and elk population remains in the upper basin.

A few miles east of where the Middle Fork of the John Day turns north, its waters are augmented by those of the South Fork. Traveling due north for fifteen miles the combined flow is further increased by the waters of the North Fork at Kimberly. Here, also, the river turns northwest and begins its course through Wheeler County. It passes through country rich in fossil remains. These are found from Rock Creek Junction to the orchards of Twickenham and include the Clarno formations of the late Eocene, which reveal fossilized vegetation and nuts, and bones and teeth of such vanished animals as eohippus, mastodon, and sabertooth tiger. Near Clarno is the recently established John Day Fossil Beds National Monument which includes Camp Hancock, a paleontology and paleobotany research facility maintained by the Oregon Museum of Science and Industry.

Clarno, directly on the John Day, was named for Andrew Clarno who settled in the valley in 1866. His son Charles admired the Columbia River steamboats so much that he built one in miniature, about forty feet long, which he navigated on the river from about four miles below Clarno to ten miles above. Later, Clarno and about twenty others attempted to take the *John Day Queen* downriver to the Columbia but the venture came to an ignoble end in the Clarno Rapids. The river here runs between Wheeler and Wasco counties and turns again directly north to enter the John Day Canyon.

From Clarno to its mouth the river flows through one of the few wild places still left in Oregon. It is inaccessible by vehicular traffic through most of its course. In high water, anglers and recreationists brave the rapids in a variety of craft, although canoes are not recommended for amateurs. But the river rewards the venturesome with incredible vistas of cliffs hundreds of feet high, accented by eagles, hawks, deer, and wildflowers.

Old shacks and outbuildings, road grades carved from the canyon walls, and other signs of homesteads now abandoned whet the boatmen's curiosity. They are all that remain of the work of latter-day pioneers who entered the canyon in the early decades of the twentieth century, then found the labor unrelenting and the profit potential insufficient for continued development.

At the mouth of the John Day, slackwater from the John Day Dam on the Columbia, completed in 1968, swallows the tributary river. It also swallows the original site of the river village of Arlington which had to be relocated above the reservoir, Lake Umatilla, which covers eighty-one square miles and holds a half million acre-feet of flood storage. That water begins in springs and snow sources high in the Blue Mountains of northeast Oregon. With the addition of John Day water the Columbia becomes the drainage system of central Oregon also.

FURTHER READING: Herman Oliver, *Gold and Cattle Country* (1961). F. Smith Fussner, ed., *Glimpses of Wheeler County's Past* (1975).

Keith Clark

The Kern River

Source: Northwest of Mount Whitney in Sequoia National Park in the California Sierras
Length: 155 miles
Tributaries: None of significance
Mouth: Flows into Buena Vista Lake in south-central California
Agricultural products: Vegetables (often called "the salad bowl of America"); cotton
Industries: Oil production; cattle ranching

The Kern River originates in Sequoia National Park in the California Sierras northwest of Mount Whitney. Its North Fork drops 5,600 feet in the sixty-two miles above Kerrville. In the forty-eight miles below that point it drops another 2,100 feet before joining a smaller and more stable South Fork. The river ends in Buena Vista Lake in south-central California, about 155 miles from its place of origin. Because it is such a turbulent river Californians have sometimes called it, in jest, the "Kern-trary."

The first European to view Kern waters was the Franciscan Padre Francesco Garces; the date was May 7, 1776, fifty-two days before the signing of the American Declaration of Independence. Padre Garces had arrived at the banks of the Kern in search of a practical overland route from Spanish settlements in New Mexico to those in Monterey, California.

"It was a large river," he noted in his diary, "which made much noise and whose waters ... were crystalline, bountiful, and palatable." He was soon to discover that the waters were also cold. Since he could not swim, a band of friendly Yokuts Indians from the village of Woila (on the site of present Bakersfield) offered to assist him in crossing. They demanded that he strip, which he did, up to a point. Modesty forbade his undressing beyond his undershirt and drawers. Then four Indians, each grasping an arm or a leg, propelled him, raft-like, through the current to the other side. Padre Garces named it "El Rio de San Felipe." The Indian name had been Po-sun-cola. Seventy years later Captain John C. Fremont renamed it in honor of Edward Meyer Kern, topographer of his expedition through the Rockies, Oregon, Nevada, and the Sierra Nevadas.

In 1853 gold was discovered in the rugged area of Greenhorn Gulch about a mile northwest of the upper Kern River. Deposits were limited, but the excitement quickly spread, creating a minor boom along the slopes of Greenhorn Mountain and the gulches whose streams emptied into the Kern.

Kern County's first town, Keyesville, resulted from Richard Keyes's discovery of what became the Keyes Mine (originally the Hog Eye). Keyesville, in the upper reaches of the Kern northeast of Bakersfield, has long since become a ghost town with its once-occupied buildings sagging and weathering into oblivion. The mines that gave to the town its moment of glory remain as gaping entrances to a labyrinth of hand-dug tunnels, drifts, shafts, and stopes that fan out through the innards of the Kern watershed.

Keyesville and its major mines, the Hog Eye, Mammoth, and the Big Blue (discovered when a Cherokee Indian named Lovely Rogers picked up a rock to heave at a contrary mule and found himself with a fistful of gold-bearing quartz) set off a chain of "discoveries." Boom towns sprouted up quickly but just as rapidly became deserted ghost towns.

Rogers's discovery created Rogerville, later to become Quartzburg; then, when Quartzburgers requested one of their denizens, a whiskey dealer whose prices were too high, to move elsewhere, Whiskey Flat came into being. When the latter became the town of Kernville, a group of miners with little taste for the trappings of civilization moved fifteen miles up the mountain slopes to create the town of Havilah. In contrast to the hum and excitement of their short-lived but rowdy existence, these towns today sleep in peaceful decay, dwarfed by the grandeur of steep mountain slopes dotted with digger pine and towering walls of granite. Their hoard of gold has long since been replaced by an even more valuable and longer-lived treasure—water. The Kern's annual run-off is 700,000 acre-feet of which eighty percent originates from melting snow along the first fifteen miles of its course. Yet when the waters reach the valley floor they are absorbed by the desert sand, and the stream ambles along, sluggishly as if it were panting in the heat.

Strangely, the largest and principal city along the Kern, Bakersfield, was built in the midst of these sandy swamps and bogs. It was in 1863 that Colonel Thomas Baker, who had purchased reclamation rights to "swamp and overflow" lands, brought his family to settle on the site of the former Indian village of Woilo. The location was a sandy island between the main channel and a slough that divided the waters of the Kern.

While Colonel Baker set about erecting a series of dams, levees, and ditches that would eventually bring the Kern to rest in a man-created Buena Vista Lake, Mrs. Baker opened in her home a school and for two years taught children of neighboring settlers without compensation.

Kern County, named for the river, was organized three years later (1866). Baker's reclamation project was to be the beginning of a vast agricultural industry that later would see 700,000 acres of land placed under cultivation. It would eventually become the "salad bowl of America" as well as one of the largest cotton-producing areas in the nation.

But before this could take place, beginning in 1880 the waters of the Kern were the object of a violent and bloody range war waged both in the field and in the courts. On the one hand were the powerful partners Henry Miller and Charles Lux who were building an agricultural empire in northern Kern County. Opposing them were James Ben Ali Haggin and Lloyd Tevis, just as intent on their own accumulation of land. Both needed the resources of the Kern to carry out their enterprises, and both are said to have recruited small armies of typical western gunslingers to protect their interests.

The "war" ended in 1888 with a legal compromise by which thirty-one corporations and fifty-eight individuals owning water rights along the river agreed to an equitable distribution and paved the way for creation of the massive Kern County Land Company, one of the West's largest cattle ranching-truck farming-oil producing operations.

In 1888 history of a gentler sort was made when a young woman, Mary Hunter, rode a buckskin pony into the county, accompanied by her mother and brother. The family joined half a dozen other families who had taken up claims on government land adjoining the U.S. Army's Fort Tejon. This family settled in a one-room cabin with calico curtains and bunks against the wall. From there young Mary set out on her pony to explore her new homeland. She made friends with vaqueros, Indians, sheepherders, and was a fascinated spectator at cattle roundups, brandings, sheep shearings and other everyday happenings in the Old West. Later, as the novelist Mary Hunter Austin, she was to make these characters live again in such works as *The Flock*, *Earth Horizon*, and her best known *Land of Little Rain*.

The way of life author Austin depicted was to be disrupted in 1888 when oil was discovered in a hand-dug pit seven miles northeast of Bakersfield. Within a short time 2,000 men were at work for twenty-nine drilling companies. Bakersfield became as boisterous a boom town as were the gold camps that preceded it along the Kern River.

Oil continued to flow, with drillers bringing in bigger and bigger gushers until at eight o'clock on the Monday morning of March 14, 1910, they brought in the all-time big gusher, Union Oil's Lakeview Gusher, a short distance from Buena Vista Lake. In its lifetime of eighteen months the well yielded nine million barrels. Even today the Kern Plain of the San Joaquin Valley is one of the world's richest oil-producing areas.

From gold boom to oil boom Kern County attracted its share of bad men. The pages of its history resound with the sound of gunshots exchanged between holdup men and stage drivers, bandits and soldiers from old Fort Tejon, and between lawmen and outlaws.

Probably the Kern's most famous outlaw was Tiburcio Vasquez, who baffled posses by swooping down with his gang on stagecoaches and freight wagons, robbing their occupants, and then retiring to a rocky hideout beyond Walker Pass. Vasquez came to a violent end in the Hollywood Hills where almost a century later his exploits would be filmed for motion picture entertainment.

For Bakersfield the era of the western outlaw ended in a blaze of gunfire on a Sunday morning, April 19, 1903. Jim McKinney, "the Old West's Last Badman," was a killer with too many notches on his gun. On that date he stopped a bullet in a shootout that resulted not only in his own death but also in that of City Marshall Jeff Packard and his deputy Will Tibbett, father of a singer of the 1930s, Lawrence Tibbett. The incident resulted in a city cleanup that put an end once and for all to the Wild West on the Kern River.

In 1953 a major flood control and water conservation project was completed at the junction of the North and South forks with a storage capacity of 550,000 acre-feet. Since then, to overcome the receding water table—a problem that has plagued cotton and produce growers—the Kern River has been linked with the Central Valley water project via the Friant-Kern Canal. It carries water from Friant Dam near Fresno 153 miles south to the Kern. Its boom and bust days are now over, and the Kern has become a working contributor to the productivity of modern California.

FURTHER READING: Bob Powers, *South Fork Country* (1971). William Harlan Boyd, *A California Middle Border: The Kern River 1772–1880* (1972).

Vivienne L. George

The Trinity/Klamath Rivers

Sources: Klamath rises in Klamath Lake in south-central Oregon; the Trinity (strictly speaking, a Klamath tributary) rises amount the Salmon and Scott mountains of northern California
Length: Klamath, 263 miles; Trinity, 136 miles.
Tributaries: Klamath: Trinity, Scott, and Shasta rivers; Trinity: South Fork River
Mouth: Klamath: into Pacific at Requa, 15 miles south of Crescent City, California; Trinity: into the Klamath River at Weitchpec, about 76 miles northeast of Eureka
Agricultural products: None of significance
Industries: Salmon fishing, lumbering, tourism, some mining

The Trinity and Klamath rivers drain much of extreme northwest California, flow through similar terrain and share much history. Strictly speaking, the Trinity may be considered a tributary of the Klamath since it flows into it from the southeast, about forty miles inland from the Pacific Ocean. The Trinity rises among the Salmon and Scott mountains of northern California and is considered as being 130–159 miles long. In its journey it slices a precipitous swath through the jagged, saw-toothed Trinity Alps, now designated a federal wilderness area.

The Klamath is, with the exception of the Colorado River which forms part of California's eastern border, the only river that rises outside the state. It originates in south-central Oregon as the outflow from Klamath Lake (Indian name: "Klamate") at the eastern base of Oregon's Cascade Mountains. It veers southwestward into California, then northwestward before it pours its waters into the Pacific. On its journey the river makes a precipitous drop, sometimes as much as 100–200 feet per mile, in its 263-mile race to the sea. Klamath country is a land of rivers, creeks, and lakes accented by the Marble, Siskiyou, and Scott mountains, a land for the most part unsettled and accessible only by four-wheel-drive vehicles. Part of the area has never been surveyed accurately and can be reached only by backpack over narrow trails.

In spite of their continuing remoteness, both the Trinity and the Klamath have a long history. In 1775, while revolutionary activity on the northeast coast was rising to crisis proportions, the Spanish were pressing their explorations of California both by land and by sea. On Trinity Sunday in the late spring of 1775 Captain Bruno Heceta sailed into a bay he judged to rank third after those of San Diego and San Francisco; he named it for its day of discovery, Trinidad. When, seventy years later, Pierson B. Reading, the first American to hold a land grant in North

Sacramento Valley, came upon a large river, he incorrectly surmised that it drained into Trinidad Bay. Therefore he gave the river an anglicant equivalent title, the Trinity, and the name has remained. The misassumption as to the location of the Trinity's mouth led to almost unbearable hardships for its first explorers from overland some seventy-five years later.

After the California gold rush, argonauts plunged into northern California where they found a terrain of rugged mountains, steep canyons, and fast-flowing streams. To serve them—since a road was at that time out of the question—a search was launched for a bay that could serve as a port for the rugged country. A botanist named Josiah Gregg, best known for his book on the Santa Fe Trail, *Commerce of the Prairies*, found himself with about forty argonauts at Rich Bar on the Trinity with winter coming on and supplies dwindling out. Ordinarily supplies were brought by boat to Sacramento, then into the Trinity Alps by pack train. But packers found it impractical during the winter to make the 300-mile round trip.

Gregg had heard Indian rumors about the "shining waters" of the Pacific, which the Indians estimated to be around "three days of a man's travel." But because for the past month winter rains had deluged the valley and heaped new snow in the mountains, Gregg cautiously allowed for a week. He organized the party to cross over the mountains, planning to use the sandy shores of the Pacific as a smoother roadway to the nearest settlements. As time neared for their departure, all but seven of the men reconsidered. Even the Indian guides refused to attempt the snow-filled passes. Nevertheless on November 5, 1849, the small Gregg party set out. The "three-day" journey stretched into two weeks before they were to discover that the "shining water" at the mouth of the Trinity was not the ocean, but the larger and more powerful Klamath. Indians at the confluence of the two streams warned the party that other Indians downriver were hostile, so Gregg's tired party turned away from the Klamath, heading west overland.

For fifty-six days they battled the mountains and valleys, always certain that the ocean must be just beyond the next mountain. After supplies were exhausted they ate the sour paste that had formed on the inside of their flour sacks due to

the continuing saturation from rainfall, later they consumed tree bark, and finally the flesh of pack horses that died on the trail. The penetrating cold and acute suffering caused by wearing sodden clothing, sleeping in hollowed-out mounds of snow and battling the ridges frayed their tempers. The group degenerated into constant bickering because Gregg, without telling the others why, insisted on slowing their already snail's pace by stopping to take precise measurements and surveys, jotting them meticulously in a notebook he carried in a rain-proof pouch along with his surveyor's instruments. His companions heaped vituperation on him, to which Gregg, who had a volatile temper, returned volleys of abusive language.

Animosity ran so deep that when they finally reached the coast on Christmas Eve, even though they were able to shoot an elk and feast upon it, the party agreed to separate on an every-man-for-himself basis. Five of the group followed the ridge of the Coast Range while Gregg and two others followed the shore line. Two weeks later Gregg's two companions reached settlements north of San Francisco babbling incoherent and conflicting stories of Gregg's death. They indicated that he had died of starvation and that they had buried him along the way.

The men's story seems improbable since Gregg was traveling through an area where berries, nuts, and edible herbs abound, even in winter. The milder surmise is that he may have died of apoplexy during one of his violent rages. A more drastic theory is that he may have been murdered by one of his party in reprisal for the same cause. The event remains an enigma since neither survivor could give the location of Gregg's grave. Historians continue to search, in the somewhat unlikely hope of finding his "watertight bag" containing his instruments and his intrinsically valuable notes.

Josiah Gregg's exploration was a failure but peripatetic prospectors plunged into the region and some of them struck it rich. The village of Weaverville grew up on the Trinity River as a result of extensive gold strikes. It is a town whose picturesque streets are adorned with wrought iron balconies and circular stairways reminiscent of the southern planters who founded it. Nestled in the Trinity Alps, it is a spot ringed with peaks on which snow remains most of the year. It was author James Hilton's inspiration for his "Lost Horizon."

During gold rush days Weaverville had a large population of Chinese who although thousands of miles from home, kept up the religious traditions of their forefathers. They built a Taoist temple, the only one of its kind in America. Today the well-preserved "Temple Amongst the Forest Beneath the Clouds" contains elaborately carved altars, gongs, lanterns, tapestries, and other artifacts, some of which are gifts from the Emperor of China, several hundred years old before they arrived by pack train at Weaverville. Now preserved as a State Historical Monument, the Temple is still used as a place of worship by Chinese Taoists from throughout California and other states.

During the heyday of its mining boom, clay banks high about the Trinity three miles west of Weaverville were the location of one of the more extensive hydraulic mining operations. These were carried on by a company of French capitalists, headed by Baron Ernest De La Grange. On the crest overlooking the mines, the Baron constructed for his homesick Baroness a reproduction of a French villa complete with stained glass windows, tasteful furnishings, and French antiques. As the operation prospered the "castle in the wilderness" became the scene of ultra-lavish socials as the baron and his wife entertained visiting noblemen from both France and Russia where the baron also held mining interests.

While the strains from the minuet drifted down from the hill, ten miles north of Weaverville Indians in the Hupa Valley might at the same time be chanting the religious rites of the Sacred White Deer dance, the Jump Dance, or a healing ceremony called "E-edovern," or Bark of the Tree dance. The latter, still performed on occasion, is an all-night ritual danced and sung in an open pit around a charcoal fire on which native herbs and bark are burned to create a healing vapor to be inhaled by sick children. The ceremony now carries the American nickname of "Brush Dance" because it appeared to early settlers that the Medicine Woman was gathering "worthless brush" for the formality.

The Hupa Valley, formed like a round bowl, flairs southward from the confluence of the Trinity and Klamath and is ringed on all sides by mountains. Its Indian inhabitants believe

they have lived in the valley "since the creation of all things," and that their valley is the center of the earth. Their Reservation is one of the few having been established on the Indian tribe's "home ground." An Army post was set up on the reservation, complete with a cannon, shipped around the horn to Arcata. Since the pint-sized post lacked the horses necessary to draw it to its destination, foot soldiers were forced to push, pull, heave and haul it the forty miles up and over the mountain. Not wishing to repeat such a fatiguing performance, two privates "invented" a cannon made from the hollowed-out trunk of a redwood tree. When the charge was lit, the explosion split the trunk end to end and the resultant backfire sent the inventors sprawling, one with a broken collar bone.

The Klamath River country is the land of the legendary Big Foot, an elusive creature whose humanoid footprints, sometimes as much as eighteen inches long, indicate a creature about eight feet tall and weighing 600–800 pounds. Occasionally these "footprints" are found in the soft dirt of newly bulldozed logging trails. In recent years the creature, purported to be the American version of the Himalayan "Yeti," has received much publicity and has been hunted by such earnest scientists as Sir Edmund Hillary. In the more inhabited areas along the Klamath travelers can find residents evenly split on whether Big Foot is or is not a figment of imagination. There are many purported sightings at a distance, but close encounters have never been reported.

And although presently both the towns of Weaverville and Willow Creek present annual "Big Foot Daze" replete with parades, merchandise bargains, and carnival atmosphere, Indians of the Klamath and Trinity Rivers stand stoically on the sidewalks, licking ice cream cones and watching the tomfoolery with disapproval. To them "Big Foot" is as much a part of their heritage as are the twin rocks at Ishi-Pishi falls which, in summer (so the Indians say) move down the Klamath to Mak-Harum falls to protect their dugouts from spills in the rapids.

For most of the Klamath's length, Indians are the only inhabitants. They live in small settlements along the banks and are divided into the Hurok (downriver people) and the Karok (up river). There is friendly and sometimes not-so-friendly rivalry between the two, with the Hupa acting somewhat as a "demilitarized zone." The three tribes meet for dance competitions and games, particularly the Stick Game, in which rival teams vie with wooden clubs to propel a smaller wood "tossle" to the scoring line. It is an "anything goes" kind of game in which arms, legs, and even skulls are fair game as the player tries to immobilize his rival while getting the stick to his own goal.

The Klamath is one of the most active salmon fishing streams in the world. Annually on Labor Day at the height of the season people pack the banks at the mouth where salmon start their run from the Pacific upstream to spawn. Fishermen stand shoulder to shoulder and sometimes as many as 400 boats maneuver for position.

The Klamath is also a rockhound's happy hunting ground. Besides colorful red and yellow jasper, fortification, and moss agate, rhodonite (pink jade) occurs in a section nine miles south of Happy Camp near the Clear Creek forest campground, and vesuvianite (an ashen grey jade) is mined some six miles up Indian Creek, a tributary that joins the Klamath at Happy Camp. Trinity River jade, in varying shades from opaque dark green to translucent apple green, occurs along that stream in the 12-mile stretch between Willow Creek to Hupa.

Much of the Trinity/Klamath country remains wilderness even today, and most of its few inhabitants hope it will remain that way.

FURTHER READING: Chad L. Hooper, *Lure of Humboldt Bay Region* (1966). Jake Jackson, *Tales from the Mountaineer* (1964).

Vivienne L. George

The Owyhee River (Oregon)

Source: Convergence of headwater streams in Malheur County in extreme southeast Oregon
Length: 300 to 400 miles
Tributaries (including headwater streams): Crooked, Rattlesnake, Antelope, Little Owyhee, Battle, and Jordan creeks; South and East forks
Mouth: Into Snake River near Nyssa, Oregon, about 45 miles northwest of Boise, Idaho
Agricultural products: (Where irrigation is provided) corn, sugar beets, onions, potatoes, carrots, hops, rye, oats, and alfalfa
Industries: Cattle ranching, tourism

From cool, sparkling springs in remote mountains, the waters of the Owyhee River, in remote southeast Oregon, tumble into the spectacular Owyhee Canyon, now partially flooded by backwater from the Owyhee Dam. The tributaries drain equally remote regions and carry names that imply desolation: Crooked Creek, Rattlesnake Creek, Antelope Creek and Little Owyhee Creek in Oregon; Battle Creek and Jordan Creek for Idaho; and from Nevada, the South and East forks. The total length of this river of the northwest Great Basin is about 400 miles; it drains about 11,100 square miles before it spills into the Snake River. It swells the waters of the Snake which channels the silt-laden waters of the Owyhee through Hells Canyon to the Columbia below Pasco, Washington.

"Sandwich Island River" the Hudson's Bay trapper Peter Skene Ogden called it when he sent Antoine Sylvailles to investigate its sources in 1826. The former name alternates with Owyhee (spelled in different ways) in the correspondence of Dr. John McLoughlin, the head of Fort Vancouver. It is Owyhee today, commemorating in that name those natives of Hawaii who professed great eagerness to see the rest of the world. Captain Thorn of the Tonquin, sent by fur tycoon John Jacob Astor to establish a trading post at the mouth of the Columbia, stopped on the way at Hawaii and took some natives on to the Columbia with him. Still other ships carried Hawaiians to the northwest coast where they worked for the North West Company and the Hudson's Bay Company as trappers, mill men, cooks, gardeners, and carpenters. Ogden's reference to "Sandwich Island River" is obliquely to the murder there, by Indians, of three Hawaiians, part of Donald McKenzie's expedition to Snake River and its tributaries in 1819.

The Snake, Malheur, and Owyhee rivers came

again under trapper scrutiny when Peter Skene Ogden moved through the Snake country in the Hudson's Bay Company expedition of 1825–1826. Those explorations were followed by those of John Work who led the Snake River fur brigades after Ogden had left the field for administrative duties. In 1831 Work's men explored and trapped the distant sources of the Columbia. His Journal entry of May 12, 1831, specifies eight men sent by him "to hunt to the Westward on the heads of the small rivers which fall into Snake River and on the Eastern fork of Sandwich Island River Southward to Ogden's River [Humboldt] and then to the heads of Sandwich Island river."

Two years later, in 1833, a group of trappers associated with Benjamin Bonneville, and including Stephen H. L. Meek, trapped the Owyhee. John Ball, Oregon's pioneer educator, described the Indian fishery he had seen on the Owyhee in 1832: "They built a fence across [the stream] near its mouth," he wrote. "Then leaving some distance above they made a weir at one side so that the fish coming down or coming out would go in, but were unable to find their way out. Then they speared them."

With the departure of organized trapping parties the Owyhee, depleted of furs, was left alone. Except for an occasional trapper the region was not revisited by large parties until a military reconnaissance in 1864. In the spring of that year Colonel Charles S. Drew was directed to investigate the feasibility of a route from Fort Klamath, above Klamath Lake, to Boise. Such a road would cut across the upper reaches of the Owyhee and intersect a road from Yreka, California, to the Boise mines.

Behind this order were three military and political concerns: controlling Indian tribes, opening the country to exploration and settlement, and forestalling any Confederate attempts at sedition in Nevada, Oregon, and Idaho Territory. Drew started in June, reaching Boise in September, having covered 431 miles. His command consisted of about sixty men including enlisted men, civilian employees, and two Indian scouts. Two wagons hauling part of the supplies were the first to make wheel tracks from the west into the Owyhee region.

The reconnaissance was generally without incident. Drew visited Camp Alvord at the base of

the Steens Mountain in southeast Oregon on August 26 and by August 31 was past the headwaters of Crooked Creek and moving toward the crossing of the Owyhee. "The descent to the Owyhee from the west," he wrote, "is gradual and smooth, the route passing among detached perpendicular portions of what was once a high volcanic table representing now, by a little stretch of the imagination, so many towers, and grand old castles, delineating the various orders of architecture, and on the whole presenting a sublime and picturesque appearance." In the reconnaissance Drew encountered both placer and quartz mining on the Owyhee tributaries. He mentioned the new mining towns of Booneville, Ruby City, and Silver City as "marts of commerce" for the region.

In April of the same year (1864) Lieutenant George B. Curry with two regiments and part of a third left Fort Walla Walla for the Owyhee, which was reached on May 14. There his force was joined by Captain E. Barry of the First Washington Territory Infantry. On May 18 they began to ascend the river. They were fascinated by weird, wind-caused formations. "Here stands a group of towers," wrote Lieutenant Curry, "there is an archway curiously shaped, yonder is a tunnel running the face of a sandstone ledge hundreds of feet from the bottom."

These were the principal military explorations of the river until General George Crook passed along its western line on his way west to wage the Snake Campaign of 1866–1868. However, in 1865 the upper reaches of the Owyhee had been scouted by Major L. H. Marshall, the commander of the military district of Fort Boise. In the late spring, between the Middle and South forks, Marshall encountered a strong band of Paiutes who ultimately forced his retreat with the losses of a raft, a mountain howitzer, and one non-commissioned officer. It is rumored that the howitzer is still there, buried in the silt of the upper Owyhee. In August the Major retrieved some of his reputation by successfully battling another Snake force on the upper Owyhee, hanging thirty-five captives from the limbs of trees. After General Crook's campaign, fear of Snake (Paiute) raids ended for all time.

John Baptiste Charbonneau died in 1866 at Inskip Ranch on Cow Creek, an Owyee tributary.

At the time he was traveling from California to Montana and had stopped off to see the Owyhee mines. Charbonneau represented the beginning and (almost) the end of far west exploration, for he was the son of Sacajawea, born in the Mandan encampment on February 11, 1804; she had carried him as an infant to the shores of the Pacific and back again.

Beginning in 1863 miners from the Boise Basin had moved west and south to the headwaters of the Owyhee. On Jordan Creek silver ledges of remarkable richness were discovered. By 1864, Silver City, Ruby City, and Booneville were all established centers. Ultimately five Owyhee mining districts came into being, yielding almost incredible riches.

The Orofino mine on War Eagle Mountain, near Silver City, yielded $2,756,128 in six years. Another mine produced $500,000 in one month. Some chlorides were 60% pure silver. By 1881, some quartz mines had been worked to 1500 feet. The bullion output for Owyhee county in 1881 was nearly $300 million.

With the cessation of most mining activity on the upper Owyhee, population withdrew and the once flourishing mining towns were deserted. Ranchers used the ranges for their cattle, and a period of stability ensued from 1890 until 1926.

Under the Reclamation Act investigations were made in 1904 and 1905 and a report filed by the United States Bureau of Reclamation in 1909 that included the estimate that 80,000 acres could be developed for irrigation under the Carey Act. The Boise-Owyhee Company proposed an Owyhee irrigation project to embrace some 135,000 acres. In that early period private irrigation companies undertook to reclaim these arid lands which would be sold to land hungry settlers. The estimated cost of the project by 1915 was $1,446,000 with Reclamation costs ranging from $50 to $68 per acre.

The project was not formally organized until 1926 when four irrigation districts entered into contract with the Bureau of Reclamation for water; by 1937 several other projects were under way. Contracts were let and work begun in 1928. The Owyhee Dam was the highest in the world when it was dedicated in 1932. The first water was delivered to project lands in 1935. Behind the great dam the Owyhee River flow deepened as the water backed up the canyon, covering ancient camp sites, petroglyphs, and artifacts of the native inhabitants along the river. By 1936 the lake, 52 miles long, filled the reservoirs to capacity, storing 715,000 acre-feet of water.

In 1949, eight irrigation districts were served by waters of the Owyhee Project for a total of 104,000 acres, some in Idaho. In that year Federal investment was computed at over $18 million. Cumulative gross crop value for the years 1935–1948 totalled $72 million. Settler-farmers moved onto the newly irrigated lands. Some were refugeees from the Dust Bowl states. Some were industrious and frugal Japanese. And the land responded to the water with remarkable crops of corn, sugar beets, onions, potatoes, carrots, hops, rye, oats, and alfalfa.

Still another benefit was the recreation afforded by the extended reservoir. The waters behind the dam were soon swarming with bass, crappie, and blue gills. Access was limited and still is to a surprising degree. Roads now lead from Nyssa to Adrian, to the dam, and from Homedale, Idaho, but the upper reaches of the Owyhee, above the reservoir, are today almost as isolated as when they were visited by John Work in 1831.

So the Owyhee, named for Hawaii, has become a cornucopia of mineral treasure and ultimately an agricultural treasure as well. Its recreational uses are still being developed. It is a river shared by three states, but Idaho and Oregon benefit most. Float trips down the upper reaches to the placid reservoir are increasingly popular.

The raft floater can lose his sense of time as he drifts downriver. Along the rocky rims he sees bands of Chukar partridges. Mule deer graze peacefully in the breaks, sharing the browse with cattle. Ducks and geese from the great Snake River flyway rest upon the waters of the reservoir. Eagles soar high above the canyons, catching the thermal updrafts. Wild horses compete for the grazing lands of domestic cattle. Nature is still dominant along the Owyhee.

FURTHER READING: Mike Hanley with Ellis Lucia, *Owyhee Trails, the West's Forgotten Corner* (1973).

Keith Clark

The Rogue River

Source: Rises on the northeast slope of Mount Maza-
ma (which crests with Crater Lake) in southwest
Oregon
Length: 215 miles
Tributaries: Bear Creek, Applegate River, Illinois Riv-
er
Mouth: Flows into Pacific Ocean at Gold Beach
Agricultural products: Wheat, stock raising, apples,
peaches, and pears
Industries: Lumbering, tourism

The Rogue is 215 miles in length and the fourth largest river within the borders of Oregon; it drains the three southwestern counties of the state, which border California. The Rogue is not a typical river. Rising in the northeast on the outer slopes of prehistoric Mount Mazama, whose empty caldera presently holds Crater Lake, the Rogue tumbles down through the remarkably deep Cascade Canyon. It then enters a plateau region called the Rogue River Valley, though most of this relatively level agricultural land is the valley of one of the Rogue's secondary tributaries, Bear Creek. In this plateau region, the Rogue itself is frequently constricted by rocky promontories or encroaching hills. Below Grants Pass, after being joined from the south by the Applegate River, the Rogue assumes its most atypical riparian form. Instead of lazily passing through a wide plain, it cuts a tortured passage-way nearly 100 miles long through the Klamath Mountain Range. On the western slopes of these mountains, as they merge with the Coast Range, it is joined by the equally wild Illinois which rises in the Siskiyou Mountains on the California border. Just five miles from the Pacific the fully formed Rogue reaches tidewater and then flows straight through bounding hills into the ocean. The unusual physical characteristics of the Rogue have determined its unique human geography.

It was comparatively late in the period of nineteenth-century exploration that the Rogue was identified as a distinct river. The Greenleaf map of the 1840s, for example, only shows the Klamath River, which actually flows through northern California, to exist in southwestern Oregon. The upper portions of the Rogue were crossed by fur trappers in the 1820s and Jedediah Smith camped at the Rogue's mouth during June, 1828. Not until 1850 was there a recorded entry of a sailing vessel into the river, by the *Samuel Roberts* of San Francisco.

The Indian population of the Rogue River basin was not large. An 1852 census by the Indian Agent, admittedly an undercount, reckoned 1,154 in the Rogue River Valley area; an additional 1,311 were counted along the lower Rogue and its coast in 1854. Some diminution of the population had no doubt already occurred by these dates.

Two language groups, the Athabascan and the Takelma, accounted for most of the Indians. They lived by the hunting of deer, elk, and small game, salmon fishing, and the gathering of acorns, grass seeds, camas, pine nuts and berries. The first of these plant foods was ground into meal for baking and porridge. Their gathering also required seasonal migration from the Indians' winter homes. On the coast the Indians' diet was enriched with shellfish, smelt, seaweed, and occasionally sea lion or whale meat. In the Rogue River Valley the less recognized delicacies of grasshopper, snail and caterpillar supplemented the basic diet of the region.

Throughout the basin the Indians lived in small patrilineally organized villages. Houses were constructed of planks set vertically in the earth and the dwelling's plank or earthen floor was generally sunken a foot or more below the surrounding ground level. The habitation was used for sleeping, cooking, and storage of food hung or in baskets. The men had special sweating houses. Canoes were apparently manufactured solely near the mouth of the river but were also used on the upper river. Deerskin breeches or pelt kilts clad the men and aprons of the same materials the women. Their attire was distinctively ornamented with woodpecker scalps and small shells; the ensembles were climaxed with basket hats.

On first contact the Indians who visited Captain Vancouver's ships in 1792 were friendly.

Their later hostility to the whites—which gained them and the river of their land the name Rogue—may have stemmed from some unrecorded ill treatment or from jealous defense of the limited hunting and gathering grounds which the rugged geography imposed upon them.

While the first whites in the Rogue area were fur trappers and, somewhat later, cattle drivers between California and the Willamette Valley, the basis of major early settlement was gold mining. The California Gold Rush quickly ran north to the Shasta region and then to southern Oregon. Those bringing foodstuffs from the Willamette Valley to the Sacramento area prospected on the way and others from the south sought golden grains and nuggets in the Rogue's tributary creeks. Success quickly rewarded their efforts when rich finds were made in 1851 on the Applegate and near Jacksonville in 1852. That boom town quickly became the largest center of population in the Oregon Territory as the ever hopeful horde let loose after 1848 was drawn to the area. Prospecting pans were soon replaced by sluice boxes along the region's creeks to wash the dirt and stones from the heavy precious metal sought by the miners.

It was to be the Rogue Indians' misfortune that the first white settlers in the area were such as these. Impatient for quick wealth and paranoid over its possible loss, the early miners were hostile to the Indians who from time to time marauded their camps or even killed isolated gold seekers who overran their foraging areas. Because the mining techniques in the area depended on plentiful supplies of water, the dry periods of late summer and early autumn or periods of severe winter cold and snow left the miners inactive and frustrated. The historian of the Rogue Indians convincingly related the outbreaks of violence against the natives to these periods of miner inaction. Thus the Indian War of 1853 took place in the Rogue River Valley during the month of August drought. So, too, did five documented massacres of sleeping Indian villages which matched the grisly scene of slaughter of the Sioux at Wounded Knee.

It was not such acts of violence, however, or the frequent cry for extermination that brought the first precipitous decrease of Indian numbers. The decline of the Upper Rogue native population from 1,154 in 1852 to 523 in 1854 was largely a result of white men's diseases, smallpox, measles, and tuberculosis, which acted on bodies undernourished because their traditional hunting and gathering patterns had been interrupted. In 1854 the Rogue River Valley Indians were driven out to the Siletz reservation, while their warriors made a last stand in the mountains of the Lower Rogue. The resisters stimulated the coast Indians to attack the miners and settlers near Gold Beach. Army contingents defeated the Indians in May 1856 and they, too, were forced to go to the Siletz reservation. That depleted assembly of a thousand lost half their number in the first year of exile. Thus in the brief span 1852 to 1857 the Rogue basin was cleared of Indians and their population reduced from well over 3,000 to a few hundred.

During the following generation the white population made a slow expansion of settlement in the region. The crowds of miners departed for new strikes in British Columbia leaving a reduced mining population augmented by numerous Chinese to search the tailings and more isolated creeks of the region or engage in lode mining. Farmers, many of whom had followed the Applegate trail across Nevada and by Klamath Lake, concentrated on wheat as their staple crop which was largely sold in northern California. They also grazed cattle and sheep. Grist and sawmills were important local resources. As mining declined, the wagon road head of passage over the Siskiyous, Ashland, replaced Jacksonville as the major population center in the basin. The German founder Abel Helman's concern that a town center be established in Ashland may also have helped to make it a focus of urban settlement. Certain it is that this town center has charmed the expanding number of visitors to the Shakespeare Festival during the last generation. This theatrical institution has made Ashland the present cultural capital of southern Oregon.

The record which the first permanent settlers wrote in diaries or their children related to historical investigators recalls the round of agricultural and domestic tasks, the brief school terms, and weekend-long dances which attracted young folk from miles around. Sparse settlement and encroaching mountains meant that wildlife remained abundant, and the hunting and fishing ambiance of Rogue River life was firmly established in this early period.

Because of its peculiar physiography, the Rogue was never a major highway of commerce, and its banks were not the locus of major population settlement in the area. Such functions were provided by the railroad. The Oregon and California line was linked with the Southern Pacific in 1887, and the direction of economic development in the basin has been north and south rather than east and west along the river. With the railroad Ashland lost place to Grants Pass, located at an old ferry crossing of the Rogue, and Medford, newly laid out around the tracks, as the population center of the Rogue River Valley.

The railroad company was not a passive instrument of population growth. It sponsored promotional writings by *Sunset Magazine* which encouraged many easterners and Californians to come to the valley, particularly to establish fruit orchards. The railroad knew their produce could find ready markets and would require its freighting capacity to reach them. Expanding fructiculture meant widespread diversion of watercourses for irrigation. The fresh influx of eastern immigrants and money gave a new tone to Valley life. Two new arrivals, Dr. C. R. and Col. Frank Ray, constructed the first major hydroelectric dam in the region at Gold Ray.

The railroad was also the means, though not impressively until the decade of the 1940s, by which the timber resources of the surrounding mountains could finally be exploited. The Rogue and its tributaries had never been satisfactory log-driving streams, but the railroad, and later surfaced trucking roads, could exploit the enormous natural wealth of the forests. Today nearly half of the employment income of the region is generated by forestry manufactures.

With the exploitation of the forests, coastal Curry County entered into the mainstream of the region's life. It had done so briefly in the mid-1850s with the working of fine grained deposits of gold in the ocean sands, but thereafter it had an idiosyncratic history. Its only industry in 1880, besides the cedar mill at Port Orford, was the Robert D. Hume salmon cannery at the mouth of the Rogue. This Scot was a pioneer in salmon propagation and conservancy and a determined fighter for control of all salmon fishing at the river's mouth. He bought virtually all of the river bottom and banks for five miles from the ocean. His alleged monopoly was broken by court decision, but he retained economic dominance of the Rogue coast until his death in 1908.

The Rogue River canyon bred a number of characters in the century after the Indian Wars, its subsistence economy prolonged by the Great Depression of the 1930s. These have been enshrined in Zane Grey's *Rogue River Feud* and the folk tales of Hathaway Jones. Jones delivered mail by mule along the Rogue River Canyon trail until he and his faithful mount plunged from it to their deaths in 1936. His tales are now the stock in trade of river guides, and old residents fondly recall his ubiquitous stories; this one gives their flavor:

> When a blizzard had formed a half mile drift which prevented Hathaway from getting the mail through, his quick wit provided the necessary remedy. Stripping the saddle off his fast riding mule, he led her over to a pine tree and started her running round and round it. He kept increasing her speed faster and faster, round and round, until she was just a blur; then she became red-hot. Whereupon he drove her through the drift where she melted a path by which Hathaway's packtrain could proceed.*

In a more serious effort to improve mail delivery on the Lower Rogue, Elijah H. Price obtained post office rank for Illahe in 1895. Frank Lowrie established an effective mail boat run on the route in the early part of this century. This mode of mail carriage has provided one of the most exciting tourist excursions in this country, especially after the introduction of aluminum hulled jet boats in the 1960s. The tourist business in the Rogue canyon began in the 1920s and expanded after 1936 when the river was closed to commercial fishing and several displaced fishermen became professional river guides.

The fact that the Rogue and the mountains from which it springs and through which it flows have retained their wild character for such a long period has meant the presence of another force which goes to form the dynamic of present life in the region. Federal agencies led by the National Forest Service and the Bureau of Land

---

* Paraphrased from Stephen Dow Beckham, ed., *Tall Tales from Rogue River* (Bloomington: Indiana University Press, 1974), p. 112. Used by permission.

Management play an important role in economic development and decision making in the region, not least concerning the character and use of the Rogue River. Another federal agency, the Corps of Engineers, has recently built several upriver dams to regulate the river's flow and reduce the destructive power of its awesome floods. The December 1964 flood released a greater discharge than the mean flow of the mighty Columbia. In the rock-girded lower Rogue canyon, the crest rose a staggering 100

feet above normal and a new concrete bridge was demolished. Whether beneficial or not, the strong presence of the federal government has led to the paradoxical confrontation of the ethic of the isolated frontiersman and the procedures of the modern regulatory state within the Rogue region today.

FURTHER READING: Stephen D. Beckham, *Requiem for a People* (1971). James M. Quinn, et al., *Handbook to the Rogue River Canyon* (1978). Kay Atwood, *Idaho* (1980).

James E. Farnell

The Sacramento River

Source: Flows out of a small lake on Mount Eddy, near Mount Shasta in the Klamath Mountains of northern California
Length: 320 miles
Tributaries: McCloud, Pit, Feather, Yuba, Bear, and American rivers; Cache and Putah creeks
Mouth: Joins the San Joaquin in a common delta into Suisan Bay, the eastern arm of San Francisco Bay
Agricultural products: Walnuts, prunes, alfalfa, sugar beets, tomatoes, rice, asparagus
Industries: Lumbering and the processing of forest products; livestock raising

Mount Shasta, its 14,162-foot peak perpetually capped with snow, stands as a sentinel guarding the northern end of the great Central Valley of California. Near Mt. Shasta, in a small lake on Mt. Eddy, are the headwaters of the Sacramento River; from that point the river flows south and west some 320 miles until it joins the San Joaquin River to empty into Suisan Bay, flows through the Strait of Carquinez into San Francisco Bay, and then finally its waters are swept by the outgoing tides under the Golden Gate Bridge into the Pacific Ocean.

In its first few miles the Sacramento is a wild river that is a delight to experienced boaters. Then near Redding some forty miles below its source, the Shasta and Keswick dams block its waters along with those of its tributaries, the McCloud and Pit, to form Lake Shasta. After

Shasta Dam the river's descent slackens noticeably and then finally, below Red Bluff, it enters the great Central Valley. From Red Bluff to the city of Sacramento the river flows a winding course through a bountiful agricultural region, along the way collecting the runoff from a number of mountain streams so that for the most of the distance it is a broad expanse of fast-moving water. The Sacramento's appearance in this area prompted many early settlers to call it the "Nile of the West." South of the city of Sacramento the river joins with the San Joaquin to form a delta region of about 750 square miles within which are a number of islands that are slightly below sea level. The rich peat lands on these islands make this one of the richest agricultural regions in the United States. In addition the 1,000 miles of waterways in the delta make it a boater's and sportsman's paradise. Here also the river helps carry the products of this productive valley to United States and world markets. The channel of the Sacramento east of San Francisco serves as an entry way for ships seeking the deep water channel that takes them to the inland port of the city of Sacramento.

Most of the Sacramento River valley has a Mediterranean climate. The summers are long and hot with abundant sunshine. Rainfall is scant and as a result irrigation is extensively practiced. There are exceptions to the dry nature

The fertility of the Sacramento Valley was renowned from the earliest days of white settlement. (Credit: Wells Fargo Bank History Room.)

of the climate. In 1861 almost constant rain in the early months of the year turned the Central Valley into a lake 250–300 miles long and 20–60 miles wide. At that time the city of Sacramento remained under water for three months.

When Europeans first settled in California an estimated 350,000 Indians lived within its present boundaries. Because of the area's geographical and cultural isolation, the tribes living in the Sacramento River valley (as elsewhere in California) still had a stone age culture. Along the Sacramento food was so abundant that the Indians there engaged in hunting, fishing, and gathering rather than in agriculture; this abundance also allowed the growth of a sizeable population. The most important staple was the acorn. It was husked, pounded into a rough meal, winnowed by tossing in a basket, and then

repeatedly washed to rid it of tannic acid. The finished product was then used to make bread or a type of porridge that was often flavored with berries.

The many linguistic groups and the location of plant and animal food influence the size of villages and their relationship with one another. Usually Indians were grouped in established village communities of 100 to 500 people. The many different languages and the localized nature of food supplies tended to keep these small groups apart. As a result the culture that developed was isolated, relatively static, and not warlike, although villages would fight to defend their community and food-gathering areas.

The relatively harmonious relations that the California Indians had with one another and their natural surroundings quickly came to an end with the coming of Europeans. The first ones to feel the effect of the clash of cultures were those located in the coastal areas. With the coming of the Spanish in the 18th century they were rounded up and place in missions. The Indians in the Sacramento Valley, however, remained "wild" until the gold rush of 1849. Then the tremendous influx of people brought them ruin. In their rush for gold, miners ruthlessly overran traditional tribal grounds, massacring thousands and destroying their food stores. One authority has estimated that seventy percent of all California Indians were killed or died of disease in the decade 1849–1859.

So devastating was the white impact on Indian tribes in the Sacramento Valley that many were thought to be extinct by the 1870s. The Yahis, a sub-tribe of the Yana, located south of Mt. Lassen, were such a tribe. They had been hunted by miners as though they were animals and it was widely believed that by 1870 no Yahi remained alive. Then in 1911 a disheveled, frightened man—apparently the last Yahi alive—was found in a stockyard near Oroville. An anthropologist from the University of California named him Ishi—the Yahi word for man—and brought him to the university's museum of anthropology. Ishi quickly adapted to his new environment, but within a few years fell victim to tuberculosis.

Even though Spain occupied California in 1769 it was not until 1808 that Ensign Gabriel Moraga led a small group of soldiers from Mission San Jose into the Sacramento River valley. It was on this expedition that Moraga gave the name Sacramento—which means "Holy Sacrament"—to the lower reaches of the Feather River, a tributary of the Sacramento. Soon, however, the name was applied to the present Sacramento River. Morago and other Spanish continued to explore and map the river valley in later years.

In the 1820s small bands of mountain men, including among their personnel Jedediah Smith, Kit Carson, and Jim Bridger, entered the Sacramento Valley in search of beaver and otter furs. In 1829 the Hudson's Bay Company sent a trapper brigade into the valley under the command of Alexander McLeod. Hudson's Bay trappers commonly called the Sacramento the Buenaventura, or "the big river," but—although it

appeared on several maps in the 1830s—the name was never widely used. The fur trapping era came to an end quite suddenly due to the scarcity of beaver and otter.

The first permanent European settler in the Sacramento Valley was John Sutter. He had emigrated to the United States from Switzerland in 1835 and reached California by 1839. In that year, with Mexican permission, he settled inland close to where the American flows into the Sacramento River. Here he successfully carried on a wide range of enterprises, ranging from fur trading to farming. "Sutter's Fort" also became a port of entry for overland immigration from the United States, both in the Mexican period and after American annexation.

In order to provide lumber for the many immigrants and for his own needs, Sutter started a sawmill in association with an American frontiersman, James Marshall. It was at this mill, located on the south fork of the American River (a tributary of the Sacramento) that Marshall discovered gold on January 24, 1848. The news soon spread and within a year 100,000 gold-seekers had made their way into California. For the next several decades gold dominated the region's economy. Before the discovery Sutter's Fort—now within the boundaries of the city of Sacramento—had been the only settlement in the valley. Soon, with claims being mined all the way from the Mariposa River in the south to the Mt. Shasta area in the north—a distance of about 250 miles—towns sprang up along the Sacramento River and its tributaries to serve the needs of the miners.

The influx of gold-seekers created a demand for transportation. Enterprising businessmen met the need by rushing steamboats from the East to the Sacramento River. Most river steamers were shipped in parts in the holds of sailing vessels but some actually made the perilous journey around Cape Horn under their own power. Some steamboats maintained regular schedules between San Francisco and the city of Sacramento. In the beginning profits were high: in the first year of operation the *Senator* yielded a net profit of over $60,000 a month. With the arrival of a few more steamers, many of them constructed in California shipyards, prices declined to a more realistic level. A notable California-built steamboat was the 1,625-ton *Chry-*

sopolis, built in 1860. The quarter of a million dollar craft was not only elegant but fast. Once, in a race with the *New World* in 1861, it made the 125-mile passage from the city of Sacramento to San Francisco in five hours and ten minutes. Smaller craft, some with a draft of only twelve to fourteen inches, plied their trade all the way up to Red Bluff, ninety-one miles north of the city of Sacramento, and on the river's tributaries. Even after the decline of gold mining and the coming of the railroad, steamboats continued to play an important role on the Sacramento carrying passengers and freight.

After the gold rush the Sacramento River valley experienced several economic transformations. Many of the early settlers were stockmen. Then in the 1860s it was discovered that a variety of wheat that could be shipped on long voyages without spoilage thrived in the Central Valley. Until the 1890s the region was one of the major wheat-producing areas in the United States. Steamers and barges carried millions of bushels to the world's markets. Some of the wheat ranches in the Sacramento Valley were truly gigantic. Dr. Hugh J. Glenn's holdings, for example, extended for twenty miles along the west bank of the river and totaled 55,000 acres. By the 1890s soil exhaustion and the competition from new wheat-growing areas in the United States, Canada, and Australia brought this bonanza period to an end. Many of the large wheat ranches were divided and a more diversified agricultural economy developed in the twentieth century.

Today the economic activity along the banks of the Sacramento River is as varied as the geographic regions it flows through. Near its source, processing industries related to forest products, and the raising of livestock, predominate. The broad, flat valley between Sacramento City and Red Bluff produces walnuts, almonds, prunes, alfalfa, sugar beets, tomatoes, and rice. The only major urban center on the river is the city of Sacramento. The delta region, where the Sacramento joins with the San Joaquin, is one of the most important fruit, nut, and vegetable

growing regions in the country, with asparagus being one of the most important crops.

The Sacramento River also contributes to the economy and well-being of the state by sharing its water. Concern over use of the river's water came early. The annual rainfall in large portions of the valley is not sufficient for dry farming and hence irrigation was used from the beginning of settlement. Farmers established local irrigation districts to dam, store, and allot water to users. As early as 1854 a state board of Water Commissioners was established to regulate water diversion from rivers for agricultural use.

These early efforts largely involved local agricultural users. In the twentieth century a new water plan was implemented. The Central Valley project was authorized by the state in 1933, taken over by the Bureau of Reclamation in 1935, and begun in 1937. Its main features were dams: the most impressive one is the Shasta, which forms a thirty-five-mile-long lake to store the run-off from the mountains, canals to carry this water to the thirsty Central Valley as far south as Bakersfield, and power transmission lines to carry electricity to factories, farms, and homes.

Later water plans involving the Sacramento Valley resulted in construction of additional dams such as the Oroville Dam which is the largest earth-fill dam in the world, and canals to shunt water to the Los Angeles area. These later plans have met with resistance from environmentalists, partially because of fears that canals through the delta would result in salt water intrusion.

Today the Sacramento River plays an indispensable role in filling the needs of the state. It carries 22 million acre-feet of run-off each year—nearly one-third of the total for all California's rivers—and four million acre-feet of this run-off is diverted for industrial, agricultural, and domestic uses.

FURTHER READING: Julian Dana, *The Sacramento: River of Gold* (1939). Theodore Kroeber, *Ishi in Two Worlds* (1961).

Erling Erickson

The San Joaquin River

Source: Rises on the slopes of the Sierra Nevada in southeastern corner of Yosemite Park
Length: 350 miles
Tributaries: Fresno, Chowchilla, Merced, Tuolumne, Stanislaus, Calaveras, Mokelumne, and Cosumnes rivers
Mouth: Into Suisan Bay, the eastern arm of San Francisco Bay , near Antioch
Agricultural products: The San Joaquin Valley is one of the wealthiest agricultural areas in the world, raising grains, cotton, nuts, citrus fruits, and almost all kinds of vegetables
Industries: Food processing

Rising high on the slopes of the Sierra Nevada at the southeastern corner of Yosemite National Park in California, the upper San Joaquin River flows southwest to Fresno County and then northwest to Stockton, and the lower river continues northwest to its mouth near Antioch. The San Joaquin is 350 miles long. It drains the rich San Joaquin Valley basin from the Sierra Nevada to the Coast Range through important tributaries like the Merced, Tuolumne, Stanislaus, Calaveras, and Mokelumne rivers, flowing to the sea through the Sacramento–San Joaquin Delta, Suisun Bay, Carquinez Strait, San Pablo Bay, San Francisco Bay, and out the Golden Gate to the Pacific Ocean. The San Joaquin has undergone a most interesting series of historical events as succeeding generations of men utilized and benefited from its use.

At the time of European contact, the Yokuts Indians lived along the wetter borders of the rivers and lakes and the tidal swamps at the lower end of the river. Tule, or fresh-water bulrush plants, furnished the dominant ground cover, often found in patches two or three miles wide along each bank. The tules supported the Yokuts' subsistence economy in many ways. Through their collecting and hunting they got food from the seeds and roots of the plant. Tules gave them huts, balsas, and rafts, and the attractive waters supplied them with fish, fowl, mussels, berries, and game. The appearance of Europeans temporarily caused the Yokuts to stiffen their opposition to incursion, and the tule lands (*tulares* in Spanish) became a sanctuary into

which to escape or in which to fight. But, with the arrival of Americans, the day of the Indian village was gone by the 1850s.

The discovery of the San Joaquin River by Spaniards came within the first years after their colonization of Upper, or Alta, California in 1769. On a land expedition in 1772 to search the shores surrounding San Francisco Bay, Captain Pedro Fages and Franciscan Father Juan Crespi first saw to the east two large rivers, later to be called the San Joaquin and the Sacramento. Other expeditions by land and by water followed under Juan Bautista de Anza (1776) and José Joaquín Moraga (1776), and the river was called the San Juan Bautista and also the San Miguel. However, Spanish imperial goals were to establish San Francisco, with its presidio and mission, as its northernmost defensive outpost, and no functional use was attached to these large rivers running from the flat plain of the Central Valley to the east. The inland rivers and Tulares lay outside Spanish control and became a sanctuary for runaway neophyte Indians and for the *gentiles*, or pagan natives like the Yokuts, who remained beyond the reach of Christendom. Expeditions were organized to recapture runaway neophytes, seek new mission sites, find new unchristianized Indians, baptize sick or dying natives, and punish those who harassed Spanish converts, buildings, and herds.

In 1806, Ensign Gabriel Moraga and Father Pedro Múñoz marched from the Mission San Juan Bautista to seek new mission sites in the Central Valley. They traveled north to the main channel of the river, and they gave it the name San Joaquin, which became permanently fixed in a short time. Moraga returned two years later, but neither his expedition nor any other ever succeeded in founding inland missions in the area. Military expeditions of a more purely punitive nature also brought Spaniards into the delta and river areas from 1811 until 1820, but the main heritage of this time was to fix geographical names on the area and to gain full knowledge, if not incorporation, of the delta and the San Joaquin River system.

When the Viceroyalty of New Spain gained

The San Joaquin River

independence from the Spanish Crown in the 1820s and the new Republic of Mexico emerged, provincial Mexican *californios* continued to treat the San Joaquin River and its adjacent lands as a marginal area where expeditions rode out to recover stolen horses and cattle and to punish unincorporated Indians. By this time, a new frontier element had appeared beginning with the American trapper, Jedediah Strong Smith. He traveled tributaries of the San Joaquin in 1827 and 1828, and his reports of rich beaver and otter pelts made to the Hudson's Bay Company at British Fort Vancouver brought Andrew Roderick McLeod and Peter Skene Ogden south to the area of present-day Stockton. Other trapping brigades followed for about fifteen years; tens of thousands of pelts were taken from the San Joaquin north to Fort Vancouver.

The Mexican government also began to view the San Joaquin River as a potential area for permanent settlement. In 1836 Jose Noriega settled a grant near Antioch close to the mouth of the river. Another grant, the Rancho del Campo de los Franceses ("French Camp"), was given to William (Guillermo) Gulnac in 1844 near the Calaveras River and Stockton. He was a naturalized Mexican citizen from New York, and he sold his stock-raising grant to Captain Charles M. Weber in 1847. These men were nominally loyal to Mexico, but their real interests lay in opening the river and the land to herding and farming. By the fall of 1847 Weber had gathered a small colony on the Gulnac grant and named their town Tuleburg, changing the name soon to Stockton in honor of Commodore Robert F. Stockton of Mexican War fame. Sending his cattle products down the river to trade for supplies with San Francisco, Weber opened a new day in the use of the river.

Trading activity grew rapidly with the Gold Rush in 1848 and 1849. Argonauts, as the California miners were called, used the San Joaquin as a road to the southern mines of the Mother Lode. People and supplies arrived by sailboats, rowboats, manual towing, and wood-burning steamships. A small bark, the *María*, owned by Weber, began commercial navigation on the river in 1848, followed soon by a schooner, the *San Joaquin*, and probably the first steamboat, the *Captain Weber*, in 1849. Stockton flourished as a supply center while other shortlived towns appeared on nearby tributaries, like Stanislaus

and San Joaquin City on the Stanislaus River and Tuolumne City on that river. Mining did not sustain the early activities and high profits for many years, but Stockton did retain its leadership as the main center on the San Joaquin for passengers and freight.

With the American acquisition of California at the end of the Mexican War in 1848, immigrants soon fell back from the mines to join farmers in tilling the rich soils of the Central Valley along the San Joaquin and its tributaries. Agricultural production and commercial activities brought expansive growth and development of the tidal plains of the San Joaquin and of the adjacent dry lands. By the 1860s crops and livestock thrived, particularly the production of bonanza crops of wheat and related products needing transportation to coastal markets. Grain was very important for the remainder of the century, and the river served the vital need for irrigation and a channel for freight and passengers downriver to San Francisco.

The steamboat dominated river traffic from San Francisco to Sycamore Point, some miles up the San Joaquin. Navigation depended on the depth of channels and the seasonal supply of water, particularly on the upper branches where the dry season ending in July and August often brought a halt to river travel due to low water levels. Stockton held its position as the central port city for its own area and for transhipment of freight from others. Sailing schooners, barges, and tugs carried significant amounts of freight too, but settlement of the Central Valley drew off more and more water and sediment from hydraulic mining in the Sierra Nevada lowered water levels so that by 1906 service upriver from Stockton was mostly abandoned. Since the 1870s, advocates of maintaining navigable channels on both the upper and lower river had existed, but, ultimately, only the Stockton Channel had survived.

Steamboats to and from Stockton thrived until the First World War. Freighting flourished, and passenger service took on new life with nightly concerts on board, ladies' night programs, improved cabins, and dining rooms that opened to both sides of the ships to enhance enjoyment of the river and delta scenery. During the war, service diminished and never really recovered in the 1920s, although in 1926 two steelhull inland steamers were built at Stockton for use on the Sacramento River. They were the *Delta King* and the *Delta Queen*, luxurious examples of river stern-wheelers, but their appearance coincided with the end of steamboating on the San Joaquin where the final passenger run from Stockton to San Francisco came on the *Captain Weber* in 1932. The *Delta Queen* still operates on the Ohio and Mississippi rivers.

While steamboating rose, flourished, and declined on the river and its branches, steady alterations occurred as growers called for reclamation and for increased emphasis on water resources for the dry but agriculturally rich Central Valley lands. Early problems were mining debris, silt deposits, snag removal, flooding, and channel straightening. Federal attention to these matters began in 1874 on the lower river and on Stockton Channel in 1885, and levees rose in the process. The United States Corps of Engineers maintained a nine-foot channel from Suisun Bay to Stockton from 1913 to 1933, when a twenty-six foot channel was dredged to turn Stockton into a deepwater channel for ocean freighters. This channel was deepened to its present depth of thirty feet in 1950, and, since 1932, it has supported the Port of Stockton as a major western inland port that served 101 ocean vessels from all over the world in 1977.

All-weather freighting over railroads, roads, bridges, and rapid, efficient trucking gradually replaced river traffic in large part. Also, the United States Bureau of Reclamation initiated the Central Valley Project (CVP) in 1935, and this vastly altered the use of water resources in succeeding years. Initially the CVP sought to divert surplus water from the Sacramento River basin southward for irrigation, flood control, improved navigation of the Sacramento River, power, halting of salt water intrusion of the Sacramento-San Joaquin Delta, and for water recreation for the public. As the management of scarce water resources continued, it led to the construction of a diversion dam, the Friant Dam, on the San Joaquin above Fresno. That project and the Friant-Kern Canal sent the mountain waters to dry areas of the valley for development of productive new agricultural lands. But, the San Joaquin River below the dam was left to drain off irrigation waste waters from newly supplied fields.

Today the river continues to serve as a basic source of water in one of the wealthiest farming areas of the world, and it supports an important inland deepwater port. It has excellent acquatic recreation, hunting and fishing, and it shelters rich sources of animal, bird, and fish life in its delta areas.

FURTHER READING: Jerry McMullen, *Paddle-Wheel Days in California* (1944). Bob Walters, *Cruising the California Delta II* (1976).

Walter A. Payne

The Snake River

Source: Among streams and lakes in the high country straddling the continental divide in southern Yellowstone Park

Length: 1,038 miles

Tributaries: Lewis, Henrys Fork, Boise, Payette, Bruneau, Salmon, Clearwater, Malheur, Owyhee, and Palouse rivers

Mouth: Flows into the Columbia River near Pasco in southeast Washington

Agricultural products: Potatoes, beans, sugar beets, grains, fruits

Industries: Food processing, hydroelectric power

High on the Continental Divide near Yellowstone National Park sparkling lakes and streams dot a forested, pristine landscape. The waters of this region flow in opposite directions. Only a short distance separates the Yellowstone and Snake Rivers, the former flowing eastward into the Missouri and Mississippi, the latter twisting its way to unite with the Columbia.

The Snake River is one of the largest of America's river systems. Draining a vast tract of land exceeding 100,000 square miles, it serves as the most important tributary of the mighty Columbia. With source waters in the 10,000 foot reaches of Wyoming's mountains, the river flows over 1,000 miles through the diverse topography of America's Northwest.

From its beginnings the Snake threads its way southward across the Jackson Hole at the eastern base of the Grand Tetons. Upon crossing into Idaho the Snake reverses direction and, as it flows in a northwesterly direction, the western face of the Tetons serves as background. Abruptly leaving the mountains the Snake crosses all of southern Idaho in a southwesterly curving arc. In western Idaho the river turns northward again, forming 200 miles of boundary between Oregon and Idaho. It likewise separates Washington and Idaho for a short distance until turning westward through Washington's fertile Palouse Hills before meeting the Columbia in the Tri Cities area (Richland, Pasco, and Kennewick) of southeastern Washington.

Of far greater significance than physical data concerning the Snake River is its uniqueness.

There is no American model for the Snake; it is both a typically great river system with farms, commerce, and cities and a wild river with cascading waterfalls, rapids, incredibly deep canyons, and, in some areas, virtual inaccessibility. No river calls upon such diverse tributaries as the Salmon, or "River of No Return," which drains the largest primitive wilderness left in America outside Alaska, and the Bruneau and Owyhee Rivers which flow through forbidding desert high country. In southern Idaho, the Snake picks its way across an immense lava plain, replete with tunnels, tubes, and cinder cones.

This geologic peculiarity prevents surface waters from reaching the Snake along its northern banks. Most of the waters from the southern exposure of the Sawtooth and Lost River Mountains of south-central Idaho simply sink into a bleak, volcanic desert. The result is an enormous underground aquifer which proves its efficiency as it comes gurgling and cascading in the form of the beautiful "Thousand Springs" from sheer rock cliffs of the Snake River Canyon. The contrast is bizarre; on the surface of this region there is virtually no water, while a hundred feet below, the water table may contain 100 million acre-feet.

The predominantly desert environment and interior course of the Snake River prevented easy discovery and exploration. Americans had discovered the mouth of the Columbia and sailed several miles upriver as early as 1792. Overland discovery of the Snake was left to Lewis and Clark in 1805 when they canoed down the Clearwater River where it joins the Snake near present Lewiston, Idaho. Before proceeding downriver to the Columbia, Clark routinely observed that the waters of the Snake were greenish-blue, while the Clearwater was "as clear as cristial."

On the return trip the following year Lewis and Clark learned from Indians that a great river beyond the mountains flowed westward across a harsh desert. Enticed by such a possibility Lewis and Clark nonetheless stuck to north-

Spectacular Shoshone Falls occur in an arid part of the Snake River Course. (Courtesy: Idaho State Historical Society Collection.)

erly routes and thus returned to St. Louis having explored only the lowest portion of the Snake. However, John Colter, a volunteer member of the expedition, became the first white man to discover and explore the source waters of the Snake as well as the mysterious Yellowstone country.

Colter, who unfortunately kept no journal, joined two trappers who sought their fortunes in the Yellowstone River country. Colter's wanderings took him into the Jackson Hole country and the upper reaches of the Snake. Exploration of the middle course of the river followed several years later when an expedition funded by fur magnate John Jacob Astor and led by Wilson Price Hunt traversed all of southern Idaho.

To avoid hostile Blackfeet Indians, Hunt's party sought a southerly route to the coast where they could deposit beaver pelts with Astor's advance party which had come to Oregon by sea. On the tranquil Henry's Fork of the

Snake, Hunt put to the river with fifteen boats and high hopes of sailing to the coast. Those hopes were shortlived. The Snake River proved so treacherous with its numerous white-water rapids, thundering waterfalls, and boulder-strewn course that Hunt abandoned what remained of his boats. The bewildered party then split into smaller groups with Hunt's main party essentially paralleling the Snake River which they had dubbed the "Mad River." In western Idaho Hunt was forced to abandon this route when he encountered the wild mountains and deep canyons of the Seven Devils country. Here the Snake cuts its way through America's deepest gorge, appropriately named Hell's Canyon, and Hunt simply retreated before such an obstacle. He later crossed Oregon's Blue Mountains and trekked overland to the Columbia. Except for the wilds of Hell's Canyon, Wilson Price Hunt had explored the middle Snake country. After eleven months of deprivation, death, and great toil, Hunt and his remaining followers reached Astoria at the mouth of the Columbia.

In the immediate decades following Hunt's expedition, the Snake River country was the scene of intense international competition between America and Great Britain. The immediate prize was of course beaver pelts but at larger stake was a great inland empire. Between 1825 and 1835 the Snake River country was a beehive of trapping and trading activity. Perhaps as many as several hundred men in the employ of British and American fur companies traversed nearly every range of mountains and tributary drainages of the Snake River. Mapping and naming practically everything of significance, trappers indeed left their impression on the land of the Snake River.

In succession came missionaries, miners, and settlers to the region. The latter group initially found little to attract them to the Middle Snake River. Stories of deep, rich soils and a favorable climate lured tens of thousands of settlers along the Snake River to Oregon during the years 1843 to 1859. One needed few signs or directions to follow the Oregon Trail; summer's dust rarely settled during those restless years. Even today deep ruts carved by thousands of wagon wheels are clearly visible in places along the left bank of the Snake.

The Snake River country was settled much as it was discovered and explored, from the lower and upper reaches first and then, most recently, along the Middle Snake. It is a historical paradox that in America's westward expansion the Snake River country was settled from west to east. Oregon-bound settlers who tried to keep the fine dust from choking them agreed that soils along the Snake were "alkali powder" and unfit for agriculture. Only with the prospect of very cheap land and irrigation schemes did the Middle Snake River become attractive.

For American settlers migrating westward there were few agricultural examples in their backgrounds to encourage the practice of irrigation. Eastern and midwestern farmers counted on the heavens to supply moisture while in the West, Indians rejected the entire idea of agriculture as women's work or unfit for people of the horse.

On the Snake River plains an agricultural miracle simply awaited the proper combination of vision, cooperative hard work, and capital. The volcanic soils are rich, the growing season is as long as 200 days, and the several mountain ranges enclosing the Snake River Plain hold great promise of water from melting snow. Despite such advantages agriculture along the Snake River did not reach successful proportions until the first part of the twentieth century when large-scale irrigation projects were begun.

Missionaries and religious colonists were the first to practice irrigation along the Snake River. On the Lower Snake near the confluence of the Clearwater and Snake Rivers, the Reverend Henry Spalding established a mission at Lapwai in 1836. He taught the Nez Perce Indians the art of cultivation and they practiced crude forms of irrigation.

Some years later Mormon colonists were ordered by Brigham Young to settle in the upper Snake River country along the Salmon River. Mormons also instructed the Indians, principally Bannocks, in the production of a variety of crops, at least those which the 5,000-foot high country would permit. The Mormons were experienced irrigationists and therefore proceeded to dig canals and laterals in order to maximize production. This was the first irrigation scheme of any size in Idaho, but the persistent Mormons could not contend with the double scourge of grasshoppers and the increasingly hostile Indians. Both the Spalding mission at Lapwai and the Mormon's Fort Lemhi were abandoned and these early agricultural toeholds in the Snake River drainage proved abortive.

Despite such experiences with the Nez Perce and Bannocks, large-scale settlement along the Snake River by whites was not prevented by hostile Indians. Long after the last Indian conflict, settlers were still reluctant to stake their future in this forbidding desert country. Even the promise of cheap land guaranteed by such federal legislation as the Federal Homestead and Desert Land acts failed to attract settlers. Investors, speculators, and private companies frequently had their hopes dashed that the region would support sizeable populations. The attractiveness of the Snake River Plains for agriculture and settlement was keyed entirely to the availability of irrigation water.

Wherever large-scale irrigation has been practiced there has been a high degree of social cooperation. Such cooperation is possible only with some conviction that the capital and labor expended will produce satisfactory results. In the case of the Snake River, the federal government provided such an assurance with the Carey Land and Reclamation acts of 1894 and 1902, respectively. Passage of the latter act began the development of modern irrigation along the Snake River and its tributaries.

Beginning with the Minidoka Project in 1904 and its American Falls Dam, the Snake River has been repeatedly tamed. One such irrigation diversion is Milner Dam, thirty miles upriver from Twin Falls, Idaho. In 1812 Wilson Price Hunt named this dangerous stretch of the River "Caldron Linn" and, after calamitous boat wrecks with the loss of critical supplies and one life, he gave up on his attempt to navigate the Snake. Today the damming of the Snake at "Caldron Linn" has provided the irrigation water which makes some of the bleakest of Idaho's desert country blossom as the rose. Today the area is known as the "Magic Valley" and boasts a prosperous agricultural economy with an expanding population.

Names like "Magic Valley" and "Treasure Valley" provide sharp contrast to earlier names like "Mad River" and "Hells Canyon." The harnessing of the Snake and its tributaries has been an economic blessing to the people who have settled along their reaches. Today there are approximately 4.5 million acres in the Snake River drainage under irrigation with an estimated additional potential of twice that acreage. Equally significant is the enormous hydroelectric generation along the River.

The region drained by the Snake is 100 percent dependent upon hydroelectric power. It is a region blessed with an abundance of cheap power as well as significant potential for more. Because the Snake River area is an energy exporter, its fate has been tied to that of both the American Southwest and Northwest.

Western tradition has it that more men have been killed over water than over women or gold. Indeed, Idahoans are very sensitive about the waters of the Snake River. Recently, when the entire West was experiencing a serious drought, the governor of Idaho threatened to bring suit against the state of Washington if that state seeded any clouds which might have deprived Idaho of urgently needed moisture. No longer does one use the term "surplus" to describe either the water or the electricity of this region. Recognition that the resources of the Snake River are finite has been slow in coming.

Whether or not ecology or environmental-mindedness is the single cause of this new conservatism is a difficult question to answer. Nevertheless, this phenomenon is very real in the Snake River region and has already profoundly influenced the thinking of planners, politicians, and certainly the private power companies. While arguments raged in the late 1950s and early 1960s over who was to build dams and where they were to be built on the Middle Snake, the environmentalists slowly took the offensive. As the environmental and ecological question of "why" displaced other considerations, future damming of the Snake River appeared unlikely.

In Southwestern Wyoming, in the Upper Snake River region, is situated the newly constructed Jim Bridger power plant. A cooperative venture between Utah and Idaho power companies, its principal source of fuel is coal hewn from the earth in nearby mines. In a region totally dominated by hydroelectric power a thermal plant is a paradox, yet it provides a glimpse into the future as far as the energy needs of the Northwest are concerned.

It is projected that thermal energy output will approximate that of hydro sometime within the next decade. Such projections suggest that the history of the Snake River over the past 150 years has gone nearly full circle. Those early explorers and trappers, who were impressed at the wildness of this river and its drainage area, would be astonished at the taming of the Snake. At the same time they would undoubtedly be amazed at those who are so determined to preserve in the river the same "madness" that the explorers saw.

FURTHER READING: The best single volume on the Snake River is the beautifully illustrated *Snake River Country*, by Bill Gulick, printed by Caxton Printers Ltd., Caldwell, Idaho, 1971. The most detailed, albeit one-sided look at the environmental issue is Boyd Norton's, *Snake Wilderness*, published by the Sierra Club, San Francisco, 1972. The latter work has a guide to the various wilderness and scenic areas in the Snake River drainage.

Robert J. Allred

The Willamette River

Source: At Springfield, Oregon, where the Coast and Middle Fork rivers converge
Length: 189 miles
Tributaries: McKenzie, Calapooya, Santiam, Clackamas rivers
Mouth: Just north of Portland into Columbia River
Agricultural products: Wheat, fruits
Industries: Lumbering, food processing, diversified industries

The Williamette River is at the center of a great part of the history of Oregon. It is the largest river wholly within the state, formed by its Coast and Middle forks where they join near the town of Springfield. It then flows northward for approximately 189 miles before spilling into the Columbia River just north of Portland, the state's largest city.

The Willamette drains an area of about 11,200 square miles in northwest Oregon. Flowing in a braided, meandering channel, the stream travels through a generally dish-shaped basin with its main valley floor situated just west of center. Foothills slope up to the rugged, mountainous terrain of the Cascade Range to the east, the Coast Range to the west, and the Calapooya Mountains to the south. The valley floor covers approximately 3,500 square miles, extending from Eugene, the state's second largest city, at its southern tip, approximately to Oregon City in the north.

The river generally lies below 500 feet in elevation. In the past, as a result of erosion, it has wandered over an area two to three miles wide. This has created secondary channels, dead-end sloughs, and oxbow lakes, which are interspersed along its course. As the Willamette makes it passage, sloping, alluvial plains are relieved by local basaltic ridges and rolling hills. About five miles above Oregon City (fifteen miles south of Portland) a range of low basaltic hills crosses the basin at New Era. There the river flows into a narrow gorge which ends at Willamette Falls in a picturesque drop of about forty-five feet.

If, in fact, the state's history has pivoted on the banks of the river, it is in large part because the floor of the Willamette Valley is so rich with hospitable land and climate. Combined with its annual rainfall of fifty inches and mild mean temperature, the valley has always attracted those interested in growing things.

The first occupants of the Willamette's banks were, of course, Indians. Indeed, Willamette is an Indian term (although the Indians did not use it for the river—they gave it no name). While the meaning of the word is now generally agreed to be lost, one early historian asserted that it originally meant "green waters" and denoted a place on the lower river's bank, just below the falls. An anthropologist, however, has recorded another meaning, "to spill or pour water."

The Indian population lived in intimate relation to the river. The Kalapuyans (k ae le pu 'yans), a dominant group upstream from Willamette Falls, provide a good study of the conditions of Indian life along the Willamette. The spring run of Chinook salmon was probably their single largest source of food. Camas (an edible root of the lily family), was pit-oven roasted and then dried and was another mainstay of their diet.

Whites had little Indian trouble in settling along the Willamette River primarily because in the period from 1829 to 1833 the Kalapuyans were decimated by epidemics, probably malaria and influenza.

The first white man to sight the Willamette River was Lieutenant William R. Broughton, a member of Captain George Vancouver's expedition which was in search of the Northwest Passage for the British crown. In the fall of 1792, Vancouver dispatched Broughton to travel up "the river of the West," the Columbia, lately discovered by the American, Captain Robert Gray. On October 29 of that year, Broughton sighted the mouth of the Willamette and duly noted the fact in his journal naming it the River Mannings, perhaps after another member of the Vancouver expedition.

The next white men to arrive at the Willamette were Meriwether Lewis and William Clark who reached the Pacific Ocean in 1805. They had unwittingly passed the Willamette's mouth as they pushed toward the coast. On the return trip, on April 2, 1806, however, they were informed by some Indians of its existence. As they again passed the river, Clark and a few of his men went back to investigate and entered the stream's mouth. In his journal, Clark called it "Multnomah. . . from a nation who reside on Wappato Island, a little below the entrance. . . ."

Clark's name for the river did not endure, as variations of the name Willamette began to appear in the travelogues, journals, government reports, and official maps of those whites who ventured into the Oregon country. Then, in 1841, Lt. Charles Wilkes investigated the area for the federal government and used the current spelling in his *U.S. Exploring Expedition* (1845) and in an accompanying atlas and charts. This usage was apparently adopted by the government and everyone else who could spell.

The initial influx of settlers along the banks of the Willamette was the beginning of a trend of population growth that has never abated. Moreover, the coming of the white man signalled an entirely new relationship between the river and man. The Indians had, as one writer put it, "lived lightly upon the land," but now the Willamette became a key to civilization as the whites knew it. This meant that its fish and game resources would be exploited more fully than ever before, that its power would be harnessed for industrial purposes, that it would be used as a commercial roadstead, that it would become a repository for human and industrial wastes, as well as a source of drinking water and recreation.

Oregon City was the first center of the new society. It was, indeed, the first town incorporated west of the Missouri River. The Hudson's Bay Company ordered the chief factor of the Company's "Columbia Department," Dr. John McLoughlin, to open a sawmill at the falls of the Willamette. As a result three log houses were built at Oregon City in the winter of 1829–30 but were burned by resentful Indians. Nevertheless the settlement managed to take root and by 1832 the first water-powered sawmill and flour mill in the territory were in operation. In 1842, in an attempt to maintain control of the locale, McLoughlin platted the town.

The tide of American immigration was, however, inexorable; in 1844 approximately 800 people arrived in Oregon City. In 1843 a provisional government was formed at Champoeg, a spot on the Willamette a few miles upstream from Oregon City, and in 1844 its legislature granted Oregon City a charter. Moreover, in 1844 the city became the territorial capital, an honor it retained only until 1852.

Because the Willamette afforded an easily tapped and cheap source of power at the falls and was a dependable, navigable access to other areas downstream, Oregon's industrial development actually commenced at Oregon City. The first furniture factory in the Pacific Northwest was located there and in 1864 a woolen mill was built. In 1866 the first paper mill on the Pacific Coast began operation there.

For nineteenth-century Americans, the competition for intrastate urban preeminence was a favored pastime. Oregon City's head start as the leading city of the territory soon dissipated as up and down the river new towns sprang up. Portland's strategic location was the strongest point in its favor. Built at the confluence of the Willamette and the Columbia, the city's location had been used by the Chinook Indians as an ideal spot for commerce and industry. Later, Americans found that they could take ocean-going ships up the Columbia as far as there. Portland became the hub for a potentially rich agricultural hinterland to the west (the Tualatin Valley adjacent to the valley of the Willamette) and the Willamette Valley itself.

By 1850 Portland had replaced Oregon City as the largest town in the Northwest. The California gold rush of 1849 was then in full swing, and Portland had become a primary beneficiary of the needs of the miners who were crowding San Francisco. Provisioning needs of the Indian wars of the 1850s and the eastern Oregon-Idaho gold rush of the 1860s sustained Portland's economic well-being. By 1860 her citizens numbered 2,874 and by the 1890s Portland was secure as the preeminent city of the state.

Salem, founded in 1840 on the Willamette about fifty miles south of Portland, had a different reaction to the California gold rush. When gold was discovered, almost fifty percent of the village's population decamped for the gold fields. Even though Salem became the territorial capital in 1852 and state capital in 1859, such prominence failed to advance its fortunes very much, nor did its central location in the Willamette Valley. It was not until 1871 when the railroad came that a new era of growth was initiated for the city.

Other cities on the upper river, such as Corvallis and Eugene, also developed as market centers, Corvallis for the dairy and fruit produce of its hinterland and Eugene mainly for wheat, lumber, and mineral products. Eugene was generally regarded as the farthest navigable point on the river. Both sustained themselves later on as homes of the state's principal universities.

Despite the sometimes spectacular economic growth that characterized it in the middle decades of the nineteenth century, the Willamette Valley remained essentially a raw frontier. In these years the river was the main highway of the valley.

The *Lot Whitcomb* was the first steamboat built on the Willamette. Constructed at Milwaukie, a town between Portland and Oregon City, by its namesake, it was a sidewheeler. The route of the *Lot Whitcomb* was Milwaukie to Astoria, on the mouth of the Columbia, and back. Initially the *Whitcomb* bypassed Portland, in the hope that this would hinder its development as a deep-sea port and as a town, making Milwaukie, of course, preeminent. But Portland's boosters retaliated by purchasing the California steamer *Goldhunter*. *Goldhunter* was actually an ocean-going vessel and, traveling between California and Oregon, gave Portland an immediate competitive advantage. Whitcomb lost out. By 1852 there were fourteen side and sternwheelers docking at Portland. So promising did river commerce appear that in the period from 1850 to 1853 the federal government spent $30,000 clearing rocks from a stretch of the river, in the belief that this would open the Willamette to the ocean-going vessels as far as the falls. The intention was never realized, but the project did aid navigation for river boats on the lower river. Steamers also plied the upper river ports for many years, but only at high water.

After locks were completed at Oregon City in 1873, allowing circumvention of the falls, thus making the river continuously navigable, they multiplied greatly. By 1878 there were perhaps twenty paddlewheelers operating on the lower

river alone. By the end of the century, the steamers were made obsolete by the improved highway and rail systems that spread through the valley. But in their heyday the boats were the most important mode of transportation in the region.

During the twentieth century the Corps of Engineers emphasized not navigation but flood control. In 1936, Congress passed legislation to rehabilitate the Willamette. The river had always been susceptible to flooding, particularly as the clayey soil of the valley does not provide good drainage. The flood of December, 1861, had been the worst such disaster; the river rose as much as nineteen feet over its banks in some locations. The years 1881, 1890, 1927, and 1964 saw high water. The Corps constructed seven storage reservoirs on the Willamette and its tributaries in order to control runoff.

One of the subsidiary effects of the flood control program was to enhance the potential for development of the river's flood plain. The result was an ever-increasing impact on the river from urbanization and industrialization. This effect was most immediately felt in the sanitary and life-supporting condition of the water.

Indeed, by 1951 the Willamette was the most heavily polluted stream in the Pacific Northwest and one of the dirtiest rivers in America. In addition to raw sewage, wastes from industries, particularly pulp and paper mills, were being discharged into the Willamette to a population equivalent of more than three million. Eight hundred thousand people resided in the Willamette Valley at the time.

Over the ensuing twenty-five years, however, much was done to correct the polluted condition into which the river had fallen. By the mid-1970s these measures had begun to show beneficial results. In the period from 1973 to 1976, the U.S. Geological Survey reported, the water quality of the Willamette basin was excellent. Oxygen levels in the water were once again high enough to sustain fish life, tracemetal levels were beneath minimum standards, and the impacts of land use and erosion on the river systems were under control.

In order to preserve the remaining stretches of wilderness on the Willamette and to assure a well-coordinated and sensible land use program in the face of anticipated high population growth in the valley, the 1973 Oregon legislature established a 150-mile length of the river between southern Lane County and Portland as a natural, historical scenic and recreational greenway. The greenway plan was also designed to protect agricultural and other economic uses of the land adjacent to the Willamette.

The greenway boundaries in each location were fixed at a minimum of 150 feet. At one spot near Oregon City, however, the boundary has been set at 3/4 of a mile. Most regulations regarding the greenway concern construction that might be visible from the river and any alterations of the river banks. Both banks of the river are protected from future development. By 1983, however, the plan was well on its way toward completion. One member of the Willamette Greenway Advisory Commission, observing a stretch of protected wilderness along the banks of the Willamette's middle fork called the greenway "... a thing that any other place in the country or maybe the world would give their right arms for." Robert W. Straub, former governor of Oregon, wrote, "once fully implemented, the Willamette River Greenway will be one of Oregon's major accomplishments."

Even as in the lives of the Indians to whom it was a central motif of existence, and to the white settlers for whom it was a key to the establishment of their own society and culture, so in the last third of the twentieth century has the Willamette River once again come to play a pivotal role in the development of the state of Oregon. Its metamorphosis from a river of the wilderness to an economic lifeline to an instrument of complex uses suggest the rich history in which it has figured so prominently.

FURTHER READING: Howard Mc K. Corning, *Willamette Landings*, 2nd ed. (1973). Arthur L. Throckmorton, *Oregon Argonauts* (1961).

Craig E. Wollner

The Yukon River

Source: **East side of Coastal Range of extreme northwest British Columbia; some consider the Yukon proper as beginning with the convergence of the Lewes and Pelly rivers at Fort Selkirk**
Length: **1,875 miles**
Tributaries: **White, Innoko, Pelly, Porcupine, Nulato, Koyukuk, Tanana, Stewart, Fortymile, Chandalar, and Klondike rivers**
Mouth: **Into Bering Sea near Kotlik**
Agricultural products: **None**
Industries: **Fishing, mining, furs**

The Yukon, fourth largest river in North America, is nevertheless one of the least known of the continent's great waterways. It is 1,875 miles from the headwaters of the Lewes—now better known as the Upper Yukon—to its estuary at Norton Sound in the Bering Sea. Seven hundred and fourteen miles of the river flow through Yukon Province in northwest Canada while the remaining 1,400 miles flow through the state of Alaska. It is the river's remoteness from civilization and the high northern latitudes through which it flows that have kept it from being better known.

As the river is something of a mystery to people of the "lower forty-eight," so also is Alaska. That enormous expanse of land, glaciers, and mountains that constitutes the forty-ninth state was acquired from the Russians in 1867. It contains several distinct geographical regions. These include the coastal zone, the high mountains that separate the great central plain, the north slope, and the Aleutian Islands. The Yukon flows through two of these. It rises on the east side of the coastal mountains of British Columbia, some of its headwaters less than fifty miles in a straight line from the sea. It flows northnortheast as the Lewes (or Upper Yukon) and is joined by the Pelly River at Fort Selkirk. It then heads northwest, crosses into Alaska and continues in the northwest direction until it briefly crosses the Arctic Circle. At that point it is joined by the Porcupine River coming in from the northeast. The Yukon then continues west-southwest across the barren central plain of Alaska to its wide estuary. On a drainage map the river appears as a great arc originating just over the boundary from southeastern, coastal Alaska, curving northwest and reaching its northernmost point at Fort Yukon in northeastern Alaska, then curving slowly southwestward to the Bering Sea.

Although the Yukon at its headwaters is a tumultuous stream (some of which is now inundated by a lake and hydroelectric facility at Whitehorse), most of it flows through the barren great central plain of Alaska, bounded on the north by the Brooks Range and the south by the Alaska Range, which includes Mount McKinley. At places the river widens into a water and island wilderness of thousands of lakes, making it difficult to follow the channel. And the Yukon Estuary is a fan-shaped plain covered with willow and brush and cut by thousands of meandering streams; again, the channel is sometimes difficult to follow. The river is frozen over from October until June, but in summer it is navigable throughout its distance in Alaska and by shallow-draft vessels even up to Whitehorse in Yukon Territory.

Although it is still remote, humans may have used the Yukon before any other river in the western hemisphere. This is because during the great Ice Age, when water was locked up as ice, the waters of the Bering Sea were lowered until a land bridge appeared between Asia and America. Primitive hunters, following game, advanced across the bridge, struck the Yukon River and, in following the easiest route, passed between the great mountain ranges until, as they approached the river's headwaters, they crossed southeastward into another great intermountain trough which carried them farther into the interior of the continent. These migrations were 10,000–25,000 years ago.

The people who stayed behind after most of the hunters had migrated southward were Indians of Athapascan stock. Five linguistic branches inhabited the Yukon River country. Fierce, tough aborigines, related to the Navajos and Apaches of the American Southwest, for thousands of years they eked out a seminomadic existence along the Yukon and its tributaries. They were primarily hunters and fishermen using snares, spears, nets, and arrows to take fish and game. Central in their wanderings was the Yukon, an Athapascan word meaning "big river."

These peoples, whose blood is increasingly mixed with that of the whites, have both profited and suffered from white domination. The few thousand Indians inhabiting the central Yukon today, and their recent ancestors, have suffered from the white people's diseases such as small pox, tuberculosis, and V.D.; they have also been exploited by the whites' lust for furs and gold. All of this changed the Indians' way of life. In more recent times the federal government has tried to educate and help these stone-age people into the modern world, improve their health, and give them some protection from predatory whites.

The first white men to penetrate the Yukon were Russians. In 1838 a creole—a person of mixed Russian and native blood—named Malakov crossed from St. Michael, a Russian settlement on Norton Sound, to the Yukon. At the mouth of the Nulato River, about fifty miles inland, he found a small Indian trading center; here a few years later the Russians maintained a fur trading post. In 1851 the post occupants were massacred by Indians, but the Russians nevertheless returned a few years later to carry on trade. The Russians had also explored above the mouth of the Tanana River, which enters the Yukon from the south.

Meanwhile Hudson's Bay Company traders working northwest from Yukon Territory were tapping the upper half of the river for furs. One trading post was Fort Yukon, just inside the Arctic Circle where the Yukon bends to the southwest and the Porcupine flows in from the northeast. The other H. B. Company post was located 500 miles upstream at a strategic point where the Pelly River flows into the Yukon. This post was dubbed Fort Selkirk. The explorer responsible for these Hudson's Bay establishments was an H. B. Co. employee named Robert Campbell; his explorations took place in the 1840s; in 1848 he built Fort Selkirk. Fort Yukon was built the year before (1846) by Alexander Hunter Murray, who had reached the site by crossing the short distance from the headwaters of Canada's Mackenzie River to the Porcupine's headwaters, and then floating downstream to where the latter joins the Yukon. Neither Murray nor Campbell nor any other Hudson's Bay officials had known that the two posts were on the same river. Fort Selkirk was subjected to Indian attack and was abandoned in 1852; Fort Yukon continued operational.

Although Alaska is far north of the forty-ninth parallel—the northern boundary of the "lower forty-eight" states—interest in the region arose in the 1860s with the completion of the transcontinental telegraph. In 1856 Perry McDonough Collins traveled across Russia and down the Amur River to the Pacific. By 1857 he was back in the States with permission from the British and Russians to construct an international overland telegraph line. Subsequently he received authorization from Congress to pursue his project. Then Collins merged his interest with the Western Union Company.

Among their plans was an expedition to survey a telegraph route across Alaska via the Yukon River. To lead the survey expedition, because he had been at Fort Yukon in 1860–61 and had collected extensively of Alaskan flora and fauna, was naturalist Robert Kennicott. He assembled a small expedition that, unfortunately, was lacking in *esprit* and was plagued by troubles. In 1866 Kennicott was found dead near the Nulato River, a Yukon tributary; he may have committed suicide.

The remaining members, Frank Ketchum and Mike Labarge, in the summer of 1866 set out from Nulato in a three-holed kayak and worked upriver to Fort Yukon and return. In November the Telegraph expedition welcomed its new leader, William Healey Dall, a twenty-one-year-old Bostonian of easy temperament and scientific turn of mind. Also joining the expedition was an English artist, Frederick Whymper. In March, 1867, Ketchum and Labarge departed from Nulato by dog sled for Fort Yukon while as soon as the ice broke up on the river, Dall and Whymper paddled to the same location. The former two went on to abandoned Fort Selkirk. When all four arrived again back at Nulato they discovered that the expedition was terminated because Cyrus Field's new Atlantic cable was a success, making a land route telegraph unneces-

sary. A few months later they heard that the United States had purchased Alaska. Nevertheless the International Telegraph Expedition mapped the great central valley of Alaska, through which the Yukon flows, for the first time.

Hardly had the exchange of sovereignty been made before American traders began probing Alaska's interior. In 1869 Parrott and Company of San Francisco launched upon the stream a small steamboat, the *Yukon*. Aboard was Captain Charles R. Raymond, U.S. Army, who informed the commandant at Fort Yukon that the Hudson's Bay post was on American soil. Forthwith, and with good grace, the H.B. people left. Parrott and Company merged with the Alaska Commercial Company in 1870, and for the next twenty years that firm dominated Alaskan, and Yukon, trade.

For thirty years after the Alaska Purchase the United States neglected the colony, and as a result lawlessness was rampant. In 1883 an American explorer, Lieutenant Frederick Schwatka, with six companions, climbed Chilkat Pass in the coastal range and came down to the headwaters of the Yukon; they then floated the nearly 2,000 miles to the river's vast, island-studded estuary. But in spite of Lieutenant Schwatka's book and occasional travel articles by others, "Seward's Ice Box" lacked attention.

Gradually, however, interest in Alaska's potential increased as prospectors climbed over the steep Chilkoot, Chilkat, and White passes of the Coastal Range to Yukon headwaters and prospected up the river and its tributaries. By the mid-1880s minor strikes had been found on the Stewart River and the Fortymile River, the latter of which is also in Canada's Yukon Territory, and at Birch Creek, about 150 miles northeast of Fairbanks in Alaska. In 1895 the Canadian Mounted Police arrived in northwest Yukon Territory, bringing to the Canadian part of the river a semblance of law and order.

Indeed, much of the Yukon's most colorful history has been made in its Canadian portion. The greatest gold strike to occur in the Yukon country was along the Klondike, a 100-mile-long river rising east of Dawson, in northern Yukon Province, and flowing west to join the Yukon. In 1896 gold was discovered in the region resulting in an incredible stampede in 1897–1898. The hardships encountered took many lives. Those bound for the region took passage to Skagway; from there they crossed Chilkat, Chilkoot, or White pass to Yukon headwaters and then floated downstream to Dawson. Others took passage in Yukon steamboats from the estuary; many of them were stranded during the winter at Fort Yukon. Probably 25,000 gold seekers and hangers-on were in the Klondike region at its height. Many of those who failed to strike it rich found placer deposits at other points along the Yukon. In 1902 Fairbanks was established on the Chena, a Yukon tributary, and remains to this day an outfitting center for the vast region.

After the gold rushes the Yukon country returned to its isolation, with an extractive economy based on metals and furs. In 1959 Alaska attained statehood. With an expanding economy in the "lower forty-eight," U.S. Army Engineers in the 1960s proposed an enormous hydroelectric project. According to a publicity agency, Yukon Power for America, the dam at Rampart Canyon would be 530 feet high and 4,700 feet long, would inundate the vast marsh and lake region known as Yukon Flats, one of the world's greatest waterfowl breeding places, and create a body of water as large as Lake Erie. Five million kilowatts would be generated by its dynamos. Nothing came of the scheme.

Then came the discovery of oil along Alaska's North Slope. Fairbanks's population swelled with pipeline workers and the Yukon was bridged to connect north and south portions of the road to the North Slope. Then, with the pipeline built, as with the gold rushes of eighty years before, the Yukon country reverted to the loneliness and remoteness that have characterized its history. Tributary streams continued to add to the Yukon milk-white water containing glacially ground rock particles in suspension. Millions of birds, thousands of moose, bear, wolves, and other animals continued to live in the great central valley, and mosquitoes swarmed by the billions. People still read Jack London's tales of the Yukon country and the poems of Robert Service, such as "The Shooting of Dan McGrew," but few readers anticipate emigrating to the magnificent, starkly beautiful Yukon River country.

FURTHER READING: William E. Simeone, *A History of Alaskan Athabaskans* (1982). Allen A. Wright, *Prelude to Bonanza: The Discovery and Exploration of the Yukon River* (1976).

Richard A. Bartlett

Index

Page numbers in *italic* indicate main discussion.

About the Editor

RICHARD A. BARTLETT is a Professor of American History at Florida State University. An authority on the Westward Movement, he has written *Great Surveys of the American West; The New Country: A Social History of the American Frontier; Nature's Yellowstone,* and is the co-author of *Freedom's Trail,* along with many articles and book reviews. Formerly employed by the National Archives and the Library of Congress, he holds a Ph.D. from the University of Colorado.